THE STRUCTURE

OF

SOCIAL ACTION

A Study in Social Theory
with Special Reference to a Group of
Recent European Writers

BY

TALCOTT PARSONS

Harvard University

THE FREE PRESS

GLENCOE, ILLINOIS

1949

PREFACE TO SECOND EDITION

Nearly twelve years have passed since the original publication of *The Structure of Social Action*. The post-war wave of interest in theoretical study and teaching in the relevant aspects of social science unfortunately found the book out of print, so that the decision of *The Free Press* to bring out a new edition is most welcome.

For a variety of reasons, it has been decided to reprint the original book without change. There is, in this decision, no implication that the book could not be substantially improved by revision. Nothing could be further both from the spirit of the work and from a number of explicit statements* in it. The author's own process of theoretical thinking has not stopped and if he were to undertake writing the book again at this time, it would come out a substantially different and, let us hope, a better book.

To present a revised version which would at all closely resemble what the book would be like if newly written in 1949 would, however, be a very heavy task. It would not only involve much actual rewriting, but, prior to that, a careful re-study and re-evaluation of the principal sources on which it was based. This would certainly be highly productive, but the problem is to balance judgment of the productiveness of such work compared to alternative uses of the time and energy it would require.

The most important consideration involved in the balance is the relative advantage to be derived from further refinement of the critical analysis of theoretical work done a generation and more ago as compared with the probable fruitfulness of proceeding with direct analysis of theoretical problems in relation to presently going empirical research interests without further refinement of critical orientation. The decision not to embark on a thorough revision of the book represents the judgment that in the present situation of social science, the latter constitutes the more fruitful channel for a major investment of time and energy.

The Structure of Social Action was intended to be primarily a

---

* See Chapter I, pages 40-41.

A

contribution to systematic social science and not to history, that is the history of social thought. The justification of its critical orientation to the work of other writers thus lay in the fact that this was a convenient vehicle for the clarification of problems and concepts, of implications and interrelations. It was a means of taking stock of the theoretical resources at our disposal. In the on-going process of scientific development, it constituted a pause for reconsideration of basic policy decisions, on principles which are serviceable in scientific work as in many other fields, namely, that "it is a good thing to know what you are doing," and that there may be resources and potentialities in the situation which in our absorption in daily work, we tend to overlook. The clarification gained from this stocktaking has opened up possibilties for further theoretical development of sufficient scope so that its impetus is as yet by no means exhausted. This is certainly true in a personal sense and it is reasonable to believe that it continues to be true for others.

The Structure of Social Action analyzed a process of convergent theoretical development which constituted a major revolution in the scientific analysis of social phenomena. The three principal authors treated in that study are by no means isolated but as contributors to the "sociological" side of the development, the added perspective of another decade does not diminish their relative stature as high points in the movement. There is an elevated range, not just three peaks, but these three peaks loom far higher than the lesser ones.

This is true on the sociological side. A major one-sidedness of the book is its relative neglect of the psychological aspects of the total conceptual scheme—a balance which a thorough revision would certainly have to attempt to redress. Here, at least, one figure in the same generation as the others, that of Freud, looms up as having played a cardinal role in a development which, in spite of the differences of his starting points and empirical concerns, must be regarded as a vital part of the same general movement of thought. Psychology is probably richer in significant secondary figures than is true on the sociological side, but no other one seems closely to approach the stature of Freud. So much is this the case that a full-dress analysis of Freud's theoretical development seen in the context of the "theory of social action"—and adaptation of the rest of the book to the results of such an analysis—would seem

THE STRUCTURE OF SOCIAL ACTION

indispensable to the kind of revision which ought to be undertaken. This would, of course, necessarily result in a substantial lengthening of an already formidable work.

There may well be a difference of opinion whether there is any figure of comparable *theoretical* stature, who is classified as essentially a social or cultural anthropologist. It is the author's opinion that there is not. Though Boas, for example, may be of comparable *general* importance to social science and an equally great man, his contributions to systematic theoretical analysis in the same stream of development are not in the same category with a Durkheim or a Freud. In a diffuser sense, however, the contributions of anthropological thinking are, however, of first-rate importance and should receive distinctly more emphasis than has been given them in *The Structure of Social Action*. This is particularly true of the relations of the structure of social action to the "structure of culture." Further clarification of these issues is one of the most urgent needs of basic social science at present.

In its fundamentals, this basic theoretical development had taken place by, let us say, twenty-five years ago. But the frames of reference, the polemical orientations, the empirical interests and the intellectual traditions surrounding the authors were so various that the actual unity of their work was accessible only with a great deal of laborious critical interpretation. Indeed, it was worse than that, for the actual differentiations had already become overlaid with a welter of secondary interpretations and misinterpretations, which made the confusion even worse confounded. One of the principal services of *The Structure of Social Action* has been, I think, to clear away a great deal of this "underbrush" so that the bold outline of a theoretical scheme could stand out with some clarity.

A better understanding of the psychological and cultural aspects, which an analysis of Freud's work and of anthropological thought might have contributed would be desirable. Allowance should also be made for awkwardness of exposition. But even with qualifications of this sort, the book reached a point on which further developments can be built. Furthermore, given certain of the interpretive keys which it provides, the original works can be much more freely and fruitfully used. In a word, the outline of a theoretical scheme and the contributions of some of its principal creators have become much more the public property of a professional group rather than remaining the exclusive possession of a small coterie of

Pareto, Durkheim, or Weber scholars, which would more likely than not be rival coteries.

Assuming that, subject to the inevitable process of refinement, the basic theoretical outline developed in *The Structure of Social Action* is essentially sound, to place its significance in better perspective, something may be said about the nature and direction of the developments which can be built upon it.

It was emphasized that the scheme had developed in direct connection with empirical interests and problems of the authors. This is true and of the first importance. But only at a few points could this empirical orientation have been said at this stage to have approached the level of being "operationally specific." One of the most notable of these, with all its crudity, was Durkheim's analysis of suicide rates. Another, on a totally different level, was Weber's attempted test of the influence of religious ideas on economic development by the comparative analysis of the relationships between the relevant factors in a series of different societies. But on the whole, the major relation to empirical problems remained that of a broad "clarification of issues," elimination of confusion and untenable interpretations, and the opening up of new possibilities.

A central problem, therefore, has been and is, how to bring theory of this sort closer to the possibilities of guiding of and testing and refinement by technical research, especially with the use of technically refined instruments of observation, and of the ordering and empirical analysis of observational data.

At least at many points, an important series of steps in this direction seems to be made possible by a shift in theoretical level from the analysis of the structure of social action as such to the structural-functional analysis of social systems. These are, of course, "in the last analysis" systems of social action. But the structure of such systems is, in the newer version, treated not directly in action terms, but as "institutionalized patterns" close to a level of readily described and tested empirical generalization. This, in turn, makes it possible to isolate specific and manageable action processes for intensive dynamic study. Such processes, that is, are treated as action in relation to institutionalized roles, in terms of balances of conformity with and deviation from the expectations of the socially sanctioned role definitions, of conflicting role expectations impinging on the individual, and the constellations of motivational forces and mechanisms involved in such balances and conflicts.

The isolation of such problems to the point of empirical manageability can, however, within the framework of a structural-functional system of theory, be achieved with a relatively high level of attainment of the advantages of generalized dynamic analysis. Treating dynamic problems in the context of their relation both to the structure of a system and the relation of the processes to the functional prerequisites of its maintenance, provides a frame of reference for judging the general significance of a finding and for following out systematically its interconnections with other problems and facts.

The most promising lines of development of theory in the sociological and most immediately related fields, particularly the psychological and cultural, therefore, seem to be two-fold. One major direction is the theoretical elaboration and refinement of structural-functional analysis of social systems, including the relevant problems of motivation and their relation to cultural patterns. In this process, the structure of social action provides a basic frame of reference, and aspects of it become of direct substantive importance at many specific points. The main theoretical task, however, is more than a refinement of the conceptual scheme of the presently reprinted book—it involves transition and translation to a different level and focus of theoretical systematization.*

The second major direction is the development of technically operational formulations and adaptations of theoretically significant concepts. The development of techniques of empirical research has been exceedingly rapid in the recent past and promises much more for the future. Such techniques can now accomplish impressive results even if the theory which guides their employment is little more than common sense. But this is a minor fraction of the undertanding they promise if they can be genuinely integrated with a really technical and generalized theoretical scheme.

It is the promise of the fruitfulness of developments in such directions as these which motivates the author not to undertake a thorough revision of *The Structure of Social Action* at this time. Indeed, such a revision does not seem to be really necessary. Whatever theoretical progress the author has been able to make

---

* For a fuller account of this focus and what it involves, see Talcott Parsons, *Essays in Sociological Therapy* (The Free Press, 1949), Chapters I and II.

since its original publication* has been built solidly on the foundations it provides, starting, of course, with the insights provided by studying the great theorists whose works it analyzes. There seems to be substantial reason to believe that this is not merely of idiosyncratic significance. Further dissemination of these contributions, even in their present form, should help to elevate the general level of theoretical understanding and competence in our profession and to stimulate other contributors to develop the most fruitful lines of theoretical advance of social science to a level so much higher as to fulfill the promise in the work of their great predecessors of the turn of the century.

TALCOTT PARSONS.

CAMBRIDGE, MASSACHUSETTS
March, 1949

---

* See Talcott Parsons, *Essays in Sociological Theory* (The Free Press, 1949).

PREFACE

In a sense the present work is to be regarded as a secondary study of the work of a group of writers in the field of social theory. But the genus "secondary study" comprises several species; of these an example of only one, and that perhaps not the best known, is to be found in these pages.

The primary aim of the study is not to determine and state in summary form what these writers said or believed about the subjects they wrote about. Nor is it to inquire directly with reference to each proposition of their "theories" whether what they have said is tenable in the light of present sociological and related knowledge. Both these questions must be asked repeatedly, but what is important is not so much the fact that they are asked, or even answered, but the context in which this takes place.

The keynote to be emphasized is perhaps given in the subtitle of the book; it is a study in social *theory*, not *theories*. Its interest is not in the separate and discrete propositions to be found in the works of these men, but in a *single* body of systematic theoretical reasoning the development of which can be traced through a critical analysis of the writings of this group, and of certain of their predecessors. The unity which justifies treating them together between the same covers is not that they constitute a "school" in the usual sense, or that they exemplify an epoch or a period in the history of social theory, but that they have all, in different respects, made important contributions to this single coherent body of theory, and the analysis of their works constitutes a convenient way of elucidating the structure and empirical usefulness of the system of theory itself.

This body of theory, the "theory of social action" is not simply a group of concepts with their logical interrelations. It is a theory of empirical science the concepts of which refer to something beyond themselves. It would lead to the worst kind of dialectic sterility to treat the development of a system of theory without reference to the empirical problems in relation to

v

which it has been built up and used. True scientific theory is
not the product of idle "speculation," of spinning out the logical
implications of assumptions, but of observation, reasoning and
verification, starting with the facts and continually returning
to the facts. Hence at every crucial point explicit treatment of
the empirical problems which occupied the writers concerned is
included. Only by treating theory in this close interrelation
with empirical problems and facts is any kind of an adequate
understanding either of how the theory came to develop, or of its
significance to science, possible.

Indeed though this volume is published as a study in theory in
the sense just outlined, the tracing of the development of a
theoretical system through the works of these four men was not
the original intention of the author in embarking on intensive
study of their works. It could not have been, for neither he nor
any other secondary writer on them was aware that there was a
single coherent theoretical system to be found there. The basis
on which the four writers were brought together for study was
rather empirical. It was the fact that all of them in different
ways were concerned with the range of empirical problems
involved in the interpretation of some of the main features of
the modern economic order, of "capitalism," "free enterprise,"
"economic individualism," as it has been variously called. Only
very gradually did it become evident that in the treatment of
these problems, even from such diverse points of view, there was
involved a common conceptual scheme, and so the focus of
interest was gradually shifted to the working out of the scheme
for its own sake.

Many of the author's debts, in the long history of the study,
which in continuity of problems extends back into undergraduate
days, defy acknowledgment, because they are so numerous and
often so indefinite. An attempt will be made to acknowledge
only those of most important direct relevance to the study as it
now stands.

Of these immediately relevant debts four are of outstanding
significance. The least definite, but perhaps the most important,
is to Professor Edwin F. Gay, who over a period of years has taken
an active interest in the study, has been a source of encourage-
ment at many points in the long and sometimes discouraging
process of its development, and has consistently stimulated the

author to the highest quality of work of which he was capable. Secondly, the author's colleague Professor Overton H. Taylor has contributed, in ways which would defy identification, at innumerable points, largely through a long series of personal discussions of the problems, particularly those associated more directly with the status of economic theory. Both have also read parts of the manuscript and made valuable suggestions. Third, Professor Lawrence J. Henderson has subjected the manuscript to a most unusually thorough critical examination, which led to important revision at many points, particularly in relation to general scientific methodology and to the interpretation of Pareto's work. Finally, much is owed to the changing group of students, especially graduate, with whom the author has carried on discussions of problems of social theory throughout much of the period of incubation of the study. In the lively give and take of these discussions many a fruitful idea has emerged and many an obscure point has been clarified.

Two other critics have been particularly helpful through the suggestions and criticisms they have given after reading the manuscript, Professor A. D. Nock, especially in the parts dealing with religion, and Dr. Robert K. Merton. Various others have read the manuscript or proof in whole or in part, and have made valuable suggestions and criticisms. They include Professor P. A. Sorokin, Professor Josef Schumpeter, Professor Frank H. Knight, Dr. Alexander von Schelting, Professor C. K. M. Kluckhohn, Professor N. B. DeNood, Miss Elizabeth Nottingham, Mr. Emile B. Smullyan and Mr. Edward Shils. To Mr. Smullyan and Dr. Benjamin Halpern, I am also indebted for research assistance.

The foregoing have aided this study in relation to the technical subject matter as such. But this is by no means all there is to the completion of such a work. In other respects two other debts are particularly important. One is to the Harvard University Committee on Research in the Social Sciences, which made possible by its grants some valuable research assistance in bibliography and the secondary literature, and stenographic assistance in preparation of the manuscript. The other is to my father, President Emeritus Edward S. Parsons of Marietta College, who took upon himself the heavy burden of going through the whole manuscript in an attempt to improve its English style.

Whatever of readability an unavoidably difficult work may possess is largely to be credited to him.

For secretarial assistance in typing the manuscript I am much indebted to Miss Elizabeth Wolfe, Miss Agnes Hannay and Mrs. Marion B. Billings, and for assistance in preparation of the bibliography to Miss Elaine Ogden.

TALCOTT PARSONS.

CAMBRIDGE, MASS.,
October, 1937.

CONTENTS

PART III

THE EMERGENCE OF A VOLUNTARISTIC THEORY OF ACTION FROM THE IDEALISTIC TRADITION

PART IV

CONCLUSION

*Jede denkende Besinnung auf die
letzten Elemente sinnvollen mensch-
lichen Handelns ist zunächst gebunden
an die Kategorien "Zweck" und "Mittel."*

Max Weber, Gesammelte Aufsätze
zur Wissenschaftslehre, p. 149.

PART I
THE POSITIVISTIC THEORY OF ACTION

Chapter I

INTRODUCTORY

The Problem

"Who now reads Spencer? It is difficult for us to realize how great a stir he made in the world. . . . He was the intimate confidant of a strange and rather unsatisfactory God, whom he called the principle of Evolution. His God has betrayed him. We have evolved beyond Spencer."[1] Professor Brinton's verdict may be paraphrased as that of the coroner, "Dead by suicide or at the hands of person or persons unknown." We must agree with the verdict. Spencer is dead.[2] But who killed him and how? This is the problem.

Of course there may well be particular reasons why Spencer rather than others is dead, as there were also particular reasons why he rather than others made such a stir. With these this study is not concerned. But in the "crime," the solution of which is here sought, much more than the reputation of, or interest in, a single writer has been done to death. Spencer was, in the general outline of his views, a typical representative of the later stages of development of a system of thought about man and society which has played a very great part in the intellectual history of the English-speaking peoples, the positivistic-utilitarian tradition.[3] What has happened to it? Why has it died?

The thesis of this study will be that it is the victim of the vengeance of the jealous god, Evolution, in this case the evolution of scientific theory. In the present chapter it is not proposed to present an account either of what has evolved or of what it has evolved into; all that will come later. It is necessary to preface this with a tentative statement of the problem, and an outline of

---

[1] Crane Brinton, *English Political Thought in the Nineteenth Century*, pp. 226—227.

[2] Not, of course, that nothing in his thought will last. It is his social theory as a total structure that is dead.

[3] See the following two chapters for an analytical and a historical account.

some general considerations relevant to the way the present task is to be undertaken, and how the present study should be judged.

Spencer's god was Evolution, sometimes also called Progress. Spencer was one of the most vociferous in his devotions to this god, but by no means alone among the faithful. With many other social thinkers he believed that man stood near the culminating point of a long linear process extending back unbroken, without essential changes of direction, to the dawn of primitive man. Spencer, moreover, believed that this culminating point was being approached in the industrial society of modern Western Europe. He and those who thought like him were confident that evolution would carry this process on almost indefinitely in the same direction cumulatively.

A good many students have lately become dubious of these propositions. Is it not possible that the future holds in store something other than "bigger and better" industrialism? The conception that, instead of this, contemporary society is at or near a turning point is very prominent in the views of a school of social scientists who, though they are still comparatively few, are getting more and more of a hearing.

Spencer was an extreme individualist. But his extremism was only the exaggeration of a deep-rooted belief that, stated roughly, at least in the prominent economic phase of social life, we have been blest with an automatic, self-regulating mechanism which operated so that the pursuit by each individual of his own self-interest and private ends would result in the greatest possible satisfaction of the wants of all. All that was necessary was to remove obstacles to the operation of this mechanism, the success of which rested on no conditions other than those included in the conception of rational pursuit of self-interest. This doctrine, too, has been subjected to increasingly severe criticism from many quarters, by no means all relevant to the purposes of this study. But another article of faith about the workings of the social world has been breaking down.

Finally, Spencer believed that religion arose from the pre-scientific conceptions of men about the empirical facts of their own nature and their environment. It was, in fact, the product of ignorance and error. Religious ideas would, with the progress of knowledge, be replaced by science. This was only a phase of a much wider deification of science. Indeed the interest of the

Spencerian type of social scientist in religion has thus been virtually confined to primitive man—the question was, how has science developed out of primitive religion? In this field, too, there is increasing skepticism of the Spencerian view.

It has been possible above to cite views on only a few questions. It is, however, enough to indicate that a basic revolution in empirical interpretations of some of the most important social problems has been going on. Linear evolutionism has been slipping and cyclical theories have been appearing on the horizon. Various kinds of individualism have been under increasingly heavy fire. In their place have been appearing socialistic, collectivistic, organic theories of all sorts. The role of reason and the status of scientific knowledge as an element of action have been attacked again and again. We have been overwhelmed by a flood of anti-intellectualistic theories of human nature and behavior, again of many different varieties. A revolution of such magnitude in the prevailing empirical interpretations of human society is hardly to be found occurring within the short space of a generation, unless one goes back to about the sixteenth century. What is to account for it?

It is, of course, very probable that this change is in considerable part simply an ideological reflection of certain basic social changes. This thesis would raise a problem, the answer to which would be difficult to find in terms of Spencerian thought. But to deal adequately with this problem would far transcend the limits of this study.

It is no less probable that a considerable part has been played by an "immanent"[1] development within the body of social theory and knowledge of empirical fact itself. This is the working hypothesis on which the present study has been made. The attempt will be made to trace and evaluate the significance of one particular phase of this process of development which can be discerned and analyzed in detail in the work of a limited group of writers in the social field, mostly known as sociologists. But before entering upon this enterprise it is necessary to make a few preliminary methodological remarks about the nature of a "body of social theory and knowledge of empirical fact." What are the main relations of the principal elements in it to each other, and in

---

[1] A term often used by Professor P. A. Sorokin of Harvard University in a sense which seems to me essentially the same as my present meaning.

what sense and by what kind of process may such a "body" be thought to be undergoing a process of development? Only then can it be stated explicitly what kind of study is here proposed and what order of results may reasonably be expected from it.

THEORY AND EMPIRICAL FACT

In the following discussion some fundamental methodological propositions will be laid down without any attempt to give them a critical foundation. It will, however, turn out that the question of the status of these views will form one main element of the subject matter of the whole study. Their soundness is to be judged not in terms of the arguments brought forward in their defense in the present introductory discussion but in terms of the way they fit into the structure of the study as a whole and its outcome.

There is, more often implicit than explicit, a deep-rooted view that the progress of scientific knowledge consists essentially in the cumulative piling up of "discoveries" of "fact." Knowledge is held to be an entirely quantitative affair. The one important thing is to have observed what had not been observed before. Theory, according to this view, would consist only in generalization from known facts, in the sense of what general statements the known body of fact would justify. Development of theory would consist entirely in the process of modification of these general statements to take account of new discoveries of fact. Above all, the process of discovery of fact is held to be essentially independent of the existing body of "theory," to be the result of some such impulse as "idle curiosity."[1]

It is evident that such terms as "fact" are much in need of definition. This will come later. At the present juncture against the view just roughly sketched may be set another, namely, that scientific "theory"—most generally defined as a body of logically interrelated "general concepts" of empirical reference—is not only a dependent but an independent variable in the development of science. It goes without saying that a theory to be sound must fit the facts but it does not follow that the facts alone, discovered independently of theory, determine what the theory is to be, nor that theory is not a factor in determining what facts will be discovered, what is to be the direction of interest of scientific investigation.

[1] A term used by Veblen.

Not only is theory an independent variable in the development of science, but the body of theory in a given field at a given time constitutes to a greater or less degree an integrated "system." That is, the general propositions (which may be, as will be seen later, of different kinds) which constitute a body of theory have mutual logical relations to each other. Not, of course, that all the rest are deducible from any one—that would confine theory to the one proposition—but in the sense that any substantive change in the statement of one important proposition of the system has logical consequences for the statement of the others. Another way of putting this is to say that any system of theory has a determinate logical structure.

Now obviously the propositions of the system have reference to matters of empirical fact; if they did not, they could have no claim to be called scientific. Indeed, if the term fact is properly interpreted it may be said that a theoretical proposition, if it has a place in science at all, is either itself a statement of fact or a statement of a mode of relations between facts. It follows that any *important* change in our knowledge of fact in the field in question must of itself change the statement of at least one of the propositions of the theoretical system and, through the logical consequences of this change, that of other propositions to a greater or lesser degree. This is to say, the structure of the theoretical system is changed. All this seems to be in accord with the empiricist methodology sketched above.

But, in the first place, it will be noted that the word "important" used above was italicized. What does an important change in our knowledge of fact mean in this[1] context? Not that the new facts are vaguely "interesting," that they satisfy "idle curiosity," or that they demonstrate the goodness of God. But the *scientific* importance of a change in knowledge of fact consists precisely in its having consequences for a system of theory. A scientifically unimportant discovery is one which, however true and however interesting for other reasons, has no consequences for a system of theory with which scientists in that field are concerned. Conversely, even the most trivial observation from any other point of view—a very small deviation of the observed from the calculated position of a star, for instance—may be not only impor-

---

[1] Of course there may be many other reasons beside scientific ones, why men are interested in facts.

tant but of revolutionary importance, if its logical consequences for the structure of theory are far-reaching. It is probably safe to say that all the changes of factual knowledge which have led to the relativity theory, resulting in a very great theoretical development, are completely trivial from any point of view except their relevance to the structure of a theoretical system. They have not, for instance, affected in any way the practice of engineering or navigation.[1]

This matter of the importance of facts is, however, only one part of the picture. A theoretical system does not merely state facts which have been observed and their logically deducible relations to other facts which have also been observed. In so far as such a theory is empirically correct it will also tell us what empirical facts it should be possible to observe in a given set of circumstances. It is the most elementary rule of scientific integrity that the formulator of a theoretical proposition must take into account all the relevant *known facts* accessible to him. The process of verification, fundamental to science, does not consist merely in reconsideration of this applicability to known facts by others than the original formulator of the theory, and then simply waiting for new facts to turn up. It consists in deliberately investigating phenomena with the expectations derived from the theory in mind and seeing whether or not the facts actually found agree -with these expectations.

This investigation is one of situations which have been studied either never at all before or not with these particular theoretical problems in mind. Where possible the situations to be investigated are experimentally produced and controlled. But this is a matter of practical technique, not of logic.

In so far as the expectations from the theory agree with the facts found, making allowance for "errors of observation," etc., the theory is "verified." But the significance of the process of verification is by no means confined to this. If this does not happen, as is often so, either the facts may be found to disagree with the theoretical expectations, or other facts may be found which have no place in the theoretical system. Either result necessitates critical reconsideration of the system itself. There is,

---

[1] Conversely, many discoveries of crucial practical importance have been scientifically quite unimportant. In the popular reporting of the results of scientific research it is generally nonscientific importance which is stressed.

then, a reciprocal process: direction, by the expectations derived from a system of theory, toward fields of factual investigation, then reaction of the results of this investigation on the theory.

Finally, verification in this sense is not the only important relation of a theoretical system to the direction of empirical investigation. Not only are specific theoretical propositions which have been directly formulated with definite matters of fact in view subject to verification. But further, a theoretical system built up upon observations of fact will be found, as its implications are progressively worked out, to have logical consequences for fields of fact with which its original formulators were not directly concerned. If certain things in one field are true, then other things in another, related field must also be true. These implications also are subject to verification, which in this case takes the form of finding out what are the facts in this field. The results of this investigation may have the same kind of reaction on the theoretical system itself.

Thus, in general, in the first instance, the direction of interest in empirical fact will be canalized by the logical structure of the theoretical system. The importance of certain problems concerning the facts will be inherent in the structure of the system. Empirical interest will be in the facts so far as they are relevant to the solution of these problems. Theory not only formulates what we know[1] but also tells us what we want to know, that is, the questions to which an answer is needed. Moreover, the structure of a theoretical system tells us what alternatives are open in the possible answers to a given question. If observed facts of undoubted accuracy will not fit any of the alternatives it leaves open, the system itself is in need of reconstruction.

A further point is of importance in the present connection. Not only do theoretical propositions stand in logical interrelations to each other so that they may be said to constitute "systems" but it is in the nature of the case that theoretical systems should attempt to become "logically closed." That is, a system starts with a group of interrelated propositions which involve reference to empirical observations within the logical framework of the propositions in question. Each of these propositions has logical implications. The system becomes logically closed when each of the logical implications which can be derived from any one

[1] In one particular aspect.

proposition within the system finds its statement in another proposition in the same system. It may be repeated that this does not mean that all the other propositions must be logically derivable from any one—on the contrary, if this were true scientific theory would be sheer tautology.

The simplest way to see the meaning of the concept of a closed system in this sense is to consider the example of a system of simultaneous equations. Such a system is determinate, *i.e.*, closed, when there are as many independent equations as there are independent variables. If there are four equations and only three variables, and no one of the equations is derivable from the others by algebraic manipulation then there is another variable missing. Put in general logical terms: the propositions stated in the four equations logically involve an assumption which is not stated in the definitions of the three variables.

The importance of this is clear. If the explicit propositions of a system do not constitute a logically closed system in this sense it may be inferred that the arguments invoked rest for their logical cogency on one or more unstated assumptions. It is one of the prime functions of logical criticism of theoretical systems to apply this criterion and, if gaps are found, to uncover the implicit assumptions. But though all theory tends to develop logically closed systems in this sense it is dangerous to confuse this with the "empirical" closure of a system. To this issue, that of "empiricism," it will be necessary often to return.

The implications of these considerations justify the statement that all empirically verifiable knowledge—even the common-sense knowledge of everyday life—involves implicitly, if not explicitly, systematic theory in this sense. The importance of this statement lies in the fact that certain persons who write on social subjects vehemently deny it. They say they state merely facts and let them "speak for themselves." But the fact a person denies that he is theorizing is no reason for taking him at his word and failing to investigate what implicit theory is involved in his statements. This is important since "empiricism" in this sense has been a very common methodological position in the social sciences.[1]

---

[1] Marshall made a very apt statement apropos of this point: "The most reckless and treacherous of all theorists is he who professes to let facts and figures speak for themselves." *Memorials of Alfred Marshall*, ed. by A. C. Pigou, p. 108.

From all this it follows what the general character of the problem of the development of a body of scientific knowledge is, in so far as it depends on elements internal to science itself. It is that of increasing knowledge of empirical fact, intimately combined with changing interpretations of this body of fact—hence changing general statements about it—and, not least, a changing structure of the theoretical system. Special emphasis should be laid on this intimate interrelation of general statements about empirical fact with the logical elements and structure of theoretical systems.

In one of its main aspects the present study may be regarded as an attempt to verify empirically this view of the nature of science and its development in the social field. It takes the form of the thesis that intimately associated with the revolution in empirical interpretations of society sketched above there has in fact occurred an equally radical change in the structure of theoretical systems. The hypothesis may be put forward, to be tested by the subsequent investigation, that this development has been in large part a matter of the reciprocal interaction of new factual insights and knowledge on the one hand with changes in the theoretical system on the other. Neither is the "cause" of the other. Both are in a state of close mutual interdependence.

This verification is here attempted in monographic form. The central focus of attention is in the process of development of one coherent theoretical system, that to be denoted as the *voluntaristic theory of action*, and the definition of the general concepts of which this theory is composed. In the historical aspect the primary interest is in the process of transition from one phase of its development to another, distinctly different, one. Of the first phase Spencer may be regarded as a late, and in some points extreme, but nevertheless a typical representative. For convenience of reference and for no other purpose this has been designated as the "positivistic" system of the theory of action, and its variant, which is most important to the present study, the "utilitarian." Both these terms are used in technical senses in this work and they will be defined in the next chapter, where the main logical structure of the positivistic system is outlined.

It is, however, a striking fact that what is in all essential respects the same system may be found emerging by a similar process of transition from the background of a radically different theoretical tradition which may be designated as the "idealistic." One dominant case of this latter transition, the work of Max Weber, will be dealt with at length. It goes without saying that this convergence, if it can be demonstrated, is a very strong argument for the view that *correct observation and interpretation of the facts* constitute at least one major element in the explanation of why this particular theoretical system has developed at all.

As has been said, interest will be focused in the process of emergence of a particular theoretical system, that of the "voluntaristic theory of action." But the above considerations indicate the great importance of dealing with this in the closest connection with the empirical aspects of the work of the men whose theories are to be treated. So for each major thinker at least a fair sample of the major empirical views he held will be presented, and the attempt made to show in detail the relations of these to the theoretical system in question. In each case the thesis will be maintained that an adequate understanding of how these empirical views were arrived at is impossible without reference to the logical structure and relations of the theoretical concepts employed by the writer in question. And in every case except that of Marshall[1] the attempt will be made to demonstrate that the conspicuous *change in his empirical views* from those current in the tradition with which the writer in question was most closely associated cannot be understood without reference to the corresponding *change in the structure of his theoretical system* from that dominant in the tradition in question. If this can be demonstrated it will have important general implications. It will be strong evidence that he who would arrive at important empirical conclusions transcending common sense cannot afford to neglect considerations of systematic theory.

The choice of writers to be treated here has been dictated by a variety of considerations. The central interest of the study is in the development of a particular coherent theoretical system, as an example of the general process of "immanent" development of science itself. This process has been defined as a matter of the logical exigencies of theoretical systems in close mutual interrela-

---

[1] This is because Marshall failed to think through the implications of his own empirical and theoretical departures from the prevailing system for the logical structure of the system as a whole and, hence, its empirical implications.

tion with observations of empirical fact and general statements embodying these facts. Hence a choice of authors is indicated which will serve to isolate these elements as far as possible from others, such as influence of the general "climate of opinion," irrelevant to the purposes of this study.

The first criterion is actual concern with the theory of action. Among those who are satisfactory in this respect it is desirable to have represented as great a diversity of intellectual tradition, social milieu and personal character as possible. The inclusion of Marshall is justified by the fact that economic theory and the question of its status involve a crucial set of problems in relation to the theory of action in general and to the positivistic system, especially its utilitarian variant.

This question is as will be seen, the most important single link between utilitarian positivism and the later phase of the theory of action. Pareto also was deeply concerned with the same set of problems, but in relation to distinctly different aspects of the positivistic tradition, and in the midst of a strikingly different climate of opinion. The comparison of the two is most instructive.

Durkheim's starting point was also positivistic, indeed by far the most explicitly so of the three. But it was the variant of the positivistic system most radically foreign to that of utilitarian individualism[1] in which Marshall was primarily immersed, and Pareto also, though to a less extent. In personal character and background more violent contrasts are scarcely imaginable than between Marshall, the strongly moralistic middle-class Englishman; Durkheim, the Alsatian Jewish, radical, anticlerical, French professor; Pareto, the aloof, sophisticated Italian nobleman; and, finally, Weber, a son of the most highly cultured German upper middle class, who grew up on the background of German idealism and was trained in the historical schools of jurisprudence and economics. These intellectual influences were of no real importance in the formation of the thought of any of the other three. Moreover, Weber's personal character was radically different from any of the other three.

Another point strongly in favor of this choice is that although all four of these men were approximately contemporary, there is with one exception not a trace of direct influence of any one on any other. Pareto was certainly influenced by Marshall in the

[1] What I have called "sociologistic" positivism. See Chap. IX.

formulation of his technical economic theory, but with equal
certainty not in any respect relevant to this discussion. And this
is the only possibility of any direct mutual influence. In fact,
within the broad cultural unit, Western and Central Europe at the
end of the nineteenth and beginning of the twentieth century,
it would scarcely be possible to choose four men who had important ideas in common who were less likely to have been influenced
in developing this common body of ideas by factors other than the
immanent development of the logic of theoretical systems in relation to empirical fact.[1]

Certain other considerations are relevant. The main concern
of the study is with the outline of a theoretical system. Its minor
variations from writer to writer are not a matter of concern to
this analysis. It is, however, necessary to work out its logical
structure and ramifications in the clearest form attainable.
Hence the choice has been made of intensive analysis from the
relevant point of view of the work of a small number of the most
eminent men. Marshall was, by many in his field, thought to be
the most eminent economist of his generation. But the interest
of the present study in him is more limited than in the others.
The other three are all generally known as sociologists. There can
be little question of their eminence in their generation in their
field. A list of the first six sociologists of the last generation which
failed to include all three names could hardly be taken seriously.[2]
This is not to say they are the only equally eminent ones, but for
the purposes of this study they are distinctly the most suitable.

In order to avoid all possibility of misunderstanding, it should
be reiterated: This study is meant to be a monographic study of
one particular problem in the history of recent social thought,
that of the emergence of the theoretical system which has been
called the "voluntaristic theory of action." It follows that there
are a number of related things which this study is not and is not
meant to be. In the first place it is not a history of sociological
theory in Europe in, roughly, the last generation. It deliberately

---

[1] In so far as there is such an influence which can be understood in terms
of *Wissenssoziologie* it practically has to be common to the whole of Western
civilization.   *Wissenssoziologie* is a term much used in Germany recently,
referring to the discipline which investigates the social factors in the development of "ideas."

[2] Professor Sorokin, asked in a gathering of eminent social scientists for
his opinion of who had been the most important recent sociologists, gave
these three names and only these.

avoids the inclusiveness with regard both to problems and to men which such a task would require. If there is anything at all in its results, it follows that the process under investigation is one element of the history of European sociological theory in that period. Then this study will constitute a monographic contribution to this history, but that is all.

In the second place, it is not a general secondary interpretation of the work of any or all of the men dealt with. Its aim is neither secondary exposition as such nor critical evaluation of them.[1] With respect to each of the theorists the aspects which this study treats are of great, sometimes of central, importance to their work as a whole. But in the treatment of none will the attempt be made to evaluate this importance relatively to that of other aspects. That must be left to other studies. Finally, in harmony with all this, there has been no attempt to discuss all aspects of the work of these men or all the secondary literature about them. Practically all the existing secondary literature about them has been read, but has been cited only where it seemed particularly relevant to the immediate context. Failure to cite is not to be interpreted as implied criticism, only lack of important bearing.[2] Also, with the texts themselves, encyclopedic completeness has not been aspired to. Nor has every passage that could be construed as relevant to the purpose in hand been cited but only enough, taken in terms of the structure of the writers' theories as a whole, to establish the points at issue.[3]

Perhaps one more word with reference to interpretation may be permitted. This study is conceived to be an organic whole, concerned with ideas which are logically interrelated and permeate the whole study. The reader should keep this in mind in weighing whatever critical remarks he may be inclined to make. Particularly in a study of this character, it is legitimate to ask that a fact cited or a statement made be taken not only in its immediate intrinsic character and meaning but also in relation to the total structure of which it forms a part.

[1] What it contains of both, which is considerable, is to be regarded as a means to an end, not the end itself.

[2] Where more than one work was "good" only the "best" for my purpose has been cited.

[3] Hence omissions are not relevant unless they definitely affect one of these points.

Residual Categories

Two or three further preliminary questions should be taken up so as not to leave the reader in doubt on some matters that are bound to arise in his mind. In the first place, one further conclusion about the character of scientific development follows from the position already taken. It is possible to have scattered and unintegrated bits of knowledge, and to assent to the "truth" of further scattered bits as they are called to one's attention. This type of knowledge does not, however, constitute "science" in the sense in which this study is interested in it.

The latter is present only in so far as these bits of knowledge have become integrated with reference to fairly clear-cut theoretical systems.[1] In so far as this has happened, two things can be said. It is at least unlikely that such a system should play an important part in canalizing the thought of a considerable number of highly intelligent men over a period of time, if it were not that the propositions of the system involved empirical references to phenomena which were real and, within the framework of the conceptual scheme, on the whole correctly observed.

At the same time the structure of the conceptual scheme itself inevitably focuses interest on a limited range of such empirical facts. These may be thought of as a "spot" in the vast encircling darkness, brightly illuminated as by a searchlight. The point is, what lies outside the spot is not really "seen" until the searchlight moves, and then only what lies within the area into which its beam is newly cast. Even though any number of facts may be "known" outside this center, they are not scientifically important until they can be brought into relation with a theoretical system.

This fact is of the greatest importance as a canon of interpretation. In studying a man's empirical work the questions asked will not merely be, what opinions did he hold about certain concrete phenomena, nor even, what has he in general contributed to our

---

[1] Much empirical knowledge which is scientifically valid is thus not science in this sense because its integration involves other centers of reference than systematic theory. Thus, much of the practical "lore" of everyday life is integrated about practical needs and interests. The facts thus non-scientifically known are capable of integration in terms of theoretical systems in so far as they are really validly known.

"knowledge" of these phenomena? The primary questions will, rather, be, what theoretical reasons did he have for being interested in these particular problems rather than others, and what did the results of his investigation contribute to the solution of his theoretical problems? Then, in turn, what did the insights gained from these investigations contribute to the restatement of his theoretical problems and through this to the revision of his theoretical system? Thus, in connection with Durkheim the real point of interest is not in his having established the fact that the suicide rate in the French army was, during a certain period, considerably higher than in the civil population. Those interested in this fact for its own sake can consult his study. The present interest is, rather, why did Durkheim study suicide anyway, and what is the significance for his general theory of this and the other facts he established in the course of his investigation of it?

Something should also be said about the general character of the process by which this awakening of new scientific interest in fields of fact proceeds, and theoretical problems shift. Every system, including both its theoretical propositions and its main relevant empirical insights, may be visualized as an illuminated spot enveloped by darkness. The logical name for the darkness is, in general, "residual categories." Their role may be deduced from the inherent necessity of a system to become logically closed. On whatever level it operates,[1] a theoretical system must involve the positive definition of certain empirically identifiable variables or other general categories. The very fact that they are defined at all implies that they are distinguished from others and that the facts which constitute their empirical reference are thereby, in certain aspects at least, specifically differentiated from others.

If, as is almost always the case, not all the actually observable facts of the field, or those which have been observed, fit into the sharply, positively defined categories, they tend to be given one or more blanket names which refer to categories negatively defined, that is, of facts known to exist, which are even more or less adequately described, but are defined theoretically by their failure to fit into the positively defined categories of the system. The only theoretically significant statements that can be made

[1] Some possible distinctions will be indicated at the end of the present chapter.

about these facts are negative statements—they are *not* so and so.[1] But it is not to be inferred that because these statements are negative they are therefore unimportant.

It is true that in the work of the mediocre proponents of a theoretical system the qualifications of their empirical deductions from theory which are necessitated by the existence of these residual categories are often ignored, or so vaguely stated as to be virtually meaningless. In the case of the dogmatists of the system their existence, or at least their importance for the system, may even be vehemently denied. Both procedures are vastly encouraged by an empiricist methodology. But in the work of the ablest and most clear-headed proponents of a system these residual categories will often be not merely implicit but explicit, and will be quite clearly stated. In this sense, the best place to go to find the starting points of the breakdown of a system is to the work of the ablest proponents of the system itself. This more than any other reason is the explanation of why the work of so many of the greatest scientific theorists is "difficult." Only the lesser lights can bring themselves to dogmatize about the exclusive importance and adequacy of their own positively defined categories.[2]

It follows from this that the surest symptom of impending change in a theoretical system is increasingly general interest in such residual categories.[3] Indeed, one kind of progress of theoretical work consists precisely in the carving out from residual categories of definite positively defined concepts and their verification in empirical investigation. The obviously unattainable, but asymptotically approached goal of the development of

[1] Perhaps the best single case this study will encounter of the role of a residual category in a theoretical system is that of Pareto's "nonlogical action." The fact that it is a residual category is the key to the understanding of his whole theoretical scheme.

[2] There are excellent illustrations of this in the history of the classical economics. Ricardo, undoubtedly by far the greatest theorist of them all, saw most clearly the limitations of his own theoretical system. His qualifications were promptly forgotten by such epigoni as McCulloch. Ricardo's work is correspondingly full of such residual categories as "the habits and customs of a people."

[3] In so far as it has had any unity at all the so-called anti-intellectualist movement can be defined residually, by the common contrast of its diverse tendencies to "rationalism." The same is true of "institutionalism" in American economics.

scientific theory is, then, the elimination of all residual categories from science in favor of positively defined, empirically verifiable concepts. For any one system there will, to be sure, always be residual categories of fact, but they will be translatable into positive categories of one or more other systems.[1] For the empirical application of any one system these residual elements will be found to be involved in the necessary data.

The process of the carving out of positive concepts from residual categories is also a process by which the reconstruction of theoretical systems is accomplished as a result of which they may eventually be altered beyond all recognition. But this should be said: The original empirical insights associated with the positive categories of the original system will be restated in different form, but unless they entirely fail to stand up to the combined criticism of theory and renewed empirical verification, they will *not* be eliminated. Indeed, as has been noted above, this is unlikely to happen. This fact is the essential basis for the justification of talk of the "progress" of science. Theoretical systems change. There is not merely a quantitative accumulation of "knowledge of fact" but a qualitative change in the structure of theoretical systems. But in so far as verification has been valid and sound, this change leaves behind it a permanent precipitate of valid empirical knowledge. The form of statement may well change, but the substance will remain. The older statement will generally take the form of a "special case" of the new.

The utilitarian branch of positivistic thought has, by virtue of the structure of its theoretical system, been focused upon a given range of definite empirical insights and related theoretical problems. The central fact—a fact beyond all question—is that in certain aspects and to certain degrees, under certain conditions, human action is rational. That is, men adapt themselves to the conditions in which they are placed and adapt means to their ends in such a way as to approach the most efficient manner of achieving these ends. And the relations of these means and conditions to the achievement of their ends are "known" to be intrinsically verifiable by the methods of empirical science.

Of course this statement contains a considerable number of terms which have been, and still are, ambiguous in general usage. Their definition is one of the prime tasks of the study as a whole.

[1] This issue will be explicitly discussed in the final chapter.

This range of factual insight and the theoretical problems involved in it, and this alone, is the theme of the first analysis. The task of the first two parts of the study is to trace its development from one well-defined theoretical system to another. The process has been essentially that just sketched, a process of focusing attention on, and carving positive theoretical concepts out of, the residual categories to be found in the various versions of the initial system.

Perhaps it is permissible to state here, or to repeat in a somewhat different form, a vital canon of interpretation for a study of this kind. It is in the nature of the enterprise that many facts and theoretical considerations that are important from any one of a large number of different possible points of view will have been neglected. A specific criterion has just been laid down of what scientific "importance" is considered to mean, and the remarks just made serve further to elucidate the meaning of this criterion. If a critic is to charge neglect of the importance of such things, he should be able to show either (a) that the neglected consideration bears specifically on the limited range of theoretical problems to which this study has been deliberately limited and that its correct consideration would significantly alter the conclusions about them or (b) that the whole conception of the nature of science and its development here advanced is so fundamentally wrong that these criteria of importance are inapplicable.[1]

THEORY, METHODOLOGY AND PHILOSOPHY

Out of these considerations grows directly another range of problems which must be commented upon briefly. It will be asked

[1] In general, pains have been taken to state legitimate lines of criticism as explicitly as possible because it is my experience, particularly in dealing with the secondary literature on these writers, that it is extraordinarily difficult for an idea or ideas which do not fit the requirements of the prevailing "system" or systems to be understood at all even by very intelligent people. These writers are persistently criticized in terms utterly inapplicable to them. The fates both of Durkheim's proposition "Society is a reality *sui generis*," which is still predominantly held to be merely an unusable "metaphysical postulate" (it started precisely as a residual category), and of Weber's theory of the relations of Protestantism and capitalism are conspicuous examples. Recent discussions of Pareto's work occasioned by the appearance of the English translation do not serve to increase optimism on this point. See the symposium of articles in *Journal of Social Philosophy*, October, 1935, and compare with the treatment in Chaps. V–VII.

whether a study of this character will find it possible to confine itself to "science" or will not find it necessary to embark upon the perilous waters of philosophy. Such a venture will, indeed, prove necessary at certain points and it is hence advisable to make a general statement of the relevant relations of these two kinds of discipline to each other and to the kind of study here attempted. Like the other statements in this chapter it will be brief and without critical foundation.

The main outline of a view of the general character of empirical science has already been presented. The distinction of science from all the philosophical disciplines is vital. It will turn out to be so at every stage of the ensuing study. But this is *not* to be taken to mean that the two kinds of discipline are without significant mutual interrelations and that each can afford to ignore the other. For the purposes of this study—not necessarily for others—it is legitimate to define philosophy as a residual category. It is the attempt to achieve a rational cognitive understanding of human experience by methods other than those of empirical science.

That there are important mutual relations of philosophy and science, once the distinction between them is established, is a simple deduction from the most general nature of reason itself. The tendency of theoretical systems in science to become logically closed is a special case. The general principle is that it is in the nature of reason to strive for a rationally consistent account of all experience which comes within its range at all. In so far as both philosophical and scientific propositions are brought to the attention of the same mind, there is in the nature of the case, a tendency to bring them into relations of logical consistency with one another. It likewise follows that there are no logically watertight compartments in human experience. Rational knowledge is a single organic whole.

The methodological principles already laid down yield a canon for use in this context as well as others. Since the present concern is with the character and development of certain specific theoretical systems in science, and the interest in these systems is scientific, philosophical questions will be treated only when they become important to these systems in the sense strictly defined. Discussion will be deliberately limited to important philosophical questions in this specific sense. But equally there will be no attempt to avoid them on the plea that they *are* philosophical or "metaphysical" and hence have no place in a scientific study. This is often a facile way of evading the clear decision of vital but embarrassing issues.

It is important briefly to indicate a few of the main ways in which philosophical questions will be found to impinge upon the problems of this study. In the first place, while scientific knowledge is not the only significant cognitive relation of man to his experience, it is a genuine and valid one. This means that the two sets of disciplines stand in a relation of mutually corrective criticism. In particular, the evidence gained from scientific sources, observation of fact and the theoretical consequences of these facts constitutes, in so far as it is sound, valid ground for criticism of philosophical views.

If, then, scientific evidence which there is reason to believe is correct and has a bearing on important problems, is in conflict with philosophical views explicitly or implicitly involved in the works studied, this will be taken as an indication of the necessity to inquire into the basis of these views on a philosophical level. The object will be to discover whether the philosophical grounds for them are so cogent as to leave no alternative but to revise the earlier impression of the validity of what purported to be scientific evidence. A number of instances of such conflicts will be encountered where philosophical ideas do conflict with crucially important and relevant empirical evidence. However, in none of these has it been possible to discover sufficiently cogent philosophical grounds for discarding this evidence.[1]

But this necessity of criticizing philosophical positions from a scientific point of view is not the only important relation of the two sets of disciplines. Every system of scientific theory involves by implication philosophical consequences, both positive and negative. This is nothing more than a corollary of the rational unity of cognitive experience. Then it is also true that every system of scientific theory involves philosophical assumptions.[2]

[1] Perhaps the most conspicuous case is the implication of a rigidly positivistic philosophy (in our sense) that "ends" cannot be real (not epiphenomenal) causal elements of action. This will be discussed at length.

[2] It may be well to note that these two terms denote two aspects of the same phenomenon. The two sets of systems, philosophy and science, are logically interdependent. Reasoning from the scientific we arrive at philosophical *implications*. But since these are not verifiable by empirical obser-

These may lie in a number of different directions. But the ones to which special attention should be called now are the "methodological." That is, the questions of the grounds of empirical validity of scientific propositions, the kinds of procedures which may on general grounds be expected to yield valid knowledge, etc., impinge directly on the philosophical fields of logic and epistemology.[1]

Indeed it is scarcely too much to say that the main preoccupation of modern epistemology from, approximately, Locke on has been with precisely this question of the philosophical grounds for the validity of the propositions of empirical science. Since all through the study questions of validity will be of pressing importance, discussions of their philosophical aspects cannot safely be neglected. This is important especially in one context. A group of methodological views will be encountered which, again for convenience of reference and that purpose alone, have been brought together under the term "empiricism." The common characteristic of them is the *identification* of the meanings of the concrete specific propositions of a given science, theoretical or empirical, with the scientifically knowable totality of the external reality to which they refer. They maintain, that is, that there is an immediate correspondence between *concrete* experienceable reality and scientific propositions, and only in so far as this exists can there be valid knowledge. In other words, they deny the legitimacy of theoretical abstraction. It should already be evident that any such view is fundamentally incompatible with the view of the nature and status of theoretical systems which is a main foundation of this whole study. Hence discussion of the philosophical grounds advanced to support it cannot be avoided.

It is in this sense of the borderline field between science on the one hand, logic and epistemology on the other, that the term "methodology" as used in this work should be understood. Its reference is thus not primarily to "methods" of empirical research such as statistics, case study, interview and the like. These latter it is preferable to call research techniques. Method-

---

vation they remain, from the point of view of the scientific system, *assumptions.*

[1] See the discussion of the scope of methodology in A. von Schelting, *Max Weber's Wissenschaftslehre*, Sec. I.

ology is the consideration of the general[1] grounds for the validity
of scientific propositions and systems of them. It is as such
neither a strictly scientific nor a strictly philosophical discipline.
It is, of course, a field where these systems are subjected to
philosophical criticism touching the grounds of their validity,
but equally it is a field where philosophical arguments advanced
for or against the validity of such propositions are subject to
criticism in the light of the evidence from science itself. While
philosophy has implications for science it is not any less true that
science has implications for philosophy.

The following example will illustrate what is meant. Prior to
Kant the epistemological question was generally put, what
philosophical grounds do we have for believing that we have valid
empirical knowledge of the external world? Kant reversed this by
stating first: It is a fact that we have such valid knowledge. And
only then he asked, How is this possible? While Kant's answer
may not be wholly acceptable, his way of putting the question
was of revolutionary importance. It is a fact, as well established as
any in empirical experience.[2] The existence and implications of
this fact must form a principal starting point for any philosophical consideration of the grounds of validity of science.

In this context three different levels of considerations may be
distinguished. In the first instance, there is scientific theory
proper. Its status has already been discussed at some length.
Its direct concern is only with the specific empirical facts, and
the logical implications of the propositions embodying these
facts for other propositions involving other facts. Theory proper,
then, is confined to the formulation and logical interrelations of
propositions containing empirical facts in direct relation to the
observation of the facts and thus empirical verification of the
propositions.

Methodological considerations enter in when we go behind this
to inquire whether the procedures by which this observation and
verification have been carried out—including the formulation of
propositions and the concepts involved in them, and the modes of

[1] As opposed to the particular grounds involved in the specific facts of the
field of science in question.

[2] If it were not a fact there could be no action in the sense in which it is
the subject of this study. That is, the whole "action" schema would have
to be discarded from scientific use.

drawing conclusions from them—are *legitimate*. We ask whether on general grounds, apart from the specific facts involved, such a procedure can lead to valid results, or our impression of their validity is illusory. The testing of scientific theory on this level is the task of methodology. This, finally, will lead over into philosophical considerations. For among[1] the grounds, real or alleged, for believing or disbelieving in the validity of a scientific procedure, there will be some of a philosophical order, which must be philosophically considered. Thus the three sets of considerations are closely interdependent. But it is none the less important to keep them *logically distinct*.[2]

Two main contexts should be noted briefly in which of necessity concern with methodological questions in the above sense will arise. One is the field of questions of the general grounds of validity of the theories of empirical science in the sense in which the term has been used here, irrespective of the particular class or kind of empirical facts involved. Any theory which claims scientific status is, of course, legitimately subject to critical analysis in these terms. On the other hand, there are those methodological questions which arise in connection with judging the validity of propositions about particular kinds of empirical facts and the particular kind of theoretical systems involved in these propositions *as distinguished from others*. Failure to distinguish adequately these two orders of methodological questions has been the source of much unnecessary confusion and misunderstanding.

[1] Note, not the sole grounds.

[2] It is one of the commonest but most serious of fallacies to think that *inter*dependence implies absence of *in*dependence. No two entities *can* be interdependent which are not at the same time independent in certain respects. That is, in general terms, all independent variables are, by virtue of the fact that they are variables in a system, interdependent with other variables. Independence in the sense of complete lack of interdependence would reduce the relations of two variables to sheer chance, incapable of formulation in terms of any logically determinate function. A dependent variable is, on the other hand, one which stands in a *fixed* relation to another such that, if the value of x (an independent variable) is known, that of y (the dependent variable) can be deduced from it with the aid of the formula stating their relation, and without the aid of any other empirical data. In a system of interdependent variables, on the other hand, the value of any one variable is not completely determined unless those of all the others are known.

The empirical subject matter with which this study is concerned is that of human action in society. A few of the main characteristics peculiar to this subject matter which raise methodological problems may be noted. It is a fact, however it may be interpreted, that men assign subjective motives to their actions. If asked why they do a given thing, they will reply with a reference to a "motive." It is a fact that they manifest the subjective feelings, ideas, motives, associated with their actions by means of linguistic symbols as well as in other ways. It is, finally, a fact that both in action and in science when certain classes of concrete phenomena are encountered, such as black ink marks on sheets of paper, they are interpreted as "symbols" having "meanings."

These facts and others like them are those which raise the central methodological problems peculiar to the sciences concerned with human action. There is a "subjective aspect" of human action. It is manifested by linguistic symbols to which meaning is attached. This subjective aspect involves the reasons we ourselves assign for acting as we do. No science concerned with human action can, if it would penetrate beyond a superficial level, evade the methodological problems of the relevance of facts of this order to the scientific explanation of the other facts of human action.[1] This study will be intensively concerned with them.

There is another, related point at which philosophical problems are closely relevant to the problems of the sciences concerned with human action in a sense in which they are not related to the natural sciences. It is also a fact beyond dispute that men entertain and express philosophical, *i.e.*, nonscientific "ideas."[2] This fact also raises basic problems for the sciences of human action. For it is, further, a fact that men subjectively associate these ideas in the closest way with the motives they assign to their actions. It is important to know what relation the fact that men entertain such ideas, and that in any specific case the ideas are what they are, bears to the equally definite facts that they act, or have acted, as they do. This will constitute one of the central substantive problems of the whole study.

There is one further aspect of the relation to philosophy which should be mentioned. It is a corollary of the immanent tendency

---

[1] Often referred to as the facts of "behavior."

[2] Nonscientific ideas will be called philosophical only in so far as they contain existential rather than imperative propositions.

of reason to a rational integration of experience as a whole, that a scientist as well as other men may be presumed to have philosophical ideas and that these will stand in determinate reciprocal relations to his scientific theories. Indeed, since eminence in scientific theory implies a high level of intellectual ability, this is more likely to be true of scientists than of most men. It is clear that the *Weltanschauung* and the scientific theories of an eminent scientist cannot be radically dissociated. But this is no reason to believe there is not an immanent process of the development of science itself,[1] and it is this that is the focus of interest here. Above all the motivation of the scientist in entering on his studies will not be treated except in so far as it is determined by the structure of the theoretical system itself with which he works. Back of this, to be sure, lie in part philosophical and other reasons for his being interested in the system at all. Consideration of these would be essential to a complete account of the development of his scientific theories. But the present task is not to arrive at an account which is complete, only at one involving the limitations which have been stated. This other would be a phase of *Wissenssoziologie* and as such falls outside the scope of this study.

Of course what has been said implies that there are points where the personal philosophical views of the men to be studied impinge upon the present field of interest. This is where they become important to the theoretical system under consideration. In so far as this is true they must be taken up not because they are "interesting" or "pernicious" or anything else as philosophical views, nor because they throw light on their holders' general motivations, but because of their relevance to the particular theoretical problems at the time under discussion. Only in this context will they be considered at all.

TYPES OF CONCEPTS

Thus far theory and theoretical systems have been spoken of in general terms as though there were no important distinctions between different kinds of theory and theoretically relevant

[1] That is, the interdependence of the two does not imply the absence of independent elements.

concepts. It is not wise to attempt to proceed with the main task without some consideration of different types of theoretical concepts and their different kinds of relation to the empirical elements of scientific knowledge. The following discussion will only outline in a preliminary, tentative way the principal forms of concept of direct significance for this study.

It is fundamental that there is no empirical knowledge which is not in some sense and to some degree conceptually formed. All talk of "pure sense data," "raw experience" or the unformed stream of consciousness is not descriptive of actual experience, but a matter of methodological abstraction, legitimate and important for certain purposes but, nevertheless, abstraction. In other words, in Professor Henderson's phrase,[1] all empirical observation is "in terms of a conceptual scheme." This is true not only of sophisticated scientific observation but of the simplest common-sense statements of fact. Conceptual schemes in this sense are inherent in the structure of language and, as anyone thoroughly familiar with more than one language knows, they differ in important respects from one language to another.

But of these conceptual schemes in so far as they are important here, three main types may be distinguished. It follows from the considerations just put forward that description of the facts involves a conceptual scheme in this sense. It is not merely a reproduction of external reality but a selective ordering of it. When scientific observation begins to transcend common sense and becomes to a degree methodologically sophisticated, there emerge explicit schemata which may be called descriptive frames of reference. These may be of greatly varying degrees of generality of application and perhaps differ in other respects. No attempt will be made to analyze them exhaustively here. They are modes of general relations of the facts implicit in the descriptive terms employed.

The spatiotemporal framework of the classical mechanics is such a schema. Thus a fact to be relevant to the theory must be described as referring to a body or bodies which can be located in space and time relatively to other bodies. A similar schema in the social sciences is that of supply and demand in economics. A fact to be relevant to (orthodox) economic theory must, in

[1] See L. J. HENDERSON, "An Approximate Definition of Fact," *University of California Studies in Philosophy*, 1932.

an analogous way, be capable of location in terms of supply and demand. It must be capable of interpretation as in some way qualifying a good or service for which there is a demand, and which is in some degree scarce, relatively to the demand for it.

It must be made clear that mere location in terms of such a schema does not by itself explain anything. But it is an indispensable preliminary to explanation. The statement that a physical body at a given time and place has a given property, say a particular velocity, does not explain why it has this velocity. That implies reference both to its other properties at this and previous times and to the properties of other bodies. The same is true of an economic fact, such as that the closing price of wheat (of a given grade) in the Chicago market was $1.25 a bushel on a given day. Above all, it does not even imply that its full explanation is possible in terms of any one theoretical system, mechanics or economic theory. For example, the velocity of a man falling off a bridge, as he is about to strike the water is a physical fact. But if the person in question is a suicide it is certainly not proved by the statement of the fact that all the antecedents of which this velocity is a consequence can be explained in terms of the theory of mechanics. Similarly, if there has been a great rise in the price of wheat in the first few days of a war, there is no proof that this fact, though it is indeed an economic fact, that is, a fact relevant to the descriptive and analytical schemata of economics, can be satisfactorily explained in terms of the factors formulated in economic theory.[1]

When this is pointed out with reference to a concrete example it seems obvious. But failure to see and to take account of it is what lies at the basis of many deep-rooted errors, especially in social science. It is the fallacy which Professor Whitehead has so beautifully exposed under the name of the "fallacy of misplaced concreteness."[2] This raises methodological issues which will be of fundamental importance throughout the later discussion.

It has already been indicated that such frames of reference may be of varying scope. It is above all to be emphasized that the same empirical facts may, according to the scientific purpose in view, be stated in terms of more than one such schema which are related to each other not only in the sense that one is a

---

[1] On the economic case, see especially Chap. IV.
[2] See A. N. Whitehead, *Science and the Modern World*, p. 75.

narrower, special case of another but by cutting across each other. It is a great service of Professor Znaniecki[1] to have pointed out that essentially the same facts about "man in society" may be stated in any one of four[2] different schemata of this character, which he calls "social action," "social relationships," "social groups" and "social personality." As far as the present interest goes the terms are practically self-explanatory. It may be noted though that the schema of social personality relates not to "psychology" but to the concrete individual, as a member of society, belonging to groups and in social relationships to others. The primary basis in this study will be the schema of action, with concrete individuals thought of as adapting means to ends. Under any one of these there may be of course a number of subschemata. Supply and demand is to be considered as a subschema of action.[3]

Descriptive frames of reference in this sense are fundamental to all science. But by no means do they exhaust scientific conceptualization. Facts cannot be described except within such a schema. But their description within it has, in the first instance, the function of defining a "phenomenon" which is to be explained. That is, of the great mass of possible empirical observations we select those which are at the same time meaningful within such a schema and "belong together." They thus serve together to characterize the essential aspects of a concrete phenomenon, which then becomes the object of scientific interest. This is what Max Weber calls a "historical individual."[4] It is particularly to be noted that this is not a simple case of reflection of external reality, but of its conceptualization in relation to a particular direction of scientific interest.

Only when such an object is given do the next problems of conceptual formulation—those associated with "explanation," in a proper sense—arise. But here two fundamental lines of procedure open out instead of one. The distinction between them is vital.

We start with the fact that a defined object of scientific interest is given, that is it is described in terms of one or more frames of

[1] Florian Znaniecki, *The Method of Sociology*, Chap. IV.

[2] This classification may or may not be exhaustive. It is not a matter for present concern.

[3] The reasons will become evident later on. See especially Chaps. IV and VI.

[4] See vol. II, Chap. XVI.

reference as stated. Theoretical explanation demands that it shall be broken down into simpler elements which shall serve as the units of one or more theoretical systems in terms of which it is to be explained. Now this breaking down may proceed not in one, but in at least *two* logically distinct directions.

On the one hand, we may break the concrete object down into parts or units. On the physical and biological levels it is easy enough to see what is meant by them. A steam engine consists of cylinders, pistons, driving rods, boilers, valves, etc. Similarly an organism is composed of cells, tissues, organs. A part in this sense is a unit, the concrete existence of which, aside from its relation to other parts of the same whole, is meaningful, "makes sense." A machine can actually be taken apart. An organism cannot be taken apart in the same sense, at least without permanently destroying its function, but a dead organism may be dissected and its parts thus identified. These two examples have in common the spatial reference, the parts are entities which can as such be located in space relative to each other.

But this is not the essential point. The same order of analysis is possible where the parts are not, as such, spatially existent, because spatial coordinates are not inherent in the frame of reference concerned. Not to speak of any other examples, a complex of actions can be analyzed into parts, such as rational acts and irrational acts, or religious acts and secular acts and the like. The test question is always whether we can conceive such an act as existing "by itself," that is as a "pure type" without involving the other types from which it is concretely distinguished. The fact that most actual concrete cases are "mixed types" is of no importance just now. Thus we can well conceive meeting a purely "Nordic" man (however the type may be defined) and need not assume a priori that he *by definition* has Mediterranean or any other non-Nordic blood.

The principal difficulty of dealing with "part" or "type" concepts of this kind arises from one circumstance. It is that the concrete entities with which science has to deal possess in varying degrees a property generally called the "organic." That is, the whole which is made up of the parts in question may to a greater or less extent be an organic whole. At one pole or extreme is the "mechanistic" case, is where all the important "properties" of the concretely functioning parts can be defined independently of their relations to the other parts or to the whole. Above all, it is the case where the part can, in fact, be concretely separated from these relations and still remain "the same." Thus we can take a steam engine apart and actually examine its pistons, record their size, shape, tensile strength, etc. We can do the same for the other parts and, provided our observations are accurate, from these observations calculate how they will operate when put together; for instance we can calculate the efficiency of the engine.

Now precisely in so far as a whole is organic[1] this becomes impossible. The very definition of an organic whole is as one within which the relations determine the properties of its parts. The properties of the whole are not simply a resultant of the latter. This is true whether it be an organism or some other unit, such as a "mind," a "society" or what not. And in so far as this is true, the concept "part" takes on an abstract, indeed a "fictional" character. For the part of an organic whole is no longer the same, once it is separated factually or conceptually from the whole. Perhaps the classic statement of this point is that of Aristotle, that a hand separated from the living body is no longer a hand "except in an equivocal sense, as we would speak of a stone hand."[2]

---

[1] The works of Professor Whitehead contain the most extensive analysis of the general concept of the "organic" which is known to the author.

[2] *Politics*, trans. by B. Jowett, Book I, p. 4. This Aristotelian formula is not by itself satisfactory. It is true that the "part" of an organic whole abstracted from its relations to the rest is an abstraction, thus is comparable to the functioning part only "in an equivocal sense." But it does not follow that in no sense are the relations between the parts important in a mechanistic system. A machine is not a machine, it does not work, unless the parts are in the proper relations to each other.

The difference can be put more precisely by reference to the concept, to be developed below (see especially Chap. XIX) of the "emergent properties" of organic systems. In the organic field descriptions of concrete systems arrived at only by what will be called the "direct generalization" of the properties of units are indeterminate as applied to the concrete reality. The gap is filled by taking account of the emergent properties of the systems, properties which are empirically found to vary in value independently of the "elementary properties." It is impossible to attempt in this introductory discussion satisfactorily to clear up these complexities. This note is introduced merely to show a recognition that the problem of the nature of the organic is complex and that the formulation in the text is to be regarded as a rough approximation which serves the purpose of calling the reader's attention to the importance of the problem in the context of this study.

But whether the concept refers to a mechanistic "part" which can be observed without essential change of properties in complete concrete separation from the whole in which it occurs, or to an organic part which when concretely separated remains a part only in an "equivocal sense," the *logical* character of the concept remains the same. It refers to an, actually or hypothetically, existent concrete entity. However much the concept of the "pure type," especially in the "organic" case, may differ from anything concretely observable, the test is that thinking of it as concretely existent makes sense, that is does not involve a contradiction in terms.[1]

The concept of any particular physical body or system of such bodies in mechanics is of this character. This is true even if it is fictional, as are a "perfect" gas, a "frictionless" machine, etc. So are the chemical elements, even though some of them are never found in nature uncombined with other elements. So also are such concepts as a "perfectly rational act," a "perfectly integrated group," etc. The scientific legitimacy, indeed the indispensability, of such concepts is not to be questioned. Without them there could be no science.

Moreover, such concepts are not restricted in their use to their definition and empirical identification as "really" parts of a single concrete phenomenon. Rather this is always the first step of scientific generalization—for such parts may be identified as common to a plurality of different concrete phenomena. Furthermore, on occasion, a great deal can be said about the behavior of these parts under certain kinds of definable circumstances. Such judgments may yield a kind of generalization which is of high explanatory value, and, within limits, perfectly valid. General statements about the possible or probable behavior of such concrete or hypothetically concrete "parts" of concrete phenomena, or various combinations of them, under given typical circumstances will be referred to as "empirical generalizations."[2]

---

[1] This is one of Max Weber's principal criteria of the "ideal type," that it should be "objectively possible" (see vol. II, Chap. XVI).

[2] In this sense the "part" which is made the "ultimate" unit of analysis is in a sense arbitrary. There is no inherent logical limit to the possible divisibility of phenomena into more and more "elementary" units. But precisely in so far as the phenomena are "organic," the more elementary the unit the more "abstract" or "empty" its concept becomes. A limit to the

What should be insisted upon is the radical *logical* distinction between these two kinds of concepts, "type-parts" and "empirical generalizations," and another kind which may, in a strict sense, be called "analytical" concepts. This kind of conceptualization really presupposes the first. For whatever concrete or hypothetically concrete units or parts a complex concrete phenomenon may be broken down into, once these units are established they will of logical necessity have general attributes or qualities.

Any particular concrete or hypothetically concrete phenomenon or unit must be thought of not as a property in this sense, but as capable of description in terms of a particular combination of the particular "values" of these general properties. Thus a physical body is described as having a certain particular mass, velocity, location, etc. in the respects relevant to the theory of mechanics. Similarly an act may be described as having a certain degree of rationality, of disinterestedness, etc. *It is these general attributes of concrete phenomena relevant within the framework of a given descriptive frame of reference, and certain combinations of them, to which the term "analytical elements" will be applied.*

Such analytical elements need not be thought of as capable of concrete, even hypothetical, existence apart from other analytical elements of the same logical system. We may say that such and such a body *has* a mass of x, but not that it *is* a mass. We may also say that such and such an act is rational (to a certain degree) but never that it *is* rationality, in the sense of a concrete thing. There are, concretely, rational acts only in the same logical sense that there are heavy bodies. Above all the distinction between type-parts and analytical elements has nothing to do with the relative degree of "organicity" of the phenomena to which they refer.[1] Where these are organic both concepts involve "abstraction" but for different reasons. The "part" of an organic whole is an abstraction because it cannot be observed existing *in concreto* apart from its relations to the whole. An analytical element, on the other hand, is an abstraction because it refers to a general

---

useful prosecution of this type of analysis does seem to be set by the relations of this kind of concept to the other two. This issue will be taken up in the final chapter.

[1] Nor with the difference between the physical and the social sciences so often correlated with the problems of the organic.

property while what we actually observe is only its particular "value" in the particular case. We can observe that a given body has a given mass, but we never observe "mass" as such. Mass is, in the terminology of logic, a "universal." Similarly we can observe that a given act has a high degree of rationality, but never can we observe "rationality" as such.[1]

[1] In order to forestall any possible confusion over these crucially important concepts the following explicit definitions may be given:

1. A unit in a concrete system is the entity which constitutes the common reference of a combination of statements of fact made within a frame of reference in such a way that the combination may, for purposes of the theoretical system in question, be considered an adequate description of an entity which, within the frame of reference, conceivably exists independently The theoretical unit is the specific combination of logical universals in specific logical relations to each other into which these statements of fact are fitted.

2. An analytical element is any universal (or combination of universals) of which the corresponding values (or combination of values) may be stated as facts which in part determine a class of concrete phenomena. "Determine" here means that a change in these values within the framework of the same universal(s) involves a corresponding change in the concrete phenomena in respects important to the theoretical system.

The distinction between unit and element is in the first instance a logical-operational distinction. Any fact or combination of facts may constitute the "value" of an element so long as this element is treated as a variable, that is, so long as the question is asked whether or not a given change in this value would alter the concrete phenomenon and how. Such values may or may not be adequately descriptive of concrete or hypothetically concrete units or combinations of them. Most elements of developed analytical systems, such as mass, velocity, are only partially descriptive of concrete entities. But where the two types of concept overlap in empirical reference, it is often convenient to speak of structural parts or units as "elements" though it takes more than one fact to describe them adequately. Thus an end, or a norm or a given condition of the situation may be an element. Confusion is likely to arise only when it is assumed that, since some elements are at the same time potentially concrete entities, all elements must be so.

There is one further possible source of confusion in this field against which warning should be given. Those features of organic systems which are emergent at any given level of the complexity of systems cannot, by definition, exist concretely apart from the relevant combinations of the more elementary units of the systems. They cannot be isolated, even conceptually, from these more elementary units in the sense of being thought of as existing independently. Hence where structural analysis must describe organic systems these emergent properties or relations of units must be included. It may or may not be expedient in any given case to employ these emergent properties also as variables. They have in common with elements such as mass the fact that the conception of "existing by themselves" is non-

It is the universal experience of science that such analytical elements, once clearly defined, will be found to have certain uniform modes of relation to each other which hold independently of any one particular set of their values.[1] These uniform modes of relationship between the values of analytical elements will be referred to as "analytical laws." Whether or not they are expressible in numerical terms is of secondary importance for present purposes. In the example from the field of action in so far as a system of action is rational, regardless of the value or degree of its rationality, it conforms to certain laws, *e.g.*, it tends to "maximize utility."

It is analytical elements in this sense which are the variables of the physical sciences. But both the term "variable" and the dominant type used in the physical sciences are apt to cause a misunderstanding regarding the relation of quantitative and qualitative aspects. In one sense, perhaps, the "ideal type" of variable is that of mass or distance, which is a property of bodies or their relations that is not only observable but measurable. That is, the only observations which may be called observations of mass may be arranged along a single quantitative scale in terms of the variation of a constant and definite unit. Where measurement is impossible, as with what are sometimes called nonmetrical variables, it is often still possible to arrange all relevant particular observations on a single scale of order of magnitude in such a way that of any two it is possible to say which is the greater and which the smaller. In addition to this, measurement involves the exact location of the observation relative to others by determining the interval between each pair in a way directly comparable quantitatively with the interval between any other pair. Thus in nonmetrical terms it is possible to say that one glass of water is warmer than another, which in metrical terms may become a difference of 10 degrees centigrade.

As applied to genuine variables of systems of broad scope, measurement is almost nonexistent in the social field, while even

---

sensical. But it depends on the exigencies of the particular theoretical system and its problems whether the same concepts find a place both in the structural and in the analytical aspects of the theoretical system.

[1] That is, these elements though independently variable are indirectly interdependent. The reference is to their uniform modes of interdependence in a system.

nonmetrical quantitative determination of order of magnitude is rare. Fortunately the logical requirements of theoretical systems permit a still further departure from the ideal type of a simple measurable variable.

It is a methodological requirement that the facts which enter into a scientific theory should be capable of determination with a degree of precision adequate for the theoretical purposes of the system. In recent years it has through Professor Bridgman's influence[1] become common to state this requirement in the form that the facts should be obtained by a clearly definable "operation." Both measurement and arrangement in order of magnitude are types of such operations, but these two categories do not exhaust the roster of scientifically acceptable operations. In addition, there are those by which observations are made which, though having in common the fact that they result from the "same" operation, are still not capable of arrangement on a single scale of order of magnitude. This means that, if order is to be introduced into such facts, it must be in terms of some kind of classification more complex than a single range of variation. But so long as the observations are the result of the same kind of operation, that is, so long as they are the concrete instances of the same general category or universal in this sense, it is permissible to treat them all as "values" of the same element. This is notably true, as will be shown, of Pareto's most famous category, the "residues," which cannot be measured, but which are arrived at by a definite operation and reduced to order by means of a rather complex classification, into which a still further complexity will be introduced as a result of the analysis of this study.[2]

It will probably be generally agreed that for the sake of simplicity and precision of results it is highly desirable that the elements of a theoretical system should be, like mass and distance, capable of precise measurement on a unitary scale. Then the question arises why some sciences, like the social, must put up with elements like Pareto's residues. The answer lies in the character of the facts which, it has been pointed out, are a matter of the concrete phenomena, on the one hand, in their relations to

[1] P. W. BRIDGMAN, *The Logic of Modern Physics.*

[2] Hence an "element" is the general concept corresponding to any particular fact or facts which may by operational observation be predicated of a phenomenon.

the conceptual scheme, on the other. This study is dealing with a particular theoretical system in a particular phase of its development. It is not asked whether other, radically different theoretical systems are possible as means of understanding the phenomena of human behavior in society. But given this theoretical system in the form in which it existed at the time when it is here taken up, certain problems regarding the facts are inherent in the structure of the system, such as the rationality or, as Pareto says, the "logicality" of action. The scheme can only be of empirical significance so far as it is possible to devise observational operations in terms of which these problems can be answered. It is simply a fact that the majority of the operations which the writers treated here have employed yield data the qualitative heterogeneity of which cannot be reduced to a single quantitative scale of variation and still fit the conceptual scheme employed. It is by no means impossible that in the course of the future development of the system much more quantification, or even possibly measurement, will prove possible.[1] But the fact that so little is as yet possible does not mean that no scientific results of any importance have been achieved. Scientific truth is not an all-or-none proposition, but a matter of successive approximation. What we have is of very substantial validity and importance even though it is very far from scientific perfection.

A "theoretical system" for purposes of this study will be held to include all three types of concepts discussed above. They are so closely interdependent that there is never a system of analytical elements without a corresponding frame of reference and a conception of the structure of the concrete systems to which it applies as made up of certain kinds of units or parts. But studies of theoretical systems may differ in the relative emphasis they lay on these three kinds of concepts. This, like any other study, must involve all three, but its central focus of interest will be in one,

---

[1] It seems to be safe to say that almost all true measurement in the social field is on a statistical level which it has so far been exceedingly difficult to integrate directly with analytical theory in the way the measurements of physics are integrated. What is measured is the resultants of a considerable number of elements, as selected in terms of the theories extant. The nearest approach to the physical science situation is, perhaps, the attempts in economics to formulate statistical demand-and-supply functions. But even here there are serious difficulties in the way of fitting available statistical facts to the definitions of elements in the theory.

the "part" or unit concept. Its interest will be in the units and their structural interrelations out of which concrete systems of action are made up. These concrete systems are all phenomena that are capable of description in terms of the action frame of reference. Analytical elements will be treated at various points, but no attempt will be made to work out systematically the definitions and interrelations of the analytical elements involved in such concrete systems of action.

The treatment of the parts or units of systems of action falls naturally under two headings, the definition and classification of the elementary units and the determination of the relevant relations of the units in systems. The latter may, for present purposes, be designated as structural relations. The main framework of the present study may, then, be considered an analysis of the structural aspect of systems of action, in a certain sense their "anatomy." It is well to call attention to the fact that in relation to the same concrete phenomena it is possible to carry structural analysis to many different levels. The mutual relations of the four schemata mentioned above[1] are primarily those of different levels on which "social structure" is described. Of these four, at any rate, the one of interest here, that of "action," may be regarded as the most elementary. The following is thus not an analysis of social structure in all possible terms, but only so far as it can be couched in terms of the action schema. Hence the title "The Structure of Social Action."

Though all structures must be regarded as capable of analysis in terms of a plurality of analytical elements, and hence the two types of analysis are closely related, it does not follow that only one choice of elements is possible in the analysis of a given concrete structure, once the latter has been adequately described. On the contrary, it is a well-established fact that various such choices are likely to be possible. If more than one work, it is, of course, true that they will turn out to be related. But this very possibility of different choices of elements explains why it is not advisable to attempt to jump directly from an outline of the structure of action systems to a system of elements. It is on the former, not the latter, level that the writers treated here converge almost explicitly upon a single system. But in their various works the way in which this system is described varies so widely that it is

[1] *Supra*, p. 30.

not possible to reduce, without a long and difficult analysis, the analytical elements to terms of a single system. Indeed this would be exceedingly arduous since only in Pareto is a system of elements explicit at all.

There is only one further introductory point needing comment. This is not and does not aspire to be a definitive work, even within the restricted scope which it has set itself. It is one of the most important corollaries of the view of the nature of science here put forward that science cannot, without external pressures, be a static thing, but is inherently involved in a dynamic process of development. Hence every publication of results, if it goes beyond matters of fact of a character which cannot have implications for the structure of theory, is, in a sense, an arbitrary fixation of a given point in this process.

A study, the objective of which is to determine whether Caesar was or was not murdered on March 15, 44 B.C., may well come to a definitive result because the fact, one way or the other, when once established, will fit into almost any conceptual scheme. This is not true of a study like the present one. Like every scientific study it can, if sound, hope to leave a permanently valid "precipitate" but cannot claim to have attained the final conceptual scheme in terms of which this precipitate may best be formulated and related to other facts.

An earnest warning is given against such premature claims to finality. The author has been more or less intensively concerned with the major works of the men treated in this study over periods ranging from six to ten years. After considerable periods of occupation in other fields, he has come back to intensive reconsideration of their works. Every time this reconsideration brought to light fundamentally important things about them which had been missed before. The most important points, for the purposes of this study, were not understood at the first reading, but generally only after repeated reconsideration.

The explanation of this fact seems to be that thinking on these matters had in the meantime been undergoing a process of development. Although the significant points had been read and, in one sense, "understood," they were not on earlier readings "important" in the sense in which they have since become because at first it was not possible to relate them to a theoretical system and the problems growing out of it. As there is no reason to believe that this process of development of thought has suddenly stopped,[1] the only justification for publishing the results of such a study at this or any other time is the conviction that the process has reached a point where the results to date, while not definitive, are well enough integrated to be significant.

The god of science is, indeed, Evolution. But for those who pay their obeisance in a true scientific spirit, the fact that science evolves beyond the points they have themselves attained is not to be interpreted as a betrayal of them. It is the fulfillment of their own highest hopes.

NOTE ON THE CONCEPT "FACT"

To forestall a very common source of confusion it is well at the outset to note the sense in which the term "fact" is to be employed. Adapting Professor Henderson's definition,[2] in this study a fact is understood to be an "empirically verifiable statement about phenomena in terms of a conceptual scheme." At present the questions as to the sources of evidence for such statements and whether it is legitimate to include such a phrase as Professor Henderson's "receptor experiences" will not be raised. In various connections these questions will come up later in the study. At present, however, it is necessary to point out only one distinction which has a significant bearing on the question of scientific abstraction. In the above definition a fact was referred to as "an empirically verifiable *statement* about phenomena." The point is that a fact is not itself a phenomenon at all, but a proposition *about* one or more phenomena. All scientific theories are made up of facts and of statements of relations between facts in this sense. But this does not in the least imply that the facts included in any one theory are the only verifiable propositions that can be made about the phenomena to which they refer. A system of scientific theory is generally abstract precisely because the facts it embodies do not constitute a complete description of the concrete phenomena involved but are stated "in terms of a conceptual scheme," that is, they embody only the facts about the phenomena which are *important* to the theoretical system that is being employed at the time. The distinction between a fact, which is a *proposition about* phenomena, and the phenomena themselves, which are concrete, really existent entities, will, if kept clearly in mind, avoid a great deal of confusion. The terms will be employed in these senses throughout the present study.

It follows from the above considerations that no phenomenon is ever a "fact" unless one is speaking in an elliptical sense. In general, a concrete phenomenon can only be described adequately for purposes even of a single theo-

---

[1] Indeed the result of critical reconsideration of various parts of the study, stimulated by the friendly criticisms of colleagues, has, since this sentence was first drafted, strongly confirmed the statement. The process has continued and will doubtless do so in the future.

[2] L. J. HENDERSON, *op. cit.*

retical system by stating a number of facts which are logically independent. Just what order of statements and how many is a question which is relative both to the empirical character of the phenomenon being studied, and to the theoretical system in terms of which it is being analyzed. For the purposes of any conceptual scheme there is an "adequate" description, the determination of a sufficient number of *important* facts. This falls, in general, far short of all the facts that it is possible to know about such a phenomenon. Even when we say "we do not know enough facts" to justify a given conclusion, we do not mean quantitatively that we cannot make a sufficient *number* of verifiable statements about the phenomenon but rather that we are not in a position to make certain *important* statements which are logically required as premises for the conclusion. What facts are important is determined by the structure of the theoretical system.

Chapter II

THE THEORY OF ACTION

It has already been stated that the aim of this study is to follow in detail a process of fundamental change in the structure of a single theoretical system in the social sciences. The remainder of Part I will be devoted to outlining the basic features of the system, in terms in which it is legitimate to speak of its continuity throughout the process, outlining the logical structure of the initial version or related group of versions with which this process starts and, finally, sketching the history of the system in Western European social thought to the point at which intensive analysis of it will begin in Part II.

For convenience of reference this conceptual scheme will be called the theory of action. The continuity referred to above consists in the retention, during the whole development, of a basic conceptual pattern which, however much its use and setting may vary with different stages of the process, is maintained in certain essentials unchanged throughout.

The Unit of Action Systems

In the first chapter attention was called to the fact that in the process of scientific conceptualization concrete phenomena come to be divided into units or parts. The first salient feature of the conceptual scheme to be dealt with lies in the character of the units which it employs in making this division. The basic unit may be called the "unit act." Just as the units of a mechanical system in the classical sense, particles, can be defined only in terms of their properties, mass, velocity, location in space, direction of motion, etc., so the units of action systems also have certain basic properties without which it is not possible to conceive of the unit as "existing." Thus, to continue the analogy, the conception of a unit of matter which has mass but which cannot be located in space is, in terms of the classical mechanics, nonsensical. It should be noted that the sense in which the unit act

43

is here spoken of as an existent entity is not that of concrete spatiality or otherwise separate existence, but of conceivability as a unit in terms of a frame of reference. There must be a minimum number of descriptive terms applied to it, a minimum number of facts ascertainable about it, before it can be spoken of at all as a unit in a system.

In this sense then, an "act" involves logically the following: (1) It implies an agent, an "actor." (2) For purposes of definition the act must have an "end," a future state of affairs toward which the process of action is oriented.[1] (3) It must be initiated in a "situation" of which the trends of development differ in one or more important respects from the state of affairs to which the action is oriented, the end. This situation is in turn analyzable into two elements: those over which the actor has no control, that is which he cannot alter, or prevent from being altered, in conformity with his end, and those over which he has such control.[2] The former may be termed the "conditions" of action, the latter the "means." Finally (4) there is inherent in the conception of this unit, in its analytical uses, a certain mode of relationship between these elements. That is, in the choice of alternative means to the end, in so far as the situation allows alternatives, there is a "normative[3] orientation" of action. Within the area of control of the actor, the means employed cannot, in general, be conceived either as chosen at random or as dependent exclusively on the conditions of action, but must in some sense be subject to the influence of an independent, determinate selective factor, a

[1] In this sense and this only, the schema of action is inherently teleological.

[2] It is especially to be noted that the reference here is not to concrete things in the situation. The situation constitutes conditions of action as opposed to means *in so far as it is not subject to the control of the actor*. Practically all concrete things in the situation are part conditions, part means. Thus in common-sense terms an automobile is a means of transportation from one place to another. But the ordinary person cannot make an automobile. Having, however, the degree and kind of control over it which its mechanical features and our property system lend, he can use it to transport himself from Cambridge to New York. Having the automobile and assuming the existence of roads, the availability of gasoline supply, etc., he has a degree of control of where and when the automobile shall go and, hence, of his own movements. It is in this sense than an automobile constitutes a means for the analytical purposes of the theory of action.

[3] For a definition and short discussion of the term normative as used in this study see Note A at the end of this chapter.

knowledge of which is necessary to the understanding of the concrete course of action. What is essential to the concept of action is that there should be a normative orientation, not that this should be of any particular type. As will be seen, the discrimination of various possible modes of normative orientation is one of the most important questions with which this study will be confronted. But before entering into the definition of any of them a few of the major implications of the basic conceptual scheme must be outlined.

The first important implication is that an act is always a process in time. The time category is basic to the scheme. The concept end always implies a future reference, to a state which is either not yet in existence, and which would not come into existence if something were not done about it by the actor or, if already existent, would not remain unchanged.[1] This process, seen primarily in terms of its relation to ends, is variously called "attainment," "realization," and "achievement."

Second, the fact of a range of choice open to the actor with reference both to ends and to means, in combination with the

---

[1] While the phenomena of action are inherently temporal, that is, involve processes in time, they are not in the same sense spatial. That is to say, *relations in space* are not as such relevant to systems of action analytically considered. For the analytical purposes of this theory, acts are not primarily but only secondarily located in space. Or to put it somewhat differently, spatial relations constitute only conditions, and so far as they are controllable, means of action. This gives a sense in which the schema of action is always and necessarily abstract. For it is safe to say that there is no empirical phenomenon, no thing or event, known to human experience, which is not in one aspect physical in the sense of being capable of location in space. There is certainly no empirical "self" known which is not an "aspect of" or "associated with" a living biological organism. Hence the events of action are always concretely events in space, "happenings to," physical bodies or involving them. Thus, in one sense, there is no concrete act to which the category of space is inapplicable. But at the same time that category is irrelevant to the theory of action, regarded as an analytical system, which of course implies that the "action" aspect of concrete phenomena never exhausts them. The facts which the theory of action embodies are never "all the facts" about the phenomena in question. On the other hand, there certainly are many concrete phenomena which so far as they are objects of scientific study are exhausted by the "physical," nonaction aspect, such as stones and celestial bodies. This "involvement" of action in the physical world must apparently be taken as one of the ultimates of our experience.

concept of a normative orientation of action, implies the possibility of "error," of the failure to attain ends or to make the "right" choice of means. The various meanings of error and the various factors to which it may be attributed will form one of the major themes to be discussed.

Third, the frame of reference of the schema is subjective in a particular sense. That is, it deals with phenomena, with things and events *as they appear from the point of view of the actor* whose action is being analyzed and considered. Of course the phenomena of the "external world" play a major part in the influencing of action. But in so far as they can be utilized by this particular theoretical scheme, they must be reducible to terms which are subjective in this particular sense. This fact is of cardinal importance in understanding some of the peculiarities of the theoretical structures under consideration here. The same fact introduces a further complication which must be continually kept in mind. It may be said that all empirical science is concerned with the understanding of the phenomena of the external world. Then the facts of action are, to the scientist who studies them, facts of the external world—in this sense, objective facts. That is, the symbolic reference of the propositions the scientist calls facts is to phenomena "external"[1] to the scientist, not to the content of his own mind. But in this particular case, unlike that of the physical sciences, the phenomena being studied have a scientifically relevant subjective aspect. That is, while the social scientist is not concerned with studying the content of his own mind, he is very much concerned with that of the minds of the persons whose action he studies. This necessitates the distinction of the objective and subjective points of view. The distinction and the relation of the two to each other are of great importance. By "objective" in this context will always be meant "from the point of view of the scientific observer of action" and by "subjective," "from the point of view of the actor."

A still further consequence follows from the "subjectivity" of the categories of the theory of action. When a biologist or a behavioristic psychologist studies a human being it is as an organism, a spatially distinguishable separate unit in the world.

---

[1] Epistemologically, not spatially "external." The external world is not "outside" the knowing subject in a spatial sense. The subject-object relation is not a relation in space.

The unit of reference which we are considering as the actor is not this organism but an "ego" or "self." The principal importance of this consideration is that the body of the actor forms, for him, just as much part of the situation of action as does the "external environment." Among the conditions to which his action is subject are those relating to his own body, while among the most important of the means at his disposal are the "powers" of his own body and, of course, his "mind." The analytical distinction between actor and situation quite definitely cannot be identified with the distinction in the biological sciences between organism and environment. It is not a question of distinctions of concrete "things," for the organism is a real unit.[1] It is rather a matter of the analysis required by the categories of empirically useful theoretical systems.

A fourth implication of the schema of action should be noted. Certainly the situation of action includes parts of what is called in common-sense terms the physical environment and the biological organism—to mention only two points. With equal certainty these elements of the situation of action are capable of analysis in terms of the physical and biological sciences, and the phenomena in question are subject to analysis in terms of the units in use in those sciences. Thus a bridge may, with perfect truth, be said to consist of atoms of iron, a small amount of carbon, etc., and their constituent electrons, protons, neutrons and the like. Must the student of action, then, become a physicist, chemist, biologist in order to understand his subject? In a sense this is true, but for purposes of the theory of action it is not necessary or desirable to carry such analyses as far as science in general is capable of doing. A limit is set by the frame of reference with which the student of action is working. That is, he is interested in phenomena with an aspect not reducible to action terms only in so far as they impinge on the schema of action in a relevant way—in the role of conditions or means. So long as their properties, which are important in this context, can be accurately determined these may be taken as data without further analysis. Above all, atoms, electrons or cells are not to be regarded as units for purposes of the theory of action. Unit

[1] But no more a completely concrete entity than an actor. It includes only those facts about this entity which are relevant to a "biological" frame of reference.

analysis of any phenomenon beyond the point where it constitutes an integral means or condition of action leads over into terms of another theoretical scheme. For the purposes of the theory of action the smallest conceivable concrete unit is the unit act, and while it is in turn analyzable into the elements to which reference has been made—end, means, conditions and guiding norms—further analysis of the phenomena of which these are in turn aspects is relevant to the theory of action only in so far as the units arrived at can be referred to as constituting such elements of a unit act or a system of them.

One further general point about the status of this conceptual scheme must be mentioned before proceeding to the more particular uses of it which will be of interest here. It may be employed on two different levels, which may be denoted as the "concrete" and the "analytical." On the concrete level by a unit act is meant a concrete, actual act and by its "elements" are meant the concrete entities that make it up. Thus by the concrete end is meant the total anticipated future state of affairs, so far as it is relevant to the action frame of reference. For instance, a student may have as his immediate end the writing of a paper on a given subject. Though at the inception of the course of action he will not be in a position to visualize its content in detail (this is true of many concrete ends) he will have a general idea, a forecast of it in general terms. The detailed content will only be worked out in the course of the action. But this visualized product, perhaps being "handed in," is the concrete end. Similarly, concrete means are those things in the situation over which he has an appreciable degree of control, such as books in his possession or in the library, paper, pencil, typewriter, etc. The concrete conditions are those aspects of the situation which he cannot control for the immediate purposes in hand, as the fact that he is limited to books available in his college library, etc. The function of this concrete use of the action schema is primarily descriptive. Facts may be of possible significance to the scientist employing it in so far as they are applicable to entities which have a place in the scheme, to "ends" or other normative elements, "means" or "conditions" of acts or systems of action. But, in this context, it serves only to arrange the data in a certain order, not to subject them to the analysis necessary for their explanation.

For the purpose of explanation a further step in abstraction is generally necessary. It consists in generalizing the conceptual scheme so as to bring out the functional relations involved in the facts already descriptively arranged. The shift can perhaps most clearly be seen by considering that one of the main functions of an analytical as opposed to a concretely descriptive scheme in this context must be to distinguish the role of the normative[1] from that of the non-normative elements of action. The problem is well illustrated by the difficulty one encounters in connection with the concept "end." As so far defined, an end is a concrete anticipated future state of affairs. But it is quite clear that not this total state of affairs but only certain aspects or features of it can be attributed to normative elements, thus to the agency of the actor rather than to features of the situation in which he acts. Thus, to use the previous example, in the process of action leading to the writing of a paper for a course, various aspects of the concrete end cannot be attributed to the agency of the student, such as the fact that there are available given books in the library, and other conditions relevant to the act. An end, then, in the analytical sense must be defined as the *difference* between the anticipated future state of affairs and that which it could have been predicted would ensue from the initial situation *without the agency of the actor having intervened.* Correspondingly, in an analytical sense, means will not refer to concrete things which are "used" in the course of action, but only to those elements and aspects of them which are capable of, and in so far as they are capable of, control[2] by the actor in the pursuit of his end.[3]

[1] Normative here means a teleological element only from the point of view of the actor. It has no ethical connotation for the observer. See Note A, p. 74.

[2] Either alteration or deliberate prevention of an alteration which would otherwise occur.

[3] A particular case of this general distinction is of considerable importance. It has already been noted that the actor is an ego or a self, not an organism, and that his organism is part of the "external world" from the point of view of the subjective categories of the theory of action. In this connection it becomes necessary to keep in mind the difference between two distinctions. On the one hand there is that so commonly used by biologists, between the concrete organism and its concrete environment. Thus in the concrete means to a given course of action it is often necessary or useful to distinguish the concrete powers belonging to the actor, that is the strength of his muscles, the manual skills he may have. from means available in his environment,

A second highly important aspect of the distinction between
the concrete and the analytical use of the action scheme is the
following. The prevalent biological schema of organism and
environment has already been mentioned. While the concrete
action schema cannot be identified with this it is in certain
respects closely analogous to it. That is, a concrete actor is conceived as acting, in the pursuit of concrete ends, in a given concrete situation. But a new logical situation arises when the
attempt is made to generalize about total systems of action in
terms of the functional interrelations of the facts stated about
them. The problem of the discrimination of the roles of normative
and non-normative elements may again serve as an example.
From the point of view of a single concrete actor in a concrete
situation the effects, both present and anticipated, of the actions
of others belong in the situation, and thus may be related to the
action of the individual in question in the role of means and
conditions. But in estimating the role of the normative elements
in the total system of action in which this particular actor constitutes a unit, it would obviously be illegitimate to include these
elements in the situation for the system as a whole. For what are,
to one actor, non-normative means and conditions are explicable
in part, at least, only in terms of the normative elements of the
action of others in the system. This problem of the relation
between the analysis of the action of a particular concrete actor

---

such as tools, etc. But on the analytical level the analogous distinction is
clearly different; it is that between heredity and environment in the sense of
biological theory. It is clear that the concrete organism at any given time is
not the exclusive product of heredity but of the complex interaction of
hereditary and environmental factors. "Heredity," then, becomes a name
for those elements influencing the structure and function of the organism
which can be considered as determined in the constitution of the germ cells
out of whose union the particular organism issues. Equally, in principle, the
concrete environment of a developed organism is not to be considered as the
exclusive product of environmental factors in the analytical sense, for to the
extent that it may be held to have been influenced by the action of organisms
upon it, hereditary factors will have played a part. In considering an organism
such as man, this is obviously a matter of great importance. Since the
biological aspect of man is of such great concrete importance, in dealing with
action it is often very convenient to employ such terms as heredity and
environment. When doing this it is always of extreme importance to keep
clearly in mind which of the two concept-pairs just outlined is applicable
and to draw only the inferences appropriate to the one which is relevant.

in a concrete, partly social environment, and that of a total action system including a plurality of actors will be of cardinal importance to the later discussion. It forms, for instance, one of the principal keys to the understanding of the development of Durkheim's theoretical system.

THE UTILITARIAN SYSTEM

Thus far the discussion has been confined to the most general features of the action scheme of thought. Though the unit act is basic in all the theoretical structures encountered here, it is not surprising that the different possible permutations and combinations on this basis should not have been exhausted in the earlier stages of the process of development of the system as a whole. In fact, by the nineteenth century a subsystem (or, perhaps better, an interrelated group of several sub-subsystems) of the theory of action dominated Western European social thought. It was built essentially out of the kind of units described but put together in a peculiar way which distinguishes it sharply from the emerging system—the principal concern of the present discussion. Since the process of emergence of the later subsystem from the earlier must be traced, it is necessary to give a fairly extensive account of the starting point of the process, so that the nature and extent of the change may become clear.

The origin of the mode of thinking in terms of the action schema in general is so old and so obscure that it is fruitless to inquire into it here. It is sufficient to point out that, just like the schema of the classical physics, it is deeply rooted in the common-sense experience of everyday life, and it is of a range of such experience that it may be regarded as universal to all human beings. Proof of this claim can be found in the fact that the basic elements of the schema are imbedded in the structure of all languages, as in the universal existence of a verb corresponding to the English verb "to do." The peculiarity of the situation with which the analysis begins lies in the fact that for sophisticated thinkers this universal material of common-sense experience has become selectively ordered in a particular way so that a peculiar conceptual structure arises which, in spite of its many variants retains certain common features throughout. The peculiarities of this structure go back to a selective emphasis on certain problems and certain ways of looking at human action.[1]

The first leading characteristic is a certain "atomism." It may be described as the strong tendency to consider mainly the properties of conceptually isolated unit acts and to infer the properties of systems of action only by a process of "direct" generalization from these. That is, only the simplest and most obvious modes of relationship of unit acts in systems—those indispensable to the idea of a system at all—are considered. They must be grouped according to whose acts they are, according to the actor as an aggregate unit. The potential acts of one may be relevant as means and conditions to the situation of action of another, and the like. It is not necessary to seek far for certain of the roots of this tendency. It is but natural that in the early stages of development of a theoretical system its adherents should work with the simplest conceptual scheme which seems adequate. It is only with the accumulation of factual knowledge and the more refined and subtle working out of logical implications and difficulties that the more complex possibilities are brought into consideration. At the stage of development closest to the common-sense level there is generally found an atomistic tendency in scientific theories.

But this natural atomistic tendency has undoubtedly been strongly reinforced by certain peculiar features of the Western European intellectual tradition since the Reformation. In the first place, the opposite, antiatomistic tendency, especially on a relatively unsophisticated analytical level, when applied to total social systems of action, has a way of issuing in organic theories of society which swallow up the individual in a larger whole. This tendency has run counter to a very deep-seated individualism which has, throughout most of Europe[2] held it strongly in check. It is true that the main burden of this individualism has been ethical rather than scientific. It has been a

[1] The following account of possible historical influences on the formation of the utilitarian system of theory is not the result of a systematic study, but is derived from certain general impressions built up relative to the subject. Moreover it is not an integral part of the study but might be omitted without disturbing its logical framework. It is introduced to aid in giving the reader a sense of the empirical relevance of what may appear to be a series of very abstract propositions.

[2] Germany is the principal exception.

concern for the ethical autonomy and responsibility of the individual, especially as against authority. But it must not be forgotten that our current sharp distinction between considerations of fact and of value is a very recent thing, especially in the social field. The great majority of the social thinkers responsible for the development of the ideas under discussion have been at least as much, generally much more, interested in justifying a course of conduct or policy which they considered ethically right, as they have been in an objective understanding of the facts of human action. The two points of view are inextricably intermingled in the history of thought.

Probably the primary source of this individualistic cast of European thought lies in Christianity. In an ethical and religious sense Christianity has always been deeply individualistic. That is, its ultimate concern has been with the welfare, above all in the next world, of the individual immortal soul. All souls have always been for it, as it were, "born free and equal." This sharply marks off all Christian thought from that of classic antiquity prior to the Hellenistic age. The spiritual absorption of the individual in the social unit which was self-evident to a Plato or even an Aristotle is unthinkable on a Christian basis, in spite of all mystical conceptions of the church as a "spiritual body."

In Catholic Christianity, however, this individualistic strain has, in its practical consequences for social thought and conduct, been considerably mitigated by the role of the Catholic Church. The latter has been considered as the universal trustee of the spiritual welfare of individual souls whose access to spiritual life is only through the sacramental dispensations of the church. The whole medieval cast of mind favored ideas of corporate unity and conceived the church as the central form of human life. With the Reformation, however, all this was radically changed. The immediacy of the individual soul to God, inherent in Protestant Christianity, gave a peculiar turn to the problems of social thought in the last age before social thought became predominantly secular in spirit. The combination of the primary ethical valuation of the individual soul and of the elimination of the sacramental church as an intermediary between the individual and God, made the freedom of the individual in the pursuit of his religious welfare and in whatever practical modes of conduct were included as appropriate means to it, a matter of prime importance. Interference with this religious freedom by the Catholic Church, on the one hand, and by secular authority, on the other, was a potential, indeed the principal, religious danger under the conditions of social life of the time. With the rise of national states at the time, it was primarily on the problem of the relation between religious freedom (the necessary condition for realization of the highest Christian values) and political obligation that attention was focused.

Under medieval Catholic conditions this problem of religious freedom naturally focused on the relations of church and state, since the church was universally recognized as authorized to speak for the religious interests of all. But under the new conditions existing after the Reformation it was the freedom of the individual, not of a corporate body, that was at stake. Although all except a few radical sects assumed that there was an objective body of revealed religious truth, no organization had a monopoly on legitimate interpretation and administration of religion. The "true" church was no longer the visible church but the invisible body of the faithful or the elect. The visible church was reduced to the status of a means of enlightenment and the maintenance of external discipline. In the last analysis the individual, and only he, was responsible for his own conduct in the sphere generally acknowledged to be supreme, that of religion. Hence the emphasis was not on the preservation of a tradition of values *common* to the members of the community, even to all Christians, but on the safeguarding of the freedom of conscience of the individual *in his differences* from others, particularly when there were attempts to coerce him into agreement with an organization or an authority. Thus, in so far as there was intensive concern with the ends of human action, particularly the ultimate ends, it was in terms which emphasized their diversity, especially as between one individual and another. This preoccupation contains the germs of what will be called the "utilitarian" mode of thinking.

A further related consequence of the Protestant immediacy of the individual to God was the corresponding devaluation of his attachments to his fellows, above all the tendency to reduce them to impersonal, unsentimental terms and to consider others not so much from the point of view of their value in themselves as of their usefulness, ultimately to the purposes of God, more immediately to his own ends. From this attitude flows a strong bias in favor of the "rationalistic" means-end analysis characteristic of utilitarian thought.

Of course individualism is by no means confined to Christianity or Protestantism, but has independent roots in our cultural heritage. Though it is true that the thought of the classic Greek polis was predominantly organic in a sense opposed to individualism, in later antiquity there emerged schools of thought closely analogous to modern individualism. Christian thought was undoubtedly greatly influenced by Hellenistic philosophy. But in the early modern period in which our modes of social thinking took shape there was certainly an important additional independent classic influence, coming through humanism. Without claiming that it stands alone, reference may be made to what was perhaps the most highly integrated and clearest of these influences, that of the later Roman law, the revival of which was one of the major features of that period.

Roman law shared the conception of the unitary corporate entity of the state which dominated Greek social thought, and hence created great difficulties in the way of finding a legitimate place in the social whole for such a body as the Catholic Church. But in a way unknown to Plato and Aristotle, yet in part influenced by later Greek, especially Stoic, thought, Roman law set over against this unitary state a body of free and independent individuals, who in their private sphere were separate and discrete. And in its later development this aspect, "private" law, came to assume a more and more prominent place.

It is, no doubt, true that among the reasons for the rapid adoption of Roman law by the secular princes of the Reformation period was their recognition of the usefulness of the unitary classic conception of the state as a weapon against the corporate entities within their own society with which they were in conflict, particularly the feudal corporations and the church. But in the peculiar religious situation which then existed, the other side of the rigid dualism of Roman law, the conception of a society of free and independent, "unincorporated" individuals could not but be highly influential. The more political authority asserted itself against corporate privileges the more, in turn, the rights of individuals were asserted against authority and the more the discreteness and separateness of these individual units was built into the basis of thought. The way in which these two independent sources of individualism became coordinated and dovetailed is very striking.

The general effect of the individualistic elements of the European cultural tradition so far as they concern the present discussion has been to emphasize the discreteness of the different individuals who make up a society, particularly with regard to their ends. The result has been to inhibit the elaboration of certain of the most important possibilities of the theory of action, those having to do with the integration of ends in systems, especially those involving a plurality of actors. The tendency has been rather to concentrate for analytical purposes on the unit act itself and to leave the relations between the ends of different acts in a system entirely out of consideration or, when they were considered, to lay emphasis on their diversity and lack of integration.

The other principal element of the subsystem of action which is of special interest here may now be approached—the character of the normative element of the means-end relationship in the unit act. There has been, in the thought with which this discussion is concerned, an overwhelming stress upon one particular type, which may be called the "rational norm of efficiency." Hence the second predominant feature of the developing system here outlined, "atomism" being the first, is the problem of "rationality" action. It would not be correct to speak of the "rationalism" of the wider body of thought since a large section of it has been marked by the minimization of the role of rational norms. But in spite of this disagreement over the concrete role of rationality there has been, on the whole, a common standard of rationality and, equally important, the absence of any other *positive* conception of a normative element governing the means-end relationship. Departures from the rational norm have been described in such negative terms as "irrational" and "nonrational." With a more sophisticated development of systematic thinking these have, as will be shown later, taken on quite specific meanings, but for the present the important thing is the fact that attention has been concentrated on this particular type of norm.

No attempt will be made to give an exhaustive historical analysis of the influences which account for this peculiar focus of thinking. Three may, however, be mentioned. In the first place, there is obviously a very solid common-sense foundation for attributing a large importance to rationality in action. We are all engaged in multifarious practical activities where a great deal depends on the "right" selection of appropriate means to our ends, and where the selection, within the limits of knowledge current at the time and place, is based on a sound empirical knowledge of the intrinsic relation of the employment of means to the realization of our ends. Every society obviously has a considerable stock of technical procedures based on an extensive body of lore. Though it may still be a problem why other practices, perhaps equally current, where the intrinsic appropriateness of the means to the end was not so evident, were not taken as a model and type case, there can be no question of the pervasiveness of the rational case in all systems of human action.

The most prominent class of concrete actions thus overlooked is that of "ritual" actions. It happens that in two of the elements of our cultural heritage already discussed there is a strong hostility to ritual and hence a tendency to minimize its importance. On the one hand, Protestantism reacted strenuously against the ritualism of the Catholic Church. Ritual of almost all kinds was proscribed as superstition which if it existed at all was an anomaly due to the ignorance or the perversity of men, not anything natural and useful. This fact, of course, coincided with a society in which the monastery with its ritual devotions was under a cloud, and for whatever reasons, attention was turned strongly to the practical affairs of secular life. Secondly, the humanistic element of our tradition was marked by a strong current of rationalism inherited from the ancient world, where superstition was also looked upon askance. Their negative valuation of ritual is one of the few points on which the Puritans and the men of the humanistic Renaissance could agree.

Whatever may have been the influences responsible for preoccupation with the problem of the rationality of action, there can be little doubt that a dominant influence in shaping the terms in which the problem came to be conceived in social thought was the emergence of modern science, especially physical science. With the waning of religious interests science and the philosophical problems hinging upon science came to form perhaps the main preoccupation of minds with a bent for systematic theorizing. And science came to be widely looked upon as the rational achievement of the human mind par excellence. So powerful an intellectual influence could not fail to leave its mark on the plastic structure of early modern social thought.

In the positive sense, then, the prominence of science in the climate of opinion of the time was one of the principal influences that led social thinkers to take an interest in the problem of the rationality of action while, at the same time, it provided the main point of reference in the formulation of what was meant by the norm of rationality itself. However much common-sense experience may have contributed, the common element in the great majority of attempts to reach intellectually sophisticated formulations of the concept of rationality is the view that action is rational in so far as it may be understood to be guided on the part of the actor by scientific or, at least, scientifically sound knowledge of the circumstances of his situation.

The simplest and most widespread concept is that which defines a particular type of norm for the means-end relationship, accepting the end as given without inquiry as to its rationality or "reasonableness." It may be stated as follows:

Action is rational in so far as it pursues ends possible within the conditions of the situation, and by the means which, among those available to the actor, are intrinsically best adapted to the end for reasons understandable and verifiable by positive empirical science.

Since science is the rational achievement par excellence, the mode of approach here outlined is in terms of the analogy between the scientific investigator and the actor in ordinary practical activities. The starting point is that of conceiving the actor as coming to know the facts of the situation in which he acts and thus the conditions necessary and means available for the realization of his ends. As applied to the means-end relationship this is essentially a matter of the accurate prediction of the probable effects of various possible ways of altering the situation (employment of alternative means) and the resultant choice among them. Apart from questions relating to the choice of ends and from those relating to "effort"—the ways in which action is more than an automatic result of knowledge—there is, where the standard is applicable at all, little difficulty in conceiving the actor as thus analogous to the scientist whose knowledge is the principal determinant of his action so far as his actual course conforms with the expectations of an observer who has, as Pareto says, "a more extended knowledge of the circumstances."

Thus far there have been laid down, with some indication of their origins, two of the main features of the system of theory on the action basis on which initial interest will be centered. It is a theory which is predominantly atomistic in the above sense, employing the "rational unit act" as the unit of the systems of action which it considers. It is unnecessary to go further in considering other features of the unit itself; it is now time to turn to the way the units are built up into systems and consider certain characteristics of the general systems thus arrived at.

The rational unit act which has been described—fictitious or not is immaterial—is a concrete unit of concrete systems of action. It is a unit which is, within the framework of the general action schema, arrived at by maximizing one important property of unit acts—rationality. By assuming that a concrete system as a whole is made up only of units of this character we get the picture of a complete concrete system of rational action. This is the simplest and most obvious mode of employment of this conceptual scheme—the assumption, often naïvely made without full realization of what it implies, that the concrete action systems being studied are simply aggregates of such rational unit acts. Even on this basis certain complications can arise, as will be seen in the next chapter. But for the present the discussion must be confined to the more general issues involved in the question of the relation of such a conceptual scheme to concrete reality.

The naïve empiricist view just stated has certain very important implications. If the concrete system be considered as analyzable exclusively into rational unit acts it follows that though the conception of action as consisting in the pursuit of ends is fundamental, there is nothing in the theory dealing with the relations of the ends to each other, but only with the character of the means-end relationship. If the conceptual scheme is not consciously "abstract" but is held to be literally descriptive of concrete reality, at least so far as the latter is "important," this gap is of great significance. For the failure to state anything positive about the relations of ends to each other can then have only one meaning—that there are no significant relations, that is, that ends are random in the statistical sense. It is by this indirect path of implication rather than by that of any positive theorem that the last defining feature of the system is arrived at—the randomness of the ends, at least the ultimate ends, of action. Though seldom brought out into the open, it will be found to be continually lurking in the background as one of the implicit logical assumptions upon which the whole structure rests.

The theoretical action system characterized by these four features, atomism, rationality, empiricism and randomness of ends will be called in the present study the utilitarian system of social theory. The term, like most of its kind, is partly in conformity, partly at variance with general usage. Unfortunately usage is not consistent and some choice must be made. What has been outlined is, however, the logical center of the historical body of thought usually called utilitarianism, though various other doctrines, partly consistent with the above, partly not, have been historically associated with it. But above all the choice is justified by the fact that it is in connection with the modern economic doctrine of utility that the logic of the situation just developed has been clearly worked out. Subject to the corrections necessitated by placing these elements in a wider system of thought which takes account of others as well, the utility elements of human action are in fact, as will be seen, those to which utilitarian theory in the above sense came relatively near doing justice.

The Positivistic Theory of Action

It has been stated that developing modern science constituted one of the principal influences in establishing a main feature of the utilitarian system of thought, its emphasis on the problem of rationality. The same influence may be followed out on a still deeper level, involving still wider issues, in relation to the question last brought under consideration—that concerning the properties of systems of action taken as wholes.

It has been stated that when combined with an empiricist view of the relation of the theory to concrete reality, the utilitarian failure to consider the relations of ends to each other amounts to the implicit theorem that they have no such relations that are important to the logical structure of the theory. That is, that relative to the considerations affecting the rational choice of means, the center of gravity of theoretical interest, they may be held to vary at random. Focusing theoretical interest on the relation of science to rational action and failure to consider other elements explicitly result in still further implications which define a wider closed system of thought of which the utilitarian must be regarded as a subsystem. This is most easily seen in connection with the subjective point of view which is throughout the decisive one for purposes of the action schema. Starting with the utilitarian case we can see that the actor is conceived as possessing a certain amount of rational scientific knowledge of the situation of his action. But at the same time it is freely granted that this knowledge is so limited as to be inadequate for the complete determination of action. Specifically, in utilitarian terms, it is irrelevant to the choice of ends. But the fact that there is *no alternative selective standard,* in the choice either of ends or of means, throws the system, with its tendency to become logically closed, into the negative concept of randomness. Then, from the point of view of the actor, scientifically verifiable knowledge of the situation in which he acts becomes the only *significant orienting medium* in the action system. It is that alone which makes of his action an intelligible order rather than a response to the "meaningless" forces impinging upon him. It should be remembered that the actor is here being considered as if he were a scientific investigator. This throws the emphasis on the *cognitive elements* in the subjective aspect of action. The peculiarity of the point of view under consideration now is that it involves explicitly or implicitly (more often the latter) the view that positive science constitutes man's sole possible significant cognitive relation to external (nonego) reality, man as actor, that is. In so far as this inference is drawn, or as the reasoning dealt with implies it as a premise, the system of social theory in question may be called "positivistic." From this point of view utilitarianism as it has been herein defined is a true positivistic system but by no means the only possible one. On the contrary, deviations from it are possible in a number of different ways, all of which remain within the positivistic framework.

The thesis may be put forward that one of the main currents of Western European social thought since its secularization in about the seventeenth century has been positivistic in this sense. In the eighteenth century the elements which go to make up this positivistic current were often and to a large extent synthesized with others so that it would scarcely be proper to call the system

as a whole positivistic. But during the course of the nineteenth
century there was, on the whole, an increasing tendency for these
elements to differentiate out and to form a closed system of their
own, becoming more and more explicitly positivistic. There has
been an increasingly clear differentiation from another trend of
thought which, though more prominent in Germany, is also
common to European culture, the "idealistic." It can safely be
said both that with the course of the nineteenth century the
two have become increasingly distinct, and that in the countries
of Western civilization the positivistic has, until lately, become
increasingly predominant. Of the positivistic system there have
been many variants, several of which will be discussed in the next
chapter, but all have remained within the same broader conceptual framework.

The main significance of the movement of thought to be traced
in Part II is that it constitutes the transition from a positivistic
theory of action to a radically different subsystem of the latter
conceptual scheme, what will be called a "voluntaristic" theory
of action. In order to understand clearly the magnitude and
nature of the change it is essential to have a clear conception
of all the principal ramifications of the system preceding it, since
this system in some degree permeated the minds of the first three
thinkers to be studied here. This is the justification for such an
extended introductory discussion, which will include in the following chapter a substantial historical outline of positivistic social
thought. This outline is introduced in order thoroughly to famil-
iarize the reader with the structure and ramifications of this mode
of thinking. Without a grasp of the various possibilities of doctrine
possible within this general logical framework and the sense of
their reality which can only be gained by following them out in
terms of the concrete history of thought, it would be difficult to
appreciate many of the implications of the main body of the
study.

Before embarking on this more extended historical sketch,
however, it is necessary to carry the analysis of the logical structure of positivistic thought somewhat further in order to complete
the outline of the scheme. The utilitarian version of positivism
is not only on the whole historically prior but forms a convenient
starting point for analysis of the logical alternatives which are
open within the framework of the wider system. If the atomism

of rational unit acts be accepted as its most distinguishing feature, it is clear that there are two fundamental respects in which a departure from the utilitarian basis can be made: in the status of the ends of action, on the one hand; in that of the property of rationality, on the other. In both respects the positivistic framework imposes certain limitations on what kinds of departures from the utilitarian position are logically acceptable. In both respects, also, these positivistically acceptable alternatives to utilitarianism fail to exhaust the logical possibilities of the more general action schema. In fact the transition from a positivistic position consists precisely in opening up those possibilities which are perfectly consistent with the general scheme of action, but which involve abandonment of the positivistic version of it. For the present, however, only those alternatives will be outlined which make it possible to retain the positivistic position.

First, then, the status of ends in the utilitarian scheme. Here the distinction between ends of action in the analytical sense and the elements of action belonging to the situation is vital and essential. In conformity with the voluntarism of the Christian background the reality of the agency of the actor was never doubted. The positivistic element consisted only in the implication that ends must be taken as given, not only in a heuristic sense for certain analytical purposes, but on the empiricist basis, with the assumption that they varied at random relative to the means-end relationship and its central component, the actor's knowledge of his situation. Only thus could their analytical independence be preserved in terms of the utilitarian scheme. But what happens when this assumption is questioned without abandoning the positivistic basis? And it was sure to be questioned, for such an assumption could hardly be considered scientifically satisfying in the long run. It is, indeed, the statement of an ultimate limit to scientific investigation, and science has always been reluctant to accept such limitations, especially when they are arbitrarily imposed a priori.

On positivistic ground there was only one possible way of escaping this unsatisfactory limitation. If ends were not random, it was because it must be possible for the actor to base his choice of ends on scientific knowledge of some empirical reality. But this tenet had the inevitable logical consequence of assimilating ends to the situation of action and destroying their analytical independence, so essential to the utilitarian position. For the only possible basis of empirical knowledge of a future state of affairs is prediction on the basis of knowledge of present and past states. Then action becomes determined entirely by its conditions, for without the independence of ends the distinction between conditions and means becomes meaningless. Action becomes a process of rational adaptation to these conditions. The active role of the actor is reduced to one of the understanding of his situation and forecasting of its future course of development. Indeed, it becomes somewhat mysterious what the function is of this rational process, how it is possible for the actor ever to err, if there is no other determinant of his action than knowledge and the conditions through this knowledge.

Thus with respect to the status of ends, positivistic thought is caught in the "utilitarian dilemma." That is, either the active agency of the actor in the choice of ends is an independent factor in action, and the end element must be random;[1] or the objectionable implication of the randomness of ends is denied, but then their independence disappears and they are assimilated to the conditions of the situation, that is to elements analyzable in terms of nonsubjective categories, principally[2] heredity and environment, in the analytical sense of biological theory. This utilitarian dilemma turns out to be of cardinal importance in understanding the theories of the writers dealt with in Part II. "Radical rationalistic[3] positivism" is, in this connection, the

[1] This is really an impossible position for there can be no choice between random ends.

[2] See below, Note C appended to this chapter (p. 82), for a statement of the status of the relation of these concepts to the theory of action.

[3] The use of the term rationalistic in this instance is somewhat dangerous, but there seems to be no better alternative. It refers not to rationalism in what is often called the psychological sense of the relative role of rational and irrational factors in the determination of the course of action. Its reference is, rather, to the use of the rational methodological schema of positive science in the analysis of action from the subjective point of view. In this latter sense the rationalistic pole is the point at which it is claimed that all the important elements of action can, from the subjective point of view, be fitted into this schema, that is, are manifested to the actor as either verifiable facts about his situation or logically cogent statements of relations between such facts. These two senses of the term rationalistic are by no means unrelated to each other, but it is none the less vital to distinguish them. For instance, Durkheim has been freely accused of falling into a

polar type of case at which utilitarianism as here defined disappears and action becomes solely a function of its conditions. It is the refusal to accept either horn of the dilemma which constitutes the departure from a positivistic basis in this respect on the part of the theories to be analyzed in Part II.

The second problem involves the status of the norm of rationality. Here, as has already been pointed out, the utilitarian position represents the polar type of case where rationality is maximized. It is the case where the actor's knowledge of the situation is, if not complete in any ultimate sense, fully adequate[1] to the realization of his ends. Departures from the rational norm must be associated with falling short in some respect of this adequacy of knowledge.[2] Now the significant thing in this connection is that on a utilitarian or, more generally, a positivistic basis, there is no other, alternative type of norm in relation to which such departures from rationality may be measured. Their

---

naïve rationalism in the former sense when, in fact, this impression is occasioned by the fact that he operates with a rationalistic schema in the latter sense, that is, in his earlier phases he is a radical rationalistic positivist of a peculiar kind.

[1] Thus, to use a very humble example, the most ignorant and unscientific housewife knows that if a potato is boiled a certain length of time it will become soft and mealy and be "done." So long as this is a *known fact* it is an entirely adequate basis of knowledge for the purposes of cooking potatoes. The point is that the fact that the housewife does not know *why* the potato becomes soft under these circumstances except in some such sense as "because it was boiled" or, *in what*, biochemically speaking, the change from being "raw" to being "done" consists, is entirely irrelevant to a judgment of the rationality of her action. Such knowledge might go far to satisfy intellectual curiosity; it would not, unless it opened up a new technique of preparing potatoes, contribute in the least to increasing the rationality of cookery. The fact that these changes take place under the given conditions is enough. Similarly if this housewife on moving to the highlands of Peru observes that potatoes are not done until they are boiled considerably longer, the fact is enough. It is not necessary to know that this is due to the lower boiling point of water at high altitudes, in turn due to the lower atmospheric pressure, etc. These details of knowledge, however interesting and important to the scientific understanding of the phenomenon, are *not relevant to judging the rationality of the action unless knowing them would alter its course* from what it would have been without that knowledge.

[2] Except in the limiting case where there is *no discoverable relation* between the correct knowledge and the course of action. This case is not theoretically important in the present context.

characterization must be purely negative. There are two current terms which quite satisfactorily describe this—"ignorance" and "error." Any failure to live up to the rational norm must be imputed to one or both of these two elements. Either the actor simply did not know certain facts relevant to his action and would have acted differently had he known them, or he based his action on considerations which a more extensive knowledge would have proved to be erroneous. He thought he knew, but in fact he did not.

The terms ignorance and error may, on a common-sense basis, be taken to mean merely the absence of adequate knowledge. But in positivistic terms they must have a more specific connotation. Since scientific knowledge is held to be man's only significant cognitive relation to external reality, then there are open only two alternatives in explaining why the actor in question was the victim of ignorance or error or both. Either this subjective fact may be the reflection of elements in the situation which are intrinsically incapable of being understood in scientific terms in their relations to action—then they are random elements and must be taken as ultimate data without further inquiry into whys and wherefores—or, on the other hand, they can be explained. The explanation must be that they are due to intrinsically understandable factors which the actor has either failed to understand or positively misunderstood. Then the only possible course for the scientific investigator is to "get behind" the actor's subjective experience, that is to abandon the subjective categories of the schema of action in favor of objective processes which may be thought of as influencing action by acting upon the actor without his knowledge or awareness of what is "really" happening.

But one point must be kept clearly in mind. It follows directly from these considerations that, if and in so far as the actor comes to know these elements in his action, and is able to act rationally relative to them, it must be in the form of acquiring scientifically valid knowledge of them, of eliminating the ignorance and error. Being rational consists in these terms precisely in becoming a scientist relative to one's own action. Short of the ultimate boundaries of science, irrationality, then, is only possible so long as actors are not in possession of the logically possible complement of knowledge affecting human affairs.

It follows further: If the explanation of irrationality on a positivistic basis must lie in factors not in fact known, but intrinsically capable of being known scientifically to the actor, then these factors must be found, on analytical generalization, to lie in categories capable of nonsubjective formulation, that is in the *conditions* of action. Thus, remarkable as it may seem, departure from the utilitarian position, so long as it remains within the positivistic framework leads in both the major problems, that of the status of ends and that of the norm of rationality, to the same analytical result: explanation of action in terms of the ultimate nonsubjective conditions, conveniently designated as heredity and environment. The difference lies merely in the account of the process by which their influence on action is exerted. In the one case it is through the medium of a rational scientific appreciation on the part of the actor of his situation; in the other, this medium is dispensed with and it is by means of an "automatic" process which, if it is subjectively manifest to the actor at all, is so only in terms which render effective adaptation and control impossible, positively only as error. This position may be called radical anti-intellectualistic positivism. Thus the utilitarian dilemma is broadened into a more inclusive form. It may, in this form, be stated in the following proposition: In so far as the utilitarian position is abandoned in either of its two major tenets, the only alternative on a positivistic basis in the explanation of action lies in the conditions of the situation of action objectively rather than subjectively considered, which for most practical purposes may be taken to mean in the factors of heredity and environment in the analytical sense of biological theory.

The principal reason for the common failure to see this implication seems to lie in the fact that thinkers have been principally concerned with what has been called the concrete use of the action schema and have failed to carry their reasoning through systematically to a general analytical plane. In the latter terms it is inescapable.

This striking result raises a fundamental methodological problem. At the outset of this chapter attention was called to the fact that the subjective point of view is central to the structure of the conceptual scheme under consideration—the theory of action. But at the radically positivistic pole of thought, whether in the rationalistic or the anti-intellectualistic form, the analytical necessity for it disappears. It is true that the facts relevant to the explanation of action are always *capable of statement* in terms at least of the concrete action schema, actually in the rationalistic case, potentially in the anti-intellectualistic, on the assumption of the actor coming to know the extent of his ignorance and the sources of his error. But the analytical categories of heredity and environment are, in the sense here used, characterized by the fact that for purposes of adequate scientific explanation they are able to dispense with subjective categories. Then in so far as they or other nonsubjective categories prove adequate to the task of understanding the concrete facts of human action, the scientific status of the action schema itself must be called into question. It may be a convenient heuristic tool, a scaffolding to use in building up a theory, but no more. It can be torn down and dispensed with at the end to the general benefit of the scientific virtues of simplicity and elegance.[1]

[1] For the general status of nonsubjective categories in relation to the theory of action see Note C appended to this chapter. For most purposes it is convenient to employ the concepts of heredity and environment as summing up the factors in action capable of formulation in nonsubjective terms. But these concepts do not enter into the fundamental definitions relative to the theory of action here laid down, and no important conclusions are based on them. They are used for illustrative, not demonstrative, purposes.

There are, however, certain implications of this situation at the radically positivistic pole. It makes, as has been said, the action schema a derivative of another one, in general a biological theory. It is clear that the latter is the more fundamental since it is applicable to concrete phenomena, such as the behavior of unicellular organisms, which cannot be described in subjective terms, since no subjective aspect is observable.

As in the case of the concept normative (see Note A below) it falls outside the scope of this study to attempt to determine whether the subjective aspect generally is ontologically "real" or derivative from some other, perhaps a "biological" reality. The only questions are whether the theory of action is derivable from known nonsubjective schemes, and whether such schemes are able to take account of all the verifiable facts which fit the theory of action. The answers may be anticipated: (1) At the radical positivistic pole the theory of action does become a derivative of nonsubjective theoretical systems, principally the biological. (2) But it will be demonstrated that the radically positivistic versions fail to take account of certain crucially important facts which will, on the other hand, be found to fit other versions of the action theory, notably the voluntaristic, which are not reducible to terms of any biological theory considered here.

It is legitimate, then, to conclude that if the version of the theory of action

This is, of course, true only at the "radically positivistic" pole of positivistic thought, and ceases to be so in so far as the utilitarian position is adhered to. But, as will be seen in the next chapter, where reasons will be entered into, there is as an adequate general explanation of human action an inherent instability in the utilitarian system. If this is so, there has been raised in radical form the question whether the preoccupation of so many generations of acute thinkers with the theory of action has not been based on delusion, or has at best been a stage of scientific development which is now happily past. This is one solution of the dilemma, and one which certainly enjoys wide acceptance at the present time. But this study will present as one of its main theses an alternative, namely to accept the incompatibility of the two principal elements here considered, the action schema and positivism, but to maintain that the evidence indicates that by freeing the former from its involvement with the latter its most valuable services to social science can best be taken advantage of. It will be the task in the following pages to present this thesis, backed by a careful analytical study of the empirical consequences of taking one or the other of these two alternatives. For scientific theory is one thing to which the pragmatic formula applies; it is justified only by its usefulness in understanding the facts of empirical experience.

EMPIRICISM

Before closing this chapter attention should be called to two important issues which will recur continually throughout the study. In outlining the utilitarian system of thought there has been occasion to speak of it as involving what has been called an "empiricist" conception of the relation between the theoretical system involved and concrete reality. It will contribute to future clarity if a few more words are devoted to the general issue of empiricism and its relation to scientific abstraction. The term empiricism will be used in application to a system of theory when it is claimed, explicitly or implicitly, that the categories of the given theoretical system are by themselves adequate to

---

which "works" best is not reducible to any of these biological theories, the burden of proof is on him who would challenge its independence. It would clearly be beyond the scope of this study to analyze critically all contemporary biological theory with a view to attempting to settle this question.

explain all the scientifically important facts about the body of concrete phenomena to which it is applied. It has been stated in the first chapter that all systems of scientific theory tend to become logically closed and this has already been vividly illustrated by what must be called the implicit consequence of the randomness of ends for utilitarian theory. The effect of an empiricist position is to turn a logically closed into an empirically closed system. That is, in a logically closed system all the propositions in the system are, on the one hand, interdependent in that each has implications for the others and, on the other, the system is determinate in that each of these implications finds its statement in another proposition of the same system. But if this system alone is held to be adequate to the explanation of all the important concrete facts known about the phenomenon in question, then the propositions must completely include all these facts and their relations. In other words, empiricism transfers the logical determinism which is inherent in all scientific theory into an empirical determinism.

Though they have been, in fact, very closely bound up together historically, by no means do positivism and empiricism in this sense necessarily logically imply one another. The doctrine generally known as scientific materialism is perhaps the most important example of a combination of the two, consisting of the theorem that in the last analysis the categories of the classical mechanics were alone adequate to the scientific understanding of reality, and that all other systems, if they were sound, were ultimately reducible[1] to this one. But though no such conclusion is inevitably bound up with positivism, the latter position places very narrow limitations on the extent to which a true recognition of the role of scientific abstraction can relieve one of the difficulties into which the empiricist, whether utilitarian or materialistic, is plunged.

This is evident in utilitarianism. It has been shown that the systems which are relevant to the understanding of human action

---

[1] Reducible means here that the propositions of one system can be converted into those of the other by logical (including mathematical) manipulation without change of meaning, that is, of important definitions of variables and relations between them. Two systems reducible to terms of each other are, logically considered, two alternative ways of saying the same thing.

and which aside from the utilitarian version of the action schema
have a place in the positivistic framework at all are those which
can dispense analytically with subjective categories. But these
are already taken account of in the utilitarian system[1] itself, so
far as it is possible to maintain its rationalistic position. The
knowledge which is held to guide the course of action is precisely
knowledge of the ultimate conditions of the situation of action,
for practical purposes, of heredity and environment. It is presumably for this reason among others that the utilitarian scheme
has withstood attack so long. For unless one has transcended
the positivistic framework, even a consciousness of the abstractness of the theory does not open up any new *theoretical* possibilities. Limitation of its empirical scope on grounds of its
abstractness leads only to supplementing it by various modes of
influence of the nonsubjective factors (in recent times mainly
forms of positivistic anti-intellectualism) and, however useful
in correcting certain empirical errors, has contributed very little
to the analytical apparatus of social theory. This has been

[1] As far as it concerns the facts of the situation of action the term "system" has been employed throughout in two different senses which should be
made clear. On the one hand, it refers to a body of *logically* interrelated
propositions, a "theoretical system"; on the other, to a body of *empirically*
interrelated phenomena, an empirical system. The first kind of system is
not only not a "real" system at all, it does not state any facts in the ordinary
sense. It merely defines general properties of empirical phenomena and states
general relations between their values. In applying the theoretical system
to empirical phenomena, data, ordinarily called facts, must be supplied.
These data constitute the specific "values" of the general categories which
make up the system of theory. If, of course, the empirically given values of
one or more variables are known, other facts can be ascertained about the
same empirical system, by applying the theory.

It is important to note that in so far as a theoretical system is abstract
the data necessary for its application to an empirical system fall into two
classes, usually called in the physical sciences the values of variables and
constants. What are constants for one theoretical system, of course, constitute values of the variables of some other. Thus in the action system the
facts of the situation of the actor in so far as they are analytically independent of action are constants. Their values must be known to arrive at
any concrete conclusions, but they are not problematical for purposes of the
theory of action. The only respect in which the facts of the situation are
affected by the theory of action is that the action frame of reference requires
that they be stated in such a form as to bring out their relevance to its
problems, that is, as means and conditions of action, not as aggregates of
atoms, cells and the like.

notably so with a school of economic theorists who have come to realize the abstractness of traditional economic theory, but have attempted merely to supplement it without any thoroughgoing critique of the positivistic underpinnings of the original utilitarian position.[1] At the same time, empiricism, backed as it has been until quite recently by what has at least purported to be the authority of the natural sciences, is one of the most serious obstacles to further theoretical development. But it is not alone sufficient to overcome this obstacle in order to be freed of the difficulties of the utilitarian and other positivistic theories to be outlined in the next chapter.

INDIVIDUALISM IN THE THEORY OF ACTION

Secondly, a few more words may properly be added about one aspect of the concept "individualism." It has been remarked that as an influence in shaping social thought it was largely in the ethical context that it has been important. But there is a very important sense in which the predominant current of positivistic social thought has been individualistic on the scientific side as well. The two aspects are closely correlated but by no means identical.

The question is whether all the facts necessary to the understanding of concrete social systems can be predicated on analytically isolated "individuals" combined with a process of direct generalization from these facts, that is, those additional facts which the most general frame of reference makes necessary to the idea of a concrete system at all. Such a system is atomistic, with, however, the "individual" as the atom rather than the unit act. Any theoretical system which is atomistic relative to the more elementary unit is necessarily so with reference to the individual. Hence the utilitarian position which has been defined by atomism in this sense as a principal criterion is inherently individualistic. So long as, in the transition to radical positivism, the same atomism has been preserved, and it has been to a very large extent, the versions to radical positivism in question have also been individualistic.

[1] See TALCOTT PARSONS, "Sociological Elements in Economic Thought," *Quarterly Journal of Economics*, May and August, 1935; also "Some Reflections on the Nature and Significance of Economics," *idem.*, May, 1934.

In these terms all the elements which have been distinguished in the foregoing discussion have been fitted into an individualistic pattern. It is quite clear that no exception to this statement could be derived from the role of utilitarian ends since these are conceived as random relative to the other elements. Knowledge, so long as it is rational, is not random, but is determined by and is a "reflection" of the things known. On a general analytical plane the facts attributable to the ends of others in the system are eliminated. This leaves those elements which are capable of nonsubjective formulation since ends and knowledge are the only elements of utilitarian theory which are not capable of nonsubjective formulation.[1]

But the way in which these elements are treated is relative to the atomism of the unit act. They include the facts of the nonsubjective environment and of the actor's own nature so far as they are relevant to the attainment of the isolated given end. Heredity, in this context is necessarily individual since it is by definition determined prior to the individual's participation in social relationships. The only logical possibility of a non-individualistic element is in environment, and this possibility is excluded by the atomistic treatment. So long as the only differences in the transition to radical positivism are the elimination of the independence of ends, and departure from the norm of

[1] The elements of a utilitarian explanation of action have been enumerated as random ends and a knowledge of the situation of action, hence they are involved in the latter categories themselves in so far as they are determinant of that knowledge. It may occur to the reader that among the determinants of knowledge are not only the intrinsic properties of the phenomena known, but also the "faculties" of the knower. What of the "reason" which would appear to be a necessary condition of rationality? The existence of such a faculty is, of course, a necessary assumption for a utilitarian theory and is only such, generally implicit and not made problematical within the range of utilitarian thought. Its existence is merely the necessary logical basis for the use of the "rationalistic" schema of the methodology of science in the explanation of action. How men came by this faculty, above all whether the analysis of action in society can throw any light on the fact or the degree of the attainment of reason, are questions never ever raised while thought has moved within this orbit. The fact that the question rose to such importance at a much later stage in the development of the theory of action, in Durkheim's "sociological epistemology" and in the German so-called *Wissenssoziologie* is of great significance, one of the most symptomatic marks of the process of change in social thought. The explicit discussion of the issue will be deferred until later.

rationality, the radical positivistic version is also individualistic.
The group of theories which vary between the utilitarian position
and the two polar versions of radical individualistic positivism
will form the subject matter of the next chapter.

It is logically possible to escape from this individualism on a
positivistic basis. One version of this possibility of "sociologistic
positivism," the "radically rationalistic" as held by Durkheim
in the earlier stages of development of his theories, will be
thoroughly explored.[1] There is possibly a basis of fact in the
view, since there is no reason to doubt that the fact of association
of individuals in collectivities has consequences analyzable in
nonsubjective terms such as those of biological theory. But the
crucial facts which Durkheim deals with as constituting the
"social milieu," though part of the concrete environment of
the concrete individual, turn out to be, when analytically considered, quite specifically couched in terms of the theory of
action, and within its structure at a point which precludes their
being treated subjectively as elements of scientifically valid
knowledge as held by the actor.

With the exception of Durkheim and his antecedents the
positivistic tradition has been predominantly individualistic.
This has tended to throw all organic and other anti-individualistic
theories automatically over into the antithetical, the "idealistic"
camp, which has served to rule them and all the facts they stated
out of court for all with a positivistic turn of mind. It is not
surprising that Durkheim, in the breakdown of his sociologistic
positivism, adopted a kind of idealism. The fact that he thus
vacillated between two modes of thought goes far toward explaining the extraordinary lack of understanding that his work has
encountered. His "idealism" alienated the positivists, and vice
versa his "positivism" equally alienated the idealists. It is
hoped, in transcending the positivist-idealist dilemma, to show
a way of transcending also the old individualism-social organism
or, as it is often called, social nominalism-realism dilemma which
has plagued social theory to little purpose for so long.

Note A: On the Concept "Normative"

Because of its association with ethical and legal points of view which are
ordinarily distinguished from those of empirical science, liberal use of the

---

[1] See especially Chap. IX.

erm normative in a scientific work calls for a word of explanation and an explicit definition.

For the purposes of the present study the term normative will be used as applicable to an aspect, part or element of a system of action if, and only in so far as, it may be held to manifest or otherwise involve a sentiment attributable to one or more actors that something is an end in itself, regardless of its status as a means to any other end (1) for the members of a collectivity, (2) for some portion of the members of a collectivity or (3) for the collectivity as a unit.

An end, for these purposes, is a future state of affairs to which action is oriented by virtue of the fact that it is deemed desirable by the actor(s) but which differs in important respects from the state which they would expect to supervene by merely allowing the predictable trends of the situation to take their course without active intervention.[1]

A norm is a verbal description of the concrete course of action thus regarded as desirable, combined with an injunction to make certain future actions conform to this course. An instance of a norm is the statement: "Soldiers should obey the orders of their commanding officers."[2]

The first remark, which though obvious, must be made, is that attribution of a normative element to actors being observed has no normative implications for the observer. The attitude of the latter may remain entirely that of an objective observer without either positive or negative participation in the normative sentiments of his subjects. The practical difficulty of carrying out this precept in the practice of scientific investigation of human behavior does not alter its status as an indispensable part of scientific methodology which may also serve as a norm toward which scientific work is to be oriented.

[1] This definition is specifically formulated so as to include the maintenance of an existing state of affairs as an end, as well as the bringing into being of a state differing from the initial situation.

[2] A concrete norm in general involves other than normative elements of action. Thus soldiers' obedience may be an indispensable means of achieving a given military objective, more generally of attaining military efficiency. But there are at least two respects in which analysis may reveal a normative element as involved in such concrete norms: (1) Among those who "recognize" this norm, whether officers, soldiers or civilians there may exist a sentiment that soldiers' obedience to orders is an end in itself regardless of considerations of military efficiency. (2) When the question is raised as to why obedience is valued as a means it will lead to following the means-end chain "upward" (see Chap. VI). The analysis will, by this procedure arrive eventually at an ultimate end, whether it be military efficiency for its own sake or an indispensable means to other ends, such as national security. Normative elements are usually involved in both modes in the same concrete norm. On the other hand, the recognition of the concrete norm may depend in part on non-normative elements such, for instance, as a hereditary tendency to submission. A concrete norm may be a "part" of a system of action, and it has already been pointed out (Chap. I) that such parts are normally capable of analysis in terms of a variety of elements.

Second, elements, in the strict sense laid down above, may be either normative or non-normative. Systems of action and their parts, on the other hand, are neither normative nor non-normative as wholes, but in general are found to involve both classes of elements, to be capable of an analysis of which the discrimination of these two types of elements will be an essential part.

The distinction of the normative and the non-normative elements of action systems is an empirical distinction on the same methodological level as many others in all sciences, such as that between hereditary and environmental elements in use in the biological sciences.[1] As employed in this study, it is thus not a philosophical distinction.

The logical starting point for analysis of the role of normative elements in human action is the fact of experience that men not only respond to stimuli but in some sense try to conform their action to patterns which are by the actor and other members of the same collectivity, deemed desirable. The statement that this is a fact, like all statements of fact, involves a conceptual scheme. The most fundamental component of that scheme is what is here called the means-end schema. The theory of action, more particularly the voluntaristic theory of action, is an elaboration and refinement of that basic conceptual scheme. From a scientific point of view, which is that of the present study, the sole question is whether this conceptual scheme "works," whether in its terms it is possible to make verifiable statements of fact which when analyzed yield important uniformities. It is not denied that it may be possible to state the same facts in terms of other conceptual schemes, in particular such as will not involve normative elements. Schemes of that character which have been advanced, such as the behavioristic scheme, are, in the author's opinion, much less adequate as tools for statement and analysis of the facts of human behavior than the action scheme. But this remains for present purposes an opinion. No attempt is made in this study to discuss such an alternative scheme critically or compare it systematically with that of action in empirical application. This study is limited to discussion of the conceptual scheme of action. The only systematic comparison here attempted is between various versions of that scheme. It will be demonstrated that the schema of action is an empirically valid conceptual scheme, in the sense above stated, that in its terms it is possible to state many verifiable facts about human behavior, and to formulate many important uniformities involving these facts. A normative orientation is fundamental to the schema of action in the same sense that space is fundamental to that of the classical mechanics; in terms of the given conceptual scheme there is no such thing as action except as effort to conform

---

[1] The two are similar in that the diagnosis in both cases is often difficult.

[2] But like many other empirical distinctions which prove useful in science it is related to certain philosophical distinctions, and the fact of its empirical usefulness may well have implications on the philosophical level. The development of such implications, beyond the point where they are important to the empirical and theoretical problems of this study, falls outside its scope.

with norms just as there is no such thing as motion except as change of location in space. In both cases the propositions are definitions or logical corollaries of definitions. But it is not necessary for present purposes even to raise the question whether human behavior is "really" normatively oriented.[1] For this study is not concerned with the philosophical implications of the theory of action except negatively to criticize attempts to rule it out of court on a priori grounds. It is confined to its scientific status in relation to the verifiable facts.

NOTE B: SCHEMATIC OUTLINE OF SYSTEM TYPES IN THE THEORY OF ACTION

In the above chapter and throughout the study a rather complex classification of types of theoretical system in the field of action is employed. In order to assist the reader in clarifying the relations of the various types to each other, it has seemed best to include a schematic outline of the classification here. The clearest way to do this seems to be by arbitrarily assigning symbols to the various conceptual elements involved, so that which ones are included in and which excluded from any given type of theoretical system can be quite unambiguously expressed in an appropriate formula. This note is not meant to be "read" but to be used by the reader for reference when he, reading the text, finds difficulty in being quite clear about the meanings and mutual relations of the various terms applied to the types of theory there discussed. This is the more necessary since this particular classification and the terminology used to describe it are not current in the literature, and are hence likely to be unfamiliar to the reader. The attempt has been made, in choosing terms, not to depart any farther than necessary from current usage, but it is impossible in a case like this, where the distinctions made are themselves not current, to employ terms the technical meanings of which will be immediately obvious.

This is a classification of subtypes of the theory of action. By a theory of action is here meant any theory the empirical reference of which is to a concrete system which may be considered to be composed of the units here referred to as "unit acts." In a unit act there are identifiable as minimum characteristics the following: (1) an end, (2) a situation, analyzable in turn into (a) means and (b) conditions, and (3) at least one selective standard in terms of which the end is related to the situation. It is evident that these categories have meaning only in terms which include the subjective point of view, *i.e.*, that of the actor. A theory which, like behaviorism, insists on

---

[1] That is to say, for present purposes the concept normative is defined only with reference to its place in a particular theoretical system, not in ontological terms. This means that its ontological status becomes relative to that of the theoretical system in question as a whole, which is, in turn, a phase of the still broader question of the status of systems of scientific theory which "work." This question is not within the scope of the present study. A few remarks on this subject will, however, be made in the final chapter (see pp. 753–757).

treating human beings in terms which exclude this subjective aspect, is no a theory of action in the sense of this study.

Let A = a unit act. A unit act consists of

S = a situation. The situation, when seen directly in its rela tions to action may consist of

C = conditions, plus

M = means, plus

i = normative or ideal elements, plus

i_e = symbolic expressions of normative or ideal elements

When the subjective aspect of action is analyzed according to the method ological criteria of science, the situation and its elements may be subjectively manifested in

T = scientifically valid knowledge held by the actor which in turn consists in

F = statements of verifiable fact, plus

L = logically correct deductions from F

t = elements which, in terms of the knowledge held by the observer, can be declared to be capable of correc scientific formulation, but in fact depart from thi standard; unscientific elements. These are

f = erroneous statements purporting to be fact

l = logical fallacies

ig = ignorance; elements objectively knowable bu without subjective manifestation.

r = elements varying at random relative to those formu lated as T and t

E = an end (for definition see previous note)

N = a selective standard relating E and S

Let Z = a system of action.

R_{el} = elementary relations of unit acts in a system, *i.e.*, thos which, so long as the system is described in terms of the action frame of reference at all, are logically implied i the conception of a system consisting of a plurality of such units existing at all

R_I = relations which are emergent in systems of such a degree of complexity that unit acts are grouped to constitut one or more of the larger, organized units called individual or actors, but no emergent properties deriving from the relations of these individuals to one another

R_C = relations emergent in respect to the relations of individuals as members of social groups, of "collectivities"

Then the most generalized formula for a system of action is as follows:

A = S (M manifested in T, t, r +

C manifested in T, t, r +

i_e manifested in T, t, r)

+E + N (defined in terms of T, t, r, i or of i_e)

+r (in role other than as manifestation of S, as i_r)

Z = $(A_1 + A_2 + A_3 \ldots A_n) + R_{el} + R_I + R_C$

With the exception of one, the voluntaristic theory of action, to which the analysis of this study heads up, all systems of interest here are defined by one or more restrictions which they place, explicitly or implicitly, on the generality of this formula. The restrictions, consisting in the suppression of the role played by certain of the elements here symbolized, may touch the analysis of the unit act or of the relations of units in systems or both.

THE POSITIVISTIC THEORY OF ACTION

A theory of action is positivistic in so far as, explicitly or implicitly, it treats scientifically valid empirical knowledge as the actor's sole theoretically significant mode of subjective orientation to his situation. Thus the significant subjective elements will be either (1) elements of valid empirical knowledge T, (2) elements which involve departures from the standard of valid knowledge in a sphere where such knowledge on the part of the actor is conceivable t or (3) elements random relative to knowledge T. Knowledge as here used is by definition knowledge of the situation, past, present or predicted future. Elements included under (2) will therefore be interpreted as stating modes in which action is influenced by the situation but with subjective manifestations other than valid knowledge. Elements not constituting either valid knowledge or manifestations of situational influences are, in a positivistic system, by definition random. The situation is by definition that part of the "external world" of the actor of which he can have valid empirical knowledge.

Then the general formula for a positivistic system is

$$A = S \text{ (manifested subjectively in } T, t, r) + E(T, t, i_r) + N(T, t, i_r)$$
$$Z = (A_1 + A_2 + A_3 + \ldots A_n) + R_{el} + (R_I) + (R_C)$$

Thus in a positivistic system the unit act is describable in terms which, neglecting the possible random elements that are not of substantive theoretical significance, can, with respect to each element, vary between two poles. The situation can be manifested in terms of either scientifically valid knowledge T or scientifically unsound subjective elements t or any combination of them. The same is true of the selective standard defining the means-end relationship. If ends constitute an analytically independent element at all, it must be with a content random relative to the situation and knowledge of it. But at one pole ends may disappear from analytical significance altogether, the concrete "end" becoming a prediction, correct or erroneous, of the future trends of the situation. The elementary relations between unit acts must be present in any system, but emergent elements of both categories may or may not be present, as indicated by the parentheses.

Positivistic systems may be further subclassified as follows, first with respect to the unit act:

A. *Radical Positivism*

Elements formulable only in subjective terms as analytically independent drop out. The concrete end and selective standard are assimilated to the situation. The general formula is

$$A = S(T, t, r) + E(T, t) + N(T, t)$$

(Formula for system as above.)

The important polar subtypes are

*A*1. *Radical rationalistic positivism.*

$$A = S(T, r) + E(T) + N(T)$$

All theoretically significant elements can be fitted positively into the methodological criteria of valid empirical knowledge.

*A*2. *Radical anti-intellectualistic positivism.*

$$A = S(t, r) + E(t) + N(t)$$

All theoretically significant elements can be fitted negatively as unscientific into the same criteria. In both cases the only place for random elements is in the situation (*cf.* Darwinian variations).

B. "Statistical" Positivism

This is a term which in strictness is applicable wherever a random element enters in. In the context of the present study, however, the only point at which this question is of substantive significance is where the concept of randomness is a mode of admitting an empirical role to normative elements without disturbing the positivistic framework. In the unit act the only places for these are in N and E. Hence the formula is

$$A = S(T, t, r) + E(i_r, T, t,) + N(i_r, T, t)$$

All the above distinctions touch only the character of the unit act. In the other basis of subclassification it is the character of the system which is at issue. An atomistic system is described only in terms of the units plus their elementary relations:

$$Z = (A_1 + A_2 + A_3 + \ldots A_n) + R_{el}$$

The following types are important here:

1. *"Individualistic" Positivism.*—The term individualistic positivism is applied to a theory that refers to a system which is either atomistic or includes only emergent relations attributable to the organization of unit acts relative to the actor as a larger unit, and which in other respects meets the definition of a positivistic system. The formula is

$$Z = (A_1 + A_2 + A_3 + \ldots A_n) + R_{el}(+ R_I)$$

2. *"Sociologistic" Positivism.*—A sociologistic system is one which, besides the emergent relations attributable to the organization of unit acts relative to the same actor, includes further emergent relations attributable to the organization of a plurality of actors in a social system, a "collectivity." Such a system is positivistic in so far as the terms in which the unit acts of which it is composed are described are positivistic. The formula is

$$Z = (A_1 + A_2 + A_3 + \ldots A_n) + R_{el} + R_I + R_C$$

For the discussion of this study the following types of positivistic system will be important:

1. "Utilitarianism," or rationalistic, individualistic statistical positivism:

$$A = S(T, r) + E(T, i_r) + N(T, i_r)$$
$$Z = (A_1 + A_2 + A_3 + \ldots A_n) + R_{el}(+ R_I)$$

2. Radical rationalistic, individualistic positivism:

$$A = S(T, r) + E(T) + N(T)$$
$$Z = \text{as above}$$

3. Radical anti-intellectualistic individualistic positivism:

$$A = S(t, r) + E(t) + N(t)$$
$$Z = \text{as above}$$

4. Radical rationalistic sociologistic positivism:

$$A = S(T, r)^1 + E(T)^1 + N(T)$$
$$Z = (A_1 + A_2 + A_3 + \ldots A_n) + E_{el} + R_I + R_C$$

THE "VOLUNTARISTIC" THEORY OF ACTION

As opposed to all types of positivistic theory the basic tenet of the voluntaristic is that neither positively nor negatively does the methodological schema of scientifically valid knowledge exhaust the significant subjective elements of action. In so far as subjective elements fail to fit as elements of valid knowledge, the matter is not exhausted by the categories of ignorance and error, nor by the functional dependence of these elements on those capable of formulation in nonsubjective terms, nor by elements random relative to these.

Positively a voluntaristic system involves elements of a normative character. Radical positivism eliminates all such elements completely from em-

---

[1] The T which is particularly important in this connection in the case which will be analyzed here, that of the early Durkheim, consists of "social facts" (see Chap. IX). Social facts are interpreted subjectively as facts about the situation of action which, through fitting into an empirically valid theory held by the actor, serve to determine his action. The facts emphasized are, however, those of the "social milieu." It cannot be doubted that the concrete actor is placed in a concrete social milieu. But on the analytical level it is quite certain that many elements of this concrete social environment are capable of formulation in terms of categories which, if not "individualistic," at least are not by definition "sociologistic," but cut across this dichotomy; thus the biological elements in the constitution of the component individuals. The question then is as to how far there is, analytically, a residuum of "social" elements, the subjective manifestation of which is a body of verifiable facts, and how far those phenomena attributable to the fact of association are, on the analytical level, elements in the "state of mind" of the actors, not, in this sense, reflections of an "objective" reality. The theory can only be upheld so far as crucially important facts concerning the phenomena studied are capable of fitting this schema.

pirical relevance. A utilitarian system admits them, but only in the status of random ends which are thus only data for the empirical application of the theoretical system. In the voluntaristic theory they become integral with the system itself, positively interdependent with the other elements in specifically determinate ways.

The voluntaristic system does not in the least deny an important role to conditional and other non-normative elements, but considers them as interdependent with the normative. The general formula for a voluntaristic system is as follows:

$$A = S(T, t, i_e, r) + E(T, t, i, r, i_e) + N(T, t, i_e, i, r)$$
$$Z = (A_1 + A_2 + A_3 + \ldots A_n) + R_{el} + R_I + R_C$$

The Idealistic Theory of Action

While the voluntaristic type of theory involves a process of interaction between normative and conditional elements, at the idealistic pole the role of the conditional elements disappears, as correspondingly at the positivistic pole that of the normative disappears. In an idealistic theory "action" becomes a process of "emanation," of "self-expression" of ideal or normative factors. Spatiotemporal phenomena become related to action only as symbolic "modes of expression" or "embodiments" of "meanings." The scientific standard of rationality becomes irrelevant to the subjective aspect of action. The means-end schema gives way to a meaning-expression schema. Non-normative elements cannot "condition" action, they can only be more or less "integrated" with a meaningful system. The general formula is

$$A = S(i_e, r) + E(i, i_e, r) + N(i, i_e, r)$$
$$Z = \text{as in voluntaristic theory}$$

It does not seem worth while to attempt to subclassify different types of voluntaristic and idealistic systems as in the positivistic system, since such distinctions are not important to the present study.

Note C: On the Content of Nonsubjective Categories in Relation to the Theory of Action

One of the principal features of the conceptual scheme analyzed in this study, the theory of action, is that it is couched in terms of subjective categories, that is, categories referring to aspects or parts of, or elements in, the "state of mind" of the actor. The question naturally arises whether this use of the subjective point of view is merely a methodological device or is essential to our scientific understanding by means of the action schema of the phenomena being studied. One conclusion of this study will be that it is more than a methodological device and that certain of the fundamental elements involved in human behavior in society are not capable of systematic theoretical formulation without reference to subjective categories unless a totally different conceptual scheme is used. At the same time it is beyond question that certain elements that make their appearance in the subjective

chema of action are also capable of formulation in terms that make no
reference to any state of mind whatever.

The most obvious case of this is a large part, at least, of the content
of the knowledge which is thought of as determining action so far as it
approaches the scientific norm of rationality. Indeed so far as such knowledge
does not refer to human beings, the judgment of the scientific validity of the
general concepts involved may be verified by the observer in situations not
involving any concrete phenomena to which a state of mind is ordinarily
imputed. And even though it is knowledge of the behavior, actual or probable, of human beings arrived at through analyzing their states of mind, a
large component in it may be reduced to terms of theories not involving a
subjective reference.

There then arises the question of the systematic classification of such
knowledge. It seems fairly evident that it is knowledge verifiable in terms
of the theoretical systems of the sciences which deal with phenomena other
than those of human behavior or culture, above all physics, chemistry and
the biological sciences. It is not, be it noted, necessary, that the knowledge
guiding action be stated in the terms normally in use among competent
representatives of these sciences, but only that it should be *verifiable* in
terms of their established theories. Moreover, for action to be rational it is
necessary only that the actor's empirically correct knowledge should be
adequate as knowledge of fact; it is not necessary for him to be in a position
to explain why the facts on the basis of which he acts are true.

At the same time, there is abundant evidence that the factors formulated
in these sciences influence the concrete course of human behavior through
mechanisms other than those involved in the process of rational taking
account of them. Whatever these anti-intellectualistic channels of influence
may be, and they are probably many, the subjectively observable results of
them will either be only indices of the effective factors, in such a manner that
meaning is irrelevant, or there will, in the limiting case, be no subjective
manifestations at all. The latter would seem to be true of various physiological processes.

For most practical purposes it seems convenient to sum up the role of
these elements of action capable of nonsubjective formulation, in both the
above aspects, as that of heredity and environment in the biological sense.
It has already been remarked that this is an analytical distinction which cuts
across the distinction between the concrete organism and its concrete
environment. Also, neither heredity nor environment is a final analytical
category for purposes of the classification of the general theoretical sciences.
What is environmental for purposes of analyzing any class of biological
organisms has its physical, chemical and biological aspects. Similarly, though
analysis of the actual mechanisms of heredity seems not to have reached
more than a relatively elementary analytical level, there is every reason to
believe that these mechanisms will prove amenable to analysis in terms of
all three of the above general theoretical systems.

But one of the most fundamental units of all social systems of concrete
action is what may be called the concrete individual. In its particular
reference to the systematic theory of action in the sense of this study this

unit appears as an "actor" which we know to be an abstraction. But so far as we know, all actors are marked by a solidarity as units with corresponding organisms. That is, there is no such thing, empirically, as an actor which is not in another aspect a living organism. There is, furthermore, much evidence that in the synthetic aspect of general biology the physicochemica aspects of this concrete entity are taken account of in much the same sense as through the role of knowledge and the other modes pointed out non-subjective elements affecting concrete action are taken account of in the theory of action. Then it would seem useful to employ, as a general formula for the role of these elements, the pair of concepts which forms perhaps the most general framework of biological theory, since it is the biological aspect which seems most immediately to impinge on the aspect of action of this concrete unit, the individual. But because this appears for many purposes convenient, it is not to be inferred that this study has become involved in the subtle controversies of biological theory. It has proved possible (see Note B above) to define all the fundamental types of theory of action employed here without reference to the concepts of heredity and environment. They play no substantive role in the central theoretical argument of the study. They serve, rather, the purpose of clarifying and making comprehensible the general meaning when it is necessary to look outside the rigid limits of the systematic theory of action into certain neighboring fields. The important lines of distinction are that between subjective and nonsubjective categories, and among the subjective those which are and which are not capable of formulation in nonsubjective terms. Any further differentiation or definition among those capable of nonsubjective formulation is a question which lies, in strictness, outside the scope of the theory of action.

Attention should, however, be called to one point which may worry the reader. In the great body of thought here called individualistic positivism in the theory of action, one main limiting type has been termed radical positivistic anti-intellectualism. What this means is, in general, the biologizing of the theory of human action so that the latter becomes essentially applied biology. So prominent has this tendency been that there is a strong tendency to infer that biological factors in social action must, in the nature of the case, be individualistic in the causal sense. There seems, however, to be no empirical justification for this view. On the contrary, there is in the evidence available here no reason to doubt that on the level of animal life where the subjective categories of the theory of action are inapplicable, the properties of collectivities involving a plurality of organisms are by no means all capable of derivation from those of analytically isolated individual organisms by a process of direct generalization. This is most likely to be conspicuous in the "social" animals, like ants. If it is true, there is further no reason why the same emergent elements of social systems should not operate on a biological level in human societies. It is, indeed, quite unsafe to postulate that all biological elements in human behavior must necessarily be individualistic or, conversely, that all those capable only of subjective formulation must be sociologistic. Just as many individualistic positivists were guilty of the first fallacy, so Durkheim was, as will be shown, guilty of the second.

NOTE D: ON THE RELATION OF PSYCHOLOGY AND BIOLOGY

Readers of the foregoing chapter may have noticed that no attempt has been made to define the place of psychological factors in the scheme of positivistic social thought. This problem apparently raises a difficulty. For it seems that in so far as human behavior is independent of the factors of its situation the elements explaining it must either be of the utilitarian order or fall altogether outside the schema of individualistic thought in the causal sense. This situation necessitates conceiving the psychological factor as linked to heredity, which would appear to eliminate it completely. For is not heredity exclusively biological? The problem does not appear to be as simple as that.

There are two logically possible positions. One is the reductive doctrine most commonly held in materialistic form. In these monistic terms the problem evaporates, for then only one conceptual scheme, that of the physical world is ultimately valid for positive explanatory purposes anyway. Then both biology and psychology become simply fields of application of these ultimate principles to particular classes of fact. This position is taken most consistently by behaviorists.

On the other hand, it is possible to hold an emergent or other non-reductive view. On this basis there arises the possibility of making a distinction of two sets of elements, both of which operate through heredity. The distinction can best be elucidated through two different approaches to the same concrete subject matter.

In so far as the organism is analyzed structurally on a biological level it is broken down into parts anatomically speaking. That is, the parts are units having a spatial location—organs, tissues, cells. Their structural relations to each other are relations in space. One organ is "next to," "above," "below," "to the right of" another, etc. On the other hand, the starting point for psychological analysis lies in modes of behavior of the organism as a whole. In so far as the units in these modes are analyzed structurally on a psychological level the parts are not anatomical parts at all, but are described in terms of non-spatial categories. It is absurd to ask whether the sexual instinct is above the intelligence or the emotion of anger to the left of the emotion of sympathy. The two types of analysis are, of course, not unrelated to each other, since they both are applicable to the same concrete phenomena in the empirical world. There is no reason why they should be completely reducible to each other.

The second approach lies on another plane. It is true that the biological level of analysis involves teleological elements. The concept of organism itself implies them. But these are teleological elements of a character which do not imply a subjective reference, though they do involve the conception of the organism as in some degree an active entity which does more than merely reflect its conditions of existence. The psychological level, on the other hand, does involve this subjective reference. A knowledge of psychology is a knowledge of "the mind" and not merely of behavior. This is not to be taken to mean that the data of psychology must be confined to introspection but that in its interpretation of the data of observation, such as behavior, linguistic and other forms of expression, it must employ concepts the definition of which involves such subjective categories as "end," "purpose," "knowledge," "feeling," "sentiment," etc.

Now these subjective categories have no meaning on the biological level at all precisely because they are not reducible to terms of location in space. When we are thinking in biological terms we are dealing with *conditions* of the subjective aspect of human action, conditions which are necessary but not sufficient. In so far as the concrete developed organism is conditioned by its hereditary constitution there seems to be no reason why its "mental traits" should not also be affected along with its anatomical structure. Put another way, the fact that mental traits are in part transmitted by heredity is no proof that they are in this respect reducible to biological categories. Heredity is a concrete category while biological theory is a system of analytical concepts.

Thus the terms heredity and environment, by which the radical positivistic factors have been summed up from the point of view of analysis of action, must be taken to include both biological and psychological[1] elements.

This conclusion holds whether the ultimate general position taken is positivistic or not, but with one important qualification. In the strictly positivistic scheme of thought the only place for a subjective reference is in the utilitarian element, at least in other than an epiphenomenal status. The utilitarian position is a peculiarly unstable one, continually tending to break down into radical positivism. The tendency of this breakdown is, in turn, the elimination of the subjective reference—the logical end result is behaviorism. This tends to reduce psychological to biological considerations.

This indeed seems to be the source of the difficulty which has occasioned this note. The opinion may be ventured that a stable place for psychology in the roster of the analytical sciences dealing with human action is incompatible with a strictly positivistic methodology. It is concerned with those elements of human nature through which man's biological heritage is related to his purposes, ends, sentiments. If these subjective elements are eliminated, as they are in radical positivism, the elements which relate them to the biological heritage become superfluous. The question of the classification of the sciences will be taken up in general terms at the end of the study.

[1] Consideration of the next paragraph will show that for a positivistic system the definition of the terms heredity and environment employed above (p. 67) is still correct.

CHAPTER III

SOME PHASES OF THE HISTORICAL DEVELOPMENT OF INDIVIDUALISTIC POSITIVISM IN THE THEORY OF ACTION

Christian thought during the Reformation period was directed toward the jealous safeguarding of the sphere of religious freedom of the individual.[1] Since this problem tended to fuse with the dichotomy of the Roman law, the problem of religious freedom tended to become identified with that of political obligation, because the only authority that could threaten this sphere was the state. From a Protestant Christian point of view the general trend of thought on this question was unfavorable to the state, for in contrast with its status in pagan antiquity the state had been robbed by Christianity of the intrinsic sanctity it had enjoyed. It could enjoy religious approval only in so far as it contributed to, or was at least compatible with, the religious interests of individuals, for these formed the supreme goal of Christian conduct.

In the problem of political obligation there were, of course, both normative and explanatory elements involved. The central Christian starting point was normative, that of deducing the consequences for conduct and policy of Christian ideals. At the same time, however, this inevitably raised the problem of knowing the empirical conditions under which such ideals must be sought, and the limitations on them imposed by these conditions. The peculiar way in which Protestant Christianity had settled the locus of religious values in the individual had an important consequence in this respect. The arguments for freedom from authority tended to become predominantly normative, only with freedom of conscience could even the opportunity for a truly Christian life be guaranteed. Conversely the argument for limitations on freedom of the individual tended to become

[1] The remarks made in note 1, p. 52 apply also to this introductory sketch.

empirical and factual, emphasizing the inexorable conditions of human life in society and the numerous ways in which a freedom gained in the name of religion could be perverted so as to endanger the stability of society itself. Far back in Christian thought the necessity of the state and its coercive authority had been explained by the Fall and the consequent sinfulness of man which necessitated a control more immediately drastic than the spiritual sanctions of religion could furnish. Gradually the sinful element of human nature was brought into the framework of a concept of natural law thought of as a set of inexorable necessities which could not be overcome by any spiritual power, at least any at man's disposal.

Thus when social thought became secularized about the seventeenth century its central problem was that of the basis of order in society, in the particular form of the sphere of individual freedom from authoritarian control in relation to the coercive authority of the state. The former sphere tended to be justified and protected by normative arguments, first from religious motives of the freedom of conscience, later in secularized form involving a *normative law of nature* the principal content of which was a set of ethically absolute natural rights.[1] Over against this the argument for authority tended to involve an attempted demonstration of the inexorable necessities of man's life in company with his fellows, above all in the form of the sinful "natural man" secularized into a deterministic human nature. Thus is seen the tendency to think deterministically in terms of the *conditions* of action. This tendency paralleled another—the seventeenth century was also the period of the first great systematization of modern physical science, it was the century of Newton. Hence there was a strong tendency to assimilate these deterministic laws of human nature, in logical type and in part also in content, to the current deterministic theories of physical nature—the scientific materialism of the classical physics. The

---

[1] On these two concepts of the law of nature and their relations in eighteenth and early nineteenth century thought, see the two articles by O. H. Taylor in *Quarterly Journal of Economics*, November, 1929, and February, 1930. The earlier history of the conception of natural law in the various phases of Christian thought and its antecedents in the thought of late antiquity is admirably discussed in E. Troeltsch, *Social Teaching of the Christian Churches.*

first great example of this type of deterministic thinking in the social field is Hobbes.[1]

Hobbes and the Problem of Order

For present purposes the basis of Hobbes' social thinking lies in his famous concept of the state of nature as the war of all against all. Hobbes is almost entirely devoid of normative thinking. He sets up no ideal of what conduct should be, but merely investigates the ultimate conditions of social life. Man, he says, is guided by a plurality of passions. The good is simply that which any man desires.[2] But unfortunately there are very severe limitations on the extent to which these desires can be realized, limitations which according to Hobbes lie primarily in the nature of the relations of man to man.

Man is not devoid of reason. But reason is essentially a servant of the passions—it is the faculty of devising ways and means to secure what one desires. Desires are random, there is "no common rule of good and evil to be taken from the nature of the objects themselves."[3] Hence since the passions, the ultimate ends of action, are diverse there is nothing to prevent their pursuit resulting in conflict.

In Hobbes' thinking, the reason for this danger of conflict is to be found in the part played by power. Since all men are seeking to realize their desires they must necessarily seek command over means to this realization. The power a man has is in Hobbes' own words[4] simply "his present means to obtain some future apparent good." One very large element of power is the ability to command the recognition and services of other men. To Hobbes this is the most important among those means which, in the nature of things, are limited. The consequence is that what

[1] In this chapter there will be no attempt to discuss all authors in terms of their general importance. A selection will be made for discussion of a few concrete theories which conveniently bring out the different logical possibilities of the general system of thought with which we are concerned. In many cases others would do as well.

[2] Thomas Hobbes, *The Leviathan*, Everyman ed., p. 24.

[3] *Ibid.*, p. 24. In Hobbes' general philosophy there is a tendency to relate the passions, through a mechanistic psychology to a materialistic basis in the laws of motion. This tendency does not, however, play any substantive role in his analysis of social action and hence need not be considered here.

[4] *Ibid.*, p. 43.

means to his ends one man commands another is necessarily shut off from. Hence power as a proximate end is inherently a source of division between men.

Nature hath made men so equal in the faculties of body and mind, that though there be found one man sometimes manifestly stronger in body or of quicker mind than another, yet when all is reckoned together the difference between man and man is not so considerable as that one man can thereupon claim to himself any benefit, to which another may not pretend as well as he. . . . From this equality of ability ariseth equality of hope in the attaining of our ends. And therefore if any two men desire the same thing which nevertheless they cannot both enjoy, they become enemies; and in the way to their end endeavor to destroy or subdue one another.[1]

In the absence of any restraining control men will adopt to this immediate end the most efficient available means. These means are found in the last analysis to be force and fraud.[2] Hence a situation where every man is the enemy of every other, endeavoring to destroy or subdue him by force or fraud or both. This is nothing but a state of war.

But such a state is even less in conformity with human desires than what most of us know. It is in Hobbes' famous words a state where the life of man is "solitary, poor, nasty, brutish and short."[3] The fear of such a state of things calls into action, as a servant of the most fundamental of all the passions, that of self-preservation, at least a modicum of reason which finds a solution of the difficulty in the social contract. By its terms men agreed to give up their natural liberty to a sovereign authority which in turn guarantees them security, that is immunity from aggression by the force or fraud of others. It is only through the authority of this sovereign that the war of all against all is held in check and order and security maintained.

Hobbes' system of social theory is almost a pure case of utilitarianism, according to the definition of the preceding chapter. The basis of human action lies in the "passions." These are discrete, randomly variant ends of action, "There is no common rule of good and evil to be taken from the nature of the objects themselves." In the pursuit of these ends men act rationally,

[1] *Ibid.*, p. 63.
[2] *Ibid.*, p. 66.
[3] *Ibid.*, p. 65.

choosing, within the limitations of the situation, the most efficient means. But this rationality is strictly limited, reason is the "servant of the passions," it is concerned only with questions of ways and means.

But Hobbes went much farther than merely defining with extraordinary precision the basic units of a utilitarian system of action. He went on to deduce the character of the concrete system which would result if its units were in fact as defined. And in so doing he became involved in an empirical problem which has not yet been encountered, as the present discussion so far has been confined to defining units and noting merely their logical relations in utilitarian thought—the problem of *order*. This problem, in the sense in which Hobbes posed it, constitutes the most fundamental empirical difficulty of utilitarian thought.[1] It will form the main thread of the historical discussion of the utilitarian system and its outcome.

Before taking up his experience with it, two meanings of the term which may easily become confused should be distinguished. They may be called normative order and factual order respectively. The antithesis of the latter is randomness or chance in the strict sense of phenomena conforming to the statistical laws of probability. Factual order, then, connotes essentially accessibility to understanding in terms of logical theory, especially of science. Chance variations are in these terms impossible to understand or to reduce to law. Chance or randomness is the name for that which is incomprehensible, not capable of intelligible analysis.[2]

Normative order, on the other hand, is always relative to a given system of norms or normative elements, whether ends, rules or other norms. Order in this sense means that process takes place in conformity with the paths laid down in the normative system. Two further points should, however, be noted in this connection. One is that the breakdown of any given normative order, that is a state of chaos from a normative point of view,

---

[1] Its main competitor is that of rationality as empirically adequate. That of order is the more strategic for the present analytical purposes.

[2] Only on a positivistic basis is intelligibility confined to empirical science. This yields the rigid dilemma: either scientifically understandable or random chaos. The limits of science are, then, to the positivist the absolute limits of human comprehension.

may well result in an order in the factual sense, that is a state of affairs susceptible of scientific analysis. Thus the "struggle for existence" is chaotic from the point of view of Christian ethics, but that does not in the least mean that it is not subject to law in the scientific sense, that is to uniformities of process in the phenomena. Secondly, in spite of the logically inherent possibility that any normative order may break down into a "chaos" under certain conditions, it may still be true that the normative elements are essential to the maintenance of the *particular* factual order which exists when processes are to a degree in conformity with them. Thus a social order is always a factual order in so far as it is susceptible of scientific analysis but, as will be later maintained, it is one which cannot have stability without the effective functioning of certain normative elements.

As has been shown, two normative features play an essential role in the utilitarian scheme, ends and rationality. Thus, for Hobbes, given the fact that men have passions and seek to pursue them rationally, the problem arises of whether, or under what conditions, this is possible in a social situation where there is a plurality of men acting in relation to one another. Given one other fact, which Hobbes refers to as the "equality of hope," the problem of order in the normative sense of a degree of attainability of ends, of satisfaction of the passions, becomes crucial. For under the assumption of rationality men will seek to attain their ends by the most efficient means available. Among their ends is empirically found to be attainment of the recognition of others. And to them under social conditions the services of others are always and necessarily to be found among the potential means to their ends. To securing both these, recognition and service, whether as ultimate or as proximate ends, the most immediately efficient means, in the last analysis, are force and fraud. In the utilitarian postulate of rationality there is nothing whatever to exclude the employment of these means. But the effect of their unlimited employment is that men will "endeavor to destroy or subdue one another." That is, according to the strictest utilitarian assumptions, under social conditions, a complete system of action will turn out to be a "state of war" as Hobbes says, that is, from the normative point of view of the attainment of human ends, which is itself the utilitarian starting point, not an order at all, but chaos.[1] It is the state where any appreciable degree of such attainment becomes impossible, where the life of man is "solitary, poor, nasty, brutish and short."

The point under discussion here is not Hobbes' own solution of this crucial problem, by means of the idea of a social contract. This solution really involves stretching, at a critical point, the conception of rationality beyond its scope in the rest of the theory, to a point where the actors come to realize the situation as a whole instead of pursuing their own ends in terms of their immediate situation, and then take the action necessary to eliminate force and fraud, and, purchasing security at the sacrifice of the advantages to be gained by their future employment. This is not the solution in which the present study will be interested. But Hobbes saw the problem with a clarity which has never been surpassed, and his statement of it remains valid today. It is so fundamental that a genuine solution of it has never been attained on a strictly utilitarian basis, but has entailed either recourse to a radical positivistic expedient, or breakdown of the whole positivistic framework.

Before leaving Hobbes it is important to elaborate a little further the reasons for the precariousness of order so far as the utilitarian elements actually dominate action. This precariousness rests, in the last analysis, on the existence of classes of things which are scarce, relative to the demand for them, which, as Hobbes says, "two [or more] men desire" but "which nevertheless they cannot both enjoy." Reflection will show that there are many such things desired by men either as ends in themselves or as means to other ends. But Hobbes, with his characteristic penetration, saw that it was not necessary to enumerate and catalogue them and to rest the argument on such a detailed consideration, but that their crucial importance was inherent in the very existence of social relations themselves. For it is inherent in the latter that the actions of men should be potential means to each other's ends. Hence as a proximate end it is a direct corollary of the postulate of rationality that all men should desire and seek power over one another. Thus the concept of power comes to occupy a central position in the analysis of the problem of order. A purely utilitarian society is chaotic and

[1] Seen as a factual order a purely utilitarian system would then be an inherently unstable phenomenon, incapable of empirical subsistence.

unstable, because in the absence of limitations on the use of means, particularly force and fraud, it must, in the nature of the case, resolve itself into an unlimited struggle for power; and in the struggle for the immediate end, power, all prospect of attainment of the ultimate, of what Hobbes called the diverse passions, is irreparably lost.

If the above analysis is correct one might suppose that Hobbes' early experiments with logical thinking on a utilitarian basis would have brought that type of social thought to a rapid and deserved demise. But such was very far from being the case, indeed in the eighteenth and nineteenth centuries it enjoyed a period of such vogue as to be considered almost among the eternal verities themselves. But this was not because the Hobbesian problem was satisfactorily solved. On the contrary, as so often happens in the history of thought, it was blithely ignored and covered up by implicit assumptions. How did this happen?

It is significant that the immediate practical animus of Hobbes' social thought lay in the defense of political authority on a secular basis. A strong government, justified by the social contract, was a necessary bulwark of the security of the commonwealth, threatened as it was by the imminent danger of the resurgence of force and fraud. It has already been remarked that in the argument over political obligation those who defend individual liberty tend to make use of normative rather than factual arguments. It is largely in this context that what later came to be the dominant stream of utilitarian thought developed, so that Hobbes was virtually forgotten. In the process of development there took place a subtle change. What started as normative arguments about what ought to be, became embodied in the assumptions of what was predominantly considered a factual, scientific theory of human action as it was. By some this theory was looked upon as literally descriptive of the existing social order; by others, more skeptically as, though not the whole truth, at least justified for heuristic purposes; and above all in either case as constituting the working conceptual tools of a great tradition of thought. Hence for present purposes it matters little which of the two positions was taken since the empirical qualifications of utilitarian theory were embodied in residual categories which played no positive part in the theoretical system itself, at least until the time of its incipient breakdown.

LOCKE AND THE CLASSICAL ECONOMICS

The most convenient starting point for the present discussion is Locke. The contrast between Locke and Hobbes is striking and illuminating precisely because of the extent of agreement in their underlying conceptual schemes. Locke also thinks in terms of a plurality of discrete individuals each pursuing his own ends independently of the others. Though there is no explicit statement that these ends are random, as there is in Hobbes' work, yet it is quite clear that Locke entertains no clear conception of any positive mode of relation between them. The only explicit treatment of ends at all is that of the natural rights which men have "by nature," independently of civil society, and which it exists to protect. But all these—life, health, liberty and possessions,[1]—are to be regarded as the universal conditions of the attainment of individual ends, not as the ultimate ends in themselves. They are the things which all rational men want as conditions or means regardless of the character of their ultimate ends. In the philosophy of Locke as well as Hobbes men are rational in the pursuit of their ends.

Nevertheless there are striking differences between the positions of the two men. As against Hobbes, Locke consistently minimizes the problem of security. To be sure, one motive for the social contract is that although men have the above rights by nature, still, if in the state of nature they are violated, there is "no recourse but to self-defense," while in civil society men will be protected in their rights by the government. There thus is a problem, but it is a highly contingent one. Men's rights might be violated but the danger is so slight that overthrow of government if it does not live fully up to its obligations to protect them is fully justified. The risk is not, as Hobbes would have maintained, too great. Thus for Locke, government instead of being the dam which precariously keeps the angry floods of force and fraud from inundating society and destroying it becomes merely a prudent measure of insurance against an eventuality which is not particularly threatening, but which wise men will nevertheless provide against. Indeed so much is this the case that security against aggression really becomes a subordinate motive of

---

[1] JOHN LOCKE, *Two Treatises of Civil Government.* Everyman ed., p. 119.

participation in civil society; its place is taken by the positive mutual advantages of association.

What underlies this difference? It is usually put as a difference in the conception of the state of nature. Instead of being a *bellum omnium contra omnes* it is for Locke a beneficent state of affairs, governed by Reason, the law of nature. Reason "teaches all mankind who will but consult it that, being all equal and independent no one *ought* to harm another in his life, health, liberty or possessions."[1] Reason is not merely the servant of the passions but the dominant principle of nature itself.

But what does this mean? Essentially that men "being reasonable" ought to, and in general will in pursuit of their ends subordinate their actions, whatever these may be, to certain rules. The essential content of these rules is to respect the natural rights of others, to refrain from injuring them. This means that the choice of means in pursuit of ends is not guided solely by considerations of immediate rational efficiency, but that "reason" in this sense is limited by "reason" in the other. Above all they will not attempt to subdue or destroy one another on the way to their end. There will be, that is, drastic limitations on the employment of force and fraud and other instruments of power. Now this limitation on utilitarian rationality is achieved by introducing a third normative component not indigenous to the utilitarian system as it has been defined. And it is this which accounts for the stability of Locke's particular type of individualistic society. It is the means of minimizing the importance of the problem of order.

By employing the term reason Locke apparently implies that this attitude is something at which men arrive by a cognitive process. It includes the recognition that all men are equal and independent and that they have a reciprocal obligation to recognize each other's rights and thus take upon themselves sacrifices of their own immediate interests. This, however, is the necessary condition of a maximum attainment of the ends of all in the long run. Thus at the basis of the position lies the postulate of the rational recognition of what Halévy[2] has aptly termed the

---

[1] *Ibid.*, p. 119.

[2] See ÉLIE HALÉVY, *La formation du radicalisme philosophique*, 3 vols. This is much the most penetrating account available of the aspects of utilitarian thought which are important for this discussion. It has been of great value in the formulation of the present historical sketch.

natural identity of interests. This is the device by which it has been possible for utilitarian thought, with few exceptions, for two hundred years to evade the Hobbesian problem.[1]

It is a fact, curious as it may seem, that Locke's more or less wishful postulation of the natural identity of interests opened the way to a highly important scientific development which, though in essence utilitarian, could never have taken place in terms of the more consistent Hobbesian version of utilitarian theory. And this is true in spite of the fact that many of its proponents went far to forget the assumptions on which the empirical applicability of their reasoning depend even with the degree of clarity with which Locke was aware of them. The mode of thinking which Hobbes employed, applying it as he did in an empiricist sense, led empirically to an intensive concentration on the problem of a minimum of security. So intense was this concentration that the sheer difficulty of attainment of this minimum far overshadowed any possibilities of positive advantage to be derived from social relationships beyond security itself. Locke, on the other hand, having pushed the problem of security aside, was in a position to pay attention to these matters, and what is much more important, to create a framework of thought within which their analysis could proceed later to far more refined stages than Locke himself attained.

[1] How far Locke's position here as against Hobbes' is a case of wishful thinking is not a matter of importance at present. There is a sense in which he was factually the more nearly right. But in terms of the utilitarian scheme there was no adequate way of formulating his correct insight that most societies would not dissolve into chaos on the breakdown of government, that hence there must be some other element of normative order than fear of governmental coercion. It often happens, in a state of scientific immaturity, that the thinker who comes nearest being factually right in his empirical views is the least theoretically penetrating. Hobbes' iron consistency in developing the consequences of utilitarian assumptions was, in spite of the fact that it led him to empirical errors, such as an exaggerated fear of the consequences of revolution, a greater scientific achievement than Locke's more "reasonable" attitude with its failure adequately to discriminate his implicit normative assumptions from established fact. Locke, that is, was right but gave the wrong reasons. It must be remembered that *scientific achievement is a matter of the combination of systematic theoretical analysis with empirical observation.* When a theoretical system is only partially adequate to the known facts a more correct factual account may be achieved by admitting theoretical errors and inconsistencies. But factual correctness is not the sole aim of science; it must be combined with thoroughgoing theoretical *understanding* of the facts known and correctly stated.

The treatment of Locke is, it should be remembered, with the sole exception of the "identity of interests," restricted to a utilitarian basis. The ends of individuals are still discrete and unrelated. Then there arises, in civil society, the possibility of the presence of any one individual being used as means to another's ends, and with the satisfactory elimination of coercive power this will entail mutual advantage. Of this mutually advantageous use as means to each others' ends there are two logically possible types. One is that of cooperation in the pursuit of a common end, however proximate. The other is exchange of services, or possessions. For a number of reasons the first possibility played little part in the tradition of thought now being considered; its attention was fastened on the exchange of services or possessions. This is probably owing primarily to the fact that with the concentration of attention on the diversity of ends, and on the unit act, the very existence of common ends even on the proximate level seemed relatively rare and unimportant. Indeed it was mainly in the transition to radical rationalistic positivism that this possibility came into its own.

In the meantime it was the phenomenon of exchange which attracted attention. And if this was to have empirical meaning beyond the mere accidental possession of diverse resources, it naturally had to become combined with a theory of specialization and the division of labor. The phenomena of specialization, the division of labor and exchange constitute the empirical starting point and focus of attention of the classical economics. One of the first formidable attempts at systematic discussion of these issues is to be found in the famous chapter on Property in Locke's Second Treatise of Civil Government.[1] It lays the foundations of the central classical doctrine, the labor theory of value, and is particularly instructive in indicating its genetic, though possibly illogical, connections with the normative aspect of the Lockean theory of the state of nature.

For, in the first instance, this chapter was a defense of private property which, it will be remembered, was listed among the natural rights of men. But property Locke found defensible because it embodied human labor; something became a man's

---

[1] JOHN LOCKE, *op. cit.*, Chap. V.

property when he had "mixed his labor with it"[1] as the celebrated phrase went. The "state of nature" defined a norm of justice for property relations. They should start with "natural equality," in other words, initial advantages should be equalized. This, of course, implied the unrealistic assumption that all men had equal access to the gifts of nature with which to mix their labor. The doctrine held only as Locke said when "there is enough and as good left in common for others."[2] But under Locke's assumptions the same standard defined the conditions of exchange both in justice and in the condition in which rational men would actually accept it. For there could be no advantage in exchange unless a man received more than he could produce in the same line of endeavor by his own labor, otherwise there would be no inducement to enter into exchange. All this would hold so long as there was no coercion, so long as each could choose what transactions he should enter into freely and on an equal basis with his fellows. Then not only would the actual distribution of property and the terms of exchange be just, but goods and services would in fact exchange in proportion to the labor embodied in them. This is the theorem which was later taken up and developed.

Its elaboration and qualification into a usable economic theory, especially as carried out by Adam Smith and Ricardo, involved many intricacies which cannot be reviewed here. Besides the possibility already noted of unequal access to the gifts of nature there were several other sources of difficulty involved in its application to the analysis of a complex concrete society. One was occasioned by the use of capital, the spreading of the production process over time and hence the deferring of consumption for the sake of a larger ultimate product. Ricardo saw very clearly the implications of this difficulty, but on the whole its consequences were obscured for the classical economists by certain peculiarities of their way of conceiving the role of capital, as "funds destined for the maintenance of labor."[3] Another difficulty is caused by the fact that for the most part production is not carried out by an independent individual, but by an organized

---

[1] *Ibid.*, p. 130.
[2] *Ibid.*
[3] Adam Smith, *Wealth of Nations*, ed. by E. Cannan, Vol. I, pp. 74–75.

unit so that the question must be raised of the terms of cooperation in its functioning. These questions need not be further
discussed now.

Only two points must be emphasized here. First, what was to
Locke primarily a standard of justice, the "natural equality in
exchange" became by the time of Ricardo primarily a heuristic
assumption which served to simplify the problems sufficiently to
make possible the development of a workable conceptual scheme.
Ricardo probably came as close as anyone in the history of the
social sciences to a purely scientific point of view. But none the
less the assumptions of Locke's state of nature were built into
the structure of Ricardo's scientific theorizing. That Ricardo
himself was not defending any standard of justice makes no
difference from the present point of view, so long as he had
nothing to put in its place as a basis in assumption for an economic theory. He himself realized the scientific limitations of
the labor theory of value with extraordinary clarity and anticipated most of the subsequent criticisms to which it has been
subjected. But he had no alternative to put forward. If not fully
satisfactory it was at least a first approximation, which was far
better than nothing. In Ricardo what may have been for Locke
an ethical limitation on scientific insight had become definitely a
theoretical limitation. It could not be overcome until there
developed a new theoretical movement. As far as economics was
concerned this took two directions. One, which Ricardo himself
in part shared, involved the breakdown of the assumption of
natural identity of interests. This will be discussed presently.
The other came much later, and was developed by people who
had for the most part ignored the first; it was the advent of the
marginal utility conception, in England through Jevons and
Marshall. This, while still consistent with the Lockean assumptions, in fact solved the principal theoretical difficulties which
Ricardo had been unable to surmount.

The second point to be emphasized is that the conceptual
scheme of the classical economics was enabled to flourish as a
serious scientific theory and more than a mere intellectual exercise precisely because it was applied to a society in which the
basic problem of order was assumed to be solved. Otherwise there
could have been no empirical interest in its problems. For
economic relations as conceived by the classical economics can

take place on a significant scale only within a framework of order by virtue of which force and fraud are at least held within bounds and where the rights of others are respected to a degree.[1] But utilitarian theory, though it operated on an empiricist basis, had no adequate way of accounting for this order. Since no more adequate conceptual scheme than the utilitarian was available at the time, it was a fortunate error that the gap was filled by what, it is now evident, was an untenable "metaphysical" postulate, that the identity of interests was "in the nature of things" and that never under any circumstances was there occasion to question the stability of such an order. Utterly dependent logically on this "erroneous" premise there grew up what is perhaps the most highly developed theoretical system in the social sciences with correct results—within certain limitations. This fact may serve as a lesson to those who are overly puristic in their scientific methodology. Perhaps it is not always wise to discard even methodologically objectionable elements so long as they serve a useful scientific function, unless one has something better to substitute. Of course the fact is that, however untenable in other respects, the postulate of the natural identity of interests was a way of stating a crucially important fact, that in some societies to an important degree there does exist an order which makes possible an approximation to the conditions required by the assumptions of classical economic theory.

From this discussion of the issue as between the Hobbesian and the Lockean versions of utilitarian thought may be seen emerging a distinction which will prove to be of great importance to the discussion which follows. It is between two classes of means in the rational pursuit of ends, those involving force, fraud and other modes of coercion, and those involving rational persuasion of advantage to be gained by entering into relations of exchange. As has been shown, the attribution of any considerable importance to the latter class is dependent on the former being kept to a degree under control. But once this control is factually given, the latter assumes a prominent position. In terms of the relative emphasis on the two classes of means, and the problems

[1] See O. H. TAYLOR, "Economic Theory and Certain Non-economic Elements in Social Life" in *Explorations in Economics, Essays in Honor of F. W. Taussig*, p. 390.

they give rise to, there can be differentiated two main phases of the development of utilitarian thought, the political and the economic, respectively. Here also a glimpse may be caught of the reasons why the question of the status of economic theory is of such crucial importance to the whole range of theoretical issues occupying this study. For, in so far as the basic action schema is employed for analytical purposes, the fact that economic action is actually empirically important must inevitably raise the question of the adequacy of the utilitarian version of the theory of action, if the contention is right that it cannot, without extraneous assumptions, account for the element of order in social relationships necessary to make this possible. Indeed, the central problem may be stated thus: How is it possible, still making use of the general action schema, to solve the Hobbesian problem of order and yet not make use of such an objectionable metaphysical prop as the doctrine of the natural identity of interests? This is why in this study the principal analysis will begin with the work of an eminent economist and continue with a sociologist to whom the question of the status of economic theory is of crucial importance. To repeat, its principal concern will be with one way of escape from the inherent instability of the utilitarian system. But before discussing this central theme it is important to analyze some of the theories which have taken the other logically possible path, the transition to the radical positivistic position.

MALTHUS AND THE INSTABILITY OF UTILITARIANISM

A convenient point of attack is to be found in the position of Malthus.[1] Without, perhaps, altogether realizing what he was doing, he made some serious dents in the armor of "optimistic" utilitarianism. In the polemics in which he was involved may be clearly seen the radically positivistic tendency just mentioned bifurcating thought into the two possible radical positivistic directions, leaving the economists stranded in the middle. That the attack was not fatal but that the classical economics and its

---

[1] All the aspects of Malthus' thought important in this context are best seen in his *Essay on the Principle of Population*, 1st ed. It has been recently reprinted by the Royal Economic Society. The best secondary treatment for present purposes is in Halévy, *op. cit.*

successors were still vouchsafed a long life without change in conceptual framework, does not matter here. The issues were clearly brought to the surface, and that is enough. That they were not met, but still ignored or evaded, in part by Malthus himself, belongs not to the logic of theoretical systems but to the history of the infirmities of man as Homo sàpiens.

In effect, the source of the difficulty was the fact that the postulate of identity of interests really amounted to a denial of one of the utilitarian cornerstones, the randomness of ends. Since both principles tended to be implicit rather than explicit, it is not surprising that there should have been vacillation between the two positions. But the tendency toward the identity of interests fitted in with another prominent element in the positivistic system, namely preoccupation with the rationalistic schema of scientific methodology in relation to action. When this rationalistic tendency is pushed through to a logical conclusion the difficulty of the conflict disappears. Then men's interests are indeed identical, for they have a common set of conditions to which rationally to adapt themselves. Thus Locke's theory of normative nature tends to fuse with the actual conditions of existence as scientifically knowable. The differentiation of the two conceptions of nature had always been more or less indistinct and wishful thinking, rationalized by the teleological optimism of deism, saw in actuality the realization of its wishes.[1] This tendency had been realized on a grand scale in the optimistic philosophy of eighteenth-century France, in the biology of Lamarck as well as the social thought of Condorcet.

But this change of position was associated with a subtle shift of emphasis in other respects. This particular rationalism could, in the current controversies over the question of political obligation, on the part of the anti-authoritarians easily develop into a form of anarchism. The contrast of human institutions with nature to the detriment of the former could lead to advocacy of the abolition of all control. Once freed of the corrupting influence of bad institutions, men would spontaneously live in accord with nature, in harmony, prosperity and happiness. For were not, so far as their reason held sway, their interests identical? There was still a further consequence of this point of view. In the

---

[1] See L. J. HENDERSON, *The Fitness of the Environment,* for certain facts which provide a partial scientific basis for this optimism.

realization of these identical interests, many of which were common to all men, was not the rational thing spontaneous cooperation? The competitive individualism of the economic order, which had come to be thought of almost as part of nature itself, began to be questioned. People saw in it no longer mainly the advantages of the division of labor, but coercion, oppression, unjust inequality. Thus in relation to economic policy this movement issued more and more in an anarchistic socialism (by no means contradictory terms) which Marx later called Utopian socialism. Partly, certainly, to meet this kind of criticism, the individualistic economists tended more directly to rationalize their preference for competitive individualism. Competition was not merely a result of men pursuing their interests independently of one another; it had a positive social function. It was a great regulatory mechanism, a check on abuses. For if one man tried to exploit another the competition of the market would force him to act reasonably or he would have to pay the price. No man could sell dear when others at no loss to themselves were in a position to undercut him. But underlying this emphasis on competition as a regulatory mechanism lay serious theoretical issues. Could it be justified as necessary out of the conceptual armory of the heritage of Locke?

It was into this intellectual situation that Malthus plunged. The anarchistic-socialistic trend of thought had recently made a dramatic appearance in England with Godwin's *Political Justice*. Malthus, like all conservative-minded men in the time of the French Revolution, was alarmed. But how were these arguments to be met? There was little enough to oppose them within the traditional deistic-optimistic natural-law body of thought. The line between Locke and Godwinian anarchism was a distressingly thin one.

The answer to Godwin, which finally emerged from Malthus' cogitations and discussions with his father, was the celebrated principle of population. Unfortunately discussion of this famous doctrine has generally been confined to the questions of whether Malthus was "right" and whether he was consistent. These are not relevant to the present discussion. In taking the position that he did, he introduced a very subtle serpent into the harmonious paradise of Locke. The whole theoretical structure threatened to crash.

Malthus' answer to Godwin was as follows: Suppose Mr. Godwin's heart's desire to be granted and all human institutions to be suddenly abolished. Suppose further the immediate result is as Mr. Godwin predicts, a Utopia of human happiness and harmony instead of Hobbes' struggle for power. What will happen? This happy state cannot last, for the inhabitants will inevitably, in obeying the dictates of nature, act in a manner greatly to increase the population. And as population increases there will gradually appear a barrier to universal happiness, the limitations of subsistence. For the food supply cannot be increased indefinitely in proportion to the amount of labor expended on its production; the limitation is inherent in a nature conceived in a highly unbeneficent sense. Faced with the prospect of starvation there is no reason to believe men will continue "reasonably" to respect one another's rights, nor, when the alternative is to eat or not to eat that their interests are identical in starvation. There will ensue a struggle for at least a minimum of subsistence. This struggle as it intensifies will become increasingly bitter and involve more and more drastic action. Indeed if nothing happens to check it, it cannot but eventuate in a state of war in which every man is the enemy of every other. (In a sense, Locke had not ignored the problem of subsistence. Retention of the fruits of labor upon the gifts of nature was only just "so long as there was enough and as good left for others." But this casual qualifying phrase of Locke's turns out in Malthus' hands to conceal a veritable serpent.) The fact is that there cannot be "enough and as good left for others." The gifts of nature will be appropriated to the hilt. And this changes the optimistic picture beyond recognition. Instead of man living in a beautiful harmony with nature, niggardly nature has played a nasty trick upon him by endowing him with reproductive instincts the exercise of which plant the seeds of his own destruction.[1] It is the same sense of disharmony that permeates Hobbes. In fact, Malthus has drastically reraised the Hobbesian problem.

But why is the actually existent society not in this dire state of an unlimited struggle for subsistence? Because, says Malthus, of the very institutions to which Godwin so strenuously objects— in particular, property and marriage. These are not the imposi-

---

[1] Malthus' attempted theological rationalization of these facts is not relevant here.

tions of the arbitrary and malevolent wills of persons in authority, nor the results of ignorance. They are the spontaneous remedy in this unpleasant situation.[1] The existing state of affairs may be bad, but it is far better than it might be without these institutions. Long before the ultimate state of chaos is reached in the process of degeneration from Godwin's Utopia, these institutional modes of regulation of conduct will spontaneously arise. Marriage is necessary so that each shall be unable to escape responsibility for his own offspring; property is the only feasible means of giving a man the means of meeting this responsibility. Only within the framework of these institutions is there adequate motivation for the "moral restraint" which Malthus held to be the only alternative to the unpleasant operation of the "positive checks." Anarchism would be all very well in the unlimited plenty of the Garden of Eden; in the hard conditions of actual life man should be thankful for the protection of institutional restraints.

The same situation provided Malthus with an apparently solid foundation for his ardent belief in competitive individualism, and relieved him of its embarassing tendency to evaporate into socialistic cooperation. Competition is not only beneficent, it is absolutely necessary, it is the *vis medicatrix rei publicae.* But what this implies as Malthus sets it forth must not escape notice. It is not beneficent under any and all conditions, but *only within the proper institutional framework*. Without an adequate check on population growth beneficent competition would degenerate into a state of war. The state which Mr. Godwin's proposals threaten to bring about is far from beneficent, yet it is highly "competitive." This brings a new note of the greatest importance into the consideration of competition. It is no longer dealt with in purely utilitarian terms. However Malthus' derivation of institutions from the pressure of population may ultimately be judged, he has dealt a fatal blow to the easy optimism of the view that competition under any and all conditions is the most desirable of all things. Malthus' doctrine of the regulatory function of institutions is, perhaps, the first major step in the development of utilitarian thought[2] in the advance beyond the

---

[1] Perhaps evidence of a twinge of conscience on nature's part for the above-mentioned "nasty trick."

[2] There were undoubtedly predecessors not in the direct line. Machiavelli is a notable example.

mere assumption of the existence of order. It is a step which had to wait for its full fruition until the movement of thought appeared which forms the central subject matter of this study.

MARX AND CLASS ANTAGONISM

Besides accounting for the spontaneous generation of marriage and property, population pressure had for Malthus a third consequence that opened up still other vistas of thought which were closed to the strict utilitarian of the Lockean stamp. That is, it would lead to a "division of society into classes of employers and laborers." The reason for this is the pressure for efficiency in production. For Locke the advantages of exchange within the framework of civil society supplied as it were the cake of human existence; for Malthus on the other hand, it was the black bread of grim necessity. While Locke thought in terms of exchange between independent individuals, for Malthus efficiency demanded the use of capital and the organized productive unit, an impossibility unless some were working under the direction of others.

Apart from any question of a tendency to justify the existing class situation, what was the implication of this view? It was that the basic disharmony between numbers and the limitations of subsistence led to a derivative disharmony within society itself, the disharmony between the interests of classes. The further implications of this were far-reaching and provided another body of explosive material within the structure of economic thought. Ricardo, by his acceptance of the Malthusian principle, carried these implications a considerable distance. Seen in terms of the logical exigencies of the Ricardian theory of distribution of wealth, Malthusianism performed an important double service. On the one hand, the development of the conception of the niggardliness of nature led to the conception of "diminishing returns," the logical basis of the Ricardian theory of rent which solved the theoretical problem raised by the full appropriation of the gifts of nature. On the other hand the theorem that there was a constant supply price of labor derived from the principle of population made it possible to draw the theoretically difficult line in the marginal product between the shares of labor and capital, by means of the famous iron law of wages. But the double disharmony thus introduced into the economic system—between the

interests of the exploiters of niggardly nature, the landlords and
all others on the one hand, between employers and laborers on
the other hand—greatly burdened the conception of a smoothly
working, automatically self-adjusting, competitive mechanism.
The disharmony between these elements and the essentially
Lockean assumptions of Ricardo's theory of value have been
acutely analyzed by Halévy.[1]

At the same time certain peculiarities of the classical system
made it difficult for at least the latter of these two disharmonies
to flower out into its full theoretical consequences. This had to
do particularly with the way in which the classical economists
conceived the capitalist employer. He did not appear primarily
as a bargainer for the services of labor. Indeed, the terms of sale
of these services were really settled by the Malthusian situation.
His role was rather that of "making advances to labor," a point
of view which issued in the wage-fund theory[2] with its fatalistic
implications. In this respect, though still in large measure on a
classical basis, it remained for Marx to draw the conclusions. To
him the fact of an organized productive unit meant an inherent
class conflict, for the immediate interests of the two classes were
completely opposed.

Once the underlying starting point was given this turn, important elements of the peculiar classical theory played into Marx's
hands.[3] This came mainly from the conception of the role of labor
in production, essentially a result of the origin of the theory in
the conception of a state of nature. According to the classical
theory at the margin labor alone was really a productive factor
while capital merely "set laborers to work." This left the capitalist employer's share of the marginal product a residual share.
Even Mill, the "high priest of Liberalism," stated, "The cause
of profit is that labor produces more than is required for its
support."[4] It was not surprising, then, that this should be
turned into a theory of exploitation, that interest and profit

[1] ÉLIE HALÉVY, *op. cit.*, Vol. III, Chap. I.
[2] On the wage-fund theory and its history, see F. W. Taussig, *Wages and Capital.*
[3] On this aspect of Marx the most illuminating discussion I have found is
A. D. Lindsay, *Karl Marx's Capital.* Lindsay, with full acknowledgment,
leans heavily on Halévy for his account of the background.
[4] JOHN STUART MILL. *Principles of Political Economy*, ed. by W. J. Ashley,
p. 416.

should be interpreted as a subtraction from the "true wages" of labor.

The permanent importance of the Marxian exploitation theory for the present discussion lies, however, not in these peculiar technicalities which are now mainly only of antiquarian interest. It lies rather in the fact that, starting as Marx did from the element of class conflict, the center of his attention was on bargaining power. Thus in a particular case he reintroduced the factor of differences of power into social thinking, which had been so important in Hobbes' philosophy and so neglected since. The particular classical trappings of the theory are of quite secondary importance and their correction in terms of modern economic theory does not alter the essentials, though it does the form of statement[1] and some of the secondary results.[2]

The Marxian treatment of bargaining power is, however, not merely a revival of the Hobbesian struggle for power. It brings into prominence an element which had been lost to sight in the conflict between the positions of Hobbes and Locke, since this conflict envisaged a rigid alternative between a state of war and a completely noncoercive harmonious order. But actual society is neither. Even though the institutional framework is strong enough to keep the role of force down to a negligible level except at certain special times of crisis, and that of fraud within limits, it still leaves the door open to certain other milder forms of coercion. This is the case with the "legal" exercise of a superior strategic position in the bargaining process. And this is all that is necessary for the main Marxian theoretical purposes even though many Marxians tend to see in the acts of government only a process of violent and fraudulent oppression of the working classes. Under institutional conditions this element may be of considerable

[1] *Cf.* Pareto's discussion of Marx, *Systèmes socialistes*, Vol. II, Chap. XV, where in spite of repudiating Marx's technical economic theory he praises him highly for his attention to the class struggle. This latter is for Pareto, however, a sociological rather than an economic factor.

[2] The error of the many modern economists who repudiate Marx altogether lies in the fact that they (rightly) criticize the outworn forms of Marxian economics without going back to the really central proposition on which Marx's most important departures from the main trend of the classical economics were based. Thus they succeed in "throwing out the baby with the bath." They have done this essentially because they have in general shared the implicit assumption of a natural identity of interests. M. M. Bober's *Karl Marx's Interpretation of History* is a good example.

importance, though perhaps not of the dominant importance attributed to it by Marx.

The reintroduction of the power factor in this form by Marx carried with it an implication of the instability of the economic system into which it came. But this instability, instead of being chaotic as according to Hobbes' theory, was the result of a power relation within a determinate institutional framework, involving a definite social organization—the capitalistic enterprise—which made it possible for it to form the basis for a theory of definite dynamic process, an evolution of capitalism. Up to this point Marx may be considered to be understandable in terms of the logical framework of English utilitarian thought, though, as has been shown, in a somewhat different way from most other utilitarians. Here, however, he tied his analysis into a theory of "dialectic" evolution largely of Hegelian origin. Marx thus forms an important bridge between the positivistic and idealistic traditions of thought. Further discussion of Marx will therefore be postponed until his relation to idealism can be taken up.[1] He is one of the most important forerunners of the group of writers, including especially Max Weber, to be dealt with under the heading of idealism. Enough, however, has been said to show that Marx's historical materialism is not scientific materialism in the ordinary sense, but is rather, fundamentally, a version of utilitarian individualism. It differs from the main trend of the latter, however, precisely by the presence of the "historical" element, which will be discussed when Marx is taken up again.

DARWINISM

It has been argued throughout that the version of utilitarian thought dominant in the heritage of Locke was, in terms of its strictly scientific elements, inherently unstable, that a modicum of stability in it was dependent on adherence to the metaphysical prop of the natural identity of interests. To give this postulate within the positivistic framework to any degree a *logically* (if not empirically) satisfactory underpinning it was necessary to make the transition to radical rationalistic positivism with all the consequences to which Malthus so strongly objected in his attack upon Godwin. But in that same attack Malthus in effect swept away the prop with far-reaching consequences, some of which

[1] See Chap. XIII.

have just been considered. It remains to inquire, however, in what direction this was leading as far as concerned the development of a general system of social theory rather than the particular problems just dealt with.

There can be no doubt that the main tendency of the Malthusian line of thinking was to oppose Godwinian rationalistic positivism with the other alternative of the radical positivistic system, positivistic anti-intellectualism, as it may be termed. In particular, Malthus may conveniently be taken to mark the beginning of a movement to interpret human action predominantly in biological terms, which steadily gained in force almost throughout the nineteenth century.

In the first place, in Malthus himself the source of all the trouble lay in what was essentially a biological hypothesis, the "tendency of population to increase." One cannot but ascribe this powerful force mainly to heredity. It is the expression of an inherited instinct which derives its importance from the sheer difficulty of controlling it even though Malthus held that, under certain conditions, it could be controlled by "moral restraint." Similarly the other term of the Malthusian difficulty, the limitations of subsistence, lay in certain ultimate features of the non-human environment. In both respects so far as the principle of population determines social conditions it is, ultimately, the effect of the conditions of action, not of men's ends or any other normative element. But so far as this is so the scope of variation open to human volition is narrowed down and the limit of a radical positivistic theory is approached. This Malthus himself did not reach; he remained too good a utilitarian. But, in part influenced by him, the tendency culminated in one of the great movements of nineteenth century thought, Darwinism, which when developed into a closed system and applied to human action in society constituted the most important radically anti-intellectualistic positivistic system ever promulgated.

The basic feature of the Malthusian situation is, of course, the assumed fact of powers of reproduction of the species far in excess of the possibilities of support in the conditions of the environment. This situation may, logically, be met in one of two ways, as indicated by Malthus' distinction between positive and preventive checks. The preventive check, "moral restraint," is indicative of the utilitarian element of Malthus' thought. On the biological plane with which Darwin was concerned this necessarily drops out; the surplus must be eliminated by the positive checks. The Darwinian name for the process is "natural selection."

Darwin differs from Malthus by applying to all species of organisms what the latter had applied only to man. But he also differed in another important respect. Malthus had been concerned solely with the problem of numbers; a certain number could attain adequate subsistence if the surplus were somehow eliminated, or of course prevented from being born. But Darwin began to pay attention to the problem of which among those present were eliminated and which survived. This necessarily implied a qualitative difference between the individuals in a population. But once given this qualitative difference, which Malthus did not consider, the process is no longer one merely of elimination, but of selection.

There is one further element necessary to complete the picture and to close the system—an answer to the question, whence the qualitative differences between individual organisms? This in the Darwinian theory is accomplished by the postulate of random variations. There is, in heredity, a continual process of variation at random about the previous hereditary type. Among these variations some are eliminated in the struggle for existence, others survive and reproduce their kind. But those which survive are not the "average"; they are a selected group so that in the process the modal type itself is shifted. It is by the combination of variation and selection that the conception of static adjustment to fixed factors, characteristic of Malthus and the other utilitarians, gives way to an evolutionary theory.

But it is essentially positivistic evolutionism. For what elements give direction to the process? Of course the conditions of the environment. It is adaptation to these conditions which constitutes the fitness which explains selection and reproduction. True, the environment alone could not produce evolution; but typically the other element is a random element, playing a role logically analogous to that of random ends in the utilitarian system. Thus the environment alone is the determining, direction-giving element.

Precisely in so far as this "biologizing" tendency, which in fact took primarily the Darwinian form, gained ascendancy there was an abandonment of the utilitarian position in favor of radical anti-intellectualistic positivism. In so far as the conditions of the environment are decisive it does not matter what ends men may think they pursue; in fact, the course of history is determined by an impersonal process over which they have no control. It should be noted that in the shift the subjective category of ends disappears and with it the norm of rationality. Darwinian variation constitutes an entirely objective element requiring for its theoretical formulation no subjective reference. Even though rational action might have, empirically, a place as one mode of adaptation to the environment, the point is that it falls out of the general framework of the theoretical system altogether and becomes a contingent phenomenon, an unimportant fact in the strict sense.

Along with this disappearance of the normative aspects of the utilitarian system, ends and rationality, goes another most important consequence; the problem of order in the sense in which it has been discussed above evaporates.[1] Without the normative elements of action order in the normative sense becomes meaningless. The only order which concerns the scientist of human action is a factual order from both the subjective and the objective points of view. Indeed, ironically enough, the order which is found to dominate this factual world is precisely that which had played the part of antithesis to social order in utilitarian thought —the "state of war." It has changed its name to the "struggle for existence" but is in all essentials the Hobbesian state of nature as the phrase "nature red in tooth and claw" indicates. But this fact is scarcely noted since, the theoretical point of view having vitally shifted, the old problem is gone. At most it is of interest, as for Huxley, only from an ethical, not from a scientific, point of view. It is unquestionably true that the economists' conception of a competitive order went far to provide the model for the biological theory of selection.[2] There too the "unfit," the high-cost producers, the inefficient were eliminated, or ought to be, though only from the market, not from life! But it must not be forgotten that in applying this model to the purposes of biological theory a deep change in its meaning was involved. For

[1] It is "solved" by being held to be meaningless.

[2] "The Principle of Survival of the Fittest could be regarded as one vast generalization of the Ricardian economics." J. M. KEYNES, *The End of Laissez Faire*, New Republic ed., p. 17.

it was one of Malthus' most important insights that only under certain specific conditions involving precisely a normative order could competition be beneficent, could it eliminate those who in terms of the social interest were the unfit. But the conditions of the struggle for existence contained no such element of order at all. They were precisely the conditions of anarchy which Malthus and his fellow economists feared.

Thus "Social Darwinism" as the empiricist application of Darwinian biology to human action may, following Pareto, be called, plays a very important part in the analytical classification of theoretical systems in the field of human action. It, or some other theory which finds the ultimate explanatory principles in the objective non-normative influence of the conditions of action, usually of heredity and environment, forms the logical end result of the process of breakdown of the unstable utilitarian system so long as it takes place within the positivistic framework and at the same time departs from the "rationalistic" schema. It will hence always be a significant question to ask about any writer, what is his position, implicit or explicit, toward this possibility in the solution of his theoretical problems, in the logical closure of his system of theory? If he repudiates this solution there are, in so far as he departs from utilitarianism, only two other positions open; either he is a rationalist in the peculiar sense developed above, hence entertains another version of the radical-positivist position, or he has abandoned the positivistic framework altogether.

Though it was undoubtedly influenced in various ways by conceptions current in social thought, both of Malthus and of others, the Darwinian movement was primarily an outcome of the biological study of nonhuman organisms. Its influence on social thought was due partly to its general ascendancy over educated minds in the latter part of the nineteenth century and to the way in which, in application to things human it fitted so neatly into the logical exigencies of the theories which are being considered. But as a social theory, it is indirect, mainly a borrowing from biology. Three other paths can now be briefly indicated by which, to a larger though not exclusive extent, the analysis of human action itself has led to the transition to a radical positivistic position, whether anti-intellectualistic, rationalistic, or a combination of the two.

Other Paths to Radical Positivism

One of the outstanding characteristics of the Darwinian movement in its application to social problems is its complete abandonment of the subjective for the objective point of view. This is implicit in the substitution for the utilitarian category of random wants or ends of that of random variations. These are objectively observable variations and the concept carries no subjective reference. The same objectivism can be noted in the first of the above-mentioned paths—through certain schools of psychology. Instead of being attributed directly to general biological factors, the uniformities of human behavior may be attributed to certain traits of the human individual—tendencies of behavior of the organism as a whole. In so far as the subjective reference is excluded these must, as has been seen, be reducible ultimately on analysis to terms of some combination of nonsubjective factors, usually heredity and environment as strictly defined in Chap. II.

It is over the question of the relative predominance of the two that the difference of opinion comes. One alternative is to lay the principal stress on hereditary tendencies of behavior; this may be called the "instinct" theory. It is not, however, an ultimate solution, but the question naturally arises further, what is the origin of these particular instinctive tendencies, why do men have these tendencies and not others? The answer, in terms of the factors of heredity and environment is in the last analysis inevitably some form of the concept of survival value. In general, this will involve a process of natural selection. The ultimate basis of the instinct theory then becomes biological, and it leads to the same result as Social Darwinism by a more indirect path.

The other alternative is that which lays stress on environment. Though naturally various versions are conceivable the movement which has been most influential is behaviorism. It is in a curiously definite way a child of the same intellectual stock as Darwinism, so much so that it might be called simply the Darwinism of individual behavior. Darwinian biology was after all mainly concerned with variations in the hereditary character of the species. Behaviorism, on the other hand, has postulated as the origin of individual traits a set of random movements. These must be conceived to vary at random about the hereditary tendencies of action which would, in the behavioristic case, be confined to a few true unconditioned reflexes. These random movements are subject to a process of environmental conditioning, by which some that meet the functional needs of the organism in its adaptation to the environment[1] are perpetuated by conditioning and become conditioned reflexes or habits and others, which do not meet such needs, are eliminated. It is clear that the random movements of behaviorism correspond directly to the random variations of Darwinism, while the process of conditioning is another form of that of natural selection.

But there still remains the residue of original hereditary traits, of "prepotent reflexes," and the explanation of these, in turn, will naturally take the form of the biological theory of natural selection. So behaviorism also ends up in essentially the same place as Social Darwinism.[2] In fact the difference between it and its bitterest enemy, the instinct psychology, is from the present point of view entirely secondary—only one of relative emphasis on environment and heredity, respectively. In addition behaviorism is by its peculiar type of analysis more closely bound to specifically Darwinian modes of thought. But the most important thing is that both ultimately reduce the interpretation of human conduct to terms of a theory of biological selection.

The two may be treated together as the principal forms of positivistic anti-intellectualism. As was noted in Chap. II, positivistic social thought has approached the subjective aspect of action in terms of the role of scientific knowledge, that is, the standard has been the *cognitive* aspect of the subjective. This circumstance has forced the reaction against rationalism, so long as it has remained within the positivistic framework, in the direction of appealing to the factors of heredity and environment.[3]   Hence Social Darwinism may be regarded as the logical end result on a positivistic basis of the anti-intellectualist movement.

[1] In so far as the environment actually studied is the concrete social environment it is clear that the behaviorist position seen as a general theory of human action involves the circular reasoning discussed in Chap. II.

[2] Naturally in most behaviorist literature the individual actually being studied is the *concrete* individual in a *social* environment. It is only in the attempt to extend the scheme to a *general* factor-analysis of human behavior that these radical biologistic consequences emerge.

[3] It is not necessary to repeat the reasons for this statement here. See above, Chap. II.

Behaviorism has a peculiar importance in this connection. Not only does it carry through the common tendency of reduction of the factors of human behavior to biological terms, but it goes further. This reduction naturally does away with the analytical indispensability of the subjective approach, since it can reveal nothing not reducible to the general terms applicable to all biological organisms; it makes the subjective "epiphenomenal." Behaviorism draws the radical consequence in its methodology— the subjective approach to it is not only superfluous but illegitimate; it is contrary to the canons of "objective" science.[1] Thus the substantive scientific theory is integrated with a methodological doctrine which seeks to make its results not only empirically correct, but methodologically inevitable—for when all reference to subjective categories is excluded from the start, the objectivism becomes a closed system.[2] In this methodological respect behaviorism furnishes the limiting type which Social Darwinism furnishes in the substantive context. In the last analysis behaviorist objectivism is the only position for a radically consistent positivist.

The movements just discussed, while they do not short of behaviorism radically exclude the subjective point of view, are on the whole couched for analytical purposes in objectivist terms. It remains to trace the principal movements by which the implications of the positivistic position have been worked out in explicitly subjective terms. Two of these may be considered relevant here. The first, which has historically been in very close relation to the economic aspect of utilitarian thought, is hedonism. Like most of the theories here considered that of hedonism grew up under the aegis of an empiricist methodology. Hence it is not surprising that in the concrete entities "pleasure" and "happiness" ambiguities have come to light later on which have split later hedonistic thought into separate schools. At the present time only one of these need be discussed.

The general logical context in which the doctrine that men are primarily actuated by the pursuit of pleasure and the avoidance of pain grew up is not difficult to see. In the first place,

[1] In the peculiar behavioristic sense which really limits the data of science in general to facts which can be stated in terms of the conceptual schemes of chemistry and physics. All others are eliminated by simply denying their status as facts.

[2] Empirically as well as logically closed.

science is seldom content to stop with the postulation of certain ultimate data. It was inevitable, above all in an empiricist atmosphere, that the question of the ultimate motivations of conduct should arise, that is, one should not only assume that men have certain wants, but that the attempt should be made to understand why they have them. .This happens above all when it is realized that within the conditions of the environment there are qualitative choices open as between possibilities of action between which it is possible to choose.

Secondly, the manner in which utilitarian thinking had concentrated on the economic aspect of life indicated the direction in which the solution of the problem might be sought. For the mechanism of competitive market relations seemed to reduce human motivation to a common denominator; all men seemed to be following a single direction of behavior, the promotion of their economic "interests." The question then was what lay at the basis of this common economic motivation. What was the nature of the common element? The problem, it should be noted, was set in terms of the means-end schema: What is the "end" of individual action?

In this context, then, it was natural to observe two things: first, that there was a distinction between things men sought and things they avoided; second, that success in attainment of the former was generally accompanied by a positive feeling-tone, while infliction against their will with things they tended to avoid was conversely generally accompanied by a negative feeling-tone. If these two feeling-tones be called pleasure and pain respectively, we have the setting of the hedonistic theory.

Then arises the question of the status of these elements in the explanation of action. One of the possible explanations is the one here relevant, genuine "psychological hedonism." This may be stated as the view that the explanation of the direction rational action takes is the *fact* that in human nature certain acts produce pleasure to the actor, others pain. Whether it be hereditary or conditioned by the individual's past experience, the connection between the particular act and pleasure or pain is to the actor a *fact* of which he must take account; it is not his *doing*, at least in the particular context. Then the performance of certain acts becomes an intrinsically necessary means to enjoying pleasure or avoiding pain.

By this means, without disturbing the rationalistic schema, the indeterminacy of the pure utilitarian position is eliminated. Given man's nature, the element of random wants is no longer there. Why he should seek a given concrete end becomes known; it is a means of gaining pleasure or avoiding pain. In our terms it shifts from the utilitarian to a radically positivistic position by reducing ends as a factor in action to terms of "conditions." It is essentially human nature which explains why men act as they do.

Like the anti-intellectualist psychologies, this is not a final position either. For there remains the problem why pleasure is attached to some particular forms of action, pain to others. It is true this could be assumed as a set of ultimate data, but there seems no valid reason to do so. The natural course is to follow the problem back still another step. The means of doing it is already at hand. The basic principle for understanding human nature (as that of every organism) is that of adaptation to environment. So the explanation of the particular incidence of pleasure and pain is that pleasurable acts are those favorable to survival of the species, painful acts unfavorable. Thus by still a third route the argument comes back to Social Darwinism.[1]

The other direction in which classical utilitarian hedonism developed may be left until the last path has been indicated by which one may arrive at the proposition that the ultimate explanation of human action lies in the conditions of its environment. It is the one already sketched in connection with Godwin.

The search for the origin of this line of thought leads back to the influence of the normative conception of the law of nature "which is reason." Making reason the law of *human* nature involves, as has been remarked, conceiving it as ruling the passions rather than serving them. This means, more directly in the terms used here, that instead of being merely the faculty for devising ways and means to realize ends, it becomes the agency of determining the ends themselves.

Now so long as the conception of nature remains explicitly normative, the sense in which the function of reason is that of adaptation to nature remains outside the present concern. It

---

[1] Hedonism is thus a combination of the two logically possible polar types: rationalistic in so far as it employs the means-end schema; anti-intellectualistic in the theory of human nature which explains its particular mode of functioning.

rests on what is, in positivistic terms, a metaphysical element outside the scope of science and inadmissible to its manner of thought. But there was a strong tendency to identify nature, in this sense, with the factors in a causal explanation of empirical phenomena. The normative and explanatory versions of the law of nature tended to merge. This was, indeed, inevitable so far as the conception of reason was the positivistic one of the "faculty manifested in positive science." Then the reality to which our reason adapts us must be that of the "facts" of our empirical external world.

In this manner then there grew up the conception of a direct rational adaptation to the ultimate conditions of action, by the determination of ends in conformity with these conditions. This tendency of thought is very prominent in the "left" wing of individualistic positivism, in the French rationalists, in Godwin and Owen, and also the Utopian Socialists. Competition was irrelevant from this point of view since each individual adapted his action directly to the ultimate conditions and no such intermediary means of making him conform was necessary. It had no function in the social scheme. Hence the emphasis of this group was on the processes of spontaneous cooperation of individuals— a strong anarchistic or socialistic trend according to whether the stress was on the advantages of freedom or of cooperation.

Thus we have one extreme radical solution of the problem of order raised by Hobbes—by denying the existence of the problem. But this view, so long as it was genuinely positivistic really only differed from the others discussed in the structure of its conceptual scheme, in its conception of the nature of the process of the determination of action—in this solution of the problem adaptation is direct through rational apprehension of the facts, in the anti-intellectualistic solution it is indirect through selection. But in both cases the end result, or the ultimate determinant factors are the same, adaptation to conditions through, in the last analysis, the influence of these conditions themselves. Indeed, in the very last analysis even the difference of process disappears, for in so far as the "conditions" ultimately form the sole determinants of action the subjective aspect becomes merely a reflection of these "facts"; it is purely epiphenomenal.[1] Thus all

---

[1] The only difference from Darwinism is the elimination of the necessity for selection. The basis becomes the Lamarckian biology with its doctrine

positivistic rivers ultimately flow into the same sea, that of mechanistic determinism.

UTILITY

But to return to hedonism, the form treated above has been called true psychological hedonism. That is, pleasure is regarded as the true cause of rational action in the form that it becomes the real end of the action, while the apparent diversity of concrete ends reduces to nothing more than a plurality of means to this one end, merely reflecting the diversity of our inherited nature and of the empirical world we live in.

On the other hand, from the same starting point, there is another possible interpretation of the significance of pleasure as associated with the attainment of ends actually sought. Pleasure, that is, may be regarded not as the real end but as the index of the degree of attainment of whatever our real end may be. Instead of making it a psychological, perhaps ultimately physiological factor in action this interpretation would make it a manifestation, in the realm of feeling, of a process the *explanation* of which is to be sought in terms of other categories. This trend of thought emerges into self-consciousness in quite recent times in the form of the modern economic concept of utility.

In these terms it is possible to say that all economic action is motivated by the aim of maximizing utility. But this ultimately means that the element of order in economic relationships is to be sought only on the level of means. The proposition is only a consequence of, or a way of stating, the postulate of economic rationality. In other words, the *immediate* end of all economic activity so far as it is economic is the acquisition of control over means to the satisfaction of wants. It is precisely in their character of convertibility as means to the satisfaction of alternative ends that goods and services can be treated in terms of this common denominator, utility. The more this character of generality applies the more purely economic a thing is. Hence the economic means par excellence, the embodiment of pure utility, is "general purchasing power," the means that is applicable to the satisfac-

---

of the inheritance of acquired characters. Lamarck was indeed closely associated with this rationalistic trend of thought, as Darwin was with positivistic anti-intellectualism.

tion of all wants whatever so far as they can be related to an economic context at all.

In its strictly utilitarian form utility thus becomes the general measure of success of rational action, that is of command over means to the satisfaction of random wants. But the wants still remain the ultimate subjective *factor* in action, not the utility. This position comes to be worked out with logical clarity by the process of purifying the concept of utility of its association with psychological hedonism, a process which has been exceedingly painful. This painfulness is, indeed, not surprising, for there is in the utilitarian version of positivistic social thought a basic instability. Hence, so long as one remains genuinely positivistic, the transition to radical positivism is inescapable. For the economist psychological hedonism has naturally been the easiest path by which to make the transition. Thus, in a *positivistic* context there is a good deal of truth in the "institutionalist" charge[1] that orthodox economic theory is logically bound up with hedonism. For in its competitive aspect at least the radical rationalistic solution is unacceptable, for it makes competition superfluous, while positivistic anti-intellectualism undermines the postulate of economic rationality, with even more serious consequences. The utility theory of economic motivation is correct and not the hedonistic theory. But this implies a radical revision of the whole positivistic framework within which orthodox economic theory grew up. The character of this revision will form one of the central themes of the treatment of the first two subjects of intensive analysis, Marshall and Pareto.

EVOLUTION

Finally, a few explicit words must be said about the place of the concept of evolution in a positivistic context. It is accurate to say that from Hobbes to the end of the eighteenth century the predominant tendency of this great tradition of thought was to think in terms of a static adjustment of fixed elements to each other. Gradually, however, the tendency emerged to think in terms of evolutionary process.

[1] See W. C. MITCHELL, "Human Behavior and Economics," *Quarterly Journal of Economics*, November, 1914.

T. VEBLEN, "Preconceptions of Economic Science" in *The Place of Science in Modern Civilization*.

The first great phase of evolutionism was on the background of radical French rationalism—perhaps the first great name is that of Condorcet. It was this movement of thought which most directly applied the methodology of positive science to the analysis of the subjective aspect of action. As long as this was confined to the role of the faculty of reason positivistically defined, the tendency was to think statically. But it soon became evident that while the faculty of reason might be static, the same was not true of its product, scientific knowledge. On the contrary it is subject to a process of cumulative increase. Action, then, is determined not by reason directly but indirectly through the rational understanding of conditions and the application of this knowledge to the guidance of action. Thus the concrete result will vary according to the state of knowledge.

From these considerations emerges a theory of cumulative social change the dynamic factor in which is the progressive accumulation of scientific knowledge, that is, a linear theory of social evolution. In its process the factors limiting the rationality of action noted in the last chapter, ignorance and error, have their place in the theory, but as characteristics of the early stages of the process, being progressively eliminated in its course. Irrationalities at any given time are indices of the incompleteness of the process.

This rationalistic theory of social evolution stands at one pole of positivistic thought. It is quite clear that by themselves random wants cannot supply a dynamic element. On a utilitarian basis the only opening is equally for the factor of increasing scientific knowledge, this time, of means and conditions. Thus in both theories the central emphasis is on scientific knowledge and its application in technology. When thought departs from the rationalistic or utilitarian poles, it must be, in a positivistic framework, in terms of some kind of positivistic anti-intellectualism.

In the absence of any dynamic factor in the ultimate environmental conditions themselves this can only be found in something which alters the hereditary type, that is, in something like the random variations of Darwinism, where the factor from which the determinate direction of change is derived is that of environmental conditions. Thus at both the rationalistic and the anti-intellectualistic poles of positivistic thought the same fundamental direction of a process of evolutionary change is given, that of better adaptation to environmental conditions. At one pole this adaptation is direct rational adaptation through application of scientific knowledge, at the other indirect by selection among variations. But in both the process is linear, by a progressive accumulation of stages of approach to an asymptotic goal. The most essential point is that these are the only possibilities open on a strictly positivistic basis. Above all the one place for a positive role of ends is in the utilitarian form, and this provides no basis for a theory of change. Hence any change in ends, not a reflection of other factors, must be considered an indication of non-positivistic elements in the thought concerned.[1]

Thus has been completed the setting of the stage for the drama of thought to be presented in this study. The first attack will be at a strategic point, that of the status of economic theory and its relation to the utilitarian position. The first theorist to be taken up will be Alfred Marshall, who from his own point of view and that of the rest of the scientific world confined his theoretical attention to economic problems. In the way in which he defined them and the manner in which he dealt with them, however, it will be found that questions of the greatest interest are raised.

The second step in the analysis will be concerned with the work of Vilfredo Pareto, who, though also an economist, supplemented his economics with a sociological theory in a way which made explicit the problem of the relation of the two disciplines and the relation of both to the whole positivistic scheme. Finally, the treatment of Pareto will be followed by a detailed consideration of the thought of Émile Durkheim, who raises the same fundamental problems in a somewhat different way, involving the status of still another logical possibility of the positivistic tradition, the sociologistic, detailed consideration of which will be deferred until his work is dealt with. These three studies will complete the treatment of positivistic social thought. It may, as suggested above, be considered as an attempt to trace, in terms of the work of these three men, what happens when the consequences of the instability of the utilitarian position are followed in the opposite direction from that of the tendency to radical positivism, with which the present discussion has been concerned.

To conclude this historical sketch, a word of safeguard against

---

[1] In Chap. IV the importance of this proposition for interpreting the significance of certain elements of Marshall's thought will be shown.

misunderstanding may be added. The theoretical concepts which have been considered here may be treated from two points of view; this discussion has been predominantly concerned with one, the one which by and large the authors of the ideas themselves have held. That is, they have been treated as general theoretical frameworks for the understanding of human behavior in society as a whole. It will be maintained, and the attempt made in considerable detail to prove, that *in this sense all of the versions of positivistic social thought constitute untenable positions*, for both empirical and methodological reasons.

This must not, however, be taken to mean that the concepts which have been developed in connection with these theories are simply wrong and hence of no use for present or future social science. On the contrary, in general each of the main categories developed has found, subject, of course, to qualification and refinement, a permanent place in the attack on the problems of human behavior. Criticism is here directed not against their adequacy for properly defined and restricted purposes, but against their claim to form the basis for adequate general theories of society. It would be a serious misunderstanding to suppose that, because positivistic social theories are here severely criticized for some theoretical purposes, it is therefore held that the concepts employed in them are invalid for any and all purposes. The attempt, rather, will be made to develop the outline of a general conceptual scheme in terms of which the important elements of validity in them may find a legitimate place and thus avoid the dangers of being lost in the general critical attack on the empirical results of their use in a positivistic context.[1]

[1] The institutionalists' repudiation of the conceptual tools of orthodox economic theory is an excellent example of this. Though often empirically right in their criticism of conclusions arrived at by use of these concepts, they are none the less disastrously wrong on a theoretical level in failing to see the possibilities of avoiding these consequences by using the same tools in the context of a different conceptual framework.

PART II

THE EMERGENCE OF A VOLUNTARISTIC THEORY OF ACTION FROM THE POSITIVISTIC TRADITION

CHAPTER IV

ALFRED MARSHALL: WANTS AND ACTIVITIES AND THE PROBLEM OF THE SCOPE OF ECONOMICS[1]

It has been shown in Chap. III that the branch of utilitarian thought which has involved the postulate of the natural identity of interests has tended to focus the center of analytical attention in the study of human action on a theory of economic relationships. This tendency issued in the classical economics, a few salient aspects of which have been very hastily sketched. In the last quarter of the nineteenth century, however, this body of thought entered upon a new phase of its development, which, while remaining within the general logical framework outlined, involved important changes in the internal structure of economic theory, so much so that Professor Schumpeter has, rightly, made a sharp distinction between the classical system of theory and modern utility doctrine.[2]

The great revolutionary discovery which marked the advent of the new era was that of the principle of marginal utility. While, as has been noted above, the place of the labor theory of value in the classical system is understandable in terms of its derivation from Locke's concept of the state of nature, at least by the time of Ricardo, there had appeared in its use for explanatory purposes difficulties of such magnitude as to occasion serious misgivings on Ricardo's part.[3] But for another fifty years the classical system retained its scientific supremacy, essentially because nothing better was found to take its place.

---

[1] The main substance of the earlier part of this chapter has been reprinted with only minor alterations from an article "Wants and Activities in Marshall" published in the *Quarterly Journal of Economics*, November, 1931. Thanks are due to the editors of the *Quarterly Journal* for their kind permission to use the material.

[2] J. A. Schumpeter, *Dogmengeschichte der Volkswirtschaftslehre, Grundriss der Sozialoekonomik*, Vol. I.

[3] See David Ricardo, *Principles of Political Economy*, Chap. I, ed. by E. C. K. Gonner; *Ricardo's Letters to Malthus*, ed. by James Bonar.

On this technical plane the fundamental difficulty was that no satisfactory approach to the value[1] problem could be found on the demand side. It was recognized that scarcity was a necessary condition of value, and that, on the "subjective" side, there were two different aspects called in the classical literature "value in exchange" and "value in use." The difficulty was to relate them to each other. In the absence of a relating principle the next best thing was to fall back on the conditions of supply. It was this missing link that was supplied by the idea of marginal utility. It rested on the insight that what was relevant to the determination of exchange value on the demand side was not the value in use of the total amount of a commodity consumed per unit of time, but the *addition to* this value—to "total utility"— which could be imputed to the last unit in the supply; that is the *difference* it would make if a small change were made in the rate of consumption. It is this increment of value in use, of utility, which is called marginal utility. Once this fundamental principle had been discovered it was logical to follow out its implications into a far-reaching reconstruction of economic theory which eliminated the principal peculiarities of the classical system. It is in this context that Marshall's relation to the argument of this study is to be understood. Marshall was the most prominent agent of this process in the English-speaking countries.

ACTIVITIES AND UTILITY THEORY

Before entering on the main theme one important characteristic of Marshall's thought should be noted—its pronounced empiricism. He deeply distrusted "long chains of deductive reasoning."[2] He consistently thought of the subject matter of his economics as that of a field of concrete phenomena—it was "a study of mankind in the everyday business of life."[3] Though not explicitly maintaining its exhaustiveness he did consistently refuse to attempt to give any systematic account of its relations to neighboring social sciences. In this empiricism Marshall was entirely at one with his predecessors and contemporaries in English economics. It had scarcely occurred to anyone that any

---

[1] "Value" in the technical economic sense, of course.

[2] ALFRED MARSHALL, *Principles of Economics*, 8th ed., p. 781. Cited below as *Principles*; all references are to this edition.

[3] *Principles*, p. 1.

other position was possible—but it is no less important in its consequences. He was, moreover, exceedingly scrupulous in his attempt to stick close to the concrete facts of the world he was studying, the worlds of business and labor of his day.[1]

But in spite of this empiricism there can be no question of the importance in Marshall's economic thought of the theory built upon the concept of utility. Though he was not the first to publish it Keynes is the authority for the statement that Marshall was an independent discoverer of the principle of marginal utility.[2] Indeed the central role of utility is necessarily implied in the conception of economics as the science of wealth. For the modern conception of wealth is based on that of utility; in so far as wealth is a quantity at all it consists of "satisfactions" or "utility."[3] The same, of course, holds good of "production," which is the production of utilities, and hence of physical commodities only in so far as they are utility bearers, or want satisfiers. On this foundation Marshall built a great structure of theory. In relating Marshall's discovery of marginal utility Keynes compares him to Watt, and says that, like Watt, "he sat down silently to build an engine."[4] The engine he built rested definitely on the new principle he had discovered, just as that of Watt did.

In this aspect the two starting points of Marshall's economic theory lie in the concept of utility and the marginal idea. One important result is the conception of consumers' surplus. But the main line of his reasoning leads him into the general value problem, where a large part is played by another of his own conceptions, the principle of substitution. This, in turn, gives a certain provisional interpretation of cost of production, in terms of utility: an interpretation substantially identical with what is now generally called opportunity cost, and by Henderson transference cost.[5] The same general analysis applied to the values of the agents of production gives the other side of the picture, the theory of the distribution of wealth, where again the leading

[1] See the memoir by J. M. Keynes reprinted in *Memorials of Alfred Marshall*, ed. by A. C. Pigou.

[2] *Memorials*, p. 23.

[3] See F. H. KNIGHT, "Relation of Utility Theory to Economic Method," in *The Methods of Social Science*, ed. by S. A. Rice, p. 65.

[4] *Memorials*, p. 23.

[5] H. D. HENDERSON, *Supply and Demand*. This, of course, is not Marshall's last word on cost. A discussion of that point will be found below, pp. 146 *ff.*

conception, that of marginal productivity, is a derivative of that of utility, since "production" in the economic, as distinct from the technological, sense consists in the allocation of means to the satisfaction of wants. Finally the whole is generalized in terms of the doctrine of maximum satisfaction; a doctrine which, in spite of Marshall's important criticism of it in terms of consumers' surplus, and of other qualifications, he recognizes as essentially valid.

This aspect of Marshall's economic thought forms a single coherent whole, a logical system, dependent on certain assumptions and generally valid within certain limits. The most important of those assumptions may be summarized as follows: (1) The edifice is built essentially on a competitive basis. He considers monopoly, but separately. The most usual connotation of the term "normal" for him is, at least in a relative sense,[1] "competitive." (2) It assumes that wants are given independently of the utility aspects of processes leading to their satisfaction, *i.e.*, that they are constants in the problem of economic equilibrium. The whole concept has reference to the satisfaction of given wants and not to the explanation of their existence. (3) It assumes that all movable economic resources are effectively mobile and divisible. (4) Action must be rationally directed toward want satisfaction. It is to be noted that it is the wants of people as consumers and not as producers which are considered as being satisfied, and that under a competitive order the two factors, force and fraud, are ruled out, partly by competitive pressure, partly by a legal authority which sets up rules of the game and penalizes infractions of them.

This utility theory accomplishes two things. First, it provides, in so far as the assumptions on which it rests are valid and usable, an explanation of why economic processes take the course they do. Secondly, it provides a norm of economic efficiency, in terms of an optimum distribution of resources and a maximum of possible want satisfaction under the conditions given. Both results are used by Marshall. It may be noted, however, that the normative use of economic concepts is peculiarly dependent on two of the above assumptions, the independence of wants and rationality. On the one hand, the satisfaction of known wants supplies the only possible norm in terms of which the desirability or

[1] Qualified principally by his treatment of the time element.

efficiency of an economic process can be judged. Once ends themselves come to vary as a function of the process of their attainment, the standard no longer exists; the argument becomes circular. On the other hand, the process of want satisfaction is itself the most general and obvious meaning of rationality of action. The very concept of rationality is meaningless without reference to given ends,[1] while nonrational want satisfaction is nonsensical except in terms of divergence from a rational type. Of course this is not to say that all action is actually rational even in such a limited sense, but only that its rationality is one principal criterion of the abstract type of action called "economic." How far Marshall believed both these assumptions to be correct for the concrete world will be discussed below.

It is not to be imagined that this element of Marshall's thought is to be found in his writings worked out as a complete logical system apart from the rest of his ideas and recognized by him as such. His empiricist bent precluded that. Nor is he always explicit in making the assumptions brought out above. On the contrary, the elements of this system are closely interwoven with other strands of thought. This is a natural result of Marshall's refusal to work out his more abstract ideas to their logical conclusions, on the plea of the fruitlessness of "long chains of deductive reasoning." It has been necessary, nevertheless, to sketch the outlines of this implicit, logical system in order by contrast to get a clear view of the other aspect of his doctrine which is of particular interest here. It is noteworthy, however, that the majority of points which Keynes lists as the main contributions of the *Principles* fit into this scheme.[2] Exceptions are: the element of time, a great contribution, but one which does not in any way affect the problems here under consideration;[3] the historical parts and, in a sense, the supposed resolution of the Ricardo-Jevons controversy, to both of which attention will be called later. Because of the predominance of the utility element in Keynes' list, and even more in the work of some of Marshall's followers

[1] This, of course, is not to say that the ends themselves must be rational or "reasonable." That would involve a wider meaning of rationality than is under consideration here. The present sense of the term makes it identical with "efficiency." See Chap. II, p. 56 *ff*.

[2] *Memorials*, pp. 41–46.

[3] In the particular theoretical sense in which Keynes means it. On a deeper methodological plane the element of time may have a vital significance.

(especially Henderson), it is legitimate to call it the backbone of his technical economic theory. Yet how far it was from dominating the whole of his thought, the course of the discussion should make abundantly clear. Finally, it is perhaps significant that Keynes does not list his treatment of the supplies of the productive factors at all, though Marshall himself makes much of it and it certainly represents a departure from the views of his predecessors in important respects.

In an attempt to dissect out elements of Marshall's thought other than this utility theory, the best starting point lies in his definitions of economics. The first he gives in the *Principles* is the one quoted above, "a study of mankind in the everyday business of life,"[1] which is surely inclusive enough. This is somewhat narrowed down by what follows: "It examines that part of individual and social action which is most closely connected with the attainment and with the use of the material requisites of well-being."[2] But Marshall cannot mean to limit himself to the "material"[3] requisites. Elsewhere he speaks of economics as a science especially concerned with the "measurement of the force of a person's motives"[4] in terms of money. "It is this definite and exact money measurement which has enabled economics far to outrun every other branch of the study of man."[5] But, however important measurability in terms of money is for Marshall in some respects,[6] the real motive for the breadth of his conception of the scope of economics lies elsewhere. Later, in his description of its field of study at the beginning of the *Principles*, he goes on to say, "Thus it is on the one side a study of wealth, and on the other *and more important side*[7] a part of the study of man. For man's *character*[7] has been moulded by his everyday work and the material resources which he thereby procures, more than by any other influence unless it be that of his religious ideals. . . ."[8] Thus he explicitly states that the study of the mechanism of want

[1] *Principles*, p. 1.
[2] *Ibid.*, p. 1.
[3] Marshall fails to define this economically ambiguous term more closely.
[4] *Principles*, p. 15.
[5] *Ibid.*, p. 14.
[6] See below, pp. 171 *ff.*, for a further discussion of this issue.
[7] Italics mine.
[8] *Principles*, p. 1. See also A. and M. P. Marshall, *Economics of Industry*, p. 4.

satisfaction, the subject matter of utility theory, is only a part of economics, and the less important part. The more important is the relation of economic conditions to human character.

Marshall found one aspect of this relation in the degrading effect of poverty on character and through it on industrial efficiency. Though the problem of poverty played a leading part in his thought,[1] his treatment of it may largely be subsumed under the utility conception. A different phase of his interest in character is of primary interest here; his belief that certain types of economic activities, pursued not for ulterior motives but mainly as ends in themselves, are the principal agents in the formation of the noblest qualities of human character and the main fields of their expression.

The concrete description of what types of activities and character he had in mind is to be found principally in his picture of "free industry and enterprise," with which they are intimately associated. They consist in two sets of virtues; on the one hand, energy, initiative, enterprise; on the other, rationality, frugality, industry, honorable dealing. With them are contrasted, on the one side, sluggishness, idle stagnation, slavery to custom, lack of ambition; on the other, luxury, ostentation, waste, unreliability. To prove that a deep-rooted belief in the absolute value and the causal importance of these qualities of character and the activities which foster and express them is the main motive of Marshall's inclusion of the study of man as well as that of wealth in his definition of economics and is the main counterweight to "utility economics" in his thought as a whole, is the principal task of the present study of Marshall's work.

As has been noted above, utility economics, strictly construed, is forced to assume that the wants whose satisfaction it studies are given as data. It is precisely on the question whether this assumption is justified that Marshall's interest in activities first comes clearly to light, manifesting itself in a manner which partly determines his stand on an important technical question of theory.

For one who carries the utility analysis as far as Marshall does, the cautious hesitation with which he deals with the subject of wants is surely remarkable. Though admitting that "until recently the subject of demand or consumption has been somewhat

---

[1] See J. M. KEYNES, in *Memorials*, p. 16.

neglected"[1] and that there is a "growing belief that harm was done by Ricardo's habit of laying disproportionate stress on . . . cost of production,"[2] he springs valiantly to the defense of Ricardo as more the victim of misunderstanding than of error.[2] He explicitly refuses to make a theory of consumption the "scientific basis of economics" and his whole treatment of wants is more conspicuous for its warnings against pitfalls than for its emphasis on the importance of his positive contributions to the study.

But what are these pitfalls? They are certainly not connected with any doubts of the soundness of the principle of marginal utility or of consumers' surplus.[3] It is not positive error of which he is afraid, but the negative error of omission. A hint of what he thinks may be in danger of neglect is given in the following remarkable passage: "It is only temporarily and provisionally that we can with profit isolate for study the economic side of his [man's] life; and we ought to be careful to take together in one view the *whole of that side*.[4] There is a special need to insist on this just now because the reaction against the comparative neglect of the study of wants by Ricardo and his followers shows signs of being carried to the opposite extreme. It is important still to assert *the great truth*[4] on which they dwelt somewhat too exclusively; *viz.*, that while wants are the rulers of life among the lower animals, it is to changes in the forms of efforts and activities that we must turn when in search for the keynotes of the history of mankind."[5]

This is apparently not merely the assertion on general grounds that the influence of activities on wants may be important; the reference to Ricardo and his followers indicates that Marshall also thought that it was the great virtue of the classical labor theory of value, as a technical economic theory, to have taken account of that fact, while the utility theory with its emphasis on demand was in danger of neglecting it. But from the technical viewpoint of economic theory, the relation of the labor theory of

[1] *Principles*, p. 84.

[2] *Ibid.*, p. 84.

[3] It should be remembered Marshall was himself a discoverer of the principle of marginal utility.

[4] Italics mine.

[5] *Ibid.*, p. 85. Note also on the same page that he consents to study wants only as "considered in their relation to human efforts and activities."

value to the utility theory is that of a less to a more inclusive and accurate explanation of a certain body of facts; *i.e.*, the labor theory is true as a special case of the wider theory, dependent only on certain additional assumptions[1] which, many later theorists feel, are more doubtful than those involved in the utility theory. Certainly Ricardo was a pure theorist. So far as can be ascertained he had nothing to say about the relative part played by wants in animal and human behavior[2]; if he had, it would certainly have been irrelevant to the comparatively narrow range of his theoretical problems. Moreover it seems sheer fiction to assert, as Marshall does, that the reason Ricardo addressed himself primarily to the problems of cost of production was his realization of their greater importance.[3] While it is true he realized demand is important, it is not true that he understood its part— in fact it was primarily his failure to understand the distinction between total and marginal utility which forced him to fall back on labor cost as a second best explanatory principle, the defects of which he himself saw very clearly. It is highly unlikely that, had he known the principle of marginal utility, he would have come to be considered the great proponent of the labor theory, as Marshall implies he would.

Then why does Marshall, whose own theoretical doctrines on the utility side would for themselves tend to alienate him from Ricardo,[4] defend him so strongly and even read into Ricardo views on non-theoretical subjects which it is exceedingly doubtful he ever held? Why is he so concerned to defend himself far beyond the requirements of economic theory against the suspicion of overemphasis on demand, and why is he so insistent on the importance of the problems of supply?[5] It is true that those problems

[1] The most important, of course, being that the cost factors other than labor enter into the marginal cost of production of all commodities in the same proportion as labor.

[2] The reasons for Marshall making this apparently curious distinction will be discussed presently. See pp. 139–140.

[3] *Principles*, Appendix I, Sec. 2.

[4] See SCHUMPETER, *op. cit.*

[5] It is, of course, possible that personal jealousy of Jevons, who published the marginal utility theory before Marshall, but who probably did not anticipate Marshall in its discovery, played a part. It is true that Marshall's review of Jevons' *Theory* is not, considering the magnitude of Jevons' achievement, couched in very generous terms. But it is always highly dubious to explain important scientific views in terms of petty personal feelings. When there is

are both extremely intricate and affect any economic policies of far-reaching scope most vitally; Marshall is interested in them for both reasons. But for the present another aspect is more important. It seems beyond doubt that a main—more probably *the* main—motive of Marshall's interest in supply, more especially in the supply of the productive factors, lies in the fact that it is there that questions involving the types of energy, activity and character manifested in economic life impinge most directly on the problems of technical economic theory.[1]

The consideration of the economic order strictly as a mechanism of want satisfaction reduces the activities involved in the process to means to an end, and the human qualities expressed in those activities to the same status.[2] But Marshall is quite unwilling to accept such implications even for limited methodological purposes; for him the development of character is the main issue of human life. Hence even in the more abstract problems of economics his interest turns largely to the questions in which these aspects of social life are most concerned. The influence of this interest extends even to his analysis of wants themselves so that he says "Much that is of chief interest in the science of wants is borrowed from the science of efforts and activities. These two supplement one another; either is incomplete without the other."[3] But Marshall does not hesitate to give his own opinion of their relative importance: "If either, more than the other, may claim to be the interpreter of the history of man, *whether on the economic side or any other*, it is the science of activities and not that of wants."[3] Even for the purposes of value theory, he definitely refuses to take wants as ultimate data without inquiring into their genesis.[4]

---

another and much deeper explanation, which I feel certain is so with Marshall, it seems futile to indulge in personalities.

[1] The case of the supply of the productive factors will be taken up in detail in the next section of this chapter.

[2] Only for certain definitely limited scientific purposes, of course.

[3] *Principles*, p. 90.   Italics mine.

[4] Only the failure adequately to consider this aspect of the case seems to enable Professor Homan to say that Marshall "made but little headway toward a scientific study of demand. As a result most of his subsequent analysis is confined to the study of supply." Paul T. Homan, *Contemporary Economic Thought*, p. 226. Whatever the defects of Marshall's study of demand, they do not form the main motive for his emphasis on supply.

Moreover, Marshall's conviction of the importance of activities is not merely asserted as an antidote to overemphasis on demand; it enters directly into his positive theory of consumption. Part of that theory, centering around the principles of marginal utility and consumers' surplus, is independent of it, but in so far as Marshall has any further positive theory it is based directly on the relation of wants to activities. First, take his doctrine of the standard of living. Instead of following his classical predecessors in including under that term all those habits of life which act as a check on population growth, he makes a sharp distinction between what he calls the "standard of life" and that of "comfort." The former means "the standard of activities adjusted to wants."[1] A rise in it implies "an increase of intelligence and energy and self-respect; leading to more care and judgment in expenditure, and to an avoidance of food and drink that gratify the appetite but afford no strength and of ways of living that are unwholesome physically and morally."[2] A rise in the standard of comfort, on the other hand, "may suggest a mere increase of artificial wants among which perhaps the grosser wants may predominate."[3] This distinction would appear quite meaningless in terms of the original theoretical uses to which the doctrine was put. But in terms of Marshall's interest in activities for their own sake, the distinction between those changes in wants which are "adjusted to activities" and those which are "artificial"[4] becomes significant.

Furthermore, a close examination of Marshall's statements on the subject of wants shows that he divides them into three categories. When he uses the term without qualification, as in the passage about the "great truth" cited above, and when he says "It is man's wants in the earliest stages of his development which give rise to his activities,"[5] the wants which rule the lower

---

[1] *Principles*, p. 689. Here, it is true, Marshall speaks of activities being "adjusted to wants." The relation is reciprocal, however, with the major emphasis, on the whole, as other passages show, on activities. Hence in classifying wants it is quite legitimate, on interpreting Marshall, to distinguish between those which are "adjusted to activities" and those which are not.

[2] *Ibid.*, p. 689.

[3] *Ibid.*, p. 690.

[4] The term artificial clearly implies a value judgment which is, however, not arbitrary but deeply grounded in Marshall's whole position.

[5] *Principles*, p. 89.

animals and man in those earlier stages are not wants in the ordinary sense, but simply biological needs.[1]

No doubt most sociologists, except those who hold that all of men's actions are determined by the biological struggle for survival alone, would agree with Marshall that wants in this peculiar sense are inadequate to explain actions. But why interpret wants by themselves so narrowly? Surely most modern exponents of utility economics do not do so.

The second category of wants includes those "adjusted to activities" which form part of a "standard of life," and the satisfaction of which "affords strength," *i.e.*, increases the efficiency of labor.[2] It is of them that Marshall speaks when he says that "each new step upwards is to be regarded as the development of new activities giving rise to new wants."[3] They are the only nonbiological wants which he would dignify with the term "natural." Moreover this naturalness consists partly in the fact that, as the above passage indicates, they are not merely "adjusted" to activities, but rather created by them. The third category, finally, includes those associated with the "standard of comfort," a rise in which "may suggest a mere increase of artificial wants among which perhaps the grosser wants may predominate." These wants appear to be wholly arbitrary, mere whims with no permanent foundation in life.[4]

[1] This is clearly evident from the context. He speaks (*Principles*, p. 87) of that "need for dress which is the result of natural causes" and of house room satisfying "the imperative need of shelter from the weather" (p. 88), both times calling attention to the fact that the actual biological need forms but a small element in the effective demand for clothing and house room. And from this he concludes that demand cannot be understood in terms of "wants" alone.

[2] "A rise in the standard of life for any one trade or grade will raise their efficiency." *Principles*, p. 689.

[3] *Ibid.*, p. 89.

[4] They are presumably expressed in the "evil dominion of the wanton vagaries of fashion" (*Principles*, footnote, p. 89) and the vulgarities of "sporting men" of which Marshall speaks at various points in highly derogatory fashion (for instance, *Memorials*, p. 102). He notes with satisfaction that "leisure is used less and less as an opportunity for mere stagnation; and there is a growing desire for those amusements . . . which develop activities rather than indulge any sensuous craving." *Principles*, p. 89. It is perhaps not going too far to see here the random wants of the true utilitarian position.

Enough has been said to show clearly Marshall's view that what raises civilized man above the animals and the state of savagery is his whole-hearted devotion to a particular set of activities, and his development of a type of character. Wants not adjusted to such activities are not ultimate ends, even for the purposes of economics, but are "artificial." The real aims of life lie in the activities pursued as ends in themselves.[1] This is what he seems to mean when he says "Much that is of chief interest in the science of wants is borrowed from the science of efforts and activities."

The Supplies of the Factors of Production

Perhaps the greatest of all controversies about the scope of economics has concerned the extent to which economics alone is competent to furnish an explanation of the supplies of the factors of production. The classical economists, confidently resting their faith in the Malthusian doctrine of population, extended their claim very far. Recently to be sure there has been a strong reaction from this view. Economists are becoming more and more disposed to turn over the burden to the psychologist or sociologist. But in this respect, as in his attitude toward cost of production, Marshall adheres closely to tradition, attempting a complete theory of population, labor exertion and saving within the framework of his economics.[2]

In dealing with the first aspect of the supply of labor, its intensity, Marshall holds there is a positive functional relation to wages. His most general statement is: "We may conclude that increased remuneration causes an immediate increase in the supply of efficient work, as a rule, and that the exceptions to this rule are seldom on a large scale. . . . "[3] It is clear from the context that he is thinking of the direct effect of remuneration on individual effort.

Of course he does not hold that this relation is universal. But the chief exception which he makes is highly illuminating: "Ex-

[1] "Work in its best sense, the healthy energetic exercise of faculties is the aim of life, is life itself." *Memorials*, p. 115. "Social good lies mainly in that healthful exercise and development of faculties which yields happiness without pall." *Ibid.*, p. 310. See also *ibid.*, p. 367. This last statement is an interesting twist of hedonistic ideas.

[2] This is an especially clear manifestation of his empiricist tendency.

[3] *Principles*, pp. 528–529. See also *ibid.*, p. 142.

perience seems to show that the *more ignorant and phlegmatic* of *races and of individuals,* especially if they live in a southern clime will stay at their work a shorter time, and will exert themselve less while at it if the rate of pay rises so as to give them thei accustomed enjoyments in return for less work than before. Bu those *whose mental horizon is wider,* and who have *more firmness and elasticity of character* will work harder and longer the highe the rate of pay which is open to them; unless indeed they prefe to divert their activities to higher aims than work for materia gain."[1]

There have usually been two explanations of the type of re sponsiveness to increased remuneration of which Marshall claim the existence. One is the hedonistic. This, however, involve difficulties in accounting for acquisition beyond a certain point except under the impossible postulate that leisure has no hedo nistic value. The very fact that Marshall assigns no limit to the acquisitive activities of the more advanced peoples makes it impossible for him to have held strictly to the hedonistic view in their case.[2] The other is the postulate of an instinct of acquisi tion, which at least has the merit of evading this difficulty. An instinct is sublimely indifferent to results. But it would indeed be strange to subject those whose "mental horizon is wider" to the domination of an instinct which failed to control the "more ignorant." Nor does Marshall do so; quite the contrary. The behavior of the "more ignorant and phlegmatic of races" is strongly reminiscent partly of hedonism, partly of instinct, but that of the more enlightened is due to a rising "standard of life" involving the generation of new wants by new activities. That, and neither hedonism nor any instinctive greed, is Marshall's explanation of the tendency of modern men to do more rather than less work when their pay rises.[3]

The exception which he makes of those who "prefer to divert their activities to higher aims than work for material gain" must not be forgotten, of course, but what seems significant is that he ascribes so little, not so much, importance to it; the strongest

[1] *Ibid.,* p. 528. Italics mine.

[2] There are various other reasons why Marshall could not have held a hedonistic philosophy.

[3] Compare Max Weber's discussion of the relation of traditionalism to the "spirit of capitalism," in *The Protestant Ethic and the Spirit of Capitalism,* Chap. II. See also below, Chap. XIV.

hing he says is that it is "not devoid of significance."[1] Any sense
f the sordidness of economic acquisition as such is totally absent.
ndeed, it can be said that on the whole Marshall saw the field of
usiness enterprise[2] as the principal opportunity for the exercise
f what he considered the noblest traits of human character. The
vealth acquired in the process was not the aim, but rather a
y-product, and one which was not without its dangers.[3]

It should be noted that inasmuch as Marshall's "activities"
rc ends in themselves, work being "the aim of life," there is no
eason to suppose that the development of activities would lead to
greater *responsiveness* of labor exertion to wage changes. On
he contrary, it should lead to an indifference to mere wages, at
east above the level necessary for full physical efficiency. But
he development of activities is not for Marshall an isolated
rocess; with it always goes an expansion of wants, adjusted to
r created by activities. It is apparently out of the reciprocal
elation of activities to the expanding wants "adjusted" to them
hat this responsiveness is derived. It is a striking fact, however,
hat the responsiveness is always conceived by Marshall in an
upward direction; *increased* remuneration leads to an *increase* of
fficient work. Though he does not say so explicitly, the reader is
ed to suppose that the opposite relation would exist only as a
esult of physiological or hedonistic causes.[4] It should also be
alled to mind that the expansion of wants that Marshall is here
hinking of involves wants of a very particular sort, wants which
are "adjusted to activities." Other wants, "a mere increase of
artificial wants," would lead to quite different results.

In his treatment of labor exertion Marshall thus retained the
basic doctrine of his predecessors, the close functional relation
between effort and remuneration, but at least for modern times
he discards their predominantly hedonistic explanation and substitutes his own conception of a rising standard of life, of wants
adjusted to activities. His treatment of the population problem
is very similar. Here again he adheres ostensibly to the doctrine
of his predecessors, but reinterprets that doctrine in his own way.

[1] *Principles*, p. 529.

[2] See D. H. ROBERTSON, "Review of Memorials," reprinted in his *Economic
Fragments*.

[3] See *Memorials*, p. 102.

[4] This would be one striking example of his doctrine that the reversal of
many economic processes does not lead back to the original result.

He starts by proclaiming the essential validity of Malthus' position regarding the supply of population.[1] Moreover, in inquiring more specifically what is meant it appears that he held the literal Malthusian position for most of history, and even today, he says "over a great part of the world wages are governed nearly[2] after the so-called iron or brazen law, which ties them close to the cost of rearing and sustaining a rather inefficient class of laborers."[3] Like most other Malthusians he does not think that in such times only positive checks operate—he has a good deal to say about several sorts of preventive checks, especially of an institutional nature.[4] But he adheres to the main point, the essence of which is a static standard of living. Numbers, not the standard, change with a changing economic situation.

But Marshall specifically denies that the iron law holds for modern Western countries. Somehow the Western world has broken through the vicious circle. Yet in summing up he holds that "other things being equal an increase in the earnings to be had by labour increases its rate of growth." In other words the supply of labor generally responds to economic causes even in Western countries. Wherein then lies the difference? Apart from any extent to which the Malthusian law may not have been superseded, the explanation lies in Marshall's interpretation, in the above phrase, of the term labor. The context shows that it cannot mean merely the number of laborers, but its "growth" in the Western world also includes the increase of efficiency which accompanies a rising standard of life. He states, "It is still true even in England today that much the greater part of the consumption of the main body of the population conduces to sustain life and *vigour*—most of that expenditure which is not strictly economical as a means towards efficiency yet helps to form habits of ready resourceful enterprise and gives that variety to life without which men become dull and stagnant and achieve little, though they may plod much."[5] So that "the earnings got by efficient labor are not much above the lowest that are needed to

[1] *Principles*, p. 179.

[2] It is hard to find any statement in Marshall without such qualification as a "nearly."

[3] *Principles*, p. 531. It is evident that the persons here referred to are the "more ignorant and phlegmatic of races" discussed above.

[4] See *Principles*, Book IV, Chap. IV, Secs. 4, 5, 6.

[5] *Ibid.*, p. 531.

cover the expenses of rearing and training efficient workers and of sustaining and bringing into activity their full energies."[1] Thus, with a rise in real wages the "quantity of labor" increases, even though numbers do not, at least in the same proportion. And wages contain little surplus above the cost of production of labor because the increase of efficiency, directly or indirectly caused by that of wages, nearly keeps pace with the latter.

The cause of this increase is again the rise to a higher level of activities. Thus Marshall, while retaining the form of the classical law that the supply of labor is a function of the demand price for it, gives it an interpretation, at least for modern Western countries, in accordance with his central doctrine of the importance of activities, and involving a radical departure from Malthus. It should be observed, too, that his interpretation is in accordance with his classification of wants. Where men are ruled by animal wants, such as the instinct of reproduction, or by a *fixed* standard of living, a "standard of comfort," the iron law holds. They escape it only through a rising "standard of life" the essential element of which is the activities to which wants are adjusted.

On the problem of the supply of capital and the motives for saving Marshall does not have so much to say as on the supply of labor, but what he does say is to be understood in much the same terms. He states explicitly, "a rise in the rate of interest offered for capital . . . tends to increase the volume of saving. . . . It is nearly a universal rule that a rise in the rate increases the desire to save; and it often increases the power to save."[2] Thus he definitely maintains the functional connection between interest and the volume of saving. But he certainly does not hold that the hedonistic desire for future goods is the principal *motive* of saving, any more than primarily hedonistic motives are instrumental in making men work. On the contrary he holds that the motives of saving are very complex and that regard for others and especially family affection play a large part.[3] To be sure,

---

[1] *Ibid.*

[2] *Ibid.*, p. 236.

[3] "Affection for others is one of the chief motives if not the chief motive of the accumulation of capital." *Economics of Industry*, p. 39. See also *Principles*, p. 227. He also admits considerable historical relativity in the motives of saving. "The causes which control accumulation differ widely in

there is a touch of the old classical notion that interest is mainly a lure to saving in the statement "While human nature remains as it is, every fall in that rate [of interest] is likely to cause many more people to save less than to save more than they would other wise have done."[1] The weight of his emphasis, however, lies on the fact that saving habits are rather marks of rationality than of hedonistic conduct.[2]

But even this does not explain why the amount of saving should be increased indefinitely with an increasing rate of interest. If an instinct of accumulation be rejected, as it undoubtedly is by Marshall, the explanation must lie in the same fundamental principle of his thought which has appeared so often. One of the qualities which develop with the increasing "firmness of character" involved in a rising standard of life, is that of more vividly realizing the future, and projecting more and more new wants generated by new activities, into the future. On this basis such a responsiveness to a rise in the rate of interest becomes understandable; though it is rather the vividness of realizing the future which is decisive in accounting for a greater *responsiveness* of savings to interest. The effect of new future wants would appear to be rather the increase of the total volume of savings, independently of changes in the rate of remuneration.

REAL COST

Its close relation to the questions just dealt with will justify a brief inquiry into Marshall's doctrine of real cost. It is clear that in the money sense he holds that value tends to be equal to marginal cost of production and that he extends this doctrine to the production of the factors themselves. Since Marshall believes they are predominantly governed by a functional relation to price he is unquestionably committed to the proposition that labor, capital and "business power" receive earnings closely proportioned to their real cost of production.[3]

---

different countries and different ages. . . . They depend much on social and religious sactions." *Principles*, p. 225.

[1] *Principles*, p. 235; see also *ibid.*, p. 232.

[2] *Ibid.*, p. 234.

[3] "The supply of each agent will be closely governed by its cost of production." *Ibid.*, p. 537.

It has been noted above that his principle of substitution gives Marshall an interpretation of real cost consonant with his general utility doctrine—an interpretation which is now usually called "opportunity cost." But this conception applies only to the cost involved in the *use* of any particular agent of production for one purpose to the exclusion of other alternative uses. It has no reference to the cost involved in the production of the resource itself.[1] But when Marshall speaks of real as distinguished from money costs of production in terms of the "efforts and sacrifices" entailed in the process,[2] his intense interest in the production of the factors themselves makes it quite certain that he does not limit the meaning of "sacrifices" to this restricted sense, and, of course, "efforts" could not very well come into the opportunity cost conception at all. What then could he mean by real cost?

First, as to labor. There have been two chief interpretations of real labor cost: the physiological and the hedonistic. The physiological sense seems to be implied in the more drastic versions of Malthusianism, though it is modified by the part played by the standard of living. In this sense it is probable that Marshall thought population and hence labor supply to be partly a mechanical function of food supply among the "more ignorant and phlegmatic of races." Moreover it is not only regarding numbers that a "steam engine" theory of the "quantity of labor" is tenable, for individual efficiency may be a function of the standard of living for purely physiological reasons. Marshall states specifically that this factor is one of considerable importance even in the England of his time[3] and certainly in the less advanced countries. Thus he holds that physiological causes are by no means negligible as factors in the supply of labor.

On the other hand, Marshall often speaks, especially when he has what he calls "conventional necessaries" and "habitual comforts" rather than strict necessaries in mind, as if the efforts and sacrifices involved in their acquisition were balanced by the pleasure derived from their consumption, so that the hedonistic theory gave an interpretation both of why men worked to an

---

[1] A difference of opinion is possible respecting what constitute ultimate resources, so that what from one point of view is merely "use" of a resource is from another production of it.

[2] *Principles*, pp. 338–339.

[3] *Ibid.*, p. 196.

extent for which the "steam engine" theory is not able to account, and of the cost factor which served as a brake on their working beyond a certain point. There are various statements in Marshall which lend plausibility to such an interpretation. For example: laborers are "paid for every hour at a rate sufficient to *compensate* them for the last and most distressing hour."[1] Such statements are the main basis for the contention that Marshall was a utilitarian hedonist. Yet they cannot account for certain aspects of his treatment of labor cost.

An attempt has been made above to prove that Marshall did not hold consistently to an essentially hedonistic view of the *motivation* to labor. If he did not it would be illogical for him to hold a hedonistic theory of real labor cost. In fact it is difficult to see that, beyond the limits of the physiological sense just discussed, and the hints of a hedonistic interpretation, he could have held that labor was attended by any real cost at all in the sense of effort causing pain, or of a sacrifice which would not otherwise be incurred—indeed how could he, while saying in the same breath that "work in its best sense, the healthy energetic use of faculties is the aim of life, is life itself"?[2] What is the aim of life, what is life itself, cannot well be interpreted as a cost which must be incurred in the attainment of ends outside itself.

How then can he make so many statements to the effect that "the money measure of costs corresponds to the real costs" (in terms of effort)?[3] The confusion seems to come from the identification of two wholly different things under the term real cost. One is simply those factors, whatever they are, which serve as a brake on the supply of an economic good and which must hence, under free enterprise, be balanced by the price. In this sense anyone who goes as far as Marshall does in claiming the functional interdependence of the price and total quantity of the agents of production is bound to say that wages of any kind of labor correspond to the real costs of producing it. But when real cost means ultimate sacrifices entailed by that production which are *compensated* by the utility of the product, such a statement has, beyond the scope

---

[1] *Ibid.*, p. 527. Italics mine.
[2] *Memorials*, p. 115.
[3] *Principles*, p. 350.

of the doctrine of opportunity cost, no clear meaning except in hedonistic terms.[1]

But it has already been shown that this responsiveness to "economic causes" which Marshall claims for the quantities of the productive factors is not, in his opinion, due primarily to either physiological or hedonistic influences, particularly in modern Western countries, but to the rising standard of life, the development of character and of a level of wants adjusted to activities. "Activities" pursued largely as ends in themselves mean, broadly speaking, an equally rapid rising standard of efficiency.[2] This amounts to saying that specifically moral factors play a part in efficiency. It must be concluded that Marshall simply did not think through the implications of this result for a theory of real costs, when that term refers to sacrifices.

The sense in which Marshall would mean the contention that wages form the cost of production of the total labor supply including numbers is analogous. The cost of bearing and rearing children is considered only partly as a "sacrifice." It is, at the same time, one of those "activities" whose development is the aim of social progress.

Much the same finally is true of the sense in which the "waiting" involved in saving is the real cost of production of capital. A definite sacrifice of present consumption is of course involved in saving, but his rejection of the term "abstinence" in favor of the ethically colorless "waiting"[3] is indicative of the fact that Marshall is not inclined to take that in too literally hedonistic a sense.[4] On the other hand, frugality is one of the leading traits of character of Marshall's ideal economic man, so that

[1] Of course any physiological doctrine of real cost is incapable of interpretation in subjective terms such as "sacrifice" in the individual-hedonistic sense. To mean anything it must refer to loss of potential economic resources on the part of the individual or the community.

[2] Even physical vigor depends not only on physical conditions but "also on force of will and strength of character." Energy of this kind is "moral rather than physical." *Principles*, p. 194. "Freedom and hope increase not only man's willingness but also his power for work." *Ibid.*, p. 197, footnote 1.

[3] *Ibid.*, pp. 232–233.

[4] "The greatest accumulators of wealth are very rich persons, some of whom live in luxury, and certainly do not practice abstinence in that sense of the term in which it is convertible with abstemiousness." *Principles*, p. 233.

the development of saving habits and a vivid realization of the future lead to increasingly rapid accumulation. Hence, while interest is the cost of production of capital in the sense that the supply varies with the rate, it can hardly be said that Marshall seriously held that this rate measured the sacrifice[1] involved in waiting, since waiting is in large measure a by-product of qualities of character prized for their own sake.

Free Enterprise

The keynote of Marshall's description and analysis of the modern economic order is what he called "free industry and enterprise."[2] Its development is for him the central problem of at least modern, if not all economic history,[3] and the understanding of its workings, results and conditions of existence and efficiency is the main task of his economic analysis.

It is a system characterized by the predominance of rather small competing firms, each under the guidance of an enterprising and resourceful businessman, who at his own risk continually experiments with various combinations of the productive factors. For the sluggishness and passive adherence to tradition of a custom-bound society it substitutes rational experimentation with new methods. On the other hand, its flexibility and freedom are contrasted sharply with the rigidity of bureaucratic organizations,[4] whether public or private. This latter type, the opposite of free enterprise, Marshall found exemplified both in mercantilist monopoly and regulation and

[1] But he does say interest is the *reward* of waiting. "Human nature being what it is we are justified in speaking of the interest on capital as the reward of the sacrifice involved in waiting for the enjoyment of material resources because few people would save much without reward." *Principles*, p. 232. This passage seems to have so definitely hedonistic a connotation that it must again be concluded that Marshall did not satisfactorily think through what he meant by real cost of waiting. But even here the emphasis is on *responsiveness* of supply rather than sacrifice.

[2] The late Professor Allyn Young (*Quarterly Journal of Economics*, November, 1927) called attention to the specifically Marshallian nature of this conception in contrast to the Marxian idea of capitalism. Compare also below Pareto's "demagogic plutocracy."

[3] See especially *Principles*, Appendix A, and Alfred Marshall, *Industry and Trade.*

[4] "If he [the businessman] is working at his own risk, he can put forth his energies with perfect freedom. But if he is a servant of a bureaucracy he cannot be certain of freedom." *Ibid.*, p. 333.

n modern tendencies to very large scale business, government control and socialism.[1]

To be sure he saw a great many defects in unmitigated economic freedom, particularly in relation to the position of the working classes. His conception of the role of the state was by no means wholly negative.[2] But nevertheless he was definitely and strongly a believer in individual freedom. He had no regrets that custom has lost its sway and was severely critical of the bureaucratic methods of large joint-stock companies, to say nothing of government enterprise.[3] The prima facie case was definitely against any further extension of the economic functions of the state.[4] Socialism he considered the most serious threat to well-being in his day.[5]

At the same time Marshall's free enterprise is by no means an unmitigated struggle for existence—a Hobbesian state of nature. It is throughout closely bound by ethical norms. Again and again he reiterates that only the great improvement in character and morality of recent times had made economic development possible.[6] But, while to some extent, this moral advance facilitates an extension of governmental functions, to a

---

[1] See, especially, large parts of *Industry and Trade,* and in the *Memorials,* "Water as an Element of National Wealth," "Some Aspects of Competition" and "Social Possibilities of Economic Chivalry."

[2] See Alfred Marshall, *Official Papers,* p. 366; *Industry and Trade.* p. 647.

[3] "Government creates scarcely anything." *Memorials,* p. 338. "We secure, so far as the influence of the Post Office reaches, most of the evils of Socialism with but few of its benefits." Letter to the *Times* (London), March 24, 1891.

[4] "Every new extension of Governmental work in branches of production needing ceaseless creation and initiative is to be regarded as prima facie anti-social." *Memorials,* p. 339.

[5] "I regard the socialistic movement as not merely a danger but by far the greatest present danger to human well-being." In a letter written in 1909. *Memorials,* p. 462. There is now "a broader and firmer foundation for socialistic schemes than existed when Mill wrote. But no socialistic scheme yet advanced seems to make adequate provision for the maintenance of high enterprise and individual strength of character." *Industry and Trade,* Preface, p. viii.

[6] "Uprightness and mutual confidence are necessary conditions for the growth of wealth." *Economics of Industry,* p. 11. The great increase in the size of businesses "would have been impossible had there not been a great improvement in the morality and uprightness of the average man." *Memorials,* p. 307. See also *Principles,* p. 7; *Industry and Trade,* p. 165.

larger extent it tends to render them unnecessary and to make a system of economic freedom workable with a minimum of regulation.

It is important to note also that Marshall's strictures on large-scale organization applied to private as well as state enterprise, though in less degree. They all tend inevitably to routine and lack of enterprise. It is significant that he ascribed the failure of monopoly to engross whole industries not so much to limits in the technical economies of large-scale production and organization as to the fact that no firm has time to reach the size necessary for monopolistic domination before the process of decay sets in and proceeds so far as to force it to give way to a new firm.[1]

The main grounds for Marshall's general adherence to the policy of laissez faire are two. The first lies in a broad deduction from his utility theory, which is generally stated in the form of the *doctrine of maximum satisfaction*. It is true that Marshall makes some far-reaching criticisms of the doctrine, noting its inconsistency with the inequality of wealth[2] and, in particular, proving that free competition results in overinvestment in industries tending to increasing cost, and underinvestment in those tending to decreasing cost.[3] But with these qualifications he holds it to be a valid doctrine on the assumptions given above as underlying his utility theory as a whole. Moreover, it is significant that he states the doctrine in individualistic terms,[4] without even considering whether it would apply to a collectivist state where the whole process of production

---

[1] *Industry and Trade*, pp. 315–316; also p. 422. At the same time Marshall had a certain tendency to minimize the importance of the combination movement. Speaking of combinations, of both employers and employed, he says, "They present a succession of picturesque incidents—but [their importance] is apt to be exaggerated; for indeed many of them are little more than eddies such as have always fluttered over the surface of progress—now as ever the main body of movement depends on the deep, silent, strong stream . . . of normal distribution and exchange." *Principles*, p. 628. "Normal" in this context seems obviously to mean "competitive."

[2] *Principles*, p. 471. He apparently thought that difficulty was becoming less serious: "The main drift of this study of Distribution then suggests that the social and economic forces already at work are changing the distribution of wealth for the better." *Ibid.*, p. 712.

[3] *Principles*, Book V, Chap. XIII.

[4] *Ibid.*, p. 502.

and allocation of resources was in the hands of a single centralized body working in the general interests. The omission is surely indicative of a laissez-faire bias.

The doctrine of maximum satisfaction was certainly for Marshall more than a somewhat dubious by-product of highly abstract theoretical speculation. He consistently refused to be led into abstract reasoning which he did not think had any practical application. Indeed on any other assumption than that the doctrine represents for him a broadly valid generalization of the main tendencies of competitive society, his acceptance of it is incomprehensible.

But its significance in his scheme of thought is more clearly seen in terms of the closely related principle of substitution, which may be considered on the whole a more limited and less drastic statement of the same principle. There are numerous passages showing that he thought the principle of substitution led to the working out of optimum combinations of resources under free enterprise.[1] The basic reason for his belief in the working out of these two principles under modern conditions is his general faith in the growing rationality of mankind. Given the overwhelming evidence that he held such a view, it is hardly surprising that he should be able to accept the two principles as substantially true of a late stage in social development.

[1] *Ibid.*, pp. 341, 355–356, 405–406, 597. But even though his faith in the working of the principle of substitution under free enterprise is far-reaching, that alone does not justify the conclusion that he held that free enterprise approximated to the general optimum condition contemplated by the doctrine of maximum satisfaction. For the principle deals immediately with the adjustments arrived at by individual entrepreneurs and is hence limited by the resources available to them. It would be quite possible for every entrepreneur to reach such an optimum adjustment under the conditions he had to face and the whole system yet not be at a maximum of satisfaction. The discrepancy would be due to the existence of obstacles to the mobility of resources. They cannot be due to lack of rationality of individual behavior since that is implied in the principle of substitution.

Since Marshall had no very strong doubts of the mobility of capital there remains that of labor, where the most serious question is that of non-competing groups. Though Marshall's opinion on that issue is obscure its general drift seems to be that whatever importance they have had is diminishing and that free enterprise, aided by compulsory education, has a strong tendency to break down such barriers. See *Principles*, pp. 217, 310, 661; *Economics of Industry*, p. 47; *Industry and Trade*, pp. 4–5.

The question at issue on this side of the problem of laissez faire is its efficiency. Taking satisfaction of consumers' wants as the only possible standard of efficiency, it appears that a system of laissez faire can, under certain assumptions, be an efficient system of organization. Moreover it happens that most of these assumptions were for Marshall far more than a set of methodological abstractions; they represented to a great extent actual descriptions of free enterprise, or of the condition toward which he thought it to be tending. This is unquestionably true of three of the four main assumptions listed above—competition, mobility and rationality—all of which he thought to be characteristic of free enterprise as distinct from other systems.

The main doubts as to whether this is the sole important ground of his adherence to laissez faire arise in connection with the other main assumption, the independence of wants. This, it has been shown, he definitely repudiates, and repudiates in the interest of the influence of activities as ends in themselves. And closer examination reveals the fact that the activities and qualities of character which Marshall prizes so highly are everywhere associated with free enterprise, while their opposites —sluggishness and stagnation, on the one hand, ostentation and luxury, on the other—are invariably associated with conditions other than free enterprise, or at least, if appearing in the same society, do not properly belong to it. In fact, though he believed that free enterprise was an efficient system of organization, his paeans of praise of the businessman who combined bold initiative and enterprise with industry, frugality and general "firmness of character" are so impressive as to leave a legitimate doubt whether he would not have favored a system which bred such characters even at the cost of a considerable loss of efficiency. His praise of Athens as against Sparta and Rome, and of the modern sea powers like England against land powers like France and Germany supports this suggestion.[1] But with characteristic Victorian optimism he, in general, held that the two aspects went hand in hand, that the interests of efficiency were not opposed to those of individual character and culture. Conversely socialism, and less drastic measures of government interference with economic freedom, meant to him both ineffi-

[1] See "Water as an Element of National Wealth," *Memorials*, pp. 134 *ff.*

ciency in the technical economic sense and sapping of the springs of enterprise through the degradation of character.[1] Nevertheless, even though the two motives work in the same direction, it is important that they should be analytically distinguished and their quite separate sources brought out.

SOCIAL EVOLUTION

After the above only a brief discussion need be devoted to Marshall's doctrine of social evolution. It is evident that he had one, as is indeed only natural in a man whose thought was being formed at the time when Darwinian ideas were beginning to make a deep impression in England. The doctrine Marshall holds is essentially unilinear, in spite of the fact that he did not think evolution was absolutely continuous and unbroken, or inevitable.[2] There is no sign of an essentially cyclical conception of social change, nor of change by a dialectic process, nor, finally, of the idea that social development resembles the growth of a branching tree.

Within the general framework of this continuous unilinear process can be identified two main elements corresponding directly to the two factors in his thought which have been traced throughout this study. As has already been noted, a leading assumption of Marshall's utility economics is rationality of behavior in the adaptation of means to ends. But the rather far-reaching rationality which characterizes his picture of free enterprise has not always existed; it has come only with a long process of evolution, resulting in a gradual widening of the scope and power of rational behavior. In common with many ethnologists of his time Marshall conceived the state of primitive man (in the sense not merely of contemporary peoples called primitive but of the original state of our own ancestors) to be one of slavish devotion to custom[3] and

---

[1] "I think the chief dangers of Socialism lie not in its tendency towards a more equal distribution of income for I can see no harm in that, but in the sterilizing influence on those mental activities which have gradually raised the world from barbarism." Letter to the *Times* (London), March 24, 1891.

[2] *Memorials*, p. 305.

[3] "In primitive times and backward countries the sway of custom is more undisputed." *Principles*, p. 640.

adherence to a compulsory uniformity of behavior.[1] The process of emancipation from custom[2] is one of the gradual differentiation of functions and the growing independence of individual action according to objectively rational[3] norms. A reverse process takes place, to be sure, in the form of the crystallization of rational ways of doing things into custom and tradition.[4] But while this reverse process with its stabilizing effect on social life is recognized there is no doubt that that of emancipation is more fundamental, so that for him evolution consists in the progressive approximation to action according to the principle of substitution, *i.e.*, to economically rational action.[5]

In these terms economic history becomes for Marshall essentially the history of the development of free enterprise. In fact the only explicitly historical chapter in his *Principles*, Appendix A, is entitled "The Growth of Free Industry and Enterprise." With all the setbacks the process is conceived as in principle continuous,[6] and the things which really need explanation are not the specific forms of behavior and organization but the removal of barriers and the development of certain arrangements facilitating exchange, communications,

---

[1] Savage tribes "show a strange uniformity of general character . . . living under the dominion of custom and impulse." *Op. cit.*, Appendix A, p. 723.

[2] Custom is not necessarily ultimate; deeper factors are hinted at: "The greater part of custom is doubtless but a crystallized form of oppression and suppression" though "every body of custom that endures contains provisions that protect the weak from the most reckless forms of injury." And further, "This force of custom in early civilizations is partly a cause and partly a consequence of the limitations of individual rights in property." *Op. cit.*, Appendix A, pp. 725–726.

[3] The "business point of view" could not have been understood in a primitive society. It is "merely one drift of the tendency to adapt means to ends." *Industry and Trade*, p. 163.

[4] Thus the case for Marshall is not wholly against custom: "The solidity of custom has rendered the supreme service of perpetuating any such change as found general approval." *Industry and Trade*, p. 197.

[5] "Emancipation from custom and the growth of free activity—have given a new precision and new prominence to the causes that govern the relative value of different things . . . ." *Principles*, p. 5. Also, "Time is on the side of the more economic methods of production." *Ibid.*, p. 398.

[6] *Principles*, Appendix A. Note his treatment of mercantilism. While he admits the rise of the absolute state meant the imposition of new restrictions on enterprise, he still claims that it removed more barriers than it created and thus the process of emancipation was continuous.

etc., such as money and credit, which are generally themselves included in the developing rationality. This is on the whole the orthodox Anglo-Saxon view of economic history: the barriers must be removed, but once they are removed, modern capitalism—or free enterprise—becomes established of itself. It needs no specific propelling force—and if it consists merely in rational conduct, why should it?

In the passage quoted above about the great truth upon which Ricardo and his followers dwelt, Marshall gives the clue to the second principal aspect of his idea of social evolution. To repeat, he asserts that "while wants are the rulers of life among the lower animals, it is to changes in the forms of efforts and activities that we must turn when in search for the keynotes of the history of mankind."[1] This might be understood merely to assert a difference between animals and man, but, evolutionist as Marshall is, he clearly means more: that there is a process of development from the former to the latter state. Later on, he says specifically, "Speaking broadly, therefore, although it is man's wants in the earliest stages of his development that give rise to his activities, yet afterwards each new step upwards is to be regarded as the development of new activities giving rise to new wants, rather than of new wants giving rise to new activities."[2]

Thus along with the development of reason goes a second evolutionary process, the development of new activities, of a rising standard of life. From this point of view the process of evolution leads to the same goal as before, free enterprise, because the higher activities are those which are fostered by such a system, where the energy and enterprise of modern Western culture is set over against the sluggishness and stagnation of former times. Of the latter type of activities there are two sorts—the primeval stagnation of a custom-bound[3] society and the comfortable uninspired routine of a government department or any very large organization. Thus Marshall conceives socialism and some aspects of large-scale organization as backward steps in evolution. This, it is readily seen, is a

[1] *Principles*, p. 85.
[2] *Ibid.*, p. 89.
[3] Thus custom forms the principal characteristic of the primitive from both points of view. Adherence to it is both irrational and an indication of "sluggishness."

very different aspect of the genesis of free enterprise from the growth of rationality. So far as the interest is merely in want satisfaction it is essentially indifferent what types of activities are employed to that end, so long as they are efficient. If collective organization is more efficient in this sense there is no reason why it should not be preferred. But if it destroys the activities and character in which Marshall believed so strongly, and which he thought were fostered by free enterprise, its "mere" efficiency becomes far less important.

But this second element in Marshall's idea of social evolution, however distinct logically, is in his own mind intimately bound up with the progress of reason. In a sense the rise in the standard of life is itself a process of rationalization. Marshall would certainly say that the modern man was more rational than the primitive creature of "wants" or custom. But it is equally clear that it cannot be simply identical with the progress of reason in a sense to which all men would assent. Why is idle "stagnation" unreasonable; why are some wants "artificial," others natural? Evidently because of Marshall's belief in an absolute goal of evolution, the development of character in his peculiar sense. The rising standard of life is really the central factor; around it as a nucleus cluster the concrete economic wants, and to it is adapted the external and social environment within the limits permitted by physical conditions.[1] Basically the selective process of business competition and the rational combination of resources derive their significance from their service to this end. This it is which enables him to speak of a "higher and nobler" life at all.

And it is fundamentally because he assumes these activities to be ends in themselves that he is an adherent of the unilinear concept of social evolution.[2]

[1] It is significant that Marshall does not go far in attributing direct importance to factors of external environment in general. He says, for instance (*Industry and Trade*, p. 158), that the United States owes less to her resources than to the exceptional force of character of her people. (See also Alfred Marshall, *Money, Credit and Commerce*, p. 5.) There are, however, numerous statements about the debilitating effects of hot climates, which are understandable when we consider the enormous importance he attributed to energetic activity. See below, footnote 1, p. 166.

[2] The sociological significance of this belief and the relation of Marshall's doctrine of social evolution to those of others will be discussed below, p. 278 *ff.*, 368 *ff.*, 563 *ff.*

The "Natural Order"

From what has already been said in various connections it is evident that Marshall considered that the principles of maximum satisfaction and of substitution confirmed on the whole the desirability of free enterprise. Moreover he goes considerably further than the more limited versions of the doctrines, which would have to do only with an optimum satisfaction of wants by means of given resources. It has been shown that the quantity of economic resources, except, of course, natural agents, varies for him primarily with "economic causes," *i.e.*, immediately with the price offered for their use. Does he go still further and claim that, at least under free enterprise, there is a tendency to the automatic production of optimum quantities of labor and capital? This step is, of course, the one to a "natural order," in which the *whole* socioeconomic equilibrium is determined in a way beneficent to mankind.

The clearest case is that of the amount of labor performed by a single laborer. There are very strong suggestions in Marshall that free enterprise does produce something very much like an optimum in this respect. Activity under such a system is continually contrasted with the sluggishness and stagnation of other societies. While there are suggestions that sometimes free enterprise tends to overwork labor, this ill effect is almost always attributed to the social environment in which it has developed, and Marshall thinks there is a strong tendency for such abuses to disappear with the removal of social factors not in harmony with free enterprise.[1] So, though Marshall never committed himself definitely, there is a strong case for believing he thought free enterprise produced an optimum of effort.

What is his attitude toward the question of numbers? One negative conclusion is certain: while he believed in a form of the Malthusian doctrine for former times and for "backward countries," he certainly thought that free enterprise had broken the vicious circle. Population under free enterprise would then be more nearly at an optimum. But would it actually tend toward such an optimum? So far as can be ascertained Marshall gives no answer. It is noteworthy that he never attempted to define the concept of an optimum of population, nor to measure

[1] *Principles*, p. 748; *Industry and Trade*, pp. 72–73.

how close actual populations came to such a standard—a task which was beginning to attract considerable attention on the part of economists in the later years of his life. While Marshall does not deny the proposition, neither does he affirm it. But there is little doubt that he felt free enterprise came nearer attaining such an optimum than any alternative.

Regarding saving, a similar negative conclusion seems justified; the more vivid realization of the future under free enterprise leads to a better situation in this respect. In fact there is no hint that such a thing as too much saving is conceivable. On the whole, therefore, it would seem that free enterprise accomplished something nearer an optimum of savings than any other system. There are clear statements that one of the great dangers of socialism lies in its probable reduction in the volume of accumulation. The evidence from this aspect of Marshall's thought again points strongly in the direction of his belief in a "natural order,"[1] even though such belief is not positively established.

But serious doubts are thrown on this interpretation from the other side. An optimum is essentially a static concept; it is an optimum adjustment to certain fixed factors. For society those factors must lie either in the external environment alone, or that plus certain given wants. But Marshall holds neither of these. In particular, he refuses to take wants as given; his central doctrine is that of a progressive growth of wants generated by new activities. From this point of view the strong tendencies toward belief in an optimum adjustment could refer only to each stage in the development of wants adjusted to activities.

Whether Marshall believed in a natural order in any more than this relative sense depends on whether he conceived the whole process to be moving toward any fixed goal. Here again there are suggestions.[2] Certainly the general direction is fixed

---

[1] "In a stationary state the income earned by every appliance of production . . . would represent the normal measure of the efforts and sacrifices required to cal' it into existence." *Principles*, Appendix H, p. 810.

[2] He says, "This doctrine of natural organization [laissez faire] contains more truth of the highest importance to humanity than almost any other." *Principles*, pp. 246–247. But in its classical form it "hindered them from inquiring whether many even of the broader features of modern industry might not be transitional," and finally it "forgot that man delights in the use of his faculties for their own sake." The last statement is typical of his

as is the main outline of the types of character he thought he saw developing. But within these limitations it seems fair to say that he thought of the process as endless.

This probability is strengthened by a striking disagreement of Marshall with his eminent predecessor, John Stuart Mill. In Mill's famous chapter on the stationary state occurs the well-known passage: "I am inclined to believe that it [the stationary state] would be, on the whole, a very considerable improvement on our present condition. I confess I am not charmed with the ideal of life held out by those who think that the normal state of human beings is that of struggling to get on; that the trampling, crushing, elbowing and treading on each other's heels, which form the existing type of social life are the most desirable lot of human kind or are anything but the disagreeable symptoms . . . of industrial progress."[1] On the other hand, Marshall says, "But indeed a perfect adjustment is inconceivable. Perhaps even it is undesirable. For after all man is the end[2] of production; and perfectly stable business would be likely to produce men who were little better than machines."[3] Need anything further be said to bring out the difference between Marshall and those holding an essentially static ideal?[4]

ECONOMIC MOTIVES

The fact that economic theory has developed largely within the utilitarian framework of thought probably goes far toward accounting for the extent to which the idea that human motivation was primarily egoistic has been associated with it. Indeed the formula of the rational pursuit of self-interest has been so widely applied that egoism has seemed to be of the very essence of the economists' outlook on human action. This tendency has been strongly reinforced by the extent to which psychological hedonism has replaced the more purely utilitarian assumption

---

attitude against a laissez-faire philosophy based on the doctrine of maximum satisfaction alone.

[1] JOHN STUART MILL, *Principles of Political Economy*, ed. by W. J. Ashley, p. 748.

[2] This, of course, does not mean that the satisfaction of man's *wants* is the end of production but rather the development of his character.

[3] *Industry and Trade*, p. 195.

[4] The ideal of utilitarianism is, of course, static.

of the randomness of ends. For if the uniformities of behavior are derived in the last analysis from the human propensity to pursue pleasure, in the nature of the case the ultimate ground of action is indifferent to the welfare of others. The tendency has been strong to tie this egoism so closely to the postulate of rationality of action as to make them appear inseparable.

On the other hand, careful consideration of the conception of utility which forms the logical basis of one aspect of Marshall's thought shows that in its strict economic construction there is no such implication of egoistic motivation. For the utility concept is concerned only with command over means to want satisfaction and is as such entirely indifferent to the specific character of the ultimate ends to which these means may be applied. The norm of economic behavior will be precisely the same whether the proceeds of acquisitive endeavor are applied to the indulgence of the appetites or to relieving the sufferings of the poor.

It is a notable and symptomatic fact that Marshall quite clearly made this separation. His insistence on the rationality of human action is very strong indeed, but far from claiming that it is essentially egoistic he leaves wide scope for altruistic elements and, what is most important, maintains that the scope of altruism is rapidly broadening with the process of evolution, that is, with the increasing effectiveness of "economic forces." There would seem then to be not merely a separation of egoism and rationality in Marshall's thought, but a reverse connection, with increasing rationality man becomes less rather than more egoistic.[1] What is the source of this?

---

[1] "Whenever we get a glimpse of the economic man he is not selfish." *Memorials*, p. 160. "The motives which induce business men to compete are not altogether sordid." *Op. cit.*, p. 281.

"The economists of today go beyond those of earlier generations in believing that the desire of men for the approval of their own conscience and for the esteem of others is an economic force of the first order of importance." *Op. cit.*, p. 285. Note that this is for him an *economic* force.

The records of history do not support the doctrine that man is "harder and harsher than he was." *Principles*, p. 6. He speaks of "the marvelous growth in recent times of a spirit of honesty and uprightness in commercial matters." *Op. cit.*, p. 303.

As compared with the seventeenth century, man "has acquired an increasing power of realizing the future—he is more prudent and has more self-control—he is more unselfish—and there are already signs of a brighter time to come, in which there will be a general willingness to work and save

It is to be found again in the role he assigns to the "activities" which for him were so important in the development of character. The keynote of this element of action is "disinterested" devotion to the technical processes of economic production for their own sake, without "ulterior motives." Holding as strongly as he did to this view, Marshall naturally could not consider his "economic man" the egoist who had played such a prominent part in traditional economic thought. His acquisitive activities simply could not be regarded only as means to his own private ends. Once having broken decisively through the utilitarian-hedonistic tendency to emphasize egoism, it is not surprising that he acquires more of an ability to see "altruistic" elements of motivation as well. But it is not to be assumed that the disinterested devotion to "activities," which is his central concern, is adequately designated by the current concept of altruism. It is impossible to go into that question here.[1]

While Marshall's position led him decisively to reject the egoism of the traditional economic man, quite the contrary is true of his rationality. Man is not only rational, but is steadily growing more so; and this is a primary mark of the advance of free enterprise. It is, of course, true that the postulate of rationality has been basic to all utilitarian thought, and equally so to its hedonistic cousin. It is entirely consistent with the assumptions of the utility element of his economic theory; it is, indeed, essential to it. But it can, at the same time, be doubted whether the conception of rationality on the "utility" level, that is, as essential to the efficient acquisition of desirable goods and

---

in order to increase the stores of public wealth." *Op. cit.*, p. 680. A further sample of statements is the following: "It is deliberateness, not selfishness that is the characteristic of the modern age." *Op. cit.*, p. 6.

Keynes says (*Memorials*, p. 9), "It would be true, I suppose, to say that Marshall never departed explicitly from the utilitarian ideas which dominated the generation of economists who preceded him. But the solution of economic problems was for Marshall, not an application of the hedonistic calculus, but a prior condition of the exercise of man's higher faculties, irrespective, almost, of what we mean by "higher." But Marshall knew very well what *he* meant by "higher." Moreover the study of economics was for him not merely that of a "condition" of that exercise but a study of the actual development of such faculties and their exercise.

[1] The question will be further developed below in connection with Durkheim (see Chap. X, p. 387).

services, exhausts its role in Marshall's thought. Indeed, again the element of activities plays a major role. But this time, instead of leading Marshall to a change from the traditional view, it strongly reinforces it. The man of free enterprise is by no means rational only for "prudential" motives. He has rather an ethical obligation to be rational. Careful, systematic administration of his resources and powers, a clear realization of the probable exigencies which the future will bring and provision for them, careful regulation of his consumption and habits of life in ways that contribute to his productivity, that "afford strength"—all these are part of the disinterested ethical attitude which is characteristic of Marshall's ideal economic man. It is true that these do on the whole contribute to the efficiency of acquisitive activities, but from the ethical point of view this efficiency is rather a by-product than the raison d'être of the attitude. The two were, of course, in harmony. Man by acting rationally secured the necessary means to satisfying his increasing wants. But this fact, as Marshall maintained it was, should not blind us to the radical difference of his account of the elements in the process from the one current in the traditional economics.

Marshall was, as has been noted, a strong adherent of economic individualism as a social policy. Ultimately this goes back to an ethics where there is a heavy stress on individual ethical responsibility. But it must be clear by this time that the reasons in his own thought underlying this attitude are not exactly of the same "individualistic" kind as those current in the traditions of thought which have occupied this study thus far. The discussion must now turn to the more general theoretical issues underlying Marshall's position.[1]

---

[1] Before turning to these more general theoretical questions, a most striking fact may be pointed out: The group of interrelated attitudes which Marshall sums up under the term "activities" bears a very close resemblance to the "spirit of capitalism" as formulated by Max Weber. It entails the same ethical obligation to work in the activities of the everyday business world without consideration of reward, entirely in abstraction from "utilitarian motives." Weber, like Marshall, considers this attitude to be a fundamental necessity for an individualistic economic order to function. This empirical agreement, of which the reader can convince himself by consulting the outline of Weber's treatment of the subject which is presented below (see Chap. XIV), is one of the most important starting points for the theoretical consequences about to be drawn from the prominence

THE PROBLEM OF THE SCOPE OF ECONOMIC THEORY

Of what importance here is the situation in Marshall's thought which has just been brought out? The element which has been called his "utility theory" may quite legitimately be regarded as a development of the elements formulated in the utilitarian system of positivistic thought with which a great deal of the previous discussion has been concerned. It consists essentially in these elements dissociated from their earlier close connection with psychological hedonism, and modified and refined by the principle of marginal utility and the developments logically derived from it. At the same time the general context in which his utility theory is developed is the familiar individualistic one suggesting at least a strong leaning in the direction of a postulate of "identity of interests." The doctrine of maximum satisfaction is held to be essentially sound, competition is on the whole beneficent and becoming more so. There is no really serious concern with the problem of order in the sense of Hobbes or with the problem of class conflict in the Marxian sense.

But this utility theory does not stand alone. It is everywhere intertwined with the theory of activities. Moreover, this other element of activities far overshadows any third element in Marshall's thinking. While there are suggestions of hedonism, and now and then environmental factors or racial qualities are invoked, these may be considered quite incidental as compared with the two central strands of Marshall's thought.

Now it is to be noted that all these other factors which Marshall treats as of incidental importance are just those which constitute the other possibilities of positivistic thought. In so far as he felt the utility element to be inadequate, it would be expected that he would follow his predecessors in having recourse to hedonism. There are, indeed, some suggestions in this direction in his writings, and some of his interpreters have gone so far as to regard this as the main logical foundation of his thought.[1] It has,

---

of this element of "activities" in Marshall's "Economic Theory." It will be referred to on a number of occasions throughout the study.

[1] It is evident that it is impossible to agree with those writers who throw Marshall and the classical economists together as hedonists and find in this sufficient cause for dismissing them as inadequate on account of the falsity of their psychological assumptions. Thus Professor Mitchell says, "The fact

however, been possible to show that this cannot be the case. Had he been a genuine hedonist he must have answered quite differently many of the questions raised above. Of a tendency to think in terms of instinct psychology there is very little evidence in Marshall—indeed no important view of his depends on it. Finally while he did not take extreme views of the power of man to control his own destiny apart from the conditions of his heredity or his environment, neither did he stress the latter factors. Certainly he did not attribute the inadequacy of utility theory by itself to its neglect of them. With one important exception[1] no single doctrine of his depends on the assumption

---

remains that the ultimate terms in Marshall's account of economic activity are pleasures and pains. . . ." (*Journal of Political Economy*, Vol. 18, p. 111). Again, ". . . he [Marshall] uses money primarily as the objective measure of human motives [which is true] and then goes below money to the bedrock of hedonism" [which is quite a different thing]. *Ibid.*, p. 207. Also Professor Homan says of Marshall, "The motives he considers are very simple and distinctly hedonistic. He only succeeded in avoiding the ethics of hedonism, not its theory of human motivation." *Contemporary Economic Thought*, p. 236. But if he was a hedonist how could he have objected so strenuously to Jevons' version of the utility theory? The fact is, as should now be abundantly evident, that Marshall was *not* primarily a hedonist, and the ultimate terms in his account of economic activities are not pleasures and pains.

[1] This is the one striking exception: he repeatedly insists on the debilitating effects of hot climates; they sap the springs of energy and make for sluggishness. Why does he make the exception? Apparently he had in mind primarily India. Because of his absolute belief in his "activities," he was blind to the possibility that Indian civilization might be simply *different* from European, guided by different ideals. He tried rather to find a place for it in his evolutionary scheme. His reasoning was: The Indians are obviously an intelligent people; their failure to develop free enterprise cannot be due to innate stupidity. It must be ascribed to some arresting agency attributable to the climate. India is not essentially different from Europe, but is in an arrested stage in the same process of development. The Indians belong to the more ignorant and phlegmatic of races. (He also had a certain tendency to minimize the differences: See his continual statements that there is more operation of "economic forces" in India than is generally supposed.) It is interesting to compare this with Max Weber's view, expressed in his study of the social implications of Hindu religion (*Religionssoziologie*, Vol. II, p. 133): "The belief that the Indians are characterized by a 'sluggishness' which is the result of the climate, and that this explains their supposed aversion to activity, is wholly without foundation. No country in the world has ever known such continual and savage warfare, such ruthless conquests, subject to so few limitations, as India." In view of Weber's totally different sociological approach it is not surprising he should come to the diametrically

of the direct influences of heredity or environment in a way seriously to limit the margin open to freedom of human action.

It becomes evident, then, that the real basis of Marshall's discontent with pure utility theory is something other than a conviction of the importance of the other factors in the positivistic repertoire. The fact is that his "activities" have no place there at all. They constitute rather a "value" factor.[1] Concrete economic actions are held to be not merely means to the acquisition of purchasing power. They are also carried on for their own sake, they are modes of the immediate expression of ultimate value attitudes in action. They are an expression of ends or wants but not in the same sense as the wants of utility theory. For the latter are, for the purposes of utility analysis, significant only as constituting the ultimate basis of demand functions. Marshall's activity values are, on the other hand, directly embodied in specific modes of activity essentially independent of demand. That is why he is so anxious to distinguish them from purely utilitarian wants, so much so that he fixes the title "activities" upon them. Indeed Marshall's threefold classification of wants, which has been found to be implicit in his treatment, is highly illuminating. First, there is the category of biological needs, a radically positivistic factor; second, that of artificial wants, which cannot but be identified with the truly random utilitarian category. Such expressions as "the wanton vagaries of fashion" surely could not convey the idea of randomness more vividly. Both these fit admirably into the positivistic scheme. But this is not true of the third class, "wants adjusted to activities." The classification directly distinguishes them from the other kinds of wants, both of which do have a place in positivistic thought.

The wants adjusted to activities are, however, not merely directly expressed in action apart from the medium of demand; they also clearly are not random. And their lack of randomness cannot be due to the factors of heredity or environment, else

---

opposite conclusion from Marshall's. That makes their agreement on capitalism all the more significant.

[1] This involves the introduction of a new term which will be of central importance to the subsequent discussion. It is better not to essay a precise definition at this point but rather to allow its meaning and bearings gradually to become evident from the context. It will be explicitly discussed later on.

they would be indistinguishable from biological needs. In fact they constitute a well integrated system, a self-consistent ideal of conduct, not merely random ethical values but the expression of a single ethic. The "economic virtues" on the two sides of enterprise and honesty are not merely discrete virtues, but a system of virtuous behavior.

It has been noted in Chap. III that on a positivistic basis a theory of social evolution must be of the linear type. Marshall's theory is, to be sure, linear but not for the same reasons. In addition to the factor of accumulation of knowledge and technical lore and fused with it is a second dynamic element, the development and progressive realization of this value system, the activities of free enterprise. His theory remains linear because there is, within Marshall's horizon, only one such value system and he never even considers the possibility that there might be others.

It was also stated in Chap. III that the utilitarian position was essentially unstable and tended to break down in one direction or the other. The important thing to note about Marshall in this respect is that he shows no strong tendency to shift from it in the direction of radical positivism. The only serious question is that of hedonism, which has been shown to be a secondary element in his thinking. There can be no serious doubt that the main supplement to the utilitarian element of his thought lies on the non-positivistic side of utilitarianism—it is a "value" element. It plays the same role in his thinking as the postulate of the natural identity of interests did in that of the early "optimistic" utilitarians, or of institutions in that of Malthus. It is by virtue of the activities element that competition can be beneficent. Marshall held that pure competition favored power to "thrive in the environment" but that there are also forces which "benefit the environment."[1] These are obviously the "activities."

But there is here one important difference from the earlier use of the related concepts. Marshall's activities do not constitute a *postulate* of the same order as that of the natural identity of interests. It is not so much a postulate as a theory—the contention that certain factors play a decisive part as *variables* in the determination of human conduct. It is a theorem which claims

[1] *Principles*, p. 396; *Industry and Trade*, p. 175.

to be verifiable by empirical observation, and even though not an entirely tenable theorem, in that it quite unjustifiably confines its attention to only one value system, this is not the question immediately at issue. The point is that this order of factor is explicitly brought by Marshall into the logical system of economic theory. It is not a matter of mere assumed data, values of constants, whether the random data of utilitarian wants, or the metaphysical postulate of earlier writers.

Moreover, the element of activities is for Marshall functionally independent. It is not, as institutions were for Malthus, a derivative of another, a biological factor.

Finally, Marshall goes distinctly beyond the position that this factor must, in general, be conceded a place, to give us some definite views of what the place is. The primary stress has been laid on one of its functions because it is the point where departure from a utilitarian model is most conspicuous. That is the treatment of value attitudes as expressed directly in action independently of demand. But at the same time, the same attitudes do also play a part through demand. There is a category of wants "adjusted to activities," which may be rephrased as "wants having the same source as activities." This raises a most important methodological point. In so far as the wants expressed in demand are a part of this integrated value system, they are not, for Marshall's economic theory, random wants. This is, of course, implied in the view that they cannot be assumed to be independent of the processes of securing means to their satisfaction. Thus from a second, somewhat different angle this factor in Marshall's thought breaks through the utilitarian schema in a non-positivistic direction.

Enough has been said to demonstrate thoroughly that Marshall has introduced a factor of a radically different logical order from any to be found within the utilitarian system or any other version of the positivistic scheme. But the theoretical importance of this fact is obscured in his work by a series of peculiar circumstances.

In the first place, the empiricism which Marshall shared with his predecessors and contemporaries tended to inhibit any attempt to work out the logical distinctions between different classes of factors in concrete economic life. This would have involved the "long chains of deductive reasoning" of which Marshall was so suspicious.

Second, the peculiar empirical characteristics of Marshall's activities were such as to obscure the radical theoretical implications. On the one hand, his limitation to one value system obligated him to retain the view of linear social evolution dominant in the predominantly positivistic thought of his time. On the other, the specific character of this one system was such as to fuse readily with the rationalistic elements of utilitarian thought into something like an organic whole. For the particular values involved laid an especially strong sanction on rationality of conduct, on careful, systematic work and the systematic selection of the most efficient means to given ends. To be sure, this valuation of rational efficiency held only within certain limits, limits defined by such terms as uprightness, honesty, fair dealing. Marshall saw no place in free enterprise for high efficiency in deliberate exploitation or deception, to say nothing of the use of force. But these limitations were not very conspicuous since on the whole they coincided with the earlier assumptions of laissez-faire economic theory involving the postulate of the natural identity of interests. Instead of excluding possible departures from the optimum conditions for free enterprise by means of a postulate, Marshall does it by means of a positive theory.[1]

Thus some of the theoretical implications of Marshall's new position have not been generally appreciated among his followers. Here it is possible merely to point out the logical grounds for claiming that such radical implications are there. But their full bearing will become far clearer when in the course of subsequent chapters concepts of the same general order are followed through their ramifications in the work of several other writers whose background and empirical theories are strikingly different from those of Marshall.

Before leaving Marshall, however, it is advisable to make explicit a particular methodological problem which consideration of his work raises. Thus far this discussion has been concerned with Marshall's thought mainly as exemplifying the logical possibilities of general social theory, as outlined in the introductory chapters. But Marshall entirely disclaimed any attempt

---

[1] Moreover he conspicuously failed to recognize that his ethical predilection for these values might have led him to an undue emphasis on the universality of their causal role and hence a neglect of alternative possibilities.

to develop a general social theory. He was an economist. Hence is raised the question of the status of economics in relation to general social theory.[1]

Marshall's conception of economics was, as has been shown at the beginning of the chapter, strongly empiricist. It was "a study of mankind in the everyday business of life." What does this mean in terms of the present analysis? The "everyday business of life" is presumably a concrete category of phenomena. There is little attempt on Marshall's part to differentiate an economic element in this concrete sphere.

He makes, to be sure, one further limitation on the approach through the "everyday business of life." That is, Marshall tells us that economics is especially concerned with the "measurement of the force of a person's motives in terms of money."[2] This may be stated more generally to the effect that economic science has in the course of a long tradition built up a scheme of analysis the central feature of which is the use of demand and supply schedules or curves. Money occupies a key position because it is the quantifying medium in terms of which demand and supply relationships are generally expressed. Thus the essential fact may be taken to be that in Marshall's view economics is especially concerned with the everyday business of life in so far as it can be brought into relation with supply and demand.

But it is necessary to make clear just what this implies. The supply and demand schema is a way of arranging relevant facts for purposes of economic analysis.[3] But the phenomena which are described in terms of the supply and demand schedules Marshall uses are *concrete* phenomena. They are, on the one hand, the register of the concrete wants of a plurality of individuals, not of ends as an analytical element in their action. On the other hand, the supply schedule is a statement of the concrete (in part hypothetical) relations of quantity supplied as a function of price.

The problem arises of determining the relation of these concrete categories to the general analysis of the structure of action, which is the central task of this study. So long as these facts are

[1] One of the best discussions of these issues is to be found in the recent book of Adolf Löwe, *Economics and Sociology.* Professor Löwe's position is, however, somewhat different from that developed here.

[2] *Principles*, p. 15; see also *supra*, p. 134.

[3] It is, in the terminology of this study, a "descriptive frame of reference." See Chap. I, pp. 28 *ff.*

taken only as data, and the analysis confined to their implications
in relation to the market mechanism, it may be argued that the
explanation of phenomena is kept on an economic plane in the
factor sense. The problems of economic science are then confined
to a set of relations of the data of supply and demand, and are not
extended to the determination of the data themselves. This is
the course taken by some later economists, of whom Pareto may
be considered representative.

But it is not Marshall's course. For him the definition of
economics as concerned with measurement in terms of money
means that it is concerned, as problematical, not merely as constant data, with all elements of human action so far as they can
be held to stand in a functional relation to price. This comes out
perhaps most clearly in his treatment of the supplies of the
productive factors.[1] It is quite clear that the explanations he
advances do not run in terms exclusively or even primarily of
the utilitarian element of action or of his own utility theory.
Population, for instance, is surely conditioned in part by biological factors. In any concrete example capital goods are limited
by the technologically relevant features of the environment and
the like. In the supplies both of labor and of capital, he has
brought into a central role his element of activities, an element
specifically outside his utility theory.

His justification for treating these as *economic* problems is in
the last analysis that they are subject to economic forces (in his
sense). That is, that these supplies are responsive to changes in
the demand for them through the price mechanism. The essential
reason for bringing in the element of activities is that on utility
grounds alone this responsiveness has become dubious. For
example, the status of the "principle of population" was much
more doubtful to him than it has been to an earlier generation of

---

[1] This view is by no means peculiar to Marshall but runs through a great
deal of, perhaps most of, economic reasoning. A recent example is the article
by J. R. Walsh, "The Capital Concept Applied to Man," *Quarterly Journal
of Economics*, February, 1935. Dr. Walsh there attempts to demonstrate (1)
that there is a functional relationship between cost of professional training
and earnings of a professional man and (2) that this proves that investment
in professional training is due to "ordinary economic motives." Even though
the first proposition be granted, the second does not follow. The first is a
statement of *concrete* fact, the *explanation* of which is still lacking in Dr.
Walsh's statement.

economists. Similarly with wants "adjusted to activities." It is through this conception that Marshall brings his peculiar value system to bear on economic phenomena through demand.

From these considerations it must be concluded that even the use of the supply and demand schema does not constitute an escape from the implication that Marshall's view of economics is essentially empiricist. For in spite of this limitation it is still an attempt at full explanation of the *concrete* phenomena thus described.[1] Indeed Marshall's own use of the supply and demand schema shows that on this basis factors other than the utility elements of action necessarily become involved. On the one hand, he gives no reason for the exclusion from economics of the other factors of the positivistic system, heredity and environment. On the other, he has himself brought into the center of the stage the element of activities.

Indeed, in spite of the limitations imposed by the supply and demand scheme, in the course of the development of economic science every one of the principal elements of human action distinguished has made its appearance and been held to play a major role in *economic* theory.[2] Marshall, by his addition of activities, has merely completed the roster. The inescapable conclusion from this fact is that on an empiricist basis there is no place for a logically separate body of principles of economics. Economics must be merely the application to a particular body of concrete phenomena of the general principles necessary for understanding human conduct. If any single name is applicable to this body of theory it is "encyclopedic sociology,"[3] the synthesis of all scientific theory relevant to the concrete facts of human behavior in society. Economics then becomes applied sociology.

This conclusion has been obscured mainly by the role in economics of the supply and demand analysis. But with the

[1] That is to say, Marshall refuses, even for the analytical purposes of economic theory, to take any of the important facts known about these phenomena as given data, as the values of constants. He attempts to bring them all within his *one* theoretical system.

[2] For a full justification of this statement see Talcott Parsons, "Sociological Elements in Economic Thought," *Quarterly Journal of Economics*, May and August, 1935.

[3] This is not the view of the scope of sociology to which the author personally subscribes. The issue will be discussed explicitly in the final chapter of the work.

"institutionalist" attack on the latter, it becomes even more evident. Indeed, combined with an empiricist methodology, the use of this schema has had some rather insidious results, of which some of Marshall's doctrines furnish excellent illustrations.

It is possible to maintain that there is an analytically separable aspect of human action which can advantageously be called the economic, though it is better to postpone an exact definition of it until the status of economics is dealt with again in a somewhat wider context in connection with Pareto. Suffice it to say that this aspect may, with certain modifications, be regarded as a descendant of the utilitarian aspect of positivistic thought. Moreover, it is roughly that formulated in what has been called Marshall's "utility theory." This logically separable utility aspect can form the basis for a logically distinct discipline, generally called economic theory, which, however, in these terms must be held to be concerned with an element or group of elements *in* concrete human action and not a concretely separable *category of* the phenomena of human action, a kind or type of action. This position avoids the empiricist consequences to which Marshall's position inevitably leads.

But this is to anticipate. For reasons which will be developed later the supply and demand schema is inherent in a science of economics thought of in these terms. But equally its relevance is not limited to elements which have a place in this abstract economic theory. Indeed in principle *any* factor which bears on human action at all may affect the concrete conditions of supply and of demand. The insidious results of the supply and demand analysis on an empiricist basis are, then, two.

On the one hand, there is the tendency to deal with factors other than the "utility," or the economic aspect in action, only in so far as they can be brought into relation with the supply and demand schema. This leads to a minimization of the role of these noneconomic factors, even in their bearing on the "everyday business of life," that is, on concrete economic activities, in so far as their influence is not exerted through the medium of an influence on the quantities demanded or supplied. This is above all true of the "institutional" element, as will be seen. Any element not subject to the peculiar kind of quantification inherent in the schema tends to be minimized. This, along with other, biographical elements, goes a long way to explain why Marshall dealt with the value factor only in the peculiar form of "activities" and tended to restrict it to one particular direction of effect, that of promoting free enterprise. This is not to say that there is no empirical justification for his treatment—on the the contrary, there is a good deal—but only that it is attended with serious biases of perspective. Consideration of other writers will show how different a picture emerges when some of these biases are dropped or altered.

On the other hand, the aspect of noneconomic elements which is subject to formulation in direct relation to the supply and demand schema tends to be exaggerated in importance. It seems a fair statement that the logical necessity Marshall felt to bring the total concrete supplies of capital and labor into direct functional relation to their prices led him seriously to exaggerate the importance of the factor of activities in the peculiar sense which he gave it. It surely seems probable that the total supply of labor is only to a small extent a function[1] of the wages paid it, and perhaps this is even more true with respect to the supply of capital.

It is true that the exact extent to which the noneconomic factors, in the peculiar combination which exists at a given time, should promote responsiveness to "economic forces," that is, for Marshall, changes of price, can only be settled by empirical investigation. Marshall's hypothesis is worth testing. But this does not mean that there should be a logical requirement for this relationship to be maximized.

Above all its maximization should not a priori be made a mark of an advanced stage in social evolution. Marshall's position really implies that noneconomic factors which do not promote such responsiveness belong only to the primitive stages, summed up in "custom." This surely involves a profound laissez-faire bias which is in need of very serious correctives.

There is in the development of social thought a principle analogous to that of "least action" in physics. When new ele-

---

[1] Part of the difficulty lies in an ambiguity of the term "function." In the true analytical sense two variables are only functionally related when a definable mode of relation holds throughout a wide range of variation in their values and in those of the other elements of the concrete situation. Marshall, on the other hand, has at best proved that over a certain period in a restricted area both wages and population have increased. He certainly presents inadequate evidence for an important functional relationship in the analytical sense.

ments appear in the course of its development, whether their origin be in new empirical observations or new theoretical considerations, they have to find a place in an existing logical framework of theory. The principle is that this will tend to take place with the least possible modification of the previous framework which is compatible with a definite recognition of the new element.

Marshall furnishes an excellent illustration of the principle. In the background of his thinking may be said to lie the framework which has been called "individualistic positivism" with special emphasis on the utilitarian variant. Seen in terms of the logical structure of this system his "activities" form a new element. It is, however, fitted in in a way to cause remarkably little disturbance of the general outline of the system. This is accomplished in two ways: In the first place, it is fitted in at a point where, it has been shown, the old system had throughout a good deal of its history required an extra-positivistic prop—the postulate of the natural identity of interests. It fulfills essentially the same theoretical function as this old prop. Secondly, the new element tends to be seen and dealt with only in such terms and aspects as relate directly to the old system and virtually fuse with it. Activities become the basis of a theory of the "progressive development of character" which promotes the concrete realization of an individualistic economy, of free enterprise. It gives a new range to "economic forces," bringing a larger and larger proportion of human affairs into functional relation with the price system.

Indeed the fusion is so complete that, abetted by the prevailing empiricist "climate of opinion" the logical character of the new element and its distinctness from the rest of the system has practically escaped detection in spite of the intensive preoccupation of more than a generation of economists with Marshall's works.

The next stage of the discussion will take up the work of Vilfredo Pareto. In spite of all the differences which appear on the surface to make Pareto the representative of a totally different world of thought from Marshall's, there is a continuity of background which makes these differences of peculiar significance here. In this entirely different context of empirical opinion it will be possible to trace some further ramifications of two vital problems. Pareto, like Marshall, starts from a point close to the positivistic system of theory. But the same order of "value" element as was involved in Marshall's activities makes its appearance in a different form and context in Pareto. Hence its status and implications can be worked out still further. At the same time Pareto again, this time explicitly, raises the empiricist question in its special application to the problem of the scope of economics. The analysis of Pareto's thought will provide an opportunity to see the problems raised by the intrusion of Marshall's activities into the positivistic Garden of Eden in a much wider perspective than before.

CHAPTER V

VILFREDO PARETO, I: THE METHODOLOGY AND MAIN ANALYTICAL SCHEME

The main outline of Pareto's empirical views of social phenomena forms a marked contrast with those of Marshall. Before entering into the methodological and theoretical bases of the difference, a brief sketch of a few points may be essayed.[1]

In the first place, Pareto explicitly and emphatically rejected the theory of linear social evolution which plays such an important part in Marshall's thought and that of his generation, above all in England. In its place he puts mainly a theory of cycles according to which social forms pass through a series of stages which are repeated again and again in approximately the same order. It is true that he does not radically deny the possibility of an underlying trend in the process as a whole, but he so strongly minimizes the elements of trend as against those which follow a cyclical pattern that it is certainly legitimate to regard his theory of social change as radically different from that of Marshall and the other evolutionists.[2]

The cyclical theory immediately throws the contemporary social situation into a totally different perspective from that of Marshall. It is no longer the culmination of a process continuous in direction since the beginning of history, but is illustrative of a phase of the cyclical movement, a phase which has often been repeated in the past and doubtless will be in the future. Above all the trends of development in the later nineteenth and early twentieth century are not to be expected to continue indefinitely or even very long in the same direction—for instance, the direction of technological "progress" and increasing economic

[1] These empirical theories of Pareto will be taken up again (Chap. VII) when the necessary theoretical apparatus for an interpretation of them has been built up. The present sketch must be regarded as preliminary.

[2] Cycles may, of course, vary in period and amplitude. Pareto also speaks of the possibility of a branching-tree type of evolution. *Traité de sociologie générale*, Sec. 216. But his specific analysis is confined to cycles.

prosperity. On the contrary, Pareto's view is that we are now in a phase where the direction of social processes is changing rapidly. The recent past has seen the heyday of individualism, humanitarianism, intellectual freedom, skepticism. The near future will very likely bring restrictions on individual freedom, intellectual, economic and political, a revival of faith in place of skepticism and an increase in the use of force. All these, with the possible exception of faith, are things which Marshall held we had *permanently* outgrown except for a few "survivals."

Marshall again had emphasized the essential harmony of the interests of individuals and groups in society. Above all he had minimized the importance of class differences and relegated limitations on equality of opportunity to the status of survivals, destined to progressive elimination. Pareto, on the other hand, lays great stress on the disharmony of class interests. Indeed he gives Marx high praise for having brought this factor into prominence;[1] although in the strictly economic field he shared the predominant English view of the untenability of most of the Marxian theories. Finally, Pareto lays great stress on the role of force and fraud in social life—an opinion he shares with Machiavelli and Hobbes. This again is in the strongest contrast to Marshall's views. The attribution of any considerable role to these phenomena is strictly incompatible with the conditions of free enterprise. These, like many other factors which Pareto emphasizes, Marshall would relegate to the early stages of social evolution. They are phenomena which are destined to be superseded with increasing effectiveness, and permanently.

Such differences of opinion on the part of men trained in scientific thinking are not likely to be a matter entirely of chance, of the fact that one "happened" to observe facts which the other did not. Neither are they likely to be mere expressions of the private and personal sentiments of the individuals concerned, essentially irrelevant to their scientific work. On the contrary, the probability is great that they stand in intimate logical relations to the main theoretical framework of their thinking. That this is, in general, true is an important thesis of the present study as a whole. The striking empirical contrast then sets a problem. Wherein do the corresponding theoretical differences lie? To answer this question it is necessary to enter into an

[1] See VILFREDO PARETO, *Systèmes socialistes*, Vol. II, Chap. XII.

analysis of Pareto's methodological position and theoretical scheme.

METHODOLOGY

Though this study does not, in general, concern itself with biographical[1] matters, it is well to note the striking fact that there were two main phases of Pareto's career before he embarked upon his *Traité de sociologie générale*.[2] He was trained in physical science at the Turin Polytechnic Institute and was for many years a practicing engineer. The interest in mathematics and physical science never left him, and both as a methodological model and as a substantive element of his thinking it must always be kept in mind in interpreting his work. Secondly, through political controversy he became interested in concrete economic questions, and through them, in turn, in economic theory. His writings in this field brought him recognition so that finally at the late age of forty-five he was appointed to the chair of Political Economy at the University of Lausanne; he was one of the leading economists of his generation. His approach to sociology and the general methodology of social science is throughout determined by the question of the status of the concepts of traditional economic theory in relation both to concrete reality and to other theoretical schemata. The two together (physical science and economics) in the close interconnections which will be traced later, determine the double major axis of his thought.

Like many of his predecessors Pareto set out to make economics and sociology positive sciences on the model of the physical sciences. But he did this with a difference. A great deal of the earlier physical science contained as substantive doctrines those which can be roughly summed up as constituting "scientific materialism," which were held to be not merely working hypotheses or approximations, but necessary truths about the concrete world. They were truths of such a basic character that no theory

[1] For a brief biographical sketch of Pareto see G.-H. Bousquet, *Vilfredo Pareto, sa vie et son oeuvre*, Part I.

[2] All references throughout this study will be to the French edition by sections, not pages, since the former are uniform throughout all the editions. English translations of Pareto's text are my own since this was originally written before the appearance of the English edition. They have, however, been checked with that edition, and, where it has seemed advisable, modified to meet it.

which did not accept them could hope to be scientific—in fact, they were held to be methodologically necessary. That is, most of the earlier methodology of science, especially physical science, was radical empiricist positivism.

This position Pareto repudiates. He is representative of a much more modest and skeptical view of the scope of science. His views are not altogether original with himself but belong in a group which also includes the names of Mach and Poincaré. He himself specifically designates both Comte and Spencer as guilty of transgressing the limits of science in spite of their protests to the contrary.[1] Above all Pareto limits his own conception to very general methodological requirements.[2] He is extremely scrupulous not to maintain the necessity or desirability of taking over the substantive concepts of the physical sciences into the social. Their theory is to be built up from observation of the facts of their own fields. Even such general concepts as system and equilibrium are in the first instance used only by analogy and he is careful to point out that analogy is not proof.[3] He is thus free at the outset at least from the "reductive" tendencies so prominent in the older positivism, a matter of great importance.

In fact, Pareto for the most part limits himself to the most general methodological considerations. To him science is best characterized by the term "logico-experimental." That is to say, there are two essential elements involved: logical reasoning and observation of "fact." Logical reasoning is by itself incapable of yielding necessary results beyond tautologies,[4] but none the less it is an essential element. It is thought of, however, as subordinate to the other element, that of fact, experimental or observed.

It is noteworthy that Pareto nowhere, in his explicitly methodological discussions at least, attempts a specific delimitation of the field of scientific fact. He does not, so far as it has been possible to determine, use the term "sense datum" or any related

[1] "Le nom de *positive* donné par Comte à sa philosophie ne doit pas nous induire en erreur: sa sociologie est tout aussi dogmatique que le Discours sur l'histoire universelle de Bossuet." *Traité*, 5. "Le positivisme de Herbert Spencer est tout simplement une métaphysique." *Op. cit.*, 112.

[2] The best general account of Pareto's methodological procedure available is that in L. J. Henderson, *Pareto's General Sociology*.

[3] *Ibid.*, 121 *ff.*

[4] *Ibid.*, 28.

term. His commonest term is *expérience*, which quite clearly
connotes verifiability and independence of the subjective sentiments of the observer. Experience is equated to observation.[1]
It is often referred to as enabling men to "judge"[2] as between
differences of opinion, so it seems legitimate to infer that Pareto's
conception is distinctly broad. A fact would include any verifiable
statement about a "thing" or "event" external to and independent of the observer in the sense that (a) its existence and
properties are not functions of his private sentiments, likes and
dislikes, in that sense are "given"; (b) as a test of this independence two or more observers when confronted with the same
thing or event will agree in the essentials of their description of
it, or can, by logical argument and pointing, be brought to agree.

It seems quite clear from Pareto's usage that the meaningful
aspect of linguistic expressions is included in the status of
experienced facts. At the very beginning[3] of his discussion he
refers to "propositions and theories" as experimental facts.[4] It
is sufficient to note that when we refer to a spoken and a written
proposition as the "same" proposition, *i.e.*, the same fact or
more strictly phenomenon, this sameness is not based on a
generalization of intrinsic elements common to (a) the sound-
wave combinations and (b) the ink marks which in the two cases
respectively constitute the symbolic medium in which the
proposition is expressed. It is a difficult question to what extent
there is any significant common element on the intrinsic level.[5]
What is common to the two sets of data is not the "sense impressions" as such in any concrete sense, but the "meaning" of the
symbols. This inclusion of meanings in the realm of experimental

[1] The nearest thing to a definition seems to be the following: "Nous
employons ces terms au sens qu'ils ont dans les sciences naturelles comme
l'astronomie, le chimie, la physiologie, etc.; et non pour indiquer ce qu'on
entend par: *expérience intime* chrétienne." *Traité*, 69.

[2] It is a legitimate interpretation that Pareto had in mind the role of what
are often today referred to as "operations." Experience is the judge because
two or more scientists performing the same operation get the same result.

[3] "Toutes ces propositions et théories sont des faits expérimentaux."
Traité, 7.

[4] Clearly not in the sense employed above that a fact is always itself a
proposition, but that the phenomena to which these statements refer may be
"theories and propositions."

[5] Such as exists presumably is to be found mainly in the order in which the
elements are related.

facts or observable phenomena is perhaps the most important thing to note about Pareto's concept of fact. Without it, propositions could not be observable. Though he nowhere makes the inclusion explicit, most of his sociology would entirely fail to make sense without it.

On a second important point Pareto is more explicit—an experimental fact does *not* necessarily embody the totality of a concrete phenomenon. The theories of logico-experimental science consist in statements of fact linked together by logical reasoning. But the facts involved in the formulation of a theory are arrived at by a process of analysis and are not necessarily complete descriptions of concrete phenomena. Indeed Pareto states that "it is impossible to know a concrete phenomenon in all its details."[1] It is no valid criticism of a theory that it does not suffice fully to explain a concrete phenomenon; on the contrary, it is a virtue.[2] The facts embodied in a theory describe elements, or aspects, or properties of concrete phenomena, not the total phenomena themselves. Thus it is quite clear that in his methodological position Pareto explicitly rejects the empiricism to be found in Marshall. Science must first analyze the complex concrete phenomena and only after it has built up analytical theories can it, by a process of synthesis, aspire to a complete scientific account of any sector of concrete reality.

While this is a general scientific doctrine it is significant that the main specific example Pareto gives is that of economic theory. He says: "Let Q be the theory of political economy. A concrete phenomenon involves not only an economic element e, but also other, sociological elements, c, g, ... It is an error to wish to include in economics these sociological elements c, g, . . . , as many do; the sole justifiable conclusion to draw from this fact is that it is necessary to add—add, I say, not substitute —to the economic theories which explain e, other theories which explain c, g, ..."[3] The way in which Pareto makes room for abstract analytical theory of the type of economic theory is not to set theory over against fact, but *to include the element of theoretical abstraction in his concept of fact itself.* If, as he often says, in logico-experimental science principles are entirely

[1] *Traité*, 106.
[2] *Ibid.*, 33, 39.
[3] *Ibid.*, 34.

dependent on the facts, this is tenable only because the facts themselves are, to borrow Professor Henderson's phrase, observations "in terms of a conceptual scheme," and are thus not complete descriptions of concrete phenomena.

For the aspects of concrete phenomena which are relevant to a particular theory are not generally given in any usable form in the raw data of experience. Indeed it is desirable to be able to observe the facts relevant to a particular theory in isolation from others. Some, though by no means all,[1] of the natural sciences can do this through the method of experiment. But this, Pareto explicitly says, is a *practical* aid to science, not a logical necessity of it. The process of abstraction in the social sciences must be carried out mainly by analysis, not by experiment. But this does not make it any the less legitimate.

The aim of a logico-experimental science is to formulate "laws." A law is for Pareto nothing but an "experimental uniformity,"[2] that is, a uniformity in the facts. But a proper interpretation of what this means must take into account the special sense of experimental fact just discussed. A law is a uniformity in the facts, but since the facts are "aspects" of the concrete phenomena seen in terms of a conceptual scheme a law is not a generalization of the necessary concrete behavior of these phenomena. In this respect two qualifications must be made: The first and more important is that in the social sciences any given concrete phenomenon is generally a meeting ground, as Pareto says a point of *entrelacement*,[3] of a number of different laws. So the complete scientific explanation of the concrete phenomenon can only be achieved by the synthetic application of all the theories involved. Except in the limiting case no one law will be directly applicable to the full explanation of concrete events. Secondly, as Pareto says, we cannot know concrete phenomena in all their details anyway, so that even this synthesis gives only a partial explanation, not a complete one. Science is always concerned with successive approximations.[4]

---

[1] Thus in the sense of being able to control the phenomena observed, astronomy, one of the most exact of the natural sciences, is not an experimental science. It relies entirely on nonexperimental observation.

[2] *Traité*, 99.

[3] *Ibid.*

[4] *Ibid.*, 106.

Thus the element of "necessity" in scientific law inheres only in its logic. As such, a law can have no exceptions.[1] What is usually called an "exception" is really "the superposition of the effect of another law on that of the first."[2] In that sense all scientific laws have exceptions. But this logical necessity, what has been called, above,[3] "logical determinism" must, just on this account, not be carried over to concrete phenomena. The logically closed system of scientific theory must not arbitrarily be made an empirically closed system. In its empirical application, on the contrary, a theory can yield only probabilities, not necessities.[4]

Some aspects of Pareto's methodological position will be taken up again later when certain of the implications of his substantive analysis are discussed. But it is now necessary to plunge into a consideration of what he does with his methodological tools. It is to be noted that the two influences which have been spoken of have already made their appearance. The modern, methodologically sophisticated physical sciences have, on the one hand, provided the general model. On the other hand, economic theory has provided the leading example of a science dealing with human behavior which has developed an *abstract* theory not directly applicable to concrete social phenomena without synthesis with other "sociological" elements. This latter case provides Pareto with the starting point for his substantive analysis.

LOGICAL AND NONLOGICAL ACTION

Though undoubtedly economic theory played a large part in its formulation as a model, it is a somewhat wider[5] category which Pareto uses to lay the basis of his analytical scheme, that of "logical action." Economic theory, as Pareto treats it, is abstract by virtue of the fact that it singles out certain variables, elements in the strict sense, for formulation in a separate system. But at

[1] "Parler d'une uniformité non uniforme n'a aucun sense." *Ibid.*, 101.

[2] *Ibid.*, 101.

[3] See Chap. II, p. 70.

[4] It has often been said that Pareto follows the inductive method. Properly qualified, this is acceptable. It is essential to note, however, that it is what Znaniecki calls "analytic induction" as opposed to "enumerative induction." *Cf.* F. Znaniecki, *The Method of Sociology*, Chap. V.

[5] He includes beside the economic "les travaux artistiques et scientifiques— en outre un certain nombre d'opérations militaires, politiques, juridiques, etc." *Traité*, 152.

the same time this subsystem of the theory of action is not equally relevant to all kinds or aspects of concrete total systems of action, but is particularly relevant to certain such aspects, those which Pareto formulates as the "logical."

It is necessary at this point to state clearly the relation of the subsequent analysis on the basis of Pareto's work to that which apparently forms the main line of Pareto's own progression of thought in the *Traité*. Though by no means unrelated, the two lines of analysis are not identical and it is essential to be clear about the difference. Confusion is especially likely to arise because the concept of logical action is the starting point for both.

Logical action is not an element in Pareto's theoretical system. He employs it, apparently, for a pragmatic purpose. His aim is, it seems reasonable to infer, to work out a way of approaching the problem of definition, observation, classification, and treatment in a system, of certain of the elements of action which are neglected by economic theory. Action which meets closely the criteria of "logicality" is, to a first approximation, that for which economic theory is most nearly adequate as an explanatory tool. Hence it is a reasonable supposition that the study of cases which involve departure from these criteria will lead to the isolation of some, at least, of the important noneconomic elements. A rigorous definition of logical action is, hence, the first step in the operation by which Pareto arrives at certain of these noneconomic elements. The procedure will be outlined presently. But once the concept has been used for this purpose, as Professor Henderson points out, both it and its correlate nonlogical drop out[1] and do not have a place in the final system.

But in defining and employing the concept of logical action in this way Pareto was led to make certain observations and distinctions which are capable of being fitted into another context, that which is of central interest here. For Pareto's concept of logical action may be taken as the starting point for a systematic analysis of the structure of the concrete systems of action to which his system of elements is applied. Pareto himself did not undertake such an analysis. But the results of his own procedure are such as at a number of different points to have direct implications for and contacts with this analysis. Indeed Pareto's results, arrived at by a different procedure, provide a striking confirma-

[1] *Pareto's General Sociology*, p. 100.

tion of the correctness of the analysis which will form the main thread of the following argument. In order to make this coincidence in results clear it will be necessary, at certain points, to go rather far into the technicalities of Pareto's own conceptual scheme.

As a preliminary it is important to note that Pareto immediately lays down the possibility of studying social phenomena from two different points of view which he calls the objective and the subjective, respectively.[1] The objective is first characterized as what the phenomenon "is in reality" and opposed to the way it appears "in the mind of certain persons." The further development of the distinction, however, especially linking the objective aspect with the way in which action appears "for those who have more extended knowledge"[2] makes it legitimate to infer that the objective point of view is that of the scientific observer, while the subjective is that of the actor. It is of great significance that at the very beginning of his substantive treatment Pareto explicitly includes the subjective point of view.

Indeed this is explicitly included in his definition of logical action: "We designate as 'logical actions' those operations which are logically united to their end, not only from the point of view of the subject who performs the operations, but also for those who have a more extended knowledge."[3] A slightly different version is given in the next paragraph: "Logical actions are those in which the objective and the subjective ends coincide."

The phrase "as it really is" in its context implies that the connection between the "operations," *i.e.*, means, and the end can be established by a scientific theory on an intrinsic basis. That is, what Pareto is seeking to do is to take as his criterion of the logicality of action the demonstrable, intrinsic "appropriateness of means to an end" according to the most extensive knowledge of the relations between means and the end that the given scientific observer can command.[4]

---

[1] *Ibid.*, 149. It is the distinction anticipated above in Chap. II.

[2] *Traité*, 150.

[3] *Ibid.*

[4] It will perhaps help to avoid a possible confusion in the reader's mind if he is here reminded again of the distinction of two meanings of the concept "rationality" which was made above (footnote, p. 64). Pareto's concept of logical action is formulated in terms of what has been called the "methodological" standard. Action is logical in so far as it conforms in certain

In his second definition of logical action Pareto used a distinction between the objective and the subjective end, making their coincidence the criterion of logicality. It is not easy to discover what he means, but the following seems to be the most reasonable interpretation: The subjective end is quite clearly that anticipated (concrete) state of affairs which the actor himself subjectively desires and supposes to be the objective of his action. In the course of action, however, he chooses and employs certain

---

specific respects with a standard derived from the methodology of science. The important point is that this way of defining the concept keeps clear of any commitments regarding the nature of the "mechanism" by which conformity with the standard comes about.

In particular it avoids a very complicated set of questions having to do with habituation. We are all aware that many of our actions which are frequently repeated and would in common-sense terms be called "rational" in fact proceed to a large extent "automatically" in that we are not forced at every step to think about the appropriateness of the next step as a means to the end. This is certainly true in a degree of all highly developed skills, and they would not be possible without it.

The important thing to note is that Pareto's concept neither affirms nor denies the importance of these facts and in particular makes no attempt to analyze them. Whether automatically habitual or not, action is to him "logical" in so far as it conforms to the standard he has set up. The conformity is present in so far as the operations as seen by an observer are logically united to their end, and the same is true as seen by the actor himself, in so far as he thinks about it. The actor probably tends to be conscious of the standard primarily when occasion arises to adapt his action to an alteration in the conditions to which he is habituated. The concept of logicality of action certainly contains the implication of a range of such adaptability.

But even here, Pareto's question is not that of the *mechanism* of adaptation to changing situations. That is a question which properly belongs in the field of what is sometimes called the psychological problem of rationality. Of course the two sets of problems are by no means unrelated to each other. But dealing with one at a time is a justifiable procedure of scientific abstraction, and in doing so it is important to keep to the one set of terms under consideration and not let matters appropriate only to the other set creep in unobserved.

It is probably true, as the progress of the analysis will bring out, that certain of the unresolved difficulties of Pareto's theory lead him to abandon strict adherence to the terms of the "methodological" problem of rationality of action, and, with the creeping in of the other, his statements sometimes give rise to serious confusion. Indeed the great majority of his interpreters have both criticized and approved his theory as if it were couched entirely in psychological terms.

means, in Pareto's term performs certain operations, which he thinks contribute to the realization of the subjective end. But this supposition will be correct only in so far as the actor's judgment of the relation of the means that he proposes to employ to the end is sound. Such a judgment involves prediction, on the basis of verifiable knowledge, of the probable effects of the alterations in the initial situation and their "automatic" consequences, referred to as means. But knowing the subjective end and knowing the means it is proposed actually to employ, it is possible for an observer with a "more extended knowledge of the circumstances" to judge whether the particular operations carried out actually will contribute to the end. This predicted effect of the employment of proposed means on the basis of the best available knowledge is apparently what Pareto means by the objective end of action. Then it can readily be seen that in so far as the theory guiding action, in its concern with the means-end relationship is scientifically sound, the two will coincide.[1] Furthermore, apart from unforeseen contingencies which can be taken care of by the statement of the objective end in terms of probability rather than necessity, both will coincide with a correct description of the state of affairs actually reached as a result of the action. On account of this fact, probably, Pareto sometimes speaks as if this, the outcome of the action, were the objective end. Where the finer distinction is not relevant he is, in an elliptical sense, quite justified in doing so. For the technical terminology, however, it is best to follow Pareto in confining the term end to the *anticipated* future state of affairs, whether anticipated by an observer or the actor himself, and otherwise to speak of the "result" or the "outcome" of action.

These considerations yield an interpretation of an important statement of Pareto, that the objective end must be "a real end, entering into the domain of observation and experience, and not an imaginary end, foreign to that domain which may, however, serve as a subjective end."[2] The objective end is always arrived at by a process of empirically valid prediction of the probable effects of certain operations in a situation. For such a prediction to be possible and to be verified by the outcome, it must lie

---

[1] In speaking of the logical action Pareto confines himself to the "direct" end. Possible indirect results are not considered (*Traité*, 151).

[2] *Traité*, 151.

"within the domain of observation." But for the actor, it would beg the question of the logicality of action to require that his subjective end should always be of this character. For the relation of means to end in his subjective belief may very well deviate from the scientifically objective standard which is the criterion. In so far as it does deviate because it has an end which falls outside the domain of observation the action is, of course, by definition nonlogical.

It is important to note that the differentiating criterion of logical and nonlogical action is a matter of the *comparison* of the results of observation from the objective and the subjective points of view. The means-end relationship must be seen first as it is to the actor—what he thinks the efficacy of his means will be—and then "as it is in reality"—as the observer's more extended knowledge leads him to believe it will, or would be. Confining attention behavioristically to the observation of the external course of events is not sufficient. Then it is impossible to know the subjective end of the action at all, which is by definition in the strict sense a subjective anticipation on the part of the actor. All that it is possible to know is the objective end or the outcome of the action. But this must, in the nature of the case, always be the "logical" outcome of the operations actually performed. For in so far as a course of events is scientifically understandable in any sense its later phases must always be, in the sense in which Pareto means it, "logically united" to the earlier. Then, in terms of the objective point of view alone all action is logical.[1]

The differentiating criterion therefore involves the subjective point of view and can be stated in two ways: (a) Action is logical in so far as the operations are logically united to their end from a subjective as well as an objective point of view. That is, in so

---

[1] Such an interpretation of Pareto's scientific "objectivism" would seem on the face of it so far-fetched as to be ridiculous. Yet, since the above passage was written there has actually appeared a critique of Pareto's theory which maintains that the distinction of logical and nonlogical action is meaningless because all action must necessarily to the scientist be "logical" for precisely the reason just stated. This is a vivid illustration of the fact that many of the views stated here as extreme, which fly in the face of common sense, really do play a part in determining thought. See Carl Murchison, "Pareto and Experimental Social Psychology," *Journal of Social Philosophy*, October, 1935.

far as the relations of means and end are concerned, they must be established *in the mind of the actor* by a scientifically[1] verifiable theory, or if the actor does not know the theory, the effectiveness of the combination must be verifiable in terms of it. (*b*) The subjective end must coincide with the objective end. Subjective end here can mean only the state of affairs that the actor desires or attempts to bring about. It can serve as an end only in so far as it anticipates the actual outcome *before* the "operations" in question; it is a "subjective anticipation." To say that subjective and objective end correspond is, then, to say that the subjective end is the state of affairs which can be scientifically demonstrated actually to come about as a result of the actor's proposed action.

The question now arises as to what is the theoretical significance of the concept of logical action. As is true of many concepts, it is significant in more than one respect. In the first place, it serves as a criterion by which Pareto is able to set aside a class of concrete actions which he does not wish to study, roughly those adequately dealt with by economic theory and closely related disciplines. Second, it serves as a criterion to classify what Pareto calls, in this context "elements" of concrete actions.[2] These are elements analogous to the chemical elements, which may exist in "pure" form, but which are more generally found compounded with others. These are the principal connections in which Pareto employs the concept.

But for present purposes a slightly different use is important. Action is, according to Pareto, logical in so far as it conforms with a certain type of norm. From the point of view of this analysis the important thing he has done is to define rigorously one of the principal types of norm governing the means-end relationship. His definition covers only the norm, however. The most important questions for further inquiry will be, what is the rest of the structure of acts and systems of action of which a norm of this character can form a part and at what point does the "logical" norm fit into this structure?

It should be clear that this is the type of norm which has played such a great part in the positivistic tradition of thought. Wherever

[1] In general this term will be used since it is less cumbersome than logico-experimental, but has, for present purposes, the same meaning as Pareto's term.

[2] Which are clearly not analytical elements in the strict sense. See *Traité*, 150.

it has appeared in a positivistic framework the latter has imposed certain limitations on its combinations with other elements, and the types of others with which it could be thought of as combined. But in the way in which the concept is defined by Pareto no such limitations are implied. For the correlative category, nonlogical action is not defined positively at all, but residually. If action as a whole be designated as A, and logical action as L, then nonlogical action is $A - L$. This is the only definition Pareto gives. If, then, it is to be possible to determine the setting in which the norm of "logicality" or, in the previous terminology, rationality, is placed by Pareto, it is necessary to follow his analysis from the concept of logical action into his treatment of the nonlogical. In doing that it is necessary to keep clearly in mind that he was leading up to one thing, a system of analytical elements, while the present analysis is primarily concerned with another, though closely related thing, the structure of action systems.

Though he does not explicitly define it, "action" seems to designate the total complex of concrete phenomena comprising the life of human beings in society in relation to each other, seen from the objective and the subjective points of view combined. For preliminary analytical purposes Pareto has no further concern with logical action. He does not resume consideration of it until he comes to his synthetic treatment of social phenomena in the latter part of the treatise. Having abstracted it he proceeds to an intensive study of nonlogical action. It is important to understand the peculiar way in which he goes about this task.

He starts by stating the following antithesis: "Logical actions are, at least in their principal element, the result of a process of reasoning; nonlogical actions proceed principally from a certain state of mind [*état psychique*], sentiment, the unconscious, etc. It is the task of psychology to be concerned with this state of mind."[1]

---

[1] *Traité*, 161. It is not altogether clear what conception of the role of psychology is implied in the last sentence of this statement. Pareto nowhere attempts any systematic discussion of the relations of the various sciences bearing on the phenomena of human behavior, except to insist upon the abstractness of economic theory. All the other sciences must be regarded as residual categories and no clear line, for instance, between psychology and sociology is to be discerned in his work. Hence it would be fruitless to pursue the question further here. It will be taken up in general terms in the final chapter.

At least at his starting point it seems to be Pareto's view that this "state of mind" is not an observable reality but is a hypothetical[1] entity called in to account for the observable facts. For human beings there are, on the contrary, two roughly and concretely distinguishable sets of observable data: "acts"[2] which he labels *B*, and "expressions *C*, of sentiments which are often developed in the form of moral, religious and other theories."[1] The state of mind he labels *A*. Thus nonlogical action is analyzed in terms of three elements: The first two, the "overt acts" *B* and the "theories" *C*, are both classes of concrete, observable data. In addition there is the "state of mind" *A* which is inferred from *B* and *C*. None of these is defined very rigorously. Perhaps the clearest statement is that *B* constitutes "overt acts," that is, those involving spatiotemporal events, and *C*

linguistic expressions associated with these acts.[3] *A*, on the other hand, is left much more indefinite. It must be understood clearly that this whole schema concerns only *nonlogical* action, that is concrete action minus the logical elements. Thus linguistic expressions are included only *in so far as they are not scientifically valid* "theories" of the relations of means and ends, overt acts only in so far as they are not the "operations" by which the "appropriate" means to these ends are applied.

Pareto's concern at this stage of the analysis is with the general relations of the three elements. As distinguished from logical action it can be said that *C* is not the cause of *B*, though "the very marked tendency men have to take nonlogical for logical actions, leads them to believe that *B* is an effect of the 'cause' *C*."[4] In fact, however, all three are in a state of mutual interdependence. Thus the direct relation *CB* exists. But precisely in so far as the action is nonlogical the more important relations are *AC* and *AB*. *C* is less important as a cause of *B* than it is as a "manifestation" of *A*, which is in the main the common origin of both *B* and *C*.

[1] *Ibid.*, 162.

[2] The use of the term "acts" is here confusing since "action" is used in the broader sense indicated above. "Behavior" would be preferable.

[3] "Chez les hommes nous observons aussi certains faits qui sont la conséquence d l'emploi du langage par l'être humain." *Traité*, 1690.

[4] *Ibid.*, 162.

A and *C*, then, are in a state of mutual interdependence, but while the relation is not entirely one of "cause and effect," for *nonlogical* action *C* is much more effect than cause. *For that very reason C* may be regarded as a relatively trustworthy index of the variations of *A*. Since *A* is a nonobservable entity[1] it cannot be studied directly, but must be studied through its "manifestations." Of the two sets of manifestations, "theories" and "overt acts," the former is the more favorable, *because its reciprocal influence on A is less than that of B*.[2] Its changes will therefore more accurately indicate changes in *A*, since these changes are to a less extent due to its own influence.

Over against the "process of reasoning" which he regards as the principal cause of logical actions Pareto has set the state of mind *A*. If the understanding of this reasoning is the best means of explaining action so far as it is logical, then the understanding of *A* is the road to the understanding of the nonlogical elements of action. But in the first case the process of reasoning was given in observable data, the scientific theories governing logical action. In the present case this is not true, so an indirect attack is necessary. But for the reasons just adduced Pareto feels justified in confining his *analytical* attention to the data *C*. Henceforth he not only leaves logical action behind but also the *B* element of nonlogical action. Until he comes back to the task of synthesis his attention will be confined to the "theories" associated with nonlogical action.

This explains a circumstance which cannot but be very puzzling to the student who, like most who have written on Pareto, interprets his subsequent analysis as an analysis of nonlogical action in general conceived as a concrete type. For following the chapter in which the schema just discussed is presented are three that deal with theories. The first, *les actions non-logiques dans l'histoire des doctrines*, is concerned primarily with an analysis of the ways in which the importance of nonlogical action has been obscured. The second, *les théories qui dépassent l'expérience*, deals with theological and metaphysical theories, while the third,

---

[1] *Ibid.*, 169.

[2] This is primarily because men's overt acts are influenced more by the particular exigencies of their immediate situation than are their linguistic expressions. Pareto is not, in the present context, concerned with the influence of "conditions" upon action.

les théories pseudo-scientifiques, treats theories which *claim* to be scientific, a claim which Pareto on analysis rejects.

Running through these three chapters, especially the last two, is a common strand of thought—the theories taken up are all analyzed from the point of view of whether they can or cannot claim to be logico-experimentally valid theories, and the claim is, in general, rejected. Hence the tendency to interpret this discussion of theories as a continuation of the methodological discussion of the first chapter, thus preparing the way for the later theory of "ideologies." But this is not the real burden of Pareto's argument. He deals with *theories* rather than "acts" because he has decided to confine his substantive analysis of nonlogical action to *C*. These three chapters constitute the inductive part of the analysis. With Chap. VI on the Residues he turns to the deductive[1] method. The methodology involved will be seen to be incidental, a *tool* in the analytical task.

But before following out the main line of the argument, one other interesting point may be remarked upon. Immediately after setting forth the *A*, *B*, *C* schema Pareto introduces a subdivision of *B*. He says,

Before the invasion of the Greek gods, the ancient Roman religion did not have any theology *C*; it was confined to a cult *B*. But the cult *B*, acting on *A* strongly influenced the actions *D* of the Roman people. More than that, when the direct relationship *BD* is given, it appears to us moderns as manifestly absurd. But the relationship *BAD* may on the contrary have been in certain cases highly reasonable and useful to the Roman people. In general, the theology *C* has a direct influence on *D* even less important than on *A*.[2]

Here Pareto subdivides the original *B* "overt acts" into the "cult" and "other acts." He does not give the concepts any greater precision but it may be surmised that the cult *B* is what may more generally be called "ritual"[3] actions, while *D* is the category of actions primarily of "intrinsic" significance. Moreover it is perhaps significant that for the purposes of the study of *nonlogical* action it is for the cult that Pareto retains the original symbol *B*, while for the others he coins a new designation. He

[1] *Ibid.*, 846.
[2] *Ibid.*, 167.
[3] For an extended discussion of ritual, see Chap. XI, pp. 429 *ff.*, below.

may have considered ritual the *central* category of overt action determined predominantly by nonlogical elements. At any rate in so far as overt acts come into his concrete material, a very large proportion are of a ritual character. This is seen partly from actual descriptions of ritual acts but still more from the fact that a large proportion of the theories he deals with are theories that "it is possible to do so and so" by ritual means. This is true, for instance, of the first large-scale example he develops, that of the "sentiment" that it is possible to control the weather magically.

But having made this distinction Pareto proceeds to drop it and have nothing further to do with it. One important reason why he dropped it is that he concerned himself henceforth analytically only with C. Hence any distinctions between elements of B were irrelevant. It is only after the results of the analysis of C are interpreted and applied to the understanding of nonlogical action as a whole that such problems become important again to his argument. But this is a lead which it will prove fruitful to follow in the subsequent analysis.

It is only here that Pareto's strictly inductive study begins. He has first abstracted the logical elements of action, leaving the nonlogical. Then of nonlogical action he has discarded the overt acts B (or B and D) leaving only the linguistic manifestations or theories involved in nonlogical action. The nucleus then of the analytical, as distinct from the synthetic, part of Pareto's treatise is *an inductive study of the theories or linguistic expressions involved in nonlogical action.*

RESIDUES AND DERIVATIONS

The method of inductive study Pareto pursues is by the comparison of large numbers of similar[1] data to separate out the relatively constant from the relatively variable elements. But before he can do this he has to identify the data. He concerns himself not with the theories involved in action generally but only with the theories involved in action so far as it is nonlogical. That is, having abstracted logical action generally he has to abstract the "theory" aspects of it from concrete theories. To do this he turns to his concept of logical action for a criterion. In so

---

[1] The similarity is clearly on the level of meaning.

far as they concern the relations of means and ends the theories involved in logical action are theories measuring up to the standard of logico-experimental science. This has been found to be the meaning of "operations logically united to their end."

Hence the theories he is interested in are those which depart from the standard of logico-experimental science, for conformity with it immediately makes the theory in question a manifestation only of the logical elements. Only in so far as theories depart from the standard are they relevant to the analysis. This is the reason for Pareto's preoccupation all through his analysis with drawing the line between scientific and nonscientific theories. The scientific standard is the one he employs for the selection of his data.

However, it is also more than that. It has been shown that action is nonlogical only in so far as it departs from the logical standard. Similarly the theories with which Pareto deals are defined only negatively as a residual category; they are theories *in so far as they do not conform to the scientific standard.* Now Pareto's methodological starting point has given him the basis of an analysis of scientific theories—they are logico-experimental —that is, can be analyzed into the two elements of statements of fact and logical reasoning.

The results of his inductive study he brings into relation to this schema. He finds that the non-logico-experimental theories can similarly be broken down into two main elements, a (relatively) constant and a variable respectively. In his final theoretical discussion he compares these directly with the elements of concrete logico-experimental theories. The latter, designated as C,[1] may be "decomposed into a part A consisting of experimental principles, descriptions, affirmations of experimental facts, and another part B consisting of logical deductions to which are also added other principles and experimental descriptions employed to draw deductions from A." Thus the line Pareto draws within scientific theories is not precisely the one indicated above but is altered slightly for his purposes. A includes only the *major* factual element of the theory, its major premise, while B includes both the element of logical reasoning from A and the minor factual elements.

---

[1] *Traité*, 803. A departure from the usage of the earlier schema which is confusing.

The theories c^1 where sentiment plays a part, and which add something to experience, which are beyond experience . . . fall similarly into a part a, consisting of the manifestation of certain sentiments and a part b consisting of logical reasoning, sophisms, and also other manifestations of sentiments employed to draw deductions from a. In this manner there is a correspondence between a and A, b and B, and c and C. Here we are concerned only with the theories c, we leave aside the scientific experimental theories C.

A clearer expression of Pareto's procedure could scarcely be asked for. a cannot by definition be a statement of fact, therefore (to the actor) it must reflect something other than the properties of a phenomenon external to the actor. To that something else which a manifests Pareto gives the name "sentiment." It is an aspect of the "state of mind" with which the analysis started. a is *always*[2] the manifestation, in the form of a *proposition* which serves as the common major premise of a group of theories, of a sentiment;[3] b, on the other hand, may involve either logical or sophistic reasoning. It is the "manifestation of the human need for logical explanation."[4] But whether the logic be good or bad it is still b so long as it is associated with an a. "a is the principle which exists in the mind of man, b forms the explanations, the deductions from this principle."[5]

"Before pushing farther it would perhaps be well to give names to the entities a, b and c; for to designate them only by letters of the alphabet would embarrass the exposition and render it less clear. From this motive, to the exclusion of every other we shall call a residues, b derivations, and c derivatives."[6] This is Pareto's explicit and only definition of residues and derivations. It is clear beyond any shadow of doubt that they are elements of the *nonscientific theories*[7] which accompany nonlogical action. It is

[1] *Ibid.*, 803. Small c here is evidently equivalent to large C of the earlier scheme.

[2] So far as Pareto remains in actual usage consistent with his explicit definitions, which is unfortunately by no means always the case.

[3] Thus while the original C was a fair manifestation of A, the new a is, because of its constancy, a still better one.

[4] *Traité*, 798.

[5] *Ibid.*

[6] *Ibid.*, 868.

[7] "Il faut prendre garde de ne pas confondre les résidus (a) avec les sentiments ni avec les instincts auxquels ils correspondent. Les résidus (a) sont la manifestation de ces sentiments et de ces instincts comme l'élévation du

very curious that in the great majority of the secondary treatments of Pareto[1] the residues have been identified with the A of the earlier schema,[2] while the derivations have been identified with the C of the same schema.[3] This persistent tendency directly in the face of Pareto's perfectly explicit words raises a problem. For mere errors are random—behind a persistent error in a definite direction there must be a cause other than error alone. It happens to be one of significance to the problems of this study.[4]

It may be said that the residue is a category which is operationally defined. It is the result which is arrived at by following a certain procedure. The initial data are a body of "theories" associated with action. These theories are critically analyzed according to the standards of logico-experimental science, and those elements in them which conform with the standard are set aside. The remaining elements are further separated into the

---

mercure, dans le tube d'un thermomètre est la manifestation d'un accroissement de température. C'est seulement par une ellipse—que nous disons—que les résidus jouent un rôle principal dans la détermination de l'équilibre social." *Ibid.*, 875. see also 1690.

[1] The principal exceptions are Homans and Curtis, *An Introduction to Pareto* and L. J. Henderson, *Pareto's General Sociology*. All three of these authors, however, recognize that there is a certain looseness in Pareto's actual usage of the term residue.

[2] *Traité*, 162.

[3] Thus, for example, Professor Sorokin: "The scheme is: A (residue) leads simultaneously to B (act), C (speech-reactions). All these speech reactions and ideologies Pareto calls derivations." P. A. Sorokin, *Contemporary Sociological Theories*, p. 50.

[4] This point had best, to avoid misunderstanding, be elaborated somewhat further. The interpretation of the residue as the A of Pareto's earlier analytical scheme is wrong in the first instance in the textual sense that he nowhere explicitly defines the residue as A while he does explicitly do so as a of the later scheme. It is, however, in part substantively right in that Pareto does not, as has been noted several times, adhere strictly to his own definition in his usage, and uses the term a good deal more vaguely. This could to a certain extent be justified in the interest of avoiding unnecessary pedantry. But, more than this, there is a marked tendency for the concept in usage to slip over into a meaning, not, to be sure, identical with A as Pareto defined it but in conformity with a particular interpretation of A as a bundle of "instincts" in the technical meaning of psychology. The original "state of mind" was, it will be remembered, defined only residually. This tendency of Pareto's own thought is one of the most important symptoms of the fact that he did not, in certain directions, carry through his analytical scheme to a point where certain fundamental problems were settled. It is one

constant and the variable.[1] After setting aside the variable elements the residues are the constant elements which are left. They are employed by Pareto as elements in his theoretical system.

The data which are arrived at by repeating this operation a large number of times in different cases are not capable of quantification in the sense which has been discussed. So after having clearly defined the concept Pareto proceeds to a classification of the residues and then of the derivations. The residues he divides into six main classes and many subclasses. It is not, however, necessary for purposes of this study to attempt an analysis or critical appraisal of this classification. A brief discussion of the first two classes will be introduced below for a particular purpose.[2]

THE TWO STRUCTURAL ASPECTS OF NONLOGICAL ACTION

The logic of the present study, on the other hand, calls for temporarily taking leave of Pareto's explicit analysis at this point in order to follow out certain implications of what has just been set forth in terms of the problems which are of central interest here. This particular line Pareto himself does not follow. About the residues, generally, he tells us only that they are "manifestations of sentiments" and that the latter, not the

---

of the principal objects of the present analysis to expose this shortcoming and to indicate how it biases Pareto's treatment of various problems and leads to difficulties for which his scheme, as he himself developed it explicitly, offers no solution.

Of the predominant interpretation, then, two things can be said. In the first place it violates the canons of careful textual criticism by ignoring the author's own definition of one of his leading concepts. Furthermore, in picking out only one of the actual tendencies in his usage it conspicuously fails to do justice to the complexity of the theoretical problems involved in Pareto's work. If he had been, as he is so often made out, a clear and decisive exponent of a definite theory—psychological anti-intellectualism in application to social phenomena—it is scarcely comprehensible that he should have defined his basic concept in one sense and used it in another. This apparent inconsistency is the most important lead into a whole range of problems, which though of course not solved by Pareto, he, perhaps more than any other social theorist, served to open up. The interpretive dogmatism this note criticizes serves only to obscure these problems and to lead thought straight back into the accustomed grooves which Pareto was getting it out of.

[1] *Traité*, 798.
[2] Chap. VII.

residues, are to be regarded as the determining forces in social equilibrium. But it will be the task of the succeeding analysis to show that among the sentiments manifested in the residues there appears, on inquiry, an important line of cleavage into two classes, with far-reaching implications for the relation of the residues to the structural aspect of systems of action.

That this distinction did not appear explicitly in Pareto's own treatment is apparently owing to the fact that he was engaged on a different task. He set up the concepts of logical and nonlogical action for a particular purpose, essentially that of defining the operation by which residues were to be arrived at. Then, having arrived at the residues he set about classifying them without, for the time being, any further regard for their relation to systems of action. When he came, however, to talk about such systems, he was led to make certain statements about them which coincide with those which will be arrived at here by a different path. These will be taken up in the following chapter. Just now it is necessary to indicate the starting points of the analysis by which these statements will be arrived at, and its relation to the previous discussion of the study.

As has been shown, Pareto defines logical action positively and leaves nonlogical as a residual category. Then he approaches the problem of defining certain of the nonlogical elements by way of the "theories" associated with nonlogical action which are, by definition, nonscientific theories. Residues are the constant elements of such theories, while derivations are the variable. The question is whether any further classification of the elements of such theories is possible and relevant other than Pareto's own subclassification of each category.

The previous analysis yields the basis of one which will here be tested out. For it is a notable fact that Pareto's concept of logical action states, as has already been pointed out, precisely the norm of rationality which has been prominent in the versions of the positivistic tradition already dealt with. It is the conformity of the subjective aspect of action with the standards of correct scientific knowledge. The nonscientific theories involve in certain respects departure from this standard. The question is, in what respects?

It has already been shown that for a positivistic theory, so far at least as the subjective aspect of action can be fitted into cognitive forms at all, all departures from the standard of scientific validity must be capable of interpretation as "unscientific" elements, that is, are resolvable into terms of ignorance and error. It is certain that some of the departures from the logico-experimental standard with which Pareto deals in analyzing the "theories" in question fall into these categories. But it is equally clear that there is another group of them which do not. Theories, or elements of them, may not only be *un*scientific, they may be *non*scientific, in that they involve entities or considerations which fall altogether outside the range of scientific competence. The "more extended knowledge" of Pareto's observer does not suffice to arrive at a judgment of their validity; they are unverifiable, not "wrong."

The question then arises of what are, in terms of the aspects of the conceptual scheme of action already laid down, the consequences of this distinction between two different modes of departure from the norm of "logicality." It has already been pointed out that the scientifically valid knowledge which most obviously can play a part in the determination of action is that of the means and conditions of action. It has also been pointed out that in so far as the concrete means and conditions constitute a "social environment" consisting of the actions, actual and potential, of other persons in the same social system, the status of elements in their action which require subjective categories for their formulation is, analytically considered, problematical. For what are objects of knowledge on the part of one concrete actor may turn out, on the analysis of the system as a whole, to be attributable to the "ends" or other subjective elements in relation to the actors taken together. At any rate, apart from Durkheim's attempt to attribute analytical independence to this social environment, emphasis on objective knowledge has predominantly consisted in emphasis on those aspects of the situation of action which are formulable in nonsubjective terms, for most practical purposes on heredity and environment. It has meant the "biologizing" of social theory in one direction, that of radical rationalistic positivism.

But it has also been shown that in so far as the subjective aspect of action has been treated from the cognitive point of view as not capable of fitting into this "rationalistic" schema, but still as positivistically relevant, it has been as "unscientific," as consisting of ignorance and error. Now in the same context the sources of ignorance and error, the elements of which they constitute a "manifestation" are these same nonsubjective elements. Emphasis on this aspect constitutes a tendency to reduce action to terms of heredity and environment, to biologize its theory, but in the anti-intellectualistic direction.

So long as analysis is confined to the considerations just outlined, a system of theory will be forced into the framework of what has been called the utilitarian dilemma. For in the logicality of action, as Pareto has defined it, is involved only the relation of means and end, no relation of ends to each other. And in so far as consideration of nonlogicality is confined to terms of ignorance and error, the determining elements of action will be found to lie in the categories of nonsubjective systems, above all heredity and environment. In these terms alone, so long as there is no explicit attention paid to the structure of total systems of action (but there is implicitly or explicitly a process of direct generalization from the elements so far formulated) a system of logical action would be a utilitarian or a radically rationalistic positivistic system, while a nonlogical system would be at the pole of anti-intellectualistic positivism.

In so far as attention is confined to the conceptual elements so far outlined, there is a strong though not exclusive tendency to lay stress, empirically, on what may be called the discrepancy of theory and practice, as a dominant criterion of nonlogicality. It is conceivable that theories should "manifest" the nonsubjective nonlogical elements in such a way that, while the theories formulate the direction of operation of the real forces, they are significant only as indices of the latter, and knowledge is not itself an independent element. But Pareto's procedure is such as to emphasize not this theoretically conceivable case but that in which the theories are at variance with the real state of affairs. Indeed there is a vast amount of argument devoted by Pareto to proof of the proposition that while we think we are doing one kind of thing in fact we are doing quite another. As a phenomenon of great importance there is no doubt that he succeeds in establishing it. But, as will be seen, this is by no means the whole burden of his argument.

Now it is a striking fact that the great majority of secondary interpreters of Pareto's conceptual scheme have fitted it entirely into this context. His criticism of the "theories" accompanying action has been held to establish the fact that they are *un*scientific. The residues are then interpreted as the constant elements in such unscientific theories. The sentiments which they manifest are those aspects of the concrete individual understandable in terms of nonsubjective categories. Above all, the central element underlying the residue is held to be an "irrational" instinct. Pareto is held to have put forward another version of the instinct psychology which has been so prevalent a mode of thought in the past generation. In so far as a more general conceptual framework is discernible in his thought, it is that of positivistic anti-intellectualism.

It is, of course, true simply by definition that among the logically possible departures of theories from the logico-experimental standard are those here classed as the unscientific. There is much evidence that such departures are of great empirical frequency and importance. Pareto naturally deals with them, and hence the elements to which this line of thought leads do play a considerable part in his thinking. Perhaps, even, he tended at times to speak in terms open to the interpretation that they were the sole theoretically important ones. Whether he was consistent or not, however, the fact remains that there is a fundamental strain in his thought which will not fit into this scheme. It is that which is implied in the view that such theories contain elements which are not only unscientific, but also *non*scientific.

In this early, analytical, part of Pareto's work there is no explicit treatment of total systems of action. For him the analysis of the isolated unit act is sufficient to establish the definitions and operations which he requires at this stage. But almost at the very beginning he makes a distinction that at least suggests another line of thought. That is, he says that while the objective end must be a "real" end, "falling within the domain of experience" this is not necessarily true of the subjective end, which may, on the contrary, be an "imaginary" end, falling outside that domain. The formulation of this distinction in terms of the contrast between entities within and without the domain of experience, or empirical observation, strongly suggests that the imaginariness of an imaginary end at least *need* not be solely a matter of an erroneous attribution of "reality" to it on the part of the actor. It is entirely consistent with his formulation to hold that the reference is to a state of affairs which is not accessible to scientific observation at all, and hence the actor's "theory" can in this respect be declared empirically neither right nor wrong.

But this distinction is not isolated. On the contrary, there runs all through Pareto's analysis and discussion of the residues and derivations a strain of argument which fits into this context. The "theories" which are thus analyzed tend to fall into two classes which it is best to treat separately here, although Pareto does not do so: on the one hand, "justifications" of why certain actions should be undertaken; on the other, ideas as to the appropriate ways and means of performing them.

The nonscientific rather than the unscientific aspect is particularly prominent in respect to the first class. With reference to justifications, which occupy a very large part of his empirical discussion, the argument is, in a large majority of cases, not that the actor gives a justification which the observer, with his more extended knowledge, can prove to be erroneous, but that either no justification at all is given or that that which is given is not subject to verification. In the first class belongs the precept he quotes from Hesiod, "Do not urinate in the mouth of a river," for which Hesiod gives no reason whatever. In the second class belong all the vast number of statements that "justice" or the "will of God" or some other such reason requires a given action.

It is, of course, true, as Pareto documents almost to the point of boredom, that the total justifications of this latter type contain, as a rule rather than an exception, other imperfections from the logico-experimental point of view than the fact that they contain statements which are unverifiable. In particular they contain a very large element of ambiguity and logical and factual error. But here the distinction between residues and derivations becomes important. For it may be said to be one of the outstanding results of Pareto's analysis that these latter features belong mainly in the derivations, not in the residues, and hence are of secondary, though not always negligible, importance.

It is in the nature of the procedure by which they are arrived at that the residues should be the explicit or implicit underlying central propositions or beliefs common to a group of such theories. They are, as Pareto at one point says, the principles underlying the actions.

Since the class of "theories" now under discussion constitutes justifications of courses of action, at least one very important class of residues from the present point of view is that which may be stated in the general form of "a sentiment that such and such is a desirable state of affairs." Such statements are residues, not because they state erroneously facts which can be stated correctly, nor because, alone, they reveal the ignorance of those to whom they may be imputed. On the contrary they are residues because they embody ends, or classes of ends of action which cannot be justified in terms of any scientific theory, that is, not because they are appropriate means to other ends, but because they are deemed desirable as ends in themselves. Such residues may be called normative residues in the strict sense of the term normative defined above.[1] The implications of the appearance of this type of element among Pareto's residues will be further discussed in the following chapter. Only one or two remarks need be made just now. First, the classification of residues as normative and non-normative is a line of distinction which evidently cuts across Pareto's own classification. It introduces a further complication into the classification by distinguishing on a plane different from Pareto's own. No attempt will be made here to follow this aspect of the question further in its application to Pareto's own conceptual scheme. But one remark may be made: Whatever the details of the classification of the residues may be, the fact that Pareto introduces an explicit classification at all implies an important theorem: that the residues are not random data for the theory of action but, on the contrary, constitute a definite element of systems of action, in an understandable state of interdependence with the others. If this theorem be admitted, it must apply to the normative as well as to other residues. This, then, is in specific contradiction to the utilitarian postulate of the randomness of ends. So far as ends enter into the category of residues as independent elements, they are not random ends, but stand in definable positive relations both to other ends in the same system, and to the other elements of action. Hence the concrete system to which Pareto's conceptual scheme applies cannot be either a utilitarian or a radically positivistic system.

A second line of implication is important. Pareto used the concept of logical action as a criterion of distinction for certain

[1] P. 75.

methodological purposes. It is logically quite possible for a concrete act, class or, even, total system of action to meet this criterion and hence be called a "logical system." But it does not follow that such act, class or system of action should involve for analytical purposes only the elements which are formulated in the concept of logical action. On the contrary the latter defines only the character of the means-end relationship, it would seem, on the assumption that the end is given. Indeed there is nothing at all in the concept to exclude the possibility that the ends of "logical acts" should not be statements of fact but, on the contrary, "manifestations of sentiments." It will be seen below that this is more than a logical possibility; it is, in fact, Pareto's explicit view at certain crucial points. Indeed it must be so, so long as the residues are held to constitute an important element of such a concrete system at all. For even though the means-end relationship be completely logical there may be, and according to Pareto are, certain ends which are not capable of justification in terms of a scientific theory, the justifications of which at least contain residues, if not derivations. In so far as this may be demonstrated to be a theorem, explicit or implicit, in Pareto's position the latter cannot be assimilated to any form of positivistic theory of action. The following chapter will contain a further elaboration of the question of the status of ends and of the elements formulated among the normative residues, in complex systems of action. Only after that has been done will the foregoing proposition be fully clear.

One principal distinguishing characteristic of an end in the analytical sense is that it is necessarily a subjective category. From the objective point of view alone it is not possible to distinguish an end from any other objectively observable outcome of a behavior sequence. But after the foregoing discussion it goes without saying that nonsubjective elements are also manifested in Pareto's residues. Why then are not normative residues simply manifestations of these nonsubjective elements? There are many considerations bearing on this question, but a very general one may be noted just now. There is no reason for distinguishing different classes of residues as elements of a system of action, unless the different classes vary independently of each other. Precisely in so far as Pareto maintains the position that a residue not only is not a verifiable statement of fact, from the subjective point of view, but cannot be replaced or corrected by such a statement from the objective, that is to say is a proposition which is unverifiable, he is making such a distinction among classes of residues. For the residues which manifest the nonsubjective elements are capable of being embodied in such statements from the objective point of view.

Of course not only Pareto's own classification of the residues, but any modification or elaboration of it introduced for present purposes, is provisional. It is not asserted that it will not ever be possible to reduce some, or even all normative residues to such nonsubjective terms. But the important point is that so long as this reduction has not been achieved Pareto's theoretical system is not a positivistic system. It involves elements which have no place in such a system and implies, as will be shown, a structure of concrete systems of action which cannot be reconciled with any positivistic system. The present concern is with Pareto's actual system and its adequacy for the facts actually under review. What may happen to it in the dim future as a result of much further investigation and criticism is not within the scope of this study.

So far the discussion of the nonscientific as opposed to the unscientific aspects of theories has been confined to the justifications of why a given course of action should be pursued at all. It has been found that some ends, those which will later be called "ultimate" ends, fit into this category. It remains to ask whether in the theories so far as they are concerned with matters of ways and means a nonscientific element also is discoverable, or whether departures from the logico-experimental standard are here reducible to terms of ignorance and error alone.

It happens that a very prominent place in this connection is occupied by Pareto's study of a certain class of concrete actions, the class *B* discussed above,[1] which would commonly be called ritual actions. Indeed so prominent is ritual in his treatment that it is quite safe to say that one of the principal empirical bases for his thesis of the importance of nonlogical action is the prevalence of ritual.

But if the way in which he treats ritual is closely observed certain important things will be noted. So far as can be discerned, he nowhere treats it in terms which suggest that the important

[1] P. 195 (as distinguished from *D*).

thing for him is the discrepancy between what men have held to be the proper course of action, and that which has actually taken place.[1] On the contrary, the problem of the discrepancy of theory and practice is nowhere stressed. It is, rather, assumed throughout that men do perform rituals closely in accordance with the prescriptions of the ritual tradition. At any rate Pareto is not interested in investigating any discrepancies that may exist. The conspicuous thing about the treatment is rather that it is couched overwhelmingly in terms of the character of the "theory." But as opposed to the case of justifications, it is here not the nature of the major premises which is at issue, but rather the character of the "combinations" of means and ends. These are not intrinsically derived from verifiable empirical knowledge, but are arbitrary.

"Arbitrary" here means, in Pareto's formula, "not logically united to their end." That is to say, when investigated by an observer in possession of the best available scientific knowledge, he can discern no reason why the operations in question should serve to bring about the realization of the subjective end; the objective and the subjective ends fail to correspond. Pareto does, it is true, provide a classification of types of such arbitrary combinations of means and end; they may be reduced to a limited number of principles such as that like produces unlike, like produces like, etc. But he does not give any general characterization of ritual except the negative one that the means-end relationship is, from the "logical" point of view, arbitrary, and that hence ritual actions are to be regarded less as means of attaining ends than as "manifestations of sentiments." In this way he does attribute great importance to them and his treatment is a great advance on the dominant positivistic tendency to treat ritual as depending solely on a form of error.

Pareto arrives at residues by the analysis of ritual prescriptions as well as by that of justifications of other actions. The question is, what is the character of the sentiments underlying these

[1] Indeed so much is it the case that the discrepancy of theory and practice is not the decisive problem in this context that Pareto on several occasions directly identifies the *means* employed with the derivations. This identification is only possible on the assumption that the derivations (which are, it will be remembered, elements of the *theories* associated with action) accurately describe the "operations" that are actually performed. *Cf. Traité*, 863, 865.

residues? They will be found to have a place at various points in Pareto's own classification of the residues. But there is to be found nowhere in Pareto's treatment any reason to suppose that normative sentiments are not involved. Indeed the concrete form in which such prescriptions occur is quite definitely that of norms. For instance, in an example Pareto uses, the Greek sailors believed that, before starting on a voyage, it was desirable to perform certain sacrifices to Poseidon. The analysis of these prescriptions into residues and derivations gives no basis for discriminating the normative from the non-normative components of the underlying sentiments. In such a case it is prima facie a reasonable assumption that both classes are involved.

It is true that seen from the logico-experimental point of view the theories involved in ritual prescriptions involve either error or unverifiable statements or both. The former element is by no means negligible. But in a positivistic context the tendency is to jump directly from proof of the existence of error to the conclusion that it is explained by a non-normative, nonsubjective instinctive drive, or something of the sort. This does not follow and in Pareto's treatment there is no justification for such an interpretation. He leaves completely open the question of what is the source of this error or of the nonscientific elements.

It is, however, possible to go a step beyond Pareto's treatment to indicate a direction of possible development in the interpretation of ritual. Pareto's definition of logical action may be regarded as defining a type of norm which, on occasion, governs the means-end relationship. In a positivistic context, it has been shown, this is the only conceivable type of norm which can be theoretically important. All deviations from it must be interpreted as manifestations of non-normative elements, generally biological. But the fact that Pareto's conceptual scheme does not fit any version of the positivistic pattern opens up the possibility that one or more other types of normative element may be relevant to understanding the choice of means as well as of ends.

The norm involved in logical action may be called that of "intrinsic rationality." The term intrinsic is chosen because it suggests an antithesis, "symbolic." It is then suggested that the choice of means to an end may involve a selective standard defined in terms other than that of intrinsic appropriateness according to a logico-experimental standard. The standard of selection may be that of symbolic appropriateness as an "expression," in that sense a manifestation, of the normative sentiments involved. This interpretation would meet the empirical criteria implicit in Pareto's treatment of ritual. For the relation between a symbol and its meaning is always, by definition "arbitrary" as seen from an intrinsic point of view. There is no intrinsic reason why the particular linguistic symbol "book" should have the meaning it does. This is proved by the simple fact that totally unrelated symbols have, in other languages, the same meaning, as the French *livre*. It is suggested that the normative aspect of the means-end relationship which is dominant in ritual actions is of the order of that involved in the relation of symbol and meaning, rather than that of cause and effect as formulated in scientific theory.

It is necessary to call attention to a distinction of two different levels on which this schema of interpretation may be employed. The more obvious is the level where his act, or his "operation," may be held to have an explicitly conscious symbolic meaning to the actor. We habitually interpret conformity with many of the rules of etiquette as expressions of a sentiment, thus greeting a person cordially on the street, as indicating friendliness. But at the same time it is quite possible for the symbol-meaning schema to be a convenient tool of understanding for the observer on occasions when it is not explicitly conscious to the actor. Thus in magic the actor's subjective attitude is generally close to that of belief in the intrinsic efficacy of the operation, but to the observer it is more conveniently interpreted as an expression of his senti-ments. Often the actor gives no conscious meaning at all to the act, as in Hesiod's prescription quoted above, and often the subjective meaning he himself gives it is at variance with that imputed by an observer.

It is not desirable to attempt to pursue the analysis of the relation of symbolism to ritual action farther at this point. The question has been posed because it shows a way in which the opening for an influence of normative elements on the means-end relationship in ways other than those involved in the rational norm, which Pareto's own scheme provides, can lead to positive theoretical results important to this study. Further consideration of the question will be postponed until Durkheim's treatment of the role of symbolism in religion is dealt with below.[1]

[1] Chap. XI, pp. 429 *ff.*

The possibility of the emergence of the symbol-meaning relationship into the field of direct sociological application calls attention again to a range of methodological problems which was merely mentioned in passing at the beginning of the chapter. There it was noted that Pareto's own formulation of the conception of scientific fact made no commitments on the question of the observability of the meanings of symbols, but that his own empirical procedure was such as to imply it throughout. It must now be clear why this is so: his central analytical task is the inductive study of "theories and propositions" accompanying action. Furthermore in treating these theories and propositions his primary concern is to analyze them on the meaningful level, to subject them to a critique from the point of view of their scientific status, their logical consistency and the extent to which they involve statements of verifiable fact. Only after this analysis has been completed is the question why such theories are produced and accepted by large numbers of men raised at all.

There can, then, be no doubt that on one level it is a methodological necessity for Pareto to admit the legitimacy of treating the meanings of symbols as facts capable of finding a place in a scientific theory and treating such facts, therefore, as verifiable.[1] But the question appears again on a still deeper level. It will be remembered that Pareto made the statement that in so far as action was logical it was understandable as resulting from a "process of reasoning," but that in so far as it was nonlogical it issued from a "state of mind." Now the implication of the first part of the statement is that if we know the process of reasoning, that is, the theory accompanying action, we have, so far as it is understandable in terms of the category logical action at all, an adequate basis for understanding the action itself. Methodologically this means that to one who "knows the language" understanding of the meaning of the symbols of which the theory is made up is sufficient for understanding the course of overt action. It is not necessary to invoke any further entity, any "state of mind," which though functionally related to these meanings, is

[1] It is interesting to note that this alone is sufficient to dispose of the contention sometimes brought forward that Pareto's position is essentially that of a behaviorist (see M. Handman's article on Pareto in *The Methods of Social Science*, ed. by S. A. Rice). Pareto's objectivism is not of the behaviorist variety, but relates only to the insistence on the verifiability of the facts which are allowed a place in science.

for the scientific purposes in hand not so closely tied to them as to make the distinction unnecessary.

Pareto in the second part of the statement infers that with respect to nonlogical action the situation is different. It would then be easy to infer that here the meanings of the symbols are irrelevant to the understanding of action, that the real source of it lay in a totally different *order* of element. Is this inference legitimate? It is strongly suggested by the formulation of the first analytical scheme, the *ABC* triangle, with its sharp separation of *C* as a category of concrete phenomena, and *A* as the nonobservable, hypothetical entity on which *C* is dependent. In other words, the question is raised of what is implied in the term "manifestation" which Pareto uses to express the relation of the residue, which is an element of *C*, and the "sentiment," which is presumably an element of *A*.

This question is closely connected with that of the status of the normative elements of action. If norms are expressed at all, that is, if they become observable facts, it is only in the form of systems of symbols. In so far then as action conforms with a norm and can to this extent be spoken of as determined by the normative element, such a distinction becomes unnecessary. Then the theory may in so far be regarded as an adequate expression of the real determinants of action. This is true, as has been shown, of the logical elements, in Pareto's sense. It would seem to follow that, to the extent that action diverged from the course normatively laid down, the theory was no longer adequate, but other factors must be brought in to explain it. This is certainly one of the main reasons for the distinction between *A* and *C*.

Indeed the discrepancy between norm and actual course of action is one main aspect of the nonlogicality of action. But it has been conclusively shown that it is not the only one. There is in addition a group of normative elements which are not included in the category of logical action but which may yet exist in logical acts. One of these, as has been seen, is to be found in the ultimate ends of action. Now in this connection there is in Pareto's treatment no reason why the residues, in so far as they formulate these ultimate ends, should not be considered exactly as adequate expressions of the real determinants of action, as is the "process of reasoning" in the logical case. This is true of the polar type where the ends are definite, specific and unambiguous and the deductions from them as to ways and means, strictly logical. This by no means exhausts the problem, as will be seen, but as a polar case it is not devoid of theoretical importance. It is indeed the polar case which Pareto treats as his "rational" abstract society which will be discussed at length in the next chapter.

In this connection there is, indeed, a reason for distinguishing the kind of forces which are determinant of nonlogical action from those formulated in the concept of logical action, but it is a *different* reason from that applying to the situation where the predominant feature is the discrepancy of theory and practice. It is not as it was there a matter of a difference in the character of the relation between the symbols constituting the theory and the real forces, for these symbols are adequate expressions of the real forces. It is, rather, a difference in the character of the entities to which the symbols refer. In the logical case it was the facts of the external world to the actor. In the nonlogical case it is in the first instance[1] the actor's own sentiments. The necessity for the distinction of A and C is that certain of the symbols of C refer to elements that do not find a place in a scientific theory. Hence the action cannot be regarded as determined only by the process of reasoning, that is by those elements capable of formulation in a scientific theory, but to these must be added another, the ultimate end of the action. This ultimate end is the "manifestation of a sentiment" *by contrast* with a statement of fact, as comes out so clearly in Pareto's formulation of the second analytical scheme.

Thus appears in another form the same dichotomy of fundamental nonlogical elements which runs all through this analysis. In one approach to it, action is nonlogical in that it fails to conform with the norms accepted by the actor. In so far the symbols of the actor's own "theory" are inadequate expressions of the real determining forces of action and it is necessary, in addition to the "meanings" of the symbols, to invoke another order of elements comprised in A, the "sentiments." But in this context sentiment means predominantly an element which works *in spite of the actor's subjective intentions*. Subjectively his theory is there-

[1] For further analysis of this problem see Chap. XI and Chap. XVII.

fore marked by ignorance and error. Finally, the source of this ignorance and error on analysis lies in the factors of heredity and environment, especially "instincts." In so far as this is what is important in nonlogical action it is the sentiment as manifesting an instinct which is decisive. And it manifests the instinct, and in turn the residue manifests the sentiment, in the sense that one is an index of the other.[1] The residue, which is a proposition, is important, not because of its meaning, but as an index of a totally different order of elements which in their relation to action are not capable of interpretation in terms of the symbol-meaning relation at all, but only that of cause and effect. Moreover, these are elements which are "external" to the actor, which it is therefore in principle possible for him to know correctly and therefore adapt his action to. This is why in this context the departure of the theory from the scientific standard is a matter of ignorance and error.

In the other context the state of affairs is quite different. Here there is, in so far no question of failure to conform with norms. What is at issue is the scientific status of certain elements of the "theories" in terms of which the norms themselves are stated. Here the relation of norm to action is essentially the same as in logical action; what differs is the source of the normative element. This is found to be not in the actor's accurate observation of the facts of his external world, but in something "subjective" to him, his sentiments. In so far as this context is relevant the residue, a proposition be it remembered, manifests the sentiment in the sense that it is the adequate linguistic (*i.e.*, symbolic), expression of this subjective element, of the actor's ultimate end or intention, or rather that aspect of it which is not derivable from scientific knowledge of his situation. Here manifestation may best be paraphrased as expression rather than index. In this sense a residue manifests a sentiment in the same sense and with the same adequacy as a statement of fact manifests an aspect of the external world. The essence of the matter lies in the symbol-meaning relationship, not that of cause and effect, or of mutual interdependence on an intrinsic level.

[1] That is, is *causally* dependent on it in the sense in which the level of mercury in a thermometer is dependent on the thermal state of the fluid into which the bulb is thrust—both are part of the same physical system in a state of mutual interdependence. See *Traité*, 875.

But why has this dichotomy remained so obscure? For one reason because most of Pareto's interpreters have been biased and have favored seeing only one side of it. But for another because empirically the case just analyzed at the other pole is indeed a polar case, at best only approached with a certain degree of approximation in concrete systems of action. So much is this so that the implications of this situation come out clearly in Pareto's own treatment only when he resorts to the methodological device of analyzing an abstract society, which is exactly analogous to the device of treating bodies as if they fell in a vacuum. The situation is closely analogous to that in which mechanics would be if all bodies on this earth were of a density relative to that of the atmosphere approximating that of feathers. Then the law of gravitation could scarcely be arrived at by a process of empirical generalization from their actual behavior in nature, or by dropping them from high places. But this would be no reason why the law of gravitation would fail to hold in such a world.

To return to the subject in hand. The nonscientific theories associated with action depart from the scientific standard in general not only in that *their major premises are manifestations of sentiments* rather than statements of fact, but also in that *the reasoning involved is to a greater or less degree sophistic*, and that *the premises themselves are ambiguous*. With reference to the residues, which are at issue here, it is above all this last feature that is important. In so far as its premises are not logically determinate it is not possible for a theory to deduce unambiguous courses of action from them. On this fact Pareto rightly lays great stress. But this does not dispose of the theoretical importance of the polar type of case in which this ambiguity is eliminated, any more than the fact that feathers fall irregularly and slowly disposes of the theoretical importance of the behavior of falling bodies in a vacuum. Furthermore, and still more important, there is no warrant for the view that all deviations from this polar case are exclusively due to non-normative elements of action. After all, a cautious methodologist of science like Pareto is careful to insist that scientific statements are approximate, not completely accurate. Scientific progress is a matter of successive approximation. Therefore the meanings of the symbols employed in scientific theories are never fully adequate expressions of the aspects of the concrete phenomena they attempt to formulate.

There is no a priori reason why the same should not be true of the residues as manifestations of sentiments. But there is a difference. The sentiment itself is a human creation. It may itself be relatively vague and indefinite, only achieving definiteness by a process of development, if at all. Furthermore there may be conflicts of sentiment which are only to a relative degree clearly formulated, and which may be concealed by indefinite residues. Analysis will reveal innumerable ways in which, remaining on the normative level itself, complexities of the kind Pareto so acutely analyzes may arise.

Thus Pareto's distinction of logical and nonlogical action can be used, not as he himself used it to define the operation for identifying the residues, but as a starting point for outlining the structure of the systems of action to which his system of elements is applicable. Consideration of the way in which he treats nonlogical action leads to the distinction of two different ways in which the theories analyzed into residues and derivations may diverge from the logico-experimental standard; they may be either unscientific or nonscientific. In so far as such deviations fit into the first category, the elements underlying them can be fitted into the framework of anti-intellectualistic positivism, the sentiments are the channels through which action is determined by the nonsubjective factors of heredity and environment. In so far, on the other hand, as the deviations are due to the nonscientific elements in the theories, this is not possible, for the residues may be the ultimate ends of action, in which event the sentiments are not reducible to biological terms, but remain "subjective." The same *may* at least be true in relation to the selective element of the means-end relationship where, as in ritual, the combinations are from the logical point of view arbitrary, but are still open to the interpretation that they manifest normative sentiments rather than instinctive drives.

All that the present chapter has been able to do is to open up the subject of the structure of such action systems, and to show that, starting from Pareto's logical-nonlogical distinction it is possible to build out the outline of the structure of the systems in two main directions. One leads to the place of the elements of the "situation," the non-normative aspect of the system, the other to ends and the sentiments underlying ends and other normative aspects of such systems. That the latter direction of analysis is clearly left open by Pareto's own formulations, marks his position off clearly from the positivistic systems which have been considered. In the next chapter three further steps will be made. First the validity of the contention that the distinction of the two different aspects of the nonlogical really is supported by Pareto's own thought will be tested by reference to certain crucial discussions of his in which this issue is, in general terms, brought out into the open. In particular, it will be shown that he could not, in these respects, have held to the view of radical anti-intellectualistic positivism which many of his interpreters have read into his thought; in short, Pareto's "sentiments" are not the instincts of psychology.

Second, on the foundations laid down in this chapter the outline of the structure of systems of action will be elaborated much further. In particular, certain questions of the relations of unit acts in a system will be considered. This development, in the form in which it will be attempted, Pareto does not undertake at all. But after he has completed his classification of residues and derivations he does, in the synthetic part of his work, consider their interaction with each other and with other elements in a social system. In discussing this he gives an outline of certain features of the social system itself, which can serve to verify the correctness of the development on the structural level to be attempted here. The result will be, third, a demonstration of a remarkable point-to-point correspondence between the outcome of his procedure and that followed here so far as the two concern themselves with the same problems.

CHAPTER VI

VILFREDO PARETO, II: EXTENSION AND VERIFICATION OF THE STRUCTURAL ANALYSIS

PARETO AND SOCIAL DARWINISM

Before entering upon the main analytical task of this chapter, further evidence may be presented for the view that the sole important theoretical result of Pareto's analysis of nonlogical action cannot be a psychological "instinct" theory or any other theory taken from the armory of positivistic anti-intellectualism. It has been shown above[1] that when the rationalism of the utilitarian position breaks down within the alternatives of the utilitarian dilemma in the direction of positivistic anti-intellectualism, an "instinct" theory or other related one is not a stable stopping place. There is always a reluctance to take such instincts or drives simply as ultimate data without inquiring further into the forces determining them in turn. When this inquiry has been pushed on on a positivistic basis it has led sooner or later to some version of biological survivalism. If this were the main burden of Pareto's thought, failure to show at least important traces of a tendency to survivalism would be most unlikely.

The most prominent version of this survivalism in the time in which Pareto's ideas were being formed was undoubtedly the Darwinian. Hence Pareto's attitude to the Darwinian theory in its social application is of great interest. The essence of the theory, it may be recalled, was a combination of two elements. On the one hand, the hereditary type of an organism is thought of as undergoing continuous variation at random about the previous type as a mode. On the other hand, these variations are subject to a selective process in terms of their adaptation to the conditions of their environment. The selective process, by affecting the ratio of survival and reproduction among the variants, shifts the modal type for the next generation in the direction of greater fitness. Since the element of variation is random it is the environ-

---

[1] Chap. III, pp. 115 ff.

220   *VILFREDO PARETO, II: EXTENSION*

ment alone which gives determinate direction to the process of evolution. In its social application it may be "social forms" which are thought of as varying. But within a strictly positivistic framework unless these are direct adaptations to environment (usually involving a rational process[1]) these forms will be thought of as functions of the hereditary human type, so that Social Darwinism becomes an application, to a special factual field, of the biological theory.

There is definite secondary testimony that Pareto was strongly attracted by the theory of Social Darwinism.[2] But he ended by decisively rejecting it as an adequate general social theory. Of this there is a perfectly explicit statement:

Social Darwinism is one of these theories. If it is maintained that the institutions of a society are always those best adapted to the circumstances in which it [the society] is placed, except for temporary oscillations, and the fact that the societies which do not possess institutions of this character will disappear in the end, we have a principle capable of extensive logical development constituting a science. . . . But this doctrine fell into decadence with the theory from which it originated—the Darwinian theory of the origin of animal and vegetable species. . . . It does not determine the form of institutions: it determines only certain limits which they cannot exceed.[3]

Thus as a general social theory Pareto found Social Darwinism inadequate. The conditions of the environment do not completely determine social forms but only set limits to variations in them which are capable of survival. Any attempt to make the theory serve for more rigorous determination within these limits is possible only on the basis of a surreptitious introduction of final causes,[4] which vitiates the theory. The implication of this position is quite clear—that besides the conditions of the environment there must be factors determining social forms other than random variations.[5] Otherwise there is no basis for Pareto's rejection of the Darwinian theory.

[1] Or a Lamarckian version of evolutionary theory.
[2] BOUSQUET, *Vilfredo Pareto, sa vie et son oeuvre*, p. 205. It is convenient to adopt Pareto's term.
[3] VILFREDO PARETO, *Traité de sociologie générale*, Sec. 828.
[4] *Ibid.*
[5] "Les formes ne sont pas produites du hasard." *Supra*, p. 206. 1770.

Such an explicit statement could scarcely be a mere aberration resulting simply from failure to consider the problem. But if it is not considered sufficient evidence of Pareto's real position on the question two other bodies of testimony may be introduced. In his discussion of social utility, of which much more will be said later in another connection, Pareto introduces a comparison of two abstract theoretical types of society. The one of primary interest here is the first, "a society where the sentiments act entirely alone without reasoning of any sort [entering in]."[1] The second is "a society determined exclusively by logico-experimental reasoning."[2]

Now on the first abstract type Pareto has the following interesting comment to make:

In the first case the form of the society is determined if we have given the sentiments and the external circumstances in which the society is situated, or even if we have given only the circumstances if we add the determination of the sentiments by the circumstances. Darwinism, pushed to its extreme, gives the complete solution of the problem by the theorem of the survival of the individuals best adapted to the circumstances.[3]

On this statement two comments may be made. First, the abstract society in question is not human society[4] but human society is in "an intermediate state between the two types just indicated."[5] The second abstract society will be discussed presently. Here it need only be said that "it is not at all (*pas du tout*) determined if the external circumstances are given."[6] Then even if the Darwinian solution were adequate for the first type this solution becomes inadequate for social theory precisely in so far as human society departs from it in the direction of the second. Hence this is another version of Pareto's critique of the Darwinian theory as applied to human society.

But second and more important it seems quite evident that the "sentiments" considered in the first abstract type are precisely

[1] *Ibid.*, 2141.
[2] *Ibid.*
[3] *Ibid.*, 2142.
[4] To be sure, Pareto doubts the complete adequacy of the Darwinian solution even on the biological level. *Ibid.*, 2142.
[5] *Ibid.*, 2146.
[6] *Ibid.*, 2143.

what would be meant by the sentiments if they constituted the nonrational psychological factor and others capable of non-subjective .formulation. In the first place Pareto states that "animal societies probably approach close to this type."[1] But furthermore this society is characterized by the absence of reasoning of any sort. The sentiments in this sense are precisely what the determinant factors of action would be in so far as the theories, the subjective aspect, are causally irrelevant to its understanding. But in so far as the sentiments are of this character there is no bar in principle to their being determined by the external circumstances through the medium of selection, at least to the extent to which the Darwinian theory is valid on a biological level.

But Pareto does not motivate his rejection of Social Darwinism here primarily by the shortcomings of the Darwinian theory on a biological level, though he mentions some.[2] It is rather because human society approaches the second abstract type. A consideration of this will indicate the nature of the principal limitation on the psychological or "drive" concept of the sentiments. He characterizes it in a remarkable passage:

The form of the society is not at all determined if the external circumstances are given. It is necessary in addition to indicate the *end* which the society[3] should pursue by means of logico-experimental reasoning.

[1] *Ibid.*, 2141.

[2] *Ibid.*, 2142.

[3] Since this chapter was written it has been noticed that the words "which the society should pursue," which are a literal translation of the French (*le but que doit atteindre la société au moyen du raisonnement logico-expérimental*) do not occur in the English edition, which says simply, "the end to be pursued by means of logico-experimental reasoning." A check reveals that the English is a correct translation of the original Italian, and that hence the reference to the society has crept into the French edition. Since its occurrence there is emphasized a note of explanation is called for. Two remarks may be made: (1) The French translation, though not made by Pareto himself, is advertised on the title page as "*revue par l'auteur.*" Moreover, Pareto is said on good authority to have been even more at home in French than in Italian. His mother was a Frenchwoman and he lived in France throughout his childhood and in French Switzerland from the age of forty-five until his death. Moreover, while at Lausanne he lectured in French and did a great deal of his writing in that language. This insertion occurs at a place which Pareto could not but have regarded as crucial. Considering these circumstances it seems unlikely that it could have been a mere slip which was

For whether the humanitarians and positivists like it or not, a society determined exclusively by "reason" does not and *cannot* exist; and this is true, not because the "prejudices" of men prevent them from following the dictates (*enseignements*) of "reason" but because the *data* of the problem they would solve by logico-experimental reasoning are *lacking*.[1] Here appears again the indeterminacy of the concept of utility.[2]

This is certainly one of the crucial passages in Pareto's work. It will be discussed again later in another context. But for present purposes the following are the important things to note about it: First what has already been remarked, that the Darwinian solution will not apply to this abstract society nor to concrete human society primarily because it neglects the element here formulated. And the reason why it will not apply is not that there are limitations in principle on the role of "logico-experimental reasoning" as such in this abstract society, but because of the absence of essential *data* for the solution of the "problem of conduct" by such reasoning. It is quite specifically stated that the inadequacy of the Darwinian theory consists in this absence of data and not the inherent limitations of human rationality as such, not men's "prejudices" (to paraphrase: not ignorance and error caused by the irrationality of human nature in the psychological sense). To suppose that these are the sole barriers to

---

essentially out of harmony with his meaning. The view is more plausible that he let it stand as a more precise expression of his meaning than the original, or that possibly he even inserted it himself. (2) More important than these matters of textual criticism is the fact that this is directly in harmony with the main line of his thought at this point. As will be shown, the whole tenor of the discussion of social utility which immediately precedes this is to build up to the conception of a common end or system of ends shared by the members of the society. He had already spoken of the society "if not as a person, at least as a unity." Moreover it is significant that in the Italian as well as the French the term "end" is used in the singular, not the plural. Since the reference is throughout to an abstract society considered as a whole, and not to an individual, it seems fair to infer that the translator simply supplied explicitly the subject which Pareto had left implicit in the original.

In view of these considerations there seems to be no reason to alter the present text, beyond stating the fact that the author was aware of the discrepancy in the two editions.

[1] Pareto here gives references to Secs. 1878, 1880–1882 which deal with the role in society of *ideal ends*.

[2] *Ibid.*, 2141. Italics mine.

a society "determined exclusively by reason," that is, by scientific knowledge, is precisely the error of the humanitarians and *positivists.*

But Pareto goes farther than to tell us that the most significant obstacle to a scientific society does not lie in the irrationality of human nature, the sentiments of the first abstract society, but that it does lie in a gap in the data of science necessary to determine[1] action. He tells us just where this gap is situated: the missing datum is "the *end* which the society should pursue by means of logico-experimental reasoning." Furthermore to confirm this interpretation he gives a direct reference to his own preceding treatment of the role of ideal ends, a treatment which can leave no doubt that it was his view that they play a major role in social life.

The importance, then, of the second abstract type of society lies in bringing out Pareto's view that the ends of action in an analytical sense are not to the actor facts of experience in the sense required of the data of logico-experimental science. But their very importance in the determination of action precludes the existence of a society "determined exclusively by reason." *This* is the central nonlogical feature of *one* of Pareto's main nonlogical elements of action—a limitation on the scientific status to the actor of the ultimate ends of action, not a limitation of the human capacity for the rational adaptation of means to given ends. Though the residues are not specifically mentioned in this discussion, it can scarcely be doubted that included under the concept residue are these ideal ends, and that the sentiments they manifest are the source of ideal ends, and are thus here *specifically distinguished* from the nonrational psychological factor.

It should further be pointed out that a "society determined exclusively by reason" is linked by Pareto with the ideals of the positivists. It is nothing other than the position outlined as radical rationalistic positivism.[2] Then Pareto has taken a position which implies the rejection as adequate accounts of human society of both radical anti-intellectualistic positivism (Social Darwinism) and the rationalistic version. If his theory belongs within the positivistic framework at all, the only alternative

[1] Data to the actor, of course.
[2] Chap. III, pp. 119–121.

open is the utilitarian. Whether his theory can be placed in this category will be discussed below.

In the meantime the description of human society as occupying an intermediate state between the two abstract societies seems to justify the conclusion that the sentiments manifested in the residues have really split into two different classes which are significant in the present context. One, the "sentiments" of the first abstract society, turns out to include principally the nonrational psychological factor, predominantly "instinct." The other, the "end a society should pursue" is of a radically different order. The two classes have in common only the fact that neither is included in the concept of logical action defined in terms of the intrinsically rational means-end relationship. Pareto by making his original starting point, nonlogical action, a residual category did not arrive at the distinction and it did not thus find a place in his formal scheme. But none the less it has emerged out of his own work. The implications of this fact will occupy most of the remaining discussion of his theory.[1]

Before proceeding to that, however, the other piece of indirect evidence of Pareto's rejection of Social Darwinism may be noted, which will again throw light on the elements of his thought. He speaks quite frequently[2] of the problem whether the residues "correspond to the facts" or to "experience." Now in the first place, this confirms decisively the above account of the genesis of the concept residue as an element of nonscientific theories. For if it is the *état psychique A* interpreted as instinct or drive, as Professor Sorokin and many others have interpreted it, the question is simply meaningless. A drive cannot either correspond or fail to correspond to facts—it is not a proposition but a phenomenon or at least an element of one. Only *propositions* can be judged in terms of such a question at all. Then for the question to make sense the residue must be a proposition.

But once given this interpretation, the genesis of the question becomes perfectly clear. Throughout Pareto has been comparing the nonscientific theories *c* with those of science *C*. In his discussion of derivations he has at great length analyzed the sources

[1] It will be noted that in the discussion of the two abstract societies ritual does not enter at all. It is more convenient to postpone a further discussion of its status which will explain this until later. See below, pp. 256 *ff.*

[2] For instance, *Traité*, 1768–1770, 1880–1881.

of the logical indeterminacy of the first group of theories by contrast with the logical rigor of the scientific theories. The element A of scientific theories, corresponding to the residues, has been specifically defined as a statement of "experimental principles." But the residue is always the manifestation of a sentiment. Hence as such it does not, by definition, "correspond to the facts" in the same sense—in so far as it did it would ipso facto pass over into the category A.

But interestingly enough Pareto does not stop with this negative conclusion. There is, he says, *some* relation to the facts which must be investigated.[1] In carrying out this investigation he remarks, "If they [the nonscientific theories] led to consequences not in general in accordance with the facts all societies would long ago have been destroyed and forgotten,"[2] such is the importance of these theories in social life. This statement seems, in the first place, to assume that such theories are not merely indices of the real forces governing society but somehow actually embody them. But at the same time it gives a hint of the direction in which the facts relevant to the discussion are to be found—by invoking the question of survival. And sure enough on the next page[3] comes the answer: "First it is evident that these [social] forms and these residues cannot be in a state of too flagrant contradiction with the *conditions* in which they are produced; *that is the element of truth in the Darwinian solution.*"[4]

What Pareto has done, assuming the extent to which action really is guided by theories, is to twist the scientific standard of truth into the pragmatic standard of prospect of success in achieving ends. A residue which is an end does not "correspond to the facts" in the same sense as an "experimental principle" because the conditions of the situation of action are not determinate but leave an important margin of variation in objectively achievable ends. But if ends are chosen without regard to the possibilities of realization in the given conditions the consequences may be fatal to the actor. The residues "cannot be in a state of too flagrant contradiction with the conditions" and the society

[1] *Ibid.*, 1768, 1769.
[2] *Ibid.*
[3] *Ibid.*, 1770.
[4] Italics mine. Here are given references to his original explicit statement on Social Darwinism (*Traité*, 828) quoted above and to the first abstract society (*ibid.*, 2142) just discussed.

survive. Thus this definitely confirms the view that some of the residues are statements of the ends of action, not themselves facts to the actor, but still in their realization subject to the limitations imposed by the conditions of the situation in which the actor is placed.

But this is not the whole burden of Pareto's argument at this point. Granting this, there is no guarantee that ends incompatible with the conditions of existence of the society will not be chosen. What then? If they are, one alternative, of course, is extinction. Pareto by no means excludes this. But there is also another: People may not follow out the logical consequence of accepting these ends with complete rigor but may stop short when the consequences are socially (or individually) dangerous. But this in turn must needs be rationalized. And this is a principal function of the derivations in so far as they depart from the rigor of strict logic. "A residue which departs from experience may be corrected by a derivation which departs from logic, in such a way that the conclusion approaches the experimental facts."[1]

The principal importance of this second argument is that it shows that even the most strikingly irrational aspect of the derivations, their defective logic, Pareto attributes in large part not to the fact that action is *independent* of subjective ends but to the very importance of their role. This is true no matter what is the source of the correction. Even if it is purely instinctive the necessity for its existence at all is sufficient proof that Pareto did not conceive the residues entirely as a psychological factor. But there is no reason to assume this extreme case, though doubtless instinct plays a part. The illogical derivation might well also be a means of reconciling a conflict between incompatible ends.[2]

Thus the consideration of Pareto's relation to Social Darwinism has confirmed beyond any reasonable doubt the interpretation that underlying the residues as main determinants of nonlogical action lay, in the context relevant to this argument, not one well-defined homogeneous element, the drive or instinct element, but at least two radically different ones. The attitude to Social Darwinism has clearly brought out both the existence of the second and its general nature, that it has a close relation to the subjective

---

[1] *Ibid.*, 1769.
[2] Unquestionably the rationalizations of modern psychopathology fit to a large extent into this context.

ends of action. The distinction between the two is so important
that, as has been seen, it has already emerged out of Pareto's
own work in spite of the fact that he had no place for it in his
main conceptual scheme. The present discussion will have no
further theoretical concern with the drive factors. Leaving them
aside it is now possible to turn to the question of certain theoretical implications of the others, the end or value factors and
the kind of conceptual scheme their adequate treatment demands.
In so doing it will develop that even here Pareto by no means
fails to furnish important hints.

The "Logical" Aspect of Action Systems

As has been stated the series of distinctions by which Pareto
defined the operation for arriving at the residues could all be
made with reference to analytically isolated unit acts without
regard to their relations in systems. Pareto himself proceeds
from the definition of this operation to an elaborate classification
of the residues and derivations, and then proceeds to apply the
results of this classification to systems of action directly. The
concept of logical action drops altogether out of his treatment.
He does not attempt to develop its implications for the structure
of the systems of action to which his elements are applicable.
It is proposed to attempt this now. After a general outline of the
structure of such systems has been developed, it will be compared
with Pareto's own description of the social system with which
he deals.

The starting point is the concept of logical action. It will be
remembered that this concept had reference only to the character
of a selective standard regulating the choice of means. It can have
analytical significance[1] only, as Pareto's discussion of the abstract
society brings out, in so far as it is formulated with reference to a
given end. The reasons for this fact emerge from the initial
analysis of the action schema introduced above. For were the
element of ends to be included in "logical action" as formulated
by Pareto it could make no difference to the outcome whether or
not action were guided by a scientific theory. The only way in

---

[1] Not in the present context necessarily as an "element" in the strict
sense but as a structural part of an act or system of action the description of
which cannot be reduced to terms of any other part or unit, or combination
of them.

which an end of action can be arrived at by the application of scientific method alone is by prediction of a future state of affairs from facts known about past states. The element which precisely characterizes an end in the analytical sense, the difference in the state of affairs the actor attempts to bring about or maintain from what could be predicted would develop from his situation were he to abstain from acting, has no place in the schema of scientific methodology used for the subjective analysis of action. It must be, to use Pareto's formula, not a fact but the manifestation of a sentiment ("that such and such a state of affairs is desirable").

This necessity, for the concept of logical action to be applicable at all in an analytical sense, that it should have reference to an end that is given, which is analytically independent of the "process of reasoning" about ways and means, is the starting point of the theoretical development to be undertaken here. Though Pareto did not go into these questions so thoroughly as to eliminate all possibility of confusion, his careful and explicit formulations are entirely in harmony with it, and are hence adequate in this respect for present purposes.

The next step Pareto did not take at all *because* he did not consider action in systems analytically, but only synthetically, for consideration of isolated acts was sufficient for his immediate purposes. But here it is necessary to take account of the undoubted fact that actions do not take place separately each with a separate, discrete end in relation to its situation, but in long, complicated "chains" so arranged that what is from one point of view an end to which means are applied is from another a means to some further end and vice versa; and so on through a great many links in both directions. Moreover, it is a necessary implication of the analytical starting point that any concrete act may constitute a point of intersection of a number of such chains so that the same act is at the same time in different respects a means to several different ends. Similarly a given end may be served by many different means. We often "kill two (or more) birds with one stone." Or, to change the figure, the total complex of means-end relationships is not to be thought of as similar to a large number of parallel threads but as a complicated web (if not a tangle). In talking of a single chain, what is done is to unravel from the web a single thread that passes through a large number of points where it is knotted with other threads. The knots are concrete acts. It is quite clear that such a chain is an analytical abstraction.

Thus, to illustrate. In the chain of progression from raw material to finished product in industry, mining is a means to securing coal, which in turn is a means to securing coke, a means to smelting iron ore to secure pig iron, a means to making steel, a means to making engine blocks, a means to making automobiles for transportation of various kinds. Each act in the chain is a means to a further end: thus smelting is a means to production of pig iron, while the coke is itself the end of an act lower down in the chain, immediately of the treatment of coal in a coke oven, more remotely of the mining of the coal. Moreover, at any stage in the process other means are needed for the immediate end than those having a place in this particular chain, thus to produce pig iron, besides coke, iron ore, limestone, all the complicated blast-furnace equipment and labor. Similarly the product at any one stage in the chain will probably enter into several future chains, thus steel may be used for automobile cylinder heads, other automobile parts, rails, railway equipment, structural steel, munitions or any one of a thousand things. The isolation of any particular chain involves abstracting from these crisscrossings of the many different chains. Generally the producer at an early stage in the process has knowledge of the ultimate uses to which the products of his stage will be put only in the most vague and general sense.

But, none the less, certain general propositions about such chains can be made. The first is that, in so far as ends are analytically independent elements in action at all, such chains must be "open," not "closed." That is, in following through the chain of means-end relationships in one direction—from means to an end, which is in turn a means to a further end, etc.—logical necessity leads sooner or later to an ultimate end, that is, one which cannot be regarded as a means to any further end according to the concept of logical action, *e.g.*, intrinsically. Similarly, followed in the reverse direction, from an end to a means, which is in turn an end for which other means are employed, etc., sooner or later elements[1] are encountered which must be regarded as ultimate

---

[1] It is most important to note that the reference here is not to concrete entities but to analytical categories. It is not necessary that it should be

means or conditions. This must be the case, for logical action, unless what appears to be an ultimate end is only, to the actor, an "experimental fact." But in that case logical action is taken to include the end element, which is contrary to the assumptions just stated.[1]

The second proposition that can be laid down about logical action in this sense concerns the relation of the ultimate ends of a plurality of chains to each other. The proposition is that, granting the initial assumption that ends are an independent element in action, the ultimate ends of different chains cannot be related to each other at random but must to a significant extent constitute a coherent system. For if ends are a factor at all it must, empirically, make a difference which of two alternative ends is pursued. To pursue one of two alternative ends involves choice between them. But if the relation between these two ends is purely random there can be no choice, or rather the choice itself must be random, a result of chance. As has been noted[2] the concept of randomness in general has no meaning, except that it is the very definition of "meaninglessness." Randomness, to make sense, must be relative to something determinate. But in terms of the alternatives offered by the concept of logical action, if the determinate element is not found in the element of ends it must be in that of conditions or means-end relationships, ultimately these conditions.[3] That is to say that in so far as the relations of ends to each other are merely random they *cannot* make a difference.[4] So again there emerges a dilemma: either the implications of the

---

possible to identify any concrete state of affairs which is wholly an end in itself and in no sense a means to a further end. The great majority of concrete states of affairs and actions involve both aspects, though in greatly varying proportions. The isolation of ultimate ends and ultimate means is a matter of analytical logic, not a classification of concrete entities which are involved in action.

[1] See above p. 228.

[2] Chap. II, p. 61.

[3] As applied to *choice* of ends since means-end relations follow logically from such choices and cannot become determinative of them without obliterating the concept of ultimate ends.

[4] Or, to introduce the concept of choice is merely to argue in a circle, because the only determinate element of the system *is* the conditions. This is another way of saying that the subjective aspect of action becomes epiphenomenal, is not analytically independent.

analytical concept of logical action are accepted, including the systematic relation of ends to each other, or the assumptions are again violated. In other words, if the concept of logical action be accepted at all the meaning of rationality must be extended from the relations of means to a single given end, to include an element of the choice between alternative ends.

This can mean nothing but that there are knowable relations between the ends, that is that they form part of the same teleologically meaningful system. Then in so far as action is logical in this sense the total action system of an individual must be related in some degree to a coherent system of ultimate ends. The question of the relations of the ends of different individuals to each other in a social system will be taken up presently.

Before that, however, the question of the possible internal differentiation of the intrinsic[1] means-end chain must be dealt with. In this connection three things can be said about Pareto. First, he definitely took the type of action usually called "economic" as at least in part the methodological model for his logical action. Second, he recognized that the economic did not exhaust the category of logical action, but that the "logical" was the broader of the two.[2] Finally, third, he did not give any systematic account of the relation of the other logical elements to the economic. He only enumerated them as "artistic and scientific works and—a certain number of military, political and juridical operations, etc."[3] This enumeration stands in striking contrast to his serious attempt to establish systematic analytical relations between logical action in general and nonlogical, and between the different elements of the nonlogical. Whence this omission?

It seems to come from the fact that he formulated his analysis in terms of isolated unit acts without reference to their interrelations in systems of action, which was, indeed, sufficient for his purpose. For so long as only the isolated unit act is considered, the logical element is, as it were, all of a piece. That is, there is only the simple relation of a single end to the relevant means.

---

[1] "Intrinsic" is here, in the sense set forth above, meant as involving a relation of cause and effect or mutual interdependence demonstrable by empirical science.

[2] It is also possible that the elements involved in the concept of logical action do not exhaust the economic.

[3] *Traité*, 152.

Once, however, consideration is extended to systems of action, two important lines of distinction emerge.

After all, logical action must necessarily involve this simple relation of means to a single end, since it is the elementary "atom" out of which is built the whole structure of systems of action. In its application to the rational aspect of the elementary atom this may be called the technological element of action or, better for general purposes, of the intrinsic means-end relationship. But to stop here means precisely an objectionably "atomistic" account of the matter from a structural point of view—and this is where Pareto in his explicit treatment of this question does stop. He proceeded to develop a system of elements.

But as soon as a system of action is considered a complication is introduced. The existence of a plurality of ends implies that certain means are potential means to more than one end. Then in so far as these means are scarce, relative to their potential uses, the actor is faced with a different order of problem from that of maximizing technological efficiency, choosing the means "best adapted" to a single given end. This problem is that of the allocation of scarce means as between their various potential uses. This is what may most usefully be referred to as the specifically economic element of logical action.[1] It must be borne in mind that in every concrete economic action a technological element is by definition involved.

The simplest way to illustrate this is in terms of individual expenditure. In weighing the question of ways and means to achieve a given end the individual will have to keep at least two sets of considerations in mind: on the one hand, what is usually referred to as the "efficiency" of a given procedure; on the other

[1] On this whole problem see Talcott Parsons, "Some Reflections on the Nature and Significance of Economics," *Quarterly Journal of Economics*, May, 1934. This treatment cannot claim to exhaust a subtle question. It gives only a very general formulation of the aspect of the distinction which is of primary significance in the present context. There is a sense in which technological efficiency involves "economy," as, for instance, a measure of the efficiency of a water turbine generator is the percentage of kinetic energy of falling water that it converts into usable electric power. Here it is a question of economizing energy in the physical sense. But this is not an economic problem until the cost in the specific economic sense of the particular mode of obtaining power enters in. Furthermore the concept of technology used here involves other than physical energy measures of efficiency. The latter is not, for instance, applicable to the technology of mystical contemplation.

hand, its "cost." Thus in building a house the question of what
kind of heating plant is to be installed will come up. There are
available, we may assume, electricity, gas, oil and coal as sources
of heat. The first two are, in relation to action the most efficient,
in that they give the most satisfactory results with least trouble
to the operator. But, at least in New England, they are apt to be
considerably more expensive than the others, especially coal.
Hence many people who would like to have them, refrain on this
account. In these terms the cost is the sacrifice of other utilities
which the extra money could have bought, assuming that the
individual's money resources are limited. This is what many
economists refer to as opportunity cost. Considerations of cost
may thus often be in conflict with those of technological efficiency;[1] we may find it necessary to choose the less efficient way
of doing a thing because it is the cheaper.

The money cost of goods and services purchasable on a market
is, of course, not an ultimate datum for economics, but itself
reflects, more or less accurately, the conditions of relative scarcity
in relation to demand in the society at large. Pricing is society's
principal instrument of economizing, of insuring that scarce
resources will not be applied wholesale to the least important
uses.

The essence of the matter is, in the present context, that the
introduction of economic considerations in addition to technological involves the relation not only of the particular unit act,
but of any one chain in which it can be placed, to the broader
web of chains that are interwoven with this one. The concept of
the economic is framed with particular reference to the importance of other chains in the "upward" direction, that is in the
direction of ultimate ends.[2]

This exhausts the analysis of logical action so long as attention
is confined to an analytically isolated individual. This individual

---

[1] In this context "technological" is meant with reference to action.
Efficiency, then, refers, from the actor's point of view, to the attainment of
an end with a minimum of "sacrifices," or doing a minimum of things the
actor would not otherwise do but for the sake of the end. It is not identical
with mechanical efficiency, for instance.

[2] On the relation of technological and economic categories see O. H.
Taylor, "Economic Theory and Certain Non-economic Elements in Social
Life" in *Explorations in Economics, Essays in Honor of F. W. Taussig*,
pp. 380 *ff.*

necessarily faces not only technological but also economic problems, since in order to act rationally he must allocate not only the resources of his environment but also his own "powers." This is what has been called "Crusoe economics." But under social conditions the importance of the economic aspect is enormously increased by two facts: One is that there is a problem of allocation of resources not only as between different ends of the same individual, but also as between those of different individuals. The other is that the resources available as seen from the point of view of any one individual include not only his own powers and the nonhuman environment but also the potential services of others. Thus among the means to anyone's ends are the actions of others. Both these elements become important through the division of labor and the consequent process of exchange.[1]

In the first place, in any society there must obviously be some mechanism by which are settled the relative claims of different individuals to command over disposable scarce nonhuman resources. There are two basic alternatives as to the kind of process by which these claims may conceivably be adjusted. Either the settlement may be simply a resultant of each trying to realize his own ends under the conditions given, or there may be some principle imposed and enforced from outside the competitive process itself which brings about a relatively stable situation in this respect.[2] But those who try to push the first alternative through as a complete solution must face a problem. As such it gives no explanation of why there should be any limitation on the means by which any one individual or group can push his claims to command over resources at the expense of others' claims. For in the absence of such limitation there is nothing to prevent the wholesale employment of a very important class of such means which may be summed up as coercive.

In so far as any one individual or group has control over elements of the situation in which another acts, in respects such as to affect the realization of the other's ends, he can use this control in such a way as to affect the other's position. Above all by threatening to alter the situation to the disadvantage of the other, he can make it "worth while" for the latter to do what

[1] And organization of production.
[2] These two are, of course, elements. There is no bar to their both being involved in the same concrete situation.

he wants, in order to avoid the threatened alterations, or "sanctions." It can easily be shown and has been shown in classic form by Hobbes[1] that this potential use of coercion would result in a conflict which in the absence of constraining forces would degenerate into a "war of all against all," the reign of force and fraud. Hence on this basis in so far as ends are real factors in action, there must be some control over the exercise by some individuals of coercive power over others, if there is to be social order[2] at all.

Essentially the same situation is revealed in even more drastic form where individuals are thought of directly as means to each other's ends instead of as competing claimants for control over impersonal resources. Indeed this is the situation that Hobbes had primarily in mind and it is the more urgent of the two.[3]

Thus when the relations of a plurality of individuals in a system of action are taken into account, the fact of the potential conflict of ends of different individuals means that the economic process of allocation becomes subject to the influence of an extraneous factor not included in the formulation of the original concept of the economic element of action above. This arises from the fact that the total complex of relevant wants (or ends does not constitute a single controlling agency as is the case with the individual. Hence on this level the problem is not merely one of allocation as such but also of determining certain of the conditions under which allocation is to take place. For an economic process to take place within a society there must be some mechanism by which a relatively stable settlement of the power relationships between individuals and groups is attained.

It is only within such a relatively stable framework of control or order that what is generally referred to as an economic system can grow up. But once such a framework exists, there is an opportunity for an extended development of the division of labor. Above all by limitations on the means by which it is possible to gain the other party's assent to a transaction, stable and regular processes of exchange go on. This process is accompanied by the

[1] Chap. III, p. 90.
[2] In the normative sense. But the fact is that society as empirically known to us has such an element of normative order as one of its most prominent distinguishing features. Hence the problem, what is the source of this order?
[3] All this has been sufficiently discussed in Chap. III.

development of techniques facilitating the processes of exchange, above all money, banking and credit. But it must never be forgotten as it so frequently has been by economists that all this is dependent on the existence of a set of controlling conditions the alteration of which may have immensely important consequences for the concrete processes. It is one of Pareto's greatest merits, as will be shown in the next chapter, not to have overlooked these considerations but to have made very important use of them.

A good illustration of the importance of such elements of order is the role of the one-price system. Most Americans simply take for granted that the great majority of goods they consider purchasing are offered, so far as the context of a given transaction is concerned, at a given set price, and that all the purchaser has to do is to decide whether he will or will not purchase, or how much, at that price. But this is an element of order which is by no means inherent in the relations of buyers and sellers as such, as anyone with experience in countries where, in certain fields at least, the system does not prevail will know. Thus an Italian cabdriver will[1] often bargain most ferociously and the poor American, used to paying what stands on the meter, will be quite lost and very often pay an exorbitant fee simply to extricate himself as quickly as possible from a difficult situation. The one-price system thus has the effect of protecting the purchaser from exploitation of his immediate necessities, ignorance or ineptitude in bargaining with a shrewd and unscrupulous seller. The talents of the latter, while by no means useless in our society, must be exercised in other spheres, somewhat removed from the final transaction involved in the purchase of consumers' goods.

All these consequences have been developed without raising the question of the relation of the ultimate-end systems of different individuals in the same society to each other. On this point again there are two alternative fundamental positions.[2] One is that these value systems vary in content at random relative to the external conditions.[3] This is the postulate with which Hobbes

[1] Perhaps Mussolini has changed all this.

[2] In principle, of course. We are developing abstract cases analogous to Pareto's abstract societies.

[3] Defined, as by Hobbes, as a system involving only utilitarian elements of action.

started and his experience with it is very instructive—in order to prevent relapse into a "war of all against all" it is necessary that there should be a controlling agency. And for the postulate to be rigorously upheld this agency must stand *outside* the social system in question. Hobbes' way of accounting for the origin of the agency, in his thought the sovereign, is really to violate his postulate, to posit a momentary identity of interest—in security —from which the social contract is derived.

The other position is to suppose a significant degree of integration of ultimate ends into a *common* system.[1] A great deal will have to be said throughout the remainder of the book about the ramifications and implications of this possibility. Suffice it to say here that it opens the way to an interpretation of the basis of order in a society which is in a sense "immanent," founded in the character of the society itself. Whether this element is to have empirical importance is essentially a question of fact and cannot be answered in terms of the present abstract analysis alone.

The argument may, then, be summed up as follows: Working out the implications of Pareto's conception of logical action in its application to the structure of social systems of action leads to a more complicated scheme than has thus far been encountered or than any atomistic theory could develop. Instead of single isolated unit acts it is necessary to think in terms of complicated webbed chains of means-end relationships. These may, however, be analyzed with reference to a limited number of major elements.

In the first place, it is a logical necessity that such chains, if ends are to constitute an analytically significant factor in action at all, must fall into three sectors: ultimate ends, ultimate conditions and means and an intermediate sector, the elements of which are both means and ends according to the point of view, means when seen from "above"—from end to means—and ends when seen from "below"—from means to end.

Secondly, with regard to the relation of ultimate ends to each other, the problem arises on three different levels of the extensiveness of systems. With regard to a single means-end chain there is no problem. When, however, the total action system of an individual is taken into account the economic necessity of allocating

[1] The present argument is concerned only with the limiting case at the pole of "perfect integration."

scarce resources as between alternative uses implies that if the action system is to be logical at all the ultimate ends must be integrated in so far into a coherent system. Randomness of ultimate ends cannot exist in a concrete system of action to which the concept of logical action in this sense[1] is applicable.

Third, on the social level of a system involving a plurality of individuals the same problem arises again. It is logically possible on the assumption of an outside controlling agency for there to be no integration of these individual systems in a common system, but failing this "*deus ex machina*,"[2] such integration is also a logical necessity of a self-contained system of logical action.

Essentially the same considerations, seen from a somewhat different point of view, lead to a threefold subdivision of the intermediate sector of the means-end chain. First there is, so far as only a single immediate end is involved, a technological element. But the consideration of the possible applicability of the same scarce means to a plurality of alternative ends introduces a second, an economic, element. In so far as logical action is economic in this sense, it has for its immediate ends two—the acquisition of control over such scarce means and their rational allocation.

But on a social level particularly the first of these,[3] the "acquisitive" aspect of economic action involves a third element. Where others are concerned coercion is a potential means to the desired control, which is not included in the economic concept as such.[4]

---

[1] This is one of the fundamental logical defects of the utilitarian theory. The point is ably developed by R. W. Souter, *Prolegomena to Relativity Economics*.

[2] It is not altogether unreasonable to refer to Hobbes' social theory as "social deism." The logical pattern is essentially the same with the sovereign in the role of god.

[3] What is, when seen from the point of view of a given individual, acquisition, becomes, from the point of view of a collectivity, allocation.

[4] The basis for this statement needs some further clarification. The economic concept has been formulated with reference to the problem of the allocation of scarce resources as between the different ends of a single individual. The question is that of the extension of these considerations to a society involving a plurality of individuals.

In the first place, the assumption of rationality is made throughout; each actor is assumed to be in possession of knowledge adequate to the situation and any possible actions. Thus any actor A can seek to gain his own ends, among other ways, by attempting to influence the action of another actor B

It also has a similar double aspect—the exercise of coercive power as a means and its acquisition as an immediate end. Hence it is possible to speak of three classes of immediate or proximate ends falling within the intermediate sector—the achievement of technological efficiency, of control over wealth and over coercive power. Each may in turn, concretely, serve as a means to the other two. The element of coercive power may be called the "political."[1]

But while each may serve as a means to the other they stand in a kind of hierarchical relationship to each other—each, with a widening of the range of conditions involved, becoming a condition of the attainment of the one before it. Thus so long as other ends are not involved technological ends are self-sufficient. But as soon as other uses begin to compete for the potential means to a technological end, their "economy" comes to be a necessary condition of the rationality of their employment for the

---

in the direction in which he wishes the action to go. On the rational basis assumed, this can be done in one of two different ways: A can use what control he possesses over the situation in which B must act to offer, conditionally on B's doing something he wants, to alter B's situation in a way which he knows will be advantageous to B. Or, on the other hand, he can use his control to threaten, conditionally on B's failing to do what he wants, to use his control to alter B's situation to B's disadvantage. In either event B is left to take his choice of the alternatives open as he sees fit. The first mode of influencing the action of others is one to which essentially the same analysis applies as to the allocation of individual resources; it may hence be called economic exchange. But for it to be at all generalized in a social system, there must be some way of limiting resort to the second method, coercion, since this is very generally, in the immediate situation, the easier, hence from A's point of view, the more efficient method. Fraud, which plays a very large part in concrete systems of action, does not belong in the present analytical context because it is only possible in so far as B's knowledge is not adequate to the situation. It is evident, however, that for there to be a high development concretely of economic exchange it also must be held in check. Knowledge which is adequate on the assumption that there will be no attempt on A's part to perpetrate fraud on B, becomes inadequate when the possibility of fraud enters in. There are various other possible modes of influencing the action of others but they are too complex to take up here.

[1] It can scarcely be said that the political element in this sense is as definitely the agreed central subject matter of political science as the economic element as above defined is of economics. The power element, however, is certainly one of the central strands running through political thought and is far more prominent there than in any other social science. The usage is hence not altogether without a basis in precedent.

end in question. The wider context in a sense subordinates the technological element of efficiency to the economic. Similarly "economy" in relation to other persons involves the settlement of the power relations to them. Until these are settled it is irrational to concern oneself with their potential services in an economic context alone.

THE THEORY OF SOCIAL UTILITY

In this long digression it may appear that Pareto has been forgotten, but such is not the case. It has seemed necessary to build up this rather elaborate scheme in order to provide a basis for the interpretation of what is in the context of this study the most interesting theoretical portion of his work, the theory of social utility. It is true that he did not push his own analytical scheme in this direction to such lengths of elaboration as these. But the thesis will be maintained that the way in which he treats the problem of social utility can only be properly understood if it is realized that it involves, seen from a somewhat different point of view, essentially the scheme just outlined.

The filiation of this theory from the problems of economic theory is very clear indeed. In the theory of social utility Pareto may be said to be attempting to work out the sociological equivalent of the economic doctrine of maximum satisfaction which has already been discussed in connection with Marshall. It is, it will be recalled, the proposition that under certain carefully defined conditions the pursuit by each individual of his own economic self-interest (that is, his attempt to maximize the means to satisfaction of his own ends) will lead to the maximum possible satisfaction of all other individuals in the same collectivity. The principal conditions are: rationality of action, mobility of resources, independence of wants of the processes of their satisfaction, competition and substantial equivalence in exchange possible only through the elimination of force and fraud and other milder forms of coercion, perhaps even of certain forms of the exercise of power short of coercion.[1]

Starting from this point Pareto proceeds by four steps to the climax of his argument. The first two concern maxima of utility in the context of economics, the last two in sociology. The nature

---

[1] The issue is too involved to go into here. Fortunately its solution does not affect the present argument.

of the distinction is one of the most important questions to be discussed. Utility in the economic context he calls "ophelimity," a term he himself coined.[1] It will be convenient to conform to his usage.

Pareto says:

In political economy we can define a state of equilibrium such that each individual obtains a maximum of ophelimity. The conditions may be so given that this equilibrium is perfectly determinate. If, however, we drop certain of these conditions this clear determinateness is lost and equilibrium will be possible at an infinity of different points for which maxima of utility for individuals are reached. In the first case the only changes possible are those which lead toward the determinate point of equilibrium; in the second other changes become possible as well. The latter are of two definitely different kinds. In the first type, which we will call P, changes are of such a character that in acting in the interest of some individuals they necessarily injure others. In the second type, which we will call Q, changes are such that they act in the interest of or to the detriment of all the individuals without exception.[2]

At a point Q in a process of change it may be possible for the change to proceed in a given direction further with an increase in ophelimity to *each* member of the collectivity. *Such* a change can be "justified" on purely economic grounds because no question of the quantitative comparison of the ophelimities of different individuals arises. On the other hand, such a change will eventually reach a limit P beyond which any further change in the same direction would increase the ophelimity of some but at the expense of others. Regardless[3] of the numbers involved on either side "it is necessary in order to decide whether to halt or to continue to have recourse to considerations foreign to economics, that is to say, it is necessary to decide in terms of considerations of *social* utility, ethical or other, *which* individuals the decision should go in the interest of, and which should be sacrificed. From the purely economic point of view once the collectivity has arrived at a point P it should stop." This point Pareto calls a maximum of ophelimity *for* a collectivity; it may be paraphrased, for the *members* of the collectivity taken *distributively*.

[1] *Traité*, 2128.
[2] *Ibid.*, 2182.
[3] *Ibid.*, 2129.

Now "if a collectivity could be considered as a person it would have a maximum of ophelimity as a person does; that is to say there would be points where the ophelimity *of* the collectivity [*as a unit*] would be maximized."[1] But such a maximum of *ophelimity of* a collectivity does not exist because among other reasons the ophelimities of different individuals are heterogenous quantities which cannot be compared. It is only because a maximum *for* the collectivity does not involve such comparison that it has a meaning for *economics*.

What does all this mean? Surely that for Pareto the economic level of analysis is concerned only with the processes of acquisition and allocation of means to given *individual* ends. So long as a given change affects all individuals in the same direction whether its effect[2] on the collectivity is to increase or decrease total ophelimity may be determined in purely economic terms. But as soon as this ceases to be true so that a comparison of the ophelimities of different individuals becomes necessary to arrive at a judgment of net effect, extra-economic considerations must be invoked, those of social utility. Note that Pareto does *not* say that the comparison cannot be made, but that it cannot be made in economic terms. It is ophelimities not utilities which are heterogeneous as such. On the technological level no problem of comparison of ends arises at all. On the economic it does arise, but economic considerations alone do not justify going beyond the individual's own system of ends to compare it with others. This tallies exactly with the preceding analysis.

Pareto proceeds now[3] to extend his analysis to the broader field of "sociology." Here his main emphasis is laid on the fact that certain changes do affect the interests of different groups of individuals in different directions. And such differences of treatment are sanctioned by the acts of public authority and otherwise. The *effect* of such acts is "for better or worse" to compare all the utilities of individuals of which the authority has knowledge. "In short it accomplishes roughly the operation pure economics performs rigorously when by means of certain coeffi-

---

[1] *Ibid.*, 2130.

[2] In the sense of whether the change means a net increase or decrease of ophelimity for the collectivity. This cannot be given an absolute or percentage *numerical* value without additional assumptions which would involve comparison of the ophelimities of different individuals.

[3] *Traité*, 2131.

cients it renders homogeneous, quantities which are heterogeneous."[1] He continues:

> In pure economics it is not possible to consider a collectivity as a single
> person; in sociology we may consider a collectivity *if not as a person at
> least as a unity.* The *ophelimity of* a collectivity does not exist, but we
> may in rigorous fashion conceive the *utility of* a collectivity. That is why
> in pure economics there is no danger of confusing the maximum of
> ophelimity *for* a collectivity with that *of* the collectivity, since the latter
> does not exist; while in sociology it is necessary to take great care not to
> confuse the maximum of *utility for* a collectivity with the maximum *of* a
> collectivity because both of them *do* exist.[2]

What, then, are these two maxima? What is their distinction
from the maxima of ophelimity and from each other? Finally
what are the theoretical implications of "both existing?"

To quote again: "When proletarians say that they do not wish
to have children who will serve no other purpose than to increase
the power and wealth of the governing classes, they are talking
about a problem of the maximum of utility *for* the collectivity."[3]
That is, the problem on this level is *distributive*, it is a matter of
settling the conflicting claims of different individuals and groups
within the community to goods which are for whatever reason
scarce—the more one has, the less there remains for others. In
every society there is such a distributive problem as between
the claims of different individuals and groups to attain their own
ends apart from or in conflict with those of others.

How does this differ from the distributive aspect of economics?
In that it involves more extensive considerations. Economic
theory in so far as it extends into the field of social relations
formulates only certain elements of these relations, those which
have to do with determining the rational allocation of purchasable
means. But this, as has been seen, is possible on the social level
only in so far as there is a relatively stable framework of social
order by which coercion is eliminated. This framework is not
primarily dependent on economic factors. As far as it concerns
the present argument the *utility for* a collectivity differs from the
corresponding ophelimity precisely in that the distributive aspect
of this framework is brought into the picture—it is a matter of

[1] *Ibid.*
[2] *Ibid.*, 2133. Italics mine.
[3] *Ibid.*, 2134.

settling the distributive relations of individuals *in general*, not merely in their economic aspect. And above all this involves not merely the distribution of wealth, but also of *power*. Without such a relatively determinate distribution there can be no social system.

Pareto says further, "We should conclude, not that it is impossible to resolve problems which consider at the same time heterogeneous utilities, but that to deal with these heterogeneous utilities it is necessary to adopt a hypothesis which renders them comparable."[1] Pareto here seems to consider together two aspects of the problem which it is important to distinguish. Here he seems to be concerned primarily with public policy, on what assumptions it is possible to decide which of two alternative measures will contribute more to the total utility *for* the collectivity. The answer is that this depends on what is the distributive standard in terms of which the authority is operating. Only when it has introduced such a hypothesis does the problem become determinate. But such a hypothesis is not based on experimental facts, for within the limits of the conditions of existence of the society there are no determinate facts in this sense. It is rather a matter of the ultimate ends of the authority which for the observer are arbitrary. "We have no other criterion than sentiment."[2]

But this "virtual" aspect is not the whole story, nor even the most important part of it for the present argument. For if this limitation on the possible "scientific" basis of public policy be granted it has a most important implication for the empirical character of the society concerned. It is not only that to judge a measure such a hypothesis is required, but in so far as (*a*) men's actions are guided by subjective ends and (*b*) their utilities, *i.e.*, their ends, are heterogeneous there must exist, in some form "enforced" if not perhaps "accepted," such a principle in terms of which their heterogeneous utilities are for practical purposes roughly reduced to a common denominator. That is, public policy cannot be wholly guided by science because men's actions in society, even when rational with reference to given ends, involve nonscientific considerations in determining the actually existing relations of these to each other. But whatever their source the

[1] *Ibid.*, 2137.
[2] *Ibid.*, 2135.

relations *do exist*, utilities *are* to an appreciable degree rendered homogeneous. Otherwise there could be no society.

Clearly, however, this is not all. The concept of the maximum of utility *of* a collectivity and its distinction from the one just discussed have not yet been accounted for. Pareto says, "In sociology we may consider a collectivity, if not as a person, *at least as a unity*."[1] What kind of a unity in addition to that involved in the maximum *for* a collectivity, for Pareto is quite insistent on the distinction?[2] The answer that is important in the present context[3] lies in a phrase which occurs in the French text of his work[4] in connection with the second of the two abstract types of society already discussed, which discussion follows directly on that of social utility.

It was, it will be remembered, a society "determined exclusively by logico-experimental reasoning."[5] Here he says, it will be recalled "The form of the society is not at all determined if the external circumstances are given. It is necessary in addi-

---

[1] *Ibid.*, 2133.

[2] Thus he says, "Even in cases where the utility of the individual is not in opposition to that of the collectivity the points of maximum in the two cases (*for* and *of*) generally do not coincide." *Ibid.*, 2138.

[3] Another sense in which the society constitutes a unity is in that its members are bound together under the same conditions of survival as a group. Anything like aggression from without or a natural catastrophe like drought, flood or earthquake affects them more or less as a unit. These considerations are undoubtedly important to Pareto's argument taken concretely. But on the analytical level of the present discussion they can be neglected since they lead to no new theoretical problems. They would be included in the ways in which any social group is limited in its variations by the conditions of its environment. Pareto's view of the status of these conditions relative to the determination of the "form" of the society has already been discussed in connection with his treatment of Social Darwinism and need not be repeated here. The other line of thought is the one which promises to bear theoretical fruit in the present context and hence it alone is followed up.

This unity on the level capable of analysis in terms of nonsubjective categories may well include a socially emergent element, ascribable to the association of individual human organisms in collectivities. The present argument is concerned only with that aspect of the "unity" of a collectivity which may be held, analytically, to be ascribable to value elements. In so far as this is the case, it is legitimate to speak of the values as being held "in common."

[4] See footnote 3, p. 222.

[5] *Traité*, 2141.

tion to indicate *the end which the society should pursue by means of logico-experimental reasoning.*[1] After his insistence on the distributive aspect of the problem of utility *for* a collectivity it cannot but be significant that he here speaks not of the "ends the *members* of a society [distributively] should pursue" but of "*the end* which *the society* should pursue." This is surely considering the collectivity as a *unity*, a unity in the sense that the society can be thought of as pursuing a single *common* end (or system of ends) and not merely discrete individual ends.

There seems to be no other possible explanation of what Pareto meant by this concept and the necessity of distinguishing it from the other. This second abstract society is, of course, not concrete human society, but that does not mean that it is empirically irrelevant. On the contrary, human society is held to be in a state intermediate between it and the other abstract type. It certainly follows that it must be Pareto's view that the "end which the society (as a unity) pursues" is an important *element in* concrete human society.

In the abstract rationalistic type of society, which Pareto is here discussing, the existence of such an end *of* a society has certain important implications for the ends of individuals. For, as used in this study, the concept end is a subjective category, it has reference to something in the state of mind of the actor. The only way in which such a concept as that of the end of a society can be given meaning in terms of this conceptual scheme is by the theorem that it is an end common to the members of the society. In such terms the different systems of ends of the different members are not only "rendered homogeneous" to a degree in the sense that principles of "distributive justice" are involved in the actual social order, but, in addition certain aspects of these individual systems may be said to be held in common by the members. In so far as this is true the end systems may be said to be integrated. That this is applicable to Pareto's abstract society seems to be a legitimate inference from these considerations and the fact that the subjective means-end schema is so central to his own analysis.

Of course it is clearly understood that "integration" in this complete sense applies only to the abstract society; in this as in other respects it is a limiting case. Certainly neither Pareto nor

[1] *Ibid.*, 2141. Italics mine.

the present author means to imply that concrete societies are in general even approximately perfectly integrated in this sense, or that their members are normally, the majority, conscious that there is any system of common ends. But whether this system be explicit or implicit, whether integration be closely or only very distantly approached, does not affect the theoretical importance of this theorem, any more than the fact that feathers fall slowly and irregularly affects the importance of the law governing the falling of bodies in a vacuum. A concrete example which comes relatively close to the experimental conditions of the theorem is that of the Calvinists of Geneva in Calvin's own time who might be said to be pursuing the common end of establishing the Kingdom of God on Earth. But this is unusual. Not only this case, but the general issue of the empirical relevance of the theorem will be discussed on various occasions later in the study.

Pareto's treatment really involves two different points in connection with the status of this element. First, like the distributive principle it cannot be "justified" by logico-experimental science. It is indeed along with the other the principal missing datum (to the actors) which accounts for why a "society based exclusively on reason *cannot* exist."[1] But, on the other hand, this is not a reason for depreciating its empirical importance. Indeed this is one of the most important applications of Pareto's principle that it is necessary to distinguish the (logico-experimental) truth of a "doctrine" (here, end) and its social utility, implying its causal importance.

With this argument there appears in Pareto's thought as an emergent phenomenon one of the most important versions of what may be called the sociologistic theorem, that society is a reality *sui generis;* it has properties not derivable from those of its constituent units by direct generalization. This takes the form here of the view that one of the central facts underlying the theorem is the existence of a *common end* (or *system* of ends) which disappears when individual actions are considered in isolation. It is no accident that this has only appeared where Pareto is concerned with general social systems of action and not in connection with the earlier analytical scheme. In the next section of the study, dealing with Durkheim,[2] there will be occasion to trace the

[1] *Ibid.*, 2143. Italics mine.
[2] Chaps. VIII–XI.

ramifications of this theorem in various forms and in considerable detail. Here the thesis may be anticipated that Durkheim eventually arrives at substantially the same version as Pareto and that it is the most nearly correct version.[1]

It is important to realize what is the main constructive principle of Pareto's theory of utility. The two types of maxima on the level of economic and of sociological analysis respectively are *not parallel* but are arranged in a *hierarchical* relation to each other. The principle of the hierarchy is that each new step involves a set of broader considerations than the last; it posits complexities of the system which are not relevant on the narrower analytical basis. What specifically defines each new step is *the inclusion of an additional fundamental structural element of the means-end analysis* as sketched above so that in the end is reached the conception of a complete social *system* of intrinsic means-end relationships at the rational pole, the whole of which is necessary to the understanding of a concrete society.

Thus no problem of utility is raised on the technological level since there is no comparison of ends involved. The problem first arises on the economic level but is here only distributive. The settlement of conflicting economic claims between individuals involves more than economic considerations because here economic considerations are subsidiary to political, those of coercive power, so that every economic distribution is possible only within a general framework of distributive justice. But all these distributive questions concern only the settlement of potential conflicts of individual claims to wealth and power without indicating the basis of unity on which the structure as a whole rests. This basis of unity Pareto finds in the last analysis to lie in the necessary existence of an "end the society pursues." That is, the ultimate ends of individual action systems are integrated to form a single *common system of ultimate ends* which is the culminating element of unity holding the whole structure together. Thus Pareto's analysis tallies at every point with the general outline of the intrinsic means-end relationship put forward above. Can such a correspondence be mere coincidence?

[1] As stated directly in terms of the action frame of reference. The social relationship schema, for instance, would require a different form of statement.

The Nonlogical Aspect of Social Systems

By this time the reader is likely to be manifesting a certain pardonable irritation. Is it not true that Pareto's central concern is with *nonlogical* action and the discussion has been running on for nearly twenty pages dealing apparently only with logical action? Is this not a case of *Hamlet* without Hamlet? If it stopped here it undoubtedly would be, but all this has been a necessary preliminary to a definitive interpretation of the structural significance of the distinction between logical and nonlogical action. This will now be attempted in an effort to show how the scheme just outlined is related to certain of the other elements with which Pareto deals.

The most favorable starting point is to recall his statement that "human society is in an intermediate state between the two types."[1] What does this imply? In order to answer the question it is necessary to consider another implication of the scheme developed from the conception of logical action. It was found, that is, that the analytical significance of the concept for present purposes rested essentially on the assumption that subjective ends constitute an effective factor in action[2]—only on this basis is it a tenable view that economics or any other science centering on logical action has explanatory significance.[3] This point of view implies that the concept of logical action not only need not refer to a class of concrete actions, even hypothetical, but that its abstractness may be of a peculiar kind. It may define a norm of what action, under certain assumptions *should* be.[4] Such a norm may be merely an ideal prescription, but it may also be relevant to the causal analysis of concrete human action. It is so relevant in so far as there is empirical evidence that men do, in fact, strive to act logically, to attain the norm. Then, however

---

[1] *Traité*, 2146.

[2] For Pareto's initial use of it as a criterion necessary to define the operation for arriving at the residues and derivations this assumption is not necessary.

[3] That is, involves analytically significant elements such that a change in their "values" will result in a change in the concrete phenomenon. In this use of the term there is no implication of the one-sided cause-and-effect relation which Pareto so effectively attacks.

[4] In the present context this does not necessarily carry any ethical implications even for the actor, and, of course, not for the observer. It may be a matter simply of efficiency.

far their action may concretely fall short of its full attainment, the norm itself may be considered to embody *one* indispensable structural element in the actual system of action and thus may have a part in determining the process leading to the outcome of action.

There are three logical possibilities of the general relation of a norm to the actual course of action. The first is the possibility that the mere existence of the norm, that is its recognition by the actor as binding, implies automatic conformity with it. The second is the opposite, that the norm is a mere manifestation, in the index sense, of the real forces governing action, but has no causal significance at all. Action is then an automatic process. Finally, there is the possibility that while the norm constitutes one structural element in the concrete action it is *only* one. There are obstacles and resistances[1] to its attainment which must be overcome and are, in fact, only partially overcome. Hence the failure of the actual course of action to correspond exactly with that prescribed by the norm is not proof that the latter is unimportant, but only that it is not alone important. The existence of this resistance and its (even partial) overcoming implies another element, "effort," which has no place in either of the other two views.[2]

It is scarcely to be doubted that unless the whole of the analysis of Pareto's work with which the discussion of this chapter has been concerned is to be thrown out, the third possibility must be imputed to him. The hierarchy of means-end relationships is a hierarchy of normative structures superposed on each other. But these normative structures do not exist by themselves but are significant to action only in relation to another set of resistant factors. This seems to be the most likely interpretation so far as they concern the present argument of the two abstract societies and the statement that human society is in a state intermediate between them. The second abstract society, including the "end which a society should pursue," formulates certain of the norma-

[1] There may also be other factors working in the same direction as the norm but independently of it.

[2] To anticipate: The first of these possibilities is, so long as the norm is a genuine independent variable and not dependent, that taken in general by idealistic theories, the second by positivistic and the third by the voluntaristic theory of action. These issues will be taken up explicitly in the final chapter of the study.

tive aspects of action-systems in abstraction from the resistant and other non-normative aspects. The sentiments and conditions of the first abstract society, on the other hand, constitute these non-normative factors as such. Only a combination of the two sets of elements gives a usable structural analysis of human society. Hence the intermediate state.

First a brief reference to the non-normative factors: They may conveniently be held to constitute the factors discussed above[1] as heredity and environment. Their effects may, of course, be studied from the objective point of view, but they are also relevant to the subjective point of view. Here, however, they may, in one relation appear as "reflections" of an external reality, as "facts" of the external world in so far as the subjective aspect is considered as a "theory." To the actor they are "given," they are independent of his subjective "sentiments."[2] This independence, on which all methodologists of positive science have laid stress, becomes, in the context of action, "resistance" to the "arbitrary" will of the actor. They are things he must take account of as necessary conditions of his action. It is obvious that an individual's own heredity falls into this category just as much as do the properties of the external environment. The subjective point of view is that of the ego[3] not of the concrete[4] biosocial individual.

In so far as it is this element or group of elements which constitute the state of mind underlying the residues, Pareto is quite right that its investigation is, in the first instance, the province

[1] Chaps. II–III.

[2] In so far, of course, as they are "correctly seen." In so far, on the other hand, as they are not, they resolve themselves to the subjective point of view into sources of ignorance and error.

[3] While the objective point of view tends strongly to take the concrete biopsychosocial individual as its unit and hence to become involved in the empiricist fallacy. See footnote 1, p. 45.

[4] A caution should be repeated on another aspect of this point. The *problem* here is precisely that of accounting for certain features of what is sometimes called the social environment. Features of his society of course form "facts" to any *concrete* individual acting *in society*. But both the "environment" and the "individual" of the discussion of this text are analytical abstractions. To treat them as concrete entities would be to beg the whole question. The point will be worked out in detail in connection with Durkheim, as it is one of the main sources of his difficulties. See especially Chap. X.

of psychology, at a still deeper level of biology and the sciences concerned with the nonhuman environment. But precisely in so far as the above interpretation of the direction Pareto's thought was taking—toward a voluntaristic[1] theory of action—is correct it precludes this from being an adequate total account of the state of mind or the sentiments. It is, on the contrary, of the very essence of the matter that action should in this connection be thought of as a resultant of these and the normative factors together. Once having determined the general status of the non-normative factors it will not be necessary to have any further specific concern with them.

It has been argued that the non-normative elements are related to action in two main ways: in so far as action is logical in providing the sources of the facts the actor takes account of; in the non-logical case in the role of drives to which the subjective aspect of action is irrelevant or at most important as a secondary manifestation.

The first type of influence is sufficiently exemplified in the way in which a mountain climber adapts himself to the nature of the terrain he is traversing at the time. He will go at a different gait according to the grade, the more steeply it goes up, in general, the more slowly he will go; he will use different techniques and take different precautions according to whether he is on rocks or on snow and ice. It is not maintained that no other factors are involved, for instance in slowing up on a steep grade the automatic physiological effect of the greater strain put on heart, lungs and muscles is involved, but in addition to this there is, as stated in terms of the action scheme, a process of taking account of the facts of the situation. For the second type of influence there are also innumerable examples. It is easiest to demonstrate this in cases where the effect is quite precisely known to science but not to the particular actor. For instance, it is well known that too rapid release of atmospheric pressure for workers on an underwater tunnel coming out of their high-pressure working chamber without going through gradual air-pressure change in an air lock, causes the very painful, sometimes fatal condition known as "the bends." It would be quite possible for an uniniti-

---

[1] Voluntaristic because as distinguished from both the positivistic and the idealistic alternatives it involves the element of effort as the mediating link between the normative and non-normative aspects of action systems.

ated visitor to such work to come right out without thinking and have to suffer the consequences. Had he known, or, if he had but had not forgotten, he would not have acted as he did. But equally the outcome of his action would have been different.

It is now necessary to go beyond the mere assertion that there are normative aspects of social systems of action, to attempt to distinguish various structurally relevant kinds of elements, and to indicate certain of their structural relations to each other, to the non-normative and to the distinction of logical and non-logical action. As involved in social systems of action, the web of intrinsic means-end chains, in so far as it is "integrated" culminates, at the ultimate end terminus of the chains, in part in a system of more or less common ultimate ends. But throughout the system, so far as it may be held to consist of intrinsic means-end chains, action may be thought of as oriented toward, and to a greater or less degree attaining, a norm of rationality in the adaptation of means to ends. Similarly in so far as the individual's action system is rationally integrated at all it is oriented to an integrated system of ultimate ends. The corresponding conception of a socially common system of ends may be held to stand in essentially the same general relation to concrete action. It formulates a state of affairs which the members of the society, so far as their own end systems are integrated with the socially common one, may be considered to deem desirable, and thus orient their action toward. In both the individual and the social cases even the clear logically precise formulation of a system of ends, to say nothing of its actual attainment, must be thought of as a limiting type. In a "completely rationally integrated society," which it may be inferred Pareto's second abstract society either is or, according to his statements about it, might be, there would be complete integration of the ends of individuals with the common system, and precision in the formulation of the ends themselves. The society to which the theorem of maximum satisfaction in economics would apply without qualification is of this type, though not the only possible example as it involves a particular kind of system of ultimate ends.[1]

Deviation from this abstract type is, then, possible in at least two different respects. On the one hand, the society may be imperfectly integrated in that the systems of ultimate ends of the

---

[1] See Taylor, *op. cit.* and Löwe, *Economics and Sociology.*

various individuals are not integrated with each other; there is conflict. Deviation in this direction, so long as individual rationality is not at issue, leads in the direction of the utilitarian type of system, with the consequence already discussed at length of the tendency for a struggle for power to develop. The actual struggle for power, so far as it may be interpreted on a rational level as a means to the individual's own ends with a clear realization of what he wants and what he is doing, may be interpreted as placing the actual system in an intermediate position between the rationally integrated and the utilitarian types. The type of clash of interest groups which is found in the attempt to influence legislation by lobbying is the kind of phenomenon which fits into this context.

On the other hand, a second kind of deviation is equally important. As far as the system of ultimate ends is concerned this touches the failure of the ultimate-end systems of individuals to receive any precise formulation at all, even sufficiently precise to bring conflicts out clearly. Whatever ultimate ends may be observable must, in this case, be interpreted as manifestations of the sentiments which Pareto was continually describing as vague and indeterminate. These sentiments, so far as they involve normative elements may be called "value attitudes" to distinguish them specifically from those in which the non-normative element predominates. Such sentiments as those in favor of "freedom," "justice" and the like belong in this category, since it is notorious (and Pareto further demonstrates it beyond doubt) that as used, even in the works of sophisticated intellectuals, they are far from attaining a high degree of precision. Nevertheless such relatively vague and imprecise value attitudes are capable of general description and classification into broad types, and can hence serve as variables. The distinctions between such classes becomes clearer the more they are seen in terms of a broad comparative perspective. This proposition will be clearly exemplified in the discussion of Weber's comparative sociology of religion below. But even where deviation of this sort is clearly demonstrable, as it generally is to a high degree, the rationally integrated type may be considered to have a normative relevance to the concrete system in so far as the value attitudes really involved will, if "rationalized," lead actors in the direction of such a system of ultimate ends as a conscious and specific norm. The danger of hypostatizing such a rationalized system is, however, so great that much caution is needed in employing the conception.

Perhaps the most essential point just now is to realize that the normative aspect of concrete action systems is not exhausted by the extent to which it is possible to demonstrate the existence of clearly formulated, precise ultimate ends and systems of them. This is no more true than the similar thesis that the role of knowledge is limited to the situations where it is precise and completely adequate. In general, the conception of a rationalized system of ultimate ends is less important empirically, except as a methodological device for bringing out certain theoretical consequences, than is that of the vaguer value attitudes.

A further differentiation may now be made in the "ultimate value" complex. Very early in his work, it will be remembered,[1] Pareto distinguished between real and imaginary ends. A real end is one falling "within the domain of observation and experience," an imaginary end one falling outside this domain. An imaginary end is by definition a state of affairs which in some respects at least is not observable. Hence, since the objective end cannot be determined when the subjective end is imaginary in this sense, in so far as imaginary ends play a part, the two cannot correspond and action is, by Pareto's criterion, to that extent nonlogical.

It is clear that the ultimate ends of intrinsic means-end chains must be, in this sense, real or, as seems preferable for purposes of this study, "empirical" ends.[2] For only in so far as an objective end is definitely determinable, is it possible to apply either of Pareto's criteria of logical action, that the objective and subjective ends correspond, or that the operations are logically united to their end. If the end is transcendental, one cannot say that the actor is in error as to the putative appropriateness of

[1] *Traité*, 151.

[2] Pareto's contrast between real and imaginary might be confusing by suggesting, what is clearly not his meaning, that the effectiveness of the latter as a subjective end is imaginary. Both types may be real in this sense. The line of distinction Pareto has in mind is not this, but is based on the criterion whether or not the observer can state a determinate objective end to compare with the subjective. "Empirical" seems adequately to express the case where this is possible, while "transcendental" is the word commonly used to denote the realm outside the domain of empirical observation. To avoid this confusion it seems best, for present purposes, to replace Pareto's terms by the terms empirical and transcendental.

means to his end, but only that there is no criterion for determining, logico-experimentally, whether the means are appropriate or not. Thus if the end be to drive, by automobile, from Boston to New York, there are objective criteria to determine what is the "right" road; it may be safely predicted that if the driver starts northeast on the road to Portland and keeps going in the same direction he will not arrive in New York. But if the end is "eternal salvation" it is not possible to determine whether the operations the actor says are leading him toward his end, such as prayer, good works and the like, actually do, since the state of being "saved" is not capable of empirical observation. In such a case the observer is limited to two things: (1) he can note that the actor says he is or will be "saved" and (2) that people who make statements of this character are, in respects which are observable, in a certain kind of state. But whether he has or has not "really" attained his end is, scientifically speaking, a meaningless question in the strict sense. It is quite impossible either to deny or to affirm.

If it be admitted that a category of imaginary or transcendental ends is empirically important, as Pareto quite definitely does[1] the question then arises, what is the nature of their relation to means, and in particular to the web of intrinsic means-end chains which has occupied so much of this discussion. There seem to be two logical possibilities. First, a given transcendental end, like eternal salvation, may be held by the actor to imply one or more ultimate empirical ends as necessary means to it. This may be, in a limiting case, a completely logical deduction from the philosophical system in terms of which the transcendental end is conceived, or it may, in varying modes and degrees, depart from the canons of strict logic. But however that may be, the "theory" cannot be entirely logico-experimental since one element at least, the transcendental end itself, is not observable, even after the action. Hence not only, as in the case of an ultimate empirical end, is the end itself given, but the link between the last empirical link in the means-end chain and the ultimate

[1] In his discussion of ideal ends (*ibid.*, 1869 *ff.*, especially 1870–1871) Pareto, contrary to his definition, seems to confuse two things under the heading "imaginary ends": (1) ends impossible of realization because of insurmountable obstacles the actor does not properly evaluate and (2) ends the realization of which cannot be verified. Only the latter are here treated as transcendental ends.

transcendental end is nonlogical, since a scientifically verifiable theory can establish an intrinsic relation only between entities both of which are observable.

Secondly, a transcendental end may be pursued directly without the intervention of an empirical end and an intrinsic means-end chain leading up to it. In so far the means-end relation cannot, by definition, be intrinsically rational. The question then arises whether it is merely arbitrary or there is a selective standard of the choice of means involved. In the previous discussion[1] it has already been suggested that there is at least one alternative selective standard, what has been called the symbolic. The term, the "symbolic means-end relationship" will be used wherever the *relation*[2] of means and ends can conveniently be interpreted by the observer as involving a standard of selection of means according to "symbolic appropriateness," that is, a standard of the order of the relation of symbol and meaning, not of cause and effect. The symbolic relation need not be explicitly conscious to the actor for this analytical concept to be applicable. There are probably several subtypes of the symbolic means-end relationship, but one will be of predominant importance in the subsequent discussion of this study, the ritual. Ritual involves, as Durkheim defined it[3] (and his definition will be accepted here) in addition to the role of symbolism, the criterion that it is action in relation to sacred[4] things. It may hence be defined as a manipulation of symbols, in some respects regarded as sacred, which operations are held subjectively to be appropriate means to a specific end. It does not follow that ritual means are applicable only to transcendental ends. Indeed the category of magic will be defined below[5] as the application of ritual means to empirical ends, thus distinguishing magical from religious ritual.[6] Further

[1] Chap. V, p. 210.

[2] Note that it is the means-end *relationship* which is symbolic. Symbols may often be efficient intrinsic means to an end, as linguistic symbols for communication of meaning.

[3] See Chap. XI, p. 429.

[4] Since it will not be of importance in the present context it is best to postpone explicit discussion of the concept "sacred" till it is taken up in connection with Durkheim (Chap. XI, pp. 411, 414 *ff.*).

[5] See Chap. XI, p. 432.

[6] A good example of magical ritual is the one cited above, of the Greek sailors performing sacrifices to Poseidon as a means of insuring good weather for a voyage. Good weather is quite definitely an empirically observable

specific analysis of the role of ritual will be postponed to the discussion of Durkheim but, for the present, a few general remarks about its relation to Pareto will suffice.

In so far as either its ends are transcendental or the means-end relationship involved is symbolic, or both, action must, according to Pareto's criteria, be nonlogical. But the reason is somewhat different from that in action involving the play of instinct and other nonsubjective factors. There the action is adaptive, the organism does the "right thing" in the situation but without subjective motivation. In the sphere here under consideration such criteria will not apply. The subjective aspect is decisive, but the theories governing action are in this case nonscientific, not unscientific because entities and relationships are involved which are not verifiable, or observable in scientific terms. These are to be clearly distinguished from such as are erroneously observed, or from sophistic logic.

From the point of view of the actor such action falls into the means-end schema. From that of the scientific observer, however, it is best conceived in somewhat different terms. The sociologist, that is, must attempt to bring all the observable facts of his field in relation to empirical entities. In these terms, then, it may be said that action involving transcendental ends and ritual may be regarded for certain purposes as "expressions" (in *one* sense, manifestations) of ultimate value attitudes. That is, their relation to the causative factor is as symbolic modes of expression —they are related to what they express essentially in the way that linguistic symbols are to their meanings. This is perhaps one explanation of the tendency noted above[1] for ritual means to be included in the derivations which are; after all, elements of symbolic expression. There is every empirical reason to believe

---

state of affairs, but Poseidon himself is certainly a sacred entity, and the quality of sacredness pertains also, in all probability, to other features of the action. Moreover the actual operations probably have a symbolic aspect in at least two connections: (1) the sacrifice, the offer of food, is a symbol of good will calling for a reciprocation, (2) the action, given belief in Poseidon and his powers, is a symbolic expression of the sailors' attitudes, a desire for good weather. Only the first symbolic aspect is apt to be at all self-conscious to the actor. A typical religious ritual is the Catholic baptism. Its end is not empirical at all but to make the child eligible for salvation. Among the means used some, at least, are definitely sacred, as the holy water.

[1] Footnote 1, p. 209.

that among the value attitudes "expressed" in transcendental ends and in ritual[1] the common ultimate value attitudes which are also expressed in ultimate common empirical ends play a major part.

Thus from a consideration of the significance of a system of ultimate common ends there emerges, to be sure, the question of its rather complicated ramifications in relation to the intrinsic means-end chain. But in addition, a consideration of the implications of the normative character of the whole intrinsic chain including ultimate ends shows that the latter must be considered as the rationalized pole of a vaguer complex of elements which may be called value attitudes that are not, however, the resistant factors discussed above, but specifically *value*[2] factors. Ultimate ends, both empirical and transcendental, as well as ritual may be regarded as "expressions" in different ways of these value attitudes.[3]

In addition, the ends themselves fall into two categories. Pareto's "real" and "imaginary," the empirical and transcendental of this discussion, which stand in different relations to action. Only empirical ends can serve directly as the ultimate ends of an intrinsic system of means-ends relationships. In so far as transcendental ends are involved, another nonlogical element enters in. This in turn may involve as one alternative another mode of means-end relationship, the symbolic, which is characteristic of ritual action. All action in pursuit of transcendental ends as such, and by ritual means, may be regarded largely[4] as a mode

[1] Ritual acts do not appear to me to be the *only* important forms of symbolic expression of such attitudes, they are merely some of the ones involving a relatively clear-cut subjective means-end relationship. There are several others that are not in the same sense primarily significant as ways of achieving ends or differ otherwise. These will not be explicitly discussed until later. Nor is of course, the common system of value attitudes the only element of action manifested in *concrete* ritual actions.

[2] This term is applied here to the whole group of normative elements in the structure of action which emerge out of Pareto's original "state of mind."

[3] While value attitudes here are conceived as an independent variable in an analytical sense they stand in functional relations to other elements besides those so far discussed. A definite statement of these relations, even for purposes of this study, will not be attempted until Max Weber's treatment of religion has been considered. See Chap. XVII.

[4] Of course in *concrete* acts of predominantly ritual character there is no reason why other elements, above all the resistant elements, should not be involved.

of expression of ultimate value attitudes. Here can be seen the possible significance of the prominence of ritual in Pareto's concrete treatment.[1] It is not *only*[2] a manifestation of instincts and drives but also one of the principal forms of the expression in relation to action of ultimate value attitudes.[3]

It is now possible to settle the question of the line between logical and nonlogical action. If Pareto be followed in two main points—that logical action is a structurally significant element of action systems and that it is the logical relation of means and end which characterizes it—then there is a clearly distinguishable portion of the above scheme to which these criteria apply: it is *the intermediate sector of the intrinsic means-end chain.*

To take another statement of Pareto's: so far as action is "determined by a process of reasoning" and this process of reasoning or scientific theory is not merely a reflection of the real determinants, then the factors of heredity and environment, the "ultimate means and conditions," must be excluded. And from another point of view also they must be excluded since it turns out that in a different connection the same factors are the sources of ignorance and error, are hence in this connection also nonlogical factors. For nonlogical action as a structural element to overlap with logical, both categories including the same elements as criteria, is surely not permissible.

On the other hand, ultimate ends should equally be excluded. They, as has been seen, may be regarded as a manifestation of value attitudes which are also manifested in a variety of other ways, notably ritual and the pursuit of transcendental ends. Thus the value-attitude factor forms the nucleus of a complex which is best treated together, and is in fact largely so treated by Pareto, as nonlogical.

If any difficulty over the status of logical action in relation to nonlogical arises it may be ascribed to the fact that Pareto did

---

[1] A more extended discussion of ritual will be found in Chap. XI in connection with Durkheim's theory of religion.

[2] Pareto of course did not maintain that it was. It would be if the "instinct" interpretation of the statements, here demonstrated to be incorrect, were adequate.

[3] One further mode of the relation of the value element to action is highly important, the "institutional." Since Pareto does not make much of it I prefer to defer its explicit discussion until we deal with Durkheim below (see Chap. X).

not define the distinction in terms of systems of action. An isolated unit act can have only one end and that end must be either excluded or included. If it is included it is easy to slip over into the consideration under the rubric of logical action of the many problems connected with value attitudes, and that tends to leave only the factors of heredity and environment, omitting the subjective reference, as nonlogical elements. If, on the other hand, the original definition in terms of the character of the means-end relationship, be adhered to without the consideration of the wider action system, the ends as such tend to drop out of separate consideration to be assimilated to the means-end relationship with the results already repeatedly discussed.

So long as the wider context is kept in mind, however, the possible objection to Pareto's definition that it eliminates the role of ends and makes the whole subjective aspect of action a dependent variable disappears. For this to be true, however, logical action as a structural category must be thought of as one part of the whole chain, or web of chains. It can, for certain analytical purposes, be abstracted from the whole as an element or group of elements, but it is easy to fall into error if it is postulated to have, even hypothetically, independent concrete existence.[1] For this can only lead either to the objectionable rationalism of the utilitarian position, or to the elimination of ends altogether as factors in action.

If logical action be thought of thus as describing the intermediate sector of the intrinsic means-end chain, another important consequence follows. Within the context of a given system of ultimate ends, the *immediate* ends of acts within the sector *are* given as facts to the actor, in much the same sense as conditions and potential means are given. This is essentially because these immediate ends are, in turn, means to something else. This is above all true of the generalized means which emerge on the economic and political levels of analysis, respectively, as wealth and power. Other things being equal, it would always be irrational not to maximize wealth and power. The question does not involve the determination of the ultimate ends of action at all. Wealth and power are potential means to any ultimate ends of

---

[1] For an example of the consequences of this fallacy see the author's discussion of Professor Lionel Robbins' work in "Some Reflections on the Nature and Significance of Economics," *Quarterly Journal of Economics*, May, 1934.

an intrinsic means-end system.[1] Hence it can be said that on these levels, within the framework of an ultimate end system these immediate ends are "given" in the sense that the postulate of rationality involves the pursuit of them.[2] In view of this striking fact it is understandable that Pareto, like many others, had a certain tendency to assume that the ends of logical action are factual data to the actor.

It is primarily these two generalized means to any ultimate ends, or generalized immediate ends of rational action, to which Pareto gives the name "interests." They have been treated here largely in terms of their place in the normative means-end system of a society taken as a unit. As such, power and wealth appear as means to the system of common ultimate ends. This is not, however, their only possible role in concrete social life. The integration of a total system of action with a common system of ultimate ends constitutes a polar type: it is not a generalized description of the usual concrete state of affairs but formulates only one extreme limiting type of concrete state.

One highly important respect in which the concrete state may depart from this limiting type of "perfect integration" is in the degree to which the ends and value attitudes of different individuals fail to be completely integrated with any common system. But in so far as this is the case it does not necessarily in the same proportion remove their actions from the logical type. On the contrary it is precisely at these two points that the lack of integration may tend to focus in the form of a struggle

[1] The only exception is the type of case where the character of the ultimate values is such as to imply the radical repudiation of wealth and power. Certain religious systems which unconditionally enjoin poverty or non-resistance are examples. This does not, however, mean that it will always be considered "reasonable" to pursue wealth and power without quantitative limit or without restriction to "legitimate" means. So far as the individual accepts a system of values, it will have implications in both respects. For example we condemn acquisitive activities which overstep the bounds of "honesty" and this is a significant limitation however imprecise the prevailing conception of honesty may be. The "other things equal" in the above statement must be taken to mean that it is irrational not to maximize wealth and power so far as the activities required to do so do not come into conflict with the requirements of the particular system of values which guides the individual in question in his action.

[2] Within limits set by the ultimate-end system. These limits will vary concretely with variations in the latter.

between different individuals and groups for power and wealth. For all have a "like interest"[1] in these generalized means to their ultimate ends even though the latter are diverse and unintegrated. In so far as ultimate ends do not directly conflict, as they sometimes do, the failure of complete integration will then be focused on the interests. Hence, as Hobbes has shown, control over these interests is a vital point in the stability of any social system.

THE STATUS OF ECONOMIC THEORY AGAIN

Finally, the analysis of this chapter has carried us considerably farther toward the answer to a vital methodological problem, that of the status of economic theory. It will be remembered that Marshall took an empiricist view of the scope of economics, as concerned with the "everyday business of life" at least so far as it could be related to the schema of supply and demand. But in his concrete treatment he included two distinct orders of considerations: on the one hand, those of utility theory, on the other of activities. Pareto, however, took a quite different point of departure, holding that "pure economics" was an analytically abstract theoretical system which, to be concretely applicable, needed to be supplemented with other, sociological elements.

It is clear as a result of the preceding analysis that Marshall's activities belong among what Pareto would call the sociological elements. They involve, predominantly, nonlogical elements of the value character. It may be said, indeed, that the central element, so far as the present conceptual scheme goes, of Marshall's activities is a common system of ultimate-value attitudes. Many of Marshall's most serious empirical difficulties result from failing to recognize that such a system of value attitudes may vary independently of the elements of utility theory, of knowledge of the situation, scarcity of resources and the motive of maximization of utility (in Pareto's term, ophelimity). The two central elements of Marshall's scheme then are to be found at quite different points of an analysis of the structure of social action systems. Pareto's conceptual scheme takes account of this separateness while Marshall's does not; hence Pareto is free of certain biases which distort Marshall's perspective.

[1] A useful term employed by R. M. Maciver, *Society, Its Structure and Changes*, p. 8.

But in addition to providing a much more definite analytical basis for the differentiation of the two major elements of Marshall's thought than was available before, the preceding discussion has made it possible to define the focus of interest of utility theory in relation to the things closest to it much more adequately than has previously been possible in this discussion. It is clear that the focus of interest of economic theory has been in action so far as it is logical. The "ideal experimental conditions" for the concrete application of economic theory are defined in part by the requirement that the logicality of the system of action is maximized. This is the much discussed postulate of economic rationality. But at the same time structural analysis of action systems has revealed that economic theory is by no means equally concerned with all the structural elements of such a system even in the limiting case of perfect rational integration. As has already been said, action is economically explicable only in so far as it is logical; hence all factors responsible for deviation from the norm of intrinsic rationality may be ruled out as noneconomic. Second, it is clear that ultimate-end systems, as variables, are also noneconomic. Every concrete system to which economic theory is applicable has such ultimate ends, but these are given data for economic theory. Third, the ultimate means and conditions of action are noneconomic factors. For the theories relevant to them are capable of formulation in nonsubjective terms, hence economic theory would not involve any independent variables relative to nonsubjective theoretical systems. It follows that the focus of interest of economic theory is in the intermediate sector of the intrinsic means-end chain.

But from the point of view of this study it has been found that this intermediate sector may conveniently be differentiated, in turn, into three subsectors. Economic theory as dealt with by Marshall and the great majority of other "orthodox" theorists clearly makes no attempt to account for the framework of distributive order in a social system, but only for certain processes which go on within such an order and subject to certain rules laid down in the order. Neither does it deal with the tendencies to break through the restrictions of the order by such means as force and fraud, but rather only considers activities so far as certain types of means are employed. On the other hand, it is not

particularly concerned with what has here been called the technological aspect of the means-end chain, though for economic
reasoning to make sense, concretely, it is necessary to assume
that technological problems have, in a measure, been solved.
This leaves, as its main focus of interest, the central subsector
of the intermediate sector. It is the point where considerations of
the allocation of scarce means as between scarce resources
become involved. Hence, for purposes of this study, economics
may be defined as "the science which studies the processes of
rational acquisition of scarce means to the actor's ends by production and economic exchange, and of their rational allocation as
between alternative uses." To this end economic theory is a
system composed of the variables which most directly account
for the degree to which any given social system of action in fact
involves a rational process of the acquisition and allocation of
scarce resources by the means designated. That this conception
of the place of economics fits in with Pareto's use of the term is
best shown by the place at which he introduced the conception
of economic utility (ophelimity) in his more general theory of
social utility.

The argument of the present chapter may, in conclusion, be
briefly summarized. First, it was the conclusion of the previous
chapter that in addition to the distinctions Pareto himself made
in his own classification of the residues, it was necessary, for the
purposes of this study, to distinguish two different orders of
structural elements of action systems which were involved in the
sentiments manifested in the residues. This conclusion was
definitely verified by considering Pareto's relation to Social
Darwinism. His qualified rejection of this doctrine showed
clearly that the sentiments involved in nonlogical action could
not be reduced exclusively to the drives of anti-intellectualist
psychology. His explicit statement about Social Darwinism was
further confirmed by his use of two hypothetical abstract
societies to only one of which the Darwinian theory would
apply. The formulation of the other showed that one main
qualification of the Darwinian theory is due to recognition of
the role of the value elements as factors in action. The same
conclusions emerged again from the consideration of what is
meant by Pareto's question, "Do the residues correspond to the
facts?" and the way he answers it.

The attempt was then made to supplement Pareto's own explicit analysis in its relevance to the present study by taking up the implications of the concept of logical action for the structure of *systems* of action involving a plurality of individuals. The result of this was a conception of integrated chains of intrinsic means-end relationships at the one end of which are found to be integrated systems, both individual and social, of ultimate ends, at the other, the ultimate means and conditions, heredity and environment. The intermediate sector, at the same time, was found to fall into three main subsections according to the breadth of the range of conditions under consideration, the technological, economic and political, respectively.

That this scheme was not merely an arbitrary construction was then demonstrated by applying it to Pareto's theory of social utility. It proved able to account for all the main elements of the theory, most of which Pareto had not explicitly developed in his original analytical scheme. Above all, the conception of "the end which the society should pursue" which Pareto found essential to that of the utility *of* a collectivity cannot be interpreted without conceiving the action system of a society as culminating in a common system of ultimate ends. This is Pareto's version of the sociologistic theorem, and its emergence marks a radical difference from the sociological individualism usual in the positivistic tradition.

Finally, the question was raised as to the relation of this system of rational types to the other parts of systems of action. It was found to constitute a system of norms which form one, but only one, group of structural determinants of action. It implies the factors of heredity and environment, in the role both of ultimate means and conditions, and of the sources of ignorance and error, the factors resistant to the realization of a rational norm. These are involved in the sentiments along with other things.

On the other hand, ultimate ends were found to be only one element of a larger complex the nucleus of which is a system of value attitudes,[1] which are also involved in the sentiments. These

---

[1] It is because Pareto's term "sentiment" includes both this and the psychological element, that it has seemed best to replace it for purposes of this study with "value attitude." This is to be understood as a concrete attitude in so far as it can be understood by its orientation to a value system which is in one aspect related to a system of ultimate ends.

value attitudes are involved in action not only as related to the ultimate ends of the intrinsic means-end chain, thus to ultimate empirical ends, but also to transcendental ends and, as elements in ritual action, in institutional control, in art, in play[1] and in other modes. This whole ultimate-value complex comprises a relatively well-defined set of structural elements clearly distinguishable both from the intermediate means-end sector and from the factors of heredity and environment.

In the context of the present structural analysis Pareto's concept of logical action is found to apply exactly to the intermediate sector of the intrinsic means-end chain. Then nonlogical action, which Pareto defined as a residual category, is found to involve two main groups of structural elements, those capable of formulation in terms of nonsubjective systems especially heredity and environment, on the one hand; the value complex, on the other. The analysis of nonlogical action on which Pareto himself embarks, leading up as it does to the concepts of residue and derivation and their classification, cuts across the present line of analysis, and hence this distinction, which is fundamental for purposes of this study, does not appear in the analytical part of his treatise. It does, however, appear in the synthetic portions, particularly the discussion of the two abstract societies. That he did not develop it analytically is primarily due to the fact that for his own purposes he had no occasion to carry the explicit treatment of nonlogical action beyond the isolated unit act to consideration of the structure of total social systems of action.

With the results of this long and somewhat arduous analysis in mind it is now proposed to come back, in the next chapter, to some of Pareto's empirical generalizations. This will be done for two reasons. First, it will confirm the above analysis, in its relation to Pareto's conceptual scheme, by an empirical verification. In this respect it will be maintained that it is impossible to understand what he does without reference to the value elements of the theory. Second, it will provide an opportunity to demonstrate that theoretical views of this character make a fundamental difference in the interpretation of concrete phenomena. This section will then be concluded with a brief consideration of the significance of the results of the analysis of Pareto for the problems of the study as a whole.

[1] These three elements will not, as already noted, be explicitly discussed until later.

CHAPTER VII

VILFREDO PARETO, III: EMPIRICAL
GENERALIZATIONS AND CONCLUSIONS

THE IDEOLOGY PROBLEM

The first empirical aspect of Pareto's work to be discussed briefly is his treatment of "ideologies,"[1] of the "theories" associated with nonlogical action. For the particular methodological reasons already outlined this study forms the central element of his own analytical treatment, but it also has its direct empirical application, which is the matter for discussion here.

Pareto's general approach to the distinction between logical and nonlogical action is, as has been shown, such as to imply that in so far as action is logical, the "theories" associated with it will be logico-experimental theories and hence that a departure from the logico-experimental standard on the part of the theories accompanying action may be regarded as an index of the role of at least certain nonlogical elements in the action itself. His first great service is, by his exhaustive critique of these theories, the revelation of their extremely wide extent. Above all by deflating the pretentions of very many such theories to scientific status he has greatly altered the view held in many circles[2] of the relative importance of the logical and the nonlogical elements of action. But this fact alone does not settle the question of the character of the relations of such nonscientific theories to overt action. As a result of the previous analysis one thing may be said with confidence: that it is a highly complex problem. But there are nevertheless to be found certain hints of the direction of its solution.

What distinguished logico-experimental theories in their relations to action was the character of the means-end relationships

---

[1] It is not expedient here to enter into the many meanings of this much used, and often abused, term. It is chosen simply as the most convenient for present purposes.

[2] Pareto stands by no means alone in this, in this sense, anti-intellectualistic current of thought.

they stated, as guided by scientifically verifiable theories in the "virtual" form. Hence the elements of departure from the logico-experimental norm may be classified as belonging to two general types: on the one hand, those concerning the status of what from the subjective point of view appear as means-end relationships and, on the other hand, those concerning elements of action falling outside the logical means-end relationship as such.

The first type of departure in turn involves two kinds of elements, erroneous observation of fact and sophistic reasoning from the observations. Either or both may be involved in any given concrete theory. In so far as the nonlogicality of a theory is of this character the tendency is, as has been seen, to regard its meaningful aspect as irrelevant and to interpret the theory itself as a "manifestation" in the sense of an "index" of something else. Then the "real forces" of action are not expressed in the theory, but the latter is like a veil covering them, which it is the business of the sociologist to tear away. In this sense the forces manifested in the theories turn out to be the "non-meaningful" categories of heredity and environment. The latter become "meaningful" in relation to the subjective aspect of action just in so far as they can be related as means and conditions to subjective ends. But from this point of view, in this context, if such relation exists to the actor it is "erroneous"; hence the "real" significance of these determinants in nonlogical action is on another level. The theories are ideologies in the derogatory sense of secondary manifestations of the real determinant forces. The practical empirical result is to "debunk" such theories, to come to the conclusion they are not in themselves important but are secondary phenomena significant only as "thermometer readings."[1]

The other type of departure involves quite different considerations. These may again be subdivided into two. The ultimate ends of action in the analytical sense, whether empirical or transcendental or both, are always "manifestations of senti-

---

[1] It is noteworthy that when he is talking in this vein Pareto often, in spite of his explicit definitions to the contrary, slips over into speaking of the *whole* of the nonscientific theories as "derivations." This seems to arise from the fact that the derivations, being the variable, contingent elements, are unimportant while the residues are (or "express") the real determinant forces. Hence the tendency to identify derivations with total theories which in *this* context, but not the other, are contingent. *Cf. Traité*, 2152–2153.

ments" and never statements of what are to the actor external facts. Hence, whenever an ultimate end is involved, for this reason alone the theory accompanying action must by definition depart from the logico-experimental standard. Here, however, by its departure from the standard above, the theory is not devalued as a factor in action. What is debunked is only its claim to scientific status. This is not, of course, to say that the residue simply is the effective force in action. The matter is by no means so simple as that, as Pareto was well aware. But the residue, the principle, is an expression of the value attitudes underlying it. It is more than an index, it embodies in its meaning at least certain aspects of these value attitudes. In its relation to action it stands in the normative relation of a logically[1] formulated end or rule which in the limiting case is a completely adequate[2] expression of the real force. But above all in relation to ultimate ends this limiting type is seldom attained, or even very closely approached. Hence there is an element of "indeterminacy" in the relation between residue and sentiment, between logically formulated end and value attitude, on which Pareto rightly lays great stress. But this does not affect the main point of the present discussion—that, however inadequately, a residue does express a sentiment, a value attitude. The relation is radically different from that in the above case.[3]

Secondly, on the value plane, the theories may depart from the logico-experimental standard by the character of the means-end relationship involved. That is, the relations established may not be merely, from an intrinsic point of view, "erroneous" but may also have a peculiar positive character—they may be symbolic or ritual.[4] As in the case of ultimate ends these relationships necessarily involve departure from the logico-experimental standard—they are from the latter point of view arbitrary relationships. But, again as in the case of ultimate ends, this

---

[1] Or pseudologically depending on the degree of precision.

[2] For the analytical purposes in hand in the same sense as is applicable in the case of logical action. *Supra*, p. 215.

[3] Perhaps this capability of "expression" by meaningful symbols is the best single criterion of a "value" element as distinguished from the factors of heredity and environment.

[4] Pure "error" and symbolic relationships may naturally be involved in the same concrete theories. But none the less the analytical distinction is vital.

fact does not imply that they are irrelevant to the understanding of the forces determining action.

On the contrary, the doctrine would seem to be the following: In so far as these theories attain the norm of rigorous logical formulation according to their own standards, they may be regarded as "adequately expressing" these forces, or, for practical scientific purposes as interchangeable with them. That is, action may be regarded as determined by the theory, the "process of reasoning," in the same sense as is true of logical action. In this context the distinction between the logical and the nonlogical elements of action does not lie on the plane of a difference in the relation of theory and of action as such, but in the character of the theories which may be held to determine action. Here the term ideology changes its meaning radically—it becomes a name not for an *unimportant* theory but for a nonscientific theory related to action.[1]

But this is strictly true only at the rationalized pole. Short of this, where most concrete theories fall, the theory is not a fully adequate expression of the real forces of action, even the value

[1] In the main logical structure of Pareto's theoretical system there is contained no definite theorem, explicit or implicit, relative to the role of ideas in action. The question is rather left open to be decided on empirical grounds in the particular case. There is, however, in the procedure by which Pareto led up to the formulation of his system, a source of what may be called an anti-intellectualistic bias. It is well to call attention to it.

In the formulation of the concept of logical action the starting point is the methodology of positive science. From this Pareto concludes that action, so far as it is logical, can be understood as proceeding from a "process of reasoning," that the meanings of the words in the "theory" accompanying action constitute a sufficient basis for understanding the action itself. This is not true of nonlogical action in general, hence the necessity of introducing into the analysis the "state of mind" A, which is distinguished from the "theories" C. Since nonlogical action is a residual category, it is not brought out that there is a type where the relation of theory and action is essentially the same as in the logical case, the only difference being in the character of the theory. It is likely to be inferred, rather, that in so far as action is nonlogical it is never possible to understand it in terms of the meanings of the words constituting the theories.

The above analysis has shown that there is no warrant for this inference in the main structure of Pareto's system. But the fact that it is indicated in his starting points helps to account both for any anti-intellectualistic bias which he may authentically show, and for the very widespread tendency of secondary interpreters to impute a radically anti-intellectualistic position to him.

factors, because of its indeterminacy. In so far as this is true it is not possible to take the theory at its face value but a complex study must be undertaken to separate out the fundamental from the contingent elements of the theory. This study is the inductive analysis into residues and derivations. It is this indeterminacy, this failure to attain the logical norm, which makes necessary such a procedure, laborious as it is, before the sociologist can gain insight into the determining forces of social equilibrium. But this necessity is *not* an index of the unimportance of value factors. Even when, as is the case short of the fully rationalized-type case, the theories cease to be fully adequate expressions of value attitudes, they still remain the best available. Particularly when they have been subjected to the analysis of separating out the residues they are more usable than any other manifestation because they are less affected by extraneous factors than are overt acts.

Pareto never attempted a classification of these nonscientific theories in terms of their relative degree of approach to the rationalized pole. A very rough classification is suggested by the distinction between "myth" and "dogma."[1] A myth is primarily an "expression," while a dogma involves the explicit statement of a principle set up as a guide to action. The latter category includes what are generally called ethical, metaphysical and theological systems.

The problem of the relation of "ideologies" to scientific theories is most acute in the case of "dogmatic" ideologies. The general distinction between scientific and metaphysical theories goes far back in European thought. To mention only one prominent case, it was made a fundamental cornerstone of Comte's thought. What is new in Pareto is not the formal distinction itself but two main uses to which he has put it.

In the first place, among more or less avowedly nonscientific theories he has, by his incisive critical analysis, shown that generally their claims to logical precision are greatly exaggerated.[2] They not only surpass experience in their basic premises, but

---

[1] Some such distinction is common in the literature. This version is owed largely to Professor A. D. Nock (unpublished lectures at Harvard University).

[2] See especially *Traité*, Chaps. IV and V, *Les théories qui dépassent l'expérience*, and *Les théories pseudoscientifiques*.

these premises are themselves, in a large proportion of cases, so lacking in precision that clear-cut, unambiguous prescriptions for conduct cannot be derived from them.[1] Hence Pareto's roundabout way of studying their relation to action is far more often necessary than would appear at first sight.

Secondly, Pareto has extended his criticism to a large group of positivistic theories which set up claims to furnish guidance to action. The theories of progress, democracy, humanitarianism and the like are for his purposes in exactly the same status as those of karma and transmigration, as Catholic dogma or the mythology of the Eskimo. They are only pseudoscientific theories, departing from the logico-experimental standard in respect both of formal precision and of the factual status of many of the entities involved.[2]

While the criticism is directed specifically against these particular modern theories the conclusion drawn, at least by implication, is broader—that all the theories which express the ultimate value elements of action are in so far nonscientific. And so long as the principal elements of action remain what they are and have been these theories will persist; however much they may change their form and take on scientific camouflage, their essential character remains unchanged.[3] "Taking the population as a whole we observe a succession of theologies and metaphysical systems rather than any diminution in the totality of these phenomena, as we have already often had occasion to note."[4]

This conclusion, due essentially to Pareto's more skeptical version of the methodology of positive science, has truly revolutionary empirical consequences for the positivistic theory of social change. For, as has been shown,[5] the latter has been predominantly a theory of linear evolution. In the anti-intellectualistic version it has become assimilated with the theory of

---

[1] They are *comme le caoutchouc*, as Pareto says.

[2] "In reality what is called the warfare of 'reason' against the positive religions is merely the warfare of two religions. In the theology of Progress history is seen as a struggle between a principle of 'evil' called 'superstition' and a principle of 'good' called 'science.'" *Traité*, 1889.

[3] "There is no such thing as a faith more scientific than another." *Traité*, I, p. 333.

[4] *Ibid.*, 1881.

[5] Chap. III.

biological evolution, and social change has been viewed as a process of cumulatively better adaptation to the conditions of the environment. This version, as stated above,[1] Pareto unequivocally rejected. In the rationalistic version, on the other hand, the dynamic element of the process of change has been the cumulative growth of scientific knowledge.

Though this element remains for Pareto, its social influence is confined to the category of logical action. Whatever dynamic process the ultimate value element may be subject to, it is by no means clear that it is necessarily one of linear accumulation[2] as in the case of scientific knowledge. In the above passage Pareto speaks of a "succession of theologies and metaphysical systems" rather than the continuous development of a single one. In fact, it seems highly probable that this view of the nature and role of ideologies has a close and important connection with Pareto's explicit rejection[3] of a linear evolutionary theory in general and espousal of a cyclical conception in its place. The investigation of the question may, then, be combined with the discussion of the cyclical theory.

Before leaving the subject of ideologies, however, it may be noted that the above discussion yields an interpretation of Pareto's very frequently reiterated distinction between the "truth" and the "social utility" of a doctrine.[4] To confuse the two is, he says, a typical error of those who can see only the logical elements of action. The standard of truth which he continually employs is that of logico-experimental science. An untrue doctrine is, then, one which departs from this standard. But in this sense the view that only true doctrines should be useful would mean that society should be "based upon reason." This, however, as has been shown, Pareto considered impossible since essential data were lacking. Hence society, so long as the value element plays a part, will always be characterized by the currency of untrue, *i.e.*, nonscientific doctrines. These doctrines moreover partly manifest, partly constitute, elements essential to the

---

[1] Chap. VI, pp. 220 *ff.*

[2] This was, it will be recalled, the version Marshall gave, without full methodological self-consciousness.

[3] *Traité*, I, 343–344, also 730.

[4] VILFREDO PARETO, *Manuel d'économie politique*, p. 31. *Traité*, I, Sec. 72, 167, 219, 249, 568, 843; II, 1621.

maintenance of the social equilibrium. Hence their suppression could not but be harmful to the society.

For these "untrue" theories to serve as efficacious motives of conduct they must be "believed."[1] But since they cannot be proved scientifically, the "truth," that is, criticism according to the logico-experimental standard, can act only as a solvent, undermining this belief.[2] Skepticism is, Pareto often remarks, an inadequate basis of action.[3] Hence knowing the "truth," that is adopting a skeptical, scientific attitude toward value questions, may well incapacitate the members of the society for action in pursuit of its end.[4]

Essentially the same considerations are relevant to understanding what Pareto meant by another of his common views— that it is very easy to exaggerate the efficaciousness of logic as a means of persuasion, of getting others to act as you want them to. One ground for this view is the common argument of anti-rational psychology: men simply do not act rationally in any

---

[1] "Rare and not very persuasive is the unbelieving apostle; on the contrary frequent and highly persuasive is the apostle who believes." *Traité*, I, 854.

Also: "Those who see in prophets only charlatans and imposters are very far from the truth; they confuse the exception with the rule." *Ibid.*, 1101. See also 1124.

"Rare are those men who are cynically agnostic, and just as rare are the pure hypocrites. Most men try to reconcile their personal advantage with the residues of sociability." *Ibid.*, 1884.

"It goes without saying that every believer holds his belief to be rational and all others absurd." *Ibid.*, 585.

[2] "Reason always weakens the sentiments of religion of the upper class." *Manuel*, p. 87. The accusations against Socrates were sound. *Ibid.*, p. 91. See also *Traité*, I, 616; II, 2341.

A highly interesting statement of the main idea involved here is the following: "The oscillations [of skepticism and faith, see below pp. 284 *ff.*] are the result of the antagonism of two opposed sets of forces—the correspondence of the derivations with reality, and their social utility." *Traité*, II, 1683. A fundamental social instability and hence a prime cause of the cyclical movements discussed in the next section is implied in the double fact that faith, *i.e.*, in a broad sense, religious belief, is indispensable to social stability, but it cannot withstand the disintegrating effect of rational, scientific criticism. Hence the tragic situation: society is doomed to oscillate forever between fanatical obscurantism and fatal instability. See also *ibid.*, II, 2341.

[3] "Discussion of ethical questions can be harmful to a society and even destroy its foundations." *Ibid.*, 2002.

[4] *Ibid.*, 2147.

sense. They are swayed by habit, by suggestion, crowd influences, etc., or by instinctive drives. Arguing with them does no good. You must place them in situations where these mechanisms will act in the desired way. This is one element in Pareto's view, but only one. Rational persuasion is also limited because to persuade anyone to do something you must not only show him how to do it, but also get him to see why he should do it at all. Where values are involved which are not facts which everyone must admit to be true or false, but which are "subjective," there is no rational means of getting another to accept the end.[1] An Indian mystic can tell an American businessman that the things of this world to which he devotes his life—money and success— are pure illusion and that reality can only be approached by sitting under a tree and contemplating. It is unlikely he can prove it to the American's satisfaction. The only recourse in such cases is an appeal to sentiments. Values are either accepted or rejected; they are not proved or disproved as facts are.[2]

Thus Pareto's treatment of the ideology problem confirms the general analysis. While one of the lines of thought involved leads to a depreciation of the role of ideas in conduct, the other does not. In the latter context the error Pareto is combating is the identification of ideas in general with logico-experimental theories. It is only the role of the latter he attacks. What may be called value ideas are, on the contrary, of the greatest importance to the understanding of the social equilibrium.[3]

[1] Among many statements is this: "No one ever became a believer by demonstration." *Manuel*, p. 77.

[2] Not only can a "religion" not be "demonstrated," *ipso facto*, it cannot be "refuted" by reference to "facts." "At one time some good people thought they could destroy Christianity by proving that Christ never existed; they have merely struck their swords in water." *Traité*, 1455.

[3] See *Manuel*, p. 128. While from the point of view of logico-experimental science we recognize that the theories of religion and ethics "are entirely devoid of precision and exact correspondence with facts, on the other hand we cannot deny their great importance in history and in the determination of social equilibrium." *Traité*, 843. See also *ibid.*, 541.

"It follows that sentiments and their manifestations [*i.e.*, ideas] are facts for sociology at least as important as actions." *Ibid.*, 219. "This reasoning applies not only to the catholic religion but to all other religions even to all metaphysical doctrines. It is impossible to consider the major part of the life of human societies up to our time as absurd." That this is in fact a theory affirming a positive though not exclusive role of ideas is defi-

CYCLES OF SOCIAL CHANGE

The cyclical theory Pareto actually developed was not meant to be an exhaustive theory of the total process of social change but was concerned predominantly with the process of change in the relations to each other and to the rest of the factors in the social equilibrium of two of the six classes of residues:[1] Class I, the "instinct[2] of combinations" and Class II, the "persistence of aggregates." However, both the fact that he selected these two and the manner in which he deals with them make it a fair presumption that he considered them of outstanding importance.

---

nitely proved by such statements as the following: "The *idealistic* theory which takes the *residue* for the cause of the facts is erroneous. But the *materialistic* [can we not say positivistic?] theory which takes the facts for the cause of the residue is equally so. In reality they are mutually dependent." *Ibid.*, 1014.

[1] No attempt has been made in this study to enter into a general critical consideration of Pareto's classification of the residues. Though a very arduous task, it would well repay the effort. The author is not aware that anyone has seriously made the attempt. One point may, however, be noted. The concept "residue" as developed in Pareto's analytical discussion in the early part of the *Traité* refers to a proposition which is isolable from concrete nonscientific theories by a process of analytical induction, and is hence an element of such theories. Even if attention is paid not strictly to the residues, but to what is manifested in them, the reference will necessarily be to analytically separable elements of action.

Pareto's own classification does not appear to have been arrived at from such an analytical basis, for when speaking of particular residues or classes of them such as those of combinations or of the persistence of aggregates, he speaks in terms which give the reader to understand that he refers to general, concrete tendencies of action (such as innovation and hostility to it). Pareto, in his text, gives no account of the process by which he arrived at the classification; he merely sets it forth and illustrates it. The suggestion may, however, be ventured that it was primarily by a process of empirical generalization in which his vast knowledge of the history of antiquity played a prominent part. There is no adequate theoretical bridge to be found in his work between the analytical approach to the concept, in the first place, and the classification he offers. Besides the kind of structural analysis in relation to his initial scheme, set forth in the last chapter, a most important line of theorizing based on Pareto's starting points would be to attempt to construct this. The fact that he did not himself do it is certainly one of the circumstances contributing to the confused state in which secondary interpretation of his work in general stands.

[2] In view of the above discussion "instinct" seems to be an unfortunate term to use here, but it would not be advisable to attempt to amend Pareto's terminology for present purposes.

The two classes of residues are not rigorously defined, but certain traits of the persons in whom each predominates occur repeatedly. The instinct of combinations residues[1] lead to the tendency to form combinations out of all sorts of disparate elements, without necessarily any foreknowledge of intrinsic relatedness.[2] With them are associated innovation, inventiveness, projecting and scheming. The tendency is to attain ends by cleverness and resourcefulness rather than by persistence and steadfastness, to use indirect rather than direct methods, to avoid overt conflict, to circumvent rather than override obstacles.

The persistence of aggregates[3] class of residues is, on the other hand, associated with essentially the opposite characteristics. It involves a stability of combinations once formed, steadfastness and directness, willingness to accept open conflict, a tendency to override obstacles and hence to use force, traditionalism rather than innovation, an absence of cleverness and resourcefulness. With this general contrast goes a somewhat more special one in matters of great social importance. Men strong in "combinations"[4] tend to value the present above the future, the immediate above the distant future, "material" over "ideal" goods and satisfactions and the interests of the individual over those of any collectivity such as the family, the local community or the state. Men strong in "persistent aggregates," on the other hand, value the future above the present, the ideal above the material, and subordinate their personal interests far more to those of the collectivities to which they belong. Hence for Pareto's theory, some of the most important properties of any given society depend upon the relative proportions in its members of these two classes of residues.[5]

But, for Pareto, the significance of the situation in this respect is greatly heightened by its relation to the class structure of a society. Class differentiation is, he holds, so fundamental that society may almost be defined as a hierarchical entity.[6] For his purposes, however, he goes no farther than to divide it roughly into two classes, the elite and the non-elite. The elite are simply

[1] *Cf.* in general *Traité*, 889 *ff.*
[2] It must be remembered this is an element of *nonlogical* action.
[3] *Cf. Traité*, 991 *ff.*
[4] *Cf. ibid.*, 2178.
[5] Or, more strictly, of the sentiments which they manifest.
[6] See especially *Traité*, 2025 *ff.*

those who greatly excel the mass in any particular respect—they always constitute a relatively small minority. The elite are, in turn, subdivided again into the governmental and the nongovern-mental elite—the former being those who directly or indirectly in important degree influence or take part in administering the affairs of government. The constitution of the elite in terms of the two classes of residues is a matter of great importance.

In society as a whole the residues change but slowly, and the classes of residues in relation to each other still more slowly, but on account of its relatively small numbers this is not nearly so likely to be true of the elite. There is in most societies a continual process of "circulation of the elite" whereby some individuals are rising into the elite and others falling out of it. In the course of this process the character of the elite may change radically in a relatively short time.

This process Pareto conceives as essentially cyclical, and he considers it in terms of three closely interrelated phases. The first concerns the status of the governmental elite as such. The starting point of the analysis is the postulate that there is in general a certain amount of class antagonism so that government is not entirely a matter of routine administration but also involves measures specially aimed at the attainment and maintenance of power. These measures tend to divide for Pareto into the two main classes of "force" and "ruse."[1] Force needs no explanation; it is the exercise, at such critical junctures as may arise, of physical coercion or the threat of it as a means of gaining assent and obedience. Ruse shades all the way from clever stratagem and maneuvering, appeal to sentiment and interest, over into outright fraud. It is quite clear that in so far as the two classes of residues in question are mutually exclusive—and they are, for Pareto, to a high degree—the men of "persistence" will tend to use force and the direct appeal to sentiments of persistence which they themselves share, while the men of "combinations" will predominantly employ ruse, the appeal to interests and the exploitation of sentiments they do not themselves share.

The cycle, then, is one of alternation in predominance in the governing elite of these two classes of residues. Pareto starts with the remark that a governing elite which is unwilling or unable to make use of force to maintain its position is an easy

[1] *Ibid.*, 2274–2275.

prey to a small, well-organized and well-led group who are ready to employ force to attain their ends.[1] Such men he calls the "lions." The cycle starts with the accession to power of such a group through the use or threat of force. These men tend to be men strong in the persistence of aggregates, with a strong "faith" which they share with their followers.

But these qualities, however efficacious they may be in bringing their bearers to power, are not so advantageous in its maintenance. Force is more advantageously used, or threatened, against the "ins" in the process of attaining power than against one's own followers and other "subjects" in the process of maintaining discipline when in power. Hence the tendency is to turn more and more to "combinations," to ruse. These same circumstances also alter the conditions of circulation of the elite. The premium on ruse as a means of government leads to the rise into the governing elite of men skilled in ruse, who never have shared the faith of the original founders of the regime. Hence the residues of persistence in the governing elite are both weakened by the fact that the exigencies of their situation call less and less for the qualities associated with them, and are diluted by the accession of a different type from below. Above all, when opposition, domestic or foreign, instead of being suppressed by force is circumvented by ruse, the tendency is for the processes of government to become more and more expensive. This fact puts a great premium on abilities which are suitable to the finding of means in ways which do not involve the use of force.

Finally, in combination with these elements, the mere fact of the ease of achieved power tends to weaken the persistence of aggregates in the governing elite. The immediate end, power, having been achieved, the more nearly ultimate ends tend to be lost sight of, and the members of the elite lie back and enjoy the fruits of their victory. This is above all true since, often, the process of weakening of the residues of persistence is accompanied by an efflorescence of the finer fruits of "civilization" which naturally is especially pronounced in the elite.

This same process, however, has its reverse aspect on the side of the governed. On the one hand, the sentiments on the basis of which the governing elite was borne into power may be outraged by the by-products of the process of dilution of the residues of

[1] *Ibid.*, 2178 *ff.*

persistence—among other things with the passing of ruse over into fraud. On the other hand the alteration of the conditions of circulation of the elite leads to the accumulation below of able men strong in the persistence of aggregates who share these sentiments and are willing to use force. The extent to which the situation becomes unstable is very largely dependent on the extent to which the elite is able to deprive the governed of their leaders. If the elite is open and allows the rise of these men, the process may go on for a very long time. But, subject to this qualification, the increasing predominance of the men of combinations, the "foxes,"[1] in the elite steadily decreases the latter's resistance to force; on the other hand, the probability of forceful opposition, from below or possibly from without, steadily increases. The result is likely to be the eventual overthrow of the governing elite and the beginning of a new cycle.

This strictly political phase of the cycle fits closely with an economic phase. Here the combinations type, the "speculators,"[2] are the economic counterpart of the political "foxes." The general change in the character of the governing elite, which naturally shades off into the nongovernmental elite, brings to the top in economic affairs an entrepreneur class of this type—fertile in projects and promotion schemes of all sorts. The immediate result of this is likely to be a burst of economic prosperity since these men take the direction of economic affairs out of the hands of the more traditionally minded. The rise of this class tends to coincide with that of the "foxes" partly because the general social milieu is favorable to both types, but also partly because of a direct reciprocal relation. On the one hand, government has an immense power over economic opportunity and its actions can be highly important means of opening the door to the speculators. On the other, the growing expensiveness of government makes the speculators equally useful to the "foxes." Hence the predominance of the two tends to coincide.

There is, in strictly economic activities, no place for a group of "lions" since the use of force as a means of acquisition takes action out of the economic sphere into the political. But there is none the less a type characterized by the predominance of the

[1] *Ibid.*, 2178.
[2] *Ibid.*, 2313.

residues of persistence—Pareto calls them the *rentiers*.[1] While not "forceful" persons, they are conservative traditionalists opposed to the innovations of the speculators. Their functional importance in the social scheme lies in the fact that they are savers, while the speculators, though often great producers, are extravagant, exploit saving and for their role in the cycle are dependent on accumulations of savings. Pareto lays great stress on this distinction between the speculator and the *rentier*—the entrepreneur and the saver—and the conflict between them, stating that it is sometimes even more important than the traditionally emphasized capital-labor difference.[2]

The *rentier* type is characterized by saving, not as a matter of rational economic calculation, but of nonlogical forces. Hence it is quite possible, and Pareto maintains it as a fact, that they are not as a class alive to their own interests. In fact their great weakness is that they are too easily exploited by the speculators,[3] so that as the cycle proceeds its speculative phase runs the danger of being brought to a halt by the exhaustion of savings. While on the political side it is the defenselessness of the regime of the "foxes" against force which sets the main limit to the combinations phase of the cycle, on the economic side it is the inability of the speculators to save. The two elements may, however, be very closely interconnected as, though *rentiers* are in general timid and easily exploited, they may in certain circumstances be aroused to political activity so that they form an important element in the support of the political "lions" against the "foxes."[4]

Finally there is a third phase of the same cycle, that of "ideologies"[5] which points the way to important elements in its theoretical interpretation. These ideologies, the "theories" of the previous analysis, may be regarded from two points of view, the intrinsic

---

[1] *Ibid.*

[2] *Ibid.*, 2231.

[3] *Ibid.*

[4] Pareto has a most interesting note (*Traité*, 2336) in which he remarks that anti-Semitism has as a "substratum" a reaction against the speculators, of whom the Jews serve as a symbol. Hence the propensity for *rentier* classes to take it up. The history of Nazi Germany admirably bears out Pareto's view (written more than twenty years ago) on this point.

[5] *Traité*, 2329 ff.

and the extrinsic, respectively. The former concerns their correspondence with facts, the latter the forces accounting for their production and acceptance in the given social situation.

While all the theories concerned are nonscientific there is an important distinction between two types. The theories of one type are *explicitly* nonscientific. They tend to depreciate the value and importance of positive science in favor of "higher" entities such as "intuition," "religious experience," the "absolute," a "true science," etc. There is always explicitly involved a different and supposedly higher realm than that of experimental fact, principles are invoked which "dictate" to the facts instead of vice versa, as in science. The other theories, on the other hand, though not legitimately scientific, are pseudoscientific. They assimilate themselves as closely as possible to science, invoke the authority of "reason" and of what purport to be factual entities. They also generally involve a polemical repudiation of theories of the former type. Hence Pareto speaks of times when the former are predominant as ages of "faith," while the predominance of the latter characterizes an age of "skepticism."

From the extrinsic point of view these two types of theories are associated, respectively, with the residues of persistence and of combinations and, of course, with the corresponding sentiments. The period of predominance of the "foxes" and speculators is also an age of skepticism—that of the "lions" and the *rentiers* one of faith.

This gives the main clue to the theoretical interpretation of the general cycle. The distinction of type of the two classes of theories shows that the two corresponding classes of residues do not, for the purposes of the present analysis, lie on the same analytical level. They are, rather, defined by the presence and absence of certain characteristics, *e.g.*, "faith" in the reality of certain nonexperimental entities. At least one main element of the persistence of aggregates is ideal ends; they may be presumed to be, very often, transcendental ends. These ideal ends may be thought of as exercising a discipline over conduct.[1] The same sentiments which are manifested in such ideal ends are also generally manifested in a large amount of ritual, performance of which for other than utilitarian motives[2] involves "faith."

[1] *Traité*, 2420.

[2] As, for instance, when a man joins a church and attends its services for the sake of the business advantages membership will bring him.

The predominance of the instinct of combinations is, on the other hand, to a large extent[1] a state of the absence of effective control by such ideal ends or value elements over conduct.[2] Here attention centers on the immediate rather than the ultimate, the satisfaction of the appetites, the pursuit of wealth and power. In other words, a high development of this class of residues places a particularly strong premium on the "interests."

The cycle of the two classes of residues then becomes one largely of integration and disintegration of faiths, of "religions," predominantly in the elite. This is indicated among other things by the form the cyclical waves take.[3] It is not a long, even swell, but the increase of intensity of the persistence residues is relatively sudden—Pareto speaks of "revolution." Then follows a gradual process of disintegration varying in length of time according to the particular circumstances, but never of revolutionary character.

Similarly the most essential reason for the element of social instability which the cycle involves is the instability of the persistence of aggregates in the elite. There are in Pareto's view three main reasons for this instability. One reason is "extrinsic" —the exigencies of maintaining power, the premium on ruse and the difficulties in the way of the use of force, operating both through influence on the actions of an elite composed originally of "lions" and through the altered conditions of vertical mobility. The other two, however, are "intrinsic," that is, concerned with the nature of persistent aggregates as such. One is the difficulty of maintaining discipline against the pressure of appetites and interests. That is, there would seem to be an inherently difficult problem of control, of keeping the interests in conformity with an ultimate value system.[4] Such a system, above

---

[1] Consonant with Pareto's general procedure these classes of residues *may* contain or manifest *any* elements left over in the residual category of nonlogical action. Just what lines are involved in his classification of residues cannot be entered into here. Hence the attribution of a specific content to any class must always be qualified as "one element in."

[2] *Traité*, 2375.

[3]

 Not

[4] Pareto here approaches on an empirical level a conception of the relation of interests to values and of the dynamic process involved which is very

all in the form of a system of institutional[1] norms is subject to a continuous "bombardment of interests" which, in the absence of especially powerful controls, is likely eventually to break it down to such a degree as seriously to endanger social stability.[2]

The second intrinsic reason lies in the instability of the "theories" which manifest the sentiments of persistence and are, at least as far as the residues are concerned, to a high degree interdependent with them.[3] That is, it is evidently Pareto's view that the only stable product of intellectual processes, of reason, is logico-experimental science. It is in the nature of the case that theories will be criticized in terms of this standard and since, by definition, they cannot meet it, they will be found wanting, and the effect of the criticism will be destructive. It will be a force tending to dissolve the aggregates in question.[4]

But such a process cannot go on to a point of stable equilibrium. For action rests on premises for which factual data are *necessarily* lacking.[5] Hence the theories associated with it cannot become really scientific theories but at best in appearance only, that is, pseudoscientific. These pseudoscientific theories, those of

---

close to that arrived at by both Durkheim and Weber. Theoretically, it leads into consideration of the "institutional" aspect of action systems which will be taken up in connection with Durkheim (see Chap. X).

[1] See previous note.

[2] See under the section "The Role of Force," pp. 288 *ff*. In this connection it is probably significant that all Pareto's empirical examples of his cycles were taken from Greece and Rome and Western society. He did not consider such societies as China, India and ancient Egypt, which have a much greater appearance of stability over long periods. Comparison with Weber's *Sociology of Religion*, above all his treatment of China and India, will prove interesting.

[3] *Supra*, p. 276.

[4] It is a suspicion worth noting that perhaps this strong sense of the inherent instability of nonscientific theories is, like the instability of institutional control, in part connected with Pareto's empirical concentration upon two particular civilizations. For instance, in over two thousand years of India's history no significant movement of skepticism of two of the basic Indian metaphysical doctrines, karma and transmigration, has appeared. The social role, of "skepticism" may well be associated with the peculiarly important social role of "reason" and "science" in Greek and Western societies. This question is, of course, not to be confused with that of the *epistemological* status of nonscientific theories. It does, however, affect the general empirical applicability of Pareto's conclusions.

[5] See Chap. VI.

"skepticism," do not indicate a state of the sentiments which is stable any more than do those which surpass experience, hence another reaction back to the pole of "faith."[1]

In this connection Pareto enters into a very revealing discussion which well illustrates the peculiar intellectual situation out of which his views emerged. In particular with reference to the medieval realism-nominalism controversy, he remarks that the realist position was entirely out of accord with the facts. The nominalist criticism brought it much closer—but it went too far. The intermediate "conceptualist" position as revived by Victor Cousin is, properly interpreted and qualified, more acceptable scientifically than either.[2]

There are two different levels on which Pareto is thinking in this connection. One is that of *general* epistemology and scientific methodology, concerned with the status of universals in general. But the other line of thought, much more important in the present context, is the following: Entities of the sort involved in realist philosophy are typical elements of the "theories" of which the residues of the persistence of aggregates are a part. Such entities are, from a general critical point of view, metaphysical, outside the range of "experience," which involves only the particular. But at the same time they are real in the sense that it is a *fact* that men believe in such entities and this fact is in a state of mutual interdependence with other social facts so that a loss of these beliefs results in an alteration of the social equilibrium. Hence the sociologist cannot treat them as purely imaginary entities in the sense that he can ignore them. They are essential elements in his problem. It is this which is the kernel of truth in realism and similar philosophies.

This is thus another way of affirming the importance *in action* of the value elements and at the same time of noting their peculiar status in respect to "factualness." They are facts to

---

[1] This situation provides a most important confirmation of the preceding analysis in that its basis must lie in the role of value elements. For there is in principle *no intrinsic* reason why a scientific theory of his own psychological equipment is not possible to the actor—the limitations on it are those of ignorance and error only. But the entities which make the theories of the phase of skepticism *pseudoscientific*, such as "reason," "progress," "science," "humanity" are *not* mere errors; they are *metaphysical* entities which "surpass experience." This is perfectly clear from Pareto's argument.

[2] See *Traité*, 2367 *ff*.

the observer, but to the actor they are not observed elements of his situation but are "subjective." This is a position to which Pareto (and, as will be seen, Durkheim) comes back again and again by a large number of different paths.

Pareto's cyclical theory thus gives perhaps the largest scale example of the interweaving of the theoretical ideas with which the analysis of the previous two chapters has been concerned, and a specific empirical subject matter. It seems not unfair to conclude that the cyclical theory confirms at least the main point of the analysis, the importance of the role of value elements in Pareto's category of nonlogical action. For, whatever other elements further analysis of the persistence of aggregates may reveal, there can be no doubt that the element of most importance to the cycle is that which appears in its "ideological" aspect as a "faith." The cycle is essentially that of the effective control and discipline over action by the sentiments expressed in such faiths, or value complexes on the one hand, the relaxation of that control opening the door to a relatively free play of appetites and interests, on the other. The latter at the same time creates conditions of instability which sooner or later put an end to this phase of the cycle.

Such ideas are by no means peculiar to Pareto. It is one of the most striking facts about the group of writers being considered in this study that with the exception of Marshall they all bring forward ideas involving a process of disintegration of the kind of social control associated with a faith. In its application to the contemporary social situation as well as to history as a whole such views surely present a sufficiently striking contrast to those associated with the concepts of linear evolution and of progress. The concurrence of the theoretical change with that in empirical outlook in such widely separate writers cannot be a matter of mere chance. Of its significance more will be said later.

THE ROLE OF FORCE

Though the cyclical theory is the *pièce de résistance* of Pareto's empirical sociological theories there are a large number of interpretations of empirical questions which would well repay discussion. Lack of space makes it necessary to confine the treatment to one more which is of peculiar interest. Persons of liberal antecedents are often impressed, perhaps more strongly than in any other way, by a kind of Machiavellian element in Pareto's thought. This takes the form of laying great emphasis on the social importance of force and fraud. To avoid misunderstanding it is worth while to inquire just how these elements fit into the general framework of his theory.

Any considerable role of force has, in recent social thought, generally been associated with "naturalistic" ideas, above all in the various versions of Social Darwinism. There is a continuity in the history of thought of this element with Hobbes' state of nature through the different permutations traced in Chap. III. Pareto's relation to Social Darwinism, discussed in Chap. VI, would make it seem probable that the prominence of force in his theory was not alone a matter of such naturalistic elements.

The considerations just dealt with give conclusive proof that such cannot be the case. For the use of force is most prominent in the case of the "lions," who are strong in the persistence of aggregates and are men of strong faith. On the contrary, those lacking in faith are very generally both unwilling and unable to use force.

What lies back of this association between idealism and the use of force on which Pareto lays so much stress but which runs counter to so much of current opinion? It goes deeply into the foundations of his thought. A leading characteristic of a faith, for Pareto, is its absoluteness. And the more intensely it is believed in, the more prominent this is. Such a faith, it is to be remembered, has definite consequences for action. The man of strong faith in general tries to make others conform to the standards demanded by his faith by whatever means are available. Force is the ultimate means when all others fail. Given the inherent limitations on securing conformity by rational persuasion,[1] the man of strong faith turns readily to force. The inconvenience, unpleasantness and risk involved do little to deter him, since in comparison with an absolute end counting the cost is almost meaningless.

The man of little faith, on the other hand, is motivated by a great multiplicity of interests. Hence there is not the same absolute claim upon him of any one end and he is far more sensitive to sacrifices and costs. He does not readily adopt

[1] *Supra*, pp. 276–277.

extreme measures, but tends wherever possible to avoid open conflict, to come to terms with opposition. Moreover, his lack of faith makes it easy for him to come to terms. This is the main basis of the association of force with the persistence of aggregates.

There is, however, one important qualification. There are certain faiths of which repugnance to the use of force is an integral part. Pareto does not go into this question explicitly but there seems no doubt that this is one element in the peculiar role he assigns to humanitarianism. He regards it partly perhaps as a sheer symptom of decadence, as its association with ages of skepticism and pseudo science would suggest, but partly also as a faith characterized by the hostility to force. The effect of this is greatly to accentuate the "combinations" phase of the cycle. For the repugnance of a humanitarian elite to the use of force puts a double premium on ruse and opens the door in an extraordinary degree to the regime of the "foxes" and the speculators.

This humanitarianism, which Pareto himself speaks of as a kind of diluted Christianity, has been a conspicuous attribute of the European elite since the eighteenth century and may be considered one important cause of the peculiar instability of the present situation, both by the extra amplitude it has given the combinations phase of the cycle, and by making the elite peculiarly defenseless, beyond what a "fox" elite ordinarily would be, against the use of force.[1]

Fraud, on the other hand, is the polar extreme into which the ruse associated with the "foxes" and the speculators shades off as the dominance of the residues of combinations becomes more complete. In "getting something out of others," which is the main point of view from which both the concepts are framed, it is no longer mere cleverness in devising ways and means but passes over into deception.

Both force and fraud are means of getting something done. They are means which, whatever their differences, have one important feature in common—the absence of certain limitations on the choice of efficient means imposed by ethical consideration

---

[1] It is in discussing humanitarianism and other related elements of contemporary liberal democracy that Pareto departs farthest from the ideal of scientific objectivity he himself has set up. This fact is not, however, of great importance for present purposes, however important it may be in a political context. There is a substantial basis of observed uniformity which is the present concern.

for the rights of others.[1] Except where forceful coercion is employed as a means of enforcing commonly accepted rules, as by the state, which does not seem to be prominent in Pareto's treatment, the appearance of either or both on a considerable scale may be considered a symptom of lack of social integration. For, on the one hand, the "lions" have occasion to use force mainly against persons or groups that do not share their faith— hence in so far as the faith is shared in common by the whole community the occasion does not arise. On the other hand, considerable limitations on the use of fraud appear to be indispensable conditions of stable social relations within a community. But there is this difference: while the faith of the "lions" tends to result in forceful coercion of outsiders it may become itself the basis of a community of values—it is in so far an integrating force. This is not true of the fraud of the "foxes" which is a symptom of a kind of individualization, the dissolution of community ties.[2]

Force and fraud are thus important both in themselves and as symptoms of the state of the deeper lying forces which Pareto speaks of as "determining the social equilibrium" which, in a somewhat different context may be said to determine the state of integration of a society. The role and significance of both has undoubtedly been very seriously minimized by the "liberal" theories of progress and linear evolution, of which Marshall may, in this respect, be taken as typical. Force frequently attends the "creative" process by which a new value system becomes established in a society in part through the accession to power of a new elite.[3] Fraud, on the other hand, attends the later stages in the breakdown of the persistence of aggregates involved in this integration and may become an important factor in the state of instability which necessitates a reintegration.

[1] They are thus the marks of egoism par excellence, though this must be qualified by the fact that the fraud may be perpetrated more for the sake of others than for the actor himself.

[2] Approaching as a polar type the state Durkheim called *anomie* (see Chap. VIII). At this point a naturalistic type of force also appears, but Pareto does not stress this since the process is generally brought to a stop before this point is reached.

[3] It may well be doubted whether this is the whole story. Some new values, like Christianity, have come in by rather a different process (see below in connection with Weber's concept of charisma, Chap. XVI).

At this point the discussion of Pareto's empirical theories may be concluded with a few brief remarks upon his view of civilization, and its place in his theories. By civilization he meant the flowering of literature, the arts, science and the like such as occurred in classical Athens or in Renaissance Italy. Such a flowering, he held, was not associated with any static state of society, but with a stage in the process of the disintegration of the persistence of aggregates in favor of the combinations residues. The "lions" are generally of such strong faith as to be fanatics. They create an atmosphere of rigid orthodoxy, intolerance, binding ritual, austerity of discipline and sometimes otherworldliness which stifles civilization. That requires an atmosphere of relative freedom, tolerance, mobility. Thus Pareto repeatedly states that a flowering of civilization is associated with an increase in the combinations residues.[1] But when the process goes so far as to break down the "barbarous" rigidity of fanaticism it soon proceeds to the point of endangering the stability of the society in which civilization flourishes. Perhaps, though Pareto does not say so, too much instinct of combinations is fatal to the arts in itself. But however that may be, a new wave of fanaticism may wipe out the creations of the previous cycle[2] which has to start over again to a large extent.

Thus according to Pareto's view of civilization, its flowering has taken place only under certain specific conditions which have been in the nature of the case of short duration and have been closely linked with occurrences that are repugnant to most lovers of the fruits of civilization. The grimness and fanaticism of the "lions" are generally a prelude, however unpleasant it may be, and the regime of fraud and corruption the usual end product of the total process.

This provides an important key to Pareto's personal values, which are by no means a main concern of this study but may be remarked upon very briefly. He was, above all else, a lover of this civilization. That is, he was in the aristocratic "cultural" rather than the bourgeois sense a liberal, a connoisseur of the good things of life, a lover of freedom in thought and action.

---

[1] Thus both Periclean Athens and the Italian Renaissance were such periods. *Traité* 2345, 2529 *ff*.

[2] See his discussion of the relation of the Reformation, which was to him such a wave, to the Renaissance. *Traité*, 2383, 2538.

But to him freedom in thought and personal conduct was far more important than in business. This fits into his background. His father spent many years in exile in the Mazzinian cause.

Pareto nowhere delivers any attack on these liberal values. He is not a lover of brute force, a glorifier of the beast of prey[1] as good in itself for its very rapaciousness. He is, to be sure, a scoffer at bourgeois morality, especially antialcoholism and sexual puritanism,[2] but this only goes with the aristocratic bent of his liberalism and is an authentic element of the liberal tradition. What distinguishes him from most of his predecessors in liberalism of, for instance, his father's generation is not his personal values but his view of the conditions necessary for their realization. He did not have faith in progress in this liberal sense and, for reasons which should be evident from the preceding discussion, was particularly pessimistic about the immediate outlook for liberal civilization in Europe. This is an Old World pessimism which it is difficult for Americans to understand. One possible reason for the prevailing hostility to Pareto in this country is that he was a "knocker" not a "booster."

GENERAL CONCLUSIONS

It remains only to sum up very briefly, in terms of the general problems of the study, this analysis of Pareto's work.

First a few brief remarks on his scientific methodology: Pareto's explicit methodology was derived mainly from his experience in the physical sciences. It did not, however, involve the older mechanistic positivism in the sense in which Comte and Spencer had held it, but a much more skeptical and sophisticated version of scientific method which attempted to divest logico-experimental science of all metaphysical elements whatsoever, with a much more rigorously inclusive standard of the metaphysical than his predecessors had.

Thus Pareto approached the theory of action without any positivistic dogmas on a methodological level which would have committed him in advance to a positivistic system of theory. He was thus spared many of Durkheim's difficulties. He was further-

---

[1] *Cf.* his interesting remarks on the relations of Athens and Rome. See *Traité*, 2362.

[2] *Cf.* especially *Le mythe vertuiste* and many remarks scattered through the *Traité*.

more immensely helped by a clear realization of the abstractness of the analytical concepts of science which was, among the subjects of this study, approached only by Weber. It may be said, however, that Pareto had a clearer conception than Weber in the more general methodological context. He was thus also spared most of the difficulties growing out of a conscious or unconscious empiricism. The main qualification of this statement is the fact that, in the strength of his emphasis on the central importance of observable fact in science, Pareto sometimes made statements which are, at least on the surface, open to an empiricist interpretation. In his most careful statements, however, the element of abstraction is always considered, and it must always be remembered that it was involved in his conception of fact itself so that, properly interpreted, the very frequent statements to the effect that scientific laws are simply "uniformities in the facts" do not involve the "fallacy of misplaced concreteness." Moreover, still more important, so far as can be seen, none of his important generalized statements and theorems can be said to be dependent on the empiricist fallacy.

To the set of methodological questions peculiar to the theory of action, rather than common to science in general, Pareto contributes a good deal less. Particularly in questions relating to the status of subjective categories, which are central to the theory of action, he took what was essentially the common-sense view of a sophisticated man of the world. In doing this he was able to get ahead without having to worry about any behavioristic dogmas, and the slight extent of methodological clarification he attempted in this field seems to have been adequate for his purposes. At the same time clarity about some of the implications of the analysis of the structure of action systems developed above in connection with Pareto calls for a further extension of explicit methodology in this direction than Pareto provided. This is particularly true in two connections. In the first place, it is necessary to accord factual status not only to the physical properties, but also to the meanings of symbols. This conclusion is involved in the use of propositions and theories as data for a scientific theory. This, in turn, opens up the possibility that such data may be interpreted as manifestations of the state of mind of the actor, not only in the sense of a mutual interdependence on the causal-functional level, but also as constituting symbolic expressions of the "meaningful" content of this state of mind. This mode of manifestation has been found to be of substantive importance to the analysis of this study at several points.

Secondly, Pareto does not clarify the methodological status of the normative aspect of systems of action. This is comprehensible since it is a problem which does not arise for the physical sciences in terms of which Pareto's methodological views seem mainly to have been formed. But it may be one reason why in classifying the residues he did not make the distinction between normative and non-normative one of the bases of his classification. Had he done so he would have come much closer to an explicit outline of the "morphological" analysis of the structure of action systems which has been developed here. As has been shown, his own system is not incompatible with this structural analysis, but its absence may be justly regarded as a limitation on the completeness of his work regarded as a treatise on general sociology.

That there is what may be called a normative orientation of action systems is one of the fundamental propositions underlying the whole analysis thus far developed. It follows that the abstractness of some of the concepts which are employed in the theory of action consists precisely in the fact that they are descriptive not of the actual observable state of affairs of overt action, but of the norms toward which it may be regarded as being oriented. Hence these concepts contain an element of "unreality" which is not involved in the physical sciences. Of course the only reason for admitting such concepts to a scientific theory is that they are in fact descriptive of an empirical phenomenon, namely the state of mind of the actor. They exist in this state of mind, but not in the actor's "external world." It is, indeed, this circumstance which necessitates resort, on the part of the theory of action, to the subjective point of view.

Both Pareto's own theoretical system and the structural analysis just built up here start from the concept of logical action. Nonlogical action then becomes a residual category, action so far as it is not defined by the logical criterion. For the study of nonlogical action there are available two main classes of concrete data. For the reasons discussed Pareto concentrates his analysis on the "theories," leaving overt acts aside. The identification of the data relevant to nonlogical action involves the comparison of all the theories associated with action with those of logico-experimental science in order to segregate out the elements which fail to conform with the scientific standard. These fall, by inductive analysis, into the two groups of the constant and variable elements, residues and derivations.

From this point Pareto went on to classify the residues and derivations without further concern for the question of the relation of the sentiments manifested in them to the structure of action systems. Logical and nonlogical action served as a scaffolding to build the beginnings of his analytical system, but he did not follow the structural implications of the distinction farther.

This is the point where the analysis of particular interest here, however, sets in. The question is, what are the implications of Pareto's definition of logical action for the structure of the social systems in which it has a part, on the hypothesis that the theory of action has independent analytical significance and is not reducible to terms of any other theoretical system making its appearance in Pareto's work? The general drift of the argument is the thesis that, in this context, there are two different classes of structural elements which are involved in the nonlogicality of action systems. There are those which underlie the *un*scientific features of the theories and those concerned with their *non*scientific aspects. Following out the first line of thought leads to the structural elements which have played the major role in radically positivistic theories, those capable of nonsubjective formulation. The most prominent of these in the secondary interpretation of Pareto have been the instincts of anti-intellectualist psychology. The elements which are involved in the nonscientific aspects of the theories are, on the other hand, those with a normative character, what has here been called the value complex. Psychological drives turn out to be one way in which the factors of heredity and environment influence concrete action, objectively as the sources of deviation from the logical type and subjectively, of ignorance and error. The other mode is that of constituting the ultimate means and conditions of action so far as it is rational.

The value element, on the other hand, stands in rather complicated relations to the others. Its most obvious place is in the role of the ultimate ends of the intrinsic chain of means-end relationships. Analysis of the implications of Pareto's treatment of social utility in this connection has brought out two important conclusions: first, that these ultimate ends are to be radically distinguished from the ultimate means and conditions of rational action. One of the main criteria of the difference is that the latter are accorded factual status which the former are denied, from the point of view of the actor, though both enjoy it from the point of view of the observer. Secondly, among such ultimate ends Pareto has made a most important distinction of two classes or elements. On the one hand, are those held distributively by individuals and groups within the society so that there arises for every society the problem of distributive justice in the allocation of means—above all power and wealth. But to be distinguished from these is the element of ultimate ends held in common by the members of the society or predicated on the collectivity as a unit. Only by virtue of these nondistributive elements does the concept, the utility *of* a collectivity, acquire a determinate meaning. This is the first appearance in the discussion of the sociologistic theorem, which will occupy a great deal of the subsequent treatment.

It is, however, quite clear from Pareto's text that this part of the theory is concerned with a rational norm, and is by no means a complete account of the facts. The first important consideration is the indeterminacy of the residues and hence also of the sentiments which they manifest. The second is the great empirical prominence in Pareto's treatment of nonlogical action of a type which falls outside the rational intrinsic means-end schema altogether—namely ritual. Neither of these sets of facts has been found, however, to be necessarily reducible to terms of the psychological drive element. On the contrary, they point to another type of element in the sentiments which has been called ultimate value attitudes, of which both ultimate ends and ritual as well as other phenomena[1] may be regarded in part as manifestations. This is quite strictly a value element in the sense of this discussion and is as such to be carefully distinguished from others, especially from nonsubjective elements which may be involved in the same concrete phenomena.

Placed in this context it turns out that Pareto's original concept of logical action can be applied to what has here been called the intermediate sector of the intrinsic means-end chain. The economic element as generally conceived by orthodox economic

---

[1] Institutions, art, play and one or two others are to be discussed below.

theory does not, however, exhaust this but must be conceived in turn as intermediate between two others, the technological and the political. It is distinguished from the former by the consideration of more than one end (and hence the element of "cost"), from the latter by the exclusion of coercion as a means to its own immediate ends so far as they involve relations to others.

There is no difficulty over the status of ends in logical action in this context since the ends of the intermediate sector are immediate not ultimate ends. Hence two statements may be made: *Given* the ultimate ends, as, for instance, in the form of the institutions of a society, these immediate ends are also to be regarded as means involved in the rational norm of efficiency. Secondly, these ends may be "given" to the actor in an even more general sense, in that the complex of social relationships can under certain circumstances focus a great deal of rational action on two sets of generalized immediate ends, wealth and power, the desirability of which as ends is a corollary of the postulate of rationality of action, to a large extent independently of the specific content of ultimate ends. These are what Pareto calls the "interests." Hence there is a very real sense in which the "ends" of the logical element of action are "given" to the concrete actor as "facts" of the situation in which he acts.

Finally, consideration of the relation of the rational norm to the other structural elements of action leads to the view that Pareto is here concerned, as his central subject matter, with what may be called a voluntaristic conception of action. To this at least three things are essential. Two of these are formulated in Pareto's two abstract societies—an ideal norm of what action should be, and a set of resistant and divergent and other non-normative factors. Not explicit in Pareto is the third element which is logically required, an element of "effort" by virtue of which the normative structure becomes more than a mere idea or ideology without causal relevance. The suspicion may be voiced that this third element has something to do with the role of ritual, but since Pareto does not deal with the question explicitly, its further discussion will be postponed.[1]

Consideration in the present chapter of some of Pareto's more definitely empirical theories has served three purposes. It has, in general, confirmed the correctness of the analysis of certain

[1] See Chap. XI on Durkheim's theory of religion.

implications of Pareto's theoretical approach, particularly with reference to the importance of the value element in nonlogical action. It has, secondly, brought to light new theoretical aspects of his thought to fill out some of the gaps of the previous analysis. And it has, finally, served to show the intimate connection between the new[1] theoretical system explicit and implicit in Pareto's work and his interpretation of empirical phenomena. As compared with Marshall and the utilitarians Pareto, though he is not alone, in both respects marks a major turning point in sociological thought. This analysis may be held to demonstrate that the two events are not independent, but are so intimately connected that they can be considered as two aspects of the same process.

The analysis of Pareto's work has brought this study an important step forward on its journey. The first concern was to outline the utilitarian position and to note its instability and tendency to break down in the radical positivistic direction. The study of Marshall served to show the connection of this logical situation with the question of the status of economics and the way in which, in the form of "activities," he introduced, as a variable, a factor of a totally different order which had in the previous discussion been present only in the form of metaphysical postulates. But by Marshall's general framework of thought this element was tied down in its theoretical consequences to very narrow limitations. It served, however, to break the positivistic circle.

Pareto approached the study of action free from positivistic dogmas. Moreover, his recognition of the concrete inadequacy of economic theory implied, in a direct way which Marshall did not provide, the inacceptability of the utilitarian position for general social theory. And having defined logical action in a way closely corresponding to the conceptions of economic theory he proceeded to a systematic investigation of some of the principal nonlogical elements of action. For Pareto, this eventuated in a complex classification of residues and derivations which, along with the "interests" and the principal facts of social heterogeneity he incorporated into his generalized social system.

But analysis of the way in which Pareto approached the study of the noneconomic elements of action, particularly the nonlogical, has made it possible to carry analysis of the structure of action systems much farther than could be done in connection

---

[1] New as compared to those already discussed in this study.

with Marshall. Not only is the general distinction of logical and nonlogical, which would separate utility theory from activities in Marshall, made, but it has been possible to make, and verify in relation to Pareto's own work, the general distinction between the normative and the non-normative nonlogical elements and, further, to carry the differentiation of the normative side of the structure to a considerable degree of elaboration. This makes it possible to gain a much more accurate view of the status of the value element which Marshall introduced with his activities. It further makes it possible to clarify greatly the place in a total system of action of those elements which have been the traditional concern of economic theory. Finally, by definitely breaking through certain of Marshall's limitations and those of positivistic theory generally, it has been possible to open up vast new vistas, both theoretical and empirical, for further exploration.

Pareto's work is not a synthesis of sociological theory, in the sense of a perfected system. It is a pioneer work. But it is throughout dominated and guided by the logic of systematic theory and goes far toward building up such a system. The general outline of this system is far in advance of any of the positivistic systems which have been discussed, and of Marshall's. Furthermore there is in it nothing essential on either the methodological or the theoretical level[1] which, from the point of view of this study, must be discarded. In this respect it is unique among those studied here. It has, however, proved possible to add to it in certain directions for the particular purposes of this study. For these purposes Pareto's system is incomplete, but is entirely compatible with everything which has here been developed. But its very incompleteness is one thing which makes it particularly useful for the purposes of this study, since it provides an excellent medium for verification of the analysis attempted here, in spite of not stating the analysis explicitly.

The discussion will now turn to a writer of a very different character, with many more positive difficulties, but a focus of interest closer to that of the present study, in the structure of social systems as such. The very differences of Durkheim's starting points, type of mind and methods from those of Pareto throw into bolder relief the substantial residuum of common results.

---

[1] This is, of course, not in the least to say that Pareto made no mistakes. But, so far as can be determined, the mistakes he made are not important, in the strict sense, to the general analysis of this study.

CHAPTER VIII

ÉMILE DURKHEIM I: EARLY EMPIRICAL WORK

In approaching the work of Émile Durkheim this study seems at first sight to plunge into a totally different intellectual world from that of Pareto. The differences of the two men were marked in almost every possible respect. Pareto was an Italian nobleman, aloof, skeptical, sometimes cynical, a man to whom moral fervor was suspect. Durkheim was an Alsatian Jew of rabbinical parentage who worked his way through an outwardly uneventful academic career in France, finishing with the attainment of the ambition of all French academic people, a professorship at the University of Paris.

The principal target of Pareto's biting critical irony was the belief in democracy, progress, humanitarianism as typically held by French middle-class, anticlerical "radicalism." Durkheim was a fervent devotee of this very belief. Pareto was a detached observer, very little concerned to say anything that could be of practical application. Durkheim held that only its practical usefulness could justify occupation with social science at all.[1]

Pareto came into sociology by way of mathematics and the physical sciences and was thoroughly conversant with their problems and points of view. His previous acquaintance in the social field had been with economics, the one among the social sciences which has been traditionally closest in theoretical form to the natural science model. Durkheim had no first-hand contact with the physical sciences beyond what a well-educated man of his time would almost necessarily have. He had no training in economics. His previous training was at the opposite intellectual pole from Pareto's—in the "humanistic" fields of law and philosophy.

Two further differences should be mentioned. Both Marshall and Pareto were undoubtedly great theorists whose theoretical

---

[1] *Cf.* ÉMILE DURKHEIM, *Les règles de la méthode sociologique*, p. 60. *De la division du travail social*, 5th ed., p. xxxix (all references in this study are to the 5th French edition, although the title is usually given in translated form).

contributions to their respective fields were eminent in a high degree. But both types of mind were strikingly different from Durkheim's. Both are characterized by a certain tentativeness, a sense of the complexity of the empirical problems they deal with, with the result that the broad, bold lines of theory are relatively little emphasized and can be gotten at only with considerable trouble. Durkheim, on the other hand, had a different type of mind, a type encountered previously in this study—in Hobbes. Durkheim possessed to a remarkable degree the faculty of persistence in thinking through the consequences of a few fundamental assumptions. There is perhaps to be gained from studying him less insight than from the study of the others into some of the subtler problems of detail in their fields, but this is compensated for by the most unusual boldness of the general outline of the theoretical system. Durkheim always refused to be diverted from the fundamental questions. His empirical observation is of the nature of the crucial experiment rather than the survey of a field. The factual element in his work is, relatively speaking, not large, but a great deal is made of what there is, and the most fundamental assumptions, shading into the field of methodology, can be brought out with a sharpness which is most useful to the present study.

It is not to be inferred from the above considerations, as many of his critics have maintained, that Durkheim was therefore a philosopher, a dialectician and not an empirical scientist at all. On the contrary, he was one of the great empirical scientists of his day. It will be one of the principal tasks of this discussion of his work to show how, at every critical point, there is the closest possible relationship between his theoretical views even on the most abstrusely methodological plane, and the problems of interpretation of empirical material with which he was struggling at the same time. Durkheim was a scientific theorist in the best sense of one who never theorized "in the air," never indulged in "idle speculation" but was always seeking the solution of crucially important empirical problems.

It is interesting to note another thing. Marshall and Pareto were empirically minded in an eminent degree, but both did their theorizing mainly on the basis of general empirical material brought together from many sources to illustrate and elucidate their discussions of principle. Neither made any important monographic contributions to social science. Durkheim, on the other hand, proved the genuineness of his concern for fact by embarking on some of the most fruitful monographic studies which sociological science has yet produced. Three are of particular importance. The first and the last were not in the usual sense original research. In both the *Division of Labor* and *Elementary Forms of the Religious Life* he used secondary material brought together for the purposes of throwing light on his own problems. In *Le suicide*, however, he did an original piece of research which will long remain a model. There are very few monographs in the social science field where the empirical and theoretical aspects are so happily combined. For on the basis of what appears at first sight to be very restricted and specialized empirical subject matter Durkheim manages to arrive at results which throw an amazingly bright light on some of the deepest and most far-reaching problems of social theory. It is a case of the "crucial experiment" at its best.

It is a curious circumstance, and one which implies a serious reflection on the current state of affairs in social science, that the great majority of the persons who have discussed Durkheim's methodological views, usually in an unfavorable sense, have completely ignored this empirical aspect of his work. They have confined their attention to his methodological writings so that the reader would not even know, except from other sources, that the man whose work was being discussed was the same person as the author of the *Division of Labor* and *Le suicide*. Yet it is impossible to understand how Durkheim arrived at these methodological views, which have been the subject of so much discussion, if they are not seen as attempts to meet the empirical problems with which he was there faced, in terms of the alternatives left open by the conceptual scheme with which he was operating. It is one of the main purposes of this discussion of his work to attempt to correct this unfortunate separation by treating both the empirical and the theoretical aspects together. To this end discussion of Durkheim's methodology will be preceded, in the present chapter, by a fairly full outline of the major features and conclusions of his earlier empirical studies. Only when the reader is aware of the problems there involved can he appreciate the significance of what Durkheim was doing in the methodological field.

One further general characteristic of Durkheim's work in contrast with that of the others may be noted. All that is of major importance for the purposes of this study in Pareto's work is to be found in his last book, the *Traité*. What precedes, especially in the *Systèmes socialistes*, is of interest primarily as indicating the gradual genesis of the ideas most fully developed in the later work. In Pareto there is only a process of gradually increasing clarity in the ideas relevant to this study. In Durkheim, on the contrary, there is a fundamental change, from one set of sharply formulated ideas to another. Hence it will be necessary, in the following discussion, to treat Durkheim's theory as a process of development. This may be divided roughly into four main stages. There was an early formative period, of which the most important document is the *Division of Labor* (1893), in which he was still feeling his way to the formulation of his fundamental problems. Second, there was an early synthesis in which he had worked out a relatively well-integrated general system of theory which seemed adequate to the empirical facts he had studied and successfully met all the important critical attacks to which he was subjected at that time. The main documents of this stage are *Les règles de la méthode sociologique* (1895) and *Le suicide* (1897).

This was followed by a period of transition in which the early synthesis gradually broke down and was gradually replaced by a different general position in systematic theory. This is documented by such writings as "Représentations individuelles et représentations collectives"[1] (1899), *L'éducation morale* (1902–1903) and "La détermination du fait moral"[1] (1907). Finally, on the basis of this new general position, there opened up a vast range of further problems, leading into new empirical fields, which was developed in *Les formes élémentaires de la vie religieuse* (1912). Durkheim never, however, was able to carry these latter investigations far enough to achieve a new general synthesis, and his work was broken off by his early death at a point where many of his fundamental problems remained unsolved. What the new synthesis would have been, had he lived to achieve it, can only be guessed, but as will be shown, there were, in his final phase, two main tendencies of thought struggling for supremacy.

Pareto carefully refrained from committing himself on explicitly philosophical problems. He did not generally follow his

[1] Reprinted in the volume *Sociologie et philosophie*.

theoretical problems and their implications into that part of the
methodological realm where they border on philosophy. Hence
in terms of the broadest framework of classification of types of
theoretical system in the social field which has been employed
here, it is not possible to classify him rigorously. It is possible
to speak of a certain positivistic bias, but certainly not to call
Pareto definitely a positivist. The origin of this bias is mainly
to be attributed to the fact that, insisting so strongly as he does on
the importance of the distinction between scientific and philosophical considerations, he refuses explicitly to be drawn into the latter
realm. He tends, therefore, to imply that all philosophical considerations are in fact unimportant to any of the problems with
which he has to deal, hence that there is an indefinite plurality of
possible philosophical positions varying at random relatively to
scientific problems and it does not matter which is held, or
whether none at all is held. This is a positivistic implication, but
it stands on the periphery of Pareto's thought.

At the same time it has been possible to show by analysis the
relevance of certain of Pareto's leading theoretical problems
to the basis of the classification. Certain of these problems involve
the range of alternatives open within the framework of the utilitarian dilemma, while others led Pareto to break through these
rigid alternatives, to admit the importance of elements having
no place in the positivistic system. Hence Pareto's work is an
excellent vehicle for exploring the possibilities of various alternatives comprised within the positivistic system and for demonstrating their inadequacy for the purposes of general social
theory. Taken as a whole, his system belongs definitely in the
voluntaristic category.

Durkheim, on the other hand, was almost always perfectly
explicit on these matters. From the beginning his early position
was explicitly positivistic; this was, indeed, held to be a methodological requirement of science itself. The essential result of his
early formative period was the working out of a sharply formulated conception of certain alternatives open within this system, and the statement of his explicit adherence to one of these
alternatives; by the time this had happened he had achieved
his early synthesis. The breakdown of this synthesis, mentioned
above, consisted essentially in a breakdown of the entire positivistic framework itself. Certain of its features, however, he

never completely shook off, and this fact largely accounts for his failure to achieve a new synthesis comparable in extensiveness and degree of logical closure to the first.

The peculiarity of Durkheim's early synthesis was that it involved an unequivocal challenge to one of the basic features of the versions of positivistic social theory so far encountered in this study, their causal "individualism."[1] From the time he achieved a clear formulation of the problems of the division of labor his attention was concentrated on a "social factor" by virtue of which society was, in his frequently repeated formula, a reality *sui generis*. In other words, Durkheim's basic problem, almost from the beginning, was that of the general relations of the individual to the social group. And in respect to this problem he adopted, also almost from the beginning, a position radically opposed to all forms of what has here been called "individualistic positivism." In so doing he was guided primarily by certain empirical insights which he felt—rightly, as will be shown— were not adequately accounted for by any of the individualistic theories. Undoubtedly, given the general positivistic framework, he adopted a reasonable position, in terms of which it seemed that an adequate understanding of these facts could be achieved. But as time went on it began to appear more and more clearly that this position involved serious difficulties, particularly on the methodological plane; it involved Durkheim in objectionally "metaphysical" assumptions. But the result of his gradual revision of his position in the light both of theoretical thinking and of further factual investigation, was not to revise his opinion of the correctness of the factual insights with which he had started, but to demonstrate more and more clearly their incompatibility with the initial positivistic framework. The outcome was to bring about a revision of the theoretical framework itself which brought it in all essentials surprisingly close to the position at which the previous discussion has arrived by consideration of Pareto's problems. It is an unfortunate fact that "Durkheim's theory" in the literature of the subject still means predominantly the earlier synthesis, and that the process of development from that point has been almost totally ignored. How incompatible this is with a fair judgment of his work and its significance will be made abundantly clear in the following discussion.

[1] *Supra*, Chap. II, pp. 72–74.

It has already been remarked that the individualistic bias of the main Anglo-American tradition of positivistic thought has had the effect that any theory which presumed to question it has almost automatically been branded as "idealistic" and hence condemned as "metaphysical." This has happened in striking fashion in the case of Durkheim, with the result that he is still predominantly known as the theorist of the "unsound" and "metaphysical" group-mind concept. There has been a still further effect: Durkheim's ideas have been held to be derived from Germany, the home of idealistic philosophy.[1] Plausibility has been lent to this claim by the fact that early in his career Durkheim spent some time studying in Germany.

It is true, as will be seen, that idealistic strains appear in Durkheim's thought, but only at the latest stage of its development. The system which was in process of formation when he studied in Germany was so specifically positivistic that any important outside influence of a non-positivistic character cannot have been very important. In so far as any influence beyond the facts themselves and the general climate of opinion is needed to account for his ideas, the most important one is certainly to be found in a source which is both authentically French and authentically positivistic—Auguste Comte, who was Durkheim's acknowledged master. Durkheim is the spiritual heir of Comte and all the principal elements of his earlier thought are to be found foreshadowed in Comte's writings. As will be shown in the following discussion, the breakdown of the positivistic system is the necessary outcome of following through to their logical conclusions the problems with which he started, with the dogged determination of a thinker of rare persistence. It is quite unnecessary and seriously misleading to attempt to account for the major features of his work as the arbitrary fiats of a *deus ex machina*, the results of an influence essentially alien to the milieu in which Durkheim lived and worked. Every element in his thinking is rooted deeply in the problems immanent in the system of thought of which Comte was so eminent an exponent.[2]

[1] See S. Deploige, *Le conflit de la morale et de la sociologie.*

[2] The one major difference between Comte and Durkheim is the fact that the latter did not share Comte's predominant preoccupation with the problems of social dynamics, but was almost wholly concerned with what Comte would have called "social statics." The problem of order is Durkheim's central problem from an early stage. Durkheim's advance beyond

The Division of Labor

Durkheim's first major work, *De la division du travail social*,[1] published in 1893, which forms a most important landmark in the history of social thought, is a book which has, beyond a relatively narrow circle, not received anything like the recognition it deserves. It is, however, a book which is far from being complete or clear in many of the most essential points, and is distinctly difficult to interpret. It contains, in germ, almost all the essential elements of Durkheim's later theoretical development, but it was a long time before the relations of all these various elements to each other became cleared up. It will be worth while here to devote to it a fairly extended discussion.

Ostensibly, as indicated by both the title and the arrangement of the material, the book is a study of the division of labor or of social differentiation and its various causative factors and concomitants. Secondarily it seems to be a study of social types since, by contrast with the differentiated, Durkheim develops his conception of the undifferentiated type. But there is no particular reason why, for purposes of the present study, a general study of social differentiation should be of greater interest than any other specialized monograph. Such a monograph becomes of interest only when it is possible to see its relation to a range of problems inherent in the theoretical system with which the present study has been occupied.

Durkheim's very first statement in the Preface to the first edition strikes a keynote which cannot but be of interest to the reader of the preceding section of this study: "This book is above all an attempt to treat the facts of the *moral* life by the method of

---

Comte consisted precisely in his following of this problem to a much deeper level than Comte had done. It is logically prior to the problem of change, and once having questioned Comte's solution, it was natural that it should take precedence. It is interesting to note that at the very end of Durkheim's career there began to appear hints of a new concern with dynamic problems. Whatever the direction in which following these hints would have led him, had he developed them, the result could not but have been radically different from Comte's version of social evolutionism. See below, Chap. XI, p. 450.

[1] This has been translated into English by G. Simpson under the title *The Division of Labor in Society* (see footnote, p. 301).

the positive sciences."[1] After the emergence into a place of such prominence in relation to Pareto's work of what has been called the value complex, an emphasis from the start on the moral elements of human action immediately arouses interest. Moreover, a number of features of Durkheim's earlier discussion serve greatly to sharpen this interest.

For early in the discussion of the undifferentiated social type, which he takes up before the differentiated, he introduces for the first time what is perhaps his most famous concept, the *conscience collective*, as that which is primarily descriptive of this type. The definition deserves to be quoted in full:[2] "L'ensemble des croyances et des sentiments communs à la moyen des membres d'une même société forme un systeme déterminé qui a sa vie propre; on peut l'appeler la conscience[3] collective ou commune." The combination of the terms "beliefs and sentiments" with the phrase "common to the members of the same society" comes very close, indeed, to the form of statement applied above to certain aspects of the value element in Pareto's thought. Moreover, in the discussion of punishment, which Durkheim takes as his principal immediate index of the state of the *conscience collective* comes a strong suggestion, sometimes explicit, of a prominent role to be attributed to the symbolic relationship in addition to the intrinsic. Punishment is primarily a symbolic expression of adherence to the common values of the *conscience collective*, and, in so far as this is the case, it is irrelevant to judge it by intrinsic standards such as its effectiveness as a deterrent to crime.

It is, indeed, true that, on the empirical level, from the very beginning of the documentation of his thought, Durkheim was deeply concerned with the role of common moral values in relation to action. Yet even in the intrinsic context this element was not theoretically clarified until after the revolution referred to above. It is equally true that one of Durkheim's most important

---

[1] *Division of Labor*, p. xxxvii. My translation.

[2] *Ibid.*, p. 46.

[3] The French word *conscience* may be translated either "conscience" or "consciousness." The ethical connotation is very generally, as appears in the present passage, more adequate to Durkheim's meaning than the psychological. The predominant use of "consciousness" in English translations is clearly indicative of an interpretative bias. It seems best here to leave it untranslated.

theoretical contributions lay in the clarification, in certain respects, of the role of symbolism in relation to action. Yet the full theoretical implications of this could not be drawn until a still later stage in his development. These two points constitute the subject matter of Chaps. X and XI below.

It is not worth while to go into their analysis exhaustively in terms of the present relatively elementary level of Durkheim's own thought. Rather, two problems must occupy the earlier stages of the development. First, what was the genesis in Durkheim's own mind of interest in the phenomena of the moral life, and by what process did he come to lay particular emphasis on the *common* value element? This problem will, in the remainder of the present chapter be followed through its development in all his earlier empirical work. Secondly, how did this interest and the empirical insights which he achieved in following it out fit into a general conceptual scheme? This is the subject of the following chapter.

Durkheim, as has just been noted, directs attention immediately to the moral elements in social life. When an author insists so strongly on a proposition it is more than likely that he holds a polemical animus against some other widely current view. One of the things which makes the interpretation of the *Division of Labor* difficult is that a clear-cut discussion of this polemical issue is not provided until the middle of the book, after the reader's mind has already been directed into other channels. For the purposes of the present discussion, however, it is best to begin with this, as it fits the needs of the present study best and there is strong reason to believe that it was the principal starting point in Durkheim's own mind of the train of reasoning that is of interest here.[1]

---

[1] The most important piece of biographical evidence is to be found in the preface by M. Mauss to the series of lectures published after Durkheim's death under the title *Le socialisme*. These lectures were delivered at Bordeaux in 1895–1896, near the culmination of the earlier period of development. M. Mauss there tells us that Durkheim's earliest preoccupation had been with the problems of economic individualism. He early came to the conclusion that the individualistic theories, including those of the orthodox economists, were inadequate to account for the situation, and Durkheim was long attracted to socialism as an alternative. He made a thorough study of socialist thought and intended to publish a book on it. In the course of the study, however, he became convinced that the socialist theories were also inadequate for essentially the same fundamental reasons. This situation constituted his principal motive for changing his field of interest and embark-

It is not until Book I, Chap. VII, that Durkheim launches into a contrast between the conception he has just put forward of "organic solidarity" and that of "contractual relations" as employed by Spencer. The latter is not, however, a concept peculiar to Spencer, but is, for Durkheim's critical purposes, a convenient form, a mode of expression, of a much broader general point of view. Spencer's contractual relation is the type case of a social relationship in which only the elements formulated in "utilitarian" theory are involved. Its prototype is the economic exchange relationship where the determinant elements are the demand and supply schedules of the parties concerned. At least implicit in the conception of a system of such relationships is the conception that it is the mutual advantage derived by the parties from the various exchanges which constitutes the principal binding, cohesive force in the system. It is as a direct antithesis to this deeply imbedded conception of a system of "relations of contract"[1] that Durkheim wishes his own "organic solidarity" to be understood.

The line which Durkheim's criticism takes is that the Spencerian, or more generally utilitarian, formulation fails to exhaust, even for the case of what are the purely "interested" transactions of the market place, the elements which actually are both to be found in the existing system of such transactions, and which, it can be shown, must exist, if the system is to function at all. What is omitted is the fact that these transactions are actually entered into in accordance with a body of binding rules which are not part of the *ad hoc* agreement of the parties. The elements included in the utilitarian conception are, on the contrary, all taken account of in the terms of agreement. What may, however, be called the "institution" of contract—the rules regulating relations of contract—has not been agreed to by the parties but exists prior to and independently by any such agreement.[2]

---

ing on the studies the results of which were published in the *Division of Labor*. As will be seen in connection with a brief account of his treatment of socialism, this biographical account supports directly the interpretation which has here been placed on the genesis of the problems Durkheim treats in the *Division of Labor*.

[1] This term is here used to designate the concrete reality, while Spencer's term "contractual relations" may designate certain abstract elements in it.

[2] Durkheim repeatedly reiterates this point. See especially *Division of Labor*, p. 192.

The content of the rules is various. They regulate, in the first place, what contracts are and what are not recognized as valid. A man cannot, for instance, sell himself or others into slavery. They regulate the means by which the other party's assent to a contract may be obtained; an agreement secured by fraud or under duress is void. They regulate various consequences of a contract once made, both to the parties themselves and to third persons. Under certain circumstances a party may be enjoined from enforcing a contract quite legally made, as when the holder of a mortgage is sometimes prohibited from foreclosing when interest payments are not made. Similarly one party may be forced to assume obligations which were not in his contract. They regulate, finally, the procedure by which enforcement in the courts is obtainable. In a society like our own this nexus of regulations is exceedingly complex.

For convenience Durkheim lays the principal stress on the body of rules which are formulated in law and enforceable in the courts. But this must not be allowed to lead to misunderstanding of his position. Even Spencer recognized the necessity for some agency outside the contracting parties themselves to enforce contracts. But on the one hand, Spencer and the other individualistic[1] writers have laid their principal stress on enforcement of the terms of agreements themselves, whereas Durkheim's main stress is on the existence of a body of rules which have not been the object of any agreement among the contracting parties themselves but are socially "given."[2] If they wish to enter into relations of contract it is only under the conditions laid down in these rules and with the consequences with reference both to eventual rights and to obligations which they define that they may do so at all. Of course if the rules were not to some degree enforced, they would be unimportant, but it is on their independence of the process of *ad hoc* agreement that Durkheim lays his emphasis.[3] Secondly, while he discusses mainly legal rules, he is careful to point out that these stand by no means alone, but are supplemented by a vast body of customary rules, trade conventions and the like which are, in effect, obligatory equally with the

---

[1] In the sense used in this discussion.

[2] See especially *Division of Labor*, p. 192.

[3] His most succinct formula is "Tout n'est pas contractuel dans le contrat." *Division of Labor*, p. 189, see also p. 194.

law, although not enforceable in the courts.[1] This shading off of law into trade practice indicates that this body of rules is much more closely integrated with the contractual system itself than the individualists would be ready to grant. The latter tended to think of the role of society in these matters, as represented by the state, as one of only occasional intervention to straighten out a difficulty in a machinery which normally functioned quite automatically without "social" interference.[2]

Why is this body of rules of contract important? In the first place, Durkheim notes that the possible consequences of the relations entered into by agreement, both to the parties themselves and to others, are so complex and remote that, if they all had to be thought out *ad hoc* and agreed to anew each time, the vast body of transactions which go on would be utterly impossible.[3] As it is, it is necessary only to agree formally to a very small part of these matters; the rest is taken care of by the recognized rules.

But the most important consideration of all is that the elements formulated in the utilitarian theory contain no adequate basis of order.[4] A contractual agreement brings men together only for a limited purpose, for a limited time. There is no adequate motive given why men should pursue even this limited purpose by means which are compatible with the interests of others, even though its attainment as such should be so compatible. There is a latent hostility between men which this theory does not take account of. It is as a framework of order that the institution of contract is of primary importance.[5] Without it men would, as

---

[1] *Division of Labor*, p. 193. There may also be rules enforced on themselves by occupational groups such as the professions.

[2] This analysis of Durkheim's is directed to the concrete nexus of relations of contract, itself. Even there, on the individualists' own ground, he found their position untenable. But he also attacks the Spencerian thesis that relations of contract tend, with the progress of differentiation, to drive all others out. Particularly with regard to the state he argues that a great increase in its functions and importance is altogether normal to a differentiated society (*Division of Labor*, pp. 198 *ff.*). Though he does not take up the problem explicitly there is no reason to attribute to him the view that social structures other than the state tend to disappear with the development of the contractual nexus.

[3] *Division of Labor*, p. 190–191.

[4] *Ibid.*, pp. 180–181.

[5] It states, says Durkheim, "the normal condition of stable equilibrium." *Ibid.*, p. 192.

Durkheim explicitly says, be in a state of war.[1] But actual social life is not war. In so far as it involves the pursuit of individual interests it is such interests, pursued in such a manner as greatly to mitigate this latent hostility, to promote mutual advantage and peaceful cooperation rather than mutual hostility and destruction. Spencer and others who think like him have entirely failed to explain how this is accomplished. And in arriving at his own explanation Durkheim first points to an empirical fact: This vast complex of action in the pursuit of individual interests takes place within the framework of a body of rules, independent of the immediate individual motives of the contracting parties. This fact the individualists have either not recognized at all, or have not done justice to. It is the central empirical insight from which Durkheim's theoretical development starts, and which he never lost.

It is clear that what Durkheim has here done is to reraise in a peculiarly trenchant form the whole Hobbesian problem. There are features of the existing "individualistic" order which cannot be accounted for in terms of the elements formulated in utilitarian theory. The activities that the utilitarians, above all the economists, have in mind can take place only within a framework of order characterized by a system of regulatory rules. Without this framework of order it would degenerate into a state of war. On this fundamental critical ground Durkheim is clear and incisive, and in this respect he never in the least altered his position. Nor did he ever abandon the basic empirical insight just mentioned, the importance of a system of regulatory, normative rules. His difficulties appeared in confronting the problem of how to fit this insight, dependent as it was on his critical position, into a conceptual scheme which would be scientifically satisfactory, yet not share the fallacies of the scheme underlying the position he had criticized.

The solution to which Hobbes turned was, as has been seen, that of the *deus ex machina*. The sovereign, standing entirely outside the system, forcibly kept order by the threat of sanctions. Even in the most optimistic of the individualistic writers short of anarchism there is at least a glimmer of the Hobbesian solution in the place reserved to the state in the enforcement of contracts. It has already been noted that Durkheim's thinking

[1] *Ibid.*, p. 181.

was not tending in these channels. While not inclined to depreciate the role of the state,[1] neither was he inclined to the radical dualism of state versus the nexus of individual interests which characterized the whole utilitarian tradition. The fact that for him the system of rules of contract shaded off from formal law into informal trade practice, while yet maintaining its regulatory character, its independence of immediate individual interests, made the rigidity of such a dichotomy impossible.

A direction was indicated by the use of the term moral to designate the central feature of the facts to which he was pointing. This was, indeed, prophetic of the line of his future development. But he did not leap immediately to the central thesis of his later work, but had to arrive at it gradually by a complicated and devious route. This delay seems to be explained by two main sets of considerations. One lay in the peculiar character of the conceptual apparatus with which he worked, in the *Division of Labor*, very tentatively, then much more clearly and decisively. That point will be discussed in full in the following chapter. But at the same time, on the relatively empirical level of the present discussion, certain things can be seen to have inhibited the attainment of the solution at which he ultimately arrived, and to have thrown his thought into another channel. Even so there tended to remain a gap between the empirical and the theoretical levels of his work. All through the earlier period his empirical insights were a good deal nearer his final position than was the theoretical scheme. The attempt to bridge this gap was doubtless an important driving force in the process of theoretical development.

In so far as the problem of order in Hobbes' sense was the logical starting point of Durkheim's study, and his approach to it was through a critique of orthodox utilitarian interpretations of a system of relations of contract, it is not difficult to understand how the division of labor and the problem of social differentiation became involved. For, especially to the classical economists, the division of labor is one of the prime features of an individualistic society. Without specialization there would be on a utilitarian basis no society at all, since it is the mutual advantages of exchange which constitute the main motive

---

[1] He did not limit it to enforcement of contracts or the other "classical" functions of the state.

for abandoning the state of nature and entering into social relationships.

Indeed it is simply a further logical step when Durkheim extends his critique of the individualistic theories from their treatment of the problem of order to their theory of the forces explaining the progress of social differentiation. Here the object of his attack is what he calls the "happiness" theory.[1] The alleged reason for the progressive development of the division of labor is the increase of happiness to be derived from each further step in specialization.

It is not surprising to find on analysis that Durkheim, like most of his opponents, failed to differentiate clearly two elements in this happiness theory. Some of his critical remarks are directed against strict psychological hedonism. Others, on the other hand, do not assume hedonism but rather what has been called here in a strict sense the utilitarian position. Taken together all his arguments are sufficient to throw very strong doubt on any theoretical system which takes as its fundamental basis the rational unit act and treats it atomistically—in the sense of the above discussion. It has already been seen that hedonism is the doctrine which, in the radical positivistic direction, calls for least modification in the utilitarian system and is hence closely associated with it historically. In the course of this critique again fundamental elements appear which cannot be properly interpreted on a theoretical and methodological level until a much later stage of Durkheim's development.

The principal argument directed against hedonism as such is that, on a psychophysiological level our capacity for pleasure is limited. With increasing volume and intensity of any stimulus, the resulting pleasurable sensation increases up to a point and then begins to decline. At either extreme pleasure is transformed into a negative feeling-tone, pain. Then in so far as it is the maximization of pleasure which explains a course of action there would, relatively soon, be a point of satiation and hence equilibrium reached. Thus such an element is entirely inadequate to explain a process which has gone on continuously in the same direction for many generations. It seems to the present writer that, in so far as to any degree a level of the psychology of sensation is adhered to, Durkheim is undoubtedly in the right.

[1] *Division of Labor*, Book II, Chap. I.

The most plausible rejoinder to his critique really leads over to another level of discussion. It is that while there is an inherent limit to the amount of pleasure derivable from what may be called the quantitative satisfaction of wants—a man can eat only so much—there is no limit to the refinements of quality. This argument really shifts the ground. For it cannot be said in any sense applicable to the psychology of hedonism that when such a qualitative change has become large it is the *same* wants that are being satisfied. In so far as this is true the happiness criterion becomes a relative one, relative to the particular system of desires under consideration. From being an inherent feature of human nature it becomes a measure of the attainment of human desire. It becomes what the economists have called "utility."

Then, the happiness principle is inadequate for the purpose in hand if, and in so far as, the system of wants is itself relative. It is this thesis, then, which really underlies Durkheim's critique of the happiness theory. The latter involves a circular argument unless it be assumed that there is one and only one possible system of human wants which throughout all history is equally relevant to all action. On either a utilitarian[1] or a hedonistic basis this assumption is accepted without question. In questioning it Durkheim has opened up a world of considerations entirely outside the range of either of these two theoretical positions. This critical position is one which points in the general direction of a large role to be attributed to value elements. As has been said, the full consequences of this insight took a very long time to develop. But, as in his critique of the conception of a system of contractual relations, his position here is sure and incisive. The basic insight he never abandoned.[2]

[1] Here because the randomness of wants implies that there is no significant relation between their concrete content, hence variation in it, and the processes of their satisfaction. For practical purposes this is the same as assuming that wants are constant.

[2] On the empirical basis Durkheim raises the question whether in fact happiness may be held to have increased with the progress of civilization. His conclusion is negative. As an index capable of objective treatment he discusses the rate of suicide, arguing that the suicide cannot be held to be happy. In this connection he calls attention to the great increase during the nineteenth century of the suicide rate in Europe, and the fact that it is much higher among the most "civilized" parts of the population, particu-

The peculiar way in which Durkheim set out to build up a positive theory of his own which would avoid the difficulties of the positions he had criticized, had the consequence of assimilating his basic problem, that of order, far more closely to that of social differentiation than is intrinsically justified. It is natural that, having laid his empirical emphasis on the existence of a body of regulatory norms, of rules of action, he should turn to law as the most promising field in which to find the facts on which to build his own interpretation. In so doing he was led to make a distinction between two types of law which lies at the basis of the peculiarities of his position, between what he called "repressive" and "restitutive" law. In the one case infraction of the legal rule calls forth punishment, in the other merely restitution of the *status quo ante.*

This distinction was in turn bound up with the distinction of two types of society, the undifferentiated and the differentiated, respectively. Repressive law is held to be an index of *common* beliefs and sentiments. It plays a part in social life in so far as the members of the community are *alike,* that is, alike in sharing the same beliefs and sentiments. Repressive law is, then, an index of the strength of the *conscience collective.* Restitutive law, on the other hand, is an index of social differentiation. In so far as the rules involved are applicable only to a specialized part of the community their infraction does not strike at the common beliefs and sentiments and does not call forth the reaction of punishment, but only a much milder demand for restoration of the damage. In the one case there is "mechanical solidarity," in the other "organic."

It is the thesis of the present interpretation of Durkheim's development that the situation just outlined must have operated to throw him seriously off the track. For it is a striking fact that it was in the conception of the *conscience collective* that the germ of most of his later theoretical development lay. Indeed it is striking to discover how much of his later position is to be found in his earliest discussion of it. The central conception is that of a system of common beliefs and sentiments, that is, the main emphasis is on its ethical or value character. In the

---

larly in the cities and the liberal professions. This is particularly interesting in that it contains the germ of his monograph on suicide, which brought him a long step farther in his theoretical development.

conception of punishment was clearly stated the view that the value elements were manifested in symbolic form as well as in connection with an intrinsic means-end relationship.[1] But this conception was associated with an undifferentiated society and mechanical solidarity. His original problem, on the other hand, had been to understand the "non-contractual element in contract." The classification he evolved had the effect of dissociating this altogether from the *conscience collective*, it was a matter of the division of labor and of organic solidarity.

It may be said that Durkheim showed the same incisiveness in his early formulations concerning the *conscience collective* as he did in his double critique of utilitarian individualism. But the gap between his critical starting points and his first sure positive insights could not be closed at once. The main line of

[1] In his discussion of punishment Durkheim makes an observation which is of far-reaching importance though its implications lead to problems which are peripheral to his own system even at the end of its development. It is that punishment is not necessarily a "rational" (meaning, it seems, calculated as a suitable intrinsic means to an end) reaction but is "passional" or, perhaps, better, "emotional." The fact that this is associated with the action of the *conscience collective* means that, in a certain sense, there is opened up a whole range of nonrational elements which are yet not adequately understood in terms of "individual psychology." The relation of this to symbolic expression is evident.

In this connection Durkheim is continually referring to the individual's dependence on the society. Though he does not explicitly make the suggestion, his whole treatment points strongly to the importance of a distinction between two radically different types of dependence which are analytically separable. One type is "emotional dependence" on other persons or on common values. The typical manifestation of this dependence occurs in that when the relationship is threatened or disturbed there is an emotional reaction (anger, jealousy). On the other hand, there is the kind of dependence the economists have in mind, the sense in which Manchester cotton workers are dependent upon Canadian wheat farmers, a matter of the intrinsic means-end relationship, in the sense that the Manchester worker eats bread, as one means to his ends, which is produced by means (wheat) under the control of another group of persons.

The ramifications of the first type of dependence have been explored most thoroughly on the individual level by psychopathology, especially psychoanalysis. The fact that this type of emotional reaction crops up at such an early stage in Durkheim's work strongly suggests that he is not, as has often been claimed, bound to a "falsely rationalistic psychology." Indeed this leads into problems which lie on the periphery not only of Durkheim's own systematic theorizing, but of this study as a whole. It will not, unfortunately, be possible to carry their discussion further here.

his development may, however, be considered to be just such a process. Gradually the *conscience collective* came more and more to overshadow the conception of organic solidarity. The distinction of social types ceased to be one between situations where a *conscience collective* did and did not predominate in action, but became a matter of distinguishing different contents of the *conscience collective* itself. As will be shown, this process was already well under way in *Le suicide*. In the process the problem of differentiation, or of social structure in any concrete[1] sense, receded more and more into the background. What mattered was the relation of the individual to the common element. But in the meantime it is necessary to take up the difficulties into which Durkheim fell in trying to keep individualistic, differentiated society and common values separated.

The problem may be stated succinctly as follows: The individualists have been wrong in maintaining that the element of order which actually exists in a differentiated society with a wide extension of exchange relationships can be derived from the immediate interests of the parties to these relationships. There is a distinct element present which Durkheim calls "organic solidarity." This element cannot, however, be the same as that which accounts for the cohesion, the solidarity, of an undifferentiated society, the *conscience collective*. What, then, is it and where does it come from? In answer to the first problem: The original tendency is, as has been shown, to hold that it is a body of normative rules governing action. But it is an indication of the embarrassment growing out of the situation Durkheim was in, that he does not proceed directly from this empirical insight in building up his own theory, except to the extent of working out a differentiating criterion from the rules of repressive law. He, rather, jumps directly to general considerations. The direction of this move is of the greatest interest to the present study.

He starts by remarking that the division of labor cannot have developed from a "state of nature," a plurality of discrete individuals.[2] Differentiation can take place only within a society. The development of organic solidarity presupposes the existence of mechanical solidarity. But he does not really get beyond this

---

[1] That is, more concrete than the structure of systems of action.

[2] The argument here to be followed is found in *Division of Labor*, Book II, Chap. II.

point. The general drift of his argument is to the effect that the division of labor itself creates solidarity. What he gives as an account of the mechanism of this process is extremely sketchy, but the reader gathers that it is in his mind primarily a matter of habituation. New practices grow up along certain lines which in the course of time become habitual. In the course of still more time ways of doing things which are habitual in turn become obligatory as binding rules.

But this is clearly from his own standpoint an unsatisfactory account of the matter. He started with the view that organic solidarity was analytically a quite distinct element from those included in the utilitarian analysis. But along this line the only addition he had made is that of the mechanism of habituation, and that raises greater difficulties than it solves. For where, in the mechanism of habit, is the element of *obligation* to be found? Yet this was, at the beginning, the nub of the question. The only real element of obligation still seems to be that involved in mechanical solidarity. In a sense reversion to mechanical solidarity represents the authentic line of Durkheim's own development. In the present context, however, it is a serious source of embarrassment.

But granting for the moment that solidarity is created by the mere process of differentiation itself, what is the source of the latter? He has decisively rejected the happiness explanation; such an element cannot account for a process which is continuous over very long periods in a single direction. Here enters the first clear intimation of the theoretical dilemma which will dominate the discussion of the next chapter. The happiness explanation, Durkheim argues, is subjective. It attempts to make use of the actor's motives. Since this is not acceptable, the only alternative is to turn to the conditions of the situation in which he acts. In this sense, then, the cause of the division of labor must be found in features of the social milieu of action. What features?

The particular feature on which Durkheim fastens is what he calls the "dynamic density" of the society. The essential reasoning behind the concept is that if there is to be differentiation of function there must be effective contact between individuals in the society. This above all means there must be a breakdown of the "insulation" between subgroups which is characteristic of what he calls a "segmentary" social structure.[1] But dynamic density is in turn dependent on the "material density" of the society, the number of individuals that are to be in contact per unit of space. Finally, material density cannot be high unless there is an absolutely large number of persons available to be in contact, unless the "volume" of the society is large. That is, in the last analysis social differentiation is a result of the increase of numbers in the society, of population pressure.

This is, to Durkheim at this stage of his thinking, the principal cause of the division of labor. It is to be seen that it is arrived at by a somewhat attenuated argument. He has, on the one hand, eliminated one possible set of factors, those capable of being summed up as individual interests. From there on he has proceeded by a process of further elimination, citing not so much positive determinants as necessary conditions. Dynamic density cannot exist without material density, material density without volume. The indeterminateness of this solution comes out vividly in his discussion of the mechanism by which increasing population pressure gives rise to division of labor. Borrowing from biological sources Durkheim describes the process as a result of the intensification of the struggle for existence. But he recognizes the fact that there is more than one possible outcome of this intensification. It might lead simply to the elimination by natural selection of a larger proportion of those born. In contrast to this the division of labor constitutes a mitigation of natural selection. It operates by differentiating out different areas within which groups of individuals are in competition with each other. Instead of each individual being in direct competition with every other, he competes only with a limited number, those in the same occupational group.

But in the course of this argument the meaning of "struggle for existence" shifts. In the Malthusian-Darwinian sense it meant essentially competition for food supply, the means of subsistence in a strict sense. But Durkheim speaks predominantly in terms of the "attainment of ends," which certainly includes much more than physical subsistence. Indeed it becomes predominantly the satisfaction of ambition, of the desire for social

[1] An adaptation from Spencer's classification of social structure. For Durkheim's exposition see *Division of Labor*, Book I, Chap. VI.

prestige. Thus the argument returns to the social milieu, but to aspects of it which are not at all obviously the simple outcome of population pressure as such. Indeed it is just the differentiating element from the Darwinian which should evidently be of primary importance here, that which accounts for the mitigation of natural selection, but that is just what Durkheim fails to throw light upon.

What is clear in the solution of the problem of organic solidarity is only the critical repudiation of utilitarian interpretations and the insight that peaceful differentiation can only proceed within the framework of order of a society. But Durkheim has conspicuously failed to account for the specific element of organic solidarity beyond the very general formula that it must lie in features of the social milieu. When he attempts to go beyond this what he ends up with is population pressure, not in any analytical sense a social element at all, but essentially biological. In so far as this is Durkheim's main line of thought it is a familiar one here; it is the breakdown of utilitarianism into radical positivism, in this case the "biologizing" of social theory. But this is not the main line. It was one which was soon abandoned. That it was entered on at all is accounted for by a combination of the empirical embarrassment just discussed and certain difficulties of the general conceptual scheme which will be discussed in the next chapter. It is of great interest as symptomatic of the peculiar situation in which Durkheim was placed in both these respects.

A hint of the direction the development was actually to take appears in the discussion of what Durkheim refers to as a "secondary cause" of the division of labor. It is what he calls the "progressive indetermination of the *conscience collective.*"[1] In the type of society dominated by repressive law, says Durkheim, there is a minute regulation of the details of action. With the progress of the division of labor this detailed regulation gradually falls away. The sanctions and the typical emotional reaction in defense of common values no longer attach to particular acts, to the employment of particular means for a given end, but only to very general principles and attitudes. This necessarily results in a far wider range of independence for individual choice and initiative.

[1] *Division of Labor*, Book II, Chap. III. My translation.

Here is an element which acts not in the direction of a break-down in the influence of the *conscience collective*, as population pressure does, but through a change in the character of its influence due to a change in its own constitution. This element heralds the changed position which is found emerging in *Le suicide*, to which the discussion must now turn.

SUICIDE

Le suicide[1] seems at first glance to be concerned with an entirely different range of problems from those of the division of labor. This is not so, however. In the respects which are of primary interest here it is to be regarded as a continuation of the same line of thinking, a new crucial experiment in a different factual field. As usually develops, in the course of the investigation the theory itself is not merely verified, but undergoes a change. It is this which is of primary interest here.

It will be remembered that Durkheim called attention to the possible significance of suicide rates in his critical discussion of the happiness hypothesis of the development of social differentiation. The monograph he published four years later is to be regarded as an intensive study following up the suggestive remarks made in that brief discussion.

After the statement of the problem and preliminary definitions the book starts with a systematic critique of previous attempts to explain variations in the rate of suicide.[2] The various theories he criticizes fall into two main classes. One type, which he dismisses very briefly, is that which employs what are ordinarily called the motives of suicide, such as financial reverses, domestic infelicity and the like. The principal empirical argument

---

[1] All references in this study are to the 1930 edition.

[2] *Suicide*, Book I. Durkheim confines himself to the rate and makes no attempt to explain individual cases. Thus he succeeds in eliminating factors in the latter which bear only upon incidence. "Rate" is here meant in the statistical sense similar to "death rate." It is the number of suicides annually per 100,000 of a given population. Factors of incidence are, on the other hand, those explaining why a given person committed suicide rather than another. Thus to take an example from another field, personal inefficiency may well explain why one person rather than another is unemployed at a given time. But it is extremely unlikely that a sudden change in the efficiency of the working population of the United States occurred which could account for the enormous increase of unemployment between 1929 and 1932. The latter is a problem of rate, not of incidence.

he brings to bear is that, in so far as these motives are ascertainable at all, when they are classified the proportions of cases falling into the various classes remain approximately constant through wide variations in the general rate. Since it is the latter which he is attempting to explain, motives in this sense may be regarded as irrelevant. The "motive" type of explanation is important in the present context because it is the principal form taken, in relation to suicide, by the utilitarian type of theory. Suicide is regarded by it as a rational act in pursuit of a definite end, and it is not thought necessary to go beyond this end. The social rate would be a mere summation of such "cases."

The other theories discussed all invoke factors in explanation which can be classified for present purposes as belonging to the categories of heredity and environment. In the first place there are what Durkheim calls the "cosmic" explanations,[1] in terms of climatic conditions and the like. He has little difficulty in demonstrating that the alleged relations between suicide rates and climate are at least open to other interpretations. Then there are race,[2] alcohol,[3] psychopathological states[4] and imitation.[5] In each case he succeeds in demonstrating, for the most part on purely empirical grounds, that previous theories embodying these factors, or any combination of them, are not capable of yielding a satisfactory general solution of the problem, though he has by no means succeeded in showing that they can have nothing to do with it.[6] Except race, they are probably of greater significance as factors in incidence than in the rate, but Durkheim certainly has not eliminated them from the latter. He has however shown that previous explanations embodying them have not so completely explained the phenomenon that a new approach to it is ruled out from the start.

The only one of these which calls for special comment here is the case of psychopathological states. It should be remembered that Durkheim was writing in the 1890's and that psychopathology has advanced enormously since then. The psychopatho-

---

[1] *Suicide*, Chap. III.
[2] *Ibid.*, Chap. II.
[3] *Ibid.*, Chap. I, Sec. V.
[4] *Ibid.*, Chap. I.
[5] *Ibid.*, Chap. IV.
[6] Sometimes he overshoots the mark but this does not affect the general soundness of his position.

logical views he criticizes are primarily those which attribute suicide to a specific, hereditary psychopathological condition and he is able to show easily that this cannot account for the significant variations of suicide rates. His arguments do not, however, apply to the "environmental" and "functional" types of mental disturbance of which our understanding has been so greatly increased in the last generation, especially through psychoanalysis and related movements. But in so far as the ultimate causes of a mental disturbance which issues in suicide are "environmental," *e.g.*, not hereditary, there is every reason to believe that the social component of the environment plays a decisive part. In fact Durkheim's analysis, especially in connection with the concept of *anomie* which will be discussed below, throws a great deal of light on these causes. Psychopathology comes in to trace the mechanisms by which such social situations affect the individual and his behavior. Thus, as has been shown by Durkheim's principal follower in this field, Professor Halbwachs,[1] the social and the psychopathological explanations of suicide are not antithetical but complementary. But at the time when Durkheim wrote neither psychopathology nor his own sociology had reached a point of development where it was possible to build the bridge between them.[2]

One thing is to be noted particularly about Durkheim's critical work in this connection. In the *Division of Labor* his critique was directed primarily against the utilitarian type of theory. There was a more or less incidental critique of explanations of the division of labor in terms of heredity[3] by which he there meant the hereditary component in differentiation of character and ability between individuals. At the same time he invoked, as has been seen, another hereditary factor, the principle of population, for his own purposes. Here is, on the other hand, a clear and self-conscious criticism of a group of hereditary and environmental[4] theories. The results of his detailed empirical criticisms of particular theories are generalized into the position

---

[1] M. HALBWACHS, *Les causes du suicide*, Chap. XI.

[2] The logic of the situation was, however, well known in the natural sciences, and had Durkheim been acquainted with them he would have been spared a great deal of trouble. Pareto would not have fallen into this error.

[3] *Division of Labor*, Book II, Chap. IV.

[4] In the technical sense of the above discussion, excluding the subjective components of the "social" environment.

that no theory either in terms of motives in the above sense, or of these other factors, can be satisfactory. The latter are specifically characterized as individualistic[1] and over against them is set, as his methodological program, the development of social factors. The social milieu is specifically distinguished from the nonsocial components of the environment of the acting individual. Correspondingly there is, in the *Suicide* no further use made of the population factor; indeed it drops out of his work altogether. The social milieu retains, however, one basic property in common with heredity and environment: as seen by the actor it is a matter of things beyond his power to control—this is the nub of Durkheim's rejection of the "motive" explanation of suicide. It remained for a long time the distinguishing feature of his sociological objectivism.

The factors in the suicide rate in which he is interested are, then, to be found in features of the social milieu. They are what he calls *courants suicidogènes*. His own positive analysis consists in the distinction between and working out of the empirical consequences of three such factors.[2] In so far as one of the three factors is maximized in importance relative to the others there are three "ideal types" of suicide called, respectively, "altruistic,"[3]

[1] Which, as has been seen is probably not legitimate. See above, Chap. II, p. 74. This served, however, the useful purpose of directing Durkheim's attention to the value components of the social environment. It was a "fruitful error."

[2] He makes room for a fourth called *suicide fataliste* but does not develop it himself, and hence it is not treated here. See *Suicide*, footnote 1, p. 311.

[3] Durkheim's use of the terms "egoism" and "altruism" in this connection calls for comment. This dichotomy is of course, deeply imbedded in modern ethical thinking, and it had already made its appearance at a number of points in the *Division of Labor*. Indeed, in a sense, egoism is inherently bound up with the utilitarian manner of thought. For in so far as men's ends are genuinely random it follows that, given the rationality of their action, others are significant to them *only* in the capacity of means and conditions to their own ends, which are by definition devoid of any positive relation to those of others except through relations to means. It has been shown how the consequences of this were developed by Hobbes in connection with the problem of power, and that Durkheim accepts the Hobbesian analysis. In this vein he repeatedly speaks of the need of control as a matter of the "moderation of egoisms." As opposed to the Hobbesian state of nature, "solidarity" implies the existence of a moderating influence, and in so far as this is "moral" and not a matter of coercion, Durkheim refers to it as an element of altruism. A society, he says implies the existence

"egoistic" and "anomic" suicide. The principal task of the remainder of the present discussion of his treatment of suicide will be to analyze these three concepts, their relation to each other and to the conceptual framework of the *Division of Labor* already discussed. The prototypes of all of them have, as will be seen, appeared in the earlier work. But the modifications from their use there are of the first importance.

The simplest case is that of *suicide altruiste*.[1] It involves a group attachment of great strength such that in comparison with claims made upon the individual in fulfillment of the obligations laid upon him by the group his own interests, even in life itself, become secondary. This leads, on the one hand, to a generally small valuation of individual life, even by the individual himself, so that he will part with it on relatively small provocation; on the other hand in certain cases it leads to a direct social mandate to suicide. In modern Western societies the case which arrests Durkheim's attention is that of armies.[2] It is a fact that the suicide rates of armies are in his data markedly higher than in the corresponding civilian populations.[3] This is a matter of the

---

of altruism. The terms "interested" and "disinterested" motivation as they appear in the *Division of Labor* seem to be synonymous with egoism and altruism respectively.

As will be seen, however, serious difficulties arise over the tendency in modern thought to interpret this dichotomy as one of *concrete* motives. Durkheim eventually overcame these difficulties, but not without a great deal of trouble and misunderstanding.

In the *Suicide* it will be seen that the terms shift their meaning somewhat. What was meant earlier by egoism is much closer to what *anomie* comes to mean. The term egoism, on the other hand, is attached to what may be called "social individualism," while altruism is attached not to disinterested motivation in general but to a particular sort of attachment to groups. All this will be discussed in considerable detail below. But the shift in meaning of the terms is distinctly confusing and it is well to warn the reader of it in advance. It is an indication of the fact that Durkheim's own thought was in a process of dynamic development throughout this period, and that he had not defined his terms rigorously.

[1] *Suicide*, Book II, Chap. IV

[2] *Ibid.*, Sec. II.

[3] It is well to remark briefly on Durkheim's use of statistics in the study of suicide rates. It has already been pointed out (footnote, p. 38) that in the social field most available statistical information is on a level which cannot be made to fit directly into the categories of analytical theory. Even on the relatively high analytical level which economic theory has reached,

peacetime situation, although when a soldier in obeying orders apart from coercion exposes himself to a risk of almost certain death in battle it would also be suicide according to Durkheim's definition. But the peacetime military suicide rate has generally been explained by the objective hardships of military life. This is not, however, satisfactory. For one thing, suicides are more common among officers than enlisted men, and surely the officer's lot is easier. Furthermore, the rate increases with length of service, while one would expect that there would be habituation to hardship so that its effect would be greatest in the first year or two. Finally, more generally there is no correlation between hardship as indicated by poverty, and suicide. Some of the poorest countries of Europe, such as Italy and Spain, have far lower general suicide rates than more prosperous countries like France, Germany and the Scandinavian countries.[2] Moreover, within a country the upper classes, especially in the cities, have higher suicide rates than the lower. This cannot be due to hardship in the ordinary sense.

---

with the, socially speaking, quite exceptional degree of quantification which economic concepts have achieved, the attempt to fill the "empty boxes" of theoretical demand and supply functions with specific statistical data has met with very serious difficulties. Durkheim's conceptual scheme in this monograph is not nearly so refined and rigorous as that of economic theory and his statistical techniques are on a crude level, sometimes even directly fallacious. In any event, it is out of the question that in the usual sense of statistical "elegance" he should be held to have accomplished rigorous statistical verification of his conceptual scheme. What is true is, rather, that by means of a very broad and elementary statistical analysis he has been able to bring out certain broad features of the facts about suicide and the variations in its rate. He relates to these broad features of the facts certain equally broad theoretical distinctions in such a way that the two, on the whole, in this broad sense, "fit." Above all there is nothing even approaching numerical exactitude in the theoretical significance of his results. But the very broadness and lack of refinement of the statistical method is perhaps an advantage from the point of view of the present interest, which is in the most general categories of the theory of action. It is almost certain that refined statistical analysis of the data by modern techniques would reveal many complexities of which Durkheim was not aware, but it is very unlikely that any such analysis would make it possible to "refute" Durkheim on the broad basis on which his analysis properly rests. Certainly the author has never seen any argument which could be seriously considered as such a refutation.

[2] *Ibid.*, Book II, Chap. V, Sec. II.

330 ÉMILE DURKHEIM, I: EARLY EMPIRICAL WORK

The explanation that Durkheim advances is quite different. What distinguishes the army in modern society is the stringency of its discipline. There the desires and interests of the individual count very little in comparison with the impersonal duties imposed upon him by his membership in the group. This situation generates an attitude which is careless of individual interests in general, of life in particular. This is manifested for instance by the ease with which the military man will commit suicide when his "honor" is impugned. Japan, a specifically militaristic society, furnishes a most striking example. The fact that in those countries where the general rate of suicide is high the army rate is relatively low and vice versa[1] strikingly confirms the view that the army rate is due to causes different from those operative in the general population.

Altruistic suicide Durkheim also finds exemplified in primitive societies, and in certain religious groups. In some of these cases, such as the Indian custom of suttee, there is a direct social mandate to suicide.

It seems quite clear that the altruistic factor in suicide is, for Durkheim, on essentially the same theoretical plane as mechanical solidarity. It is a manifestation of the *conscience collective* in the sense of group pressure at the expense of the claims of individuality. But even here there is a slight shift of emphasis. It is no longer similarity which is the central point, but subordination of individuality to the group. It is not because the army is an undifferentiated group that it has a high suicide rate, not that there is no difference between officers and men or artillery and infantry, but because of the character of the discipline imposed. Already Durkheim is moving away from the identification of the problem of "solidarity" with that of social structure. Altruistic suicide is a manifestation of a *conscience collective* which is strong in the sense of subordinating individual to group interests, and which has the particular content of a low valuation of individual life relative to group values.

With "egoism" the explanation is more complicated, and there is a much more radical shift from the position of the *Division of Labor*. There are two main groups of empirical phenomena in connection with which Durkheim strongly emphasized this element. In the first place, he is much struck by the relation of

[1] *Suicide*, p. 255.

suicide to family status.[1] In general, married persons have distinctly lower suicide rates than unmarried, widowed and divorced. This difference is greatly increased by the presence of children and in proportion to the number in the family. The decisive factor with which Durkheim emerges after eliminating various others, especially selection, is the attachment to a certain type of group as a mitigating influence.[2] People are, to a point, less liable to commit suicide in so far as their relation to a group of others is, in the sense noted above, one of emotional dependence. But so far as the formulation of the concept of egoism is concerned this leaves us with an essentially negative conclusion. Egoism seems to exist as a factor in suicide so far as people are freed from such group control, while altruism exists so far as the group control is excessively strong in certain respects. This leaves the relation of egoism to *anomie* distinctly unclear.

But in the discussion of the other body of data, those concerning the relation of suicide to religious affiliation, something much more definite emerges. The striking fact is that the rate for Protestants is very much higher than for Catholics.[3] The relation holds when a number of other factors are eliminated,[4] as for example, nationality. For instance, in both German and French Switzerland the Protestant rate is much the higher, and in Germany the rate is much lower in the largely Catholic sections of Bavaria, the Rhineland and Silesia than for the country as a whole. What is the explanation of this striking fact?[5]

It lies, according to Durkheim, in the Protestant attitude toward individual freedom in religious matters. The Catholic,

[1] *Ibid.*, Book II, Chap. III.
[2] *Ibid.*, Book II, Chap. II.
[3] There is no necessary inconsistency in Durkheim here. In interpreting the data on suicides among Catholics he ascribes a low suicide rate to attachment to a group, whereas in interpreting the army suicide data he appears to ascribe high suicide rates to the same cause. The difference is quantitative. There is an optimum intensity of group attachment which the Catholic with a large family comes close to. Too strong an attachment, an increase far beyond this optimum, leads to an increase (the army rate) as does too weak an attachment (the Protestant rate).
[4] The principal exception is the relatively low rate for England, a predominantly Protestant country. Durkheim takes account of this, *Suicide*, Book II, Chap. II, Sec. III.
[5] The case of the Jews is interesting since for the period of Durkheim's data they had far the lowest rate of all. *Suicide*, Book II, Chap. II, Sec. II.

precisely in so far as he is faithful, has laid down for him a system of beliefs and practices which his membership in the church prescribes for him. He has no initiative in the matter; all responsibility belongs to the church as an organization. The very state of his soul and chances of salvation depend on his faithful adherence to these prescriptions. The case of the Protestant, on the other hand, is very different. He is himself the ultimate judge of religious truth and the rightness of conduct deduced from it. The church is in a very different relation to him. It is an association of those holding common beliefs and carrying out common practices, but as an organized body it does not have the same authority over the individual in prescribing what these beliefs and practices shall be.

It is, then, in the relation of the individual to the organized religious group that Durkheim sees the decisive difference. In one sense the difference consists in the fact that the Catholic is subjected to a group authority from which the Protestant is exempt. But this negative aspect does not cover the full extent of the differences. For the essential point is that the Protestant's freedom from group control is not optional. It is not a freedom to take his own religious responsibility *or* to relinquish it to a church as he sees fit. In so far as he is a Protestant in good standing he *must* assume this responsibility and exercise his freedom. He cannot devolve it on a church. The obligation to exercise religious freedom in this sense is a fundamental feature of protestantism as a religious movement. It may be said that this exemplifies quite literally Rousseau's famous paradox, as a Protestant a man is, in certain respects, *forced* to be free.[1]

This is surely not simply a matter of the effects of differentiation of function due to population pressure. Indeed it comes exceedingly close to being a manifestation of the *conscience collective*. For religious freedom in the above sense is a basic ethical value common to all Protestants. In so far as a man is a Protestant at all he is subjected to a social, a group pressure in that direction. But the result is a very different relation to the religious group as an organized entity from that of the Catholic. He is under pressure to be independent, to take his own religious responsibility, while the Catholic is under pressure to submit himself to the authority of the church. But this decisive differ-

[1] JEAN-JACQUES ROUSSEAU, *Du contrat social*, ed. C. E. Vaughan, p. 16.

ence is *not* a matter of the action of the Catholic being influenced by the values common to Catholics while the Protestant is emancipated from the influence of those common to Protestants; the freedom in question is freedom in a different sense. The difference lies in the different *content* of the different value systems. It may safely be inferred that in so far as the high Protestant suicide rate is due to egoism it is a result of the hold over the individual of a *conscience collective*, a system of beliefs and sentiments common to Protestants, which are not shared by Catholics.

This system of beliefs and sentiments does not operate by directly enjoining the Protestant to take his own life. On the contrary, for Protestants and Catholics alike suicide is a mortal sin. But by placing the Protestant in a particular relation to his religious group, by placing a particularly heavy load of religious responsibility upon him, strains are created of which, in a relatively high proportion of cases, the result is suicide. Durkheim throws little light on the actual mechanisms by which the result is produced in the individual suicide. But he has established the fact of the relationship beyond doubt.

Later in the book[1] Durkheim generalizes this insight and puts forward the view that the leading common moral sentiment of our society is an ethical valuation of individual personality as such. This is the more general phenomenon of which the Protestant version of religious freedom and responsibility is a special case. In so far as this "cult" is present men are under strong social pressure, on the one hand, to "develop their personalities" —to be independent, responsible and self-respecting. On the other hand, they are equally under pressure to respect others, to shape their own actions so as to be compatible with others attaining the same development of personality. There can be no doubt that on the empirical level Durkheim has here reached a solution of the problem of the "non-contractual element in contract." The fundamentals of the system of normative rules governing contract and exchange by virtue of which "organic solidarity" is possible, are, in certain respects at least, an expression of the cult of individual personality. This is not a matter simply of freeing the individual from ethical restraints imposed

---

[1] *Suicide*, Book III, Chap. I. Definitely foreshadowed in the final chapter of the *Division of Labor* (see especially p. 403).

by society, it is a matter of the imposition of a different *kind* of ethical restraint. Individuality is a product of a certain social state, of the *conscience collective*. It is true that Durkheim leaves us there. He does not attempt to explain in turn what is the source of the cult of the individual; he is content with establishing its existence. But by contrast with the *Division of Labor* he has accomplished a great work of clarification. No longer is the common-value element tied to a state where there is similarity of individuals and lack of differentiation. Above all the freedom itself which is the basic prerequisite of a "contractual" society is seen to be capable of being related positively to a *conscience collective*. With that, all attempt to derive organic solidarity from differentiation as such drops out, and with it the "biologizing" tendency which appeared in the population thesis. What changes this involves in the conception of the social milieu will be taken up in subsequent chapters.

This has been worked out by Durkheim with exemplary clarity in connection with one empirical phenomenon, the differential suicide rates of Protestants and Catholics. By implication it clarifies the confused thought regarding the family as a protection against suicide. For in so far as the individual responsibility and independence inherent in the cult of personality has tended to break down certain types of emotional dependence on the family group, to prevent people from marrying and to lead to divorce as well as to affect relations within the family, it is legitimate to speak of an egoistic component in the suicide rates of persons excluded from family ties. The whole matter is, however, much further clarified by the development, by contrast with egoism, of the concept of *anomie*, to which the discussion must now turn.

Anomie already had a part in the *Division of Labor*, but a relatively minor one descriptive of one of the "abnormal" forms of the division of labor,[1] that is, one in which organic solidarity was imperfectly realized. In the *Suicide* it occupies a far more prominent place and the concept itself is much more completely worked out, hence its discussion has been deferred to this point. From a relatively minor position it has been elevated to a factor in suicide *pari passu* with egoism and altruism.

---

[1] *Division of Labor*, Book III, Chap. I.

As in the other two cases there is a body of empirical fact which was particularly important to Durkheim in framing the concept. It is the fact that there are quite large variations in the rate of suicide concomitant with the business cycle.[1] It would surprise nobody to learn that panic and depression were also accompanied by increases in the suicide rate; disappointment and suffering due to financial reverses and losses seems a plausible, common-sense explanation. The surprising thing is that the same is true of periods of unusual prosperity, and the fluctuation from the average rate over a long period, or its trend, is of about the same magnitude. Hence Durkheim questions that even the increase of suicides in depression is due to economic hardship as such, especially in view of the lack of general correlation between suicide and poverty already mentioned. The probability is that the increase, both in prosperity and in depression, is due to the same order of causes.

That cause Durkheim finds in the fact that in both cases large numbers of people are thrown with relative suddenness out of adjustment with certain important features of their social environment. In depression expectations relative to the standard of living, with all that implies, are frustrated on a large scale. In that of unusual prosperity, on the other hand, things which had seemed altogether outside the range of possibility become for many people realities. At both extremes the relation between means and ends, between effort and attainment is upset. The result is a sense of confusion, a loss of orientation. People no longer have the sense that they are "getting anywhere."

Durkheim's analysis goes yet deeper. The sense of confusion and frustration in depression seems not so difficult to understand, but why is the reaction to unusual prosperity not increased satisfaction all around, as any utilitarian point of view would take for granted as obvious? Because, Durkheim says, a sense of security, of progress toward ends depends not only on adequate command over means, but on clear definition of the ends themselves. When large numbers are the recipients of windfalls, having attained what had seemed impossible, they tend no longer to believe anything is impossible. This is, in turn, because human appetites and interests are inherently unlimited. For there to be satisfaction they must be limited, disciplined. It is as an agency of

---

[1] *Suicide*, Book II, Chap. V, Sec. I.

breakdown of this discipline that prosperity is a cause of suicide. It opens up the abyss of an endless search for the impossible.

This discipline which is indispensable to the personal sense of attainment, and thus to happiness, is not imposed by the individual himself. It is imposed by society. For it to serve this function, however, the discipline cannot be mere coercion. Men cannot be happy in the acceptance of limitations simply imposed by force; they must recognize them to be "just"; the discipline must carry *moral* authority. It takes the form, then, of socially given moral norms by which ends of action are defined. If anything happens to break down the discipline of these norms the result is personal disequilibrium, which results in various forms of personal breakdown, in extreme instances, suicide.

In the present context the relevant norms are those concerned with the standard of living. For each class in society there is always a socially approved standard, varying within limits to be sure, but relatively definite. To live on such a scale is a normal legitimate expectation. Both depression below it and elevation above it necessitate what Durkheim calls a "moral re-education" which cannot be accomplished easily and quickly, if at all.

Durkheim also attributes to the same thing a part in the higher suicide rate of the widowed and divorced as against the married. The breaking of the marital tie, like the removal of limitations on the standard of living, puts men's standards in flux, creates a social and personal void in which orientation is disorganized. The result is the same sense of frustration, insecurity and, in extreme cases, suicide.

What are some of the theoretical implications of the concept of *anomie?* In the first place, in setting *anomie* explicitly over against egoism, Durkheim has completed the process discussed above. Instead of the *conscience collective* being contrasted with organic solidarity, there now are two types of influence of the *conscience collective,* and set over against *both* of them the state where its disciplining influence is weak, at the polar extreme altogether absent. In so far as this weakening of discipline is present, the state of *anomie* exists.[1] The freedom from collective

[1] *Suicide fataliste* is related to the situation where the pressure of the *conscience collective* is excessive. Though Durkheim does not develop the possibility it might well have something to do with the high rate of suicide in armies, along with "altruism."

control, the "emancipation of the individual" in the cases of egoism and of *anomie* are on quite different levels. Above all the development of individual personality is not a mere matter of the removal of social discipline, but of a particular kind of such discipline.

In discussing the institution of contract, Durkheim was calling attention to an aspect of the normative regulation of action which is relatively "external" to the acting individual. It can to a point readily be treated as a set of given conditions of action. But the type of discipline formulated by contrast with *anomie* is of a much more subtle kind. It concerns not only the conditions under which men act in pursuit of their ends but enters into the formulation of the ends themselves. Moreover, it is only by virtue of such a discipline that an "integrated personality" exists at all.

This amounts to carrying the Hobbesian problem down to a deeper level. The level of social instability which Hobbes analyzed presupposes a plurality of individuals who are capable of rational action, who know what they want. But this is itself an unreal assumption. The man in the state of nature could not even be the rational being the utilitarians posit. Durkheim's sociological analysis is not merely relevant to the elements of order as between individuals, to the power problem, but has extended further into the elements of order in individual personality itself.

With this a fundamental methodological point is already foreshadowed, but it was long before Durkheim attained anything like methodological clarity on it, as on many other implications of this insight into the *anomie* problem. This is that the analytical distinction between "individual" and "social" cannot run parallel with that between the concrete entities "individual" and "society." Just as society cannot be said to exist in any concrete sense apart from the concrete individuals who make it up, so the concrete human individual whom we know cannot be accounted for in terms of "individual" elements alone, but there is a social component of his personality. The various ramifications of this problem on the methodological level will occupy a good deal of the subsequent discussion of Durkheim's work.

To sum up, then, the change from the *Division of Labor* to the *Suicide:* The element of a system of moral beliefs and sentiments common to the members of a society, the *conscience collective*, has been freed of its confusion with lack of social differentiation, with similarity of social role. *Pari passu* with this has come the realization that the non-contractual element of contract is just such a system of common beliefs and sentiments, that this is an essential element in the basis of order in a differentiated individualistic society. Modern "individualism" including the egoistic component of suicide is not a matter of emancipation from social pressure, but of a particular kind of social pressure. In both cases it is primarily a matter of the discipline to which the individual is subjected by his participation in the common beliefs and sentiments of his society.

At the same time the concept of *anomie*[1] emerges into a position of much greater prominence. With it the disciplining function of the *conscience collective* is extended from the relatively external action of rules governing action to the constitution of the ends of action themselves, and thus into the very center of individual personality. This brings Durkheim's empirical insight to a point far in advance of his general conceptual scheme. Before entering into the intricacies of that scheme and its development, however, and the sense in which the *conscience collective* may be called a "social" factor, it will be well to note briefly two other connections in which the empirical fundamentals of Durkheim's position at this period are vividly brought out.

OCCUPATIONAL GROUPS AND SOCIALISM

The new emphasis on the importance of the common normative regulation which resulted from the study of suicide and its connection with the concrete group forms the theoretical background of Durkheim's best-known proposal for social reform—the reestablishment in most occupations of organized professional groups on the analogy of gilds. It is significant that this

---

[1] One striking result of the greater prominence of *anomie* in the *Suicide* is that Durkheim became much more pessimistic about contemporary European society. In the *Division of Labor* Durkheim, while questioning the Spencerian explanation of the stability of contractual society, did not doubt the fact. There are only the relatively slight reservations contained in his discussion of the "abnormal" forms of the *Division of Labor*. The investigation of suicide seems to have opened his eyes to the great empirical importance of *anomie*, particularly in certain strategic places such as commerce, the liberal professions and the great cities.

proposal does not appear at all[1] in the *Division of Labor* as such. It is first made in the final chapter of the *Suicide*[2] and then developed at length in the well-known Preface to the second edition of the *Division of Labor* written *after* the publication of the *Suicide*.[3] With the amount of differentiation in our present society there is no longer any group larger than the family to which the individual has a close and intimate relation, and even the family is unmistakably declining in its power of control over individuals. The state, on the other hand, which has steadily grown in power and importance, as an essential element in the process of growth of individualism,[4] is too distant and impersonal to perform the function. Its control tends to be more and more that of impersonal law backed by the sanction of physical coercion. But what is needed is a control by moral authority.

Since occupational differentiation is the dominant characteristic of modern society, it is logical to take the occupational group as the unit and endow it with an ethical control over its members which will serve to discipline the unlimited expansion of their individual interests. The regulatory codes of these groups will of necessity vary from one to another, since no one code can apply to all the different conditions in need of regulation. But each one will impose common specific norms on its members. Each will be in a sense a group characterized by mechanical solidarity. This Durkheim saw as the most hopeful practical means of checking the growth of *anomie*. Given freedom of choice of occupation it is not inconsistent with the basic tenets of our individualistic ethics.

His advocacy of organized occupational groups has often led writers to classify Durkheim as an adherent of the syndicalist movement. It is not without interest, before closing this chapter, to enter briefly into his relation to socialism in general as well as to syndicalism, because it was in the same period, 1895–1896, shortly before the publication of *Le suicide* that he delivered his course of lectures on socialism, though it was not published until 1928. It is extremely interesting to note that Durkheim,

[1] Though there is some discussion of professional ethics and a note of their absence from business.

[2] *Suicide*, Book III, Chap. II, Sec. III.

[3] As is proved by references given to the *Suicide*, *Division of Labor*, pp. i, xix, xxxiii.

[4] A basic difference from Spencer's thought.

like so many of the eminent minds of his generation, was deeply interested in the socialist movement and stirred by the problems it raised. He and Pareto wrote on it directly and at length, while both Marshall and Weber were greatly influenced indirectly.

The theoretical discussion centers around a basic distinction—that between socialism and communism. In the sense in which Durkheim uses the term, communism is a doctrine advocating a rigid control over economic activities by the central organs of the community motivated primarily by a sense of the dangers of uncontrolled economic interests to the higher ends of the community. Underlying this is the conviction that uncontrolled acquisition of wealth tends to release the passions or appetites, which in the interest both of the individual and of society must be controlled. Plato's *Republic* is the archetype of communistic writings. Since this is an ever-recurring problem of human society in all times and places, communistic ideas are not bound to any particular social situation but appear sporadically in all sorts of conditions.

Socialism, on the other hand, is a doctrine advocating the *fusion* of the economic interests with the controlling organs of the community. Applied to the present situation of Western society it is not so much control *by* the state as fusion *with* the state. Underlying it is precisely an economic view of society. There is no necessity felt for controlling the economic element in the interest of something higher. The difference of socialism from utilitarian individualism is entirely over the question of what are the best means to maximize wealth. There is no questioning of the desirability of maximizing wealth as an end—no question of its conflicting with other ends. This is possible because socialists are ethically and philosophically utilitarian individualists. This is the ultimate basis of the socialist doctrine of economic determinism.[1]

Socialism, unlike communism, is a phenomenon peculiar to our own modern social situation, because it could not develop as a serious movement without the previous existence of a highly developed governmental machine capable of taking over the complex administrative functions inherent in the modern type of economic order.

[1] The Marxian version of this doctrine will be further discussed below (see Chap. XIII).

Of course these concepts of Durkheim's are abstract, and he readily admits that in the modern socialist movement concretely considered there are communistic elements. In particular he defines socialism so narrowly as to exclude the element of equality, which undoubtedly plays a very large part in the concrete movement, but must in his terminology be relegated to communism.

Apart from the intrinsic interest of the subject matter, and whether or not his views may be acceptable, Durkheim's discussion of socialism again reiterates the basic distinction between the economic and other utilitarian elements—the pursuit of *individual* want satisfaction and the quite different "social" element which, looked at from the individual point of view, is a constraining, controlling factor. This distinction may be regarded as the really fundamental starting point of Durkheim's sociological thought. He is a communist rather than a socialist.

It is particularly significant that, as has already been noted,[1] Durkheim's preoccupation with socialism was very early, antedating the *Division of Labor*, although he did not come to a systematic exposition of his views until later. In particular, one of the main reasons why he ventured into the unknown paths of sociology was his conclusion that socialist economics failed to meet the issues raised by the theory of laissez-faire individualism. From Durkheim's point of view, as from that of Pareto and Weber, socialism and laissez-faire individualism are of the same piece—they both leave out of account certain basic social factors with which all three are concerned.

Enough has been said to demonstrate the great part played in Durkheim's earlier thought by the problems of economic individualism in a broad sense. His reaction against the scientific doctrines underlying it—not so much the state of fact—and the interpretation of modern Western society implied in these doctrines set him on the track of alternative views. In his earlier phase he considered, but ended by decisively rejecting, two such alternatives. One was that presented by socialistic economics which he decided offered no real alternative (in his terms) at all but was another expression, somewhat more nearly adapted to the factual situation, of the same basic doctrines. The other, biopsychological determinism, appeared in the thesis that the

[1] See above, footnote 1, p. 310.

division of labor was primarily the result of pressure of population. But this harmonized badly with many elements even of the *Division of Labor* and in the development of his ideas through the *Suicide* was definitely dropped and plays no real part in his later thought. There was left a "social" factor on which his attention was concentrated. Negatively, this was radically distinguished from those formulated either in utilitarianism or in heredity and environment; positively, it was described mainly as "the constitution of the social milieu" or sometimes as "social structure."

This social factor and its status Durkheim subjected to a systematic methodological treatment, analysis of which is the next task of the discussion. It must, however, never be forgotten that this methodology was by no means abstract philosophical speculation, but was dictated at every step by the problems and difficulties arising out of the empirical work, just sketched. The omission of this connection by so many persons who have discussed Durkheim's methodology has given an impression of dialectic sterility in reality quite foreign to Durkheim's nature.

CHAPTER IX

ÉMILE DURKHEIM, II: THE METHODOLOGY OF SOCIOLOGISTIC POSITIVISM

The discussion of the previous chapter has shown that in his earlier empirical work Durkheim was vitally, even primarily, concerned with certain problems which had been raised by the theories above called the "utilitarian," as formulated above all by Spencer. The *Division of Labor*, so far as it is of interest here, is to be understood mainly as a polemic against the utilitarian conception of modern industrial society. Moreover it is principally in its critical portions that Durkheim's argument here is really sure-footed and incisive. When it comes to building up a positive theory of his own, he is, as has been shown, uncertain and wavering at many points, and it was some time after the completion of the *Division of Labor* before his main direction of thought in terms of the alternatives offered him by contemporary conceptual schemes was settled.

It will provide a striking confirmation both of this interpretation of the earlier empirical work, and of the thesis that Durkheim's methodology was directly dependent on and concerned with these empirical problems, if it can be demonstrated that there is a close parallel in Durkheim's thought on empirical and on methodological questions. Indeed this is precisely what the present chapter will attempt to show. In the early methodological work there are two main strands of thought. The one, polemical, is a criticism on the methodological level of the conceptions underlying utilitarian individualism. The other, his own positive doctrine, is a development of the general positivistic tradition with which most of the argument of this study has so far been concerned. He soon came to a clear repudiation of the doctrine of all versions of individualistic positivism as well as utilitarianism, and in place of both built up an essentially positivistic system of another kind. This system formed a relatively stable equilibrium and dominated his thought in the middle period, but because it contained serious elements of inadequacy in relation to the facts gradually broke down. The process of its breakdown must, however, be reserved for discussion in subsequent chapters. The task of the present one is to trace the main elements in its genesis and to outline the system at the height of its development.

THE UTILITARIAN DILEMMA

It is necessary at this point to recall some of the essential methodological features of the "utilitarian" system. Its central principle is the explanation of conduct in terms of the rational pursuit of the wants or desires of individuals. It has thus a teleological character quite unacceptable to the radical positivist. It attempts none the less to be scientific in a positivistic sense. This is achieved in essentials by extruding the factor of wants entirely from the field of scientific problems by making, explicitly or implicitly, certain assumptions.

Wants, that is, are assumed to be subjective in a double sense. On the one hand, each individual creates his wants on his own initiative—they are outside the range of "natural" determinism;[1] on the other hand, they are private to each individual. What any one may want has no necessary relation to the wants of others. The relations of individuals to each other are thought of entirely on the level of the extent to which they are significant to each other as a means to and conditions of attaining each other's ends.

This double subjectivity of individual wants has an important consequence. In positivistic terms to be outside the realm of natural determinism has a specific implication—that of exemption from "law." This, in turn, means that wants are thought of as varying at random in the strict statistical sense, since this is the negation of natural law—that is, of uniformities in the behavior of things.

Thus the utilitarian position takes individual wants as "given data," as some economists like to say, but in a special sense. They are not first studied empirically, to find out what individuals do in fact want in order then to raise the question as to what uniformities are to be found in these facts. On the contrary,

---

[1] Of course, as has repeatedly been pointed out, this position shades off into one of radical determinism—psychological hedonism is one of the main transitional phases.

it is arbitrarily assumed, none the less effectively if by implication, that there *are*[1] no such uniformities which are significant to the theory.

Under these assumptions, then, a realm of "law," a set of uniformities, as factual order in human behavior, can be derived from only two possible sources. One of these, the one on which the utilitarians laid the greatest stress, is the uniformities of the means-end relationships involved in rational action of this type on the part of a plurality of individuals whose actions are means to each others' ends—above all the economic laws of the market. Hence the central place of economics in the utilitarian tradition of thought. The other lies in the situation of action—especially the nonhuman environment and individual inherited human nature. As has been seen, the line between these two types of explanation is the line between utilitarianism and radical individualistic positivism. In the concrete history of thought there are many gradual transitions between them.

Before going into Durkheim's relation to these ideas another fundamental distinction must be recalled to mind which affects the whole current of thought here under discussion—the distinction between objective and subjective in the special senses of "from the point of view of an outside observer" and "from the point of view of the person thought of as acting." It is quite clear that the basic schema of the utilitarian analysis takes the latter point of view—only on the assumption that individuals do pursue ends and that the latter are effective factors in action does this analysis make sense. But their specific content is eliminated from the scientific problem by the assumption that they are random—but not, of course, their general role in concrete action, which remains the very basis of the whole conception.

On the other hand, the whole of positive science is concerned with the observation of "fact" by the scientist. In the physical

[1] On the generally prevalent empiricist basis this is to be taken literally, as it certainly was by Spencer, whom Durkheim directly criticizes. For the purposes of an abstract analytical economic theory, on the other hand, it is possible to say that whatever uniformities of wants do exist are irrelevant for the particular scientific purpose in hand. But even here it is necessary to observe great caution as to just what kind of abstraction from the uniformities of wants is permissible. For some of the difficulties, see TALCOTT PARSONS, "Some Reflections on the Nature and Significance of Economics," *Quarterly Journal of Economics*, May, 1934.

sciences the relation is relatively simple since only the relation
of one observer, the scientist himself, to one set of facts, the
phenomena he is studying, is in question. In the sciences dealing
with human conduct unfortunately there are two further compli-
cating problems: The first is the status of the subjective aspect
of the persons whose conduct is being studied—is it part of the
world of fact to the observer at all, and if so in what sense? This
is, of course, the behavioristic problem. The second complication
is much less often seen. Once the legitimacy of the study of other
peoples' "states of mind" is admitted, the further complication
arises as to what, to the actor, constitutes "fact" of his external
world and what not—the whole set of questions revolving about
the application of the "scientific" standard to the analysis of
rationality of action. This set of problems will be found to be as
decisively important for Durkheim as it was in relation to Pareto.
But like most persons growing out of the positivistic tradition,
Durkheim does not explicitly deal with these problems and has
the common tendency to shift without warning from the point
of view of the observer to that of the actor and back again. Any
clear analysis of his thought must, as a first requirement, keep
the distinction clear and continually in mind.

As has been pointed out, Durkheim's most fundamental criticism of utilitarian individualism was on the ground of its inability
to account for the element of normative order in society.[1] In the
first place since wants themselves are assumed to be random, this
element of order cannot be derived from them. Spencer then
sought to derive it from contractual relations. Durkheim's central
thesis is that the elements formulated in the common utilitarian
conception of contract, held by Spencer, the elements involved
in the *ad hoc* pursuit of an individual interest as a means to its
fulfillment, are incapable of accounting for the stability of a
system of such relations. As he came to think later on, a state of
purely contractual relations would not be order[2] but *anomie*, that
is, chaos. It is unnecessary here to recapitulate Durkheim's argu-

[1] *The Division of Labor in Society*, Book I, Chap. VII. Although the title
is given in translated form, all references are to the fifth French edition.

[2] As has been noted above, in the concept of order two radically different levels must be distinguished. An "order of nature" in the sense of the
physical sciences is simply a set of phenomena involving uniformities of
behavior which can be formulated in terms of "laws." This implies no
necessary relation to human purposes. The struggle for existence or the war

ment for this thesis. He thought necessary a further element which he then called "organic solidarity," something analytically distinct from the complex of individual interests.

It is only to this point that his thought is really clear in the *Division of Labor*. It is most important to keep in mind the fact that this polemic is the starting point of his whole position. He has so far accepted the most fundamental basis of utilitarian thought—the subjectivity of individual wants in the peculiar sense pointed out, involving the assumption of their random variation. Given this starting point, he thought of an individualistic explanation of human conduct as finding the element of order in the relations of means to these subjective ends. This is what Durkheim has initially rejected, not the underlying assumptions as to the fundamental nature of individual wants. He thus identified an individualistic explanation with one in utilitarian terms. Having rejected the utilitarian explanation he seeks his own in terms of factors "exterior"[1] to the individual. This may be considered the original genesis in Durkheim's of the famous criterion of "exteriority" as a distinguishing mark of "social facts." It obviously implies a special connotation of the term individual to which these forces must be "exterior."

The original sense of the term constraint,[2] the other main criterion of social facts, is to be understood similarly. As the wants of the utilitarian were thought of as subjective or internal

---

of all against all may perfectly well constitute order in this sense. Its antithesis is a state where events occur at random, that is, are not subject to analysis by science. On the other hand, the antithesis of the order of which Durkheim is here thinking is precisely this war of all against all, as he explicitly states. His order implies not merely uniformities in events but a control of human action with reference to certain norms of ideal conduct and relationship, *e.g.*, the "institution of contract," of a legal order. In his earlier work Durkheim, like other positivists, did not clearly grasp the distinction in theoretical terms, though his empirical observation quite definitely has reference to the latter type of order. The theoretical implications of this clearly perceived state of fact form, over a long period, one of the central themes of his theoretical work. It is the main path leading to the breakdown of his positivistic system. Of all that more will be said in the following chapter. The order relevant to the present discussion is to the actor a "normative" not merely a "factual" order, though to the observer it is a factual order only.

[1] *Règles de la méthode sociologique*, pp. 6 *ff.*; 2d ed., Preface, pp. xiv *ff.*

[2] *Ibid.*, pp. 6 *ff.*; 2d ed., pp. xx, *ff.*

so also were they "spontaneous." The realm of wants was by definition outside that of deterministic law—the wants are internal to the individual—hence they are to be thought of as his own spontaneous creation. If an explanation of conduct in terms of these wants is unsatisfactory, then the factors invoked to take their place must, from the point of view of the individual, be the opposite of spontaneous, that is they must "constrain" him in his actions.

So much can be understood in terms of Durkheim's direct critical relation to utilitarianism. The methodological framework into which he fitted this critique comes from the other element mentioned at the opening of this chapter, the methodology of positive science. Its significance for Durkheim in this early stage of his thought is to be found in the interpretation of his first rule of method—social facts are to be treated "*comme des choses.*"[1]

The more obvious meaning of this is that the *sociologist* must treat the facts of social life as "things"—as referring to objects of the external world—as observable facts. This is in conformity with the epistemology lying back of the whole development of positive science with its emphasis on the empirical, observable element. Now, as Durkheim himself states, the distinguishing characteristic of the empirical element is its objectivity, its independence of the subjective inclinations, sentiments or desires of the observer. A fact is a fact whether we like it or not. As he says[2] it offers "resistance" to any alteration on the part of the observer. A fact is precisely distinguished by the criteria of exteriority and constraint—it is from scientific methodology that these criteria have been derived.

All this amounts only to the program of making sociology a "positive" science, a program by no means peculiar to Durkheim, but common to the whole positivistic tradition and to other positions as well. True, at a later stage the sense in which social facts are "observable" becomes an important problem. But the principal result of this attitude in the present connection is to give Durkheim a bias in favor of the use of facts of the objective verifiability of which there can be no question, such as division of labor, suicide rates, legal codes, etc., while

[1] *Ibid.*, pp. 20 *ff.*
[2] On *choses* generally see *Règles*, 2d ed., pp. xi *ff.*

he is suspicious of such "subjective" entities as "ideas" and "sentiments."[1]

The main present interest, however, is in another aspect of the matter. The utilitarian position which Durkheim criticizes is stated, in its methodological aspect, in terms of the subjective point of view, that of the actor. It is only natural that he, like Pareto, should apply his scientific methodology in this context, as well as the other, as many have done before and since. The criteria of exteriority and constraint are, in fact, applied primarily in this context—it is exteriority to the *actor* not the observer which is the basic distinguishing[2] criterion of *social* fact.

Then thinking of social facts as *choses* comes to have a double meaning. Not only are the facts of the social phenomena he is studying part of the external world, of "nature," to the sociological observer, but also human conduct must be understood in terms of factors, forces which to the individual who acts also may be thought of as *choses*, as stubborn facts which cannot be altered in conformity with his own private wishes or sentiments. That is, after all, the antithesis to the wants of the utilitarians, which are both spontaneous and subjective, while *choses* are not spontaneous but given, not subjective but exterior. If wants will not suffice as an explanation of conduct, the only alternative lies in factors which are in the category of *choses* in this sense.[3]

---

[1] Durkheim is not at this stage fully conscious of the importance to his thought of the subjective point of view, and hence often argues at cross-purposes. Some interpreters have even attributed to him a behavioristic "objectivism" which would exclude subjective categories altogether. This interpretation is, however, altogether incompatible with the central structure of his theoretical scheme even at this early stage, to say nothing of its subsequent development.

[2] That is, distinguishing social fact from utilitarian wants. This is what is meant by exterior to the "individual," an element of the external world of the individual as actor. See *Règles*, 2d ed. pp. xiv.

[3] Since this epistemology thinks in terms of a rigid dualism: objective-subjective, phenomenon-idea, etc. If a thing does not fit into one half, by definition it must belong in the other, since there is no further alternative. This mode of thought is of great importance for Durkheim at a number of points. It will readily be seen that this is what has above been called the utilitarian dilemma, so long as the alternative is couched in positivistic terms.

THE "SOCIAL" FACTOR

Thus far virtually nothing has been said about the social element, or society as a reality *sui generis,* which occupies such an important place in Durkheim's thought and in the discussion of it. The foregoing is, however, a necessary preliminary to understanding what he meant by that famous formula. The considerations just adduced were apparently prior in his own mind to any sharply specific concept of the social, as is proved by the course of his thought from the *Division of Labor* to the *Suicide* already sketched. As has been shown, his explanation of the division of labor is not in terms of what to his later theory is a "social" factor at all, but of a biological factor—the principle of population. The above discussion offers an explanation of how he could have fallen into such a curious position. For seeing that this starting point was polemical, any alternative which did not share the difficulties of utilitarianism was prima facie acceptable. Durkheim started as a radical dualist. There were the two worlds of the individual and the nonindividual, a distinction which was originally identified with that between the subjective and the objective as held by the epistemology of positive science, and at the same time with that between the "wants" and the facts or "conditions" of the external world relevant to their satisfaction.

Thus, since it was objective, the biological factor fitted into his category of the nonindividual. It was something "exterior"[1] to the individual ego which "constrained" him. The "facts of life" were part of the external world of *choses* to the actor as well as the observer, to be taken account of, not altered at will.[2] At this stage it is scarcely proper to speak of Durkheim, in methodological terms at least, as a *social* realist at all—only as a radical positivist by contrast with utilitarian teleology.

---

[1] The discussion to this point has already made clear that "exteriority" for Durkheim even in the earliest phase cannot be taken in the spatial sense. Such a naive interpretation of his "realism" is quite unacceptable and those critics who read it into him explicitly or by implication are knocking down a straw man. It is meant here in the *epistemological* sense in which the body is part of the external world. The ego is not a spatial entity, an "object." Perhaps, however, Durkheim did not sufficiently guard himself against this misunderstanding.

[2] As already noted this is the main dichotomy in terms of which he is thinking throughout the *Division of Labor.* See above, p. 311.

The completion of the methodological system of *sociologistic* positivism came as the counterpart of the empirical development already discussed between the *Division of Labor* and the *Suicide*. In the latter book, as has been noted, Durkheim extends his criticism to include another whole category of factors which, besides the "utilitarian," he also classes as "individualistic," that is, the "cosmic" environment and the attributes of the individual human being in so far as they are derived from heredity—his organic constitution and his psychological mechanisms. Thus he also decisively rejects the claims to adequacy of explanations of suicide in terms of the external environment, of race, of psychopathological factors, and of imitation. This may be regarded as primarily an empirical finding derived from a critical study of theories which had attempted this kind of explanation.

But it had the decisive methodological result for Durkheim of introducing a radical distinction between two categories of "natural" objects, of *choses*—the individual[1] and the social.[2] Or to put it somewhat differently, for the purposes of social science the category of "individual," that is, that which was not acceptable as an explanation of "social facts," was expanded from the original narrow and special utilitarian meaning to include in addition all those elements which "individualistic positivists," whether their bent were environmental, biological or psychological, had invoked in the explanation of human conduct, largely like Durkheim in opposition to utilitarianism. That is, Durkheim had come to reject all the factors most generally in favor in the predominantly individualistic Western thought of the nineteenth century.[3] The parallelism of his history in this respect with that of Pareto must strike the reader. In the thought of both the driving force of the change may be said to lie primarily in the

[1] It is not correct to say physical since Durkheim held that both the organic and the psychological levels of existence were syntheses *sui generis*, that is, involved "emergent" phenomena.

[2] It is to be noted that the category "social" is arrived at by a process of elimination, is thus a residual category.

[3] This situation may be represented graphically in the following manner: There are three overlapping terms—"subjective," "objective" and "individual." The social becomes the residual category—that element of the objective which is not individual. At this stage there is no such thing as a subjective realm which is not also individual.

realization of the empirical inadequacy of "individualistic" theories as revealed by their own critical analyses of them and their own empirical investigations.

That this is so is further suggested by the fact that for Durkheim his category of the "social" was still at this stage defined negatively rather than positively; it was a residual category. Moreover, it is still more striking that his negative and critical position remained unchanged throughout his subsequent career, while the positive ideas he had at this time changed radically.[1]

The main features of "social facts" as they were developed by Durkheim at this time, then, were as follows: In terms of his critical attitude to utilitarian individualism he had developed the two criteria of exteriority and constraint. From the methodology of science he derived the category of *choses*. Social facts were thus *choses*, to both the observer and the actor, characterized by exteriority to and constraint of the actor.

But in the original senses all these criteria turned out to be too broad. *Choses* included the facts of the physical, biological and psychological levels of reality. *All choses* were "exterior" to the individual as actor[2] and exercised "constraint" upon him in the sense that they were what they were regardless of his wishes. By what criteria then did he narrow these categories so as to eliminate the factors he had rejected?

Durkheim's essential analytical problem is to define the nature of the "social factor" in human behavior. To this end he has a clear critical position worked out: it cannot fit into the category of ends as formulated in utilitarian theory. Positively he has certain criteria formulated in terms derived from scientific methodology; by contrast with that of ends in the utilitarian sense, it must constitute to the actor a category or element of *choses*, of verifiable facts of the external world, which are in this particular sense "exterior" to him and "constrain" his action.

But the further critical repudiation for his theoretical purposes of all the elements reducible to terms of heredity and nonsocial

[1] Principally this circumstance has misled many critics into treating the different phases of his work as homogeneous for all theoretical purposes.

[2] Whether the category of *choses* from the two points of view is identical in extent, above all whether things could be *choses* to the observer which were not such to the actor, *e.g.*, his ends, feelings, ideas, etc., Durkheim fails to say. It does not seem that at least at this stage he was aware of the problem, which is, as has been remarked, that of behaviorism.

environment[1] complicates the situation. For these elements turn
out to fit the original criteria which are derived from a critical
antithesis to random wants. The conditions of the environment
and the hereditary component of "human nature" are *choses*
in Durkheim's sense: they are "exterior" to the actor as an
ego, and they "constrain" him, he must take account of them
in his action if it is to be rational. The social element then becomes
a residual category. It is that category of *choses* to the actor
which are not reducible to terms of heredity and nonsocial environment. To this purely negative definition is added one positive
criterion. It is clearly an element attributable analytically to
the fact that the individual stands in social relationships to other
human beings. For the analytical abstraction of an isolated
individual eliminates this element.

The problem is how to arrive at something more than a residual
definition of the social factor so that the situation does not merely
take the form x equals y minus z, while at the same time remaining
within the general analytical framework just sketched. That is, it
is required to define positively an element which meets the criteria
of exteriority and constraint and is yet not reducible to terms of
heredity and nonsocial environment.

As has already been noted there was one positive clue available;
it clearly has something to do with the fact of the association
of individuals in a system of social relationships. This clue plus
the empirical insight that certain facts are not capable of explanation without invoking such an element forms the basis of Durkheim's first attempt to draw the line positively rather than
residually. It is what may be called the "synthesis" argument
and is purely formal; in other words, it is based on general grounds
rather than the specific facts of the empirical phenomena that
he has been studying.

In essence this argument is a challenge to the view which has
above been called atomism. The world of experience contains
many organic entities in the sense that the functioning whole has
properties which cannot be derived by direct generalization from
the properties of the units or parts and their elementary relations,
taken in isolation from their concrete involvement in the whole.
The breakdown of a complex concrete entity by unit analysis
destroys in such a case certain features of it, which can only be

[1] In the analytical sense employed throughout this discussion.

observed in the whole. For Durkheim this doctrine of synthesis[1] is a general doctrine with a far wider application than to the social case. In developing it he makes extensive use of analogies to the social case, especially from the fields of chemistry and biology. It can hence scarcely be said to solve his theoretical problem, but only to lead to a somewhat clearer statement of it in certain respects. It is clearly not enough to know that certain vital elements in social theory are not taken account of in atomistic theories; it is necessary to know further just what they are, what are their relations, logical and functional, to the elements formulated in the theories he has rejected, what are the mechanisms by which they influence concrete human action. Above all this argument has no necessary relation to the action frame of reference, but is applicable to all empirical reality. To make it the essential basis of a sociological theory in terms of the action schema is a glaring example of what Professor Sorokin aptly calls the fallacy of "logical inadequacy."[2] It is to explain a body of fact with properties clearly differentiating it from others, in terms of a schema applicable to the others in the same way. This is to ignore the scientific importance of the differentiating facts, as between, for instance, human society and a biological organism, or even a chemical compound.

But, granting these limitations, there is no exception whatever to be taken to the argument. The concrete entity society is beyond all possible doubt in this sense an organic entity, or, as Durkheim usually says, a reality *sui generis*. Atomistic theories are in fact empirically inadequate, as in some important cases Durkheim's own empirical work has clearly proved. Except that it does not go far enough, valid objection can only be raised through what is undoubtedly a misinterpretation, but one against which Durkheim did not adequately protect himself. It is the view that the "individual" which is the unit of the synthesis and the "society" which results from it are concrete entities, the concrete human being known to us, and the concrete group. In this sense it is scarcely more than a truism that society is simply the aggregate of human beings in their given relations to one

---

[1] It is most elaborately developed in the essay, "Représentations individuelles et représentations collectives," in *Sociologie et philosophie*, though it is reiterated throughout his work.

[2] P. A. SOROKIN, *Contempory Sociological Theories*, p. 29.

another. But the "individual" of Durkheim's argument, as became increasingly clear with the progress of his development, is not this concrete entity, but a theoretical abstraction. In the simplest sense it is the fictional human being who has never entered into any social relationships with other human beings. This "unit individual," like the unit act of the previous discussion, does not exist as a concrete entity, and may not be identified with the concrete human being. To do so is to fall into the fallacy of atomistic social theories. The above discussion of Durkheim's treatment of *anomie* should surely be sufficient to dispose of this interpretation.[1]

That this interpretation has been put forward again and again is, probably, due mainly to two circumstances. On the one hand, like almost all other social scientists of his time, and the great majority to this day, including his interpreters, Durkheim had not reached full methodological clarity on the nature of analytical abstraction. In so far as an empiricist tendency remained, it was fatally easy to slip over into a mode of expression which seemed to imply that society as an analytical category independent of the individual was in fact a concrete entity. Of this tendency Durkheim was by no means free and a great many passages may be cited from his work which tend to confirm this interpretation. But it is so clearly contrary to the main current of his thought that no one who has grasped the latter could possibly entertain it seriously. But this tendency was, as will appear presently, greatly accentuated by other difficulties which appeared when he attempted to go beyond the formal synthesis argument to a more specific criterion of the social factor. The trouble here was not due to general methodological unclarity, but to certain difficulties in trying to fit the facts of his empirical studies into the conceptual framework just outlined. They persist until the scheme itself has been radically modified, then disappear.[2]

[1] It is evident that this interpretation is closely associated with that of "exteriority" as meaning spatially external. For if society is a concrete empirical entity separate from the individuals who make it up it must occupy a different position in space. The fact that this criterion is formulated by Durkheim so definitely in the epistemological, not the spatial, context is a strong argument against the other misinterpretation just discussed.

[2] This type of abstraction, that of "fictitious" units or parts of organic entities, does not, it has already been pointed out (Chap. I, pp. 31 *ff.*), exhaust the matter of abstraction. Indeed if society be considered a fictitiously

The second argument by which Durkheim attempts to draw the line between social and nonsocial *choses* is by means of the formula that "social facts are facts about psychic entities." In the Preface to the second edition of the *Règles* he states[1] quite explicitly that in maintaining that social facts are to be treated *comme des choses* he does not mean that society is a "material" thing, but that social facts are facts with the same title to reality and objectivity as those referring to material things. It is not only not material, but "psychic." As combined with the synthesis argument this yields the view that the "psychic," including but not exhausted by the "social," is an emergent order of empirical reality due to the association in particular ways of material elements.

Durkheim gives us little in the way of precise characterization of these two categories of the material and the psychic and their mutual relations. The psychic entities he finds it useful to employ are *conscience* and *représentations*, which will be discussed presently. The category material he appears to take for granted as a matter of common knowledge.

But before entering into the connotations of these two terms it may be pointed out that the fact that he places social facts on the psychic level involves Durkheim, partly explicitly, partly by implication, in two methodological problems which have thus far been avoided. The first is the behavioristic problem.

It has already been noted that in talking about social facts from the point of view of the observer he had a certain objectivist bias. In his rejection of what are ordinarily called motives of action, he tended to concentrate his attention on data which did not in any obvious way involve subjective categories for their observation and interpretation. The leading examples are the written legal codes employed in the *Division of Labor*, and the statistical data of *Le suicide*. Secondly, he uses the term "fact" in such a way as not to distinguish it clearly from phenomenon, the

---

posited concrete entity, the same fundamental difficulties remain. They can be overcome only by thinking in terms of an analytically separable group of elements which cannot even in a fictitious sense be thought of as existing concretely. This methodological issue will be fully discussed below. See in Chap. XIX the discussion of the methodological status of "emergent properties."

[1] *Règles*, 2d ed., p. xi.

confusion to which reference has already been made.[1] In this connection he is always careful to point out that the data he is using do not constitute the social factor but are indications of its state. Thus is raised the problem which was discussed above[2] in terms of Pareto's concept of "manifestation."

One possible line of solution of this problem has given rise, as one of several sources, to the prevailing interpretation of Durkheim's position on the problem of "social realism." It is that only objective data such as legal codes and suicide statistics are empirically observable. But by Durkheim's own testimony these do not constitute the "social reality"; they are only manifestations of it. What then is it? Since it cannot be observed it would seem to be a metaphysical entity. And since only observable things are capable of scientific treatment this metaphysical entity is not a proper object of science. It is a psychic entity, a "mind." In so far as minds are observable at all it is obviously only the minds of individuals. The "group mind," on the other hand, is merely a metaphysical assumption; its employment is scientifically unsound.

The source of this interpretation so far as it concerns the present context lies in following out one line of implication of Durkheim's arguments. But because he had not fully worked out two basic methodological problems there was more than one line left open. The one in question would be excluded by what is, from the point of view of this study, an acceptable solution of both these problems. The first is the general problem of empiricism. As long as this is left unsettled, he has not excluded, as the use of the term fact indicates, the interpretation of the social reality as either an actually existent or a hypothetical concrete entity. In both cases, since it is, by definition, analytically distinct from individual reality and since only individuals and aggregates of them exist concretely as objects of experience, it must be a metaphysical entity. This difficulty can be overcome only by treating the social reality as one, or a group, of analytical abstractions. Then social facts are always facts referring to the concrete entity society which is made up of concrete individuals. Social facts and individual facts both refer to the *same* class of concrete entities. But that is no reason whatever for denying the legitimacy of the analytical distinction.

[1] See note appended to Chap. I.
[2] See p. 215.

The problem arises in a somewhat more special form with reference to the factual status of subjective categories. In calling the social element psychic Durkheim has by implication admitted this, but not analyzed the implication far enough. Carried only to this point the argument is left hanging in the air. A psychic reality presumably cannot be located in space. In this way the erroneous interpretation first discussed is disposed of. But so long as the question of the character of the abstraction involved is not settled there exists approximately the following situation: Only "material facts" are observable. Certain of these, however, are capable of interpretation as manifestations of a certain order of psychic reality, the "social." This, however, is not in the same category of observable facts and becomes as it were a disembodied mind. But all minds known to experience are aspects of entities of which "bodies" at the same time are also aspects. This implication of disembodiment seems to be one of the principal sources of the charge of metaphysics.

And to this question is closely related the second problem. If the social reality is psychic, but does not exhaust the category of the psychic, by what criteria is the line between it and other psychic realities to be drawn? This involves the problem of the relation between the social and the psychological.

In certain general terms Durkheim presents an admirable discussion of this issue; but in more specific terms he gets into serious difficulties. Psychology, he says, deals only with the general powers and faculties of the human individual. But the latter's psychological equipment is general and plastic. The specific forms of mentality found in concrete life cannot be accounted for in terms of these general faculties alone; it is necessary in addition to study the individual in terms of the social milieu in which he lives. A "psychologistic" social theory is therefore inadequate.

No exception is to be taken to this. The question is just how the action of the social milieu is to be conceived, just how the social element differs from the psychological. This is where the third attempt to draw the line comes in; it comes down to something more specific than the characterization of the social as psychic. The social is present in so far as human action is determined by the *conscience collective* by contrast with the *conscience individuelle*. What does that mean? In Chap. VIII the *conscience collective* has already been discussed at some length. It was originally defined as a body of "beliefs and sentiments" common to the members of a society. In its original use on the empirical level the disinterested, moral character of these beliefs and sentiments was strongly in evidence. *Conscience* it would seem, should be translated "conscience," not "consciousness."[1]

But that discussion reckoned without the necessity that Durkheim was under of interpreting the *conscience collective* in its relations to the general methodological and theoretical scheme now under discussion. To it social facts are objective facts, not only to the sociological observer, but also to the actor himself. The interpretation at which Durkheim arrived is a consequence of attempting to extend the "rationalistic" schema of scientific methodology from the conditions of action involved in heredity and nonsocial environment to the social as well. This procedure has certain peculiar consequences.

In so far as Durkheim's thought runs in this channel *conscience* appears to lose its connotation of the ethically normative and to be identified with another term he frequently employs, *représentations*. The *conscience collective* is made up of *représentations collectives*. In this context the translation of *conscience* as consciousness seems more appropriate than as conscience. But what does all this mean?

COLLECTIVE REPRESENTATIONS

The phenomena of the external world are "reflected" in the mind of the scientist in systems of data and concepts. These are his "representations" of the external world. Durkheim's famous category of representations is undoubtedly simply a name for the scientist's subjective experience of the phenomena of the external world. Then according to the schema already thoroughly discussed, in so far as action is determined by a rational process, by the facts of the external world, such as those of heredity and environment, it will, as analyzed from the subjective point of view, appear as determined by the actor's representations of the external world, in exactly the same sense as that in which Pareto spoke of action, so far as it is "logical," being determined by a "process of reasoning," a scientific theory.

Then what is the meaning of the distinction between individual and collective representations? In the present context it is

[1] See footnote 3, p. 309.

perfectly clear. Individual representations make up the actor's knowledge of those phenomena of his external world which are independent of the existence of social relationships—in the analytical terms of the present study, of heredity and environment. Collective representations, on the other hand, are his "ideas" concerning the "social environment," that is, those elements in his external world which are attributable to the fact of association of human beings in society. Action is thought of as determined by the social factor, through the medium of men's rational, scientifically verifiable knowledge of their own *milieu social*, of the "social reality."

Several things are to be remarked about this peculiar way of looking at the problem. In the first place, it involves a radical shift of emphasis from the original definition and context of use of the *conscience collective*. The latter concept originally referred to a body of beliefs and sentiments held in common; the collectiveness of it consisted in the "in commonness." *Now* the collectiveness consists in the nature of the "reality" exterior to the individual to which the individual's "representations" refer. It is not a subjective community of belief and sentiment which is the source of solidarity, but rational orientation to the same set of phenomena in the environment of action, an "objective" source of uniformities. It is a curious circumstance that in this fundamental respect, as will be shown in the next chapter, Durkheim's development carried him through a complete circle. He ended where he began at the conception of a common subjective element.

Secondly, here is to be found the source of what has often been referred to as Durkheim's "falsely rationalistic psychology."[1] It is, in fact, not a psychology at all, but a case of what has been referred to above as rationalistic positivism. It results from attempting to apply the methodological schema of science to the interpretation of action from the subjective point of view. The only peculiarity of Durkheim in this respect is his explicit attempt to account for what his synthesis argument has designated as the social factor, society as a reality *sui generis*, in terms of this schema. It is not a rationalistic psychology in the ordinary sense at all, but it does involve what may be called a "cognitive bias."

[1] See C. E. GEHLKE, "Émile Durkheim's Contributions to Sociological Theory." *Columbia Studies in History, Economics and Public Law*, 1915.

One may ask, why not *sentiments collectives* instead of *représentations collectives?* If it were a matter of a common subjective element, there would be no objection. But in so far as the external world impinges upon the individual, and can affect his action in a manner accessible to analysis in terms of the schema of scientific methodology at all, it must be through the cognitive process. The only alternative would be in terms of a psychological anti-intellectualism, reducible from the subjective point of view to terms of ignorance and error. Such explanations Durkheim has already explicitly rejected. The role of representations is inherent in the whole structure of his conceptual scheme. In so far as action is not determined by subjective elements in his peculiar sense, and not by heredity and nonsocial environment either directly through rational adaptation or indirectly through drives and conditioned reflexes, it must be in the manner that he states.

Third, this situation yields still a third source of the metaphysical "group-mind" difficulty. For in this interpretation collective representations do not themselves constitute the social reality; they are representations *of* it. In the case of individual representations there is no difficulty as to "where" the empirical phenomena which are the objects of the representations are to be found; they are the phenomena of the body and the nonhuman environment. But where is the corresponding "reality" to which collective representations refer? We observe only its "manifestations," subjectively in the representations themselves, objectively in such phenomena as legal codes and suicide statistics. But the "thing itself" we do not observe. It is a psychic reality, therefore in some sense a "mind." But the subjective point of view is that of the individual actor, and in so far as we observe *his* mind it is only representations *of* the social reality we find, not the reality itself. It must, then, be a separate entity, but one withdrawn forever from empirical observation. Hence it is a metaphysical assumption with no scientific justification.

This is, indeed, a legitimate implication of the position Durkheim has here taken. It is a difficulty which is real and indicates that something is wrong. But what is it and where is its source to be found? Two main possibilities seem open. From the point of view of the traditional positivistic theoretical system Durkheim's scheme has the peculiarity of attempting to squeeze in between the horns of the utilitarian dilemma, yet without altering the fundamentals of the system itself, a third element not included in the usual formulations. One alternative then is the view that this attempt is itself the source of the trouble. This new element does not belong and should be extruded again. But this entails a further consequence: the *empirical* grounds on which Durkheim criticized, relative to his own empirical problems, the two horns of the utilitarian dilemma must be erroneous. In some form or other the theories he has rejected must be adequate to the facts. His own impression to the contrary must be due to a misinterpretation of the facts themselves. This is, in short, the line most of Durkheim's critics have taken.

But there is an alternative. Durkheim's critique of utilitarian and radical individualistic-positivistic theories may be correct. The facts which he has found to be incompatible with either of these two systems or any combination of them may have been correctly interpreted. In that event the source of the difficulty must lie, not in arbitrarily obtruding a foreign element into a sound conceptual scheme, but in failing to carry the modification of the conceptual scheme itself far enough to do justice to the factual insight already arrived at. This is the alternative which the present study will follow. Durkheim's difficulties at this stage were real. But both his own development and the progress of sociological science lay in not going back to the older positions and wiping out his innovations. His empirical criticisms of the consequences of the older positions in certain fields have never been satisfactorily answered and are, in the opinion of the present writer, unanswerable. But they could only be justly evaluated by carrying out a radical reconstruction of the whole conceptual scheme with which Durkheim had been working up to this point.

The case is similar to one already discussed, is, indeed, a special aspect of it. It has been shown that in terms of the elements explicitly formulated in a utilitarian system of social theory and logically compatible with it, Hobbes' interpretation of an individualistic order was right, that of Locke and his successors wrong. Nevertheless the actual situation was not a state of war held in check only by a coercive sovereign, but a state of relatively spontaneous order. Hobbes was theoretically right, but factually wrong. The theory on which Locke operated could not satisfactorily account for the facts he saw, hence the necessity of resort to an implicit metaphysical assumption, that of the "natural identity of interests." Only at a much more advanced stage of theoretical development was it possible to replace this with theoretical elements belonging to the system itself.

Similarly, at this stage of his development Durkheim's critics are theoretically right, as were those of Locke. Durkheim's early conception of the "social reality" in relation to action is wrong. But Durkheim was factually right; the theories of individualistic positivism do not account for the facts. As in Locke's thought, the metaphysical element in Durkheim's thought is an index of the necessity for theoretical reconstruction. Unlike Locke, Durkheim himself proceeded with this task and made great progress with it, though he did not complete it. It will be the task of the greater part of the remainder of this analysis of his work to follow this process of reconstruction. The group-mind concept as it and its genesis have been presented here, is not "Durkheim's theory"; it is the product of one stage in the development of that theory. Moreover, for present purposes it is not important in itself— indeed erroneous theories are never important in themselves. Nor is it important simply to point out that they are erroneous. It is important as the starting point of a development which without it cannot itself be understood.

Finally, fourth, a few words may be said about one of the principal sources of the difficulty. In a sense Durkheim is arguing on two different levels at once. In the general synthesis argument and in his general remarks about the inadequacies of psychological interpretations he is making an analysis of general application. The "social" element is that element of the total concrete reality of human action in society which is attributable to the fact of association in collective life. It includes the empirical features and properties of action systems in so far as they cannot be understood in terms of the nonsocial environment and of a human individual thought of in abstraction from social relationships. Similarly on the "psychic" level, it includes those features of concrete "mentality" which cannot be abstracted from the concrete social situation and history of the individual and thereby attributed to the inherent necessities of human nature. The social reality on this level is clearly an analytically separable element, or group of elements. It is not a separate concrete entity.

When, on the other hand, he is arguing in terms of the conceptual scheme just outlined, thinking of the actor as knowing the conditions of his action, the tendency is to consider a *concrete* individual acting in a concrete environment. The elements of action being considered are not general analytical elements, but concrete elements. Above all there is nothing to prove that the concrete social conditions are attributable exclusively to the fact of association. The social environment of a concrete acting individual is thought of as all the conditions relevant to his action which involve other concrete individuals. There is the strong tendency for the object of reference of collective representations to be the total concrete society as seen by a given concrete actor. But this clearly cannot be generalized for theoretical purposes— the result is a vicious circle. It would be open to the same criticism which Durkheim himself applied to the happiness theory. For it would mean taking as the explanation of the action of one individual, the very thing which is to be explained in the case of the others who constitute the social environment of the one. In other words, to explain in such terms the action of any one, it is necessary to assume that the action of all the others has already been explained, which is to beg the question of a general theoretical explanation of human action altogether. Indeed it is in attempting to evade this difficulty, without resorting to any "subjective" elements, still adhering to the canon that social facts must refer to *choses* to the actor, that the metaphysical group-mind difficulty arises. For unless the question is to be begged, the social milieu to which collective representations refer cannot be the concrete social environment of the concrete actor. But again, this is only one of two possible alternatives. The other is to discard the rigid requirement that the social element *must*, on a general analytical level, be included in the category of facts to the actor. This is, indeed, the way out, and the only way compatible with Durkheim's empirical results, but to arrive at it and to evaluate its consequences was by no means a simple task.

The general argument of this chapter may then be summed up as follows: Durkheim's early work in empirical fields had had a polemical orientation. The *Division of Labor* was, in the first instance, directed against the kind of interpretation of an individualistic order, a system of relations of contract, which had been dominant in the utilitarian tradition of thought. Over against the individualism of this interpretation Durkheim had set the view that society exercises a positive regulatory function of the first importance, essential to the stability of such a system of relationships. On the methodological level the same polemical orientation took the form of a critical repudiation of explanations of human action in terms of their motives, in the sense of the rational pursuit of given ends. This type of explanation was branded as subjective and teleological, in a sense objectionable to Durkheim, as supposedly incompatible with the canons of positive science.

The analytical schema which Durkheim set over against the rejected utilitarian was twofold. On the one hand was a semi-behaviorist objectivism which advocated the study of objective facts as against subjective motives. The two types of such facts which played a large part in Durkheim's own empirical work were legal codes and statistics of suicide. But this was the less important. As the basis of an analytical scheme for the interpretation of these objective facts he retained the subjective point of view, and within it adopted as his basic frame of reference the schema of scientific methodology. In these terms he conceived the social factor as operating through the medium of the actor's objective knowledge of it, a mode of thought with which this study has already been intensively concerned. Social facts are to be treated *comme des choses* in this sense, they are exterior to the actor in the sense of belonging to the "external world" and they "constrain" him in the sense of being outside his personal control, constituting thus a set of conditions to which his action must be adapted.

But this set of criteria, derived from scientific methodology by contrast with the subjectivity and teleology of the utilitarian schema, turned out to be too broad. Not only social facts but also those of heredity and the nonsocial environment meet them equally well. But explanations of social phenomena in such terms Durkheim had, after his brief adventure with population pressure, decisively rejected as inadequate to his facts. Such concepts as egoism and altruism as causes of suicide are not reducible to these terms. Social facts then become a residual category and the basic problem of his theoretical scheme is that of drawing the line between it and nonsocial *choses*.

So long as the scheme of analysis at present under consideration is retained, this is attempted in three steps, ranging from the general to the specific. First comes the synthesis argument, derived from the suggestion that this group of elements is in some sense attributable to the fact of association of individuals in social groups. The particular type of synthesis is further specified as psychic rather than material. Finally, within the psychic realm it is as collective representations that the significant element is identified. The emphasis on representations is not the result of a psychological rationalism, but is inherent in the peculiar structure of the conceptual scheme with which Durkheim is here operating. For it is basically a cognitive scheme; what is important is the actor's knowledge of the situation of his action.

On all three levels difficulties arise. On the synthesis level positive difficulties are not very important; the main one is the formalism of the argument, hence its logical inadequacy to the problem. When the social reality is, however, further specified as a psychic reality, the difficulty of relating it to the objective facts of suicide statistics and the like is more acute. Finally, in connection with the concept of collective representations, the problem of the empirical reference of the representations becomes crucial, and there is thus raised the metaphysical group-mind difficulty. This clearly indicates that there is something wrong with Durkheim's scheme. What it is, is the principal problem to be followed in the remainder of the discussion of Durkheim.

But, recognizing the difficulties of Durkheim's position, it should not be forgotten that he has not arrived at this position by any process of gratuitous error. In the first place, he has provided a thoroughly serious critique, backed by crucially important empirical evidence, of two major groups of theoretical interpretations of human action in society. These theories are not capable of accounting for certain facts the importance of which cannot be doubted. Secondly, in building up his own alternative he has made use, in a highly ingenious fashion, of the conceptual materials which have formed the basis of a great tradition of scientific thought and have been amply proved to be of empirical usefulness in many connections. There must be particular reasons why they will not work in the present instance; presumably he has not carried the process of theoretical reconstruction far enough.

One of the main difficulties in Durkheim's earlier work in the methodological field and in the interpretation of it has been, it has been shown, a failure to be clear on the issue of empiricism. He has not sufficiently guarded himself against the interpretation that the social reality of which he speaks is a concrete entity separate from individuals. The crudest version of this is the interpretation that it is a spatially separate object. But even on subtler levels the same difficulty arises. It is, however, quite safe to say that this interpretation in all its forms is incompatible with Durkheim's main line of argument even at this stage. It is quite clear, for instance, that society does not commit suicide in the sense in which that term is used in Durkheim's monograph. The social is an element or group of elements in the causation of the behavior of individuals and masses of them. Equally the "individual elements" do not constitute the concrete human being, but a theoretical abstraction. By the same token the same analytical categories are applicable to the understanding of the action of a single individual and of individuals in the mass as stated in rates of suicide, or in terms of changes in social structure. Durkheim did not fully realize this implication.

A still further implication Durkheim apparently did not realize at all, that there are two different levels of scientific abstraction; these he tended to confuse. While the full consequences of this fact cannot be brought out till later, a brief mention of its application to the present context is essential. The one level of abstraction is involved principally in the synthesis argument. It requires the discrimination of two elements in the concrete entity "society," the "individuals" and the *emergent properties* of the whole formed by their association. The former constitute units of this whole. As is true of all organic entities, the units in abstraction from their functional relations to the whole are different from the concrete individuals actually functioning in the whole. But whether or not they can be experimentally isolated, as chemical elements can be isolated, their separate existence as concrete entities in such isolation is conceivable—it makes sense. The abstractness of the individual in this meaning of the term is that of a fictional concrete entity. On the other hand, the same is not true of the emergent features of the organic entity. Precisely because they are emergent, to think of them as isolable in the form of another concrete entity, even a fictional one, does not make sense. Thus even on this level the two terms of the analysis, individual and social, are not on the same plane. For society cannot in principle exist except as a synthetic product of the association of individuals. On all this Durkheim is quite clear.

But heredity and environment and random utilitarian wants, with which Durkheim has contrasted social facts are not individuals, even the abstract fictional individuals arrived at by isolating them from social relationships. They are categories on a different analytical plane. They are, in the context most important to the present discussion, structural elements of a total social system of action, seen analytically, as a whole. If the status of the concept social reality is to be methodologically clarified it cannot be made to refer to a class of concrete things, even fictional entities like Durkheim's "individual," but only to such analytical categories. Whether the threefold classification of the latter at which Durkheim has so far arrived is satisfactory is not at present the question. But by this time it is quite clear that, methodologically, his classification must stand or fall on this general analytical level. But unfortunately this analytical character of Durkheim's social reality is, at this stage, only implicit and not methodologically clarified. This fact provides one of the principal openings both for justified criticism and for confusion and misinterpretation, in relation to his work. This is particularly true since the majority of those who have attempted to discuss this phase of Durkheim's work have had no clearer conception of the nature of analytical abstraction than he himself had.

ETHICS AND THE SOCIAL TYPE

There is another range of problems of a general methodological nature where the difficulties of Durkheim's position at this stage are brought out with peculiar vividness. Before closing this chapter it will be well to devote to these a brief discussion. It is the range of questions involved in the relation of science and ethics, and the basis of practical social policies. Durkheim, like all thoroughgoing positivists directly repudiates the view that sociology, or any other positive science, is concerned only with knowing and cannot provide a basis of action. On the contrary, its sole justification will lie in its becoming an instrument of human betterment.[1] Back of this lies the view that it is possible

[1] *Règles*, p. 60.

to develop a fully scientific ethics so that scientific theories become not merely indispensable elements in the determination of rational action, but alone adequate to it.

But this program of developing a scientific ethics raises difficult problems. At first sight the two disciplines seem to be poles apart. The attitude of the scientist is essentially that of the observer; he is concerned with *given* phenomena. It is true that modern scientific methodology has become sufficiently sophisticated to realize that the scientist is more than a purely passive mirror of the external world, a photographic plate. Scientific investigation is itself a process of action; it is the pursuit, not of knowledge in the abstract, but of particular knowledge of particular things. With reference to data it is a selective process, selection being determined both, as has been seen, by the structure of theoretical systems and by extrascientific considerations. But nevertheless, the aim of science is to reduce to a minimum the elements which do not lie in the facts themselves. Its development approaches an asymptote where they are eliminated. The concept of fact, as involving constraint, resistance to everything except its own intrinsic nature, is fundamental to science. In this sense the orientation of the scientist is, in the nature of the case, passive.

The orientation of ethics, on the other hand, is essentially active. Its center of gravity lies in the creative role of the actor, his ends. Freedom of choice is basic to ethics; whatever determinism it accepts lies in the field of the consequences of having made a given choice. Moreover this creative element in ends does not, as has been shown, constitute a set of facts of the external world as seen by the actor. All attempts to reduce the normative elements of action to the category of scientific theory alone end only by eliminating this creative element altogether. Action becomes merely a process of adaptation to a set of conditions. With all this the reader is familiar.

If the distinction between science and ethics is so radical, what then makes such a bastard product as a "scientific ethics" plausible at all? This seems to be primarily explained by three facts. First that all action takes place in certain given conditions over which the actor has no control. Then one of the primary requirements of rational action becomes the accurate understanding of these conditions in their bearing on the action—and this element of action, of course, *is* scientific knowledge or the common-sense precursor of it. In certain contexts of action, such as the technological, this element becomes of predominant importance; in all action its importance is very great. So the positivistic attention to it is far from being merely wrong.

Secondly, however, what is from the point of view of analyzing the general structure of action, or the action of an individual in analytical isolation, not part of the situation but a normative element, becomes, when a concrete individual acts in a *social* environment, in one sense part of the situation. The past and probable future actions of other individuals are part of the environment, the set of conditions, under which any one individual must be thought of as acting. And in so far as that action has been or is likely to be determined by normative elements, these enter for him into the situation. In other words, what is a set of facts of the external world to an observer—*other peoples'* ends to an actor who is observing the actions of other people—is not a set of facts of the external world to the same actor or to others when their own ends are in question. The fallacy of the positivistic position is easy to detect once the distinction between the points of view of the observer and the actor is clearly made. Those elements in the situation of a given individual's action which are attributable to the ends of other individuals are, when the argument shifts to terms of the *general* analysis of action, still interpreted as conditions because the change of point of view is not perceived. Thus the major part of the role of ends or other normative elements in action in general is squeezed out.

There remains only the "area of freedom" of the *concrete*[1] individual. Looking at him from without, this can be further reduced by the perfectly correct observation that his own *concrete* ends or the other concrete norms governing his action are by no means wholly or even substantially his own creation, but that every individual is a creature of the society in which he lives— his desires are determined by the conditions, the fashions, customs, ideas and ideals of his time and place. This may be, indeed generally is, true to a far greater extent than the individual himself realizes.

[1] It follows then from the above considerations that the role of normative elements for human beings in general is much greater than that for the single concrete individual. This fact is one main source of the plausibility of exaggerated anti-intellectualist psychologies, especially when combined, as is usual, with an empiricist bias.

The essence of scientific ethics,[1] then, is to turn an active into a passive relation. Instead of the phenomena of the external world being capable of use as means to the realization of an end or, at worst, limitations on action, they are thought of as the direct determinants of action. Hence, particularly from the point of view of the actor, the watchword becomes "adaptation."

All this Durkheim shares with other positivists. His departure from them lies in his addition of another category of facts or conditions to which action is and should be adapted. Individualistic positivists in their "ethical" phase laid emphasis on the external environment and human nature in various relations and aspects. Since these will not suffice, Durkheim adds the third category—social environment. The term he most frequently uses, the *milieu social*, is characteristic of this mode of thought. The social reality is precisely thought of as an *environment*, as an external reality (in the above specific sense) *to* which the individual *reacts* or which *acts upon* him. It is to the facts of this reality that he must adapt himself.

But in carrying out this line of ethical thought Durkheim runs into certain characteristic difficulties—two of which may be briefly noted. One of the principal objectives of all ethical thought has been the attainment of universal norms of human conduct. Only in terms of such principles would it seem possible to judge different kinds of conduct in terms of the dichotomy of right and wrong. But Durkheim is forced, primarily by empirical evidence, to abandon any such attempt. The facts of the social milieu do not appear to be organized in terms of any single set of principles comparable to the laws of the physical world or of biological selection. The principles of conduct, then, are not universal but are peculiar to each society—to each "social type," as Durkheim calls it.[2] On a positivistic and at the same time sociologistic basis it becomes impossible to transcend the relativity of actual and historic codes of ethics. What is right for one

[1] Ethics in any sense must, of course, retain some vestige of the subjective point of view of the actor.

[2] It is not maintained that this is inevitable, that there are no such laws governing the social world. It is Durkheim's view that is here reported. From an ethical point of view, however, he chose *at this stage* the lesser evil, since to penetrate from the relatively concrete social type to the deeper analytical laws of action would have brought to light the difficulties of his positivistic ethical position now being discussed (see *Règles*, Chap. IV).

society is not so for another. Each type has a "moral constitution" of its own which must be discovered by empirical study.

In the history of social science the appearance of this relativism of social types in Durkheim is a positive contribution of the first importance. It means an end to attempts to minimize the divergence of historical moral rules in favor of a search for a single set of central principles.[1] That it should emerge from a strictly positivistic source is particularly significant. But that does not make it any the less embarrassing from an ethical point of view, for to most ethical thinkers, including positivists, the failure of ethics to transcend the historical relativity of actual ethical codes is the failure of ethics itself.

This dilemma leads, indeed, to the second difficulty which crops up in various forms as it does for all "scientific" ethics. It is the inability to distinguish adequately between fact and ideal. In Durkheim perhaps the most interesting phase is his explicit attempt to set up a distinction between normal and pathological social states[2] which he rightly states to be essential if his ethics is to be of practical use. He takes as his point of departure the biological analogy of health and disease but proceeds to a particular interpretation of it. Disease, the pathological, is, he says, "accidental," it consists in those phenomena which are not bound up with the structure and function of the species as a type. Similarly with society, social states which are "contingent," which are not bound up with the social type or logically implied in it, are pathological. Then by a further jump—the normal is that which is of *general* occurrence while the pathological is particular, exceptional.

All these statements are full of ambiguity. Surely in the physiological realm disease is a fact— a highly important one. To say that the facts of disease are to a physiologist accidental in the sense that their causation is not to be understood in terms of the same laws as that of normal phenomena is surely not admissible. And why is it not possible for a whole species—at least all the members available for observation, to be diseased? Then disease

---

[1] It can easily be seen that Durkheim here introduces the positivistic equivalent of the "romantic" motion of a specific *Geist* peculiar to each culture. It is, hence, along with Pareto's "end which the society should pursue" an important symptom of convergence between the two traditions. Among other things it implies the unacceptability of linear evolutionism.

[2] *Règles*, Chap. III.

becomes the general fact and health the exception. The biological analogy of health is a trustworthier guide than the criterion of generality—which Durkheim undoubtedly adduces because it is empirical. But if generality is not satisfactory, how is it possible to get behind it and still remain on a scientific level? Most positivistic systems of ethics do so by saying that not the momentary existing state of facts is decisive, but rather conformity to the general conditions of existence of the species. So those who lay the main emphasis on biology generally arrive at the criterion of survival value. But survival of what? There is none but the empirical answer—the species—why it should not give way to some "higher" species is not explained.[1] This species is not the general fact but rather a normative type which to be sure is in this case defined largely, but never wholly, in terms of the adaptation to the conditions of its environment. Never do these conditions admit of only one kind of life.

Durkheim is in a similar situation. His criterion of generality will not work, so he has to fall back on his doctrine of the social type. But much more than the biological moralists he is clear that this is not completely determined by the nonsocial conditions of its existence but has a specific irreducible character of its own—for that is the very essence of his doctrine of the reality *sui generis* of society.

This shuts off in principle the solution of survival value. He does not, naturally, deny that a society, like a biological organism, must meet certain conditions of its existence or perish. But to treat it entirely in terms of these conditions would violate his basic principle.

Then he is, on a scientific level, left to the empirical observation of the society—and to remain empirical he takes the criterion of generality. But since this will not work, in struggling with its difficulties he goes, quite typically, in two different directions. In so far as he tries to remain really positive he is again and again forced back to the equivalent of the criterion of survival value.[2]

[1] Unless it be held that this should and does happen in terms of some empirically observed law of evolution. This simply drives back the problem one stage further. There is still the "creative" tendency of evolution left unexplained in terms of environment.

[2] This is essentially the same tendency as came out in another connection in his invoking of population growth as an explanation of the division of labor and reflects the same fundamental situation.

But he is aware of the dangers of this and more and more decisively turns to the other alternative. After all, what is needed is a principle of selection of the facts since from the point of view of ethics all the facts cannot be normal—if so the concept of the pathological is a contradiction in terms.[1] But the real difficulty of the criterion of generality is that it fails to yield such a principle of selection—for taken in its literal empirical meaning it is merely a simplified statement of *all* the relevant facts. The principle of adaptation to conditions being barred, one other is left open. The social type consists not in the generalizations applicable to the totality of facts known about a society but in the body of normative rules—custom and law—governing men's conduct in the society. Thus the term type (the use of which by Durkheim, in the first place, is probably significant of an important undercurrent of thought) regains its more usual meaning of a *standard*, not an average.

The employment of the schema of scientific methodology as a framework for the analysis of action from the subjective point of view was very probably dictated in large part by the requirements of a scientific ethics. For ethics must, in so far as it is to yield practically applicable rules of conduct, take the subjective point of view of the concrete individual. A scientific ethics must, in turn, be capable of fitting all the elements which are determinant of conduct into this schema.

So long as the social facts to which action is to be adapted remain an undifferentiated, unanalyzed concrete totality there is little difficulty in this scheme. But in the course of his development Durkheim was forced into such an analysis by the inherent logic of the situation. The issue comes to be between a set of conditional elements whose factual status to the actor is unquestionable, but which with increasing certainty must be differentiated out from the social reality in an analytical sense. Of this, in turn, the factual status to the actor becomes, on an analytical level, increasingly dubious. The criterion of generality may be regarded as an attempt to maintain it. But with the appearance of the difficulties of this criterion, as just outlined, there is an increasing tendency for the social reality to be identi-

---

[1] This is, in essence, the same difficulty as that of Professor Murchison over Pareto's concept of logical action (*supra*, p. 190). The methodological basis is the same in both cases.

fied with the social type, and the latter in turn, not with the concrete state of affairs in the actor's social environment, but with the *normative* aspect of it, with the body of common rules recognized as binding in the society. This development constitutes a long step in the direction of the issue of Durkheim's thinking to be stated in the following chapter. At the same time it is still plausible from the ethical point of view, to regard this body of rules as a set of external facts. Their normative character has only half emerged and only becomes fully clear by considering the analytical point of view of a total action system. The consequences of this will be developed in the next chapter.

But even at this stage there can be plainly seen a reversion to Durkheim's earliest preoccupation, as in the *Division of Labor*. He is brought back to the "legalistic" way of looking at things, in terms of the relation of an individual to a rule which he either obeys or violates. This tends to become the basic model for the relation of the individual to the social reality, not that of an actor to the external conditions of his action which he does not obey or violate, but rather comes to know and then either adapts himself to, or fails to do so. This was to be the direction of his future theoretical development. His famous statement in the *Règles* that crime is a "normal" phenomenon[1] may be taken in this sense. It is not normal in the sense of being desirable. But it is "logically implied in the social type" in the sense that the conception of action in relation to a body of normative rules implies the possibility of their violation. So long as this mode of relation persists, some men will violate such rules some of the time; there will be crime.

One of the principal difficulties was that at this stage the terms of his treatment of suicide had not been integrated with this schema. Since in Western society suicide is contrary to established rules, the causes of suicide appear to be altogether apart from the motivation of the individual. They are "impersonal" currents of social change, *courants suicidogènes*, which apparently cannot be fitted into such an analysis. This fact is one basis of the tendency of Durkheim at this stage to assimilate social to "naturalistic" causation. It was not until a good deal later that this gap could be bridged. As will be seen, the analysis of *anomie* constituted an approach to the solution of the problem.

[1] *Règles*, pp. 80 *ff.*

CHAPTER X

ÉMILE DURKHEIM, III: THE DEVELOPMENT OF THE THEORY OF SOCIAL CONTROL

The development of Durkheim's conceptual scheme subsequent to the *Suicide* can best be treated in terms of two main currents of thought. The first, which may be called the theory of social control, forms the subject of the present chapter. The empirical insights which are its main basis go back to the *Division of Labor* and certain parts of the *Suicide* and its main content is a development of the implications, theoretical and methodological, of these insights rather than an addition of new empirical elements. The most comprehensive and systematic statement of the new position is found in *L'éducation morale*.[1] The second current implies a shift in the center of interest—to an increased concern with religion—and culminates in *Les formes élémentaires de la vie religieuse*. Its theoretical analysis is devoted to a quite different aspect of concrete social life. Since its chronological place is later, and it depends in part on the other development and since only after this study did Durkheim attain the sharpest realization of his radical methodological changes, treatment of it will be reserved to the next chapter.

As has been said, it is primarily the central factual insight of the *Division of Labor* which forms the starting point for the phase of his development now under consideration. Empirical insights are often well ahead of theoretical and especially methodological formulations of their implications, and in the present instance this is certainly true of Durkheim. It will be recalled that in his criticism of the utilitarian conception of contractual relations he sets over against their view that the stability of a contractual system involves only an *ad hoc* conciliation of interests his own insistence that a vital part is played by a system of binding rules embodied in the institution of contract; without them, indeed, a stable system of such relations would not be conceivable. Thus the emphasis on the normative rule as an

[1] See also "La détermination du fait moral," in *Sociologie et philosophie*.

agency controlling individual conduct, for which it was so difficult to find a place in his earlier methodology, is from the start in the center of empirical attention.

The basis of this general thesis finds perhaps its clearest theoretical formulation in the discussion of *anomie* in the *Suicide*. There, not merely contractual relations but stable social relations in general and even the personal equilibrium of the members of a social group are seen to be dependent on the existence of a normative structure in relation to conduct, generally accepted as having moral authority by the members of the community, and upon their effective subordination to these norms. They not merely regulate the individual's choice of means to his ends, but his very needs and desires themselves are determined in part by them. When this controlling normative structure is upset and disorganized, individual conduct is equally disorganized and chaotic —the individual loses himself in a void of meaningless activities. *Anomie* is precisely this state of disorganization where the hold of norms over individual conduct has broken down. Its extreme limit is the state of "pure individualism"[1] which is for Durkheim as it was for Hobbes the war of all against all. Coordinate with and opposite to[2] the state of *anomie* is that of "perfect integration"[3] which implies two things—that the body of normative elements governing conduct in a community forms a consistent system[4] and that its control over the individual is actually effective—that it gets itself obeyed.

Back of this lies a fundamental theoretical distinction which becomes sharper and sharper in Durkheim's mind. On the one hand, there is the element of chaotic, undisciplined impulse and desire—the "individual" element in Durkheim's sense; on the other hand, the normative rule; in order that the whole conception of normative control may make sense in the way in which Durkheim thinks of it these two elements must be kept radically heterogeneous in principle.[5] For unless in "individual" desires there were this inherently chaotic "centrifugal" quality the need

---

[1] Correlative with "disorganization of personality."

[2] As a polar antithesis.

[3] *Supra*, pp. 247, 337.

[4] This aspect of integration significantly enough Durkheim scarcely takes notice of at all.

[5] Which naturally does not exclude both being involved in the same concrete phenomena; it is an analytical distinction.

of control would not be present at all. Moreover it is important to note that the analysis is couched in terms of the subjective point of view of the actor. It is a question of the relation of his desires, his subjective impulses or ends, to certain disciplining, controlling factors. Without the dichotomy of the two sets of factors Durkheim's whole critique of utilitarianism falls to the ground.

THE CHANGING MEANING OF CONSTRAINT

But where does all this fit into his methodological system? Its slow emergence into the central place with its complex implications can but be followed in terms of the changing meaning of the term "constraint."

As was stated in the last chapter, the starting point of the concept is—by contrast with the utilitarian conception of an "arbitrary" individual want, desire or motive—taken from the point of view of the actor. Then any element in his action is a constraining element which is not spontaneous or arbitrary, but which is part of the general "given" situation in terms of which he must act—which is thus beyond his control. Thus it seems to lay emphasis on the situation as opposed to the ends of action. Now, from this point of view any element which forms a part of the determinism of external nature exercises constraint over the individual and the term constraint has a tendency to become identified with causal dependence in general.

But this tendency quite clearly involves erasing all the most important distinctions of Durkheim's early analysis. It has been shown how, by his doctrine of "social realism" he was forced to throw out one category of causal forces—all those which, though in this sense constraining the individual, were causally independent of his social relations. But having done that, he was at first content to let things rest just there and at least to allow the implication that the remaining category of *social* forces constrained the individual in the same way. Being, at the time he wrote his *Règles*, presumably preoccupied with the objective study of suicide statistics, he seems, for the time being, to have lost sight of the problems raised by his treatment of normative rules in the *Division of Labor*,[1] and for the immediate theoretical

---

[1] The treatment of *anomie* which forms the main point of continuity with the earlier problems seems from internal evidence to have been thought

purposes in hand this negative formulation (even with the positive implications pointed out above) seemed to suffice. But in the treatment of *anomie* and the theoretical discussions of the final chapters of the *Suicide* (as in the Preface to the second edition of the *Division of Labor*) the problems of the role of normative rules came back into the center of his attention and remained there for a long time.

But on a "social" level this implication of the constraint of rules as acting on the individual simply like a physical force does not seem adequate. As his treatment of crime as a "normal" phenomenon implies, one cannot even think of normative rules without implying the possibility of the individual violating them. One may violate the law but one does not violate a physical force—presumably one does not violate a *courant suicidogène*. What is the status of the latter remains for the present a mystery, but in connection with such phenomena as the law Durkheim soon began using the term constraint in another sense.

This is the sense which would generally be understood without explanation when the term is applied to human conduct—that a person's will is constrained by the application of sanctions—that is, that he is coerced. In a late passage[1] Durkheim clearly distinguishes in this respect between a sanction and what may be called the "natural" consequences of an act. He puts the distinction in terms of the difference between the individual's relation to a rule of health and to a rule of law. Violation of a rule of health carries its own consequences automatically without human intervention. If, for example, a man does not eat sufficient food, he dies of starvation. Rules of this sort do constrain human action in a sense. This is simply one way of stating the fact that action is subject to conditions. But a sanction is a consequence of an act the occurrence of which is dependent in some sense on human will, though not that of the actor. To say that if a man commits murder he will die (probably) in the electric chair is very different from saying that if he does not eat he will starve. For in the former case he will not die unless someone *puts* him to death—his death is not an automatic consequence of the act of murder taken by itself.

---

out later than those of *égoisme and altruisme*—probably *after* the *Règles* was written.

[1] *L'éducation morale*, p. 32.

This distinction, elementary as it may seem,[1] is a most important step for Durkheim. While it enables him to maintain his original critical starting point that the constraining element is independent of the actor's will, he no longer implies that it is independent of *all* human will as he did at first. On the contrary, it is precisely the fact that it is an expression of human will which distinguishes social from natural constraint.[2]

At the same time the existence of the rule, and still more of the probability that its violation will bring down the sanctions behind it, is most certainly a set of facts of the first importance to the concrete actor, facts which are given and are independent of his will. It is significant that at this stage Durkheim seems to think of a rule and its sanctions as morally or emotionally neutral to the actor. The actor is thought of as if he were a dispassionate and objective scientist. Just as the conditions of biological existence are unalterable facts of the external world which it would be foolish either to approve or to resent, so are the rules of conduct of one's society and the things that will happen to one if one violates them just facts. His attitude is one of calculation. Here the "individual" is still thought of in utilitarian terms as pursuing his own private ends under a given set of conditions. The only difference is that the conditions include a set of socially sanctioned rules. This "attitude of the scientist" is surely another and a main aspect of what so many critics have incorrectly called Durkheim's "peculiar rationalistic psychology." For this calculating "individual" is to Durkheim still the concrete individual at least so far as his subjective aspect is concerned.[3]

The role of sanctions in this conception of the relation of the individual to rules is more implicit than explicit. Durkheim's main problem was to find a way to fit the conception of a normative rule into his positivistic methodology with the least possible modification. This was accomplished by thinking of the rule as a phenomenon of the external situation of the acting individual. The sanction becomes involved only by implication since, assum-

---

[1] It is one of those "obvious" things which all of us, in our preoccupation with a line of thought, forget to take account of.

[2] It is a particular case of the general distinction between the point of view of the actor and the observer.

[3] It is by no means necessarily true that the concrete individual as seen in this way is coextensive with the biophysical unit of the behaviorists, for instance.

ing this ethically neutral attitude of the scientist which was derived from the previous methodology, there is no other possible motive of obedience to the rule than avoidance of sanctions.[1]

There is a further empirical reason why this peculiar way of conceiving rules should have appealed to Durkheim. The first system with which he was concerned was that involved in the institution of contract—a set of rules governing predominantly economic activities—precisely those with which the utilitarians had been mainly concerned. But that is just the category of activities where the element of normative regulation is most definitely divorced from the immediate means and ends of action. Moreover, the immediate end of most economic activities, acquisition of money, is in itself to a considerable degree morally neutral, and it is easy to extend this attitude to the regulations to which the businessman must submit, whether embodied in law or in business custom, which then appear as conditions of action, which he must simply accept as facts. So long as the emphasis is on this aspect and no attempt is made either to analyze the forces behind enforcement of a norm or to raise the question of the motives of *habitual* obedience, this appears a fairly adequate account of the matter.

But there are certain difficulties if the analysis is pushed farther. It is all very well to think of social rules as given facts to a single concrete individual. But to the sociologist they are not given data in the same sense—they are just what he is trying to explain. Naturally Durkheim's first task was the demonstration of their existence and importance to action. But he cannot rest content with that. What then is their source and what is the nature of the force which constrains?

The direction he takes in answering this question is really implied in his analysis of *anomie*. There he was led to take another great step, the implications of which bring him to the next great phase of his development. Up to this point he has always thought in terms of the utilitarian dilemma—from the subjective point of view action must be explained either in terms of "individual"[2]

---

[1] Since the concern here is with regulatory rules which generally run counter to the immediate self-interest of the individual, the motive of "positive" interest is of secondary importance.

[2] Which to the utilitarian are *concrete* wants. It was just this tacit assumption Durkheim had to break down.

ends or wants, or in terms of the objectively knowable conditions. Durkheim has hitherto accepted this so that it has simply gone without saying that, since he rejects the utilitarian solution, his social factor has to fit into the category of conditions. Now he makes the far-reaching empirical observation that since individual wants are in principle unlimited, it is an essential condition of both social stability and individual happiness that they should be regulated in terms of norms. But here the norms thought of do not, as do the rules of contract, merely regulate "externally," *e.g.*, as the conditions of entering into relations of contract[1]—they enter directly into the constitution of the actors' ends themselves.

This really involves a complete rejection not only as before of the utilitarian solution of the dilemma, but of the dilemma itself. The individual elements in action are no longer identified with the concrete subjective individual, but the latter is recognized to be a compound of different elements. The element of ends as it appears in the means-end schema is no longer by definition "individual" but contains a "social" element. This is so important a step for Durkheim that in fact it constitutes a radical break with positivistic social theory—for in following its implications farther and farther he had to alter his original methodological position out of all recognition.

First of all, it opens the door to a new conception of the relation of the individual, and hence of constraint, to the normative rule. The normative element need no longer be thought of as a "condition" of action on the same level to the actor as other conditions, in this peculiar sense, as a fact to be taken account of. Its "constraint" over the individual may not merely differ from that of the "natural" consequences of an act in that the consequences have been "arbitrarily" placed there by a human agency other than that of the actor. In *this*[2] sense Durkheim altogether ceases to think of conformity with the norm as secured mainly by the desire to avoid the probable "external"[3] conse-

---

[1] For utilitarians who, like Hobbes, lay stress on authority as against freedom, the demand for regulation touches the *expression* of wants, not the constitution of the wants themselves. Durkheim's "authoritarianism" is of quite a different order.

[2] It is important to proceed here with great caution because most of these terms are full of possible ambiguities.

[3] That an act is performed out of a sense of duty alone does not mean its omission is devoid of *all* consequences. Qualms of conscience are certainly consequences and often most unpleasant ones.

quences of its violation. In the present analytical terms this means essentially that the element of social constraint is transferred from the category of conditions to that of normative elements.

Once this has been acknowledged it would seem that there were still two alternatives logically open. It would, that is, seem possible to interpret this in a "naturalistic" sense—that ends are constrained in the sense that they are inborn biological or psychological instincts—or that, behavioristically, they are conditioned into us[1] by our environment.

But from two points of view this alternative is unacceptable to Durkheim. Looked at objectively it leads him right back to the "individualistic-positivistic" factors he has already rejected. The return is direct if they are thought of as determined by biological heredity. If, on the other hand, they are thought of as acquired by conditioning, either the conditioning agency lies in the last analysis in the nonhuman environment, which is unacceptable, or it is the *milieu social*, in which case the problem of its origin and specific character still remains.

From the other, the subjective point of view, the difficulties become still greater, in fact decisive. For from this point of view all "external" factors as of heredity or environment are necessarily, in terms of action, elements of the conditions. But the very essence of Durkheim's new position is to drive them out of this category.[2]

There remains then only the abandonment of all the attempts and the acceptance of the view that the essence of constraint is the moral obligation to obey a rule—the voluntary adherence to it as a duty. This is the path Durkheim follows more and more decisively until his later works dealing with this subject become in this respect quite clear and consistent.

To be sure this is a special sense of the term constraint and one very different from that originally entertained by Durkheim. Some even would say that it is not constraint at all, since it involves voluntary adherence to a rule, which is precisely the

[1] That is, man in general, not any particular concrete individual.

[2] It is again evident how confusing is the empiricist bias which identifies ends in the analytical sense with *concrete* ends. Of course into what people concretely want, elements of both hereditary and environmental determinism enter. "Ends" as a causal element in action cannot be a concrete category.

opposite of constraint. In terms of the ordinary connotations of the terms this would seem to be a valid objection, but matters of terminology should not be allowed to obscure really important issues. Individualistic modes of thinking are so deeply imbedded in our culture that such confusion is very difficult to avoid. For the usual distinction between voluntary adherence and constraint carries the connotation of the utilitarian dilemma. Yet this is just what Durkheim has transcended. He has precisely distinguished, as the utilitarians did not, between voluntariness and arbitrariness. While, on the one hand, adherence is voluntary, on the other hand, that adherence is binding on the individual. But it is binding not from physical necessity but from moral obligation.[1]

[1] Even so acute a critic and original a thinker as Piaget (*Moral Judgment of the Child* and "Logique génétique et sociologie," *Revue philosophique*, 1928, pp. 167 *ff*.), who has come nearer to a just appreciation of Durkheim's work in these aspects than any other writer, seems to fall into this error. In the contrast he draws between "constraint" and "cooperation" he seems to exclude from constraint the purest type of voluntary acceptance of moral obligation. This involves an unduly narrow interpretation of Durkheim's meaning. Piaget's constraint, involving what he calls "moral realism," is found where the voluntary acceptance applies not so much to the rule of conduct as such as to an authority promulgating it—especially for Piaget that of a parent. But it seems quite clear from Durkheim's later writings (which Piaget quotes) that he did not mean to exclude the type of moral discipline involved in Piaget's "cooperation." He does insist, however, that constraint is always a *discipline* and not the mere assertion of individual desire in the utilitarian sense. This is, indeed, the real justification of the application of the term constraint. Piaget has pointed out an important distinction between two different types of genuinely moral discipline at which Durkheim unfortunately did not arrive, at least so clearly. But this contribution is not the basis for a criticism of Durkheim's final position but rather a supplement to it.

One reason, perhaps, why Piaget does not see this is his apparent failure fully to realize that even in connection with cooperation there must be an element of inculcation of norms. The social necessity of a moral consensus and of its continuity from generation to generation makes this inevitable. This does not, however, in the least mean that "reciprocity" is excluded. For Durkheim the individual (in *his* special sense, of course) is completely amoral. Hence to speak of morality without constraint is a contradiction in terms. One may suspect that Piaget has not used terms in quite the same way and has not been sufficiently careful to distinguish his usage from that of Durkheim, which is, as we have seen, often somewhat difficult.

Durkheim has in this proposition arrived indirectly and still by implication at one of Pareto's most important results—precisely the fundamental

Thus in following out the problem of control Durkheim has progressed through the conception of control as subjection to naturalistic causation and that of avoidance of sanctions, to laying primary emphasis on the "subjective" sense of moral obligation. The element of constraint persists, with a changed meaning, in the sense of obligation. In so far as he has that sense the actor is not free to do as he likes, he is "bound," but it is a totally different mode of being bound from either of the other two.[1]

It is, however, a disciplining, controlling element. The chaos of the "individual" element in human conduct is unmoral. It is given "form," is capable of issuing in order, in so far as it is brought into relation with a normative system. It is true that in certain situations and respects the attitude of the individual to these normative elements may be the morally neutral one of calculation, but that does not exhaust the matter. The normal concrete individual is a morally disciplined personality. This means above all that the normative elements have become "in-

---

reason for the necessity of "constraint" in moral action, in the determination of ends, is that analytically ends are not and cannot be scientific facts to the actor. They are therefore arrived at by a different process from that of the "spontaneous" recognition of the facts of the situation in which the actor is essentially passive. Constraint in the new meaning is simply a term for this nonscientific process. This again illustrates the decisive part played in modern social thought by the methodology of science as a standard, positive or negative. Pareto and Durkheim are agreed that the theories underlying the ultimate motivation of action are *not* scientific theories. It took Durkheim, however, a long time to work out the implications of this insight. Durkheim's moral constraint amounts to the definition of a normative element of action other than that of "efficiency" as definable in terms derived from the methodology of science.

[1] Professor Sorokin, in quoting Tarde with approval in the following passage, evidently places a quite unduly narrow interpretation on the criterion of constraint, seen in terms of its place in the course of the development of Durkheim's sociological thought as a whole: "When Durkheim says that only the phenomena which are compulsive are social phenomena, he unreasonably limits their field. Here Tarde's criticism is . . . valid. In this case, says Tarde, it seems that only the relationship of the conqueror to the conquered . . . and the phenomena of compulsion would be social phenomena. Meanwhile all instances where there is free cooperation . . . are to be excluded from the field of social facts. Such a conception of social phenomena is evidently fallacious." See P. A. Sorokin, *Contemporary Sociological Theories*, pp. 466–467.

ternal," "subjective" to him. He becomes, in a sense "identified" with them.[1]

From the beginning of the formulation of his problems in the *Division of Labor* Durkheim had been preoccupied with the problem of control. He has gone through a process of distinguishing different kinds of controlling elements, and has finally fastened his attention on the role of certain of the normative elements. But within this category he has gone farther to distinguish those normative elements which act in a manner closely analogous to external conditions, from a different category. These two classes of normative control are distinguished, not by any objective but by a subjective criterion, that of attitude. The content of the rules may be the same. The distinction relevant in the present context is not on this level, but lies in the mode of relation of the actor to them. By contrast with the morally neutral attitude associated with the sanction concept of constraint and with norms of "efficiency" generally, emerges the attitude of moral obligation, of a specific respect toward the rule.

There will be occasion later on to inquire further about the basis of this attitude of respect. At this stage of Durkheim's thought it is certainly simply a fact. It provides the basis of a solution both of the Hobbesian problem, and of the problem of order on the still deeper level of the theory of *anomie.* That men have this attitude of respect toward normative rules, rather than the calculating attitude, is, if true, an explanation of the existence of order. How far this attitude is, in turn, a function of other elements of their action is a problem which for the present may be left unanswered.

At present the problem in hand is that of the consequences of the emergence of this element into prominence for the structure of Durkheim's theoretical system. The fundamental and immediate consequence is to transcend the utilitarian dilemma. The "subjective" can no longer be exhausted by the element of random wants in the utilitarian sense, since the latter cannot become a basis of normative order. The utilitarian conception in turn therefore cannot exhaust the concrete wants of the concrete individual.

A further consequence is that at this later stage of Durkheim's thought duty or constraint is not the only leading characteristic

---

[1] They are, in Freudian terminology, "introjected" to form a "superego."

of morality. While accepting the central importance of the idea of duty, he criticizes the Kantian ethics as one-sided on account of paying sole attention to duty.[1] There is, he says, also the element of the good, of desirability. A moral rule is not moral unless it is accepted as obligatory, unless the attitude toward it is quite different from that of expediency. But at the same time it is also not truly moral unless obedience to it is held to be desirable, unless the individual's happiness and self-fulfillment are bound up with it. Only the combination of the two elements gives a complete account of the nature of morality.

The way in which the two are related in the development of Durkheim's thought is highly significant. The fact that his original starting point was the utilitarian dilemma had distracted attention from one aspect of morality—the good and the desirable—for desire was at that stage associated with the utilitarian conception of "arbitrary" wants. Hence he turns to the other aspect, duty, thinking of the two as mutually exclusive. Unquestionably, given the starting point, it was sound insight. But as his conception of the nature of constraint changed, the whole problem changed with it. When the utilitarian dilemma was finally superseded, the old alternatives disappeared. It was no longer a question of concrete ends or desires *against* external constraining factors, but the constraining factors actually enter into the concrete ends and values, in part determining them. And since normative rules, conformity with which is a duty, become an integral part of the individual's system of values in action, it ceases to be strange to think of them as also desired. This rigid ethical dualism of duty and the good is an aspect of the old utilitarian dilemma, and once the dilemma is dropped does not need to be maintained. The most fundamental criticism of utilitarianism is that it has had a wrong conception of the concrete human personality. So not only desirability, but even happiness, comes back—as a concrete state of the individual who is integrated with a set of social norms.

Furthermore the emergence of moral obligation involves a long step in overcoming what has above been called the cognitive bias in Durkheim's thought. The mode of influence of the di, ciplining element on action is no longer conceived as exclusively through the actor's knowledge of an external reality. It is true

[1] See "La détermination du fait moral," in *Sociologie et philosophie*.

that obedience to norms, even from a sense of moral obligation, certainly involves cognitive elements. The content of the norm and its consequences for conduct must be intellectually understood. Certainly part of the failure of concrete action to live up fully to the requirements of the norm is ascribable to defective understanding. But the attitude of respect is something in addition to this cognitive element, distinguishable from it. No longer is the analysis of action from the subjective point of view in terms of an exclusively cognitive schema, that of positive science, admissible. A whole new field, that of attitudes, emotions and the like is opened up. The ego is no longer merely a photographic plate, a registry of facts pertaining to the external world.

It also follows that there is a parallel shift in the meaning of the criterion of exteriority, if, indeed, it does not become completely meaningless. For originally it had reference precisely to elements in the external world in this cognitive sense. But in so far as the actor maintains an attitude of moral obligation toward it, the norm to which his action is oriented is no longer exterior in the same sense. It becomes, in the Freudian term, "introjected" to form a constitutive element of the individual personality itself. Indeed, without this moral element there would not be what we mean by human individuals, personae, at all. In its older sense exteriority is no longer applicable. Though Durkheim did not altogether cease to use it, it played a far less prominent part in his later than in his earlier work.

The theory of moral obligation was arrived at by Durkheim by a process of analysis of the action of the concrete individual from the subjective point of view, not of mass phenomena like suicide statistics. What is its relation to the methodological problem of the status of "society as a reality *sui generis*," and to collective representations?

The answer to the first question is perfectly clear. The general framework of analysis which has been employed throughout is left intact. The social is not to be identified with the utilitarian random element of wants, nor with heredity and environment— both these are to Durkheim "individual."[1] It is a psychic, not a material element. What happens, then, is that the system of

---

[1] It has been noted that this position with respect to heredity and environment is not tenable (Chap. II, appended note, p. 84). This thesis derives from the peculiar structure of Durkheim's earlier conceptual scheme.

norms of moral obligation *becomes* the social element as such. This is, in one main aspect, the end of the long quest for a characterization of the social element, the social reality. The solidarity of individuals is the unity of allegiance to a common body of moral rules, of values. The state of order to be contrasted with the disorganization of *anomie* is the moral order. Indeed this solution, in terms of his general scheme, answers all his previous pressing problems, though it gives rise, in this particular context, to further difficulties of its own. These difficulties will be discussed presently.

First, however, it is necessary to carry the implications of the new position one step farther. It is evident that in these terms the integration of a social group consists in the common recognition on the part of its members of a single integrated body of norms as carrying moral authority. A society, as Durkheim expressed it, is a "moral community" and only in so far as it is such does it possess stability.

Durkheim still continued to employ the term collective representations in this new context. But it has radically altered its meaning from that discussed in the previous chapter. It is not a system of ideas *about* an existent empirical reality exterior to the minds of individuals. It is rather a body of ideas which themselves form the effective factor in action, that is, the effective factor is itself present "in the minds of individuals," not merely a representation *of* it. To be sure the ideas are still conceived as representations of something. But this something is not a contemporaneously existent observed empirical entity, but is in part a state of affairs which will come into being or be maintained in so far as the normative elements in fact determine the actual course of action. It is not a present, but a future state of affairs in the empirical world to which they refer. It is this, in one aspect,[1] which makes it impossible to fit such ideas into the category of scientific fact. And in so far as the realization of this future state of affairs is attributable to the active agency of the actor and not merely to heredity and environment, it is also impossible for it to be a matter of predicted fact.

The collective representations include then *common* ideal norms. Their social aspect consists no longer primarily in the

[1] Ultimate ends do not, however, exhaust the nonscientific ideas important to action. Others will be discussed in Chaps. XI and XVII.

common reference of the symbols employed to the same empirical reality, as we have, in a sense, "collective representations" of the sun, but it may consist in the fact that as ideal norms, they are morally binding on the various members of the collectivity called a "society."[1] In the formula already employed, Durkheim arrives at the position that a common value system is one of the required conditions for a society to be a stable system in equilibrium. It further follows from the new position that, as has been remarked, the features of this value system relevant to action cannot be exhausted by its cognitive aspect. For to understand a norm and its consequences for action is not *ipso facto* to acknowledge it as morally binding. In addition to the cognitive element there is that of the attitude of respect. Hence the formula collective *representations*, even in the new meaning, is not by itself adequate to describe the social reality in so far as it is thought of as a part of the structure of systems of action. From being a homogeneous entity it has already begun to differentiate into a plurality of independent elements. In view of its genesis as a residual category this is by no means surprising.

ETHICAL DIFFICULTIES

The discussion may now turn to the question of the difficulties involved in Durkheim's new position, involving as it does the identification of the social element with that of moral obligation toward normative rules. Granted the correctness of his general analysis of the role of moral obligation in action, does it follow that the norms to which persons either in fact *do* subscribe from disinterested moral motives (or with ethical legitimacy *may*) must be *social* norms, must be those shared with even the majority of the other members of the community? After all, the leading modes of moral action admired by philosophers are often those involving defiance of the general code of the community.[2] The identification of the moral and the social seems in danger of elevating social conformity into the supreme moral virtue.

The criticism is justified. The conclusion does not follow in strict logic. There is no proof offered that the category of moral action is exhausted by its social aspect. Above all to deny the possibility, importance or even desirability of resistance to social

---

[1] With this change the metaphysical group-mind problem evaporated.
[2] Socrates is a prominent example.

pressure on moral grounds is surely dangerous. But the fact that Durkheim's position here is open to criticism must not be allowed to obscure the fact that he has attained a profound insight into aspects of social life very generally neglected—especially by utilitarians and positivists. The few critics who have understood at all what Durkheim meant have generally laid the main stress on one side of the relationship—that morality is a *social* phenomenon. For present purposes, and in terms of Durkheim's own scientific development, much the more important is the other side—that society is, at least in one of its principal aspects, a *moral* phenomenon in the strict sense that Durkheim has given the terms. The essential facts underlying this proposition may be formulated briefly as follows:[1] The analysis of human action shows that it cannot be understood apart from a system of ultimate values. These ultimate values are, in terms of the means-end relationship, their own justification and not means to any further ends. At the same time they assume to the individual a character of obligation, for being good, not merely *for* something, *i.e.*, as means, but in themselves; the general obligation to pursue the good is to pursue them.[2]

Moreover for any given individual, if the conception of rational action is to have any meaning at all, his ultimate values must be thought of as organized in a systematic hierarchical relationship to each other. Given the fact of actual freedom of human choice and the absence of any preestablished harmony, the abstract possibility exists of an indefinite plurality of such systems of values. But precisely since they are thought of as ultimate and thus in a sense absolute (to the actor), the existence of an indefinite plurality of such systems in the same community of individuals who have to share a common life would be incompatible with social order—would be the war of all against all.

[1] In terms, to be sure, somewhat different from Durkheim's own but in general consistent with the essential discoveries he has made while at the same time freed from some of his unfortunate implications.

[2] To try to justify them in scientific terms always involves circular reasoning. At the same time the feeling of obligation to pursue the good seems to be one of the ultimate characteristics of human beings which cannot be explained away. Attempts to do so lead to the same result only in another form. It is a "formal" property of action systems analogous to the conception of utility. It is inherent in the very conception of action itself.

So at least to the extent necessary to guarantee the minimum of order there must be a sharing of systems of values; there must be a system of *common* values. This must be a vital feature of the life of any community though its importance may vary from the guarantee of a bare minimum of order to the state of perfect integration where all action is to be understood as the complete realization of such a system of values. Durkheim has clearly shown empirically that beyond a certain point the extension of *anomie* is dangerous to physical life itself.

Moreover, the role of normative systems gives an explanation for what was to Durkheim earlier an unexplained empirical fact—the diversity of "social types." For while the members of a given community must to a certain degree share a single system of normative values, there is no a priori reason to believe that all communities will share the same system. In fact they do not on the whole to anything like the same degree that individuals within a community have done so.

Put in this way, the essential facts underlying Durkheim's theory can be accounted for without the objectionable implications. Above all, it still leaves room for individual recognition of a source of moral authority outside the value system shared with the community as a whole, without at the same time minimizing the enormous importance of moral conformity to the stability of society.

But in such a situation it is not important merely to separate truth from error in an author's work and to correct the error while retaining the truth. In discussing the work of a man of Durkheim's caliber it is instructive to inquire how he came to fall into the error and how it fits into his whole system of thought. How, then, did Durkheim come to *identify* society and moral obligation?

It is certain that even as late as the *L'éducation morale* Durkheim did not at all self-consciously question his general positivistic position, however illogical its maintenance might be in view of these developments. Such important and deeply rooted modes of thought die hard, especially in the mind of so tenacious a thinker as Durkheim. Thus he tends still to maintain the proposition that society is a reality *sui generis* in the full positivistic sense. This involves the empirical "reality" of the analytically distinct social factor not only to the sociological observer, but also to the acting individual. And still maintaining this, he fits it into the general scheme of analysis outlined above. There are the well-established realms of nature, roughly to be termed heredity and environment, to which he adds the third, the social. He is continually arguing by elimination—such and such a thing cannot belong to either of the first two categories, therefore it *must* belong to the third.[1] That the third is a *moral* reality appears as merely a specification of its nature and nothing more, unless its consequences are developed farther than Durkheim consciously did. The term "reality" still connotes an aspect of existent empirical nature from *both* the objective and the subjective points of view.

He has not yet seen the central difficulty of this position, largely because he has not systematically made the above distinction and thought through its implications. Unquestionably his position is correct if it is properly qualified. To the observing scientist the moral ideals held by the persons he observes and the rules of action growing out of them are without doubt real factors in action, the nature and effects of which are subject to the rational analysis of science. After all, that is what Durkheim and most other scientists really mean by nature—a set of phenomena subject to scientific analysis. In this sense a *science des moeurs* is perfectly reasonable and possible—it is what Durkheim means by sociology in its central part. But this is to be thought of as an explanatory science, not a normative one, even though the phenomena it has to explain are norms in their relation to human action. It is not concerned with explaining the moral validity of norms, but their causal efficacy.

The fact that in this science, as in any other at a given stage of their development, certain facts about the phenomena it studies are left unexplained—are ultimate data—is not a valid reason to deprecate its scientific achievements or potentialities. For all the empirical sciences are in this respect in the same situation. The empirical element in any body of knowledge is necessarily a nonrational element—as truly as mystical insight. All the scientist can do is to point and say, *that* is what I mean. The function of theory in a science is to reduce this empirical element to a minimum—and theoretical advance consists precisely in

[1] See *L'éducation morale* and "La détermination du fait moral" in *Sociologie et philosophie*.

finding a rational explanation for facts which had previously to be taken solely on an empirical basis. In the early work of Durkheim the diversity of social types is such an ultimate empirical fact which was later made explicable.

In general, as has been said, Durkheim's *sociological* doctrine here is sound and its importance can scarcely be overestimated. Much of the difficulty and confusion has arisen because of the fact that, like all positivists, he has not been concerned *solely* with a sociological doctrine, but also with an ethical theory in the positivistic sense—that is a *scientific* ethics. This prevents him from carrying out the analysis far enough to give him a really consistent general system of theory and methodology. For it is a requirement of scientific ethics that all the elements of action except logical reasoning should be facts of the external world in the scientific sense *to the actor*. But as has been pointed out again and again this view is utterly inconsistent with the nature of the factor of ultimate values in action[1] (as a *factor*, not as *concrete* ends or other concrete elements). Durkheim, however, does not really see this inconsistency as yet—the preceding analysis, while working out what may be considered quite legitimate implications of his position, at this stage really runs ahead of his own thought. This was necessary in order to get at the most significant content of it.

There is, however, a possible compromise position which is, in fact, the one he takes. If ends as well as the other elements of action must be thought of as facts, and if the distinction between the points of view of the actor and of the observer is not really clearly made, there is one category of ends which comes relatively near fitting these requirements—those actually embodied in the recognized governing norms of a concrete community. For to the observer the existence of these common norms as norms is an observable fact. They are to be found embodied in codes of law, in religious doctrines, in concrete custom. The essentially normative character to the actor is obscured by this relative concrete existence.

At the same time, to the actor, which is the point of view that matters for ethics, such norms are also relatively like facts.

---

[1] In terms of the system of theory under discussion in this study. The ontological question is, as has been remarked several times, outside of its scope.

In so far as they do actually govern the community life they are established facts—their violation brings external consequences, in the form of sanctions, as well as internal. Above all, so long as attention is centered, as it must be for *ethical* purposes, on the situation of the *concrete* individual and not on the *general* analysis of the elements of action, again the distinction of fact or condition and norm is obscured. On the other hand, those ethical ideals of individuals which are not shared by the community do not meet these requirements and tend to be thrown out of consideration.

This is essentially the path by which Durkheim, even though going so far in recognizing the true nature of normative control of individual action, was able, on the one hand, to maintain so much of the positivistic position in ethics: on the other, was led to elevate the *social* norm to a position of exclusive validity and throw out individual ethical independence. Thus he is in the unfortunate position of falling between two stools. He has gone so far away from true positivism that he no longer satisfies the real positivists and utilitarians as to his scientific soundness— to them he is a metaphysician. To the ethical idealists, on the other hand, he is guilty of the repression of their dearest tenet, individual moral autonomy, and hence is worthy of epithets even so harsh as materialistic.

But in spite of these legitimate ethical objections the immense sociological importance of Durkheim's work must not be lost sight of. He not only gained great insight into the nature of social control, but also into the role and importance of moral conformity. For it is a fact that social existence depends to a large extent on a moral consensus of its members and that the penalty of its too radical breakdown is social extinction. This fact is one which the type of liberal whose theoretical background is essentially utilitarian is all too apt to ignore—with unfortunate practical as well as theoretical consequences.[1] Thus Durkheim is able to offer what this type of liberal theorist entirely lacks—an explanation of why increasing diversity of ethical opinion should be

---

[1] It does not in the least follow from this that such a consensus must, should or except in a very limited degree *can* be maintained by coercion. Durkheim himself continually reiterated the importance of spontaneity for truly moral action. From his position it is illegitimate to deduce a facile justification of Nazi methods of control of opinion.

associated with social instability, *anomie*, rather than, as such liberals would tend to assume, an increase of happiness.

The immense importance of his achievement is, however, no reason to adopt an attitude of uncritical adulation and refrain from pointing out difficulties. In spite of his recognition of the specific character of moral phenomena, Durkheim's tenacious adherence to positivistic modes of thinking tends to make him continually minimize the magnitude of the difference between them and the other facts of nature with which positive science deals. Two aspects of this difference which he does not adequately emphasize at this stage may be pointed out briefly here.

In spite of the possibility that norms, including ethical ideals, may be treated as empirical phenomena by the observer, it must never be forgotten that they are phenomena of a very peculiar sort—that they are to the acting individuals *norms, ideals.* What is observable about them is not the state of concrete existence to which they as propositions refer, but the fact that the individuals acting look upon such a putative state of affairs as desirable and hence they can in a significant degree be thought of as striving to actualize it.[1] But whether, and the degree in which, it is actualized is not a question the solution of which is given in the mere existence of ideal norms as such, but remains a problem. It depends upon the *effort* of the individuals acting as well as upon the conditions in which they act. This active element of the relation of men to norms, the creative or voluntaristic side of it, is precisely what the positivistic approach tends to

[1] The difficulty may be put in terms of a double distinction between the meaning of the terms ideal and real, the identification of which is the most serious source of confusion. To the observer, as to the actor, the distinction is vital. To both an ideal is in a sense a reality—that is, it is a fact that the actor entertains such and such an ideal. But an ideal, since it is a norm of *action*, has a double aspect. In its factual aspect an ideal exists but its reality is not, as it were, exhausted in its mere existence; at the same time it refers both to a desirable *future* (including maintenance for the future of the present state of affairs) state of empirical affairs—*outside* itself—and to the *present* subjective state of the actor, the former to be actualized (in part at least) through the action with, of course, the possibility of failure. As a reality of the *external* world an ideal exists to the observer, but *not* necessarily the future state of affairs to which it refers. To the actor, on the other hand, it exists *as* an ideal but not as an actuality of the external world in any sense. The only way for that to happen is for it to be realized in action— that is for it to cease to exist as an ideal. It is absolutely necessary in the interest of clear thinking to keep these distinctions continually in mind.

minimize—for it thinks in terms of the passive, adaptive, receptive attitude embodied in the ideal of an empirical scientist.

From this bias Durkheim certainly is not free, even at this later stage. It is essentially this which is back of the implication so often attributed to him of identifying the *status quo* with the ideal. For unless the greatest of caution is observed, the treatment of ideals as facts is in great danger of idealizing whatever facts may happen to be known. The only way to avoid this danger is continually to insist on the peculiar character of ideals as elements in action and their radical distinction from the elements of the actor's situation, the "conditional" elements.

It follows from these considerations, not only that an empiricist methodological position is untenable in the sciences dealing with human action, but that the abstraction involved in some at least of their most important concepts is of a peculiar kind. For the most fundamental feature of the change in Durkheim's position which has been discussed is the shift of the "social" elements from what is, in subjective terms, a "factual" or conditional to a normative status. It is this which makes the distinction of the objective and the subjective point of view so vital, for it introduces a lack of symmetry between the two as to the status of the normative elements. They constitute, from the objective point of view, factual elements, otherwise they would not be observable and would have to be denied a place in a body of scientific knowledge. But at the same time, from the subjective point of view their status is radically different, it is as "ideal," normative elements which, if they have a factual reference at all, is not to an actually existing, but at most to a factual state of affairs which could not be brought about or maintained without effort. Its realization is conditional on the actor's either bringing about certain changes in the present state or preventing certain changes from taking place.[1]

---

[1] As was noted at the beginning of the analysis (Chap. II) a future reference is essential to the action schema. But the essential analytical distinction between the normative and the conditional elements is between those aspects of a given future state of affairs which can be predicted would come about without intervention of the actor, and the differences of the "actual" from this hypothetical state of affairs which are attributable to the actor's intervention in the situation. Only these *differences* can be imputed to normative elements. There are two main ideal types of situation to which this analytical distinction is applicable: (1) where the predicted state of

The difference between normative and non-normative elements comes out most vividly in the kind of concept that refers to a fictitiously or potentially concrete entity or state of affairs. A normative concept is not abstract only in the sense that, for instance, the conception of a frictionless machine is abstract, that, for purposes of the analysis in hand, it *does not* at the moment exist. It is further abstract in the sense that *if* it did, or could, exist apart from action in the particular concrete context in question, it could not have normative significance, for a normative concept always refers factually to a state of affairs which in some respects requires action to bring about or maintain. At least in the terms employed by the theory of mechanics, the *idea* of a frictionless machine can have no influence on the behavior of wheels, rods, cylinders and valves; this idea does not operate to reduce the amount of friction except through the mind of an engineer, that is by a process of action. But there is every reason to believe that the idea of "equality" influences the behavior of human beings and actually in certain respects operates to reduce the degree of inequality. Thus the concept of "social type" which became so important to Durkheim does not refer in the first instance of the specific structure of the actually existent nexus of social relationships, but rather to the nexus of normative elements *in* the concrete society. It is there that some, at least, of the more important differentiating elements are to be found. The divergence of social types as Durkheim treats them is predominantly a matter of the divergence of common value systems. Unless this peculiar normative character of so many concepts of the theory of action is kept clearly in mind, confusion inevitably arises.

Another difficulty which may be pointed out refers to the manner in which the relation of the individual to the social reality is conceived. As has been seen, the traditional positivistic

---

affairs will constitute a continuation of the initial state, and the end is to alter this state of affairs in certain respects; (2) where it is predictable that, if the actor ceased to intervene as he has been doing, the initial state of affairs would automatically change, but the end is to maintain it unchanged. In this latter case what can be ascribed to normative factors is the difference between the continued initial state of affairs and what it *would* have become had the actor withdrawn his intervention in the "natural" course of events. Of course actual concrete cases are made up of many different permutations and combinations of the elements formulated in these two types.

mode of analysis is to take a *concrete* unit and study the action upon it of forces from "outside." When this is applied to the human individual in the social sciences, it leads to the attempt to take the *concrete* individual and study the action of social forces upon him. Thus society comes to be thought of as an environment, such that if it is not actually spatially separate from the individual he is at least definable as a concrete entity apart from it. In subjective terms it constitutes to him a category of facts.

But if the social becomes a constitutive element in the individual's own concrete personality then his relation to society must be thought of in quite different terms. He is not placed in a social environment so much as he *participates* in a common social life. In this specific sense the relation must be thought of in organic, not mechanistic terms. Without a well-defined system of values shared to some degree with other members of the community the concrete individual is not thinkable. This goes beyond the vague general concept of an organic relationship. The specific moral element defines it much more closely. But again it is necessary to take care in interpreting this. What is shared is not merely the empirical fact of certain common features of concrete behavior. Back of this and in part explaining it is the sharing of common ideals and norms of which the common behavior is at best a partial actualization. Thus again the normative element must be brought into play. In biology an organ is thought of as standing in a purely "factual," not a normative relation to the organism as a whole.[1] There is a functional relation between part and whole. In the case of the social factor the individual is not merely in this factual sense a part of society, but shares also in a community of values the "existence" of which is necessary to and partly explains his factual, functional role.

The Role of Institutions

These difficulties show that Durkheim had by no means reached a final conclusion in his development, but only a way station. Before his death he took one more major step. But that step was so closely associated with his study of religion and his interest in quite a different set of empirical problems that even

---

[1] It seems, however, that the "type" of a species does imply a teleological element somewhere.

its application to the theory of social control is best postponed to the following chapter. Before proceeding with that it may be helpful to set forth briefly but systematically the main positive outline of Durkheim's theory of social control at this point. He was so preoccupied with the growing points of his theory that he was apt to give the impression of dropping other elements—at any rate he never explicitly related them all to one another. Furthermore, on account of the difficulties just discussed, it is necessary to resort to a certain amount of construction and to put things somewhat differently from the way in which Durkheim himself did. But in doing so the attempt will be made to remain true to the fundamental ideas of his theory.

The best approach is to follow Durkheim's development to a certain degree backward. Logically the priority belongs to the things at which chronologically he arrived last. The logical starting points are these: that a major element in human action analyzed in *general* terms is the ultimate-value system. This value system is manifested for an individual in one respect as ultimate ends which come to be formulated more or less explicitly in an organized system, the organization of which will disclose upon analysis a limited set of principles governing conduct. Applied to the permanent regulation of conduct in a set of relatively settled conditions, such a value system also becomes embodied in a set of normative rules. They not only serve directly as the ends of specific acts and chains of them, but they govern as a whole, or in large part, the complex of action of the individual. For a very large number, in fact the great majority of actions, they do not define the immediate ends but rather define modes and conditions under which actions in the pursuit of immediate ends should or may be performed. Thus there emerges from a consideration of Durkheim's treatment the distinction between two modes of the relation of values to concrete action, first as defining the immediate ends of specific action chains, second as embodied in a set of rules governing a complex of specific actions. Durkheim was much more immediately concerned with the latter relation than with the former.

The conditions of the coexistence of a plurality of human beings in the same physical space are such that, if normative elements are important at all, for them to be actuated by a random plurality of ultimate values is impossible. Hence negatively it follows that the ultimate values of the individual members of the same community must be, to a significant degree, integrated into a system common to these members. Furthermore there is, as Durkheim and others, notably Piaget, have shown, much positive evidence that not merely are already existent systems of ultimate values integrated in a social system, but that the ultimate values of individuals themselves are developed in the processes of social interaction. Thus Durkheim in his discussions of *anomie* and in *L'éducation morale* has shown that many or most individuals when deprived of a relatively stable system of socially given norms undergo a personal disintegration which destroys the moral quality of their conduct. Similarly Piaget has shown that not only moral attitudes but even the logical thought on which morality depends only develop as an aspect of the process of socialization of the child. This evidence confirms the negative proof of the impossibility of a truly utilitarian society.

The moral reality with which Durkheim's sociology has been concerned is, then, this system of ultimate values common to the members of the community in its relation to their individual actions. Since external conditions are by no means wholly determinant of specific social forms, in general it is a priori probable that each social community will, apart from genetic and diffusionist relations to others, be characterized by a system in many important respects peculiar to itself. Moreover this system will stand to the individuals under it in the above double relation—first, as defining the direct ends of specific acts and complexes of them, second as a body of rules governing the complex of actions no matter how diverse their immediate ends. The further these immediate ends are removed in the means-end chain from the system of ultimate values sanctioning the system of rules, the more the rules will tend to appear to the individuals subject to them as morally neutral, as mere conditions of action. And since the ends of the great majority of practical activities are very far removed from ultimate values,[1] there is a strong tendency to evasion. For, by itself, the attitude of expediency

[1] The degree to which this is the case depends on a number of different conditions. It is most conspicuous in the type of situation Durkheim analyzed in the *Division of Labor*—a system of pure relations of contract. It becomes far less conspicuous in a different type of situation, that of *Gemeinschaft*, which will be discussed briefly below (see Chap. XVII, appended note).

which considers a rule as a morally neutral "condition" contains no motive of obedience. Just as we attempt to remove physical obstacles to the realization of our ends in so far as that is within our power, we tend in certain circumstances to do the same with social obstacles.

As Durkheim throughout, and quite correctly, maintains, the capacity of individual desires for expansion is, in the absence of normative control, unlimited. The demand for more and more means to satisfaction, especially the peculiar abstract means— power and wealth—knows no assignable end. From this it follows that the system of normative control is continually subjected to a "bombardment of interests." A weakening of control through moral authority tends to call forth a substitute in the form of sanctions—a substitution of unpleasant, external consequences to supply a motive of obedience in place of the internal moral sense of duty. Thus from Durkheim's final meaning of constraint the logic of the situation leads back to the second. There can be no doubt that both play their part in the actual functioning of social norms.

But it is necessary to enter a little more fully into their relation to each other. The difficulty of constraint in the sanction sense as a basis for the enforcement of a system of norms as a whole is that it cannot be generalized. The Hobbesian theory is the classic attempt to do it—and it breaks down, in part under the necessity of organization for applying the coercion, which cannot itself rest on coercion in the same sense. So Hobbes is forced to fall back on a very unrealistic degree of enlightenment of self-interest at the crucial point of the formation of the contract with the sovereign—and then an element of *legitimacy* derived from this contract which transcends constraint in the sanction sense.

The principal basis, then, of the efficacy of a system of rules as a whole lies in the moral authority it exercises. Sanctions form only a secondary support. Durkheim brings this out most strikingly in his interpretation of the role of punishment.[1] The theory of punishment corresponding to the sanction version of constraint is, of course, the deterrent theory. The function of punishment is held to be to prevent the violation of rules through

---

[1] In especially *L'éducation morale*, pp. 181 *ff.* and "Deux lois de l'évolution pénale," *L'anneé sociologique*, Vol. V.

fear of the consequences. But Durkheim shows empirically that to a very large extent punishment does not bear this character. It is rather a symbolic expression of the community attitude toward the crime—a severe punishment is a mode of reaffirming the sanctity of the norm the criminal has broken. It is of symbolic, not utilitarian, significance—a relationship which will be found, in the next chapter, to be of the greatest importance to Durkheim. If this were not so, the severest punishments would be attached rather to the crimes which tend most strongly to be committed than to those considered more serious, which is by no means empirically true.[1]

From this also another important consequence follows. In so far as the true attitude of the criminal toward the rule is the morally neutral one of calculation of consequences, the more nearly will sanctions, efficiently applied, act as real deterrents. But in so far as a rule is accepted as a moral obligation, this attitude of calculation is lacking. In general, for the ordinary citizen his abhorrence of murder is so strong that he could commit it only under such powerful emotional stress that calculation would be entirely out of the question. Durkheim's theory of punishment fits this case for which the deterrent theory entirely fails to provide. And in regard to crime in well-integrated communities, it is certainly the most important case.

But the vital distinction between these two types of constraint should not lead to the misinterpretation that they are mutually exclusive in concrete life. For if Durkheim's theory of punishment is correct, the severity of punishment is due mainly to the fact that a strong general conviction of the sanctity of a rule, the strength of moral attachment to it, calls forth a correspondingly strong reaction against its violation. Then an "integrated" social situation, one in which individuals are strongly attached by a sense of moral obligation to its governing body of rules, will tend to be characterized by strong sanctions for obedience to them. The existence of these sanctions is thus not necessarily an index of the tendency to violate norms—it is, rather, the opposite. In such a society, if a single individual or small numbers of

---

[1] For instance, it is very doubtful if among the normal "respectable" population the murder rate would appreciably increase were all punishment for murder abolished. Fear of the electric chair is probably negligible as a deterrent.

them adopt the morally neutral attitude to the norms, it is still generally to their interest to conform to them.[1] In fact, two reasons for the appearance of severe sanctions, in a sense opposite, must be distinguished, as Durkheim did in essentials in an important article.[2] On the one hand, they are an index of the strength of the *conscience collective* (in this case definitely "conscience," not "consciousness"); on the other, of the breakdown of control through moral authority and the growing necessity for a substitute.

Thus in every society there is such a body of normative rules of action, the embodiment of ultimate common values. In one main aspect the integration of the society is to be measured in terms of the degrees to which these rules are lived up to from motives of moral obligation. But besides this there is always the motive of "interest" which, looking upon the rules as essentially conditions of action, acts in terms of the comparative personal advantage of obedience or disobedience and acceptance of the sanctions which will have to be suffered.

Once a body of rules is firmly established in authority it can remain intact through a considerable shift in these motives— for there develops an interlocking of interests in the maintenance of the system. But the ultimate source of the power behind sanctions is the common sense of moral attachment to norms— and the weaker that becomes, the larger the minority who do not share it, the more precarious is the order in question. For this interlocking of interests is a brittle thing which comparatively slight alterations of conditions can shatter at vital points. A social order resting on interlocking of interests alone, and thus ultimately on sanctions, is hence hardly empirically possible though perhaps theoretically conceivable, given the order as an initial assumption. For, on the one hand the greater the need for sanctions, the weaker the ultimate force behind them; on the other, the conditions of human social life being what they are, alterations of sufficient magnitude to shatter such a brittle

---

[1] It is the failure to see this relationship clearly which vitiates much of the theoretical reasoning of B. Malinowski's extremely interesting *Crime and Custom in Savage Society*. The interlocking of individual interests is certainly present and is a factor in maintaining conformity with norms, but that does not prove it is the primary basis of the system of normative control as a whole. Malinowski's criticism of Durkheim is entirely misplaced.

[2] "Deux lois de l'évolution pénale," *L'année sociologique*, Vol. V.

and unstable order can scarcely be avoided for very long except perhaps in cases of an exceptionally high degree of insulation from disturbing forces.[1]

Thus the outcome of this phase of Durkheim's development has been the emergence, in outline, of a theory of social control on the basis of the action schema. From widely divergent initial starting points his scheme has evolved to a point where it corresponds in all essentials with that which was developed above in connection with Pareto's theory. The difference lies not in the outcome, but in the process by which their respective conclusions were arrived at. Pareto started with the analysis of the individual act in terms of the means-end schema. Out of this emerged in the analysis of his work first the vital distinction between the normative and the non-normative elements of systems of means-end relationships. Only after a much further development of the logic of conceiving systems of such relationships as a whole, did the conceptions of a common system of ultimate ends and of the ends of a collectivity arise. The resulting conception of a social action system has definitely transcended

[1] The "contradiction" between the two aspects of the earlier phase of Durkheim's work as exemplified in the difference between his interpretations of suicide and of crime pointed out at the close of the last chapter can now be resolved. The fundamental thing is the relation of the individual to a norm constraining him in one of the two principal ways. But this is only the simplest "atomic" unit out of which an interpretation of such social phenomena is built up—consisting of the relation of a single individual to a single well-defined norm. When the added complication of the relation of a plurality of individuals to a more or less well-integrated system of common norms is introduced, other indirect effects are developed. There are several ways in which these can bear upon suicide. The clearest perhaps is that of *suicide anomique*. There the situation is that, since, for whatever reason, the individual is no longer sufficiently well integrated with a system of norms which, above all, define his ends of action and value attitudes, there is no organized discipline over his unlimited desires and the ultimate result is a sense of frustration which in extreme situations issues in suicide. The causation here is by no means exclusively "naturalistic" in that the normative element is entirely essential but, on the other hand, there is no reason to suppose that the sucide is conscious of the true cause of his act. What he is conscious of is an immediately intolerable situation. But this situation is compounded among other things out of the relation of this and many other individuals to ultimate values and norms.

The cases of suicide *egoiste* and *altruiste* are somewhat different. Here it is not a matter of the failure of normative control, but rather of a peculiar kind of control. In the first it is again a matter of the creation of a particular the "atomism" so closely associated, historically, with the employment of the intrinsic means-end schema.

Durkheim, it is true, also started with certain elements of the intrinsic means-end analysis, and the "scientific" standard of rationality. But his line of reasoning from this starting point almost immediately diverged from that of Pareto, not to converge again until a much later stage. The sociologistic theorem was to him the initial result of his first critical orientation to his problems. His early attempt was to fit this into the initial subjective schema by means of distinguishing the social reality as an independent category of facts concerning the external world as seen by the actor. This approach inherently obscured the specific character of the normative elements. But through the series of steps which have been traced, it gradually proved to be untenable and gave way, though not completely, to a radically different mode of analysis. In the first place, the fact that he laid emphasis on the empirical importance in the determination of action by a body of normative rules, necessitated a radically different way of conceiving the "reality" involved from that of the factual conditions of action. The full consequences of this step could not, however, be drawn, until in place of a morally neutral "scientific" attitude to the rules, which implied the avoidance of sanctions[1] as the dominant motive of conformity,

---

kind of situation—a very heavy religious responsibility, for instance, which often proves too much for the individual. Here, even though the act is in violation of one norm, the religious prohibition of suicide, it is caused in part by the indirect effects of the relation to others. In the case of altruistic suicide a similarly intolerable situation is created, but there is also at the same time often a direct *social* pressure to the act itself, as in suttee or hari-kari.

Thus the "naturalistic" aspect of Durkheim's *courants suicidogènes* turns out to be, like that of economic laws, a matter of the ramifications of the indirect effects of action in terms of, and individual relations to, the normative elements. In this particular case it is primarily in their aspect of normative rules rather than, as in the economic case, immediate ends. It is thus not necessary in order that norms may act as "causes" of phenomena for them to serve as the direct conscious motives of all the individuals they affect. A repudiation of teleology in this simple sense does not force one to accept naturalistic causation as the only alternative.

[1] Or seeking positive advantage. Durkheim's choice of sanctions as the dominant element of "interest" is a historical accident. It makes no difference in the present context.

appeared the attitude of respect, the acceptance of moral obligation. This step definitely carries over the social element for
analytical purposes from the objective category of facts, or
conditions of action, to a subjective, normative status. The
element of constraint remains only in the form of the sense of
obligation, that of "exteriority" in that it is a system of binding
norms not private to a given individual, but common to the
members of a society. Thus Durkheim's methodological schema
was brought back into conformity with the original definition
of the *conscience collective*.

To regard the essence of at least one principal integrating,
order-giving element of social system as lying in a system of
common values is directly in conformity with the outcome of
Pareto's reasoning. But Durkheim's different approach determined the fact that he emphasized a different mode of relation
of this value system to individual action. It was but natural
that Pareto, thinking in terms of means-end systems at the
rational pole, as in his second abstract society, should formulate
the integration of action systems most sharply in the concept of
the "end which the society should pursue." Durkheim, on the
other hand, started from the consideration of the social conditions
of individual action. Among these he found a crucial role to be
played by a body of rules, independent of the immediate ends of
action. In the end these rules are seen to be capable of interpretation as manifestations of the common value system of the community; it is because of this that they are able to exercise moral
authority over the individual. In so far as the immediate ends of
particular acts are removed from ultimate ends by many links of
the means-end chain, even though these ultimate ends be in
conformity with the common system of ultimate values, there is
need for a regulatory system of rules, explicit or implicit, legal or
customary, which keeps action, in the various ways detailed
above, in conformity with that system. The breakdown of this
control is *anomie* or the war of all against all.

This body of rules governing action in pursuit of immediate
ends in so far as they exercise moral authority derivable from a
common value system may be called social institutions.[1] It is

[1] It is noteworthy and significant for understanding the main line of
Durkheim's thought that at this stage he is exclusively concerned with the

an element of which the relations to the structure of action systems are not explicitly brought out in the work of Pareto.[1] The role Durkheim ascribes to social institutions is not, however, in contradiction to the analytical scheme which has emerged from the above discussion of Pareto's work, but constitutes a most valuable supplement to it, capable of fitting into the same theoretical system.

On two occasions Durkheim himself defined sociology as the science of institutions.[2] This definition indeed corresponds closely to this phase of his thought. At this time he was inclined to think that the institutional aspect of the social reality in this sense was the one of predominant importance. But this view reckons without the still further phase of his development, to which the next chapter will be devoted. There he made a still further major step in widening the scope of the analytical outline of the structure of action to include elements closely associated with the conception of the social element at which he had arrived, but not at all adequately dealt with in his earlier development, nor indeed in any branch of the tradition out of which he grew.[3]

---

relation of institutions to individual motivation, not to social structure. The latter relation, so important to the *Division of Labor*, has completely dropped out. It will reappear in this study in connection with the work of Max Weber below.

[1] It is presumably largely involved in the persistence of aggregates and the residues of sociability.

[2] *Règles*, 2d ed., Preface, p. xxiii; *Les formes élémentaires de la vie religieuse*, footnote, p. 523.

[3] What may be regarded as a classic statement of the true positivistic view of institutions radically inconsistent with Durkheim's is that of F. H. Allport: "In the Natural Science sense institution is not a substantive concept at all." The facts usually pointed to are to Allport simply complexes of habits. In his terms Allport is quite right since the whole concept of normative control has no meaning from a "natural science," that is, a positivistic point of view. The "institutional fallacy" of which Allport speaks is in truth a twin brother of the "group fallacy," in fact turns out to be the same thing. See his article in *Journal of Social Forces*, 1927, and his book *Institutional Behavior*, 1933.

Chapter XI

ÉMILE DURKHEIM, IV: THE FINAL PHASE:
RELIGION AND EPISTEMOLOGY

Durkheim's interest in the phenomena of religion goes back to the earliest part of his career. It played an important part in the discussion of mechanical solidarity in the *Division of Labor*. It is again prominent in the treatment of the relation between religion and suicide. At a relatively early date, in Volume III of *L'année sociologique* he essayed a definition of religion. But it was not until 1912, some fifteen years after the appearance of his last previous major work, that he published a comprehensive study in the field.

From quite early he had a general feeling that religion and social life had a peculiarly intimate connection.[1] But it was not until the development of his theory of social control had proceeded to the point to which it has been followed in the last chapter that the way was really opened to make a satisfactory place for religion in his sociological system. Not only did he then fit it into his system; in turn, the study of it became the major empirical factor in the modifications which lead up to the final phase of development of his general theoretical structure.

It is a noteworthy fact that Durkheim shared this feeling of the intimate connection between religion and society with the other two most important figures of this study, Pareto and Weber. As has been seen, religion, rather vaguely understood, came to be for Pareto a principal element in nonlogical action. It was certainly one of the main elements that had been neglected by the theorists whose stress had been on logical action, most notably those advancing technological and economic interpreta-

---

[1] It is interesting to note that in an open letter replying to Deploige's accusation that his social realism was "made in Germany," Durkheim denied the charge and said that the largest influence on his thought besides that of Comte had come from the English historians of religion, especially Robertson Smith. This was dated 1907. See S. Deploige, *Le conflit de la morale et de la sociologie.*

tions. Similarly Weber, reacting against Marxian historical materialism, found the central element that they had neglected to lie in systems of religious values. But Weber's background was different from that of the others. What is interesting in the present context is the fact that the two theorists with whom this study deals who were most intimately related to positivistic thought, Pareto and Durkheim, both, in their later phases particularly, became absorbed in the sociology of religion.

This interest is, indeed, most significant. In the positivistic thought of the eighteenth and nineteenth centuries the tendency undoubtedly was to depreciate the importance of religion either in general, or with the advent of the theory of evolution, for the later phases of the evolutionary process. It has been seen that this interest was involved in Pareto's arrival at a position which was radically out of harmony with the positivistic system with which much of his thought had a close affinity. The same is true of Durkheim. While, as the last chapter has shown, in other connections he had already gone far in this direction, it was his study of religion which completed the process and, as it were, made his break with positivism irrevocable.

For this study, instead of making a comprehensive comparative survey of historical religions, Durkheim chose the method of the crucial experiment, the intensive study of a limited body of facts, those of Australian totemism. The present concern is not primarily with the particular aspects of this particular factual material but with the general ideas he developed in his study of it. It is unnecessary for present purposes to be drawn into the empirical controversies which have arisen over his detailed interpretation of the Australian material[1] or even over the place of totemism in the evolution of religion in general. It

---

[1] This statement is not to be taken to mean either that facts do not matter in general or that facts are unimportant to the subsequent discussion. It is rather that the facts which are important to this discussion are not among those which are controversial. Only certain very broad contentions of fact are involved. The really crucial ones are, as will be seen, (1) that there is a basic distinction of attitude toward the classes of things which Durkheim designates as "sacred" and as "profane" and (2) that sacred things have a symbolic significance. Neither of these propositions has been successfully attacked in relation to the Australian material. On the other hand, such matters as the details of kinship systems or of particular rituals are not important to the present argument.

does not matter greatly whether Durkheim is right in his contention that totemism is the most primitive of all religions, for the present interest is in the fundamental elements common to all human action in society, primitive or not.

It is worth while to remark that here again Durkheim has written a monograph which, like *Le suicide,* is of an extraordinary sort. While ostensibly studying only a narrowly technical empirical material which might be thought to be of little general interest, he manages to make it the vehicle for unusually far-reaching theoretical reasoning. So, while *Les formes élémentaires de la vie religieuse* is in one aspect a technical monograph on Australian totemism, it is at the same time one of the few most important works on sociological theory. It is, of course, the latter aspect which is of interest here, but before entering into its content it may be suggested that Durkheim in these two instances has set a model of a type of monographic study which might well be more frequently imitated. In fact only when a monograph is at the same time an essay in theory can it be the highest type of empirical study. Durkheim had the faculty of combining the two aspects in a way which provided models for future sociologists. Unfortunately it is unlikely that many will attain this preëminence in the combination.

RELIGIOUS IDEAS

Theoretically there are two different though intertwined elements in the *Formes élémentaires,* a theory of religion and an epistemology. The theory of religion will be dealt with first, as it forms the indispensable connecting link between what has gone before and the epistemology.

There are two basic distinctions from which Durkheim departs. The first is that of sacred and profane.[1] It is a classification of things into two categories, for the most part concrete things, often though by no means always material things. The two classes are not distinguished, however, in terms of any intrinsic properties of the things themselves, but in terms of human attitudes toward them. Sacred things are things set apart by a peculiar attitude of respect which is expressed in various ways. They are thought of as imbued with peculiar virtues, as having

---

[1] *Les formes élémentaires de la vie religieuse,* pp. 50 *ff* All references in this chapter are to the second French edition.

special powers; contact with them is either particularly advantageous or particularly dangerous, or both. Above all man's relations to sacred things are not taken as an ordinary matter of course, but always as a matter of special attitudes, special respect, special precautions. To anticipate a result of the later analysis, sacred things are distinguished by the fact that men do not treat them in a utilitarian manner, do not as a matter of course use them as means to the ends to which by virtue of their intrinsic properties they are adapted, but set them apart from these other profane things. As Durkheim says,[1] the profane activity par excellence is economic activity. The attitude of calculation of utility is the antithesis of the respect for sacred objects.[2] From the utilitarian point of view what is more natural than that the Australian should kill and eat his totem animal? But since it is a sacred object, this is precisely what he cannot do. If he does eat it, it is only on ceremonial occasions, entirely set apart from workaday want satisfaction. Thus sacred things, precisely in excluding this utilitarian relationship, are hedged about with taboos and restrictions of all sorts. Religion has to do with sacred things.

The second fundamental distinction is that between two categories of religious phenomena—beliefs and rites. The first is a form of thought, the second of action. But the two are inseparable, and central to every religion. Without knowing its beliefs the ritual of a religion is incomprehensible. That the two are inseparable does not, however, imply any particular relation of priority—the point at present is the distinction. Religious beliefs, then, are beliefs concerning sacred things, their origin, behavior and significance for man. Rites are actions performed in relation to sacred things.[3] A religion for Durkheim is "an integrated (*solidaire*) system of beliefs and practices relative to sacred things, that is separate and taboo, which unite in one moral community called a church all those who adhere to it."[4] The last criterion is one which will be dealt with later, as the process by which it has been arrived at cannot be understood without a further analysis of the other criteria.

[1] "Le travail est la forme éminente de l'activité profane." *Formes élémentaires*, p. 439.
[2] *Ibid.*, p. 296.
[3] What this implies will be discussed below, see pp. 429 *ff.*
[4] *Formes élémentaries*, p. 65.   My translation.

As has been found to be the case with all Durkheim's previous thought, the point of departure here is again a critical attitude. At the outset of the book he remarks that so persistent and tenacious an element in human life as religion is inconceivable if the ideas associated with it are pure illusions,[1] that is, do not "reflect any reality." And so he starts with a critique of the schools of interpretation which have, on the one hand, made religious ideas the primary element of religion and, on the other, have sought to derive these ideas from men's impressions of the empirical world. This will be recognized as the typical approach of his earlier scheme—the question what, from the point of view of the actor, is the "reality" reflected in the ideas, the "representations," in terms of which he acts.

The two classes of theories on which Durkheim concentrates his critique are those he calls "animism" and "naturism."[2] In both cases the first burden of his criticism is that they violate the above criterion, that they reduce religious ideas to illusions. For they make them out to be prescientific explanations of phenomena which are susceptible of satisfactory explanations in terms of science—on the one hand, of psychology; on the other, of physical science. The phenomena of dreams and of the more striking natural events such as great storms, volcanic eruptions and eclipses are nothing mysterious to the modern man and require no supernatural explanation.

Starting from this point of view Durkheim might be expected to follow out his usual argument by elimination. Since neither the facts of psychology nor those relating to external nature can be the facts involved in religious ideas, and since these ideas cannot be merely primitive unscientific versions of these facts, there must be a third category of facts which they do on the whole correctly reflect. And since in observable nature there is only one other such category, the social, the reality reflected in religious ideas must be the social reality—hence Durkheim's thesis of the social character of religion.

This is, indeed, one strand of Durkheim's argument and a permanent one. But it is the one which is carry-over from the earlier stages of his thought and is therefore in need of correction as a result of the analysis of the last chapter. This elimination

[1] *Ibid.*, p. 3.
[2] *Ibid.*, Chaps. II and III.

argument must, however, be kept in mind as it is intimately intertwined with another which will form the main concern of the following discussion. Only by seeing the two in their interrelation can some of the important features of his theory be understood.

At the beginning Durkheim has laid down his fundamental distinction of sacred and profane. He is therefore not merely concerned with the question of the reality of the entities "represented" in religious ideas as such but also with the source of their peculiar character of sanctity. So, intertwined with the illusion argument, is to be found a second strand of criticism of the theories of animism and naturism. Not only do they fail to demonstrate that there is a set of real facts underlying religious ideas, but the facts they do adduce fail above all in that they cannot serve as the source of the property of sacredness. We know the "true" explanation of dreams in individual psychology. But there is nothing sacred about the "individual" as such, i.e., the object of psychology. He is a bundle of egoistic desires, impulses and sensations, which are not the objects of any peculiar respect. Similarly, the "true" explanation of the events of external nature deprives them of their character of sacredness. All are reducible to terms of natural laws which are from the point of view of the scientist morally and emotionally neutral.

More generally the peculiar respect which is the distinguishing characteristic of sacred things has no place in the merely cognitive "attitude of the scientist" which comes so often into Durkheim's thought and seems to be his starting point in his search for the reality underlying religious ideas. This attitude of respect cannot but strike the reader of Durkheim by its close relationship to the individual's attitude to the regulatory norms toward which the actor feels a sense of moral obligation. There is the same disinterestedness, the same divorce from the attitude of calculation of advantage. The distinction of sacred and profane belongs to this later phase of Durkheim's development and is not part of his true positivistic system. It is the counterpart of the distinction between moral obligation and individual interest.

But just how are the two pairs of concepts related? Or are they simply the same thing expressed in different words? There appear to be two striking differences. The starting point of Durkheim's analysis of social control was the existence of a more or less concretely homogeneous set of phenomena, the moral rules of custom and law. Such rules are distinguished by their intrinsic characteristics from other phenomena of interest to the sociologist—for instance, suicide rates. They are prescriptions as to how men are expected to behave in certain circumstances. Though rules are not physical phenomena, they are empirical objects recognizable by their intrinsic properties. This is not true of sacred objects as a class.

Moreover, secondly, while the interpretation of the causal role of moral rules involves a considerable modification of the positivistic conception of causation in terms of "natural determinism," yet there remains a certain substantial similarity. Since the analysis of their role is reducible to terms of the intrinsic means-end relationship, there is undoubtedly an intrinsic relation between end, means and normative rule somewhat similar to that between physical cause and effect. Rationality of action, that is, depends on a knowledge of the intrinsic properties of the means, and the predictable consequences of conformity with norms.[1] The recognition of the role of ultimate common values in action does not disturb this basic schema.

But in both respects the interpretation and explanation of sacred things involve difficulties. This is seen immediately in the attempt to draw the distinction between sacred and profane. As Durkheim says, the concrete objects to which sanctity is attached seem to have nothing in common except their sanctity. They may be inanimate objects, plants, animals, natural events, spiritual beings, mythical personages, rules, modes of behavior and what not. So he entirely abandons the attempt to draw the line in such terms, and falls back on the attitude of men toward these things. As far as intrinsic properties are concerned, anything may be sacred. Anything *is* sacred so long as people believe it is; it is their belief which makes it sacred.

It has been said that Durkheim criticizes the naturistic and animistic theories of religion on the ground that they could not account for the element of sacredness in sacred things. But he gradually goes further to see that there is a deeper reason for this inability. What they are really trying to do is to find as the

[1] This concrete end is in one aspect a forecast of a future state of affairs in the empirical world. "Realization" hence must be thought of in terms of the intrinsic properties of the phenomena of the empirical world.

source of religious attitudes empirical phenomena the intrinsic properties of which command this attitude of peculiar respect. Hence in naturism the concentration on the unusual and imposing or terrifying aspects of nature, such as the storm and the earthquake.

But Durkheim ultimately decides that the important reason why these theories fall down, a reason which underlies their various empirical inadequacies, is that they conceive the problem of the source of sacredness wrongly. The source lies not at all in the intrinsic properties of the concrete sacred object; it is rather, as he often says, "superposed" upon these properties.[1] That is to say, the relation of sacred object and attitude of respect is not one of cause and effect. The sacred object is a symbol. And the essence of a symbol is first that its importance, value or meaning is not inherent in the intrinsic properties of the symbol itself, but in the thing symbolized, which is by definition something else; secondly, that in so far as it is a symbol it has no intrinsic causal connection with its meaning, the thing it symbolizes, but looked at in such terms the relation between them is arbitrary, conventional.[2]

If this be true it puts the problem of the origin of the sanctity of sacred things on an entirely different basis. The question is no longer that of finding a category of things of which the peculiar intrinsic properties may serve as the "reality" which accounts for the belief in the sacredness of things. Indeed, in general, the question why at a given time and place some concrete things are sacred and others not becomes of secondary interest. The important question is, rather, what is the other term of the symbolic relationship, since a symbol implies a thing symbolized? This also opens the door to an explanation of a very puzzling problem—that of finding some unity in the perplexing empirical variety of sacred things. For, from this point of view the fact of their empirical heterogeneity may not matter— the unity and order may lie in the things symbolized, not in the symbols.

The implications for action cannot be taken up in detail until Durkheim's theory of ritual is considered. But it may be noted now that the starting point corresponds to that of his

[1] *Formes élémentaires*, p. 328.
[2] *Ibid.*

treatment of religious ideas. Just as in the interpretation of religious ideas Durkheim abandons the attempt to discover an intrinsic causal relation between the kinds of things held sacred and the "cause" of their sacredness, so he also abandons the attempt to discover an intrinsic means-end relationship in the actions of religious ritual. It is not, for instance, to be regarded as a rational technique of multiplying the totem species, but its significance lies on a different plane; it is symbolic. In both cases the fundamental error of the other theories has been to confuse the intrinsic and the symbolic relationships. This confusion is one of the basic sources of the prevalent positivistic view of the irrationality of religion—for symbolism has no place in the positivistic scheme of analysis: science cannot provide the model for it.

It is true that Durkheim, arguing in his positivistic vein, is seeking for the "reality" underlying religious ideas. He holds they cannot be representations either of the external environment or of "individual" human nature (of heredity) for, in the first place, if they are they must be held to be erroneous representations and hence liable to disappear under scientific criticism. Secondly and more important, these categories of reality cannot be the source of the peculiar quality of respect which is the distinguishing characteristic of sacred things. But if religious ideas are not sheer illusions, they must correspond to an external, observable reality. There is such a one, society, which moreover meets the fundamental requirements of Durkheim's analysis.

For respect is the attitude engendered by something which stands to us in the relation of moral ascendancy.[1] Mere physical force may arouse fear, but not respect. Society is a moral reality and is the only empirical entity which can meet the requirements of the problem and which has moral authority over man. This is the path by which Durkheim arrives at his famous proposition —that God or any other sacred object is a symbolic representation of "society."

Perhaps no proposition could awaken more instantaneous indignation in religious circles than this. The man who has started out to vindicate the permanence of religion against those who would dissolve it into illusion emerges with an even more objectionally "materialistic" view than those he criticizes.

---

[1] *Ibid.*; pp. 296–297.

For what does his formula amount to but making of religion a worship of the flesh, of what is merely human?

It is better, before too hasty a judgment is delivered, to inquire a little more closely into the implications of this position. The identification of religious "reality" with society is so profoundly shocking largely because it is assumed that everyone knows without further inquiry what society is—it is a part of "nature," something entirely distinct from the divine. But as was seen in the last chapter, the gap between the social element and the rest of nature had been progressively widening for Durkheim. The distinction between moral authority and individual interest is not merely one of degree—it is radically qualitative. Durkheim would be ready to admit that the social-moral reality is in an important sense ideal.[1] What is the effect of the identification with the source of religion on this situation? Does it assimilate society farther back to "nature" or does it widen the gap?

Unquestionably it widens it. Already it has been necessary to conclude that the collective representations, in so far as they constitute the cognitive element in a common value system exercising moral authority, do not stand in the same relation to the "external world" as do those elements in the subjective which constitute scientifically verifiable knowledge of the means and conditions of action. The underlying reason for this has been found to lie in the normative character of the value elements in relation to action. That which is of normative significance must, in the nature of the case, be analytically distinguished from any elements which play a role in the situation of action.

So far Durkheim's attention in this connection has been confined to rules of action such as those involved in the law of contract. It is true that these have a cognitive aspect in the sense that the rules may be formulated; the words in the formulation have meanings which can be understood as can the meanings of other words, and the propositions thus stated have mutual logical implications in the form of relations of logical consistency or lack of it, and implications for action as such. But all this does not imply any reference beyond the propositions themselves except to the hypothetical state of realization of the norms.

---

[1] *Cf. ibid.*, p. 605. "Il faut donc se garder de voir dans cette théorie de la religion un simple rajeunissement du matérialisme historique: ce serait se méprendre singulièrement sur notre pensée."

Now Durkheim turns to a different category of cognitive elements associated with action, "religious ideas." These are not as such norms of action. Their content is neither a set of norms nor a future state of affairs, but involves existential references to what are to the actor contemporaneous things, persons, entities. The ideas concern the behavior of these things and their relations to man. They are "sacred things."

Religious ideas as such need not have any immediate relation to action. In so far as they bear on the present discussion they do contain not a system of norms but a system of existential propositions. One fact about them stands out in Durkheim's treatment, that they deal with sacred things. And sacred things are defined by the identity of men's attitude toward them with that which is observed toward norms toward which men recognize moral obligation. This identity of attitude is the bridge between the two categories of cognitive elements.

But Durkheim carries the analysis one step farther. Some of these sacred things are, concretely, empirical objects, observable by ordinary scientific procedures, such as stones, pieces of wood, articles of clothing, places, courses of action. The peculiarity of this class is that when taken in isolation from the action context sacred things are found to differ on an intrinsic level in no discoverable respect from things of the same class which are not sacred. Sacred stones are not as a class separable by chemical or mineralogical analysis from profane stones. Then the sacredness is a property, as Durkheim says, "superposed" upon their intrinsic properties. Furthermore, another class of sacred things are not empirically observable at all. Such are spirits, gods, mythical personages and the like. From these facts Durkheim concludes, as has been noted, that the sacredness is understandable not in terms of any common intrinsic property of the sacred things, but in terms of a peculiarity of their relation to men, the symbolic relation.[1]

[1] Attention should be called again to the point noted above (p. 211) that there is more than one way in which the symbolic mode of interpretation may be employed in relation to action. The simplest is the case where a given act, or thing, is, to the actor, an explicit symbol. Such is the case with most ordinary linguistic expression. In the more sophisticated religions, particularly on the part of their more sophisticated adherents, there is a vast proliferation of this self-conscious symbolism. But it is quite clear that there is no prima facie reason why this level of symbolism is the

420 EMILE DURKHEIM, IV: RELIGION AND EPISTEMOLOGY

So far Durkheim's position seems perfectly acceptable. The difficulty arises at the next step, that of specifying the symbolic reference of religious ideas, their meaning. For symbols cannot be symbols unless there is another term of the relationship. For his own answer Durkheim reverts to a mode of thought he had already superseded. He tries to think of the religious symbol as capable of assimilation to the symbols involved in scientific propositions as constituting part of a fact the meaning of which is to be found in an observable feature of the empirical world. The result of this is to drive him back to what is in essence another version of the type of theories which he has already rejected. Religious ideas must, then, be distorted representations of an empirical reality which is capable of correct analysis by an empirical science, this time sociology.

But the whole trend of the analysis of the structure of action developed in this study has been to question the legitimacy of assimilating all, even of the cognitive aspect, of action as seen subjectively to the methodological schema of science. To do so is, ultimately, to eliminate the creative role of the actor through the role of the normative elements of action. Pareto came to an explicit repudiation of this view in his dictum that a society "based upon reason" does not and cannot exist. The analysis

---

more significant for the understanding of action. Such conscious symbolic systems may, as Pareto brings out for a number of cases (see his treatment of the Roman religion, *Traité*, 167) be significant largely as secondary rationalizations or derivations. But that element which analysis reveals as underlying such symbolism, a residue or sentiment, may, in turn, be susceptible of symbolic interpretation, an act or an "idea," may be a "meaningfully adequate" mode of expression of a sentiment or value attitude, even though the actor is not in the least conscious of the connection. Though psychoanalysts are doubtless guilty of many extravagances in their symbolic interpretations, there seems to be little doubt of the soundness of the underlying view that many of our actions and expressions are to be interpreted as symbolically related to implicit or even repressed sentiments or complexes. It is this latter mode of occurrence of the symbolic relationship in action which is of primary significance in the present context. It should be obvious that where there is an explicit symbolic interpretation of his actions on the part of the actor it need not agree with that which would be imputed by the observer. Indeed, it would do so only in a limiting case which might be referred to as that of "symbolic rationality." In that case, as in that of "intrinsic rationality" the actor's own explicit "theory" could serve as an adequate explanation of his action without resort to anything like a residue-derivation analysis to get at the fundamental elements.

of the previous chapter has, in bringing out Durkheim's gradual realization of the normative character of the social element, assimilated his view closely to that of Pareto. The doctrine at present under discussion must be regarded as a reversion to Durkheim's earlier positivistic schema. Analytically regarded the reference of religious ideas cannot be to any empirical reality at all, if they are to be held to represent the principal existential cognitive element of the ultimate value complex.[1] In effect this procedure forces Durkheim back from a genuine analytical position to one of empiricism. Instead of the common normative element, the "society" which is symbolized in religious ideas becomes the concrete social group. For this is, indeed, an empirically observable entity. The concrete individual is in a position to observe it, to be assimilated to the situation of a scientist. This is the principal source of the interpretation of Durkheim in this connection as a religious materialist. It is the direct counterpart of the difficulty discussed in the last chapter in connection with the question of moral conformism.

Positivism has been defined for purposes of this study as the doctrine that positive science is man's sole significant cognitive relation to external reality. In the present case Durkheim is remaining true to the positivist position. The only way to escape its difficulties, including a resuscitation on still another level of the group-mind difficulty, lies in a direct challenge to the fundamentals of this position. Durkheim's basic tenet that religious ideas have symbolic significance is not tenable on the view that their reference is to an aspect of empirical experience capable of scientific analysis. Neither is it tenable on the view that the reference is to nothing at all, for a symbol without a meaning ceases to be a symbol. There is, however, a third possibility, namely, that the reference is to aspects of "reality" significant to human life and experience, yet outside the range of scientific observation and analysis.

For the view that ideas which do not meet the criteria of scientific methodology in fact play a very large part in relation

---

[1] This statement refers to the theoretical scheme of the theory of action. Though it may have metaphysical implications it is not itself a metaphysical proposition and these implications, whatever they may be, lie outside the scope of this study. The reader is asked to bear this in mind throughout the following discussion.

to human action, not only in the sense that they are ubiquitous, but also that they stand in significant relations to the real forces governing action, this study has, especially through the discussion of Pareto's work, brought abundant evidence. It may hence be taken as an established fact. Then there are only two alternatives open in the explanation of this fact: (1) either these ideas must be fully accounted for in terms of ignorance and error or (2) there must be a significant element altogether outside the range of scientific methodology. In the terms in which Pareto made it possible to formulate the former of the two alternatives, it has already been shown to be unacceptable. If there is one certain conclusion to be derived from his work it is that in his opinion the nonscientific theories were not only nonscientific through ignorance and error but through the part played in them by "non-experimental" entities. Durkheim has put forward another possibility of interpretation in harmony with the same alternative but one which involves, as has been shown, insuperable difficulties. It seems reasonable, then, to explore the implications of the second.

It will be noted that the "reality" which would then constitute the symbolic reference of religious ideas has been defined only negatively, as a residual category. It is *non*empirical. Moreover care has been taken not to define it as a concrete object, or system of them. The statement is, rather, confined to aspects or elements of concrete reality. All that is required positively is the proposition that the situation of man as actor is such that orientation to the nonempirical aspects of the universe, of his life and experience, is significant. It cannot be laid aside as an "unknowable" and forgotten. One further proposition about his relation to the nonempirical will be put forward before the study is brought to a close. But in such a field it is extremely important to proceed with all possible caution and to avoid commitments not rigorously necessitated by the logic of the situation.

One immediately pressing question has not yet been answered. Why does symbolism play a part in man's relations to the nonempirical aspects of reality, different from that which it plays in relation to the empirical? To answer this it is necessary to analyze the structure of knowledge somewhat further. Just as the means-end relationship seems to be fundamental to all consideration of action from the subjective point of view, to all "doing," so the subject-object relationship is equally fundamental to all cognition. It cannot be thought away without turning human experience into a meaningless jumble.

Now all knowledge, all cognition, is subjectively a complex of symbols generally linguistic, with meaningful relations to each other. Scientific propositions are no exception to this rule. But in this case there is involved only what may be called a simple symbolic relation. The symbol "stone" refers, through the medium of a complex of organized sense perceptions, immediately to a class of concrete empirical objects distinguished by certain criteria. But if a stone is at the same time a religious symbol there is a double symbolic reference when the word "stone" or a particular of the class is spoken or thought, first a reference of the word to the object, second that of the object in turn to that which it symbolizes. In the case of an imaginary entity the situation is in essentials the same, except that the immediate reference of the original linguistic symbol is not mediated through sense data in the same way. Zeus is not experienced in the same sense as a stone.

The explanation of this double incidence of symbolism in the nonempirical field seems to be the following: The very fact that "nonempirical reality" is not capable of being scientifically observed shows that there is not available in the same sense an empirical object of the external world to serve as object of reference of the subjective symbol. In so far, then, as "experience" of this reality is to be fixated in cognitive symbols functionally analogous to those of scientific propositions one of two courses is open. Either the "meaning" is attached to an actual object of empirical experience which then becomes a material symbol, or an "imaginary" object is constructed. That there is a need to think in terms of such cognitive symbols, to "visualize" and concretize the content of "religious experience," must apparently be taken simply as a fact about human beings as we know them. There is, however, evidence that on certain philosophical and mystical planes this intermediary symbolism tends to be altogether dispensed with. An analysis of the social setting and consequences of such tendencies might well throw light on the reasons why the intermediary symbolism in fact plays such a prominent role in human life.

The discussion may now return to the question of the relation of religious ideas to action. A distinguished historian of religion has defined religion as "the active attitudes of men to those parts of their life and environment which do not to them appear to be wholly controlled, conditioned or understood by human agency, and all that they do, say or think in virtue of such attitudes."[1] Religious ideas, then, may be defined as "those ideas men hold relative to the aspects of their life and environment which are to them unknown and thought to be unknowable by the ordinary procedures of positive science or the corresponding common-sense empiricism, and toward which they are under the necessity of taking up an active attitude."

Religious ideas, then, may be held to constitute the cognitive bridge between men's active attitudes and the nonempirical aspects of their universe. Action is not only "meaningfully oriented," as the positivist inevitably concludes, to reality as rationally understood by science but to the nonempirical as well. Rational techniques, as analyzable in terms of the intrinsic means-end schema including the role played by empirical knowledge in that analysis, may be regarded as belonging to our orientation system toward empirical reality. Religion, on the other hand, is one human mode of orientation toward the nonempirical. The specific content of religious ideas is no more completely determined, probably not nearly as much, by the intrinsic features of the nonempirical than is scientific knowledge completely determined by the "external world." In both cases there is a "subjective" element, the knower is not a purely passive register of given experience. But whatever the difference of degree there is a formal similarity in the relationship.

In the religious, as in the technical case, the subjective element is capable of formulation in terms of active attitudes. But where does the social element come in? There can be little doubt, if Durkheim's view of the relation between the sacred and moral obligation be accepted, that it is the ultimate-value attitudes of the previous analysis which are significant in this context. Then religious ideas are to be regarded as partly determinant of, partly determined by, men's ultimate-value attitudes. Since the nucleus of the social element in a normative sense lies in the existence of a common system of value attitudes, it is

[1] Professor A. D. Nock, in lectures at Harvard University.

to be expected that these will, in turn, be associated with a common system of religious ideas. Thus Durkheim, in his definition of religion, refers to "an integrated system of beliefs which unite in one moral community all those who adhere to it." It is through their relation to the moral community, to the common value system with all that the reader of the foregoing analysis will have come to understand as implied in that conception, that religious ideas possess sociological significance. This is the element of truth in Durkheim's formula that religious ideas constitute a symbolic representation of society.[1]

From the point of view of this study, then, it is not possible to agree with Durkheim's view that the ultimate "reality" in general symbolized in religious ideas is the reality "society" taken either as a concrete entity or as a factor in the latter. What is true is, rather, that it is in terms of what we call religious ideas that men attempt a cognitive apprehension of the non-empirical aspects of reality to which they are actively related. For the reasons above outlined, on the one hand, these ideas tend in a peculiarly high degree to employ symbols as modes of expression; on the other, in so far as they are held in common by the members of a society, they partly determine, partly constitute "rationalizations" of the common ultimate-value attitudes[2] which have been found again and again to be such funda-

[1] The predominant attitude toward these ideas we generally designate as "belief." In most ordinary speech this is usually, linguistically at least, closely assimilated to the attitudes we assume toward scientific and empirical propositions. But Professor Nock holds the opinion that one who knows the facts well enough to penetrate behind this linguistic similarity can discern, empirically, a distinct difference between these two attitudes—that is, men do not in general "believe" their religious ideas in quite the same sense that they believe the sun rises every morning. This empirical distinction, if Professor Nock is right about it, provides an important verification of our analysis, as so important an analytical line as this should scarcely go without a direct trace in the empirical facts.

Professor Malinowski ("Magic, Science and Religion" in *Science, Religion and Reality*, ed. by J. Needham) has, I think, satisfactorily demonstrated the existence of such an empirical distinction in the senses in which primitive men believe in the efficacy on the one hand of magical manipulations, on the other of rational techniques. This case is, I think, closely analogous to the one now under consideration. Malinowski's view in this respect has been widely accepted by anthropologists.

[2] The relative predominance of these two elements constitutes one of the most important criteria of classification of religious ideas. In these terms it is

mental elements in the determination of men's action in society. Ultimate-value attitudes, religious ideas and the forms of human action constitute a complex of elements in a state of mutual interdependence, to put the relation in Paretian terms.

This may be considered a statement in terms more acceptable than his own of the immensely important scientific truth in Durkheim's view. The fundamental sociological importance of religious ideas lies in the fact that it is primarily in them that the intellectual formulation, part determinant, part expression, of the cognitive basis of common ultimate-value attitudes is to be found. His theory constitutes at the same time an affirmation in new terms of the sociological importance of this element, and the elucidation of a new relation in which it is manifested in concrete social life. What was formerly, to Durkheim at least, only seen in the relation of ethical norms governing conduct in intrinsic terms is now seen also to be expressed in those symbols which have heretofore so often been held to have no relation at all to the intrinsic problems of conduct but to form a mere excrescence, an aberration explicable only as the result of erroneous prescientific ideas of empirical reality.

After all the foregoing discussion it requires little argument to show how Durkheim arrived at his equation of the religious reality with society. For he had, in spite of the development traced in the last chapter, never explicitly or in any way consciously abandoned his positivistic position. That meant that no status whatever could be allowed to elements of reality not susceptible of empirical scientific treatment from the points of view both of the observer and of the actor. The worlds of the "individual" and of external "cosmic" nature will clearly not fit his empirical requirements—this is the outcome of his critique of animism and naturism. Then, these two having been disposed of, according to Durkheim's frequently recurrent argument by elimination, there is only one further possibility left open: it must be the social reality. All this fits into familiar grooves, hence the question does not need further comment.

Looked at from the point of view of the observer the identification of society with the object of reference of religious ideas retains a certain degree of plausibility. It is certainly true that

---

possible roughly to distinguish the two types, "dogma" and "myth." *Supra*, p. 273.

it is at least partly in relation to the social aspects of life, and not exclusively either to the cosmos as scientifically apprehended or to the forces formulated in individual psychology nor, finally, to random individual whims, that our significant determinate relations to nonempirical reality are predominantly arrived at and stereotyped. Moreover, of the factors which bear upon *concrete* social life, it is those which are in Durkheim's sense the distinctively social, the common ultimate-value attitudes which are in closest relation to religious ideas. Hence the empirical incidence of religious ideas on action is, in fact, largely social.

But even looked at in these "objective" terms it is clear that the fundamental significance of Durkheim's "equation" (which cannot be accepted as a simple equation with one variable on each side, but rather as a much more complex function) is not in the relating of religious ideas to a known "material" entity but rather the reverse—it is his proof of the great extent to which the empirical, observable entity "society" is understandable only in terms of men's ideas of and active attitudes toward the nonempirical. If the "equation" is to be accepted at all the significant way of putting it is not "religion is a social phenomenon" so much as "society is a religious phenomenon." This is naturally the more strikingly true when one realizes that Durkheim's reasoning is applicable not to the concrete phenomenon society so much as to the abstract social factor. This, defined as a system of common ultimate-value attitudes, is indeed inseparable from religious ideas. Thus the charge of "materialism" is not justified. Durkheim arrives at the equation of religion and society by emphasizing not the material aspect of religion, but rather the ideal aspect of society.

But the full methodological import of this theory is not clear until one turns to the subjective aspect, which he did not do in any systematic way—else the remaining positivistic elements of his thought must have collapsed under the strain. For it is clear from the foregoing that to the actor *no* empirical reality in the scientific sense underlies religious ideas.[1] It is the essence of the position here taken that a system of ultimate values points *beyond* the realm of the empirical altogether and so far as these are associated with ideas they are nonscientific ideas.

[1] In so far as what have been religious ideas are replaced by scientific theories, the theories in question cease *ipso facto* to be religious ideas.

This is, then, a vindication of the general views of partisans of religion but, to be sure, in formal terms which do not furnish an apology for any one system of religious ideas.[1] This fundamental implication is obscured to Durkheim and those of his interpreters who have failed to see it, by two circumstances or, rather, two aspects of the same circumstance. His positivism, with its general "objectivist" bias, correctly seeing the existence as an *empirical* reality not only of society in the concrete sense but also of his social factor, common ultimate values, thinks of the actor as also perceiving and adapting himself to such a reality—and naturally thinks of it as the same in the two cases, the social.

This confusion is aided and abetted by the typical positivistic failure, noted several times already, to distinguish the point of view of a single *concrete* actor acting in a concrete society, from that of actors in general in abstraction from concrete society. For to the former the ideas in question do have behind them a "constraining" reality in the sense that the symbols which compose them are related to the source of sanctions which may be imposed on the individual, that is, the attitudes of other individuals in the same society.

It must not, of course, be forgotten that what gives Durkheim his main clue to the social relation of religious ideas is the identity of the attitude of respect held toward them with that held toward moral rules. That is perhaps the most fundamental substantive sociological proposition of Durkheim's theory of religion. But when this is put in positivistic terms the argument is as follows: The attitude of respect implies a source of respect. We cannot respect symbols as such because of their intrinsic properties. Therefore there must be a "something" they symbolize which is its source. Now "society" is the only empirical entity which exercises *moral* authority, hence it is the only possible source of the attitude. As a result of the above discussion, proposition must be revised. The attitude of respect is as an empirical phenomenon characteristic of our attitudes toward at least *some* of the nonempirical aspects of reality with which we are concerned. This attitude becomes attached to the symbolic entities in terms of which we represent this reality to ourselves. At the same time it is also attached to the moral rules in terms of which these same value attitudes relate themselves intrinsically

[1] Also subject to the qualifications noted above, footnote 1, p. 421.

to conduct. This circumstance indicates a close relation between the two phenomena.

Durkheim's argument taken in his own terms and not the revised terms just put forward has one serious weakness which he apparently did not, at least clearly, see. If the reality underlying religion is an empirical reality, why should religious ideas take symbolic form in a way in which scientific ideas do not? Why could that reality not be represented directly by the theory of sociological science? He was consistent enough to maintain that in principle the source of religion could[1] and thus to approach Comte's later position that sociology should furnish the theology of a new religion. But this can only be regarded as the ultimate consequence of a positivism pushed to the last extremities. It hardly carried conviction even to Durkheim himself. But a less doggedly persistent thinker would hardly even have dared suggest the idea. Moreover it opened up philosophical difficulties of an extremely serious nature. For so long as different systems of religious ideas are thought of as merely different systems of symbols the idea that in some sense a unitary reference of these symbols exists is not excluded. But if they are to become literal scientific representations of the ultimate reality, this fact, combined with Durkheim's relativism of social types, puts him in a dilemma. If he adheres to the unity and universality of scientific reason, then he is faced with a complete ethical and religious relativism—the only way to escape the latter would appear to be to abandon the former, but with even more serious consequences. This in fact, he was inexorably led to do in his sociological epistemology.[2]

RITUAL

But before turning to the sociological epistemology the other side of Durkheim's theory of religion must be dealt with. It will be remembered that he defined a religion as "an integrated system of beliefs and *practices* relative to sacred things." What place then do the practices hold and what is their relation to the ideas?

---

[1] *Formes élémentaires*, pp. 614–615; see also *supra*, footnote 1, p. 427. In that case the problem of the source of sacredness would have to be solved all over again.

[2] See below, pp. 441 *ff.*

In the positivistic tradition one proposition about so-called religious practices has been predominant—that they are "irrational." This may, for present purposes, be taken to mean merely that they are different from actions analyzable in terms of the intrinsic means-end schema. They are, to be sure, actions which appear from the subjective point of view in terms of the relations of means and end. To the performer they are quite strictly ways of "doing" things. But wherein lies the difference to an observer?

Obviously, in terms of the analytical scheme of this study, it must lie at one or both of two points, in the character either of the ends pursued, or of the relation of means to them. Now the intrinsic means-end schema implies, as has been seen, two things: that the end involved is an empirical end—one the attainment of which is scientifically verifiable—and that the means-end relationship is intrinsic, that the means will bring about the end by processes of scientifically understandable causation. Now in Australia and elsewhere there exists a very large category of practices which fall outside the intrinsic means-end schema in terms of the latter criterion. But some of these do so merely because of the ignorance of the native of the conditions of his life. This is not the type Durkheim is concerned with. These practices are distinguished from rational technical procedures not only by a negative but also by a positive criterion; they are what he calls "rites" or ritual practices. That is, they are practices "in relation to sacred things."

Now this relation to sacred things implies a fundamental difference from rational techniques not merely in the negative sense of "irrationality" but in two positive ways. First, it involves the attitude of respect which Durkheim has employed as the basic criterion of sacredness throughout.[1] They are practices which are specifically isolated from the ordinary utilitarian occupations of everyday life. They possess, as Professor Nock puts it,[2] a specific quality of "otherness." They must be performed under special conditions; the performers must be placed in a special state, etc. All these characteristics, it must be noted, are specifically irrelevant from any utiliarian point of view. In

---

[1] Which Professor Radcliffe-Brown calls the "ritual attitude." See "The Sociological Theory of Totemism," *Proceedings of the Pacific Science Congress,* Java, 1931.

[2] In lectures at Harvard University.

so far as these activities have, as they very often do, either an empirical end or a utilitarian function, these special precautions bear no intrinsic relation to the accomplishment of the end—as in the Intichiuma ceremony regarded as a means of multiplying the totem species.

But the second point is no less important. As has been seen, for Durkheim the importance of sacred things for human interests is not intrinsic but symbolic. But what defines ritual practices is precisely their relation to sacred things. Hence it is a basic error even to attempt to fit such actions into the intrinsic means-end schema, for their very definition precludes their having a place in it. In so far as sacred things are involved in action, the means-end relationship is symbolic, not intrinsic. What Durkheim has done, then, is to widen the means-end schema to include a fundamental normative component of action systems which the positivists discarded as being merely "irrational." Ritual actions are not, as the latter maintained, either simply irrational, or pseudo rational, based on prescientific erroneous knowledge, but are of a different character altogether and as such not to be measured by the standards of intrinsic rationality at all.

But why, then, does ritual exist at all, and what is its role in social life? Here Durkheim's theory may, in its advance over those of the schools he criticizes, be regarded as constituting a scientific achievement of the first rank. Again it seems best to put its essence in terms consonant with the analytical position here arrived at and then return to consider their relation to Durkheim's.

In the first place, it has been shown that religious ideas may be held to constitute systems of symbolic representations of sacred entities, the "reality" underlying which lies in the nonempirical aspects of the universe. Now it has also been noted, following Professor Nock, that our relations to these nonempirical aspects are not merely cognitive, but also involve active attitudes. In fact it may be suggested that it is only proper to speak of a religious as distinct from a philosophical idea in so far as such an active attitude is involved.[1] Religious ideas are ideas in relation to action, not merely to thought. These active attitudes imply the necessity of "doing something" about the situation in which

[1] Thus religious ideas are to philosophy as the cognitive aspect of the intrinsic norm of rationality is to science.

they occur. As has been shown, in part this takes place in intrinsic terms. The active attitudes, which have been called ultimate-value attitudes, constitute a source of the ultimate ends of action in the intrinsic realm, and of the ethical norms regulating such action. But these elements do not, by definition, relate our attitudes to the universe as a whole, but only to its empirical aspect.

The active attitude, the impulse to "do something," does not, however, limit itself to this aspect. But by definition doing something outside this realm is meaningless in intrinsic terms. Given the existence of a system of "knowledge" of the nonempirical aspects of reality, however, it is quite comprehensible that this should become the basis of systems of *action* in relation to it, in a manner *analogous* to intrinsically significant action. And since this knowledge takes the form, predominantly, of a system of sacred symbols, the corresponding action takes the form of the manipulation of such symbols, that is, of ritual. Thus ritual is the expression in action as distinct from thought, of men's active attitudes toward the nonempirical aspects of reality.

According to this view, ritual action may appear wherever men take, or are forced by their circumstances to take, an active attitude to things not wholly understandable in empirical terms. Now where men's empirical knowledge is incomplete and/or their control of processes is imperfect, it *may appear to them* that the attainment of certain of their empirical ends is dependent, *besides* their technical manipulations, on forces which fall outside the empirical realm. This is particularly apt to be true in so far as there is, on the one hand, present in the society in question a developed system of representations concerning nonempirical entities, on the other, no well-developed, highly rationalized conception of an "order of nature" in the empirical sense. And since such societies are also apt to be "primitive" in the sense that their rational techniques are not very highly developed and they are hence forced to live near the margin of subsistence, their vital interests are likely to be very closely involved, their "active attitudes" strong. Hence a widespread tendency to employ ritual means for the attainment of empirical ends. This may be called magical ritual.[1] It is a technique for attaining empirical

[1] For Durkheim's discussion of magic *cf. Formes élémentaires*, pp. 58 *ff.* He makes the distinction from religion turn rather on that between

ends, employed not in place of but in addition to rational techniques. For the reasons just adduced it would be expected to loom largest in primitive societies and to diminish greatly in importance with increasing empirical knowledge, increasing control over nature and the development of the idea of an order of nature.[1]

But, it has already been pointed out, these active attitudes are not merely oriented "backward" over the intrinsic means-end chain, and the realm of empirical ends, but also "forward" in the direction of active relations to the nonempirical aspects of the universe. In so far as in this relation these active attitudes issue in action which is susceptible of analysis in means-end terms at all, the ends become transcendental, while the means become ritual means.[2] There is, then, another category of ritual actions which constitute a direct expression, apart from any immediate relation to the intrinsic realm or to empirical ends, of ultimate-value attitudes. This, as distinct from the magical, may be called religious ritual.

Now precisely in so far as among value attitudes, in general, those common to the members of society are important, the religious rituals of that society can be thought of as ritual expressions of these *common* value attitudes. This, put in somewhat different terms, is the fundamental truth in Durkheim's basic proposition of the interpretation of religious ritual—it is an expression of the unity of society. The same argument holds here as above about the way in which Durkheim arrived at this proposition. Society is to him the reality underlying the symbols of religious ritual because it is the only empirical reality which, as of a moral nature, can serve as the source of the ritual attitude. Therefore religious ritual is an expression of this social reality. This proposition may be modified to the form that religious ritual is (in large part) an expression of the common

---

interested and disinterested motives than that between empirical and transcendental ends. This has the effect of placing all ritual in the service of common ends in the religious category and leads to the denial that magic may be a socially integrating force. There is no space to pursue the issue farther here.

[1] This is not to say that in so far as this gap in empirical knowledge and power of control is not closed, even if magic does disappear, other nonlogical phenomena may not arise to fill the gap. Fashion and faddism have a place in this context.

[2] It is not meant that ritual means are the *only* possible ones.

ultimate-value attitudes which constitute the specifically "social" normative element in concrete society. In these terms Durkheim's proposition is undoubtedly correct and the fruit of a profound insight.

This brings the argument to a point where it is possible to evaluate the significance of the third main element of Durkheim's definition of religion—"a body of beliefs and practices relative to sacred things which *unites in a single moral community, called a church, all those who adhere to them.*" It should be clear from the above discussion that those who profess the same beliefs and practice the same rites may be regarded by virtue of these facts as possessing a common system of ultimate-value attitudes, that is, as constituting a "moral community."

Not on the basis of the definition alone, but rather on that of the whole argument of Durkheim's theory it may be maintained not only that those who have a common religion constitute a moral community, but that, conversely, every true moral community, that is, every "society," is characterized to a certain degree by the possession of a common "religion." For without a system of common values, of which a religion is in part a manifestation, a system adhered to in a significant degree, there can be no such thing as a society. Durkheim's treatment of *anomie* may be held to have definitely established this.

This proposition is, of course, not to be taken to mean that what we call concretely a society is always characterized by a single perfectly integrated "religion," also taken in the popular sense. As elsewhere, Durkheim is here dealing with a limiting type. In respect to its religious ideas and practices, as in other respects, a concrete community may be to a high degree internally differentiated, and may also attain the norm of perfect integration to a greater or less degree. But every community, if it is more than a mere "balance of power" between individuals and groups, constitutes such a moral community in a significant degree, and as such may be said to have a common religion.[1] Hence also religious division may be held to be a significant index of internal division within the community.

---

[1] Hence Durkheim's reference to the "cult" of individual personality as characteristic of contemporary society was not altogether inappropriate. Doubtless it would, on investigation, be found to have its rituals or their functional equivalent.

Durkheim's view that every religion pertains to a moral community in this sense and conversely that every community is in one aspect a religious unit is entirely acceptable. But it is doubtful whether it is expedient in general terms to refer to this moral community even in its religious aspect as a "church." It seems preferable to follow Max Weber[1] in reserving the term church for an *associational* aspect of community organization for religious ends. Where the moral community in question does not take the form of an explicit association for religious ends it seems best not to use the term. Moreover, in Durkheim's usage it runs the danger of being confused with the *concrete* community. But within the concrete community there arise many associations in relation to different interests. The church is best thought of as only one of these, and not as the community as a whole, even in its moral aspect.

So far ritual has been considered only as an index of the common value attitudes, the social factor. But is it only an index or does it have functions? Is it not in a state of mutual interdependence, and not merely one-way causation, with these attitudes and the other elements of the concrete complex?

Durkheim's view is quite definitely that it does have such functions, and the way in which he develops it and its implications beyond his own explicit formulation are of the greatest theoretical interest.

For by the common ritual expression of their attitudes men not only manifest them but they, in turn, reinforce the attitudes. Ritual brings the attitudes into a heightened state of self-consciousness which greatly strengthens them, and through them strengthens, in turn, the moral community. Thus religious ritual effects a reassertion and fortification of the sentiments on which social solidarity depends. As Durkheim sometimes puts it, it recreates the society itself.[2]

But why is this fortification and recreation necessary? The argument Durkheim advances is strikingly analogous to that put forward in the previous chapter to explain the necessity of institutional control. It will be recalled that the latter necessity arises out of the comparative remoteness and latency of the ultimate-value attitudes with reference to the immediate action

---

[1] See below, Chap. XV.
[2] *Formes élémentaires*, pp. 323, 493, and especially 498.

elements of a very large proportion of actions. Combined with the centrifugal tendencies of immediate "interests," the insatiability of individual wants taken alone, this gives rise to a situation where control of these actions is necessary in the interests of order and stability. Similarly, as Durkheim points out,[1] for a great deal of the time the tribe in Australia is dispersed over a wide area in tiny family groups, absorbed in such immediate interests as food getting. In these circumstances not merely are ultimate-value attitudes remote and latent; the immediacy and urgency of other elements in action tend to submerge them. Hence the necessity in periodic reunions for a mode by which they can be brought back to the center of consciousness and thus reendowed with full strength, revivified and recreated.

In Durkheim's view, then, religious ritual is far from being a mere manifestation. Though it has no empirical end and there is no intrinsic means-end relationship involved, its functional importance is very great. For it is through the agency of ritual that the ultimate-value attitudes, the sentiments on which the social structure and solidarity depend, are kept "tuned up" to a state of energy which makes the effective control of action and ordering of social relationships possible.[2] Put in terms of common religious parlance, the function of ritual is to fortify faith. In defense of this view Durkheim calls to witness the opinion he holds to be that of the great majority of religious believers everywhere.[3]

These considerations are involved in what some interpreters of Durkheim have thought to be a certain anti-intellectualism in his theory of religion which stands in rather strange contrast to what some (sometimes the same writers, *e.g.*, Lowie[4]) have called his "naive rationalistic psychology." This has generally taken the form of accusing Durkheim of an undue reliance on the concepts of crowd psychology.

The situation underlying this interpretation is the following: Durkheim, after all, remained a positivist. From this point of view, recognizing that empirically religious ideas consisted (whatever they *ought* to be) predominantly of references to

[1] *Ibid.*, p. 497.
[2] *Ibid.*, pp. 574, 597–598.
[3] *Ibid.*, p. 596.
[4] R. H. LOWIE, *Primitive Religion*, pp. 159–160.

symbolic entities, Durkheim is inclined to depreciate the importance of particular religious doctrines. After all, they refer to symbols and "mere" symbols are not intrinsically important— that is, the particular symbol, however important the role of symbolism in general may be. But this seems not to be true of a particular ritual act. In its concrete context it can be empirically proved to be of great functional importance.[1] Hence the tendency is to think of ritual as the primary element of religion[2] and religious ideas as secondary rationalizations, explanations, justifications of ritual.

This impression is confirmed by the empirical emphasis which Durkheim places on the state of "effervescence" so noticeable on the occasion of many of the great collective ceremonies.[3] There can be no doubt of the fact of this state of excitement but it is highly dubious whether to Durkheim it was a case of crowd psychology; indeed there is no justification for such an interpretation. For in the first place the theories of crowd psychology refer to phenomena which typically appear in an *unorganized* assemblage of persons. But as Durkheim repeatedly insists it is the very essence of ritual that it is minutely organized.[4] Even in the cases, such as the funeral ceremonies, where the emotional outbursts are most violent, every detail of the action is prescribed in tradition, who is to do it, when he is to do it and precisely how.

This interpretation appears to have arisen from two things: the emphasis on the state of effervescence, and the fact that ritual does not fit into the intrinsic means-end schema. To the conventional positivist any action which in this sense is irrational and is accompanied by emotional excitement is crowd psychology when it takes place in a large assembly of people. But surely enough has been said to show that Durkheim's theory of ritual is not anti-intellectual crowd psychology—in fact it is not psychology in any sense.

It is, however, in all probability true that in the concrete effectiveness of ritual in its social functions the factor of physical propinquity is of considerable importance. Indeed Plato and

[1] Perhaps the same can be said of a particular symbol *in its concrete context.*

[2] "Il y a dans la religion quelque chose d'éternel; c'est le culte." *Formes élémentaires*, p. 615, *cf.* also p. 575.

[3] *Ibid.*, p. 571.

[4] *Cf. ibid.*, p. 568.

Aristotle in justifying their drastic limitations on the size they considered desirable for a polis might well have added to the criterion of capability of all its citizens meeting in a single assembly within earshot of a single speaker, that the number should be small enough so that all could be present, either as actual participants or spectators, at a single common ritual. Such ritual was in fact a striking empirical characteristic of the polis. But this fact does not in the least prove that the specific theoretical contribution of Durkheim consists in his analyzing the psychological reactions arising from the factor of physical propinquity of large numbers of people. The main importance of his thought lies elsewhere.[1]

This general interpretation of the function of ritual, combined with the related idea of the function of institutions, to which attention has just been called, has implications of far-reaching methodological importance which must now be taken up.[2]

One of the distinguishing characteristics of the positivistic phase of Durkheim's thought was, it will be remembered, the tendency to think of the actor under the analogy of a scientist— primarily in a cognitive relation to the conditions in which he acts. This tendency was found to underlie the emphasis on representations in his earlier methodology, and also the conception of the social element as a *milieu*, an environment. Now in the traditional methodology of science (the more evident, the more it has leaned in an empiricist direction) the scientist has been predominantly thought of in a passive role. With the emphasis on the objectivity of the facts of the external world, their independence of the subjective state of mind of the scientist, the decisive element in knowledge has been this objective fact. The task of the scientist has been to "adapt" himself to it.

---

[1] It is clear that magical ritual has similar functions in reinforcing the actor's energy and confidence in his ability to surmount obstacles. But since Durkheim does not treat it explicitly these questions will not be entered into here. Suffice it to say that the current views of the role of magic held by certain functional anthropologists constitute an important confirmation of Durkheim's general theory of ritual. *Cf.* Malinowski, "Magic, Science and Religion"; R. Firth, "Magic in Economics," *Primitive Economics of the New Zealand Maori*, Chap. IV.

[2] A recent report of anthropological fieldwork in Australia forms an excellent verification of Durkheim's theory of ritual. *Cf.* W. Lloyd Warner, *A Black Civilization*.

When this point of view is applied to action the primary emphasis tends to be placed upon the acquisition of the knowledge that guides action, thought of in these passive terms. And since the actor is thought of as a scientist the tendency is further to think of action itself as following automatically upon the acquisition of this knowledge. Not that this is proved, but rather the structure of the scheme of thought is such as to divert attention from the problem of how knowledge becomes translated into action. This logical situation is probably the real basis of the criticism so often made of Durkheim that he held conformity to social norms to be automatic, meeting with no resistance.[1]

But from a very early period there was a strong contrary tendency in his thought. It is really already present in the way in which he framed the empirical problems of the division of labor—as a problem of control. On this empirical level it reaches full development in the treatment of *anomie* in the *Suicide*, where a set of inherently chaotic, insatiable impulses and desires is thought of as being subject to the control of a system of social norms, but at the same time as resisting control.

It took a long time, however, for the implications of these empirical insights to break through the hard crust of Durkheim's positivistic methodology. Indeed the main theme of this study of his development has been to trace the process by which this has taken place. The first great step was the recognition of the active role of a system of ultimate values in relation to the intrinsic means-end chain, as ends of action and as institutional norms. His theory of religion has made another great contribution in the same direction, that of the direct expression of ultimate-value attitudes in religious ideas and in ritual. This has involved the discovery of the fundamental importance of symbolism and the symbolic means-end relationship in its part in human life and action.

Now the methodological implication just referred to should be clear. This whole aspect of Durkheim's thought points in the direction of what has been called a voluntaristic conception of action—a process in which the concrete human being plays an active, not merely an adaptive role. This creative element is theoretically formulated in the conception of ultimate values, value attitudes, ends, or whatever form the value element takes,

[1] *Cf.* B. MALINOWSKI, *Crime and Custom in Savage Society*, pp. 55–56.

or the mode of its manifestation in relation to social life. However, it may still be possible to think of this element as automatically self-realizing in the sense that a cognitive understanding of ultimate values, or moral acceptance of them is enough— realization in action follows. The theory of ritual necessitates a final and decisive rejection of this position. For Durkheim's view of the functions of ritual implies the necessity of still a further element, what is generally called will or effort. So far from being automatic, the realization of ultimate values is a matter of active energy, of will, of effort, hence a very important part may be played empirically by agencies which stimulate this will.[1]

As applied to the problem of the methodological status of sociology in Durkheim's terms the above considerations imply the following: In his attempt to define the "social" reality, the social factor, he has come to concentrate on the element of common ultimate values. But merely fixing on this element is not enough; it is necessary to see it in its context, in its relations to other elements of concrete social life. The voluntaristic conception of action just characterized implies that this cannot be accomplished merely by understanding its nature; social processes cannot be understood, as Durkheim's earlier formulations would indicate, by apprehension of the properties of the social element alone. The latter must rather be seen as a *component of a system of action*. Sociology should, then, be thought of as a science of action—of the ultimate common value element *in its relations* to the other elements of action. This is the position to which the main line of Durkheim's thought was pointing. In his sum-

---

[1] As the main function of ritual is to stimulate faith, that of faith, in turn, is to stimulate will. "Car la foi est avant tout un élan à agir et la science, si loin qu'on la pousse, reste toujours à distance de l'action." *Formes élémentaires*, p. 615. See also, p. 598: "C'est donc l'action qui domine la vie religieuse par cela seul que c'est la société qui en est la source."

Durkheim proceeds to reconcile the fundamental difference of action and science and hence of the ideas which guide action from scientific ideas by saying that action is faced with the immediate necessity of doing something; it cannot wait for science to perfect itself. Hence the ideas guiding action must "run ahead" of science. This is the way in which he reconciles the distinction with his old positivism. There is, no doubt, some empirical truth in this view, but, as we have seen, the difficulty is too deep to be thus disposed of. In a sense this represents an element of Durkheim's thought leaning in the direction of pragmatism.

mary account of the theory of religion[1] he came very near its explicit statement, above all in his view that the central importance of religion lies in its relation to action, not to thought. But it never quite broke through. The principal reason is apparently that this main current was counteracted by another. This other is connected with his sociological epistemology. Only after that has been discussed and its motives understood will it be possible to get a complete picture of the conflicting currents of Durkheim's final phase.

EPISTEMOLOGY[2]

The early Durkheim was, it will be recalled, a positivistic scientist whose general leaning was in the direction of an empiricist epistemology like most of the other positivists. It is true that he never explicitly maintained or defended genuine empiricism. But his emphasis was on the central role of empirical fact, not on the difficulties involved in the definition of fact or the qualifications that might be necessitated by the recognition of these difficulties. His definition of empirical fact, of *choses*, in the *Règles* was simple and unsophisticated. Moreover, he had also a strong empiricist tendency in the sense that he did not explicitly note the necessity of distinguishing between the empirical reference of analytical categories and concretely existent entities. As it has been shown, this failure lies behind much of the group-mind difficulty.

It has also been pointed out that Durkheim's substantive theory developed along lines which made the maintenance of this empiricist tendency difficult so far as the methodological implications of much of what Durkheim was doing are concerned. This implied above all that analytical categories, including that of social facts, could not be identified with any concrete entities. This interpretation was verified in the most striking manner when Durkheim finally saw that the "individual" factor could no longer be identified with the concrete individual

---

[1] *Formes élémentaires*, pp. 599 and 615, as noted above.

[2] The main account of Durkheim's epistemological theory is to be found in the *Formes élémentaires* interwoven with the treatment of religion. The preliminary stages of his thought are, however, recorded in the article written in collaboration with M. Mauss, "Quelques formes primitives de classification," *L'année sociologique*, Vol. VI.

"consciousness," that is, the concrete individual from the subjective point of view. The social factor was then no longer to be sought "outside" this concrete entity, but as one element or group of elements explaining it. This tendency was progressively intensified until, in the *Formes élémentaires*, Durkheim is found explicitly stating that society exists only in the minds of individuals.[1] This represents the logical outcome of his whole development, and also the final abandonment of his objectivist bias. It is of especial interest here because it represents a close approach to Weber's doctrine of *"verstehen"* which will be discussed below.

These considerations do not, however, amount to explicit epistemological discussion,[2] which Durkheim did not attempt until the *Formes élémentaires*. Here he introduces an explicit criticism of the radical empiricist position which comes to the conclusion that valid knowledge cannot be accounted for on an empiricist basis.[3] The apriorist school has been essentially right in its critical attack on empiricism and in its insistence that valid knowledge involves something beyond the empirical element— "categories" which are equally essential to knowledge, but are qualitatively distinct from, and not derivable from the empirical.

So far Durkheim simply takes over the discussion of the problem of epistemology in current philosophy and pins his allegiance to the apriorist side of the controversy. But it is here that his own particular theory begins. He grants that the apriorists are right, that the categories are essential and not derivable from the empirical element. This school is then left in a dilemma, says Durkheim, for, having thrown out an empirical explanation

[1] *Formes élémentaires*, p. 521. It "consists exclusively of ideas and sentiments."

[2] The problems of epistemology are, of course, philosophical not scientific problems. The justification for embarking on a discussion of Durkheim's epistemological views at this point is that these are intimately bound up with his system of scientific theory which has been under consideration. Analysis of his epistemology will illuminate some of the implications and difficulties of his scientific position, some of which are due to the influence of certain philosophical ideas on his scientific thought. These ideas are hence important to the argument in the strict sense. But it is still true that the present interest in them is not "in themselves," but rather in their relation to the theory of action.

[3] *Ibid.*, pp. 18 *ff.*

of the categories, they really have no explanation at all. To say the categories are a priori conditions of all knowledge is to give up the problem. It is, of course, precisely the position that on an empirical basis the problem is insoluble. And it is this to which Durkheim objects.

But what alternative has he but a return to the traditional empiricism? He says, in effect, the old empiricism took account only of a part of empirical reality. The older epistemology was concerned with the source of validity in our knowledge of the physical world. This knowledge comes to us through the sense organs, that is, the body. But in these terms only the cosmic and individual elements of the empirical world are taken account of; the third category of elements, the social, is entirely omitted. Thus the apriorist school has failed to prove its contention that, since it has exhausted the possibilities of empirical derivation of the categories, there is no recourse left but to the a priori. On the contrary, an "empirical" explanation is eminently possible—the source of the categories is in the social reality. This is the central proposition of Durkheim's famous sociological epistemology. What is to be thought of it? Philosophically, indeed, it is to the present writer completely untenable. Yet no phase of his thought gives deeper insight into the methodological problems with which Durkheim was struggling than this.

In the first place, it should be noted that the old dualism of "individual" and "social" has now appeared in three different forms or aspects—the distinctions of "interest" and "moral obligation," of "profane" and "sacred," and now, finally, of "empirical" and "categorical." But this last carries the most radical implications of all. The pursuit of immediate ends, and profane activities were both thought of as involving, as indispensable elements, valid scientific knowledge. But this now turns out to be itself dependent on the social factor—for without the categories there is no knowledge. Durkheim seems to think in terms of an "architectonic" hierarchy of relations of chaos and order in the normative sense. The chaos of sense impressions is organized into the order of valid knowledge by the categories. But the instrumental use of knowledge in the pursuit of immediate ends produces a new potential chaos which is reduced to order by institutional norms. Finally the fortuitous chaos of concrete symbols is given order by the common reference to the social reality. Thus society, for Durkheim, is more than merely the principle of order in the relations between human beings, it is the principle of order in the universe as a whole. But what are the methodological implications of all this? Particularly what are its relations to the previous analysis?

As has been repeatedly pointed out the "dialectic" of Durkheim's thought appears to work out in terms of the attempt to reconcile a contradiction, that of the view of society as an empirical reality, a part of nature, on the one hand, and the view of society as distinct from the other elements of nature, on the other. The main tendency has been progressively to widen the gap between it and the rest of nature. This epistemological doctrine may be regarded as the definitive break. There can be no more radical difference possible than that between empirical and a priori. As in the case of religion, the striking thing about Durkheim's position here is not his new view about the categories but about society. Society has become the thing the idealist philosophers are talking about.[1] It consists as he says "exclusively of ideas and sentiments,"[2] and not, it may be further said, merely of "ideas" but of *the Idea*, for the categories are the very matrix out of which particular ideas are formed. It consists not merely of "representations" but of ideas in the technical philosophical sense.[3] Society becomes not a part of nature at all, but, in Professor Whitehead's phrase, of the world of "eternal objects."

And yet Durkheim will not let go of his positivism. This "society" is still held to be an observable reality, is still the object of a positive science. It is still held to be empirical. But none the less this implies most far-reaching differences from anything the older positivism would regard as admissible. For the entities Durkheim here observes exist "only in the mind" of individuals—and not at all in the world of physical space, or time. Moreover, since the mechanism of sense perception is held to be purely individual, ideas in this sense cannot be perceived by the senses but must be directly apprehended, undoubtedly by some kind of "intuition." Indeed Durkheim directly states with reference to the category of force that "the

---

[1] "Thus there is a realm of nature where the formula of idealism applies almost literally; that is the social realm." *Formes élémentaires*, p. 327.

[2] *Ibid.*, p. 521.

[3] See especially *ibid.*, p. 328.

only forces we can directly apprehend are moral forces";[1] since the categories cannot come to us through the senses, that of force must be of social origin.[2]

If this is partly true it is stated in what are for sociological purposes unduly narrow terms. For the effect of identifying society with the world of eternal objects is to eliminate the creative element of action altogether. Their defining characteristic is that the categories of neither time nor space apply to them. They "exist" only "in the mind." Such entities cannot be the object of an explanatory science at all. For an explanatory science must be concerned with events, and events do not occur in the world of eternal objects.[3] Durkheim's sociology in so far as he takes this direction, becomes, as Richard puts it, a "work of pure interpretation."[4]

In fact Durkheim in escaping from the toils of positivism has overshot the mark and gone clean over to idealism.[5] There are certain reasons why this should be easy for him. Eternal objects have the same fixity independent of the observer as the empirical facts of the positivist, a similar objectivity is possible with reference to them. The observer can maintain the same passive attitude.

Moreover, the whole tendency of Durkheim's development has been to center attention on the element of common values. His "subjective" positivism has given him a bias in favor of conceiving these in cognitive form, as "representations." He has always been looking for a reality formulable in cognitive terms.

[1] *Ibid.*, p. 521.

[2] This position seems to be based on a misapprehension. Ideas come to us through the interpretation of sense impressions, *e.g.*, of a printed page as having symbolic meanings. This is not "direct apprehension."

[3] This does not mean that an empirical science must have a historical-genetic orientation, as opposed to the development of a generalized theoretical system. It means, rather, that it is concerned with the establishment of causal relationships, and the only means of demonstrating causal relationship is by the observation of independent variation. Variation is a category which implies a temporal frame of reference, a phenomenon cannot vary except by a temporal process. Such a process is an event.

[4] See GASTON RICHARD, *La sociologie générale*, pp. 44–52, 362–370. Richard is one of the few secondary writers who is acutely conscious that Durkheim's thought underwent a profound change.

[5] In his definition of the subject matter of sociology, of course, not necessarily in general philosophy.

So it seems but natural that he should turn to the element of ideas in common values, rather than to sentiments or value attitudes. It fits in very well with many of the leading tendencies of his previous thought. As opposed to a voluntaristic theory of action there is much in common in formal terms between positivism and idealism.

But these considerations give the clue to the deepest criticism of Durkheim's new position. Just as positivism eliminates the creative, voluntaristic character of action by dispensing with the analytical significance of values, and the other normative elements by making them epiphenomena, so idealism has the same effect for the opposite reason—idealism eliminates the reality of the obstacles to the realization of values. The set of *ideas* comes to be identified with the concrete empirical reality. Hence the central feature of the category of *action*, its voluntaristic character, the elements of will, of effort, have no place in such a scheme. Indeed one very important reason why Durkheim was attracted by idealism was that he never really outgrew his empiricism. He could never clearly and consistently think of social reality as *one factor* in concrete social life, but always tended to slip over into thinking of it as a concrete entity. Then since "ideas" cannot be dissociated from the latter, it must *consist* of ideas.

The effect of this tendency of Durkheim's thought is to regard the aim of sociology as that of studying the systems of value ideas *in themselves*, whereas the position put forward above calls for a quite different study, that of these systems *in their relations to action*. Each of the elements which have been found to be involved in the "ideal" expressions of ultimate-value attitudes may be, and indeed is, studied "in itself" by a discipline concerned with the systematic interrelations of ideal elements with each other, institutional norms in jurisprudence, religious ideas in theology, artistic forms in aesthetics, ultimate ends in ethics. But sociology is not, as this phase of Durkheim's final position would logically imply, a synthesis of all these normative sciences. It is, on the contrary, an explanatory science concerned with the relations of all these normative elements to action. It deals with the same phenomena, but in a different context. At its final stage, Durkheim's sociology stood at this parting of the ways. Both paths represent escapes from positivism, but in terms of the tendency of sociological thought analyzed in the present study, especially in the following section, the idealistic phase must be regarded as an aberration, a blind alley.

It is clear that Durkheim's sociological epistemology involves inextricable philosophical difficulties, though to analyze them is not a central concern of this discussion. It has been pointed out that one of his leading empirical theories is that of the relativity of social types. The different ultimate-value systems which constitute the defining elements of different concrete societies are so radically different as to be incommensurable. For this reason he was forced to define normality with reference to the social type alone, thus ending in a complete ethical relativism. His theory of religion, by associating it with the social type, relativized another great body of phenomena.

Now his epistemology has brought the basis of human reason itself into the same relativistic circle, so as to make the previous relativism itself relative, since the relativism of social types is itself a product of a system of categories which are valid only for the particular social type. This is a doctrine which may be called "social solipsism." It involves all the skeptical consequences which are so well known in the case of individual solipsism. It is, in short, a *reductio ad absurdum*.[1]

---

[1] This fundamental philosophical difficulty of trying to derive the source of empirical knowledge from empiricist considerations probably accounts for the frequent appearance in Durkheim's arguments of attempts to indicate concrete factors in the derivation of the categories—the category of space is derived from the arrangement of the clans in the camp, that of time from the periodicity of the tribal ceremonies and other activities, etc. As Dennes (W. S. Dennes, "Methods and Presuppositions of Group Psychology," *University of California Studies in Philosophy*, 1926) correctly remarks, this argument doubtless has considerable truth in it when it is applied to the problem of the historical genesis of our concrete subdivisions of time and space, etc. But it is quite untenable and irrelevant on the epistemological level, and open to all the criticisms Durkheim directs against the older empiricism. Moreover, there is no reason why spatial and temporal aspects of external nature should not also be important in determining the historical genesis of our concrete concepts of the categories.

In fact Durkheim continually vacillates back and forth between what is really another version of the old empiricism, merely adding certain concrete considerations, and an idealism which takes society out of the world of empirical phenomena altogether. This vacillation is understandable in terms of the logical situation analyzed here. He surely had not reached a stable position.

The voluntaristic theory of action, recognizing that the specific "social" element involves reference to the "ideal" but thought of in its relation to action, while it at the same time involves a reference beyond its logical formulations to the nonempirical aspects of reality, avoids these intolerable consequences. It leaves room for an epistemology of a genuine realist nature, but involving nonempirical elements which are also nonsociological. For "society," to be the object of an explanatory science, must participate in empirical reality. But such participation does not preclude significant relations outside it.

Indeed Durkheim's difficulties are highly instructive. He penetrated so deeply as to demonstrate that only on the basis of something akin to the voluntaristic theory of action propounded here is it possible to escape the positivist-idealist dilemma so long as the action schema is adhered to at all. And it seems abundantly clear that neither horn of the dilemma provides a satisfactory methodological basis for a science of sociology or for any other social science. Durkheim, by the very tenacity and almost "stubbornness" of his thinking, has so thoroughly explored the logical implications of these two positions as to make the outlines of the situation clear for future generations. It should be less difficult in the future to avoid the maze of methodological difficulties in which he became involved.

Before leaving Durkheim, one further issue of great importance may be touched on. It cannot but strike the reader of his works how conspicuous by its absence from his thought is any clear-cut theory of social change. This is a fact of great significance in terms of the methodological considerations just discussed. His only notable hypothesis in that field was his attempt to explain increase in the division of labor in terms of population pressure. It has been shown how unsatisfactory that was. In all his later thought, with one notable exception which will be noted presently, the problem is altogether outside his field of interest.

The essential explanation of this is to be found in Durkheim's idealism. It is true that in explicit terms this latter doctrine did not emerge until the end of his career. But this was the culmination of a long development. Almost from the beginning he had thought in terms of the category of substance rather than of process. He had always been looking for the reality manifested in social facts. From quite an early date this search began to converge on a system of values, whether thought of as norms, ends or representations. And the tendency was to consider these in terms of their intrinsic characteristics, and of intellectual formulation. Thus it became increasingly evident that Durkheim was thinking of the social element as a system of eternal objects. Now the very essence of such objects is timelessness. Hence the concept of process, of change, is meaningless as applied to them in themselves.[1]

Another important consideration is that Durkheim from an early stage was primarily concerned with the problem of order. The decisive element of order he found in common values as manifested above all in institutional norms. But the very prominence of the problem of order in his thought meant that when he dealt with value elements he was primarily concerned with the element of *order in them*. That is, he was concerned with their aspect as a stable system, their intrinsic properties as eternal objects. It has been shown how fruitful of significant results this approach can be.

But its fruitfulness lay largely in the field of definition of certain of the categories of sociological analysis, much less in that of the functional interrelations between them. The tendency was to conceive these categories as fixed and timeless and the growing prominence of eternal objects in the picture accentuated this tendency. The voluntaristic conception of action, on the other hand, lays stress precisely on these relationships. And it is in the functional interrelationships between basic elements that dynamic process is mainly to be found. The eternal objects concerned are mainly intellectual formulations of nonempirical reality, of attitudes and of norms. In all these cases the intellectual formulations are partial, imperfect, often symbolic, and hence to a considerable extent unstable in relation to their referents. Complex processes of change no doubt do take place in these relations. Similarly the value attitudes and the intellectual formulations associated with them stand in various complex relationships to the ultimate conditions and the other

---

[1] A part in this situation is no doubt played by the fact that Durkheim's idealism was more in the direction of static Cartesian rationalism than of Hegelian dialectic. The issues between these two traditions of thought cannot be entered into here.

components of action systems some of which have been sketched in the course of the discussion. It is in such interrelationships that the dynamic processes of social change are to be found. Their analysis is one of the great tasks of sociological science. Durkheim's approach was inherently unfavorable to the solution of these problems. But his achievement must not on that account be depreciated. For he accomplished a great deal of the fundamental spade work which is an indispensable preliminary to the construction of a theory of social change. To have such a theory it is necessary to know what it is that changes. Toward that knowledge Durkheim made a great stride forward.

It is noteworthy that at the very end of his work Durkheim did introduce a hypothesis in this field. It was that in the effervescence of great common rituals, not only are old values recreated, but new ones are born. And along with the periodic effervescence of seasonal ceremonies he noted the occurrence of prolonged periods of general effervescence, periods in which, as he says, for the time being the "ideal becomes real."[1] It is in such periods, as for instance the French Revolution, that new values are created. This was hardly more than a suggestion. But in this, and the implied distinction between quiescent and effervescent periods, there was the germ of a theory of social change, perhaps of cyclical type. That at the end of his work his attention was turning in this direction seems to be an important confirmation of the thesis that there were not one but two main tendencies in the last phase of Durkheim's thought, since this fits directly into the context of a voluntaristic theory of action. Perhaps it is even an indication that this was the predominant direction in which he was moving and that the "idealism" was only a passing phase. Unfortunately Durkheim did not live long enough to answer the question for us.

---

[1] *Cf.* the extremely interesting article "Jugements de valeur" et jugements de réalité reprinted in the volume *Sociologie et philosophie*. Many of the aspects of the later phases of his thought come out with especial clarity here. In particular in developing the theme of its title he lays stress on the difference between scientific ideas and those guiding action. This brings out the voluntaristic tendency of his thought more clearly than anywhere else except certain parts of the conclusion of the *Formes élémentaires*. The reader is referred to it for general comparison.

CHAPTER XII

SUMMARY OF PART II: THE BREAKDOWN OF THE POSITIVISTIC THEORY OF ACTION

Before proceeding to consider a group of writers whose methodological background is an outgrowth of idealistic philosophy, it seems best to summarize briefly the main outline of the process which has formed the subject matter of this part of the volume and to formulate as clearly as possible the main conclusions which may justifiably be drawn from it.

THE POSITIVISTIC STARTING POINTS

In the terms which are most significant here, the starting point of the movement is what has been called the utilitarian position characterized by atomism, rationality, empiricism, and the assumption of random wants, and hence a view of social relationships as entered into only on the level of means to the actor's private ends. This is to be regarded as a branch of the wider system of positivism. It is an inherently unstable position which is closely related, as has been seen, to "radical" positivism and is continually tending to be transformed into it. For critical purposes the two may be regarded as phases of the same great body of thought.

What makes the utilitarian system so crucial for purposes of this study, rather than such doctrines as those of environmental or biological determinism, is the circumstance that in connection with this stream of thought the means-end schema occupies a central place in a way which embodies the methodological schema of positive science. It forms, hence, a strategic point at which to begin a historical analysis of theories about the structure of action from the subjective point of view. For the same reasons, among the social sciences economics occupies a crucial position. Indeed, in so far as the conceptual scheme of utilitarian individualism emerged from general social philosophy to form the methodological framework of a special social science, it was predominantly the economics of the classical school and its successors.

Finally, the other main, closely related starting point is methodological empiricism. Though clear self-consciousness is rare in this connection, the tendency throughout is to think of the analytical concepts of science as corresponding directly to observable *concrete* entities, and a classification of the social sciences, if such exists, as corresponding to the different concrete spheres of social life. The movement of thought which has just been analyzed may be considered as taking this double departure from utilitarianism and empiricism, and partly by direct criticism, partly only by implication, moving progressively away from both starting points until a point is reached where the whole logical position is radically changed.

MARSHALL

In these circumstances it was not altogether fantastic to begin an analysis of the methodology of the theory of action with a treatment of the work of an eminent economist. One of Marshall's outstanding traits was his strong empiricist bent. He repeatedly refused to undertake any systematic abstraction beyond his "one-at-a-time" method. His conception of economics was thoroughly empirical—a "study of man in the everyday business of life."

Analysis of what he actually did under this comprehensive heading, however, has revealed, in analytical terms, two radically distinct elements, what he called the "study of wealth" and "a part of the study of man." The former has been called in this study "utility theory." As formulated in terms of the conceptions of marginal utility and productivity, consumer's surplus, the principle of substitution and the doctrine of maximum satisfaction, it constitutes a strictly utilitarian element.[1] Its underlying postulate is that of rationality in the adaptation of means to individual ends. It constitutes the logical center of his economic theory proper—and is the element in which lie Marshall's main theoretical contributions to economics.

---

[1] Making allowances for the changes which the elements of the immediate sector of the means-end chain undergo as a result of being transferred from the utilitarian framework to that of the more comprehensive theory of action which has been developed above.

If this were all, Marshall would belong entirely in the history of technical economic theory and would not concern the present study. But this element does not stand alone. The "study of wealth" is inseparably intertwined with another element, the "study of man," a theory of the relation of activities to the processes of production and acquisition of wealth. While Marshall touches here and there on environmental and hereditary factors and has certain tendencies to hedonism, analysis of his concept of activities reveals the fact that its nucleus is a value element, a system of common ultimate-value attitudes expressed directly in those actions which are at the same time, from another point of view, wealth-getting actions.

To a certain extent, notably in his refusal to accept "wants" as given data for economics,[1] Marshall's theory of activities modifies the picture of concrete society which most utilitarians have considered normal, but for the most part it is directly fused with it. In fact, in considering Marshall's version of the doctrine of *laissez faire*, it has been found that the ultimate ground for his support of it lay not mainly in his belief in its superior "efficiency," though he did, with certain qualifications, hold such a belief. But on the whole more important was his feeling that only "free enterprise" offered a suitable field for the expression of the qualities of character which he valued on ethical grounds. Economic activities are thought of, and sanctioned, more as a mode of expressing and developing such qualities than as a means to the maximization of satisfactions.

This view of Marshall's is important in two principal respects, empirical and theoretical. Here, with a minimum of self-consciousness of its methodological implications, is a clear expression of the view than an "individualistic" society is not concretely to be understood exclusively or even predominantly in terms of utilitarian want satisfaction. It involves rather as a basic element certain common values, among them freedom as an end in itself and as a condition of the expression of ethical qualities. Essentially the same view is also very prominent in others of the writers here under consideration, Durkheim and, as will be seen, Weber.

[1] It may be suspected that Marshall's objection to this doctrine lay not so much in the "givenness" of wants as in the implied assumption of their random nature.

But this view of modern economic individualism is fraught with fundamental theoretical implications. It points to a general belief in the importance of the element of common values, not only somewhere in society, but in direct connection with "economic" activities themselves. Marshall, without realizing it, was here indicating a most important direction for the development of social thought. His view was, empirically, in a high degree correct for nineteenth century free enterprise. Hence it was impossible to go back to a rigorously utilitarian interpretation of the concrete phenomena. There were then, respecting the status of economic theory, only two directions of thought left open. Marshall's empiricism dictated his choice of one of them. It was that economics should be conceived as a science concerned with the complete understanding of concrete economic activities. Hence this theory of activities becomes a part of an economics having as its subject nothing less than the "study of man in the everyday business of life." As has been shown elsewhere,[1] this path leads to the conception of economics, from a theoretical point of view, as an encyclopedic sociology in which all the elements bearing on concrete social life have a place, with the result that the separate identity of economic theory as a discipline is destroyed.[2]

PARETO

The other path is the one which the present treatment has followed, the attempt to define economics as an abstract science of one aspect of, or group of elements in, social life. One of the first to attempt this with methodological self-consciousness was Pareto. Thus consideration of Marshall's work has served the purpose, first, of bringing out the empirical importance of the element of common values even in an individualistic economic order. At the same time, it has raised the question of the methodological status of this value element in relation to economics, and hence the whole question of the scope of economics in relation to

[1] See TALCOTT PARSONS, "Sociological Elements in Economic Thought," *Quarterly Journal of Economics*, May and August, 1935.

[2] This consequence becomes particularly clear in the case of Marshall's faithful disciple, R. W. Souter. See Talcott Parsons, "Some Reflections on the Nature and Significance of Economics," *Quarterly Journal of Economics*, May, 1934.

this study. This leads, in turn, to consideration of the whole question of the subjective analysis of action in terms of the means-end schema and its relation to the classification of the social sciences, the status of sociology in particular. These are the main elements of the methodological problem of this study.

Pareto takes a long step beyond Marshall in the direction of elucidating these problems. Like Marshall, he was initially, in social science, an economist. But they differ in two important respects. Pareto was, in the first place, much more sophisticated in his methodology, and was hence not so liable to the kind of empiricism which characterized Marshall. Secondly, his cast of mind, particularly as influenced by his historical learning, made him see the modern economic order in an entirely different perspective. What to Marshall was "free enterprise" was to Pareto "demagogic plutocracy."

Pareto's greater methodological clarity enabled him to work out a *system* of economic theory as an abstract discipline. At the same time his historical perspective precluded his following Marshall in fusing with this "utility" theory all the other significant elements into a simple evolutionary theory deduced from a broadened economics. This was impossible because so many of the nonutility elements which seemed to be important to Pareto were either irrelevant to the "economic" or could be shown to be analytically independent of it. This was especially true of the use of force, and the complex of elements he summed up as the "sentiments." So Pareto took the opposite course from Marshall, logically isolating the economic element in a theoretical system of its own, and supplementing it with a sociology which took account systematically of certain noneconomic elements and synthesized them with the economic in a final general picture.

Pareto set about this task by employing a starting point which fitted directly into the main analytical scheme of the present study, but he employed this starting point for a somewhat different purpose from that which has been the main concern here, the direct formulation of a system of analytical elements of action, rather than an outline of the structure of action systems. Hence the paths soon diverge, but it has been possible to show that they converge again when the application of the structural analysis here developed to Pareto's own formulation of the total system is considered.

This common starting point is the concept of logical action. Since it is defined in terms applicable to the isolated unit act there is no basis in the definition itself for discrimination of economic from other logical elements of action. The defining characteristic is the relation of action to a scientifically verifiable "theory" such that "operations are logically united to their ends" and may, in so far, be understood as proceeding "from a process of reasoning." Nonlogical is, then, a residual category, comprising everything not included in the logical.

The character of the "theory" is that which is definitive of logical action. Pareto continues his concentration on theories in his study of the nonlogical. In so far as these theories do not fit into the methodological schema of logico-experimental science they are subjected to an operational analysis according to which the relatively constant elements are separated from the relatively more variable, the residues and derivations, respectively. From this point Pareto proceeds to classify the residues and derivations and then to consider their mutual relations with each other and with the interests and social heterogeneity in systems.

Application to Pareto's scheme of the type of analysis already developed here shows that the analysis into residues and derivations, and Pareto's own classification of them, does not explicitly take account of a line of analytical distinction which has been found fundamental to the theory of action, that between the normative and non-normative elements, the "conditional" elements capable of nonsubjective formulation and the "value" elements. Both classes are contained in the sentiments which are manifested in the residues. This line of distinction has, however, been found not to be inconsistent with Pareto's scheme, but rather to constitute an extension of it in a direction which Pareto had not himself followed out. Indeed definite starting points for such a distinction can be found in Pareto's own analysis. First, there are two different kinds of reason why a theory relevant to action can depart from the scientific standard: because it is *un*scientific, involving ignorance and error, and because it is *non*scientific, involving considerations outside the range of scientific competence altogether. Many concrete theories involve both kinds of departure, but that is not an objection to the analytical distinction. More specific analysis has revealed that at least two types of elements can be included in the nonscientific category—the ultimate ends of action and the nonexperiential entities invoked in explanation of why they should be pursued, and certain elements of a selective standard in the choice of means which are yet nonscientific (those involved most conspicuously in ritual actions). It has furthermore proved possible to verify this analytical distinction by consideration of Pareto's treatment of the subject of Social Darwinism and of the question, do the residues correspond to the facts?

An attempt was then made, taking Pareto's definition of logical action in its structural context as a starting point, to develop explicitly an outline of certain of the main structural features of total social systems of action. This is an enterprise which, in a similar manner, Pareto never undertook at all. The first step beyond his own formulation was the conception of chains of intrinsic means-end relationships. These were found to involve a differentiation into three "sectors," ultimate ends, ultimate means and conditions, and the "intermediate sector," the components of which are both means and ends according to which way they are looked at, from "below" or "above." Secondly, it was found impossible to consider these chains as isolated except for certain analytical purposes. They form, rather, a complicated "web" of interwoven threads, such that every concrete act is a point of intersection for a number of them, which segregate out both above and below it in the time axis.

It then became evident that action must be considered as oriented not only to the higher ends in the same chain, but also at the same time to those in other chains as well. In so far as this simultaneous orientation to a plurality of different alternative ends involves the problem of allocation of scarce means between them, a distinct aspect of logical action has been separated out, which has been called the economic, as distinguished from the "technological" where only one end, or chain of them, is involved. That the concept of "choice" between alternative ends should have a meaning it was found that the ends themselves must be related in terms of a more or less integrated system, so that the ultimate ends of different chains do not vary simply at random.

All this has been developed without consideration of social relationships. When the latter are introduced on the plane of logical action the Hobbesian problem of order is raised. For when the potentiality of mutual use for each other's ends exists the question arises as to how the terms of the relationship are settled, and among the possible factors in its settlement is coercion. Economic considerations alone can settle these terms only if a framework of order controlling coercion is present. Problems relating to this framework of order in its connection with the role of coercion constitute another clearly differentiated aspect of the intrinsic means-end system, the "political." Finally not only does the ultimate-end system of an individual constitute a more or less integrated whole, but, except for the limiting case where order is imposed entirely externally, the same can be said of the collectivity, which is to some degree integrated relative to common values.

The distinctions made in the course of this analysis of the systems of norms of intrinsic rationality have been found to correspond to those Pareto made in his discussion of social utility, so that the latter may be held to verify the analysis carried out here. In addition a distinction between two different aspects of value integration has been made, in the relation of a framework of distributive order involved in discussing the utility *for* a collectivity and that of the ends pursued by a collectivity, which must be considered in talking of the utility *of* a collectivity. The latter, the ends *of* a collectivity, so far as the concrete ends are attributable to value factors, will be found to involve common ultimate ends.

Pareto's two abstract societies may, then, be held to formulate, on the one hand, the system of rational norms relevant to a social system of action; on the other, the conditional elements. Though the former are all, in a sense, rational, certain elements of them are nonlogical since it has been shown that the term logical action is applicable only to the intermediate sector of the intrinsic means-end system.

But the normative or value aspect is found to be involved in concrete systems of action not only at the rational pole, but also in other respects. The indeterminacy of the sentiments is not wholly an index of the importance of conditional, drive elements, but consideration of the value aspect of the phenomenon has led to the formulation of a broader, less definite concept than that of ultimate ends, namely ultimate-value attitudes. There is much evidence in Pareto's own treatment that this element of the sentiments is of great importance in the immense field of ritual actions as well as in relation to the intrinsic means-end chain, and possibly elsewhere.

Thus while Pareto himself proceeded from the concept of logical action to discriminate certain nonlogical elements of action systems without explicit treatment of the structural aspect, it has been possible here, taking the same starting point, to develop the implications of logical action for the structure of a social system. This structure has been found to be far more complex than any dealt with by a positivistic theory of action, or by Marshall. In particular it has been possible to show that economic theory does not focus attention on this whole structure, but only a part of it, one part of that included in logical action. Marshall's simple fusion of this with an undifferentiated category of activities was far from doing justice to the complexity of the situation, and necessarily involved him in serious biases.

By contrast with the theories of individualistic positivism from which this analysis has started, there are perhaps two primary theoretical results of the analysis of Pareto's work. Though he did not himself explicitly undertake to do so, it may be concluded that his work conclusively demonstrates, within the framework of the action schema, the basic importance of what have here been called the value elements. This is one of the primary difficulties of positivistic theories—they tend to eliminate this basic class of factors from consideration. In relation to Pareto it has been possible to go far beyond simply asserting that they have a place, to elucidate in a great many respects exactly what that place is, what specific relations, at least on the structural level, exist between the value elements and those included, on the one hand, in the scientific standard of rationality, on the other, in the nonsubjective categories (heredity and environment). Secondly, Pareto's treatment turns out quite definitely to transcend the "individualistic" bias of the positivistic theories treated above. He has explicitly stated the "sociologistic theorem" in terms which certainly involve value elements, and, in so far as they do, would make one of the elements transcending individualistic "atomism" the sharing by the members of the society of common value attitudes and ends. In the context in which this theorem emerges in Pareto's thought it is directly connected with those elements, the value elements, which are directly incompatible with positivistic systems of theory. It culminates, in explicit formulation in his work, in the concept of "the end which a society should pursue."

All this in turn has empirical consequences of the first magnitude. It leads to a conception of the contemporary social situation, and of the nature and trend of the main processes of social change, which is in the most striking contrast with the views on the same subjects of Marshall and his utilitarian predecessors. These empirical views of Pareto cannot be interpreted as the result merely of temperamental traits, as expressions of his personal "sentiments," but are directly connected with the logical structure of his theory as here analyzed. His work strongly confirms the thesis of the intimate connection between empirical problems and even the most abstract methodological considerations.

Finally, Pareto's development, which at first sight has close affinities to positivism, was definitely in the direction of a voluntaristic theory of action. He was pointed in the right direction in this respect by starting his analysis of the action of individuals in terms of the means-end schema. For this his background as an economist may be held largely responsible. The version of the theory of action at which he arrived is sociologistic among other things because the individual is seen to be to a greater or less degree integrated with others in relation to a common value system. But owing to the approach from which he started, Pareto was never tempted to conceive this "social" element as a metaphysical entity in either a positivistic or an idealistic sense. On this account he was spared many of Durkheim's difficulties. His work thus provides one of the most promising points of departure for the type of theory in sociology and the related social sciences in which the present study is interested. Progress in this direction lies not in repudiating Pareto, as so many have thought necessary, but in developing what he had begun to a more advanced stage in certain directions.

DURKHEIM

Durkheim also started from the same critical attitude. But unlike the other two he criticized utilitarianism not in relation to economic theory but, at once more generally and more empirically, by raising the question of the interpretation of an individualistic social order. His *Division of Labor* is more analo-

gous to Marshall's discussions of free enterprise than to his
technical discussions of economic theory. But Durkheim came to
the same general conclusion as Marshall, that there are involved
in relations of contract elements other than those formulated in
utilitarian terms—the "non-contractual element in contract."
In interpreting what was involved in this concept he came,
empirically, to center his attention on a system of normative rules
governing the activities and relations of individuals.[1]

His second important empirical monograph, *Le suicide*, dealt
with what was ostensibly a quite different range of problems, the
understanding of the factors involved in suicide rates. Underlying it, however, was a continuation of his study of contemporary
society, and it had a direct theoretical continuity with the
Division of Labor, which has been traced in detail. The first
important result of this was the empirical demonstration of the
importance of what he there called "social factors" in suicide.
In the process of arriving at this demonstration he drew into his
critical range a whole group of theories which had been ignored
in the *Division of Labor*, those which attempted to interpret
social phenomena exclusively in terms of the external environment and biological heredity.

At the same time the particular form that his social factors
took strongly suggested again emphasis on the role of obligatory
norms. This was particularly true of the concept of *anomie* as
formulated in the *Suicide*. But the methodological implications
of these empirical insights were not clear at this stage. In particular it seemed difficult to reconcile the subjective treatment
of contract, of crime, etc. with the objectivism of his concept of
"*courants suicidogènes.*"

At this stage, largely in the *Règles* but also in the theoretical
portions of both the *Division of Labor* and the *Suicide*, Durkheim
developed a methodological position to which the name "sociologistic positivism" has been given. Its starting point was a
critique of the utilitarian position with its conceptions of the
subjectivity and spontaneity of individual wants. In this connection Durkheim accepted the empiricist-utilitarian identification of the "individual" factor with the concrete desires of
individuals. His own starting point was definitely positivistic as

[1] This was a distinctly different emphasis from that of Marshall, who was
concerned with the "activities" themselves.

expressed in his methodological requirement that social facts be treated *comme des choses* from the points of view both of the actor and of the observer. That is, social facts must be thought of as reflecting an "external" reality, objective in contradistinction to the subjectivity of the utilitarians' wants, "determined" as against the "spontaneity" of the latter. This is the original meaning of his two famous criteria of social facts, "exteriority" and "constraint." He thus set over against utilitarian teleology a positivistic determinism of the traditional sort. His position implied acceptance of the utilitarian dilemma and naturally, in view of his critical attitude, he took the antiutilitarian alternative.

But it soon appeared that, in view of empirical considerations, these criteria were too broad. For, above all from the subjective point of view, they did not exclude heredity or the "cosmic" environment. Hence the necessity, brought out particularly by the critical parts of the *Suicide* and by his critique of "psychologism" in the *Règles*, of finding criteria by which to differentiate the social from the nonsocial (in that sense "individual") factors which were from the actor's point of view exterior, constraining *choses*. This attempt is couched in terms of (1) the synthesis argument, (2) the idea that society is a "psychic" reality and (3) the attempt to specify its nature further in terms of the concepts *conscience collective* and *représentations collectives*.

The idea that there must be a social reality distinct from the other two had, in terms of methodological formulation, been arrived at indirectly by an argument of elimination in terms of a rigidly positivistic conceptual scheme. The foregoing three arguments must be considered as groping attempts to arrive at a satisfactory formulation acceptable to this scheme, without direct positive reference to empirical evidence and hence without carrying the conviction of direct and positive empirical insight. At this stage Durkheim's main empirically fortified insights so far as they could be brought to bear on this conceptual scheme were negative and critical. All these factors unfortunately, combined with what was at best a half-outgrown empiricism, created a logical situation in which Durkheim was with considerable plausibility open to the criticism that his social reality was a metaphysical entity without empirical relevance. At best it was superfluous, at worst positively misleading. Since most of the critics have themselves been positivistic empiricists, this criticism has taken such firm root that it is the dominant feature of the current opinion of Durkheim's work today. This circumstance has had the unfortunate effect of obscuring both the positive value of the results at which Durkheim had already arrived, and still worse, of blinding the great bulk of social scientists to the fact of the process of internal development which Durkheim's position underwent from this point on and to its immense importance. To the great majority of sociologists Durkheim is still cited as the leading holder of the "unsound" "group-mind" theory. It would be difficult to discover a more striking example of the way in which preconceived conceptual schemes can prevent the dissemination of important ideas.

In tracing Durkheim's evolution away from this system, the first major stage consists in his working out the implications of some of the main empirical insights of the *Division of Labor* and the *Suicide*. From thinking of constraint as naturalistic causation Durkheim gradually came over to the legalistic view of it as a system of sanctions attached to normative rules. This view made it possible to retain the main outline of his previous conceptual scheme, for the actor was still thought of primarily in the role of knowing the conditions of his action. It meant, however, that these conditions were no longer in true positivistic fashion thought of as altogether independent of human agency in general, but only that of the individual concrete actor.

The next step was arrived at partly by pushing the analysis of the action of a concrete individual farther, partly by working out the implications of the conception of constraint as sanction. Its essence was the perception that the primary source of constraint lies in the moral authority of a system of rules. Sanctions thus become a secondary mode of enforcement of the rules, because the sanctions are, in turn, dependent on moral authority. This step brings Durkheim to the conception of the "social" element as consisting essentially in a common system of rules of moral obligation, of institutions, governing the actions of men in a community. It involves a rigorous distinction between the conceptions of individual "interest" and moral obligation. It is here that Durkheim finds the analytical basis he has long been seeking for the distinction between "individual" and "social." The critical attitude toward the utilitarian position is retained, but what is set over against it is vastly different.

The methodological implication of this development is far-reaching. For heretofore Durkheim has been seeking, from the subjective point of view, to fit in the social factor as one element in the subjective schema of rational action as analyzable wholly in terms of the methodology of science. "Ends" and the other normative elements he has previously identified with utilitarian wants. But now the whole "social" factor swings over from the category of "facts" or "conditions" to the normative side. This is a radical departure both from the alternatives presented by the utilitarian dilemma and from Durkheim's empiricist bias. For ends and norms are no longer merely individual but also social. Moreover, the social factor can no longer be considered a concrete entity, for one of its modes of expression is as a factor in the concrete ends and norms of individuals. Thus in terms of the great dichotomy of this study, the social factor becomes a normative, more specifically, a value factor, not one of heredity and environment. Durkheim's attempt to rehabilitate the positivistic position on a sociologistic basis has definitely failed. His sociologism has turned out to be fatal to his positivism.

In his definitely positivistic phase, Durkheim already set forth the conception of a plurality of qualitatively distinct social types. It will be remembered that he made this the basis of his definition of social "normality." At that time he put it in terms of a social milieu or social structure. This social structure is now seen to be formed mainly by a common system of normative rules which, however, are not completely autonomous but, in turn, rest upon a system of ultimate common value attitudes.

Thus Durkheim, proceeding from the analysis of "social facts," especially mass phenomena, arrives by a quite different path at essentially the same position Pareto reached by the analysis of individual action. It may, then, be concluded that the two are essentially different modes of approach to the same fundamental problems. Both lead to the "sociologistic" theorem when it is correctly interpreted to refer to an element in concrete social life and not to a concrete entity. Moreover, both lead to essentially the same conception of one aspect of it as a value element, a system of ultimate common values. In Pareto, owing to certain peculiarities of his logical scheme, the distinction between heredity and environment, on the one hand, and the value elements in nonlogical action, on the other, emerged only by implication after following out the consequences of his thought in a direction different from that which he himself took. In Durkheim, on the other hand, the point of distinction from heredity and environment was clear at a very early stage. His problem was, rather, to define the nature of the social element. The outcome was that the empirical line between the "individual" and the "social" nonutilitarian elements came finally to be identified with that between heredity and environment and the value elements.[1]

Finally both Pareto and Durkheim retained a place for the utilitarian elements of action. But the position at which both arrived implies an important change in the way in which this is conceived. The emphasis on the importance of a common system of ultimate values precludes the identification of the concrete ends of individual action with the random wants of utilitarianism. The conception indicated is rather that of long, complicated interwoven chains of intrinsic means-end relationships culminating in relatively integrated individual systems of ultimate ends, each of which in turn is to a relative degree integrated in a common system. This common system is related to the subsidiary intermediate sector of the chain in various complex ways formulable for present purposes mainly (1) as supplying the ultimate end of each chain and (2) as forming the source of the moral authority of institutional norms. But the common value system is never the source of all elements in the concrete immediate ends of the intermediate sector.[2] There are other elements of various kinds, many of which may be held to have centrifugal tendencies. Hence there is a place for a set of factors the behavior of which roughly corresponds to Pareto's "interests" and hence also the necessity for control of these interests is understood.

As a result of these considerations it may be argued that the correct way to conceive the methodological place of the sciences dealing with elements falling within this intermediate sector is not to treat them (as has so often been done) either as sciences dealing with concrete departments of social life or (a much subtler error) as abstract sciences dealing with hypothetical concrete

---

[1] There is here a difficulty in that there is no good reason to deny the existence of an emergent social element on the biological or psychological level. See Chap. II, pp. 72 *ff*.

[2] There is no reason to deny a role to instinct or other "irrational" elements.

societies in which the sole motives of conduct are technological efficiency, or maximization of wealth or of power. On the contrary, technology, economics and politics should be conceived as sciences dealing systematically with groups of elements analytically separable from the total complex of action, for systematic theoretical purposes in abstraction from immediate consideration of the others, but not on the assumption that the others do not exist or even are unimportant. For none of these structural elements can exist concretely apart from the others. The view of the proper abstraction for the social sciences here put forward is not that of a series of hypothetical concrete systems, but rather of abstract analytical systems each of which assumes as data the main outline of fundamental structure of concrete systems of action including the elements other than those immediately dealt with by the science in question.

Durkheim, however, having arrived at this conception of the place of the "social" as the common value element in action in its relations to the intrinsic means-end chain, did not stop there. In his study of religion he went farther, opening up quite new fields. In the distinction of sacred and profane he found another mode of expression in a different set of relationships of essentially the same elements formulated in the previous distinction of moral obligation and interest. The same attitude of respect which excludes calculation of utilitarian advantage is observed toward both the sacred object and the moral rule.

But since sacred objects are often concrete, even material things, the problem of the origin of their sacredness presented peculiar difficulties. Durkheim, unlike the adherents of previous schools, solved this problem by the theorem that the relation between sacred things and their source was symbolic, not intrinsic. The identity of attitude indicated a close relation between moral rules and this source. Thus Durkheim arrived at the proposition that sacred things were symbolic representations of "society."

This use of the symbolic relationship opened the door to two great lines of thought. It led to a view of the nature of religious ideas which, as a result of the analysis presented above, may be interpreted to imply that the common value system is not merely as in Durkheim's previous thinking, related "backwards" to action in the intrinsic means-end chain, that is, action in relation to the empirical aspect of reality. At the same time there is an organized mode in which men relate themselves and their values to the nonempirical aspects of reality. For the reasons discussed, symbolism plays a peculiarly important part in this relation.

This relation is not, however, merely a passive cognitive one, but involves active attitudes and action. This action takes the form of ritual, which may thus be held to be an expression in symbolic form of ultimate-value attitudes. Thus Durkheim has added a whole new normative category to the structure of action, giving it a systematic place in his thought, in addition to the categories which have found a place closer to the positivistic tradition. Ritual, however, is more than an expression. In his theory of the function of ritual as a stimulant to solidarity and energy of action, Durkheim has given added impetus to the movement of his thought in the direction of a voluntaristic theory of action, involving a system of ultimate values, but studying them in their complex relations to the other elements of action. In fact the results of his theory of religion seem to point strongly in this direction, especially in the emphasis he laid on the importance of the cult as compared with religious ideas.

This trend of Durkheim's thought as well as many other aspects of it is, in general, in accord with that of Pareto's. But Durkheim's methodological starting point and process of development were such as to lay emphasis on the structure of action systems and thus he came to differentiate much more clearly than did Pareto some of the different structural elements that were thrown together in the latter's great category of nonlogical action. Thus, in the first place, Durkheim made, much more clearly though from a different point of view, the distinction between heredity and environment and the value elements. Then within the latter category, in addition to the pursuit of an ultimate common end or system of ends, Durkheim elucidated the peculiarities of the institutional aspect of the role of values in action, and finally of the role of ritual, both magical and religious. In this respect his explicit discussion of the role of symbolism is most important. Though Pareto had a great deal to do with ritual, his direction of interest was not such as to lead him to attempt to bring it into so clear a systematic relation to other structural elements of action as did Durkheim.

With Durkheim's treatment of institutions and of ritual, the outline of the main relations of the "social" factor of ultimate common values to action may, so far as they may be formulated in terms of the strict means-end relationship, be regarded as complete. There are other relations but their systematic analysis must await the introduction of somewhat different points of view. These other aspects have more to do with the role of the diffuser value attitudes than with that of the rationally formulated ends and norms. There is much suggestive material along these lines in Pareto, more than in Durkheim, for the former in his emphasis on the nonlogical was, in some connections, apt to stress those things which to the actor failed to fit at all into logical categories. But for reasons adduced already, Pareto did relatively little to fit these things into a systematic scheme of the structure of action.

Finally, Durkheim in his sociological epistemology and other related elements of his thought went off also, in his last phase, in another direction than that of a voluntaristic theory of action, namely toward an "idealistic sociology." Starting as he did with the passive search for an observable reality to fulfill the requirements of his social facts, he tended to think of the actor as if he were a scientist observing society and adapting himself to it. This scheme was originally developed in a positivistic context. When the social factor came more and more to be thought of as a value element, the retention of the same schema tended to make him see it as a system of "ideas," that is, of eternal objects, which the actor passively contemplates. This tendency culminated in his sociological epistemology where he identified the social factor with the a priori source of the categories, thus finally breaking the bond which had held it as a part of empirical reality.[1] But once having done this it was impossible for him to get back again to empirical reality. He vacillated between a reversion to the old empiricism and an idealistic position which, combined with his doctrine of social types, would produce an impossible solipsistic skepticism. It was in the conflict of these two main tendencies of his later thought, and in the midst of the philosophical difficulties which the latter raised, that Durkheim's career was cut short. What the outcome would have been, had he lived, can only be surmised.

[1] Though he did not himself admit that it was such a break.

It is worth while, finally, to call attention to an important difference between Pareto and Durkheim. Durkheim, in the part of the field of present interest, relating particularly to religion and ritual, stated explicitly several very important theorems which are not to be found in Pareto's work. But in order to arrive at those theorems and to clarify their methodological setting it was necessary for both Durkheim himself and the present study to become involved in a complex critical discussion of certain methodological and philosophical questions. They could not have been stated at all in terms of Durkheim's initial conceptual scheme, and his later statements need considerable correction before they can be fitted into a scheme which is not open to some of the very serious methodological criticisms that have been leveled at Durkheim. This is not true of Pareto. From the point of view of the present study Pareto's scheme is incomplete, but there are neither methodological nor substantive obstacles to its extension in the directions attempted here. It is a question of taking Pareto's starting points and working from them. Whatever Pareto's errors may be, and there is no reason to believe they are not many, they have not proved to be important to this analysis; it has not been necessary to reject anything. Pareto's freedom from methodological dogmatism derived from philosophical presuppositions stands in marked contrast to Durkheim's status in this respect, and accounts for Pareto's being spared many of Durkheim's most confusing difficulties.

This summarizes the argument of the first main part of the study. It seems legitimate to conclude from it that neither the radical positivistic position nor the related utilitarian view is a stable methodological basis for the theoretical sciences of action. Marshall came from the very midst of the utilitarian tradition and, without meaning to do so, modified it out of recognition. The other two attacked it explicitly and successfully. Both of them tended at times to react from it in the direction of radical positivism, but for both that involved difficulties from the consideration of which they emerged with the conception of a common system of ultimate values as a vital element in concrete social life. Durkheim went beyond this to work out some of the most important modes of its relation to the other elements of action.

This process may be interpreted to constitute a definite internal breakdown of the positivistic theory of action in the work of two men strongly predisposed in its favor. In this breakdown the sheer empirical evidence played a decisive role along with theoretical and methodological considerations. It is a process in many ways analogous to the recent internal breakdown of the conceptual framework of the classical physics.

But what is to be built on the ruins? Two alternatives can be seen emerging—an idealistic theory and a theory which would group a number of analytical sciences under the voluntaristic concept of action. The latter tendency is predominant in Pareto and became, at least, prominent in the later Durkheim. But in Durkheim's work it was in conflict with the other. In this situation it is natural to turn to the home of idealistic philosophy, Germany, and to see what the tendency of thought has been there. In general, it may be held that while in the Latin and Anglo-Saxon countries the primary issue has been between positivism and the voluntaristic theory of action, in Germany it has been between the latter and idealism. Some aspects of this latter issue will form the main theme of Part III of this study.

PART III

THE EMERGENCE OF A VOLUNTARISTIC THEORY OF ACTION FROM THE IDEALISTIC TRADITION

CHAPTER XIII

THE IDEALISTIC TRADITION

METHODOLOGICAL BACKGROUND

Like every other great tradition of thought, the idealistic is highly complex, composed of many interwoven strands. As in the earlier case of the positivistic tradition the present sketch does not and cannot pretend to render an exhaustive historical account, even in outline. It must, rather, content itself with selecting, by the ideal-type method, a few major strands which are particularly relevant to the problems of this study.[1]

For the purposes of this study, it is unnecessary to trace the idealistic tradition back to a period earlier than that of Kant. Few thinkers have ever displayed so many facets to a variety of interpreters. It is proposed here only to call attention to a few salient points. In England and the United States it is customary to regard as Kant's principal contribution his solution of the dilemma presented by Hume's epistemological skepticism. This is one major element and a few words must be said about it by way of introduction to the others, which are of more immediate concern.

The empirical knowledge with the validity of which the epistemological discussion of modern philosophy, at least down to relatively recent times, has been primarily concerned, has been that of the physical world, embodied in the classical system of physical theory. It was its validity which Hume's skepticism attacked and in which Kant restored confidence. Kant quite definitely shares this preoccupation with the physical world. Perhaps the clearest indication of this is his inclusion of space, by which he clearly meant the physical space of the classical

---

[1] For purposes of this study the two most useful general accounts are in H. Freyer, *Soziologie als Wirklichkeitswissenschaft* and E. Troeltsch, *Der Historismus und seine Probleme.* The recent work of Friedrich Meinecke, *Die Entstehung des Historismus* may also be mentioned, though it has appeared too late to influence the formulations of the present chapter.

mechanics, as an indispensable schema of intuition, a logical prerequisite of empirical knowledge of any sort. Phenomena for Kant are things or events *in space*.[1]

Kant's answer to Hume involved, however, the repudiation of the naïve empiricist realism which had characterized the earlier physical scientists, the "simple faith" of which Professor Whitehead speaks,[2] which had been broken down by the epistemological criticism culminating in Hume. Kant did not, of course, return to this but reestablished the validity of physical science by reducing physical bodies and events to the status of "phenomena," depriving them of their more substantial metaphysical reality by making them relative to another order of being, the "ideal."

But in this process of "relativizing," the classical physical system remained intact, and remained, for the phenomenal world, an empirically closed system. Man, to be sure, participated in this phenomenal world, not only as knowing subject but also as object, as a physical body. But this did not exhaust man; he also participated in the world of ideas and of freedom. The tendency of Kantian thought was thus toward a radical dualism reaching its most acute point of focus in relation to man—at the same time a physical body and a spiritual being. Hence the Kantian scheme favored the reduction of all phenomenal aspects of man, especially the biological, to a "materialistic" basis, and produced a radical hiatus between this and his spiritual life—a hiatus which still persists in the rigidity of the line customarily drawn between the natural sciences and the sciences of culture or of mind (*Geist*) in Germany.

[1] There are really two issues involved in this Kantian position. One is whether there are in human experience of the empircial world *concrete* entities which do not exist in space or have a spatial aspect. The negative Kantian position on this issue is probably acceptable; certainly it produces no difficulties in the present context. It is rather the second issue which is here important, which is whether theoretical systems analytically applicable to the empirical world, to phenomena in the Kantian sense, must always be couched in terms of a spatial frame of reference. Since in Kant's time the view of analytical abstraction here put forward was not known, his view that all phenomena are observed "in space" strongly tends to be combined with the view that theories which analyze them must involve also spatial categories. It is this latter tendency which creates the dichotomy at present under discussion.

[2] A. N. WHITEHEAD, *Science and the Modern World*, pp. 27–28.

For Kant the Practical Reason fell definitely on the noumenal, not the phenomenal side of the line. This meant that man as an active, purposive being, an actor, was not to be dealt with by the sciences of the phenomenal world nor even by their analytical, generalizing methods. In this sphere man was not subject to law in the physical sense but was free. An intellectual apprehension of his life and action could be attained only by the speculative methods of philosophy, especially by a process of the intuition of total wholes (*Gestalten*) which it was illegitimate to break down by "atomistic" analysis.

In the post-Kantian development of idealism it was this element which was in the center of philosophical attention. By the time of Hegel the phenomenal world was not merely made relative to, and to a high degree dependent on, the ideal—it was practically absorbed. Since what to the idealistic philosopher was interesting about man, his action and his culture, was radically excluded from the phenomenal sphere, interest in man was guided away from general theorizing on the model of the physical sciences, but it was by no means extinguished. If one was forbidden to analyze, one could at least record human acts and their effects in their concrete wholeness. One could also philosophize about these actions and events in terms of their significance for the totality of human development.[1] Hence the tendency for the idealistic interest in human action to issue in two main directions—detailed, concrete history on the one hand, the philosophy of history on the other—which have undoubtedly been the main lines of social thinking and research in Germany since the great days of idealistic philosophy.

The two lines have, of course, been by no means completely distinct. And they have shared with each other several fundamentally important characteristics. In the first place the common filiation from the idealistic horn of the Kantian dilemma has resulted in a common opposition to positivistic trends of thought, to anything in the nature of a "reduction" of the facts of human life and destiny to terms of the physical world or to biological terms. This tendency has, as has been remarked, found its clearest expression in the sharp methodological distinctions drawn

---

[1] That both these procedures in the end involve analysis is a fact which may be neglected for the moment.

between the "natural sciences" and the disciplines concerned with human action and culture.[1]

Secondly, *general* analytical theory has been associated with these objectionable positivistic views—hence the tendency to repudiate it for purposes of the nonnatural sciences. Perhaps the clearest expression of this was the almost universal German hostility, throughout the nineteenth century, to the classical economics, *Smithianismus*, as it was frequently called.

What is perhaps the deepest methodological basis of this conflict has lain in the empiricism common to both great traditions of thought. As long as this persists, the two are, indeed, irreconcilable if any attempt is made to apply them to the same concrete subject matter. The only way to avoid conflict is to keep the fields of their application rigidly distinct, as is done in the usual German distinction between the natural and the sociocultural sciences.

Though empiricism is common to both traditions, it is important to realize that it is not the same thing in the two cases. Positivistic empiricism has been predominantly a matter of the "reification" of theoretical systems, to use Professor Cohen's phrase,[2] or of the "fallacy of misplaced concreteness," to use Professor Whitehead's. Its starting point has been the possession of a general analytical scheme which, for a certain body of fact, works. This circumstance has been interpreted to mean. methodologically, that the concrete reality was "reflected" in the conceptual scheme, adequately for all scientific purposes. It has carried with it, inevitably, the implication of determinism. The logically closed system of theory becomes, in an empiricist interpretation, an empirically closed system. This is true regardless of its content, whether it is the system of the classical mechanics or of the classical economics.

The question of determinism has been, understandably enough in terms of the Kantian background, one of the focal points of the conflict. From the idealistic side the determinist implication has not been taken to indicate a methodologically unsound way of relating the general analytical scheme to concrete reality which could be overcome by correcting the fallacy of misplaced

---

[1] The most prominent names in this connection are W. Windelband, H. Rickert and W. Dilthey.

[2] *Cf.* MORRIS R. COHEN, *Reason and Nature*, pp. 224–228, 386–392.

concreteness. On the contrary, the empiricist interpretation has been accepted without question. Then since it was equally accepted as a fundamental fact that human action could not be mechanistically determined in this sense, the inference drawn was that no general analytical system of theory was applicable to this concrete subject matter at all. A corollary of human freedom was the unique individuality of all human events, in so far as they are "spiritual."

Hence "idealistic empiricism" has not been a deterministic reification of systems of analytical theory, but has involved a repudiation of all such theory in favor of the concrete uniqueness and individuality of all things human. It is in this sense that "historicism" has been the predominant tendency of German social thought on an idealistic basis. Since the general analytical level of scientific comprehension is a priori excluded, things human can be understood only in terms of the concrete individuality of the specific historical case. It is a corollary that all the important things cannot be known from a limited number of cases, but each must be known by and for itself. History is the indispensable road to fullness of knowledge.

It has previously been noted that this tendency has worked out in two main directions. One is the interest in the concrete detail of historical processes for its own sake. This is a persistent strain of German nineteenth century thought, receiving perhaps its most striking methodological formulation in Ranke's famous dictum, that the business of the historian is to render the past *wie es eigentlich gewesen ist*, that is, in all its concrete detail. It has constituted a major element of almost all the monumental works of German historical scholarship in many different fields, and has been thus a major motive in the production of one of the great intellectual movements of the nineteenth century. Methodologically, however, it can scarcely be said to have created a school of theory in social matters—it rather issued in a negation of theory in general.[1]

But there were excellent reasons why this could not remain the sole, or even the predominant, trend of idealistic social thought. Kant himself had, in spite of his idealism, certain strong "individualistic" elements, particularly in the ethical aspects of his

---

[1] As brought out with especial vividness in the famous *Methodenstreit* between Schmoller and Carl Menger.

thought. It may be surmised that this, with its emphasis on freedom in its relatively individualistic Kantian sense, predisposed Kantians to a certain "particularistic" mode of treatment of human action, emphasizing the uniqueness of the particular human individual, and the freedom from determination by circumstances of his particular acts.

While perhaps Fichte in one phase of his thought represented the culmination of this branch of idealism, the Hegelian branch, which was much more influential, went in a different direction. Its emphasis was on the element of "objectivism" in idealistic philosophy[1] as against the greater "subjectivism" of Kant. In application to human affairs this led to a kind of "emanation" theory. Instead of being treated by and for itself an individual human act or complex of action tended to be interpreted as a mode of expression of a "spirit" (*Geist*) sharing this quality with multitudinous other acts of the same and other individuals. Thus to Hegel human history was the process of "objectification" of the single unitary *Weltgeist*.

The result of this tendency was to arrange human activities in relation to comprehensive "collective" or "totality patterns." Historical attention was focused not on individual events or acts but on the *Geist*, which constituted their unity.

Under these conditions the "historical" trend of thinking was, however, preserved intact. The unifying concept under which discrete empirical data were subsumed was not that of a general "law" or analytical element, as in the positivistic tradition, but rather a particular, unique *Geist*, a specific cultural totality clearly distinct from and incommensurable with all others. It is in this emphasis on the importance of historically unique cultural systems, and the tendency to treat all empirical data in relation to such systems that the main trend of German social *theory* on an idealistic basis is to be found.

The various fields in which this tendency has worked out are too numerous and complex to detail here. Perhaps the first prominent one, outside of history proper, was that of jurisprudence, where the famous historical school starting with Savigny applied this historical method to the analysis of systems of law, above all, Roman law. Instead of treating it as the Roman

---

[1] *Objektiver Geist* is the German term. This element was present in Kant but in a position of different relative emphasis.

jurists themselves did, in relation to a universal natural "reason," they saw it as a self-contained system expressing a certain *Geist* which could be formulated in terms of a limited number of principles.[1] But this system was radically distinct from other legal systems, for instance, that of Germanic law.[2]

There was a similar movement in the German historical school of economics[3] especially in its earlier phase. They held that the classical economics did not constitute, as its proponents claimed, a set of universally applicable principles of economic life, but was rather the expression of a particular *Geist*, that of liberalism, individualism, commercialism, *Manchestertum*. Hence its usefulness is confined to the social circumstances where the particular "spirit" in question is predominant; it is not of general application. Hence the attempt to work out in contradistinction other alternative economic systems, such as that of the Middle Ages.

In the Hegelian form the background of this "historicism" was a rigidly monistic idealism which in historical application required a unified conception of human life and history as a whole. The bridge between this final unity and the historical uniqueness of particular historical epochs and cultures was provided by the "dialectic" which left room for qualitative differences in the stages of "self-realization" of the *Weltgeist*, each stage standing in certain respects in antithesis to the preceding one.

This movement, however, has also gone through what was, in a certain sense, a "positivistic," critical stage. This has taken the form of a skeptical attitude toward great speculative constructions on the Hegelian model. As is usually the case, however, such criticism has attacked only certain elements of the thought system, leaving others intact. In this particular instance it was mainly the continuity of structural principle as between cultures which was attacked. But the underlying mode of thinking, the attempt to organize data about the concept of a *Geist* and the unique "system" associated with it, was left undisturbed. The result is that the particular historical epochs or their "spirits"

[1] *Cf.* as an explicit recognition of this the title of Jhering's work: *Der Geist des römischen Rechts.*

[2] See for instance Gierke's great work, *Das deutsche Genossenschaftsrecht.*

[3] This school, under Schmoller's influence, tended strongly in the direction of a complete empiricism.

remained in a state of disconnection, a *Nebeneinander*. The dogma
of individual uniqueness is pushed to the point of breaking all
theoretical continuity with others. So in place of a theory of
dialectic evolution on the Hegelian model there emerges a complete historical relativism. History becomes a succession of such
unique and essentially unconnected systems. On the empirical
plane one of the first radical representatives of this relativistic
view is Dilthey.[1] Since his time the same tendency has been
carried still farther onto the epistemological plane by the recent
movement known as *Wissenssoziologie*.[2]

As has already been noted, this emphasis on the whole, the
totality of a cultural system, has involved a repudiation of the
type of analytical theory inherent in the conceptual structures
of the positivistic tradition. The prevailingly empiricist temper
which has characterized both parties to the controversy has only
served to intensify this repudiation, since it is unquestionably
true both that these theories, of the classical economics for
instance, have failed to do justice to certain of the concrete
facts, and that an important and valid correction of them could
be arrived at by viewing the phenomena concerned from the
point of view of cultural totality.[3] Thus the prevailing German
view has been very far from completely lacking its own empirical
justification.

At the same time this repudiation of general analytical concepts
and the corresponding emphasis on organic totality has forced
German theory into methodological paths which were highly
dubious from the point of view of those interested in analytical
theory. For, on the one hand, science could not be limited to the
isolated observation of discrete individual facts and phenomena—
particular acts and events—as one branch of German empiricism
would require. At the same time, there was no general analytical
theory in terms of which to organize particular discrete observations, and to evaluate their scientific significance. Hence the

[1] Spengler also gives one of the more radical instances of this view.

[2] Perhaps the best-known representative is Karl Mannheim. *Cf.* his
Ideologie und Utopie, translated by Louis Wirth & Edward Shils as *Ideology
and Utopia*. For a general sketch of the literature of the movement, see E.
Grünwald, *Das Problem der Soziologie des Wissens*.

[3] From the above analysis it will be clear that one main reason for this is
the fact that the phenomena are in fact "organic," a fact obscured by the
"atomistic" tendencies of utilitarian and positivistic social theories.

necessity for recognizing a source of knowledge with little place in the repertoire of science as generally understood—a kind of "intuition" for the peculiar structures of wholes which could neither be "observed" in the usual operational sense, nor constructed by the ordinary theoretical processes.[1]

The methodological conflict has been the more irreconcilable the more definitely positivistic thought has been "mechanistic" and "atomistic," and, indeed, throughout a good deal of its history these characteristics have been strongly marked. The stock German criticism of the ideas of the "enlightenment," of utilitarianism, positivism, rationalism, has run in these terms. Over against this has been set some version or other of an "organic" view. Germany has been preeminently the home of "organic" social theory all through the nineteenth century and up to the present.

The dichotomy of "mechanistic," "atomistic" or "individualistic" and "organic" is stated, however, in exceedingly general and formal terms. It denotes scarcely more than the most formal general relations of parts or units to a whole. In the course of the development of German thought a more specific account of what is involved has gradually emerged.

The issues between German idealism and Western European positivism have been more than merely methodological in the above formal sense. They have concerned differences over the substantive factors invoked in explanation of human action. The original Kantian dualism laid down a sharp distinction between the sphere of "nature," of phenomena, of determinism, on the one hand, and that of freedom, of ideas, of *Geist*, on the other. The main line of German social thought has been concerned with the latter sphere. This means that its "organicism" has not been mainly a matter of the biological analogy, though this has sometimes appeared, but has lain in this sense in the ideal sphere.

The essential "reality" then, the determining factors in human life and action, has tended to be found on this level. There is, however, a radical distinction between this order of reality and that dealt with by positivistic thought, or given in Kant's world of phenomena. The latter is a complex of elements func-

---

[1] Hence the tendency for the "hard-boiled scientific" wing to run off into the historical particularism noted above. Schmoller is a conspicuous example.

tionally or causally related to each other. This conception involves at least the postulate of process *in time*—for underlying every conception of causal relationship is that of variation. Two entities are causally related if, and in so far as, a *change* in one will result in a change in the other. Change in this context certainly implies temporal process.

An "ideal reality," on the other hand, implies a complex of elements mutually related to one another—constituting hence a "system"—but this mode of relationship is of a radically different character from the causal—it is a "complex of meanings."[1] Thus a scientific theory is a complex or system of propositions *logically* related to one another.[2] Similarly an artistic "form" constitutes a structure of elements, in the case of a symphony, for example, of sound combinations, related to each other, not logically, but still "meaningfully." There is, to use Professor Köhler's[3] term, a certain mutual "requiredness" such that it is quite evident when a "false" note is struck, as it is possible to detect, in a theory, a logical fallacy.

Whatever else they may be, these meaningful relations of the elements of a system are not causal relations. Two circumstances may be noted to bring this out. In the first place, the relation to time is fundamentally different. Logical relations are timeless as is the form of a work of art. This is not to say that such systems do not have an origin in time in one sense—of the time of their creation.[4] Nor does it mean that time is irrelevant to the form of concrete symbolic expression, as in music or poetry. What it means is that the system of meanings "in itself" is atemporal. The relations between the elements of the system are not relations in a temporal process but are of a radically different order.[5]

---

[1] *Sinnzusammenhang*, in the expressive German term.

[2] In discussing these things it is both important and difficult to keep two levels of discourse distinct, that of the ideal system "in itself" and its relations to action. Thus in the first sense a change in one proposition of a system of scientific theory results in changes in other propositions of the same system. But though there are in the logical sense "inevitable" implications, it is not in the real world inevitable that they should be drawn. To the actor correct logic states a norm conformity with which is problematical.

[3] WOLFGANG KÖHLER, in William James lectures at Harvard University (unpublished).

[4] That is, in their relation to action.

[5] This is brought out by the fact that the "same" meanings may be

Secondly, the relation to action is entirely different. As has been shown at great length, causal relations are relevant to rational action in the role of conditions and means. In so far as causal relations subsist between elements of his situation the actor is thereby "conditioned" in the sense that attainment of an end in the given situation depends on his "taking account of" these relations. Meaningful relations, on the other hand, condition action[1] in one sense, but not in the same sense. Their role is normative—they express relations between various elements and aspects of an ideal toward which action is oriented. In elaborating a theory for instance, there is nothing in the conditions of his situation to prevent the theorist from making a logical error—what prevents him is, rather, his effort to conform his action to the norm of logical correctness. Similarly, in playing a musical theme it is perfectly "possible" objectively for a pianist to strike a "wrong" note. He avoids doing it because it would contravene the normative requiredness of the musical form.

It has already appeared in the course of the present analysis of action that at least two modes of relation of "ideal" elements to the spatial and temporal aspects of experience are significant to action, whatever others further analysis might disclose. Normative elements may, that is, be related to action and thought, first, in an intrinsic context and, second, as one term of a symbolic relation.

The first relation is that which lies closest to positivistic modes of thought, since for thought processes the elements of scientific methodology constitute such a norm, especially the logical, and in so far as action is rational, in the sense employed throughout this study, the same elements are normative not only to thought but also to action. Or, better, thought, considered as a process of attaining knowledge, is one case of a much larger category of actions oriented to logical norms. In this context the meaningful elements of action become, in the terms of a voluntaristic theory of action, of causal significance, for it is only in terms of orientation to such norms that a measure

---

expressed in two different symbolic media, one of which does and the other does not require temporal order. Thus Euripides' plays and Phidias' sculpture may be said to express roughly the same things.

[1] That is "make a difference" in it.

of independence of the processes of action from their conditions is conceivable.

The second mode of relation, the symbolic, has come into prominence especially in connection with Durkheim's treatment of religion. At the polar extreme there ceases to be any intrinsic relation between the particular symbol and its meaning; certainly the relation is not that between the non-normative elements of a situation and a norm. In this context spatiotemporal phenomena of all sorts are capable of interpretation, not in terms of their intrinsic properties and their causal relations, but as symbolic expressions of meanings or systems of meanings. In so far as phenomena are interpreted in this context, it means dispensing with the causal explanation of the natural sciences altogether.

For the connection between a particular symbol and its meaning is in the causal sense always arbitrary. It can be known only when a key is provided to open the door, when the "language" is known. The only intrinsic element common to symbols and their meanings is that of order. And this can never be grasped by the isolated study of particular symbols, but only in terms of their mutual relations in systems.[1] This fact undoubtedly constitutes one of the basic reasons for the "organicism" of German social thought, its hostility to any attempt to break down the concrete whole analytically.   Both modes of relation of the ideal or meaningful to the spatiotemporal play a prominent part in idealistic social thought, with, however, a tendency for the symbolic to take precedence over the normative.

In the course of time this basic distinction between causal and meaningful relationships has come to be embodied in methodological terms. As distinct from the analytical methods of the natural sciences, that of the sciences of "Culture" has been given the particular name *Verstehen*. Under this somewhat difficult concept, which owes more perhaps to Dilthey than to anyone else, the most important meaning for present purposes is its reference to

---

[1] That the "key" is necessary even here is brought out vividly by the experience of archaeologists with inscriptions. Before the discovery of the Rosetta stone Egyptian hieroglyphs had been known for a long time. There was no mystery about their physical properties: nothing significant has been added to our knowledge in this respect. What was needed was their meaning, which was provided by a translation of these symbols into a known language—Greek. For lack of such a key many inscriptions such as the Minoan and the Mayan can still not be deciphered.

the grasp of symbolic relationships. An entity is *verstanden* when it is given a place in a system of meaningful relationships, by which it acquires *Sinn*. If it is itself an ideal entity, for instance, a proposition, this takes place directly. If not, if it is rather a spatiotemporal object or event, the method of *Verstehen* involves a further step—this entity must by symbolic interpretation be assigned a meaning which makes it congruent to such an ideal system.

As will be seen these considerations by no means exhaust the concept of *Verstehen*, particularly as employed by Weber. Another fundamental aspect is its reference to "subjective" phenomena. In so far as "meanings" may be said to have an empirical spatiotemporal "existence" at all it is "in the mind."[1] There is unquestionably an exceedingly close connection between the apprehension of meaningful relations as such, on the one hand, and the study of the subjective aspect of action, on the other. Here only a reference is made to the relation. It will have to be discussed at considerable length in connection with Weber.

If, however, the above interpretation of the main line of German idealistic social thought is correct, the chronic conflict of that thought with that on a positivistic basis is not surprising. Against mechanism, individualism, atomism, it has placed organicism, the subordination of the unit, including the human individual, to the whole. Against essential continuity in its field of study, which has looked upon particular cases as instances of a general law or principle, it has emphasized the irreducible qualitative individuality of the phenomena it was studying and has issued in a far-reaching historical relativism.

But underlying these differences is a still more fundamental one. Positivistic thought has always directed its efforts to the uncovering of intrinsic causal relationships in the phenomena; idealistic thought to the discovery of relations of meaning, of *Sinnzusammenhang*. With this difference has gone that of method—on the one hand, causal theoretical explanation, on the other, interpretation of meaning, *Sinndeutung*, which has seen in the concrete facts of its field symbols, the meanings of

---

[1] Or "embodied in symbols" which, since they have a meaning, imply an understanding mind. Still another aspect is the subjective understanding of action and its motivation in relation to normative elements. See below, Chap. XVI, pp. 635 *ff*.

which are to be interpreted. The order and system of social phenomena has been a meaningful,[1] not a causal order at all.

Given the empiricist bias characteristic of both traditions, a mutual aggressiveness was inevitable. The positivist has persistently tried to "reduce" ostensibly meaningful systems to a causal basis, to make his causal analysis cover all intellectually apprehensible relationships; the idealist, on the other hand, has with equal insistence tried to absorb causal relationships into meaningful systems. Both have been imperialistic in the sense of attempting to make their own methodological principles cover the whole field of things knowable, at least in relation to human beings.

Earlier in this study the attempt has been made in the course of a long analysis to bring out certain fundamental difficulties of a completely positivistic version of the theory of action, and to demonstrate to what extent the positivistic theory of action has itself become involved in these difficulties and in so doing has transcended the rigidly positivistic basis, developing at least partly in an idealistic direction. The task of the present section will be to follow the reverse process and show some of the inherent difficulties of a completely idealistic position, and how positivistic elements have come into the idealistic tradition. It will not, however, do merely to say that both the positivistic and the idealistic positions have certain justifications and there is a sphere in which each should be recognized. It is necessary, rather, to go beyond such eclecticism, to attempt, at least in outline, an account of the specific modes of interrelation between the two. It is in this connection that the voluntaristic theory of action assumes a place of central importance. It provides a bridge between the apparently irreconcilable differences of the two traditions, making it possible, in a certain sense, to "make the best of both worlds."[2]

It should almost go without saying that the category "systems of meaning," or "meaningful complexes," is not homogeneous

---

[1] The term sounds somewhat awkward in English but seems to be the best available translation of the German *sinnvoll* and its various related words.

[2] It should be clear to the reader that in the view put forward here action is precisely the point of articulation in human experience between the causal-functional and the symbolic-meaningful elements. Hence a dogmatism which assigns exclusive validity to either one is unsuitable in this field.

but covers a number of different types. It is not intended anywhere in this work to attempt thoroughgoing analysis which could issue in an exhaustive classification. Certain distinctions will, however, naturally emerge from the general theoretical framework of the discussion to be more precisely formulated later on. At the present juncture, however, one fact should be noted and its significance suggested. One such type of meaning complex has been of paramount importance in relation to the positivistic tradition, namely scientific theory. A most important result of the above analysis of Pareto's work was to develop a clear distinction between it and another type which is also highly significant for action, that is, value ideas.

It is not fortuitous that in so far as the idealistic tradition has been concerned with human action it has been upon the latter that the principal stress has been laid. If the *Volksgeist* or other *Geist* has been held by various schools to be the central determinant of a concrete system of action or relationships to be analyzed, its content will generally be found to consist in normative value ideas, a set of conceptions of what human actions and relationships *should* be. Furthermore the actual treatment of historical cases will be found to bring out the close affinity of these value systems to other meaning systems such as religious and metaphysical ideas and artistic styles, all of which stand in sharp contrast to scientific theories.

In the discussion of Durkheim the significance of this basic distinction has already been commented upon. Scientific theories constitute the closest connecting link between the causal and the meaningful elements of reality because, while the theories as such are systems of meaning, the symbolic references involved are to systems of intrinsic causal relationship. This is not in the same sense true of the other types of meaning system—they can, in fact, be arranged in a series extending from purely scientific theories at one end to what are "pure forms of expression" at the other, in which intrinsic elements are of *only* symbolic significance. Certain types of art form constitute the clearest example of the second category.

THE PROBLEM OF CAPITALISM

So far the discussion of the idealistic tradition has been confined to a bare logical outline with only sporadic references to particular developments of thought in specific fields. Before closing this chapter the main stages of development of one particular historicotheoretical problem—capitalism—will be sketched both to illustrate the way in which the logical distinctions of the foregoing discussion are involved in a particular subject matter, and because it forms the central empirical focus of Weber's work, which will be taken up in detail in the two following chapters.

The disposition to consider the modern economic order as a historically unique system of relationships expressing a particular *Geist* was already strong in the earlier historical school of economics. As has been noted, the classical economics was thought of as an expression of this *Geist* and hence as applicable only to this particular set of relationships, those of an "individualistic" order. But by far the most important thinker to work out a *theory* of the modern economic order on a historical basis was Marx.[1] It is the Marxian system which has formed the central focus of the German discussion of capitalism.

MARX

Marx is not generally considered as belonging to the historical school of economics as such. He is, in the respects of importance here, a direct descendant of Hegel. Whatever may be the conflict involved in the difference between Hegelian idealism and Marxian materialism, in certain essential respects Marx took over a Hegelian mode of thought. Like Hegel he worked out a philosophy of history conceiving human development as a single process toward a determinate goal, though both the goal and the character of the process differed from Hegel's account. But also like Hegel and unlike the positivistic evolutionists he conceived the process not as continuous in a single line, each stage constituting in certain respects a quantitative increase over the previous stage, but as dialectical. That is, while there is continuity in the process as a whole, each stage forms a well-marked "system" distinct in principle of organization from the others, and arising in direct conflict with its predecessor in the series. While in a

---

[1] For purposes of the present discussion it is not necessary to attempt to distinguish in Marxian thought the specific contributions of Marx from those of Engels. The reader may, if he prefers, substitute "Marx-Engels" for "Marx" in the following pages.

continuous process the delimitation of stages is arbitrary, this is not the case in a dialectic process.

As has been noted,[1] for his own purposes Marx took over the main framework of the classical economic theory. But, characteristically, he turned it from an analytical theory of the economic aspect of social phenomena in general into a historical theory of the functioning and development of a particular economic system, the capitalistic. There is relatively little light to be found in Marx on what economic theory would be required by other systems, such as the feudal or the socialistic. But in spite of this it is entirely clear that the capitalistic system is definitely distinct, not merely as a stage, but in principle, from both its predecessor and its putative successor in the dialectic process.

The classical economic theory had been put forward on an empiricist basis—which Marx did not question. Hence it necessarily involved elements of social organization—what some modern writers would call "institutional" elements. But in those he chose to emphasize, Marx differed strikingly from the principal classical theorists. Their main concern was with the phenomena of division of labor and exchange as between discrete individuals, each producing a complete commodity for the consumers' market; this was at least the main institutional starting point. Marx, to be sure, took over the conception of a plurality of competing productive units, but centered an attention which, in spite of strong suggestions in Malthus and Ricardo, was new in its intensity and emphasis on the theoretical consequences, on the internal structure of the productive unit.

Here, of course, what mainly interested him was what Malthus had referred to as the "division of society into classes of employers and laborers." There was thus an internal conflict of interest within the basic unit of the system, the capitalistic enterprise. This was the class conflict, involving a power relationship between the classes.

Thus it was its class structure based, in turn, upon the organization of the unit of production, which primarily characterized the capitalistic system for Marx, and it was this element which he generalized beyond the capitalistic system to make the systematic unifying principle of the whole evolutionary process. It was, on the one hand, its specific class structure which char-

[1] See Chap. III, pp. 107 *ff*.

acterized each social system, this class structure in each case being founded in the "conditions of production." Each system is dominated by a class but at the same time requires, and in its own development creates, another class which, in turn, destroys it. Thus, on the other hand, it is class conflict which constitutes the dynamic element of the evolutionary process and forms the contradiction between any one system and its predecessor or successor as the case may be. It is this element, a form of the power element of the previous discussion, which gives the Marxian theory its dynamic cast as against the equilibrating tendency of "orthodox" economic theory.

It is now possible to approach the question of what can be meant by *materialism* in the Marxian sense. The experience of this study has certainly been that it is always helpful to attempt to understand a writer in terms of the polemical oppositions of the thought of his time. Marx's own polemics were aimed mainly in two directions, against Hegelian idealism and against the Utopian socialists. But before taking up the implications of this double polemic it is well to eliminate one possible and rather frequent misapprehension. Marx did not use the word materialism in the familiar positivistic sense of reducing social phenomena causally to terms of the nonhuman environment, as natural resources, or of biological heredity or some combination of both. This interpretation is definitely precluded by the historical features of the Marxian theory. To be sure, natural resources are of fundamental importance in it, as is also nationalism with whatever racial basis may underly it, but in both cases the importance derives from the relation of these elements to a particular form of social organization. They cannot, however, account for the social organization itself, since these factors have not *changed* in the process of development of the capitalistic system. There is a fundamental element in capitalism independent of men's biological needs, their other biologically inherited traits or their external environment. Marxism is a social doctrine.

Marx made the famous remark that Hegel was standing on his head and he, Marx, set him right side up. What does this mean? Only that the dynamic forces of history are not to be found in the immanent self-development of a *Geist* in the Hegelian sense, but in a different sphere, that of men's "interests." Materialism is here to be understood by contrast with the specific Hegelian sense of idealism. It is as such a residual category and not to be identified with the prevailing Western sense of the same term in the common phrase scientific materialism.

The other related epithet most frequently applied to Marx, *determinism*, acquires its meaning largely by contrast with Utopian socialism. The Utopians, of whom Owen and Fourier may serve as examples, belong mainly to a phase of the movement of thought discussed above[1] as radical rationalistic positivism. In relation to the irrationalities of contemporary social conditions they were characterized by a belief in the overwhelming power of reason to show men the "true" conditions of their happiness, independently of the particular situation a given individual happened to be in. Then all that would be necessary to change a social system would be to appeal to the "reason" of individuals, above all of those in positions of responsibility, to show them the irrationality of the present order and the reasonableness of the alternative proposed.

To this Marx opposed his view of "interests." There is, in Marx, no suggestion of a radical anti-intellectualism of the positivistic variety. Indeed, he could not have accepted classical economic theory had he taken this position. Men acted rationally for him, even if in a somewhat limited sense more suggestive of Hobbes than of Locke or Condorcet. But they acted rationally within a given concrete situation and within such a situation the rational norm itself necessitates certain lines of action, precluding others. Men, precisely because they do act rationally, will follow their "interests" as defined for them by the situations in which they are placed.

It was inherent in the conceptual framework of the classical economics that strong emphasis should be thrown on the positive advantages of the division of labor. By comparison with the state of nature it was a more efficient way of securing means to want satisfaction. The mechanism of competition was thought of more in this light and less as a mechanism of control; and even when it was considered as the latter, it was thought of more as a check on possible abuses than on anything else.

Marx, through his doctrine of interests, elevated not only competition but the whole structure of the economic order into a

[1] Chap. III, p. 119–121.

great control mechanism, a compulsive system. This is the essential meaning of Marx's conception of economic determinism. It is not a matter of psychological antirationalism, but of the total consequences of a multitude of rational acts. On the one hand, the system itself is the resultant of the myriad of individual acts but, on the other, it creates for each acting individual a specific situation which compels him to act in certain ways if he is not to go contrary to his interest. Thus for Marx exploitation was to be blamed on neither the unreasonableness nor the plain selfishness of the individual employer, but the employer was placed in a situation where he must act as he did, or be eliminated in the competitive struggle.[1]

Thus, while "liberal" theory focused its main attention on the superior efficiency of an individualistic order, Marx stressed its compulsive aspect and through this the total structure of the system. The system itself would be thought of as self-acting. Once the individuals involved in it are placed in the situations that are given, their actions are "determined" so as to maintain the system as a whole, or rather to drive it forward on the evolutionary course, to end at last in its self-destruction.

The peculiar forms of compulsion found in the capitalistic system are not universal, but are limited to its particular conditions, to its specific combination of the "conditions of production." Under feudalism, exploitation of labor in the capitalistic enterprise was not the dominant feature of society, and with the advent of socialism it will cease to be. The essential question of Marxism, then, is, what are the factors accounting for this situation which results in capitalistic determinism? This raises again the question of materialism.

The materialistic view, in the Marxian sense of the term, is that the compulsive discipline in one system, the capitalistic for instance, is a development from the similarly compulsive conditions of the preceding system. History constitutes from this point of view an unbroken chain of such deterministic systems. Whatever the degree of their incommensurability with each other, and of the importance of class conflict as the propulsive dynamic force in the dialectic process, the causal link is unbroken and each system by the process of its own "immanent "breakdown

[1] An excellent discussion of this aspect of Marx is to be found in Sombart's *Der proletarische Sozialismus.*

inevitably gives birth to its successor in the series. Naturally this conception implies an original historical element in the sense of an originally deterministic set of conditions of production out of which the whole thing flows.

It should be emphasized again that the determinism of the theory lies not on an individual-psychological, but on a social, level. It is the situation which dictates a given course of action; in a different situation all would be changed. Many Western critics of Marx have thought to detect an insoluble contradiction between the determinism of his historical materialism and the advocacy of an active revolutionary policy. Indeed, if his materialism were of the positivistic variety this would be the case— but it is not. It arises out of the *resultant* of innumerable rational acts, each act presupposing a given situation. Marx's difference from the classical economists is merely this: In the first place he threw his attention from the rational process itself back to the situation which dictated its course. Secondly, with the aid of the dynamic element supplied by the conception of class conflict[1] he saw what the classical economists did not see, that the fundamental character of these situations was subject to historical change. He thus introduced an element of historical relativism of the first importance.

But his conception of social causation remained essentially that of the classical economists; it was, in the terminology of the previous discussion, essentially utilitarian, with the addition of the historical element. It shares with them the complete preoccupation with means and conditions of action, hence the corresponding implicit assumption of the randomness of ultimate ends.

Marx took over the main "economic" elements of the classical theory, including the conception of a self-regulating competitive system. But, as has been stated, he differs in his emphasis on a particular form of social organization. Hence he invoked for the dynamic part of the theory, elements *not* central to the main framework of classical theory. It is interesting to note what these are: One is industrial technology, the development of which is to be thought of as a continuous linear process. Of course the orthodox economists were by no means oblivious of this, but they thought of it only in its bearing on productivity, while for Marx

[1] In combination with technological advance.

its main significance lay in its relation to social organization, starting with the structure of the productive unit. Thus there is one dynamic factor of a linear character.

The other is, of course, the class struggle. This it is which, in its particular combination with the technological and the economic, characterizes a given economic system and constitutes the element of discontinuity; because the class structure of each is different, the different systems cannot be compared. This is, however, at bottom a type of power element in the above sense,[1] a power relation on the basis of a given situation.

Thus Marxian economic determinism is a matter not of economic causation alone in the specific sense arrived at in the previous discussion but of the total intermediate sector of the intrinsic means-end chain, a combination of technological, economic and political determinism. It is materialistic only as *opposed* to idealistic in the Hegelian sense. It has no necessary implication of materialism in the usual positivistic sense.[2]

It is true that there is also another element in Marx—that expressed in his revolutionary side. The proletariat is characterized, in the first place, by a particular interest in the capitalistic order. But there is a fundamental difference between the case where this interest is dormant, expressed only in attitudes to immediate situations, and the case of class consciousness. At the class-conscious level another factor enters the situation, the organized concerted action of the proletariat to overthrow the existing order and establish socialism. This looks very much like a common value element. Why does it not play a part in Marx's general view of history instead of entering only at this one point?

In the first place Marx was after all an evolutionist. In such a context there is nothing inherently unreasonable in thinking of a given phenomenon as emergent at a fairly well-defined point in the process. And his view of human nature did not logically preclude the possibility of this *Sprung in die Freiheit*. But, secondly, Marx himself undoubtedly shared to a large extent the rationalistic-anarchistic philosophy of the Utopian socialists whom he criticized. He differed from them in possessing a far

---

[1] *Cf.* Chapter III, p. 109.

[2] Modified of course by the instability of the utilitarian position which has been analyzed.

greater degree of realism about the process by which the goal could be reached. The appeal to reason could not be effective regardless of social conditions, but only when it corresponded to an interest. And only at this stage of the total evolutionary process did the particular basis of interest exist.

But there is one and only one goal. Marx was in a sense a sociological relativist—but by no means an ethical relativist. And his ethical absolutism unquestionably meant the focusing of his whole system of thought, in its pragmatic aspect, on the conditions for the realization of his own ideal. In this respect it is logically the exact counterpart of the Hegelian system, with different content.[1]

SOMBART

As has already been noted, the Marxian theory in the broader aspects which have been under discussion here[2] has formed the focus of the discussion of capitalism in Germany. In closing this chapter a brief outline may be presented of one prominent issue of the discussion, the theory of Werner Sombart, which may be said in a sense to have assimilated the main content of Marx into the framework of orthodox historicoidealistic thought. Then in the next chapter Weber's treatment of the same set of problems will be taken up in more detail. It differs in important respects from that of both Marx and Sombart.

The subject of Sombart's life work has been the study of a single, historically unique economic system—modern capitalism.[3] In the process, however, Sombart has not considered himself merely as a historian but quite definitely as an economic theorist. But in his view there is no such thing as general economic theory applicable to the facts of any time or place, but only the theory of an indefinite plurality of economic systems, each separate from the others. Sombart himself gives us only the theory of one particular economic system, capitalism, in all its ramifications, and to throw it into relief, a sketch of two pre-

[1] On this aspect of Marx *cf.* Troeltsch, *Hiztorizmus*, pp. 314 *ff.*

[2] It is noteworthy that in Germany only the socialists have been much preoccupied with the technicalities of Marxian economic theory. His broader influence has been exerted almost entirely in such fields as the problems of capitalism and historical materialism.

[3] Documented mainly in Sombart's massive work, *Der moderne Kapitalismus*, 2d ed.

capitalistic systems, self-sufficient economy and the handicraft system.

The economic system is not for Sombart a historical phenomenon which he merely describes, but an "ideal type"[1] which he employs for the understanding of the concrete historical process. For him the radical discontinuity of economic systems applies only to the type. The concrete process itself is continuous, representing a gradual shading off of systems into each other.

But however much Sombart may emphasize the abstract theoretical character of his concepts, the fact remains that their reference is individual and historical and not analytical and general.[2] The economic system capitalism is useful not in general but in the analysis of the facts of only one historical epoch. In this respect Sombart has drawn the radical conclusion appropriate to following the historical-idealistic tradition.

He is equally radical in the other main aspect of his work—his theory of causation, which is a direct polemical answer to Marxian historical materialism. There are, he says, three aspects of an economic system: a form of organization, a "spirit" (*Geist*) and a technique. With one notable exception he takes over the Marxian description of the system (that is, its ideal type) but he differs profoundly in his interpretation of the relations of its elements, giving definite priority to the spirit, which, he says, has created the form of organization for itself. It is worth while to outline briefly the particular concepts in order to illuminate the general theoretical issue.

On the organization side the system is characterized, on the one hand, by the character of the unit which makes it up, the capitalistic enterprise, and, on the other, by the kind of relations between these units. The enterprise is internally organized by division into two main classes, the owner-managers on the one hand, the propertyless wageworkers on the other. Their relations to each other are typical competitive-market relations. The total complex of enterprises forms a closed, self-sustaining system.

---

[1] See below Chap. XVI for a more extended discussion of the ideal type in connection with Weber.

[2] Here, of the two elements of Marxian thought, he has self-consciously taken over one. Marx took over classical economic concepts when they were useful to him without bothering too much about their methodological status.

The immediate end of each enterprise must above all be profit making, whatever the private motives of the individual participants may be, for the competitive process focuses all capitalistic activities on profit and makes its attainment the measure of success and the condition of survival.

Thus Sombart agrees with Marx on the compulsive character of the system. Its competitiveness and acquisitiveness are not matters of the private motives of individuals but of the inexorable conditions of the situations in which individuals are placed.[1] Moreover he also agrees that this has not always been characteristic of all economic systems; it was not true, for instance, of the handicraft system.

But this compulsiveness applies only to the fully developed system where its *Geist* has become "objectified" or "institutionalized." But Sombart differs radically from Marx in his interpretation of how this has come about. Instead of this objective form of organization being a resultant from previous similar forms, it is the creation of a *Geist*. The principles of this *Geist* are acquisitiveness, competition and rationality.

For Sombart this *Geist* has two aspects, the spirit of enterprise and the bourgeois spirit.[2] The former accounts for the first two principles. Its principles are by no means confined to the economic sphere but its working there is a phase of the great movement of the Renaissance. Its distinguishing characteristics are individuality, initiative, energy and a struggle for power. It is the same spirit which has created the modern state, science and exploration.

Economic enterprise, however, is a peculiarly favorable field for this spirit, because acquisitive activities once loosed from the bonds of traditionalism do not contain, on the one hand, any inherent limit; on the other, are inherently competitive. And only in this field has the Renaissance spirit created so tightly knit an institutional system.

Another interesting difference from Marx is the way Sombart pushes his thesis of system discontinuity into the field of tech-

[1] It is instructive to note the similarity of this to Durkheim's approach to the problem of constraint.

[2] See *Der Bourgeois*, trans. by M. Epstein as *The Quintessence of Capitalism;* see also Talcott Parsons, "Recent German Literature on Capitalism, I, Werner Sombart," *Journal of Political Economy*, December, 1928.

nology, the central stronghold of positivistic, linear evolutionism. The technology of developed capitalism is not, he holds, merely more "advanced" than that of the precapitalistic era; it rests on radically different principles. Where the latter was traditional, it is rational; where the latter was empirical, it is scientific. Handicraft technique rested on empirical rules, that is, rules embodying particular experiences traditionally handed down without reference to general principles. Capitalistic technique, on the other hand, consists mainly in the application of theoretical scientific knowledge to particular problems without reference to tradition.

Finally, the class struggle is far less prominent in Sombart than in Marx. This is not essentially because Sombart fails to recognize its organizational basis in the structure of the capitalistic enterprise—on the contrary, he does so quite explicitly—but because he has a quite different conception of the process of the development of capitalism. For Marx it was the progressive emergence of the contradictions inherent in the material basis; for Sombart, on the other hand, it represents the progressive objectification of the *Geist*, that is, the gradual transformation of subjective attitudes into a compulsive institutionalized system. This is the process which forms the central theme of Sombart's treatment. Moreover, his work is not oriented "forward" to the emergence of the successors of capitalism, but is concentrated rather on the system itself; ethically he looks backward, if anything.

This brief sketch of Sombart's theory of capitalism should serve to bring out certain points. In concrete subject matter, and most of the descriptive characteristics of the system, the origin of the theory lies in Marx. But not only does it agree with Marx in emphasizing the historical character of the system; it goes far beyond him both in eliminating everything but its historical character and in bringing the interpretation of the latter away from Marx's materialism back into the main line of German historicoidealistic methodological thought.

This is accomplished principally by the role he assigns to the "spirit of capitalism." This entity is given the sole creative role except for certain limiting conditions. The concrete activities of men in the system are "expressions" of this *Geist*, not, as in orthodox economic theory, means of want satisfaction. Moreover, this *Geist* is not thought of as one element in a process of complex interaction with several others; it acts alone.

Indeed, Sombart is still in a certain sense an empiricist. His theory is not, to be sure, a direct description of the total concrete phenomenon of capitalism; it is an ideal type. But it is not analytical in the sense of the previous discussion; it states the "essence" of the concrete facts. Apart from the fact that more than one system can be identified in the same situation, what is omitted is contingent in the sense of not being significant for *any* social science theory whatever. It is an "economic" theory but not, like Pareto's, abstract in the sense that for concrete adequacy it requires supplementing by other theories dealing with other elements in the same concrete phenomena. That is why Sombart is under the logical necessity of including in his system even such an apparently foreign element as technology.

Thus in the Marx-Sombart conflict is to be found for this study the statement of a fundamental issue. As far as it is possible to read a factor theory into Marx's materialism, it involves essentially the elements dominant in the utilitarian tradition. Sombart, however, attacks Marx on the ground of his not being able to account for the facts of the objective compulsive system which was Marx's own empirical starting point. The outcome of the above analysis of the internal difficulties of the utilitarian tradition is a position empirically favorable to Sombart's criticism.

Moreover, in Sombart an element has emerged which fits in with the previous analysis of his study. His *Geist* is unquestionably a common value element. But the methodological framework in terms of which he treats it is "imperialistic" as are all empiricisms. It makes the total concrete phenomenon of capitalism, so far as it can become an object of the social sciences at all, a "manifestation" of this *Geist*. It thereby altogether eliminates the utilitarian factors. Hence Sombart's perfectly logical and definite repudiation of orthodox economic theory.

Weber, on the other hand, was a thinker steeped both in the idealistic tradition of thought and in the particular empirical problems of Marx and Sombart. He transcended, however, the Marx-Sombart dilemma in a way consonant with the general scheme of analysis developed in this study. To him, then, it will now turn for more intensive consideration.

Chapter XIV

MAX WEBER I: RELIGION AND MODERN CAPITALISM

A. Protestantism and Capitalism

The peculiar circumstances under which Weber's work on the relations of Protestantism and capitalism has come to the attention of English scholarship have given rise to a widespread but erroneous impression of his intellectual character. His association with what has been widely interpreted as a dramatic and radical thesis in historical interpretation has favored the view that he was the type that takes a simple idea and drives it to extremes, concerned only with bold outlines and showing a sovereign disdain of meticulous detailed factual study. He has often been interpreted as a "philosopher" or "theorist" in the derogatory sense of one who makes the facts fit his theories rather than the reverse.

It is true that Weber could on occasion formulate his views very sharply, particularly where a polemical element was present in the situation. But this by no means exhausts his character. Anyone who attempts to understand his sociological work in its completeness to any degree cannot fail to be impressed, and to a great extent bewildered, by the enormous mass of detailed historical material which Weber commanded. Indeed so vast is this mass, and much of it so highly technical in the various fields from which it is drawn, that an ordinary human being is under very serious difficulties in any sort of critical analysis, since a real factual check on Weber's work as a whole would probably be well beyond the powers of any single living scholar. Weber's was, what is exceedingly rare in the modern age, an encyclopedic mind.[1]

---

[1] While obviously the main interest at present is in Weber's central sociological theory and methodology, which transcends any particular concrete field, in the case of a man who covered such a vast range of factual material, the opinion of his work on the part of specialists in these fields is particularly important. Three opinions, given orally to the author by eminent scholars in different fields, all of whom hold a high opinion of

Without accepting the common adverse evaluation, it may well be held that Durkheim's mind was of the type Weber has often been held to have.[1] The above treatment of his work shows that he was always concerned, on the theoretical plane, with relatively simple bold outlines and clear-cut alternatives. The incisiveness of his thinking in this sense is a rare quality. This is not a criticism, but high praise. Durkheim's was almost the pure type of theoretical mind. This is not, of course, to say that he misused facts or was lacking in empirical insight—the above discussion should disprove any such misconception. But given the starting points of certain empirical problems, his central interest was theoretical. Like most great theorists his subsequent factual interest was mainly intensive rather than extensive, of the order of the crucial experiment.

Weber's was a very different type of mind. Its theoretical component, important as it was, coexisted with an omnivorous appetite for detail and for piling up masses of fact. It is only at certain crucial points that the bold outlines of a theoretical system stand out clearly above the mass of detail—and they must be brought out by following his interest from a clearly defined starting point step by step. That is what will be attempted here. But in doing so, it will be necessary to emphasize the theoretical as distinct from the historical aspect of his work. The element of abstraction, even "construction," in this is the more

---

Weber's competence in the respective fields with which they deal, may be quoted. Professor E. F. Gay, a specialist in Economic History, regards Weber as "one of the few most stimulating and fruitful minds of the past generation in the field of economic history." Professor W. E. Clark, a specialist in Indic Philology, holds Weber's treatment of Hinduism and Buddhism to be "the most satisfactory existing attempt to treat the Indian religio-social system as a whole." Finally, Professor A. D. Nock, whose field is the History of Religions, speaks of Weber's work in that field as "not merely work of great ability, but of genius."

Against these views is to be set the adverse opinion of a number of historians on the capitalism-Protestantism issue. As the present author has already attempted to show (*Journal of Political Economy*, October, 1935) at least one—not atypical—case of this criticism (see H. M. Robertson, *The Rise of Economic Individualism*) is based on a serious misunderstanding of Weber's work.

[1] Durkheim did not disregard facts but was intensively concerned with a small body of crucial facts rather than extensively with a vast body of information.

unavoidable because, like Durkheim's, Weber's work was left unfinished. It is not a rounded system, logically perfected and finished, but a great pioneer work. Therein, as also in the cases of Pareto and Durkheim, lies much of its interest.

The historical aspect of Weber's work is indeed understandable not only from whatever hereditary proclivities he may have had, but also from his intellectual background. His main formal training was in jurisprudence under the aegis of the historical school, particularly Goldschmidt and Mommsen. Probably his original interest in economics was largely dictated by dissatisfaction with the "formalism" of the Neo-Kantian *Rechtsphilosophie*.[1] Preoccupation with the details of legal history opened his eyes to the importance of economic and other nonformal-juridical factors in the development of legal systems. Moreover, his shift from jurisprudence to economics came at the time of the definite ascendancy in Germany of the historical school in the latter discipline, especially the particularistic empiricism of Schmoller. And, at Heidelberg, he succeeded an eminent historical economist, Knies.

Thus his primary background of training and interest lay in the detailed, empirical tradition of German historical thought, a subject discussed in the last chapter. From it doubtless more than any other source he derived his rigorous standards of objectivity in historical research. But, as has been seen, it was difficult to avoid all theory, and the most eminent members of the historical schools had always gone beyond mere observation and recording of detailed fact to the organization of facts under concepts. But in the historical tradition this took place largely in terms of the total system of a given cultural epoch, as for instance in Mommsen's *Römisches Staatsrecht*. Weber's was too actively theoretical a mind to remain indefinitely immersed in detailed historical research for its own sake. His own theorizing started, however, from the basis of the historical tradition, though it was eventually to transcend it.

As has been noted, his early studies in the field of legal history became more and more preoccupied with the "material" factors involved in legal development—material in the Marxian sense.

---

[1] Which may well help to explain the sharpness of his attack on Stammler. *Cf. Gesammelte Aufsätze zur Wissenschaftslehre*, pp. 291 *ff*. Cited below as *Wissenschaftslehre*.

His doctor's thesis already had an economic slant, as the subject, "Trading Companies in the Middle Ages,"[1] shows. Perhaps the culmination of this earlier phase of his work lay in the essay *Agrarverhältnisse im Altertum*[2] which stressed the material factors, but mainly those of military organization rather than the economic in a narrower sense.

Already in this period a strong trend of historical relativity was evidenced in his work, as for instance by his attack on Eduard Meyer's use of "modern" economic categories such as "factory" to describe the economic conditions of the ancient world.[3] But with these general trends the earlier period remained on the whole one of disconnected historical studies with a rather definite materialistic bias. A changed orientation came in rather dramatic fashion with Weber's recovery from the nervous breakdown which forced his retirement from all scientific work for about four years and from university teaching until almost the end of his life. This new orientation[4] resulted in the investigations which will occupy this discussion. It took three main directions: first an empirical concentration on a particular historical-social phenomenon—"modern capitalism"; second a new anti-Marxian interpretation of it and its genesis, which ultimately issued in an analytical sociological theory; and third a methodological basis for the latter which developed parallel with it. All three will be extensively treated. The first of the three, the problem of capitalism, descriptive and explanatory, will be treated in the present chapter and the next, the methodological basis of the studies of capitalism in Chap. XVI and, finally, in Chap. XVII, the broader theoretical system involved in, and emerging out of both.

THE PRINCIPAL CHARACTERISTICS OF CAPITALISM

Under the influence of the historical tradition of thought it was only natural that the systematization of the results of detailed historical studies from various epochs should be directed

---

[1] Reprinted in *Gesammelte Aufsätze zur Sozial und Wirtschaftsgeschichte*.
[2] Originally written for the 3d edition of the *Handwörterbuch der Staatswissenschaften*, but reprinted in the above volume.
[3] *Aufsätze zur Sozial und Wirtschaftsgeschichte*, p. 8.
[4] For the biographical aspect in this as in other connections see **Marianne Weber's** distinguished and charming *Max Weber, Ein Lebensbild*.

in the first instance to the working out descriptively of concrete systems of social structure and relationships. Thus Weber's empirical interest following his earlier economic bent came to be focused on the phenomena of the modern economic order considered as a socioeconomic system.[1] Like Marx and Sombart, he insisted upon its uniqueness in history, that nothing like this system had been seen at any other time or place.

Undoubtedly the main starting point of Weber's descriptive treatment was Marx. Marx's writings and the discussions of capitalism and socialism revolving about them were making a profound impression in Germany in Weber's formative period, but typically enough it was the "historical" Marx and not the Marx who was most closely related to the classical economic theory. In many of the descriptive categories applied to the capitalistic system, Weber concurs with Marx.

Thus he certainly thought of an organized capitalistic enterprise as its basic unit, an enterprise which, whatever the diversity of technological and organizational elements involved, was primarily oriented to the attainment of profit, to the exploitation of opportunities of acquisition in a system of market relationships. To at least a certain degree this fact alone justifies calling the system as a whole "acquisitive" in that the competitive element inherent in a system of market relationships was such as to make profit not only the immediate end but also the measure of success, indeed, in the last analysis, of the ability of an enterprise to survive. Thus *in* the system once established profit had to be an end, in fact the ruling end of action within the system of capitalistic relationships as such no matter what the ultimate individual motive above might be. The system then is not merely acquisitive; it is compulsive and "objective" in much the same sense that it was for both Marx and Sombart.

So much follows from this most general and formal concept of "capitalism" as a system of profit-making enterprises bound together in market relationships. Such enterprises or even systems of enterprises are by no means peculiar to modern Western society. Indeed Weber does not hesitate to speak of "capitalism" as existing at many times and places, and, according to the source of the opportunities for profits, as of many different

---

[1] *Cf.* TALCOTT PARSONS, "Capitalism in Recent German Literature, II, Max Weber," *Journal of Political Economy*, February, 1929.

kinds. In this respect the difference of the modern West from other societies is only a difference of degree, though a highly significant one. It is probably only here that Weber held there had been anything approaching the "capitalistic organization of society as a whole"[1] which is necessary for the compulsory acquisitiveness of the system to emerge in its full consequences. But this by no means exhausts the matter.

In the first place, Weber is careful to distinguish capitalistic "acquisitiveness" in general from that which is merely an expression of greed or psychological instinct of acquisition. The latter is by no means peculiar to modern society or even to societies with a high development of any kind of capitalism. What characterizes capitalistic acquisition is rather its "rationality."[2] It is acquisition, the pursuit of gain in a "continuous, rationally conducted enterprise."[3] This may well involve a high degree of disciplining and tempering of the acquisitive impulse.

But furthermore modern capitalism has certain specific traits which distinguish it clearly from that of other times. As an identifying characteristic Weber definitely excludes the "capitalistic adventurers," men who, however continuous and rational their enterprise, conduct it on an adventurous, speculative basis without ethical restraint. These have existed at all times and places wherever the opportunity has presented itself. What is characteristic of the modern West is rather what Weber calls "rational bourgeois capitalism." In what does this consist?

Weber like Marx started from the conception of an organized productive unit, the enterprise rather than the isolated individual of the early economists. But in his interpretation of the important features of this unit he made an important departure from Marx. In his conception of the role of the wage-earning laborer he agrees with Marx that only modern Western capitalism has "centered on a [formally] free wage-earning class separated from ownership of the means of production."[4] And the existence and situation

---

[1] *Gesammelte Aufsätze zur Religionssoziologie*, Vol. I, p. 4. Cited below as *Religionssoziologie*.

[2] In a specific sense to be worked out in the course of the discussion. Weber is very careful not to oversimplify on this point.

[3] *Religionssoziologie*, Vol. I, p. 4.

[4] *The Protestant Ethic and the Spirit of Capitalism* trans. by Talcott Parsons, p. 21. Cited below as *Protestant Ethic*.

of this class, the proletariat, accounts for the peculiarities of the modern socialist movement, expresses a class conflict unlike those of any other times.[1]

But though there is this agreement the center of interest of the two economists is different. For Marx it lay in the conflict of interest of the two classes as such; for Weber in the specific social type of organization as such.[2] The central feature of rational bourgeois capitalism is the "rational organization of free labor." This is, in turn, an example of a more general, fundamentally important type of social organization which Weber calls in a special sense of the term "bureaucracy."

Bureaucracy, as Weber uses the word, is a rather complicated phenomenon.[3] It involves an organization devoted to what is from the point of view of the participants an impersonal end. It is based on a type of division of labor which involves specialization in terms of clearly differentiated functions, divided according to technical criteria, with a corresponding division of authority hierarchically organized, heading up to a central organ, and specialized technical qualifications on the part of the participants. The role of each participant is conceived as an "office" where he acts by virtue of the authority vested in the office and not of his personal influence. This involves a clear-cut distinction in many different respects between his acts and relationships in his official and his personal capacity. It in general involves separation of office and home, of business funds and property from personal property, above all of authority in official matters from personal influence outside the official sphere.

The office is conceived of as a profession or calling (*Beruf*)[4] which involves a certain impersonal devotion to the tasks of the office imposing obligations on the incumbent. The typical form of remuneration is salary which is looked to not so much as a "reward" or as the equivalent of "sacrifice" as it is a guarantee of a scale of living consonant with the social position of the official

[1] *Ibid.*, p. 23.

[2] This difference of emphasis cannot be due to Weber's general lack of appreciation of the class struggle or more generally of the power factor. The later treatment will show that Weber gave much attention to these phenomena.

[3] See *Wirtschaft und Gesellschaft, Grundriss der Sozialoekonomik*, Vol. III, pp. 650 *ff*. Cited below as *Wirtsch. u. Ges.*

[4] *Ibid.*, p. 651.

according to his rank. Above all bureaucracy involves discipline. A bureaucracy is, Weber says, "a mechanism founded on discipline."[1] It is the fitting of individual actions into a complicated pattern in such a way that the character of each and its relations to the rest can be accurately controlled in the interest of the end to which the whole is devoted. The importance of discipline lies in being able to count on the individual doing the right thing at the right time and place.

Bureaucracy is by far the most efficient known method of organization of large numbers of persons for the performance of complicated tasks of administration, and its spread is to a considerable extent accounted for by this sheer superior efficiency.[2] But at the same time it is dependent on the existence of rather special social conditions,[3] the absence of which may constitute a very serious barrier to its development, no matter how great the objective need.

The occurence of bureaucracy even on a large scale is, of course, by no means confined to modern capitalism. Weber notes[4] six conspicuous historical cases: Egypt of the New Kingdom, the later Roman Empire, the Chinese Empire,[5] the Roman Catholic Church, the modern European state and the modern large-scale capitalistic enterprise. Of these the last two are, technically speaking, distinctly the most highly developed cases, above all, in differentiation of specialized training and in independence of method of remuneration (money salary) of all nonbureaucratic influences.

A conspicuous fact about modern capitalistic bureaucracy is its relative independence of that of the state. The large firm has not had its mode of organization imposed on it from without by the state, nor has it to any conspicuous extent grown up in imitation of state bureaucracy. The latter everywhere owes much to military influences, since the modern army is of a pronounced bureaucratic character as opposed, for instance, to the armies of feudalism. But it is a conspicuous fact that two of the most

---

[1] *Ibid.*, p. 651.
[2] *Ibid.*, pp. 128, 660.
[3] Which cannot be treated in detail here except at one or two points.
[4] *Wirtsch. u. Ges.*, p. 655.
[5] As will be seen below, this case involves certain elements differentiating it very sharply from Western capitalistic bureaucracy. See Chap. XV.

pronouncedly capitalistic countries, including the earliest, England and the United States, are precisely those among all modern great powers in which the armies have had the least influence on social structure, as compared with the principal continental European states. These facts definitely point to capitalistic bureaucracy as essentially an independent growth.

It is, of course, true that a relatively highly developed state structure has existed wherever capitalistic bureaucracy on a large scale has appeared, and appears to be a necessary condition of it, for the latter requires internal peace and order, mobility and other circumstances. But these may be present wherever capitalism develops at all in modern times without any strong bureaucratic component.

A certain amount of division of labor and specialization of function is possible on an "individualistic" basis without highly organized productive units. This was broadly true of the stage of handicraft industry and of the putting-out system. Moreover the sheer objective requirements of efficiency have constituted an important factor in the more stringent organization of the productive unit which has in general meant its approach to bureaucratic forms.

But at the moment the question of the explanation of capitalistic bureaucracy is not at issue. The present concern is, rather, to point out that under the more general category of capitalism, the subtype in which Weber is primarily interested is "rational bourgeois capitalism" and the principal characteristic of the latter is "bureaucratic organization" in the service of pecuniary profit in a system of market relations. It is this, highly developed and quantitatively widespread, which Weber considers to be the principal distinguishing feature of the modern Western economic order. It is the center about which other elements are grouped and from their relation to which they derive their main significance.

This is by no means to say that he denies the existence or even the importance of many other features of this order which are much discussed. Technology is obviously most intimately related to bureaucratic organization since it is responsible for much of the elaborate division of functions. The enterprise is oriented to a market which in the absence of control is competitive; hence the role of the price mechanism is definitely included in Weber's concept of capitalism. The high development of technical means of facilitating exchange such as money, credit, banking, organized speculation, finance is there, though by no means stressed. Finally there is no attempt to deny the importance of class relations. What characterizes Weber's treatment is rather a relative shift of emphasis brought about by bringing into the center of attention phenomena which had previously been left on the periphery and hence considered of relatively little theoretical significance. Roughly, for Weber, bureaucracy plays the part that the class struggle played for Marx and competition for Sombart.

This shift has one most important concrete result: in contradistinction to Marx and most "liberal" theories, it strongly minimizes the differences between capitalism and socialism, emphasizing rather their continuity. Not only would socialistic organization leave the central fact of bureaucracy untouched, it would greatly accentuate its importance. This important difference of perspective is, indeed, closely connected with Weber's attempt to appraise the modern order in terms of a very broad comparative framework.

In concluding this preliminary discussion, it should be pointed out that Weber has thus far been treated only on the descriptive level. The very difference of his descriptive terms from those used by Marshall in talking about free enterprise or even by Marx and Sombart, indicates that description is not simply a matter of "letting the facts speak for themselves." It involves rather an element of selection and emphasis among the facts which amounts to a judgment of their theoretical importance. But nevertheless both capitalism and bureaucracy are for Weber concrete phenomena. To be sure, they are stated in the form of "ideal types," which involves a certain form of abstraction, but even though "ideal" they are none the less concrete within the frame of reference.[1]

The main point to be noted is that there are "bureaucratic" organizations even though they do not fully conform to the type, and that these are typical of capitalism. One misunderstanding must, however, be warned against. The distinction between "rational bourgeois" and "adventurers'" capitalism is not to be taken to apply to economic systems as a whole, but only to elements of such systems. It is not even a distinction of classes of

[1] See Chap. XVI for an extended discussion of the concept "ideal type."

concrete enterprise, but rather of types of action and relationship within the enterprise. A brokerage house, for instance, which is engaged, for its members and its clients, in the wildest speculation on the stock exchange, may well have, on the part of the clerical force who execute the orders, a highly developed rational bureaucratic organization. The "rationality" which is so prominent a feature of bureaucracy to Weber applies mainly to the internal functioning of the enterprise rather than to its market relations, though it may be extended to the latter sphere.

In this descriptive aspect of his treatment of capitalism Weber, allowing for the difference of "accent," is in rather close agreement with Marx. His emphasis on the "compulsive" aspect of the system implies agreement beyond mere description; it involves a thesis concerning the determination of individual action within the system, namely that the course of action is determined in the first instance by the character of the situation in which the individual is placed, in Marxian terminology, by the "conditions of production." This implication Weber recognizes quite explicitly.[1] The system, once fully developed, is self-sustaining by virtue of its compulsive power over individuals. Whether it is going on to self-destruction by virtue of any specific laws of its own development as Marx held, Weber omits to say; on this point he is agnostic.

But here the agreement between them stops. While in a certain sense a "materialistic" view was adequate to the description of the fully developed capitalistic system, it was not, Weber held, adequate to the explanation of its genesis. For this purpose entirely different forces must be invoked. At the opening of the new period of his thinking Weber came quite decisively to the view that an indispensable (though by no means the only) element in the explanation of the system lay in a system of ultimate values and value attitudes, in turn anchored in and in part dependent upon a definite metaphysical system of ideas. This constituted, for the particular case in hand, a direct polemical challenge to the Marxian type of explanation.

The remainder of the present chapter and, more indirectly the next, will be concerned with the attempt to outline Weber's proof of the above thesis. But first it may be useful briefly to indicate the main steps in the process, following the line of logical rather

[1] *Religionssoziologie*, Vol. I, pp. 203–204; *Protestant Ethic*, pp. 54–55, 72.

than temporal continuity, though here the two correspond fairly closely.

Weber nowhere attempts to deny the importance of what Marx called the "material" factors of social change. Hence for his critical purposes it is not necessary to discard them, but only to refute exaggerated claims of their sole adequacy. Scattered throughout his whole work there are critical remarks to this effect on a number of particular points. Yet his main line of proof is not critical but positively inductive. The principal steps may be outlined as follows:

1. Having established his descriptive account of the phenomenon "modern capitalism," he proceeds to point out that there is empirically associated with it a set of values (in Pareto's terms, part of a "state of mind") which may be approached through the study of linguistic expressions. This Weber attempts to formulate systematically, but descriptively, as the "spirit" (*Geist*) of capitalism. This is taken as a set of mental attitudes directed toward economic activities as such.

2. A hint as to deeper connections of these particular attitudes is given by certain statistical facts bearing upon the relation between religious adherence and occupational grouping in parts of Germany, which brought out the tendency of Protestants to outnumber Catholics in the ownership and leadership of capitalistic enterprise, and in the branches of higher education leading to scientific, technical and business careers as compared with the "humanistic" branches. These facts constitute too small a sample to furnish "proof" but furnish rather guiding lines for further inquiry. Weber took them as such; his own further attempt at proof took another course. Subsequent studies of this character have, however, confirmed his views.[1]

3. This is followed up by establishing a close relationship, a "congruence" on the "meaningful" level, between the mental attitudes in question, the spirit of capitalism, and the ethics of the ascetic branches of Protestantism, as well as a relative lack of relationship with Catholic ethics and those of Lutheran Protestantism. This involves demonstrating the "correspondence"

---

[1] See the additional facts, which strongly confirm Weber's position, summarized in the forthcoming study by R. K. Merton, "Science, Technology and Society in Seventeenth Century England," to be published in *Osiris, History of Science Monographs*, Vol. IV.

or mutual congruence of two rather complicated systems of value attitudes. In view of this complexity the number of distinguishable elements in a rather specific relation to each other is so great that, on grounds of probability, sheer chance in effecting congruence is practically excluded and hence a close functional relationship becomes highly probable. This says nothing about causal priority, but the fact of temporal relations strongly indicates a preponderant causal role of the system of religious attitudes, since it existed prior both to any high degree of development of the spirit of capitalism as such and to any high development of the actual socioeconomic organization. Hence on these grounds alone there is a strong case for imputing to the ethical values of Protestantism an important, though not exclusive, causal role.

4. Weber not only establishes this congruence in general terms. He also shows, by analysis of Protestant writings, that there is a gradual process of transition from a religious position which though showing certain important similarities with the spirit of capitalism yet certainly would not have sanctioned it, to one which yielded direct ethical justification of acquisitive activities without limit so long as they were "righteous." Moreover, not only is the process of transition itself traced, but an understandable motivation for it is provided through Weber's analysis of the relation of Protestant theological ideas to the religious interests of believers. So long as there is no direct demonstration of the derivability of these religious attitudes and ideas from "material" factors this yields a further strong presumption in favor of the view that they constitute an important independent element in the process of modern economic development. That is, the actual system of economic activities is of a character which one would expect to develop on the hypothesis that it had been importantly influenced by the Protestant ethic by the process that Weber traces. This is where Weber stops in his essay on *The Protestant Ethic and the Spirit of Capitalism.*

5. But he is not satisfied with this. His inductive study turns from the method of agreement to that of difference. This takes the form of an ambitious series of comparative studies all directed to the question, why did modern rational bourgeois capitalism appear as a dominant phenomenon *only* in the modern West? What are the differentiating factors that account for its failure to appear in other cultures? The comparative study is couched

mainly in terms of the Marxian dichotomy of "material" and "ideal" factors. The general upshot is the thesis that at the relevant stages in the development of cultures the material conditions in China, India, Judea compared favorably, from the point of view of capitalistic-bureaucratic potentialities, with those of our own medieval and early modern times, while in each culture the "economic ethic" of the dominant religious tradition concerned was directly antagonistic to such a development. On the other hand, in Protestantism (to a less extent in Christianity as a whole) the economic ethic was directly favorable. This conclusion confirms the functional relationship between Protestantism and capitalism. Furthermore, on the one hand, it decreases the probability that the spirit of capitalism is merely a reflection of the material conditions, in other words, is a dependent variable and, on the other hand, it increases the probability that a main differentiating element lies on the value plane. This is a perfectly valid scientific method provided, of course, that Weber's allegations of fact are correct. A closer approach to "proof" is probably not attainable in a field of empirical theses of similar dimensions. But closer consideration of the methodological question involved must be postponed to Chap. XVI. The present task is to sketch the main outline of Weber's empirical argument.

THE SPIRIT OF CAPITALISM

What Weber calls the "spirit of capitalism" is a set of attitudes toward the acquisition of money and the activities involved in it. It is, of course, an attitude which strongly endorses such acquisitive activities but not in any and every form; among positive attitudes it is a quite specific one. In the first place, the capitalistic attitude is clearly distinguished from all attitudes toward acquisition as a necessary evil, which is justified because it is an indispensable means to something else. There is a great range of the latter type of attitudes all the way from condemnation of such severity as to leave little room except for the barest necessities, to a relatively complete "worldliness" that, giving free reign to enjoyment and the gratification of the appetites, cannot but approve the necessary means to these ends. This qualified sanction of worldly activities has, of course, been variously motivated, sometimes as in the case of medieval Catholicism by otherworldly religious interests; at other times, in the classical Greek ethics for instance, by a humanistic theory of harmony.

In contrast with all these, the spirit of capitalism looks upon such activities not as a means or a necessary evil, but as an ethically enjoined end in itself. To earn money is an ethical obligation for its own sake.[1]

Secondly, this ethical sanction is not applied to acquisition only within certain quantitative limits, until "enough" has been earned—there is no standard of satiety—but, rather, the pursuit of gain is enjoined without limit. This characteristic sharply marks off the spirit of capitalism from the attitude of "traditionalism" which Weber regards as in certain respects its principal antithesis. He emphatically denies that an endlessly expanding bundle of concrete wants is the normal situation for mankind. The normal situation is rather that rationally acquisitive activities are oriented to a traditionally fixed standard of living. The "economic principle" normally takes the form of satisfaction of these traditional needs with the least possible exertion. For example, the normal reaction to a rise in piece rates is not a desire by harder work to earn more but, rather, by less work to earn the same amount as before.[2] It is only in capitalistic areas that this kind of traditionalism has been to any marked extent broken down. The result is that to this extent acquisition has been freed from any definite limit and becomes an endless process. This attitude toward acquisition is "rationalized," in the form in which Weber is interested in it, by holding it to be an ethical duty for its own sake.

Another way in which the spirit of capitalism forms an antithesis to traditionalism is in its relation to the actual processes of acquisitive activities. Here instead of accepting ways of doing things as handed down, the capitalistic attitude is at every point to reorganize its procedures systematically in terms of the total task. Only the ultimate end, maximization of money, is "sacred"; the particular means are not, but are chosen anew according to the exigencies of each particular situation.[3] This double antithesis to traditionalism gives the spirit of capitalism, so far as it may be assigned causal influence at all, a strongly dynamic character which is highly important for Weber's purposes.

---

[1] Sanctioned beyond this only by transcendental considerations.

[2] See *Protestant Ethic*, pp. 59–60; in general on the concept of the spirit of capitalism, Chap. II therein.

[3] *Cf. Protestant Ethic*, pp. 67–69.

This attitude toward acquisition is correlated with a particular attitude toward labor, whether its immediate end be acquisitive or not. Labor also is not looked upon as a necessary evil, whether because of its traditional origin in the curse of Adam or for any other reason. It is carried out with the same sense of positive ethical obligation, as a field for directly realizing the highest ethical aims of man. The capitalistic attitude toward labor is what Veblen calls the spirit of "workmanship." One of its most conspicuous symptoms is the *ethical* feeling against early retirement from active work. A man who does not "produce" as long as he has health and strength, no matter how well he can afford to retire, is somehow neglecting his ethical responsibilities.

Finally, the "spirit of capitalism," although devoted to unlimited acquisition and emancipation from traditionalism both in goal and in process, still by no means implies emancipation from discipline and control. On the contrary, it gives approval to acquisitive activities only under a very stringent discipline and control. It is here that the line between Weber's spirit of capitalism and the "adventurers'" spirit (the undisciplined impulsive greed of gain) is to be drawn.[1] As against this the spirit of capitalism enjoins systematic, continuous rational honest work in the service of economic acquisition. Such work is necessarily subjected to a strict discipline which is quite incompatible with giving free rein to impulse.

The relation of all this to bureaucracy should be evident. Bureaucratic organization requires a "disinterested" impersonal devotion to a specialized task and a readiness to fit into the rational requirements of a complicated scheme of coordinated specialized activities regardless of tradition. This equally involves a rigid submission to discipline within the limits of the task. The spirit of capitalism is for Weber a special case of the "professional spirit" (*Berufsgeist*) which is the specific attitude required for the efficient functioning of bureaucracy. It is that special case where the impersonal task, to which disinterested ethical devotion is directed, contains the unlimited acquisition of money as a basic component.[2]

[1] *Ibid.*, pp. 56–58, 69.
[2] Directly as for managers of a business, or indirectly as for most of its employees. Typically in the latter case it is not their own financial interest but that of the firm which is decisive.

In all this treatment, Weber's historical approach comes out strongly in his insistence on the uniqueness of the attitudes concerned. While they are so well known to us that we tend to take them for granted as simply "natural," such is by no means the case. In all the essential respects discussed Weber maintains that the capitalistic attitude is highly exceptional. Most ethical teachers, religious and otherwise, have sanctioned acquisition, if at all, only as a means to an end or as a necessary evil, never as an end in itself. The rule in fact as well as in theory has been traditionalism, broken through to a greater or less extent by an amoral, undisciplined greed for gain, the basis of adventurers' capitalism. The theoretical importance of this thesis of historical uniqueness lies in making the origin of the spirit of capitalism itself problematical. If it were the rule at most times and places it might be explained simply as "human nature." To such an interpretation Weber's whole treatment is directly opposed.

Calvinism and the Spirit of Capitalism

Having established a set of descriptive categories by which to distinguish the spirit of capitalism from other related attitudes, Weber is finally faced with the theoretical problem of its origin.[1] He readily admits that a fully developed capitalistic system is to a large degree capable itself of generating these attitudes in the people living in it—through selection and direct influence.

What he doubts is its capability to generate itself out of markedly different conditions without an independent, widely spread mental attitude favorable to capitalism. For this doubt he gives, among others, two general critical grounds: (1) While, given the "conditions," the standards of selection, the theory of selection can account for the particular types of individuals attaining a given position, it cannot account for the origin of the standards themselves.[2] (2) A "form of organization" alone is not enough to create the attitudes concerned. It is possible for a definitely capitalistic form of organization to be administered in a thoroughly traditionalistic spirit.[3] Only when it is combined with a

---

[1] The problem is essentially causal rather than historical. The methodological problem of the relation of the two will be discussed in Chap. XVI.

[2] *Protestant Ethic*, p. 55.

[3] *Ibid.*, p. 63 *ff.*

capitalistic spirit can a completely capitalistic situation be spoken of.[1]

But these critical considerations serve only to open the door to Weber's positive proof that the "spirit" forms a fundamental causal factor in the genesis of the concrete capitalistic order and is not merely a "reflection" of its "material" elements. The first step in this proof is the establishment of the congruence of this set of attitudes with those deriving from a set of ideas which were widespread prior to the large-scale development of rational bourgeois capitalism. This he finds in the religious ethic of what he calls the "ascetic" branches of Protestantism.

The starting point is the consideration of the attitudes toward worldly activities of the various branches of Christian ethics, in particular activities largely oriented to economic acquisition.

Catholic ethics, at least from the Middle Ages on, was by no means completely hostile to the things of this world. Its dualism was by no means so radical as that of the Christianity of antiquity. The society of Christendom was, at least to a relative degree, blest with a religious sanction, was a *res publica christiana*.[2] There are, however, two fundamental reasons why this relative sanction was not a powerful stimulant to the spirit of capitalism. In the first place, the medieval view considered "callings" in relation to their religious value in terms of a hierarchy, the apex of which was the religious life as lived in the monastery. Acquisitive activities, on the other hand, were not far from the bottom of the list of those approved at all, and precisely in proportion as they tended to become capitalistic they were more and more under suspicion. This suspicion tended strongly to press capitalistic activities in the amoral, "adventurous" direction.[3]

Secondly, and largely explaining this suspicious attitude, the whole burden of medieval religious pressure was thrown on the side of traditionalism in relation to worldly callings. The medieval "organic" social ideal thought of society as a hierarchy of classes,

---

[1] Thus for Weber's descriptive concept, at least of *modern* capitalism, the form of organization, with which his general concept starts, is not enough. The total concrete phenomenon includes a given concrete set of attitudes.

[2] *Cf.* especially E. TROELTSCH, *Social Teaching of the Christian Churches*, Vol. I, Chap. III.

[3] As, above all, in the Italian Renaissance.

each in its proper divinely ordained place, each with its function for the whole. The duty of each individual was to live according to his station and to perform his traditional tasks. To such a view any break in tradition was ethically dubious. Moreover, capitalistic activities also ran counter to the strongly personal type of social relations which received the main religious approval. Related to this, in turn, was the universal sanction of charity, an attitude definitely antagonistic to the formal contractual "justice" under which capitalism thrives most.[1]

In one field, however, Catholic ethics achieved something approaching the modern conception of the "calling," namely in the place it gave to labor in the monastic discipline. As distinguished from mortification, contemplation and purely ritual devotions, Western monasticism has always been conspicuous for the role of rational labor as an ascetic exercise, and as such was distinguished from any sort of oriental counterpart. This attitude toward labor, though, of course, not generally devoted to acquisition or, if at all, certainly not for the benefit of the individual monk, was indeed in the line of "bureaucratic" development. But the very fact that it was a phenomenon of monasticism and that the way of life of the monk was so sharply distinguished from that of the laity prevented it from being generalized.

One of the fundamental results of the Reformation was to eliminate the monastery from the sphere of Protestant influence. And with this went an increase in the stringency of ethical discipline expected of the lay Christian in his daily life. The extent of this and its practical implications, however, varied greatly with the different branches of the Protestant movement.

For Weber's purposes the important distinction is that between Lutheranism, on the one hand, and what he refers to as the ascetic branches of Protestantism, on the other. The essential limitation on the capitalistic implications of the Lutheran ethic lies in the fact that it failed to break through the limitations of traditionalism.[2] This was due in the last analysis to the peculiar combination of Luther's basic doctrine of salvation by faith alone, which made any ascetic valuation of worldly activity smack suspiciously

---

[1] Other relevant features of Catholic ethics will be brought out by contrast with those associated with the doctrine of predestination(see below).

[2] *Protestant Ethic*, Chap. III.

of salvation by works, with his version of the conception of Divine Providence which placed a powerful sanction on the established traditional order of things in this world. The general result was the injunction to remain in the calling and station in which you are placed and faithfully to perform the traditional duties appertaining to it.

This is not, of course, to say that the Lutheran doctrine did not contain an important departure from the Catholic position in the general direction of an attitude to worldly activities more favorable to capitalistic bureaucracy. It did so above all by erasing the religiously privileged position of the monk and transferring religious approval to all "legitimate" worldly occupations essentially on an equal footing with each other. This may be considered the common basis of all Protestant attitudes. But the traditionalistic[1] tendency of Lutheran ethics prevented its developing further in a direction more favorable to capitalistic bureaucracy.

Among the ascetic branches Weber rested his theory mainly though not exclusively on Calvinism and for the sake of brevity the present discussion will be confined to it.[2] The discussion of the relation of Calvinism to the spirit of capitalism will throw light upon the Lutheran position and make clear the ethical differences between the two.

It is perhaps well at the outset, however, to state specifically the general relations in which Weber tried to place the three entities, the spirit of capitalism, the concept of "calling" of a given religious movement and the basic religious ideas and attitudes of that movement. The spirit of capitalism has already been outlined. The concept of the calling is one manifestation in a particular context of the typical attitudes associated with a religious movement toward the participation of its adherents in worldly activities. The spirit of capitalism, as Weber formulates it, involves a particular kind of calling attitude toward a certain

---

[1] And also its closely related authoritarianism. It may be argued that this favored a set of attitudes more favorable to *state* bureaucracy than to that of independent capitalistic enterprise. This may well have something to do with the peculiarities of German capitalism and the fact that it developed later than in England.

[2] In this respect the Calvinist position is to be regarded as the extreme polar type, the other ascetic movements are in various respects mitigations of its rigor.

class of such activities, those involving economic acquisition. This is the principal point of articulation for Weber's purposes between the spirit of capitalism and the system of religious ideas in question.

It would, however, be a serious misinterpretation to suppose that Weber's argument for a causal relation between the spirit of capitalism and the ethics of ascetic Protestantism rested on the concept of the calling as such, especially if the latter is taken to mean, in turn, the explicit statements made by adherents of this movement of the desirable attitude toward worldly activities. Such statements form one body of evidence but only one. The concept of the calling Weber sees, in turn, as a manifestation in one direction of a set of attitudes in which the structure of the system of religious ideas in question *taken as a whole* forms a central element. As Weber puts the position in the most general terms:[1] it is "interests" not "ideas" that in conjunction with the conditions of the situation in which they are placed determine immediately the conduct of men. Among these interests are those concerned with the religious status of the individual, in Protestant terms, the "state of grace." The importance of religious ideas lies in the fact that in particular ways they canalize these interests, and hence relevant action in pursuit of them. According to the conception of the universe held, the interests in grace or salvation will be or can be pursued in very different ways. Weber's concern with religious ideas is based on this fact. He is interested in the practical attitudes that large masses of men take toward their everyday activities. These attitudes, so far as religion is concerned, he tries to see in the perspective of the religious ideas with which they are associated. But it is not the mere verbal injunction to certain kinds of conduct, delivered by representatives or leaders of religious bodies, to which these masses of men adhere, on which Weber's argument depends.[2] It is, rather, the structure of the total system of religious ideas *in its relation* to men's religious interests. Both the injunctions of religious leaders and the practical attitudes of the masses are to be understood in relation

---

[1] *Religionssoziologie*, Vol. I, pp. 252–253.

[2] A conspicuous example of this misinterpretation is the book of H. M. Robertson, *The Rise of Economic Individualism*. See the critical note, TALCOTT PARSONS, "H. M. Robertson on Max Weber and His School," *Journal of Political Economy*, October, 1935.

to this system. It is by no means necessary for Weber's purposes to assume it is the personal or institutional authority of these leaders as such which is the decisive factor.[1] These considerations have unfortunately often been neglected in discussing Weber's work.

Furthermore, with this is closely associated another highly important point. Weber's interest is by no means confined to the *logical* consequences of the initial system of religious ideas, or to the directly expressed wishes of religious leaders for practical conduct based on them. He is, rather, concerned with the *total consequences* of the religious system. This involves two important points: First, the relevant consequences are, as he puts it, "psychological" rather than purely logical. The logical consequences operate, but not alone; they must be taken in conjunction with the constellation of interests involved, which may, as between two equally possible logical alternatives, bias action in the direction of one, or even inhibit the development of the full logical consequences in certain other directions.

Secondly, the influence of a system of religious ideas on practical attitudes is to be regarded as a real process in time, not a static logical deduction. In the course of it the system of ideas itself may also undergo change. In fact, as will be pointed out, the Protestant attitude toward economic acquisition underwent a steady process of change, and it was only in the later stages that the full consequences relevant in the present context emerged. Above all Weber insists that the original Reformers themselves were by no means filled with the spirit of capitalism.[2] Their concern was solely religious and they would have sharply repudiated the attitudes taken by their successors. But this does not in the least disprove that these later attitudes were in an important degree the consequence of the religious ideas put forward by the Reformers.

With these general considerations in mind the discussion may now proceed to the specific Calvinistic[3] system of ideas and its

[1] He explicitly states he is not mainly concerned with *church* discipline but with the *direct* religious motivation of the individual (see *Protestant Ethic*, p. 97).

[2] *Protestant Ethic*, p. 91.

[3] Weber defines "ascetic" Protestantism as including (1) Calvinism, (2) Pietism, (3) the sects growing out of the Baptist movement, (4) Methodism. For lack of space the present discussion is confined to Calvinism.

relation to economic activities. For present purposes the Calvinistic theology may be said to consist of a body of five logically independent yet empirically interdependent propositions. They are independent in that they do not directly imply one another; any one of them could be fitted into other theological systems. But they are logically compatible with each other, mutually limiting the inferences which can be drawn from any one while the others are adhered to, and taken together they cover all the main metaphysical problems of a theology; they constitute a meaningful system.

The propositions are, schematically, as follows: (1) There is a single, absolutely transcendental God, creator and governor of the world, whose attributes and grounds of action are, apart from Revelation, completely beyond the reach of finite human understanding. (2) This God has predestined all human souls, for reasons totally beyond possible human comprehension, either to eternal salvation or to "eternal sin and death." This decree stands from and for eternity and human will or faith can have no influence on it. (3) God for His own inscrutable reasons has created the world and placed man in it solely for the increase of His glory. (4) To this end He has decreed that man, regardless of whether predestined to salvation or damnation, shall labor to establish the Kingdom of God on Earth, and shall be subject to His revealed law in doing so. (5) The things of this world, human nature and the flesh, are, left to themselves, irreparably lost in "sin and death" from which there is no escape except by divine grace.

All these elements play a prominent part elsewhere in Christian thought and history; only their specific combination and the rigorous consistency in drawing their theological consequences are specifically Calvinistic. This system of theology yields one of the few logically consistent solutions of the problem of evil in history,[1] by declaring it beyond the reach of finite human intelligence, hence relegated to the inscrutable will of God. Logically the elements need not be thus combined. A transcendental God might conceivably have made grace dependent on good works rather than deciding it by predestination; he could let sinners go their own way to perdition on this earth rather than subjecting them to His law. He could have created the world for man's happiness rather than His glory.

[1] *Religionssoziologie*, Vol. I, pp. 246–247.

But given this system what are its implications for practical conduct?

In the first place, the complete transcendence of God and the hiatus between fleshly and divine things exclude the mystical attitude of union with the divine spirit, absorption in it. This fact is, in turn, reinforced by the conception of submission to the *law*[1] for the glory of God, and the corresponding interpretation of predestination in relation to the things of this world as assigning to the elect the task of building and maintaining the Kingdom of God on Earth in accordance with divine will. God's main relation to man becomes that of will, and man is above all an instrument, obedient or recalcitrant as the case may be, of the divine will. The net effect in Weber's view is to direct religious energies in the active, ascetic rather than the passive, mystical direction.[2] God cannot be approached at all; He can only be served. And, on account of the fundamental dualism, this service cannot be in the direction of indulgence in the things of the flesh, or of adaptation to it; it must lie in that of *control* over the flesh, in its subjection to a discipline for the glory of God. This is what Weber means by asceticism.

One further consequence of the transcendence of God and the resultant dualism is highly important. Since the finite world is a creation of God and a manifestation of His will, the best way to know Him is to study His works. Just as He wishes to submit man to a law, so in a different but related sense is order the key-note of His nonhuman works. His decisions stand for eternity; He does not continually alter them and interfere with the order of nature. At the same time nature is nature and God is God. Hence sanctification of natural things is idolatry.

This belief in divine order has two corollaries—a faith in the order of nature, which is undoubtedly a highly important motive in the development of modern science,[3] and a strong hostility to ritual as involving superstition and idolatry. God is too completely transcendent to be adequately embodied in concrete

---

[1] Of course the revealed divine law, not that of earthly authorities. The two may on occasion be held to be in acute conflict with each other.

[2] See below Chap. XV, pp. 570 *ff.*, for a discussion of the more general bearings of this distinction, which is fundamental to Weber's sociology of religion.

[3] See the study of R. K. Merton, cited above, p. 511.

sacred things or acts. Only in the specific ways revealed by Him does He intervene in the order of this world—primarily through the action of His predestined saints. Thus ascetic activity in the service of God's will is diverted away from ritual channels of expression into active control over the intrinsic relations of the world.

Thus the believing Calvinist would tend to regard himself as an instrument of God's will called to act in accordance with it in the great task of increasing the glory of God by living according to His law and helping to establish the Kingdom of God on Earth. This action could not, moreover, consist primarily in ritual observances but rather in ethical control over the world in the service of an ideal. Thus already there was a general orientation in the direction of practical worldly activity. This was, of course, reinforced by the general Protestant repudiation of monasticism with its consequent subjection of all to the same law and the same ethical standards, and the necessity of doing the will of God in the ordinary occupations of everyday life, not withdrawn from them in the monastery.[1] Moreover the strict construction of the doctrine of predestination was that election was to be recognized by no external signs whatever. Hence conviction of damnation was no ground for failure to live up to the highest standards, since one did not know his fate, and furthermore God's will demanded the subjection of all alike to His law.

This problem of knowing one's state of grace brings out the more specific consequences of predestination for conduct. The authentic Calvinistic position was, as just noted, that election could not be recognized by external signs. But even more important was the implication of the tenet that the acts of the individual could have no influence on his state of grace since the latter had already been determined from eternity. Then precisely in so far as the whole religious question was taken seriously, as the *interest* in salvation was strong, the individual was placed in a terrific position. His acts could not influence his eternal fate; hence the whole pressure of his religious interest was to *know* whether he was saved or damned.

---

[1] What Weber calls worldly asceticism (*innerweltliche Askese*) as distinguished from the otherworldly asceticism of the monastery (*ausserweltliche*). "Otherworldly" here does not imply so much orientation to the "hereafter" as refusal to participate in the ordinary daily life of the average, not especially religious person.

It is here that for Weber the "psychological" as distinct from the purely logical consequences appear. Given a serious interest, he holds the pressure was too great for the mass of men. Under this pressure it was the first doctrine which gradually gave way. It gradually came to be held[1] that good works, while they could not influence salvation, could be interpreted as *signs* of grace. A good tree could not bear evil fruit. Then gradually the elect came to be identified with the "righteous," those who did the will of God, and the damned with "sinners," those who failed to obey His will.

Before following this line of development further, however, certain other fundamental consequences of the doctrine of predestination in its Calvinistic context should be noted. As has been stated elsewhere,[2] a certain "individualistic" character has been fundamental to Christianity from the beginning and this was greatly strengthened by the Reformation. Calvinism represents the extreme of the development of this individualistic element in one particular direction.

For, in the first place, its extreme antiritualism cut off the individual far more drastically than Luther ever did from the protecting, guiding hand of church and priest, which was felt especially in the confessional. According to predestination there was no help for him; no earthly agency whatever could have any influence on the state of his soul. But at the same time the *one* fundamentally important interest to him, deprived of this comforting intermediary, was his eternal fate and the one important relation, that to his God. But this relationship to his God in the "secret places of his heart" had to be separated from relationships to any human being. Moreover, in this situation other human beings were not merely useless to him, they might be positively dangerous, since however virtuous his outward conduct, any other human being, even the closest relative or friend, might be one of the damned. The net result was, as Weber puts it, an unheard-of "inner isolation of the individual,"[3] which placed him squarely on his own responsibility in all things, and involved a radical devaluation, not to say mistrust, of even the closest human ties. God always came first.

[1] From Beza on.
[2] Chap. II.
[3] *Protestant Ethic*, p. 108.

Secondly, this inner isolation in combination with the other aspects of the doctrine of predestination, had an extremely important implication for the rationalization of conduct. Conduct acceptable to God had to be in direct obedience to His will, and could not be the result of any human motivation or interest. But since individual good works could not affect grace, and outward conduct could at most be a sign of grace, the conduct enjoined could be judged only as a *total coherent system*, as the expression of the *kind of man* one was, not as a plurality of disconnected acts. The Catholic could receive absolution for particular sins, and receive credit for particular good deeds. For the Calvinist there was possible no such release from pressure, and hence there was an incomparably greater drive to the rational systematization of conduct.

The following are a few of the more specific practical implications of these convictions: The inner isolation, the suspicion of all things merely human and worldly, the abhorrence of "idolatry"[1] turned the energy of the Calvinist into the service of impersonal ends. They also made him share the general ascetic suspicion of the rich and mighty of this world, and even sometimes made the Calvinistic movement dangerous to established authority when the latter involved a personal homage which suggested idolatry. At least the strong tendency was to "mind his own business" and to hold aloof from the struggle for worldly power, except when it was a matter of fighting God's battles directly—as in the case of Cromwell's army.

The Calvinist turned rather to pursuits where he could labor, soberly and rationally, in a calling acceptable to God. Independent, solid, honest business was a particularly suitable field.

One cannot say that the Calvinistic ethic or any of its legitimate derivatives ever approved money-making for its own sake or as a means to self-indulgence, which was, indeed, one of the cardinal sins. What it did approve was rational, systematic labor in a useful calling which could be interpreted as acceptable to God. Money was, certainly in the beginning, regarded as a by-product and one by no means without its dangers.[2] The attitude was, that is, an ascetic one. But even this served capitalistic

---

[1] A fundamental Puritan concept.

[2] See the many examples Weber brings forward in *Protestant Ethic*, Chap. V, especially the quotation from John Wesley, p. 175.

interests since, on the one hand, work in economic callings would serve to increase earnings but, on the other, the fear of self-indulgence would prevent their full expenditure for consumption. It was, as Weber says,[1] a case of "ascetic compulsion to save." Acquisition was not only promoted, but was "freed from the bonds of traditionalistic ethics."[2] After all, traditions themselves were only human; to respect them where they stood in the way of the work of God was idolatry.

Moreover, it is clear that the changed attitude to labor noted in connection with the spirit of capitalism here receives an adequate motivation. No longer is the necessity to labor the curse of Adam, a punishment for original sin. Nor is it merely an ascetic technique in the sense of a means of combating the temptations of the flesh. All these are negative motivations. The Puritan ethic added a positive one of basic importance. Labor in a calling, with no other earthly aim than "doing a good job" according to the intrinsic requirements of the situation, was a positive command of God, the first duty of one who was eager to do His will. It was a God-given opportunity to take part in the great task for which God has placed man in this vale of tears, the building of the Kingdom of God on Earth. For the true believer such work was not an unpleasant necessity to which he must grudgingly submit. It was the highest fulfillment of his own deep religious interests.

However, the more extreme asceticism of the position was gradually weakened by the results of the "psychological" process noted above. From the admission that righteous conduct was a legitimate sign of grace (since a good tree would not bear evil fruit) it was not a very long step to the view that success in a worldly calling could be regarded also as a sign of grace so long as it was righteous success and not attained by means at variance with the law. For would not God bless His chosen ones in this world as well as the next?[3] In its economic context this doctrine could supply an excellent justification for the successful man,

---

[1] *Protestant Ethic*, p. 172.

[2] *Ibid.*, p. 171.

[3] At approximately this point it may be said that there enters in an element of "secularization" which is a different thing from the direct religious influence. See below, Chap. XVII, p. 685, for a brief discussion of the place of this element in Weber's thought.

giving him a good conscience about his gain and being one important source of a kind of conspicuous self-righteousness on the part of circles with a Puritan background.

Finally the doctrine of predestination performed another signal service to the consciences of successful businessmen. They did not need to worry too much about the lot of the unfortunate in this world, since it might well be interpreted as a sign of God's displeasure with their conduct, especially if the misfortunes of the unfortunate could in any way be attributed to idleness[1] and failure to work. Puritanism had no place for the easy Catholic attitude toward charity. It organized what charity it allowed to remain as a severe discipline on a rational basis.

There can be no doubt that in his treatment of the ethics of ascetic Protestantism Weber has in general succeeded in his task of finding a system of ultimate-value ideas "adequate" to the spirit of capitalism as he himself formulated the latter conception. All its leading traits find their counterpart in the Protestant attitude properly interpreted. Above all the "irrational" element in which the peculiar capitalistic "rationalism" is centered,[2] so incomprehensible from any hedonistic point of view, has found a meaning. What other explanation of it has accomplished this fundamental thing?[3]

The effect of the juxtaposition of the two attitude systems is to bring into even sharper relief than in his original formulation the "ascetic" aspect of capitalism in Weber's theory. It is, indeed, very largely on the empirical significance of this element as a fact that the importance of Weber's theory rests. Some critics go so far as to hold in effect[4] that it is entirely an invention of Weber's. This view is not justifiable, but naturally it cannot be disproved without an elaborate argument. Attention may, however, be called to the fact that Weber is by no means alone among recent writers in noting the *concrete* importance of this element, however much they may differ from him in their explanation of it.

---

[1] "Sloth" is a very common Puritan term.

[2] *Protestant Ethic*, pp. 76–78.

[3] For a general theoredical discussion of the status of this explanation and the role of religious ideas in it see the note appended to this chapter.

[4] Thus H. M. ROBERTSON, *op. cit.*

It has already been pointed out[1] that Marshall's emphasis on "activities" has very similar connotations. There is no other explanation of the prominence of the concept in Marshall's work than his conviction that an ethical element radically distinct from hedonistic want satisfaction is essential to free enterprise. Durkheim also, though in a somewhat different connection, thought ethical discipline essential to the working of an individualistic economic order. Besides these, two others may be mentioned. Professor Carver[2] lays great stress on the importance of what he calls the "workbench philosophy," the devotion to work for its own sake, including "business." To him pure "economic individualism" in Dr. Robertson's sense certainly implies the "pig-trough philosophy" which he so sharply combats. Finally, in Veblen, who, on the one hand, strongly depreciated hedonism and, on the other, elevated to a position of central importance what he called the "instinct of workmanship,"[3] there is at least an implied recognition of the same fundamental facts. In his emphasis on the importance of "technology" evidently there lies more than the "technological element" of the previous analysis.[4] It involves also a specific attitude toward the task, an attitude of "workmanship," to use his term. Is not that regarding the task as a "calling" in Weber's sense? These four cases seem to be the more significant because they come from very different intellectual backgrounds and have no direct relation to one another nor to Weber. Is such an agreement simply fortuitous?

The establishment of "congruence" between the Protestant ethic and the spirit of capitalism does not, however, in itself constitute proof that the religious system is an important factor in the genesis of the capitalistic attitude and through it of concrete rational bourgeois capitalism. Nor does it demonstrate the quantitative order of this importance. This is the more true, in view of the fact that Weber himself not merely grants, but emphasizes the importance of, other quite distinct factors,

[1] Chap. IV.

[2] T. N. CARVER, especially in *The Religion Worth Having*.

[3] *Cf.* T. VEBLEN, *The Instinct of Workmanship*, and Talcott Parsons, "Sociological Elements in Economic Thought, I, Historical," *Quarterly Journal of Economics*, May, 1935.

[4] Chap. VI, above.

for instance, modern science, a rationalized legal system, rational bureaucratic administration in the state. None of these factors were, he holds, primarily creations of ascetic Protestantism though they may have been helped by it.

There are a number of ways in which Weber attempted to prove the causal relation of Protestantism and capitalism. After very briefly reviewing the rest, however, the main attention will be devoted to one, by means of the *comparative* sociology of religion, both because it is methodologically the most important and because, in spite of the fact that Weber himself laid by far the greatest stress on it, it has been almost completely overlooked in the English discussion of Weber's theory.[1]

First, as has been noted, there is a small amount of statistical evidence available concerning the correlation between religious affiliation and position in the social structure. This on the whole confirms Weber's hypothesis. What he used, however, was not derived from his own researches,[2] and his own work did not take this direction. He used this material more as a pointer to the significant problems than as proof. Secondly, the temporal relations of the Protestant ethic, on the one hand, and the spirit of capitalism, on the other, are such as strongly to suggest a causal relationship. That is, the Protestant ethic on the whole mainly preceded the spirit of capitalism in the same areas and social classes. Indeed in so far as the causal factors are on the "ideal"

---

[1] In part no doubt because the material has not been translated into English, but mostly for deeper reasons, because most of the participants in the controversy have not clearly seen the nature of Weber's problems. In general, more space and care have been devoted to Weber's theory of capitalism than to the empirical theories of the other writers treated in this study, because it has been the object of sharp controversy, involving very serious misunderstanding of Weber's work. It is necessary to set all this right in order not to obscure the theoretical and methodological significance of Weber's work, which will occupy Chaps. XVI and XVII. In general, it is only fair to evaluate Weber's treatment of the relations of Protestantism and capitalism in the light of his sociological work as a whole, including both the comparative sociology of religion and his general theory and methodology. Similarly, the reader should evaluate the attitude of this study toward Weber's theory in terms of its relation to the total methodological and theoretical framework of the study as a whole, and not *alone* in terms of *ad hoc* factual considerations.

[2] The study which he used most is M. Offenbacher, *Konfession und soziale Schichtung*, Tübingen, 1901. It was suggested by himself.

side this conclusion seems inevitable. But a materialistic case can be made against it on the ground that they might both be creations of the same set of material conditions at different stages of their development. It is also possible, though extremely improbable, that the congruence was purely fortuitous.

But in the most important of these three methods of proof, Weber goes beyond demonstrating the congruence of the two sets of attitudes. He builds an empirical bridge between them by tracing in the writings of Puritan leaders the internal development of the Protestant ethic itself. In the beginning the Protestant ethic was so exclusively interested in religious problems as to be strikingly otherworldly. In Calvin's own Geneva the result was a highly theocratic state of an almost socialistic type, characterized by an extremely stringent church discipline. From this point, partly no doubt under the influence of material conditions—Calvinists in a minority, for instance—the development was in a more and more individualistic direction. Instead of an immediate authoritarian, if necessary forcible,[1] introduction of the Kingdom of God on Earth, the emphasis was more and more on the duty of the individual to do God's will in his calling.

Moreover the tendency was increasingly to a direct approval of acquisitive activities under the proper conditions. Then action in a business calling, so long as it was sober, honest, rational, "useful" work, came to be looked upon as one of the most righteous things a man could do, and its fruits, "honestly" acquired riches, as the direct sign of God's blessing.

Weber not merely traces this evolution, but maintains (indeed, demonstrates) that it is not solely a process of "accommodation" to the necessities of a world recalcitrant to religious control. On the contrary, a major factor is a genuine "dynamic" of the Protestant ethic itself, the result of following *religious* interests in the situation in which the men of that time were placed. This is brought out above all by two circumstances. Devotion to a capitalistic calling was enjoined for *positive religious motives.*[2]

---

[1] As Cromwell attempted to carry out.

[2] This is so important it may be pointed out again. It is *not* Weber's thesis that Protestantism influenced capitalism through religious *approval* of acquisitive activities, expressed by preachers or otherwise, but because the religious *interests* of the believing individual directed his action in that direction. The distinction is highly important, both empirically and method-

The attitude was not permissive. Second, the later Puritan doctrine was not one of approval of any and every form of acquisitive activity under any conditions, but only under a very strict discipline. The original ascetic element, the main element for Weber, had by no means disappeared but remained intact in the somewhat altered context. This result no ethic of accommodation could have achieved.[1]

The articulation between the two was thus fully established. The development did not, however, stop here but proceeded still farther on the path of secularization.

In the line of development with which Weber is concerned this is not altogether a matter of relaxation of discipline, of concession to "moral laxity,"[2] but of gradual dropping out of the religious background of the attitudes concerned and in place of the religious substituting a utilitarian[3] motivation. It is only here that the "pure" spirit of capitalism, as Weber illustrated it from the writings of Benjamin Franklin[4] is to be found. But even here the central ethical element, the ascetic devotion to impersonal tasks for their own sake, is intact.

The gist of Weber's *causal* argument here may be put as follows: The empirical material (the writings of Protestant leaders down through the seventeenth century) shows a process of development toward the stronger and stronger sanction of individualistic acquisitive activities. Is this accommodation or is it an independent development of the religious ethic for *religious* reasons? Weber argues for the importance of the latter element on the ground that such a development is meaningful within the framework of the system of religious ideas; it is not

---

ologically. The two have generally been confused by Weber's critics. Dr. H. M. Robertson (*op cit.*) is an excellent example.

[1] This is not to say either (a) that no attitude of disinterested devotion to a calling is conceivable apart from the influence of the Protestant ethic or (b) that accommodation had played no part in the development of the spirit of capitalism. But Weber seems to have shown, with a high degree of probability (1) that the Protestant ethic played an important part in the development of *this* particular set of disinterested attitudes and (2) that they *could not* have been *exclusively* the products of "capalistic interests." That they were, is Robertson's central thesis.

[2] Though this no doubt also happened. See Chap. XVII.

[3] Not necessarily in the technical sense of the above discussion. See pp. 51 *ff.*

[4] *Protestant Ethic*, pp. 48–50.

only possible in the sense of not conflicting with essential elements of it, but it is in accord with strong religious motives inherent in the system of religious ideas itself in relation to the world. Furthermore the element of concrete capitalism in which Weber is interested is not at odds with this later ethic; it may on the contrary to a large extent be interpreted as the direct expression of these motives in practical conduct.[1]

But this, as Weber himself clearly states,[2] is "only one side of the causal chain." His book on the *Protestant Ethic and the Spirit of Capitalism* was expressly concerned only with this side. In spite of many scattered suggestions which, if all brought together, would form quite a respectable theory, Weber does not there, nor anywhere else in his work, attempt any systematic analysis of the other side with respect to this specific empirical subject matter. This would have to be done to exhaust the possibilities of empirical proof. But, instead, he turns to another line of investigation. He turns from the "method of agreement" to the "method of difference," to use Mill's term. Instead of continuing to ask directly what specific forces account for the appearance of rational bourgeois capitalism in the modern West, he asks inversely, why did anything like it *fail* to appear in any of the other great civilizations of the world?

NOTE ON THE ROLE OF IDEAS

At a number of points in the preceding chapter and below there is raised the general theoretical question of the role of ideas with particular reference to whether Weber's treatment is vitiated by any bias in the direction of rationalism. It is therefore well to insert at this point a general statement of the problem as it appears up to this point in the study, in particular attempting to relate Weber's approach to it to the previous discussion of Pareto.[3]

Weber's attention is focused on religious ideas in their relation to the motivation of action in what is ordinarily thought of as the secular sphere. The starting point of the analysis is the allegation of fact that, in the groups

[1] That is, in more general terms, there is a high degree of correspondence between the kind of socioeconomic organization that would be expected on the hypothesis that the development of the system had been importantly influenced by the Protestant ethic and the actual state of affairs. This certainly puts the burden of proof on the one who would radically deny its influence.

[2] *Protestant Ethic*, p. 23.

[3] Chap. VII, pp. 269 *ff*.

under consideration, the adherents of the Calvinist movement in the sixteenth and seventeenth centuries, there was, generally, a strong religious interest in salvation. Assuming, then, that these Calvinists were to an appreciable extent motivated by their interest in salvation, that they may be thought of as trying to attain it or to make certain of it, the question arises as to what bearing this fact will have on their actions in the secular sphere, particularly the economic. The comparison of the three religious groups, the Catholic, Lutheran and Calvinistic, shows that the interest in salvation, which may be attributed to all three groups, does not suffice to account for the differences in the direction of secular activities in which Weber has become interested. It is, rather, necessary to take into account other elements in the religious context. Weber sets about doing this by asking the question, what kind of action can, to the adherent of such a movement, be appropriate as a means of attaining or proving salvation? This depends upon the "situation" in which the believer is placed, and in particular on certain features of this situation, namely the structure of religious ideas in relation to which the interest in salvation is carried out in action. For the Catholic whose interest in salvation is strongest the indicated course is to renounce the world and enter a monastery. For the one whose interest is less intense, it is to be faithful to tradition in the station in life in which he is placed, and to lay up merit for himself by an accumulation of discrete good works, particularly of ritual devotion and charity. For the Lutheran the monastery is excluded; for him the line of action is faithful performance of the traditional duties of his station in life and obedience to the duly constituted authorities. The Christian is held to be placed in a world of sin which he cannot, in general, hope to reform. Sin, which is inevitable, is to be expiated by sincere penitence and the pious resolve to do better next time. The Calvinist, finally, is exhorted to labor in a calling, soberly and rationally, in order to bring about the Kingdom of God on Earth. He is neither to renounce the world and retire to a monastery nor to accept the traditional order, but, so far as it falls within his calling, to attempt to make over the world according to the dictates of righteousness.

These differences of attitude are also matters of fact. Weber contends that he has demonstrated that they are, respectively, the typical attitudes toward secular activity, particularly economic, of members of the three religious groups. Weber then proceeds, sketchily for the Catholic and Lutheran religions, in detail for the Calvinistic, to show that, given the initial interest in salvation, each of these attitudes becomes meaningful on the hypothesis that the actor to whom it is attributed is a believer in the system of religious ideas associated with the attitude. Thus according to the Calvinistic position: Good works cannot be a means of attaining salvation, but only a sign of election; predestination precludes the former. Meritorious conduct, furthermore, cannot consist mainly in ritual devotions since these would involve the sanctification of worldly things, in other words, idolatry. Tradition cannot be sacred since that also would be idolatry. Mysticism is excluded by the absolute transcendentality of God. Finally, the sinfulness of the flesh excludes a hedonistic attitude. Activity in the world should be directed toward rational mastery of the flesh in the interest of the glory of God, not use of the things of this world for self-indulgence and hedonistic gratification. The Calvinist works *in* the world, but neither *of* nor *for* the world.

Finally Weber's analysis not only establishes the meaningfulness of the attitude which he describes as worldly asceticism in terms of the Calvinistic theology, but he also demonstrates the congruence of this attitude with that of the spirit of capitalism with relatively minor alterations. The conspicuous thing about the spirit of capitalism is that it is a set of attitudes not clearly related to a developed system of religious or metaphysical ideas. The transition between these Weber has traced genetically, showing the existence of many connecting links.

But for the moment the genetic aspect of the question may be left aside. Granting his statements of fact are correct, it can be definitely held that Weber has demonstrated that there is a mutual relation on the meaningful level between (1) the particular form that the interest in salvation took predominantly among Calvinists, (2) the system of religious ideas summed up above as the Calvinistic theology and (3) the ascetic element in the system of attitudes which he described as the spirit of capitalism. Apart from genetic considerations what light, if any, does his analysis throw on their causal relations?

At this point it may be illuminating to try to state the relation of this problem to Pareto's conceptual scheme. Weber, being unacquainted with Pareto's work, did not carry through formally any residue-derivation analysis of his material. He is, however, interested in trying to understand what certain people do by analyzing what they say, and since their "theories" are largely nonscientific it seems an excellent case to which to apply the Paretian analysis.

It should be remembered that the residue is an operational concept. A residue is that which is arrived at by following the particular procedure that has been described in Chap. V. It is a relatively constant element of the linguistic expressions associated with action so far as they have no place in a scientific theory. In these terms if the linguistic expressions of Calvinists so far as they bear upon secular activities are analyzed they will yield not one, but several residues. One will be the residue of salvation, the manifestation of the "sentiment that men should act in such a way as to further the attainment and ascertainment of the state of grace." Associated with this among Calvinists, to form a "complex," will be certain other residues, namely the five major premises of Calvinistic theology discussed above. Since these are metaphysical propositions, not statements of empirical fact, they are nonlogical and may in the present context be treated as residues.

Now the Paretian operation as such contains no specific theorem relative to the role of ideas in general. It contains only the negative theorem that in so far as the residues constitute an important independent variable in a social system, changes in that system cannot be held to be determined by scientifically verifiable theories alone. But it has been shown above[1] that a residue, which is a verbal proposition, may vary all the way from a logically precise statement of a meaning which may stand in the same causal relation

[1] *Supra*, p. 212 *ff.*

MAX WEBER I: RELIGION AND MODERN CAPITALISM

to action as a scientifically verifiable theory to the case at the opposite pole, where it is an index of other forces, and its reciprocal influence on them is as negligible as is that of a thermometer, generally, on the system the temperature of which it indicates. The fact, then, that by the Paretian operation it is possible to arrive at the principal elements of Weber's analysis of Calvinism as residues proves nothing as to whether or how far the religious ideas are causal factors or merely "manifestations" of something else. That remains a question to be answered by further analysis of the particular facts.

It is, however, possible to extend the Paretian analysis in a manner which at first sight would seem to throw doubt on Weber's thesis of the causal role of the religious ideas. That is, it is possible to include the verbal expressions not only of Calvinists, but of those that fit Weber's description of the spirit of capitalism, in terms which do not involve any explicit religious motivation. Then some, at least, of the residues of the previous phase of the analysis, those with a specifically "religious" content, turn out, for the material being considered, to be less fundamental than others—those involved in the worldly ascetic attitude. That is, they become, in the wider context, derivations. Their place from the time of Benjamin Franklin on tends to be taken by other secular derivations, like that of the usefulness to social survival of the "workbench philosophy," or of the value of "activities" and the like. It must be remembered that the distinction between residues and derivations is a relative one and that what is in a narrower context a residue may in a broader become a derivation. This is, indeed, quite sufficient to disprove a naive "emanationist" view of the mechanisms of the influence of nonscientific ideas. The residues of worldly asceticism are clearly not simply "tied" to the Calvinistic theology in such a way that given the one the other can be inferred without further investigation. This, however, in no way disproves a significant functional relation between them. But to get farther with the problem it is necessary to bring still further considerations into the discussion. In Weber's work there are two different lines of analysis which serve to carry the argument beyond this point.

The one which fits most closely into the Paretian analysis will be discussed in some detail in the next chapter. This will broaden the comparative basis of the analysis still farther. On the basis of his comparative study of religions Weber comes to the broad conclusion that certain types of religious ideas are associated with certain types of attitudes toward secular activities. The most pronounced development of worldly asceticism is to be found in the culture which has or has had, a system of religious ideas emphasizing the transcendentality of God, the sinfulness of the flesh, etc. The farther attitudes depart from this type in the direction of either indifference to the things of this world or uncritical acceptance of tradition, the more they are associated with such religious ideas as the immanence of God, and the absence of a radical dualism of divine and worldly. Attitude and idea are, then, in all probability in close functional relation with each other, though perhaps also they may both be manifestations of sentiments lying still deeper. But this line of argument could injure Weber's position only by proving that it had not carried analysis so far as it could be carried, not by demonstrating positive error in Weber's work so far as it has gone.

The other line of analysis is one with which Pareto himself did not deal. It is that of introducing genetic considerations into analysis of the particular case. In genetic terms it may be possible to demonstrate causal connections which, in the then state of general theory could not be demonstrated in terms of such a general analytical framework as Pareto's.

The main points to be kept in mind are the following: The Calvinist theology, with its related ethical attitudes, existed in Western Europe prior to an extensive development of rational bourgeois capitalism. The theological ideas in question give, from the actor's point of view, an adequate meaning to these attitudes, and to the actions of which they constitute the residues. Not only is this the case, but Weber has traced historically, and made motivationally understandable, a process in the course of which, though certain central ascetic residues have remained essentially unchanged, they have moved in their direct relations to action steadily farther in the direction of closer congruence with the spirit of capitalism. Furthermore, he has traced a process of secularization by which the religious elements have gradually lost their importance, and he has made the probable motives for this understandable. The result of this genetic analysis is greatly to strengthen the probability that the system of religious ideas has had an important influence.

Finally there is a set of very general considerations which will be discussed in the following chapter and in Chap. XVII. Though for certain proximate purposes the attitude manifested in a residue may be taken as an explanatory factor, it is always possible to attempt to push beyond this to inquire into the forces at work in its genesis. In so far as value elements are involved it is relevant to ask whether such an attitude is, to the actor, meaningful in terms of his total conception of the world. The general tendency to rational integration of systems of action, discussed above,[1] is sufficient basis for this. Then in so far as a given system of ideas has existed for a long time in a society at strategic points, it is a reasonable hypothesis that it exerts a steady influence in the direction of canalizing attitudes in such a way that they will become, in terms of such a system, meaningful. This is the more true, the more the society in question is one characterized by the persistence of aggregates, by strength of "belief."

The question of the role of religious ideas, which is involved in so acute a form in Weber's work, is in part a phase of the broader question, which is of central interest to this study, of that of value elements. The clear distinction made by both Pareto and Weber between scientific and nonscientific ideas has cleared the way considerably. Part, at least, of the latter form a cognitive element in the value complex. The status of such ideas has been clarified by the above discussion of Durkheim's treatment of religion. Weber goes still further in clarifying it. But it seems quite apparent that the cognitive constitute only one group of elements in the value complex. Knowing, or believing, is not, as such, doing. In addition an element of effort of some sort is needed. The actor does not take toward his ideas the emotionally neutral attitude of the scientist which has played such an important part in the

[1] *Supra,* p. 21.

discussion of Durkheim. But while the ideas of the value complex are concretely bound up with other, noncognitive elements, there is no reason why they should not be analytically distinguished from them. Moreover, Weber has brought a great deal of evidence to show that while believing is not, *ipso facto*, doing, what one believes has much to do with what one does.

CHAPTER XV

MAX WEBER II: RELIGION AND MODERN CAPITALISM (*Continued*)

B. The Comparative Studies

The vehicle of Weber's comparative investigation is the series of studies on the "Economic Ethics of the World Religions."[1] Weber declared his intention[2] of including Confucianism, Buddhism, Hinduism, Judaism, early Christianity and Islam. Unfortunately it was left unfinished at his death and only four were in a condition to be published in any form. Owing to limitations of space, attention will be confined to the results of two of them, the studies of Confucianism and Hinduism, since they strikingly illustrate what are theoretically the most important types.

But before entering upon a discussion of them it is necessary to say a word about the character of the whole series. Here, as distinct from the essay on the *Protestant Ethic*, Weber deals with both sides of the causal chain. But the series is not to be understood as a general "sociology of religion" if by that is meant a systematic study of all the interrelations of religion and society. Nor is it even a general study in the correlation of religious and economic phenomena, as has sometimes been maintained. Both these interpretations would contravene one of Weber's fundamental methodological principles, which will be discussed in the next chapter.[3] It is, on the contrary, definitely oriented[4] to

[1] "Die Wirtschaftsethik der Weltreligionen," *Gesammelte Aufsätze zur Religionssoziologie* (cited below as *Religionssoziologie*), Vol. I, pp. 237 ff., Vol. II and Vol. III.

[2] *Religionssoziologie*, Vol. I, pp. 237–238. Many of the results are systematically put together in the section "Religionssoziologie," Part II, Chap. IV, pp. 227–356 of *Wirtschaft und Gesellschaft* (*cited below as Wirtsch. u. Ges.*).

[3] *Wertbeziehung.*

[4] That is, in the central argument. About this are gathered all manner of subsidiary problems partially independent of the main one. See A. von Schelting, *Max Webers Wissenschaftslehre*, pp. 283–284.

the problem of modern capitalism in the above sense. It is primarily a comparative study of the ethics of other religions in respects relevant to the spirit of capitalism and the ethics of ascetic Protestantism. This is equally true whether the relevance is by agreement or by contrast. It is this fact which justifies dealing with it in the present context.

As Dr. von Schelting points out,[1] methodologically the "ideal" procedure for Weber would have been to work out cases of social development where *only* the element of religious ethic differed from the situation in Western Europe. Unfortunately that is not to be found in concrete fact and would involve a degree of positive[2] construction of which Weber was highly suspicious.[3] What Weber does is to sacrifice methodological precision in favor of the concreteness to be gained by dealing with actual historical instead of hypothetical events.

In general terms, then, the situation is approximately as follows: In the cases which will be discussed Weber succeeds in demonstrating that the economic ethic associated with the religion in question is fundamentally different from that of ascetic Protestantism in its implications for economic activities. This fact is correlated with the further one that in the areas in which the ethic in question has been predominant, no development has taken place which is at all comparable with that of Western rational bourgeois capitalism. Thus there is established a prima-facie connection between the lack of capitalistic development and the character of the religious ethics in question since, as compared with that of ascetic Protestantism, they must, so far as they influence action at all, be held to constitute directly inhibitory forces.

The principal methodological difficulties in approximating an accurate estimate of the concrete importance of the religious ethic in the development of types of economic system, arise at two points. In the first place, the "observable" economic ethic of a religion is a concrete entity. Weber is perfectly frank to admit that in the course of its development such an economic ethic is certainly[4] influenced both in its character and in the fact

---

[1] VON SCHELTING, *op. cit.*, pp. 285–286.
[2] The methodological issue will be discussed in the next chapter.
[3] See VON SCHELTING, *op. cit.*, p. 267.
[4] See *Religionssoziologie*, Vol. I, p. 238.

of attaining ascendancy by "material" factors, above all by the social character of the class who constitute its bearers, but also by other factors. The differentiation of these from the *Eigengesetzlichkeit* of the religious system can never be arrived at historically since that would lead to a regress beyond the point where historical evidence is available. The only recourse is to analysis.

Secondly, the elements in the concrete social system other than the religious ethic which may be considered as favorable or unfavorable to capitalistic development do not, in any two cases which can be compared, directly correspond. China lacked some of the important hindrances present in the West while, on the other hand, the West had certain nonreligious favorable elements not present in China.

The practical limitations are such that certainly no quantitatively exact proof is empirically possible. Weber attempts an approach to it in the form of estimates of probability in terms of the known laws governing the behavior of each element. Thus, on the one hand, he attempts to estimate whether the concrete economic ethic could have resulted from the operation of nonreligious factors, above all whether it could be a reflection of "material interests."[1] In this it should be remembered that evidence for *Eigengesetzlichkeit* in the religious sphere is just as much entitled to be considered seriously as is evidence from the other side.[2] On the other hand, judgments must be made of the probability that in the modern West the favorable factors could have overcome the unfavorable without the intervention of the religious ethic, while in China and India the opposite would have happened. Here it is Weber's judgment that in both China and India the *combination* of nonreligious factors was at the crucial time at least as favorable to capitalistic development as in the Western situation. Hence the strong probability that in this respect a principal *differentiating* factor with respect to

[1] As noted above Weber does not attempt this systematically. For a collection of the main arguments he deals with at various points, see von Schelting, *op. cit.*, pp. 291 ff.

[2] On the question whether the Protestant ethic can be considered a product of "accommodation," see above, and Talcott Parsons, "H. M. Robertson on Max Weber and His School," *Journal of Political Economy*, October, 1935.

capitalism lay in the religious element of the economic ethic. It should be noted particularly that the reliability of these admittedly complex estimates of probability increases greatly with the broadening of the comparative perspective and hence the clarification of the different elements and of their possible relations to each other. Therefore the total result of Weber's comparative study becomes much more reliable than the judgment of any one particular case can be from its own data, taken alone. This is a well-recognized methodological principle.

CHINA

The "classical" Chinese social system[1] when compared with our own presents a curious combination of similarities and dissimilarities. On the side of social structure as such, there are two fundamental aspects—what is often called the "familistic" organization and the "political" superstructure. As is widely known, the mass of the Chinese people has been closely organized in kinship groups, to the modern sociologist strongly reminiscent of many primitive societies. The basic unit is the patrilineal exogamous clan[2] which is broadly coterminous with the local village group. It is, in turn, subdivided into smaller household groups. In general these familistic groups stand in the closest connection with the soil, and are religiously sanctioned by the highly developed system of ancestor worship.

The Chinese family system stands in perhaps the sharpest contrast with that which has been progressively developing in the United States, interestingly enough a country of typically "Puritan" background. The Chinese family group exhibits an exceptionally high degree of collective solidarity; the principle of parental authority and "filial piety" is exceedingly strict, requiring both obedience on the part of children and a high degree of ritual respect. Finally it is the extreme antithesis to the modern American independence of women. The family, not the individual, is the unit of Chinese society.

While there is a relatively high degree of differentiation of wealth among family groups, there has been since the imperial time in China no rigidly hierarchical class system as in medieval

---

[1] Roughly since the consolidation of the Empire down to quite recent times.

[2] For Weber's discussion, see *Religionssoziologie*, Vol. I, pp. 373 *ff.*

Europe, above all nothing even approaching a caste system.¹ There has been at least a formal equality of opportunity in choice of occupation,² in fact in practically all relations outside the familistic ties. In this respect the Chinese situation has resembled that of Western capitalistic countries³ with the same *order* of limitation on substantial equality of opportunity— through the effective privileges of wealth and superior social status. In all this the striking difference from the modern West is the position of the familistic groups.

The Chinese imperial "state"⁴ had two main aspects. On the one hand, it was a theocracy, in a sense differentiating it radically from any Christian political structure. The emperor was the "Son of Heaven" and was conceived of as the principal inter- mediary between the divine order of things and that of human society. A break in the harmony of the latter could be laid to his ritual inadequacy. Thus the emperor formed the center of the ritual interests of China.⁵

But this religious aspect did not lead, as it might have, to the placing of political power in the hands of a hereditary priest- hood of which he was the head. Under the emperor stood a special class of bureaucratic administrators, the mandarins. In certain respects the Chinese political system carried bureaucratic prin- ciples through to a point scarcely reached anywhere else, but in others it differed radically from the type important for bourgeois capitalism.

The mandarins were a class of men with literary training whose eligibility for appointment to office was based on the passing of a series of examinations. Thus in spite of the extent to which fac- tually personal favor and other modifying elements entered in, there was definitely an impersonal objective standard of qualifi- cation. Favoritism was confined largely to the matter of selection among available candidates, since the number of eligibles was always much larger than the number of offices to be filled. More- over, certain other highly important bureaucratic principles were radically carried through. The official could not be stationed

¹ *Ibid.*, p. 389.
² *Ibid.*, p. 390.
³ Though developed much later in Western countries.
⁴ See *Religionssoziologie*, Vol. I, pp. 314 *ff.*
⁵ The mandarin as his local representative also had ritual functions.

in the province where his family was resident and his term in the same office was rigidly restricted to three years. Thus in spite of a high degree of independence of control from above, offices never became hereditary or politically dangerous to the central authority. Feudalization was effectively prevented. The mandarins as a class, but no few great families among them, monopolized offices. The class was never closed and each new accession to office depended on appointment from above.

At the same time there were fundamental limitations to a full bureaucratic development. In the first place, the bureaucratic principle was confined to a small group of high officials. The much larger number of subordinates necessary to carry out effective administration were not subjected to general bureaucratic discipline but their appointment, payment and control were left to the individual mandarin. He was naturally highly dependent on these subordinates with their knowledge of local conditions. They in turn were likely to be in league with local interests, such as the prominent familistic groups, gilds and village organizations. Hence the administrative system was not in a position to put through radical policies against powerful local interests and was forced to leave an extraordinary amount of autonomy to the local groups. The bureaucracy remained a superstructure and did not penetrate deeply into the social structure to achieve a direct control of the individual as the modern Western state bureaucracy has done.

Secondly, the mode of payment of officials under the tax-collection system was a limitation. The mandarin was obligated to turn over to the central government a certain quota of taxes. But the costs of his local administration, including his own remuneration, were met from taxes he himself set and collected. This fact and his limited term of office led him to get as much as possible out of his position while there was time.

Finally, it was not a *specialized* bureaucracy: there were no special technical qualifications for particular offices and the necessary training was not at all specialized or technical. A knowledge of the classics was required, the same for everyone. The object was not to fit a candidate for the particular technical requirements of a given office but to insure that he was a sufficiently highly cultivated gentleman to be worthy of the exalted position of a mandarin. This circumstance obviously increased the official's dependence upon subordinates and was an important hindrance to the extension of the bureaucratic principle into the details of routine administration. It remained what Weber calls a patrimonial bureaucracy.

Between the mandarin class and the familistic group there was room for the development of a considerable amount of specifically economic enterprise. With variations at different periods craftsmanship developed highly and a large amount of mercantile trade, often on a considerable scale, and in each case with powerful craft gilds. But in spite of the occasional large scale of enterprise nothing approaching the modern Western industrial capitalism was ever developed. In spite of a great deal of technological invention, techniques remained traditional and industrial production was mainly on a handicraft basis. The large-scale organization of trade was not associated with a corresponding organization of production as in the West.[1]

At a very early time China had permanent peace over a wide area. It had relatively few restrictions on internal mobility and trade.[2] It had an unusual degree of equality of opportunity and freedom in the choice of occupation. It was practically free from such restrictions on economic development as the Catholic prohibition of usury.[3] Finally the state recognized and left a very high degree of autonomy to organizations of economic interest such as the gilds. If, as is often thought, absence of restricting circumstances alone could bring about a modern capitalistic development, surely it should have happened in China long before the modern era.[4]

When the economic ethic is considered the paradox becomes even more striking. For probably there is no ethic in the world

[1] There were, Weber says, three main sources of accumulation of private wealth: (1) the political exploitation of office and tax collection, (2) government contracts and tax farming, (3) commerce. See *Religionssoziologie*, Vol. I, p. 393.

[2] *Ibid.*, p. 390.

[3] *Ibid.*

[4] The principal hindering circumstances of not *directly* religious origin Weber mentions were (1) the absence of a solid, formal legal structure, (2) the absence of corporate autonomy of towns, (3) defective monetary development. See especially *Religionssoziologie*, Vol. I, pp. 391 *ff*. Transportation facilities were always primitive, though probably no more so than in medieval Europe.

which has any pretense to religious status which is more definitely utilitarian and worldly than that of China. Above all, nowhere else in the world has there been a more strikingly positive valuation of wealth among all classes of society. In prudent care for the interests of this world and lack of interest in any other, perhaps no people has ever surpassed the Chinese. Moreover this worldliness or utilitarianism is combined with a kind of rationalism. It involves a far-reaching repudiation of the irrational aspects of religion, above all orgiastic and transcendental elements. Wherein then lies the difference from the utilitarian rationalism of the Protestant ethic?

The predominant[1] ethical system of China which gives a definite clear-cut attitude toward the world is the Confucian orthodoxy.[2] It is important to recognize that this came to be the specific ethic of the mandarin class—that of the polished, educated gentleman. Confucianism is conspicuous for the fact that it is almost purely an ethical doctrine, a collection of practical precepts without any explicit metaphysical foundation. Confucius would have nothing to do with metaphysical speculations; they were to him useless and vain. There is no definite interest in a future life, and no concept of salvation. The doctrine is concerned with conduct in this life for its own sake with no concern beyond that except for a good name.

Its worldliness does not, however, sanction a lack of discipline. On the contrary its rationalism involves a particular kind of discipline. The central underlying conception is that of a harmony or order. The universe itself constitutes such an order ruled by "Heaven" and human society is a microcosm of the world order. The higher, educated man seeks to live in accordance with this order. To do so involves abstention from any kind of loss of self-control which might endanger his equilibrium.

There is no such thing as a radically evil principle; there is no "sin"—only error, the failure to become the most perfect "gentleman" possible with one's inheritance and opportunities. The rational man will avoid display of emotion, will be always self-controlled, dignified, polite. He will always observe the proprieties of any situation most punctiliously. His basic aim

[1] On the whole becoming increasingly so with time. See *Religionssoziologie*, Vol. I, p. 454.

[2] *Religionssoziologie*, Vol. I, pp. 430 *ff*.

is to live in harmony with a social order which is generally accepted and to be an ornament to it.

His duty is not to shoulder other people's responsibilities, not to be concerned with the state of society generally, but to attend to his own concerns. These include two main elements—his self-development as an educated gentleman and his relations to others. In the latter connection the primary emphasis is on certain specific personal relations, above all those of piety.[1] The central Chinese virtue is filial piety, and the attitude of the official to his superior should be as that of a son to his father. In fact Confucius conceived the whole of society as a network of such personal relationships and his injunction to each was to see that his conduct was right in his *own* relationships. He should not set up to be his brother's keeper. The contrast with the Puritan concern for the conduct of all is striking.

The order with which the Confucian gentleman sought to live in harmony was a definite concrete order. In the Confucian ethics no motive is given for an attempt to alter its main outline. This fact is the source of one fundamentally important set of attitudes, those toward the "religious" practices and beliefs of the society. They fall into two categories.

On the one hand, the state structure itself, of which the mandarin was a part, was a "sacral" structure. The emperor and his officials were the carriers of the state cult and, as in classical antiquity, religious duties of a ritual character were part of the accepted duties of public office. Confucianism simply accepted these things as a matter of course. One did not combat them but neither did one inquire into their meaning—that would be fruitless metaphysical speculation. They were part of the order. There was, in spite of its rationalism, as Weber says, not the slightest Confucian tendency to rationalize these things in an ethical sense. Similarly, to the duties of filial piety so strongly stressed there belonged an elaborate ritual aspect which was also simply accepted without any attempt at ethical rationalization.[2]

On the other hand, there has always been in China, as elsewhere, an enormous amount of popular magic and superstition. This also the Confucian gentleman accepted but in a different way. He did not himself participate in it because it was beneath

[1] *Ibid.*, pp. 445–446.
[2] *Ibid.*, p. 453.

his dignity, but at the same time there was not the slightest attempt to drive it out. It belonged to the life of the uneducated mass.[1]

The conception of the means to perfection expressed the same idea—acceptance of the given. Perfection was attained by a study of the classics.[2] What marked off the gentleman from the vulgar mass was not birth or wealth but classical learning. It is important to see how different this conception of learning was from the modern Western. It never occurred to anyone that the classics could be improved upon. Learning was not dynamic but static according to a constant norm.

This combination of circumstances could not but foster traditionalism. The rationalism of the Confucian ethic was genuine enough. It was also a rationalism of this world; it would have nothing to do with transcendental things. Within the framework of the Chinese society it placed an unquestioned value on the good things of this world, above all on wealth, long life and a good name. But its rationalism was limited by the fundamental traditional acceptance of an existing order, above all of the traditional religio-magical elements of it, whether state cult, ancestor worship or popular magic. Moreover, the ideal of the Confucian gentleman was a traditional static ideal, the basis of which was assimilation of a traditionally fixed body of literary culture, the classics. Confucian learning entirely lacked the dynamic quality of Western science. Finally, the dominant ethical value of Confucianism, as Weber says, its only absolute duty, "piety,"[3] was itself a traditionalistic virtue. It enjoined *acceptance* of the order of the fathers and the duly constituted authorities and proprieties. There was no sanction of rebellion against this order in the name of an abstract ideal. Confucian rationalism was that of dignified adaptation to a traditional order. Its discipline was the avoidance of all disorderliness and the self-discipline of the dignified gentleman. It was, as Professor Sorokin says,[4] "a prudent policy of sound conservatism."

But this is precisely what the ethic of ascetic Protestantism was not, as should be abundantly evident from the above dis-

[1] *Ibid.*, p. 443.
[2] *Ibid.*, pp. 451 *ff*.
[3] *Ibid.*, p. 445.
[4] P. A. Sorokin, *Contemporary Sociological Theories*, p. 695.

cussion. It was rather a distinctly revolutionary force. Its animus was not adaptation of the individual to a social world uncritically accepted. It was an injunction to make over his world, as far as lay within his power, in the name of a transcendental ideal— to establish the Kingdom of God on Earth. It was, as Weber succinctly puts it,[1] not a doctrine, like Confucianism, of rational adaptation *to* the world, but of rational mastery *over* the world. Archimedes is reputed to have said, "Give me a place to stand and I will move the world." The Confucian ethic failed to move the world precisely because its worldliness denied it a place to stand outside the world. The Protestant ethic, on the other hand, had such a place to stand, its transcendental God and its conception of salvation. In precisely the *ascetic* aspect of its ethic lay its driving force.

From this basic difference follow a number of more special differences. On one hand, from the worldliness of Confucianism followed its acceptance of tradition, even more its sanctification of it. On the other hand, from the transcendental basis of the Puritan ethic followed the absolute unsanctity of tradition.[2] To the Puritan, Chinese filial piety would be a sheer case of idolatry of the flesh; the state cult, pure "superstition." The only sanction of earthly things was their conformity with the will of God. Puritanism carried out one of the most radical possible extremes of elimination of magic from the world;[3] Confucianism left the deep-rooted popular magic untouched. This difference is, in turn, part of one of Weber's most fundamental theses, that everywhere traditionalism is the rule in the earlier stages of a given social development.[4] It is so powerful that it requires forces of exceptional strength to break through it even appreciably, and only when that has happened are certain kinds of social development, like that of rational bourgeois capitalism, possible. Not only did the Confucian ethic, in spite of its worldly rationalism, entirely fail to do this; on the contrary it provided a direct and powerful sanction of the traditional order.

Without any pretense of exhaustive treatment two other important differences may be pointed out. One of the fundamental

[1] *Religionssoziologie*, Vol. I, p. 534.
[2] *Ibid.*, p. 527.
[3] "Entzauberung der Welt," *Religionssoziologie*, Vol. I, p. 513.
[4] The general theoretical issue will be taken up below (see Chap. XVII).

requirements of modern bureaucratic structure is specialization of function and, with it, specialized technical knowledge, legal or scientific. This is one of the features of modern Western bureaucracy that the mandarin bureaucracy conspicuously failed to develop. Such specialization inevitably involves renunciation of a completely rounded personality. With us specialization has been bitterly attacked in the name of humanistic ideals. The Puritan ethic went far to break through this barrier by its conception of man as the instrument of God's will. His own highest self-fulfillment lay in playing his part, even though it be a highly specialized part, in a calling. The Confucian gentleman, on the other hand, was no "instrument" in any sense,[1] but an end in himself, a fully rounded, harmonious "work of art." Far from there being positive motives to specialization there was strong inhibition against it. Moreover, for the Confucian the only personally valuable knowledge was that of the classics, not of technical specialties. The Confucian was a humanist.

Secondly, another of the fundamentals of our modern Western social order is its ethical "universalism." To a very high degree both in theory and in practice our highest ethical duties apply "impersonally" to all men, or to large categories of them irrespective of any specific personal relation involved. For instance, the duties of honesty and fair treatment are held to apply to business dealings with everyone, not only with one's relatives and personal friends. Indeed, without this universalism, as Weber repeatedly points out, it is difficult to see how the modern economic system could function, for on it rests the essential confidence which must underlie such business relationships as the maintenance of contracts and quality of goods.[2]

In this respect the Puritan ethic represents an intensification of the general Christian tendency. It has an extremely powerful animus against nepotism and favoritism.[3] To this the Confucian ethic stands in sharp contrast. Its ethical sanction was given to an individual's *personal* relations to particular persons—and with any strong ethical emphasis *only* to these.[4] The whole Chinese

---

[1] See *Religionssoziologie*, Vol. I, p. 532.

[2] See above, Durkheim's treatment of the conditions of a contractual system, Chap. VIII.

[3] *Religionssoziologie*, Vol. I, p. 531.

[4] *Ibid.*, p. 527.

social structure accepted and sanctioned by the Confucian ethics was a predominantly "particularistic" structure of relationships.[1] This left relationships outside this category in a realm of ethical indifference, with a general unwillingness to assume ethical obligations. Since most economic relationships in a market system are of this outside character the tendency for any break in traditionalism was to take the form of emancipation from ethical limitations, of "adventurers' capitalism," not the ethically disciplined acquisition typical of rational bourgeois capitalism.

Finally, while it is in general true that Confucianism rejects metaphysical speculation, there is a predominant current of Chinese thought, within which it belongs, which shows a strong contrast to the Western, and is relevant to the general question of the basis of religious ethics. The Confucian philosophy implied the presence of principles of order in the universe; the social order is but an aspect of a cosmic order. But unlike the predominant Western view the basis of this order is immanent and, in the last analysis, impersonal. There is no analogue to the Judaeo-Christian transcendental, personal God, the creator and ruler of the world. In Chinese thought this order came to be formulated in terms of the conception of Tao which was common to the Confucian and most of the other schools.

This fact is connected with another to which Weber attributes the greatest importance, namely, the complete failure of a class of prophets like the Jewish to arise in China, whose "mission" it was to impose an ethical obligation to a transcendental ideal in the name of such a transcendental God.[2] Such prophecy he held to be a main source of the break in traditionalism in the West in favor of an ethical rationalization of the world. Indeed this prophetic attitude was incompatible with a pantheistic system of ideas. It is true that Confucian orthodoxy does not stand by any means alone in Chinese religious thought. But its principal competitor, Taoism, did not lead in the Western direction of ethical rationalization, but rather, farther away. Taoism[3] embraced two main tendencies. On a high level of intellectual sophistication it was a mystical, contemplative doctrine. Instead

---

[1] We shall come back to these problems below (see Chap. XVII, appended note).

[2] *Religionssoziologie*, Vol. I, p. 516.

[3] *Ibid.*, pp. 458 *ff.*

of seeking to uphold the ideal of a polished, worldly gentleman, like the Confucian, the Taoist held that the highest activity of man was the contemplative grasp of the essence of the universe—a path obviously leading directly away from any sort of active ascetic mastery over the world. Indeed, given the pantheistic background of Chinese thought, Weber held, there are only these two possibilities of a rationalization of the "knowing" man's attitudes toward the universe—either the Confucian worldly "adaptation" to the world order within society, or the Taoist mystical, contemplative, asocial attitude. On the other hand, the vulgarization of Taoism resulted in a tremendous proliferation of magical superstition. There is a close parallel to these two tendencies of Taoism in Buddhism. This suggests a similar metaphysical basis and may well help to explain the receptivity to Buddhism in China.[1]

INDIA

Indian society and religion may be treated somewhat more briefly than the Chinese since in both respects the contrast with

[1] In view of this discussion it is impossible to agree with Professor Sorokin's contention that Weber failed to establish an adequate distinction between Puritan and Confucian rationalism in respects relevant to rational bourgeois capitalism. The reasons he advances in his very brief discussion are inadequate to the conclusion and only take account of a small part of Weber's treatment. They have all been met in the above discussion. See P. A. Sorokin, *Contemporary Sociological Theories*, pp. 694–695.

Professor Sorokin also holds (*ibid.*, p. 696) the Japanese reception of Western economic organization in the later nineteenth century to be important empirical evidence against Weber's position. While Weber did not deal with Japan at all thoroughly (in any way comparably to his treatment of China) he was by no means unaware of the problem. Professor Sorokin's point does not seem conclusive for two reasons: In the first place, he attributes to Weber a view he did not hold—that modern capitalism could not *exist* or be adopted without the Puritan ethic. Weber's thesis is that it could not have been *developed spontaneously* without the assistance of these religious forces. There is a great difference between the possibility of a non-Protestant culture being able to assimilate rational bourgeois capitalistic forms from without, and its producing them spontaneously. The former is exemplified by Japan, and there is no statement in Weber that such a thing is impossible (see passage quoted below from *Religionssoziologie*, Vol. II, p. 300). Professor Sorokin gives no specific reference to support his imputation of that view to Weber.

Secondly, among different non-Protestant cultures there may be a great variation in the formidability of the obstacles to reception of such capitalistic the Western situation is much more obvious and there is little danger of failing to distinguish the religious ethic of Hinduism from that of Protestantism. India is the proverbial home of otherworldliness in the everyday sense of the term.

To the Westerner the most striking feature of the Indian social system is caste.[1] While some are perhaps inclined to regard caste as primitive, nothing could be farther from the truth. To any degree such as its development in India it is an absolutely unique phenomenon. Moreover, in its full state of crystallization it does not belong to the early stages of Indian history but definitely to the later. It is a product of a long process of development.[2]

Though in some respects in its recent form, as revealed by the Indian Census Reports, caste presents an extraordinarily

---

forms. Without having investigated the question thoroughly the opinion may be ventured that in certain important respects these obstacles have been distinctly less formidable in Japan than in either China or India (*ibid.* p. 359). For instance, an able distinction thesis at Harvard University (E. C. Devereux, Jr., *"Gemeinschaft* and *Gesellschaft* in Tokugawa Japan"* [1934, unpublished]) has maintained the presence of important indigenous religious elements in Japan of a *"universalistic"* as against a *"particularistic"* character [in the sense used above, p. 550] which probably went far to neutralize the imported Confucian elements. Weber also notes the presence in Japan of a political structure of quite a different character from that of the Chinese. "A population in which a class of the Samurai type played the predominant role could not—apart from all other circumstances—evolve a rational economic ethic *from its own resources.* Nevertheless the terminable relation of fealty, which created firm contractual relations in law, provided a far more favorable basis for 'individualism' in the occidental sense than for instance the Chinese theocracy. Japan could adopt capitalism as a completed thing with relative ease, even though it could not itself produce its *Geist."* (*Religionssoziologie*, Vol. II, p. 300. Italics mine.) See also *ibid.,* p. 376 (compare the last sentence with Professor Sorokin's "According to Weber this is impossible." *Op. cit.,* p. 696).

Hence in the absence of supporting evidence, which he fails to provide, it seems that Professor Sorokin's categorical statement of the seriousness of the Japanese case as against Weber's position cannot be accepted. The Chinese and Japanese cases are the only empirical points he raises against the comparative parts of Weber's sociology of religion. His methodological objection will be discussed in the following chapter.

[1] The general problem of India is treated by Weber in *Religionssoziologie*, Vol. II, caste and the other features of the social system in Vol. II, Sec. I.

[2] According to the best contemporary opinion the full crystallization cannot be placed before A.D. 700 and possibly took place as late as A.D. 1300. *Cf.* E. A. H. Blunt, *The Caste System of Northern India.*

heterogeneous picture, there is in it an element of order which definitely entitles it to be called a system.[1] It is composed of a very large number of rigidly endogamous, generally local, hereditary groups arranged in a hierarchy of relative inferiority and superiority. The ultimate endogamous units are the subcastes but these are for the most part grouped in larger, more or less well-defined units, the castes proper, those in the same caste maintaining at least the fiction of equal social status with each other.

Though by no means without exception, the caste groups are usually characterized by a hereditary occupation so that the division of society into castes is roughly a functional division of labor on a hereditary basis. A great many of the caste names, though by no means all, designate this occupation.

Furthermore the castes are conspicuously characterized by ritual barriers. The prohibition of *connubium* itself has a prominent ritual aspect as does, perhaps even more, the other most prominent single criterion, the prohibition of commensality. There is an extraordinarily elaborate system of ritual rules governing the preparation and consumption of food and personal contacts. On the whole these rules are sharply differentiated according to caste and are different for the members of any one caste according to what other castes are involved in a given situation. There are only a few all-Hindu ritual elements such as the sacredness of the cow; for the rest the ubiquity of ritual serves to make the castes a congeries of ritually watertight compartments.

In the hierarchical aspect there is a certain element of vagueness, in the sense that it is not always possible to place every single caste or subcaste in relation to all others, but the general outline of the hierarchy is clear enough. The apex is the Brahman caste and the main criterion of caste status is that of the relation of the particular caste to the Brahmans. And the criteria are on the whole of a special type—ritual relations. The status of a caste is primarily determined[2] by such considerations as what things and under what circumstances (food for instance), a Brahman of good standing will take from a member of that caste, what kinds of contact will occasion purification rites on the part

[1] Which will be sketched as an "ideal type," many of the details being neglected.

[2] In the sense of criterion, not the causal sense.

of the Brahman and what kinds of ritual services the Brahman will perform for members of the caste in question.

As has been stated, this caste structure in its present or recent form is not an inheritance from ancient India but has developed into its present form in the course of a long, slow process. At various times it has been affected by a number of different elements. As the oldest literary sources reveal, a class division into conquerors and conquered created and repeatedly reemphasized a color line. There were also differentiation of occupation and of organized occupational groups; differentiation of wealth; reception into the single system of many different ethnic groups with differing cultures, sometimes with, sometimes without, special occupations. These and, no doubt, many other circumstances have played a part.

One dominant fact, however, requires explanation. The pivot of the specific hierarchical form seems to lie in the undoubted and unchallenged social supremacy of the Brahman caste—a priestly caste. Not only are they the top, but other castes are ranked with reference to them and *on their terms*, ritual terms, which are the professional concern of the Brahman. This has happened in spite of the fact that the Brahmans did not at any historical period command an organized religious association in any way comparable, for instance, with the medieval church. In fact explicit caste organization varies in inverse relation to the rank of the caste—the panchayat or caste council is most highly developed among the lower castes.[1] Moreover, though many Brahmans have acted as ministers and advisers of princes in both lay and spiritual matters, they have never as a caste held political authority in their own right, but only as individuals by appointment of others. Finally, though often wealthy, their position certainly does not rest upon wealth as such independently of the prestige of their religious position and services. And they have by no means uniformly been the wealthiest caste. No other priesthood in history has such an achievement to its credit.

Other aspects of the social structure may be briefly noted. India has always been primarily an agricultural society[2] and the typical local unit is the village. It is, however, unlike the Chinese village, not made up of a group of blood relations but in any

[1] See BLUNT, *op. cit.*
[2] *Religionssoziologie*, Vol. II, p. 1.

given village a number of different caste groups are typically represented. But in spite of caste barriers the village organization has in general been highly integrated and stable with, as in China, a large amount of self-government as against superior political authority.

This points to a highly important contrast between both India and China, on the one hand, and the modern West, on the other. India like China produced imposing political structures, though not nearly so stable over long periods. They both developed patrimonial bureaucracies and disciplined armies, but never a full modern Western bureaucracy. China approached nearer to such an organization than India. And—a most important fact— in India, as in China and in the same sense, the state remained a "superstructure." It did not penetrate in its administrative functions directly to the individual[1] but, rather, stopped at the caste, village and other groups, leaving them essentially intact with a large degree of self-government.[2]

As in China, in India there developed craft and merchant gilds, at one time very powerful, a very considerable trade even over long distances, and high skill in craftsmanship. There was a considerable capitalistic development in trade, in war supplies, tax farming, and considerable accumulation of wealth through these and other channels. But at no time did this development approach the rational bourgeois capitalism of the West.

It is quite clear that the caste system, with its extreme of both vertical and territorial immobility and its ritually sanctioned hierarchy of traditionally stereotyped occupations, constitutes an almost insuperable barrier to such a development, certainly to a spontaneous development from indigenous sources. And such capitalism of this character as exists in India today is clearly a European importation.

But clearly the problem is not the incompatibility of caste with modern capitalism. It is, rather, why the Indian development took this direction. For not only has a rigid caste system not always existed there, but especially in the time of the growth of the great religious systems there was in India a great deal of

---

[1] As Weber puts it, administration was "extensive" rather than "intensive."

[2] It may be noted that an opposite development was a striking feature of both the polis of antiquity and the modern Western state.

social flexibility, certainly comparing favorably with medieval Europe. The question of Brahman supremacy was at that time by no means settled, least of all in the Buddhistic period. Furthermore there were a number of elements hostile to a traditional crystallization of castes; apart from the economic elements mentioned Buddhism was at least indifferent to caste. Warfare with its unsettling effects was rife at almost all periods. Moreover, India was repeatedly subject to foreign conquest with impacts on the class structure even more unsettling than internal war.[1]

The dominant religious system of India in recent times is generally referred to as Hinduism. It is necessary, however, to exercise care not to read into it our own Western ideas of what constitutes a religion. In the first place, there is no Hindu "church" one may join. The only way to become a Hindu is to be born into a caste which is recognized as Hindu. This recognition is not based upon any dogmatic propositions of belief but primarily on ritual practices. Above all a caste must observe the sacredness of the cow and avoid eating beef and recognize, in general, the religious authority of the Brahmans, which is above all ritual. India has its sacred books, especially the Vedas, and a good Hindu would never think of questioning their sanctity, but his attitude is one of general, undefined respect, not of subscription to any specific articles of faith contained in them or deduced from them.

The Hindu has, to be sure, religious duties for failure in which sanctions may be visited upon him. But these lie in the realm not of doctrine, but of *dharma*. Dharma can perhaps best be translated as duty. It consists essentially in the traditional obligations of everyday life, including above all ritual obligations. Some dharma such as not eating beef and respecting Brahmans is common to all Hindus, but for the most part it consists in the traditional duties of one's station in life, above all one's caste. So long as one does not violate these, he may think as he pleases. But for such an offense as marrying outside one's caste one may be "excommunicated," that is, expelled from the caste.[2]

---

[1] For a summary of circumstances favorable to capitalism in India see *Religionssoziologie*, Vol. II, pp. 2–4.

[2] A very serious penalty indeed when the caste system is intact. It is then nothing less than "social death."

What the Hindu is bound to by his feelings of religious duty then is the traditional social order, above all in its caste structure. Hinduism as a "religion" is but an aspect of this order with no independent status apart from it.

As has been said, there is no binding dogma in the Christian sense. More than that there is a bewildering variety of religious ideas and practices, of gods and cults, and means to salvation recognized as Hindu. But underlying all are certain definable elements. In the first place, there is a fundamental religious relativity. There is no way of life alone religiously acceptable, and no one exclusively valid approach to the divine. No Indian cult would think of the Western *extra ecclesiam nulla salus*. On the contrary, there are in principle many ways suitable for different kinds and classes of persons, adapted to their abilities and needs, which all lead ultimately to the same goal. In this religious sense India presents probably the most radically individualistic situation known to history.

But there is a more specific content of ideas, those of transmigration and karma.[1] Each soul has existed from eternity, is definitely not the creation of a god and passes through an unending series of rebirths. Karma, on the other hand, is the doctrine that each act of such an entity has permanent indestructible effects on the fate of the actor's soul which can never be evaded. The two combined yield a completely closed rationalization of the problem of evil—one of the three most consistent, Weber says, in history.[2] These doctrines are, to be sure, not dogmas in the sense that they are enforced by a church, but they are religious ideas common to the whole Hindu community, nowhere seriously attacked within it. As such they have stood intact for many centuries.[3]

The relation to practical motivation emerges with one further element, the association of karma and transmigration with dharma and through it with the place of the individual in the

---

[1] "These and only these are really 'dogmatic' beliefs of all Hindus." *Religionssoziologie*, Vol. II, pp. 117 *ff*.

[2] *Religionssoziologie*, Vol. II, p. 120. The others are that of Calvinism and the dualism of Zoroastrianism.

[3] As already noted (Chap. VII, p. 286) this is an interesting case for Pareto's thesis of the inherent instability of "nonlogical" theories. The reason certainly does not lie in restrictions on intellectual freedom.

caste structure.[1] According to the good or bad acts of the individual in past incarnations the causality of karma will determine the place of his rebirth in the caste hierarchy. For purposes of the theory this hierarchy is extended below human society into the animal world, and above it so that one may be reborn a god— with the implication that the gods are not immortal but are really only superhuman. Finally in this context good and bad can have only one meaning. Good is the faithful performance of dharma, of the traditionally stereotyped duties of one's caste position; bad, failure in this.[2]

Once this connection was made, in so far as the motives of action were religious at all, it was effectively turned in the direction of the traditional performance of caste obligations and hence the maintenance of the caste structure. The religious interest of the individual could never be in the upsetting of the system but only in the improvement of his chances of a better incarnation *within* the system. And the sole means to ensure this lay in complete conformity with the system in all its details of traditionally prescribed conduct. It was in a sense a conception of "calling" but with the utmost possible stress on traditionalism.[3] Indeed a more completely watertight and effective[4] sanction of traditionalism could scarcely be devised.

This whole conception of the individual's religious duty implied, and to a considerable extent doubtless had its origin in, the still deeper character of Indian religious thought. The latter was, along with caste, totally unknown to the classic Vedic literature which gave a religious outlook closely related to the Greek. But in the course of development the Vedic gods themselves tended to lose importance as compared with the objective efficacy of the ritual of sacrifice. This tendency seems to have centered attention on the objective impersonal order of the ritual forces, and philosophic speculation adumbrated the meaning of this ritual.

Whatever the historical process may have been, there is no doubt that by the period of Brahmanism[5] the doctrines of karma

[1] *Religionssoziologie*, Vol. II, p. 118. A product, as Weber here says, of Brahman intellectualism.
[2] There is thus, as in China, no concept of a radically evil principle.
[3] The Lutheran case raised to the nth power.
[4] In so far as religious "interests" operate at all, of course.
[5] Historians habitually divide Indian religious development into three

and transmigration had appeared and were bound up with an impersonal pantheistic conception of the principle of order in the universe, which excluded any possibility of a personal, transcendental creator-god. The ultimate order including souls was eternal and uncreated, the gods themselves of only subordinate significance. "God" was to be found within the order, not outside and above it. The Western conceptions both of creation and of grace[1] were radically excluded. In the orthodox Vedanta school of Brahmanism only this impersonal unity was recognized as real; everything else was "maya," illusion.

The process by which this extraordinary Brahmanic rationalization of the universe came to fit so perfectly a peculiar social system was certainly not a simple one. The theory was the creation of a highly cultivated intellectual class and its dissemination on the purely ideal level to the point at which its basic doctrines become the common property of a vast population, the majority illiterate, must have been a slow process. And this dissemination is the necessary condition of its serving as the canalizing framework of the religious interests of the masses.

A number of suggestions have been advanced by different writers to explain the caste system, the most important emphasizing the roles of occupational differentiation and of the racial difference between conquerors and conquered. The latter is especially notable because it involved a color line. Both undoubtedly contributed, but both are common enough elsewhere without having given rise to caste. The color line, however, could not fail to accentuate the hereditary principle and to gather about it magical and ritual elements in the culture, emphasizing what Weber calls the principle of *Gentilcharisma*.[2]

Another central element, Brahman supremacy, was by no means original. In the feudal period the Brahmans were often held inferior to the highly cultivated Ksatriya aristocracy. Their

---

main periods: (1) the Vedic period, from the Aryan invasions to about 1000 B.C., (2) Brahmanism, from 1000 B.C. to about the beginning of the Christian era, and (3) since that time Hinduism. Professor W. E. Clark, in lectures at Harvard University.

[1] The idea of such "arbitrary" interference with the cosmic order would shock the Indian mind.

[2] *Religionssoziologie*, Vol. II, p. 125. The concept of charisma will be discussed below.

supremacy was a result of various complicated changes in the social balance of power. Among these were the tendency of the patrimonial rulers to ally with the Brahmans against the feudal forces. The position of the Ksatriya was deeply shaken by the long series of foreign invasions, of which they, as warriors, bore the brunt. The Brahman literature was stereotyped and given influence by the Mohammedan conquests.[1] Patrimonial administration, especially fiscal, tended to strengthen the solidarity of existing groups.[2]

One force which conceivably might have broken through the whole traditionalistic system and which, indeed, played a very large part in the West, the influence of the urban trading and handicraft classes, failed to do so. To be sure, they became organized in gilds and were at times powerful and prosperous. But, on the one hand, they never succeeded in making the towns independent corporate units with an independent military basis, as in the West during the Middle Ages. And, on the other hand, they were crushed by the growing patrimonial states to which their power became dangerous.[3]

The Brahman theory was an incomparably fine bulwark of authority, especially for a regime of foreign conquerors. Once the Brahmans were in the saddle of power and influence, without which there would have been no caste development,[4] the Brahmanic religious philosophy had the opportunity to do its work. The other elements adapted to it were already there, and the dangerous competition of the old Ksatriyas and the gilds, was broken, so that a long slow process of pressure of ideas in a constant direction leading to the formation of a caste system could go on. Without many nonreligious conditions the Brahmanic religious ideas could not have had their influence.[5] But equally, without this peculiar system of ideas, none of these conditions,

---

[1] On all these points, see *Religionssoziologie*, Vol. II, p. 125.

[2] *Ibid.*, p. 127.

[3] *Religionssoziologie*, Vol. II, pp. 127–128. Weber lays great stress on this independent corporate character of the Western city, a trait common to the polis and the medieval town, but unknown in the Orient. See especially the extremely interesting study, "Die Stadt," *Wirtschaft und Gesellschaft*, Part II, Chap. VIII.

[4] *Religionssoziologie*, Vol. II, p. 131.

[5] On the general theoretical issue of the role of ideas involved here see above, note appended to Chap. XIV.

nor even the whole combination of them including the supremacy of a hereditary priesthood, would have produced the caste system. And this system of ideas is to be explained "as a product of rational ethical thought, not of any sort of economic conditions."[1]

While the general pantheistic basis and the doctrines of karma and transmigration formed the common foundation of all the main movements of Indian religious philosophy, religious interests were by no means confined to the means of bettering an individual's prospects in the cycle of rebirths. On the contrary, while this was the preoccupation of the mass, the elect have for many centuries been concerned with the problem of "salvation" in a much more radical sense. But what salvation could mean, what one was to be saved from and for is understandable only in terms of the underlying metaphysical position.[2]

As has been noted, the immanent pantheistic conception of divinity precluded that of a radically evil principle. There could be only "imperfection." It precluded equally eternal rewards and punishments for finite merits or faults. Such Christian ideas would appear to the Indian mind nonsensical. Salvation could not be from "sin" in the Christian sense, nor for eternal bliss. Salvation was rather radically different, from karma. Indian pessimism is founded on the conviction of the senselessness and transiency of all things worldly. Even the most meritorious conduct could only result eventually in rebirth as a god, and that too was transient, fated to death and the repetition of the whole process. Permanence, essential stability, "eternal life" could be attained only by escape from the whole thing, not only from this life but from all other conceivable "lives."

In India there have been many paths to salvation but they have only one goal. In so far as they lead to "higher" religious aims than merely better prospects of rebirth, they are all directed to escape from involvement in this world altogether, they are all otherworldly in this specific sense.[3]

The means employed have been many, but may be divided into the two great categories, the ascetic and the mystical. The latter is the predominant trend and, finding its highest value in

---

[1] *Religionssoziologie*, Vol. II, p. 131.

[2] The general treatment of these doctrines of salvation is to be found in *Religionssoziologie*, Vol. II, Sec. II.

[3] *Religionssoziologie*, Vol. I, p. 359.

contemplation, its attitude to the things of this world is, in principle, one of indifference. The importance of this world is so radically devalued that from this source there is no possible motive for a remaking of the world in the name of an ideal. The world is not combated as dangerous except as a source of diversion from true interests. But no more positive relation to it is possible than that of the passive acceptance of things as they are.

India is known as a classic land of asceticism. But this asceticism is always and necessarily on this basis what Weber calls otherworldly. Its combat with the flesh is in the interest of destroying its power to divert the soul from contact with the absolute. The flesh is to be mastered, not that it may be used as an instrument, but that it may be rendered harmless. There is, in the basic Indian position, no motive for the active "worldly" asceticism which is the essence of the Protestant ethic.[1]

Buddhism was in a sense an anti-Brahman and anticaste movement. Its opposition, however, does not lie in its departure from the basic Indian religious position in the Western direction, but in carrying it to still more radical conclusions than the Brahmanic philosophy. It represented the contemplative type par excellence. In its extreme of indifference to the world, and in its prohibition for the fully qualified person, the monk, to become involved in it in almost any way, it supplied no direct sanction of any social system but was specifically asocial. But for just this reason it could not serve as a basis of a rational economic ethic.[2]

THE SYSTEMATIC TYPOLOGY OF RELIGION

Weber's comparative sociology of religion did not consist only of a series of separate studies of "cases" which serve to bring out religious elements inhibiting the development of capitalism elsewhere than in the modern West. It is mainly preoccupied with the problem of capitalism and its main theoretical framework focuses upon it. But out of it emerges a general system of religious typology which gives the final breadth to the perspective of the religious aspect of the problem of capitalism. It is possible to

[1] *Ibid.*, Vol. II, p. 360.
[2] For lack of space no treatment is included here of the later popular developments of Hindu cult-religion. They do not in any fundamental way affect the general relation to capitalism. For Weber's treatment see *Religionssoziologie*, Vol. II, Sec. III, pp. 316 *ff*. The same is true of the popularization of Buddhism, see *ibid.*, pp. 251 *ff*.

give here to complete the preceding presentation only a bare sketch of some of the major concepts.[1]

Even a sketchy presentation of this systematic typology is not possible without some reference to Weber's general conception of historical development which will be treated more fully below.[2] It was his view that in what is relevant to his analysis there is something like a point of common origin for processes of religious development, a general "primitive religion." The various possible types of "developed"[3] religious system are then to be thought of as arising by a process of differentiation from the common starting point. They represent possibilities which are to a large extent mutually exclusive. The present concern is not, however, with the historical applications, but with the logical relations of the different type elements.

For the "primitive" type it is not, Weber thinks, possible to differentiate religious and nonreligious elements on the basis of rationality as such or of the character of "ends." The ends are in general worldly and a certain relative rationality applies to religious and magical actions as well as to secular techniques. The distinction in such terms is rather one brought in from the point of view of modern views of nature and not to be found in the primitive material itself.[4] The fruitful starting point is rather the observation that religious as distinct from secular actions involve qualities, forces, etc. which are exceptional, removed from the ordinary (*ausseralltäglich*), to which a special attitude is taken and a special virtue attributed. This exceptional quality Weber calls *charisma*.[5] It is exemplified in such conceptions as mana.

---

[1] The places where this is most systematically set forth are the "Zwischenbetrachtung," *Religionssoziologie*, Vol. I, pp. 536–573, and the section "Religionssoziologie," *Wirtsch. u. Ges.*, Part II, Chap. IV. See also on the Asiatic religions, *Religionssoziologie*, Vol. II, pp. 363–378 and in general the "Einleitung," *ibid.*, Vol. I, pp. 237–275.

[2] Chap. XVII.

[3] These terms are purposely put in quotation marks. They are here relevant only to the process in which Weber is interested.

[4] But see the view of Malinowski quoted above, p. 425.

[5] *Wirtsch. u. Ges.*, p. 227. A term coined by himself. The similarity of this concept to Durkheim's *sacré* is striking, as is that of the general approach of the two men to these problems. The theoretical significance of this similarity will be fully discussed below (see Chap. XVII).

From this conception of things "set apart" can easily arise that of a "world" of entities different from that involved in the ordinary affairs of everyday life—in this sense and only this, a "supernatural" world. The ways in which these entities may be conceived and the character of their relations to the "natural" world are most various. They may, for example, be distinguished as "personal" and "impersonal," but Weber does not for present purposes lay great stress on these distinctions; the important thing is the difference of attitude toward these entities, however conceived, from that toward everyday things. They tend to issue in two types of entity; in so far as this supernatural world is involved in the individual personality itself, it becomes the "soul," or if outside the individual, "gods" or "demons." Whether or not the conceptions are anthropomorphic is of secondary importance. The ordering of the relations of these entities to men is what Weber designates as the realm of religious action.[1]

One further element of this complex is important. This quality of special apartness, charisma, is often attributed to objects, acts, human beings, which in other respects belong to the everyday world or are closely related to it. This quality is in some sense a manifestation of these supernatural forces or entities. Some distinction between the natural and the supernatural elements in these concrete things is imperative. Among the possible interpretations of the relation of the two elements is that the former symbolizes the latter. As Weber says, "Now not only do things play a part in life which are merely there and happen, but also which have a 'meaning' and are there because of this meaning. With this, magic, from the direct action of forces, becomes symbolism."[2] However different the "native" interpretation of this may be from our own self-conscious symbolism, here is an element of fundamental importance.

From this basal idea Weber draws one of his fundamental theses, that the first effect of "religious ideas" on action including economic action—an effect everywhere present—is to sanction the stereotyping of tradition.[3] "Every magical procedure which has been 'proved' efficacious is naturally repeated strictly in the successful form. That is extended to the whole realm of sym-

[1] *Wirtsch. u. Ges.*, p. 229.
[2] *Ibid.*, p. 230.
[3] *Ibid.*, p. 231.

bolically meaningful actions. The slightest departure from the approved norm may vitiate the action. All branches of human activity get drawn into this circle of symbolic magic."[1] While there are specific acts and complexes of action which are in Durkheim's term typically "profane," that is not true of any of the great spheres of conduct, economic or political activity, love or war. In so far as these are brought into relation with charismatic forces they become traditionalized. As Weber says, "The sacred is that which is specifically unalterable."[2]

The above characterization is that of only a very broad basis of "primitive" religion. In a large number of different respects there can, on this general basis, be variations of different types and developments in different directions. Weber treats them at considerable length and with at least the beginnings of a systematic classification. There is no space here to follow through these complexities. There may be, however, great variations in the character of the supernatural entities involved, their relations to each other, to men of different classes and to the nonhuman world. There may be variations in the ways in which these sacred traditions are maintained and transmitted, by word of mouth or in written form, in the degree of specialization as between those who do and do not have especially intimate relations with sacred things and the relations of specialists such as the magician and the priest to other classes in the community.

However important these differences may be in other connections, they do not touch what is for Weber the central question of the way out of traditionalism. Religion remains on this level an aspect of the general social community and on the whole sanctions the general structure of this community and its practices, including ritual.[3] What is lacking is a rationally systematized attitude toward the religiously significant aspects of life.

Once the level of symbolism is reached the question arises of the "meaning" of things and events of this world. Rationalization

---

[1] *Ibid.*, p. 230.

[2] *Ibid.*, p. 231. Points bearing on the theoretical explanation of this have already been discussed above (Chap. XI) and will be further elaborated below.

[3] This is a type closely resembling what Professor A. D. Nock calls "cultural" religion.

of these discrete meanings into a coherent system, an inclusive interpretation of the world as a whole and man's place in it, is an "immanent" need of the intellect once the question of meaning is raised. It is as one of the points where this question is most acutely raised that Weber lays such great stress on the problem of suffering, more broadly that of evil.[1] This leads up, by the process of rationalization, to the great theodicy conceptions.[2] But this rationalization is deeply inhibited by traditionalism. For the traditionalistic situation will inevitably have assimilated and given its traditional sanction to very diverse elements which cannot all be accepted in *any* single rational system.[3]

Hence a carrying of the rationalization process beyond a certain point involves a break with traditionalism and, conversely, every sharp break with traditionalism involves rationalization —for the breaker of tradition is by his very act forced to define his attitudes toward that with which he has broken. When such breaks with tradition involve religious elements, that is, when the breaker claims charismatic authority, Weber calls the process "prophecy" and the personal agent of it a "prophet."[4] It is with prophecy and its implications and effects that the main body of his sociology of religion is concerned. The prophet is significant as the initiator of a great process of rationalization in the interpretation of the "meaning" of the world and the attitudes men should take toward it. The possible attitudes they can take Weber holds to be conditioned by the structure of ideas which results from this process.

As has been pointed out, Weber is interested in systems of religious ideas as *differentiating* elements in social development. Underlying this interest is his basic thesis that the process of religious rationalization is not predetermined by its immanent nature in *one* particular direction, but that it can proceed in a limited number of possible directions according to various circumstances. Though the subtypes are numerous, the major directions can be reduced to two—a dualism, which runs through all of Weber's work on this subject.

[1] *Religionssoziologie*, Vol. I, pp. 241 *ff.*
[2] *Wirtsch. u. Ges.*, pp. 246 *ff.*
[3] This is a theorem which Weber maintains is proved by a vast body of factual evidence.
[4] *Ibid.*, pp. 250 *ff.*

Weber defines the prophet as "a purely personal[1] bearer of *charisma* who by virtue of his 'mission' preaches a religious doctrine or a divine command."[2] He is always one who has a mission, who feels himself in particularly close connection with a "supernatural" entity or order. And he undertakes his mission without authorization by any human agency, in fact in conscious opposition to all such agencies. Jesus' words, "It is written . . . , but *I* say unto you . . . ," the opposite, are typical. Of the two forms of mission, a command, if it is to make sense, implies a doctrine but a doctrine need not imply any commands.

It is on this basis that Weber distinguishes his two fundamental types of prophecy. Either the prophet feels himself to be the instrument of a divine will, bringing in the latter's name a concrete command or a norm with which people should comply as an ethical duty. This is ethical prophecy[3] (Mohammed, Jesus). Or he is one who by his personal example shows others the way to religious salvation (Buddha), what Weber calls exemplary prophecy. But whichever type is involved, prophecy always implies "first for the prophet, then for his followers a unified attitude toward life gained by a deliberate meaningful stand taken toward it."[4] Human action must, to realize religious interests, be in conformity with the coherent meaning of the world implied in such a stand.

The ethical prophet feels himself to be the instrument of a divine will. As such a part of his mission is to give men ethical norms with which they are expected to conform. And by definition these norms are different from the existing traditional state of affairs. The rationalization of this situation leads in a particular direction. The will of which the prophet is an instrument, the source of the new norms, cannot be merely a manifestation of the immanent order of the world as it is. Only the conception of a transcendental personal God,[3] concerned with, but not in his essence involved in, the existing cosmic and human order, can be adequate to ethical prophecy. This is not to say that such a conception of God arose only as a "rationalization"[5] of ethical

---

[1] He is not "legitimized" by any human authority, especially neither by tradition nor an "office."

[2] *Wirtsch. u. Ges.*, p. 250.

[3] *Ibid.*, p. 255.

[4] *Ibid.*, p. 257.

[5] In the derogatory sense.

prophets, or vice versa, but that they are phenomena mutually interdependent. Thus Weber holds that the pantheistic conceptions of India and China, once firmly established,[1] were enough to prevent the development of ethical prophecy.

On the other hand, such a pantheistic conception of the divine as an immanent principle of order is related to the emergence of the exemplary prophet. A norm or command to change the world is out of the question, but not an attempt to live in harmony with it. And there is no inherent reason why traditional modes of achieving this "harmony" should be beyond criticism; indeed they certainly are not. In the sense of a path to salvation, an exemplary prophet may well have a new doctrine that is not traditional, and others may follow his example and his teaching of the doctrine.

There is one immediate social implication of the appearance of a prophet. If his prophecying is efficacious he gathers about him a community[2] of disciples. The fact that prophecy itself involves a break with traditionalism means that the relation of both the prophet and his followers to the society in which they appear is highly problematical, especially to the bearers of its religious tradition, but also to other elements. Moreover, in the course of its own development, this community or *Gemeinde* inevitably undergoes changes within itself, particularly the change of leadership from the founder to his successors. In all these matters a large number of different possibilities are open according to the character of the prophet and his doctrine and to the circumstances. But the main fact is that prophetic religion is a source of social organization independent of the immanent development of the traditional order. It may also itself become retraditionalized, but not necessarily so. Religion thus becomes not merely an aspect of a social community, but the basis of one.

The social implications of a prophetic movement, both within its *Gemeinde* and without, depend, in relation to the character of the prophecy and the system of ideas it involves, on the means it takes to the realization of its religious interests. These again fall into a dichotomy of two main types which Weber calls asceticism and mysticism. Their significance, however, only becomes

---

[1] "Established" may, in Paretian terms, be taken to mean "turned into residues."

[2] "Gemeinde," *Wirtsch. u. Ges.*, pp. 257 *ff*.

understandable on the basis of Weber's view, already noted, that *no* traditional order can be made to conform completely to the requirements of *any* fully rationalized conception of the meaning of the world. Hence it is inevitable that certain elements at least of the worldly order will come into conflict with religious values.[1] It is this conflict that indeed forms the basis of the need for "salvation."

In this conflict there are in principle two generally possible attitudes compatible with a consistent rational view. It is obvious that the world cannot be simply "accepted." Then worldly things can, so far as possible, be controlled, mastered in the interest of the religious idea. Or, on the other hand, they may be radically devalued and become indifferent. In Weber's terminology the former course is the ascetic, the latter the mystical.[2] Each may, in turn, be subdivided into worldly[3] and otherworldly types.

Both are carried through in a radical form only by a minority of religious virtuosos.[4] The unequal religious qualification of men is a fact on which Weber lays great stress.[5] The ascetic type of salvation is associated with ethical prophecy. The individual feels himself to be an instrument of God's will. He must hence, in terms of the latter, subject the traditional ethical code to a radical criticism, and set for himself ideals far above those of the mass even of "good" men. The "world" becomes sinful, in the extreme case radically evil, something to be combated and, if possible, controlled.

According to circumstances this may take one of two directions. The "world" to be fought and mastered may be only within oneself—for such a person there are no positive duties beyond that. Then the ascetic will flee the world, as hermit or monk. Or, where this retirement from the world is excluded as it was in Protestantism, the only recourse is to control, not only oneself, but also the rest of the world, which still, however, remains

---

[1] *Wirtsch. u. Ges.*, pp. 330 *ff.*; *Religionssoziologie*, Vol. I, "Zwischen-betrachtung."

[2] *Wirtsch. u. Ges.*, pp. 310 *ff.*

[3] "Worldly" here means remaining within the order of society, not an inner attachment to "worldly" goods. "Otherworldly" involves, on the other hand, a break with the everyday social order.

[4] A term Weber frequently uses.

[5] *Wirtsch. u. Ges.*, p. 310.

sinful. Otherworldly asceticism is also compatible with the pantheistic background as a means of mastering the interfering desires and interests of the flesh, thus rendering them harmless.

On the other hand, the end of salvation may be the attainment of an exceptional higher "state," through "mystical experience." This is attained only by a minority, using a systematic technique, that of "contemplation." The interests of the world can appear only as disturbances. To one with such an experience there can be no positive relation to such interests; they can only be avoided. The result is indifference to the world, attained either by avoiding it as far as possible—"otherworldly mysticism"—or living in it but not of it, allowing no inner attachment to it—"worldly mysticism." The connection of this attitude with the immanent, impersonal conception of the divine is evident.

The relations of these different roads to salvation to the different elements of social life are by no means simple and cannot be analyzed here. But in general it can be said that the farther over on the mystical side the position is, the more difficult it is for a stable social organization to grow up on a religious basis, even a *Gemeinde*, without a reversion to traditionalism, and the less influence the system of religious ideas will have on the life of the society except indirectly in stereotyping tradition. Buddhism represents the extreme in this direction.[1]

On the other hand, the farther over the position is in the ascetic direction, the more the opposite is true under certain conditions. Otherworldly asceticism may become radically antisocial, but the worldly asceticism of Protestantism represents the extreme of possible religious interest in shaping the organization of life in this world in the image of a rationalized religious ideal.

Weber sharply rejects the view that these rationalized systems of religious ideas can be understood as the creation of any "material" conditions.[2] They are, on the contrary, the outcome of the immanent *Eigengesetzlichkeit* of solving the problem of the meaning of the world from different starting points. He does, however, allow a very considerable role for nonreligious factors in the concrete processes by which they develop and in the particular

---

[1] That is, in its asocial character. It did not provide so strong a sanction of "lay" traditionalism as did Brahmanic Hinduism.

[2] This statement is made many times.

directions the development takes. A few of the main relations may be noted.

In the first place, the emergence of prophecy itself, and hence the start of the whole process, is to be attributed in a large degree to social situations. Above all, where the traditional values have been shaken and overt conflicts arisen, a strong stimulus is given to "taking a stand." In fact prophets have often been related to social conflicts. Secondly, when a society is differentiated, the problems of the meaning of the world will not be entirely the same for all classes of society. Just as the social significance of a system of religious ideas lies in its canalization of interests, so the kinds of ideas one will turn to will depend on the kind of problems one is faced with. Not in the sense that class interests determine religious ideas, but that some types of class situation make its members more receptive to a given line of religious thought than to another—or to the idea of salvation at all.[1] Third, the chances for a given religious doctrine to gain a predominant position in a culture are bound up with the position in the social "balance of power" of the class who are its principal bearers. This has been illustrated above in the case of the Brahmans.

On the other side it must again be made clear what is Weber's conception of the mode of influence of systems of religious ideas on practical life and through that on social structure. Society is not in any sense merely an "emanation" product of the religious idea. The process is, on the contrary, highly complex. The central theoretical concept is that of religious "interest." Ideas are effective in action because they determine the directions of practical activity in which the interests can be pursued.

But the very conception of interest implies another factor. Human action is subject not only to "ideal" but to real conditions. Moreover the rationalization that is the characteristic of these religious systems involves sacrifice of many potential values which are more or less embodied in social institutions. The process is, then, one of highly complex interaction between these various elements. In the process a selective influence at least may be exercised on the course of the development of the religious system itself. Finally, the elements of potential conflict, especially between religious interests and the "world," which are absolutely

[1] See *Wirtsch. u. Ges.*, pp. 267 *ff.*

fundamental to Weber, ensure that the process shall be highly dynamic. Nothing is more unjust than to accuse Weber, because he insisted on the social importance of religious ideas, of a naïve monistic "emanation" theory of the mode of their influence.

The Protestant ethic can now be set in the broad perspective of Weber's comparative treatment of religion. Certain fundamental features were common to the religious developments of both China and India, however much these two may differ from each other. Rationalization of religious thought in both cases went in the immanent, impersonal, pantheistic direction, starting from the conception of an impersonal order of ritual forces, tao and rita. Connected with this is the fact that in neither development did there appear a movement of *ethical* prophecy, setting up ethical standards in opposition to the traditional order.

Another circumstance on which Weber lays great stress was that the rationalized religious ideas in both areas were the creation of cultivated intellectual classes.[1] In both the status of the class and its highest religious good were bound up with "knowledge," not the empirical knowledge of modern Western science but knowledge of a totally different order. It was either the knowledge of a literary tradition, as in China predominantly, or a mystic gnosis.[2] In either case faith, in the Christian sense, was excluded. And since this knowledge was accessible only to the cultivated few there was a great chasm between the sophisticated religion of the elite and the religion of the masses. The latter was not shaken out of its state of magical traditionalism; it remained "primitive."

In China, in keeping with the character of the mandarin class who were the bearers of the Confucian tradition, the rationalization process took an entirely worldly direction. All metaphysical speculation was rigidly avoided. But precisely on this account a radical rationalization of the meaning of the world did not arise at all. Rationalization remained confined to adaptation to a given order of things. This order itself, including its ritual and magical elements, was left unquestioned. There was hence no motive for salvation by escape from it, and equally no Archimedean point from which to undertake its radical reconstruction. Confucian rationality is that of prudent conservatism, adaptation

---

[1] In contrast to Christianity.
[2] *Religionssoziologie*, Vol. II, pp. 364 *ff.*

to a given order. In so far as sophisticated minds departed from this worldliness it was not in the direction of worldly asceticism but of Taoist mysticism, the counterpart of the Indian movements.

In India, on the other hand, the radical rationalization did take place in the hands of the cultivated intellectuals. This process yielded the doctrines of karma and transmigration. For the masses, linked with the caste hierarchy, there resulted only the sanction of an extreme of traditionalized immobility; as Weber says, "the one completely logically consistent form of an 'organic' theory of society which has ever arisen."[1] For the elite, on the other hand, salvation could lie only in turning away from the things of this world in mystical contemplation and other-worldly asceticism. The traditional order was either left untouched as in Buddhism or radically sanctioned as in Hinduism. In both religions, to use Weber's words,

> . . . the layman [in China the man without literary schooling] to whom the gnosis and hence the highest religious goal is denied, or who repudiates it for himself, acts ritualistically and traditionally in the pursuit of his everyday interests. Everywhere the unlimited acquisitiveness of the Asiatic is famous as unequalled, and on the whole rightly. But it is an "acquisitive impulse" which is served with all possible means of deception and with the help of the ubiquitous recourse to magic. There was lacking precisely what was decisive for the economic life of the West—the rational disciplining of this impulsive character of acquisition and its incorporation into a system of rational ethical conduct in the world. This was brought about by the "wordly asceticism" of Protestantism carrying the beginnings of a few related predecessors to completion. For such a development the necessary elements were lacking in the Asiatic religions.[2]

The differences of the ethic of ascetic Protestantism from the religious ethics of both China and India should now be clear. In Weber's typology it is the extreme logical antithesis of the Buddhistic, more generally that of Indian mysticism. China lies between. In its radical Calvinistic form the Protestant rationalization of the world combines the following elements: (1) the transcendental God, (2) predestination, involving the complete cutting off of the individual from salvation by his own efforts including the gnosis of mystical contemplation, (3) the sinfulness

[1] *Ibid.*, p. 367.
[2] *Ibid.*, p. 372.

of the flesh leading to the most radical possible tension between ideal and real, (4) the conception of man as the instrument of God's will in building the Kingdom of God on Earth with its tendency to guide religious interests in the direction of active ascetic mastery over the world in the interest of an ideal, finally (5) the complete corruption of the world which implied the absolute devaluation of traditionalism, especially magical, ritual or symbolic. If *any* system of religious ideas could constitute an active social force, surely it was this.[1]

PROTESTANTISM AND CAPITALISM: SCHEMATIC SUMMARY

In conclusion, the question may again be raised of the sense in which Weber may be said to have "proved" his original thesis that the Protestant ethic was one basic factor in the development of Western rational bourgeois capitalism, and though not standing alone, an indispensable one. As a result of the above unavoidably long discussion the following conclusions as to Weber's position seem to be justified:[2]

1. By contrast with other civilizations, rational bureaucratic organization and closely related forms are major elements in the distinctive social structure of the modern West.

2. There is a congruence of the ethic of ascetic Protestantism with the bureaucratic rational bourgeois element of modern Western capitalism and its *Geist*.

3. There is a lack of congruence with the spirit of capitalism of the ethical implications of the major Asiatic religions. In so far as they have had an influence on secular social life it *could not* have been in a rational bourgeois capitalistic direction. In the thesis that the Protestant ethic was the only religious ethic which could have had such an influence, there is a gap left in the present presentation, which has not taken up the ethics of Judaism, Islam and the non-Protestant branches of Christianity. This gap was by no means left completely unfilled by Weber himself

---

[1] Calvinism and Buddhism represent the antithetical polar extremes of Weber's classification so far as his empirical material goes. Whether they are maxima in any more general theoretical sense need not be discussed.

[2] Compare with the formulation of von Schelting, *Max Webers Wissenschaftslehre*, pp. 287 *ff.* Though the position stated here was arrived at for the most part independently of Dr. von Schelting, its formulation was aided by his work and the agreement in the general interpretation of what Weber had and claimed to have proved is most gratifying.

though just this part of his work was left unfinished at his death. He unquestionably planned to fill it completely. In general, it may be said without presenting supporting evidence that all these three religious ethics are less unfavorable to capitalistic development than the Asiatic religions, especially since the conception of a transcendental God was common to them. But also each of them contained serious obstacles to the full force of the Protestant type of thought. But, after all, Protestantism was the product of a long process of development continuous from early Judaism.

4. In general there is a high degree of correspondence between what, on the basis of "ideal-typical" construction, the concrete social influence of the three religious ethics treated here would be expected to be, and the actual empirical state of affairs. This is strong prima-facie evidence for the reality of such influence, placing the burden of proof on anyone who would question it.

5. In a considerable part of the field, though not in all, Weber has been able to trace the unfolding of the actual processes and mechanisms by which this influence has probably been exerted. This greatly strengthens the prima-facie case referred to in point four.

6. Weber has not established and never meant to establish that other than religious elements have not to a highly important degree been involved both in the concrete process of development of a religious ethic itself, and in that of its influence on concrete social affairs.[1] On the contrary, such an interpretation is directly opposed to Weber's whole fundamental position in sociology, which as will be seen is a voluntaristic theory of action and not an idealistic theory of emanation. The attempt has been made to set forth typical examples of the different ways in which he held nonreligious elements to be involved. But this is only a sample. Anyone who reads his work carefully can be easily convinced that Weber was anything but a naïve oversimplifier.

7. On the matter of quantitative imputation of the religious as against other factors Weber has not arrived at any conclusion (such as that the causation of modern capitalism was 47 per cent Protestant) nor did he claim to have done so. Indeed on methodological grounds such a claim could, in problems like those Weber

---

[1] Even if he does not say so explicitly, Professor Sorokin's language is often such as strongly to suggest this erroneous interpretation. See, for instance, *Contemporary Sociological Theories*, pp. 678, 680, 682.

was dealing with, have no meaning. A phenomenon is not "compounded" in a given proportion of the "variables" which are used to explain it. And even the values of these variables are like most in the social field reduced not to quantitative terms but, like Pareto's residues, to a classification.

But this does not mean that Weber's work has not increased our scientific knowledge of the relations between religious ideas, action and social structure. For, the above points combined with his estimates of the net favorableness and unfavorableness of the constellations of nonreligious elements justify the conclusion that the Protestant ethic was a major factor in the capitalistic development, that it was a necessary though not sufficient condition, and more generally that religious ethics constitute a major factor in the differentiation of the characters of the great civilizations from each other.

That these judgments of the favorableness and unfavorableness of the *total* nonreligious situation are estimates, not rigorous proofs, Weber would be the first to admit. But so must any empirical judgment of such scope arrived at by such an analytical procedure be.[1] Weber has left us, by his interpretation of the evidence, with a balance of capitalistic predisposition on the whole in favor of the oriental countries, especially China. In order seriously to damage his general position it would be necessary to turn the balance a long way in the other direction. In any event this can be done only by a detailed critical examination of the empirical evidence on which Weber's judgments were based, and whatever additional relevant evidence may now be available. This is entirely beyond the scope of the present study, but the opinion may be ventured that none of the critics of Weber's general position has done it. The burden of proof rests upon them.

On this basis, then, it seems justified to accept Weber's theory of the relations of Protestantism and capitalism, in the only sense in which it is ever justified to accept a scientific theory. Within the limits of its own claims, it is in conformity with all the facts with which the present author is acquainted. The facts brought against it in the critical literature will not stand examination with respect both to their factual correctness as such and to their relevance to and importance for Weber's problems. Aside

[1] Weber certainly did not exhaust the analytical possibilities. The methodological question will be discussed in the next chapter.

from those brought forward explicitly by critics, none have been advanced that are, in the present writer's opinion, damaging to his position. This, of course, does not mean that Weber's, any more than any other scientific theory, should be held immune from continual retesting in terms of any new facts that may come to light. The attempt to discover these would, however, be clearly outside the present scope. The present discussion has been concerned with the status of the theory on empirical grounds. In the latter part of the next chapter will be brought forward methodological considerations that do affect the theory, not in the validity of its central thesis, but in its form of statement and in certain implications.

This discussion of Weber's treatment of religion and capitalism, prolonged though it is, is at best a poor substitute for the extraordinary richness of the original work. The attempt has been made to state the main outline of Weber's position. But of necessity most of the supporting evidence and many relevant considerations have been left aside. This discussion is the "ideal type" of an "ideal type." Its inadequacies, many of which are inherent in the nature of the enterprise, should not be blamed upon Weber. The discussion now turns to the methodological position that lies at the basis of Weber's empirical research.

CHAPTER XVI

MAX WEBER, III: METHODOLOGY[1]

Weber devoted even more explicit attention to methodological problems than did Pareto and much more than Durkheim, a circumstance which is fortunate since it brings out explicitly many things important for the present context which would otherwise have to be elicited by analysis. No more than with respect to the other thinkers will there be attempted here a critical estimate of Weber's *total* significance to the social sciences either on the methodological side or on any other. But a good share of his methodological work is of peculiar relevance.

Like the other principal figures of this study, indeed like the work of most creative minds[2] in science, a good deal of Weber's methodological work has a distinctly polemical element. But it is perhaps even more prominent in his case than in that of the others; so that most of his methodological views were developed in directly polemical essays. Indeed he never wrote a general statement of his methodological position except in very brief form,[3] apart from an immediately polemical context. This fact makes understanding it as a whole difficult and in the absence, until

---

[1] It is indeed fortunate that there is available for the purposes of this chapter the excellent secondary study, already referred to, by Dr. Alexander von Schelting, *Max Webers Wissenschaftslehre.* Secondary work of such quality is distressingly rare in the field this study has covered. The present writer is greatly indebted to Dr. von Schelting's treatment at many points and will follow him closely, especially in the first part of the chapter. Although in general there is close agreement with Dr. von Schelting as far as he goes, it seems, as will appear, that he neglects certain of the limits of Weber's "methodological self-interpretation" which are vital for present purposes. See also the present writer's review of Dr. von Schelting's book in *American Sociological Review*, August, 1936.

[2] Scientific "prophets," as it were.

[3] The most important is in Chapter I of *Wirtschaft und Gesellschaft*, reprinted in *Gesammelte Aufsätze zur Wissenschaftslehre* (hereafter cited as *Wissenschaftslehre*), pp. 503–523.

quite recently,[1] of really authoritative secondary interpretation helps to explain the large amount of misunderstanding and controversy that has arisen over it.

The justification for dealing with Weber in connection with the "idealistic" tradition lies in the fact that, though his own position does not fall there, his polemical starting point is in opposition to some of the commonest methodological doctrines of that school.[2] The doctrines which he attacks may be classified roughly under two headings, which, following Dr. von Schelting, may be called objectivism and intuitionism.[3]

Underlying the whole discussion is the common German distinction, remarked upon above,[4] between the "natural" sciences and the sciences dealing with human action and culture, which can be traced back to the Kantian dualism. In terms of positive influence, Weber's own position owes most to Rickert.[5] It will not, however, be necessary here to investigate in detail the question of its genesis, but only to state its main outline. Hence its antecedents are relevant only as a means to the understanding in general of the situation from which he started.

In the above discussion of the background of the idealistic tradition the tendency was noted for idealistic social thought to run in two main directions.[6] The two sets of methodological doctrines within the group of social sciences which Weber attacks correspond roughly to these two. Common ground for both is the denial that the sociocultural sciences can make use of "general laws"[7] of the logical character of those occupying unquestioned status in the natural sciences. The difference of the two schools is over what they consider to be the reasons for this alleged fact. Weber's quarrel with both is essentially over this issue. He still holds to the distinction of the natural and social sciences, but

[1] Dr. von Schelting's book was published in 1934.

[2] Just as the polemical starting point of Durkheim is the "utilitarian" position.

[3] Weber's polemic in this context is documented mainly in the series of essays on *Roscher und Knies und die logischen Probleme der historischen Nationaloekonomie,* reprinted in *Wissenschaftslehre,* pp. 1–145.

[4] Chap. XIII.

[5] HEINRICH RICKERT, especially *Über die Grenzen der naturwissenschaftlichen Begriffsbildung.*

[6] Chap. XIII, pp. 475 *ff.*

[7] Called by Rickert "nomological" knowledge.

radically denies that it can rest on the exclusion from the latter of general explanatory concepts.

One of the two main idealistic trends was in the direction of historical "particularism." This view is that the historical and social sciences should concern themselves only with the detailed facts of particular human acts and not attempt to build up *any* general theories. Weber, of course, denied neither the desirability of detailed historical research[1] nor the possibility of legitimate empirical criticisms of particular systems of systematic theory which had been set up in the social sciences, for instance, that of the classical economics. What he attacked was, rather, the elevation of this "tendency" into the methodological dogma that systematic theoretical thinking could not legitimately be used in the social field. Indeed he went a step farther than criticism of this view, to maintain that every demonstrable judgment of historical explanation rested implicitly if not explicitly on such general, theoretical concepts.

The search for a basis for this dogma led to the view that it was founded in the fact that the objective nature of the subject matter of the social sciences was such as to make generalization about it impossible. Human action was held not to be subject to regularities in the sense that the phenomena of nature are. Since general concepts formulate such regularities they cannot be applicable to such a subject matter. Hence the necessity for research being confined to particular description, and explanation, if attempted at all, involving only the specific temporal antecedents of a given event, without reference to general principles.[2]

This position was put in the form that historical reality is "irrational."[3] General concepts, on the other hand, are rational, and the two cannot meet. Weber, in the first place, accepts the proposition that the completely concrete historical reality is of infinite diversity and complexity so that in the full richness of its concreteness and individuality it cannot be grasped in terms of any system of abstract concepts. But he denies both that this constitutes a ground of difference from the natural sciences and

[1] He himself was a distinguished contributor to it.

[2] This is the necessary implication of radical empiricism in the one direction, as is "intuitionism" in the other. See below.

[3] See *Wissenschaftslehre*, pp. 64 *ff.*; von Schelting, *op. cit.*, pp. 182 *ff.*

that it is in any way relevant to the problems of the *logical* nature of scientific categories. All "raw" experience is of this character. What we formulate as scientific laws about "nature" is not the total concrete reality even as humanly "experienceable" but certain particular aspects, which can be expressed in abstract concepts.[1] Precisely the same is true of the subject matter of human action. Whatever the basis of difference between the two groups of sciences (and Weber believes there is one) it does not lie on this plane. It must lie in the principles according to which, among "experienceable" elements of reality, "facts" are to be selected which are significant for a given scientific purpose. This lies, in Weber's opinion, in its logically relevant respects; not in the objective nature of the "reality" a science deals with, but in the "subjective" direction of interest of the scientist.

With this are connected two other important points. First the goal of "adequate" knowledge in a given field can never be to know "all the facts," that is, the total concrete reality; such a goal is impossible.[2] A standard of adequacy of knowledge must be relative to the scientific purpose in hand. Whatever it is, it falls short of "all the facts." Secondly, it follows from these considerations that *logically* the natural and social sciences are in the same situation with respect to the standard so often applied, predictability. In neither case is it ever possible to predict future states of affairs in all their concrete fullness of detail. Weber uses the example of the distribution of fragments of a boulder shattered by falling in a storm.[3] No science known to man is capable of predicting the exact size, shape and position of every fragment after a storm from data available before the storm. Nor does anyone want to know. Predictability in the natural sciences seems to be high because our *interest* is predominantly in the aspects of natural events formulable in terms of known abstract laws. Our interest in human affairs is generally on a different level. In any case predictability is always relative to the extent of abstract generalization, and where this exists predictability follows. Weber is careful to point out how much of actual social

[1] In this antiempiricist interpretation of the logical nature of natural laws Weber, writing about thirty years ago, was a pioneer in a movement which has since become predominant.

[2] Pareto, it will be remembered, expressed the same view. See Chap. V, p. 183.

[3] *Wissenschaftslehre*, pp. 65, 67.

life is completely dependent on the ability to predict with reasonable accuracy the reaction of others to a given stimulus. For example, how much "militarism" would be possible if officers could not depend on obedience to commands, that is, predict the behavior of their soldiers after the commands had been issued? Indeed it was in just this predictable aspect of social life that Weber had a peculiar interest.

But driven from this position the objectivist may fall back on another and say that there is a certain mystery about men and their actions. Nature has no secrets to the scientist; there is nothing mysterious about her; but human action is not "understandable";[1] it is in that sense "irrational."

To this Weber replies by turning the tables. Far from the natural sciences having the advantage in understandability, in principle the reverse is true. For in nature we can only observe the external course of events and discover elements of uniformity. This is equally possible for human behavior but *in addition* the scientist is able to impute motives to men, to "interpret" their actions and words as expressions of these motives. That is, we have access to the subjective aspect of action. In so far as the facts of human action give access to this, they carry a peculiar quality of their own (*Evidenz*).[2] This is the first appearance in Weber's methodology of the fundamentally important concept of *Verstehen*.[3]

This fact constitutes an objective difference between the subject matters of the two groups of sciences, and one of central importance. Weber does not, to be sure, make it an absolutely rigid difference in the sense that such elements are included in one concrete subject matter and rigidly excluded from the other, a position that would involve an empiricism quite foreign to his thought. There is, on the contrary, a gradual shading off toward teleological elements as in biological and perhaps even physico-

---

[1] *Wissenschaftslehre*, pp. 67 *ff.*; von Schelting, *op. cit.*, pp. 185–187.

[2] This is because they admit of interpretation as symbols. More of this later. It is to be noted that here also Weber's position is very similar to Pareto's.

[3] The impossibility of finding immediately understandable motivation for action in this sense is one of our main standards of mental abnormality (see *Wissenschaftslehre*, p. 67). It may, however, be possible to discover understandable motives of abnormal behavior on a deeper level of analysis, as by psychoanalysis.

chemical phenomena.[1] But the analytical distinction is none the less fundamental.

At the same time Weber insists that for the questions at issue this difference does not constitute the basis of a *logical* distinction of the two sets of sciences. In the field of *Verstehen* as well as of *Begreifen*,[2] general concepts have a real place, and valid empirical proof is dependent on their use, implicitly or explicitly. This raises an issue to which we shall return later.

Finally, the "irrationality"[3] of human action may be attributed to the freedom of the will—an argument of good Kantian origin, used particularly by Knies.[4] This Weber answers by again turning the tables, and in the process he uses a very interesting argument. If this were true, he says, we should expect the sense of freedom to be associated primarily with "irrational" actions, those involving emotional outbreaks and the like. On the contrary, however, the reverse is much more nearly true. It is when we act most rationally that we feel most free, and the curious thing is that, given the end, rational action is to an eminent degree both predictable and subject to analysis in terms of general concepts. The sense of freedom[5] in this case is a feeling of the absence of constraint by emotional elements.

There can be no doubt about the correctness of Weber's point and its significance is far-reaching. For the general concepts involved in the analysis of rational action in this sense (*Zweck-rational*, as Weber calls it) formulate general relations of means and ends. And these concepts are of a logical nature strictly comparable to the general laws of the physical sciences, indeed to a large extent, in such fields as technology, they involve the direct application of such laws. Thus at this early critical stage of Weber's methodological work has appeared the concept with

---

[1] *Wissenschaftslehre*, p. 91.

[2] In German *Verstehen* has come to be applied to the situation where a subjective motivational or symbolic reference is involved, while *Begreifen* is employed for the "external" grasp of uniformities where no such additional evidence is available.

[3] See *Wissenschaftslehre*, pp. 64 *ff.*; von Schelting, pp. 189 *ff.*

[4] It is as Dr. von Schelting points out not the only type with which a sense of freedom is associated.

[5] The good old term passion expresses this—it is something to which we "succumb," in the presence of which we feel helplessly carried along by forces beyond control.

which this whole study started, that of the type of rational action which involves the means-end relationship as verifiable in terms of scientific generalizations. For him, also, rationality in this sense plays a central role, methodologically as well as substantively. And it is especially interesting that its methodological role comes out in critical opposition to an idealistic theory.

By thus emphasizing the susceptibility of rational action to general causal analysis, Weber by no means intends to convey the impression that "irrational" action is not understandable (*verstehbar*) or is not also subject to such analysis. On the contrary, he most emphatically states that it is. Rational action is used primarily because of its peculiar relevance to the freedom argument.[1] Nor is Weber in the least concerned to deny that freedom of the will exists—only that it can be the basis of a *logical* difference between the natural and the social sciences, more specifically a basis for excluding general concepts from the latter.[2]

Out of the critical discussion of "objectivism"[3] has arisen not only a defense of the use of general concepts in the social sciences,[4] but a number of the important elements of Weber's own methodological theory of the latter. First through his attack on the radical empiricist position (in the terminology of this study), he has insisted upon the abstract nature of these general concepts and hence the necessity for another term of reference in their formation than the sheer "reflection" of the experienced reality. This Weber finds to be of the general order of a "subjective" direction of interest of the scientist.[5] Secondly, the subjective aspect of action as the object of *Verstehen* has made its appearance, and third, the central role of the concept of rationality of action involving a relation of means and ends. This last is particularly

[1] Rational and irrational here clearly have a narrower meaning than in the other two contexts.

[2] It is a metaphysical problem which Weber thus shows is not important to his methodological context.

[3] Not Weber's term, but one introduced by Dr. von Schelting first in his earlier study.

[4] One of the most striking statements is "So ist eine gültige Zurechung irgend eines individuellen Erfolges ohne die Verwendung 'nomologischer' Kenntnis der Regelmässigkeiten der Kausalen Zusämmenhänge, überhaupt nicht möglich." *Wissenschaftslehre*, p. 179.

[5] Involving a choice of variables.

important in that Weber shows its relevance to be not merely substantive but to go down into the deepest methodological roots of social science. Rationality of action and systematic scientific theory are inseparably linked. The development of science is a process of action, and action is in part an application of science.

Intuitionism

Under the term intuitionism a highly diverse group of methodological doctrines may, following Dr. von Schelting,[1] be grouped together. The present sketch, like his own analysis, in no way pretends to do justice to the great philosophical systems which in one way or another stand back of these doctrines. It is, rather, concerned with a single fundamental methodological point— whether these doctrines may claim to have established the possibility of valid scientific knowledge of the phenomena of human action without reference to general concepts. It is this claim which Weber attacks.[2]

In their predominant trend the intuitionist theories may be held in the main to constitute the methodological rationalization of the collectivist branch of German historical thought.[3] This, it will be remembered, was concerned with the grasp of total cultural *Gestalten* as wholes in their unique individuality. Moreover, in the cultural-social field it has been linked with the theory of *Verstehen*. The essence of these cultural totalities has been found in some kind of "meaningful" system of which the concrete facts constitute an expression or a manifestation. The elevation of this tendency into a methodological dogma has involved two main propositions which are not inseparably linked in logic. One is that "generalization" in the field of human affairs can only mean the grasp of these cultural totalities in all their uniqueness and individuality. The other is that this grasp takes the form of an immediate "intuition"[4]—a direct grasp of meaning without the intervention of concepts in any form. It is this latter, more radical proposition which Weber directly attacks. His relation to the other is more complex.

---

[1] von Schelting, *op. cit.*, pp. 195 *ff.*

[2] The principal names Weber himself deals with are Wundt, Münsterberg, Lipps, Simmel, Croce.

[3] See Chap. XIII, pp. 478 *ff.*

[4] *Einfühlung* is one of the commonest German terms, *Nacherleben* another.

In this connection there are a number of arguments brought forward by Weber. Three are important to this discussion. First, he maintains that the intuitionists confuse two distinct things: (1) the processes by which valid knowledge is arrived at and (2) the logical grounds of its validity.[1] He fully grants that our knowledge of important historical relationships is not arrived at exclusively, or even predominantly, by logical deduction from known facts, but that "flashes of insight" play an important part. But, in the first place, this fact is by no means confined to the genesis of knowledge of human action or phenomena to which the method of *Verstehen* is applicable; it is true generally. Secondly, the psychological (rather the subjective) mode of origin of a piece of knowledge is logically quite heterogeneous from the grounds of its validity. The latter need become explicit only when it is necessary to demonstrate the truth of a proposition.[2] And this last will always be found to involve general concepts.

Secondly, the intuitionists confuse the "raw data of experience" with "knowledge."[3] This point brings the argument back to the previous discussion of objectivism. In this particular context the important thing is that the "whole" which is picked out and set forth is never a simple reproduction of immediately given experience. It involves selection and systematization of the elements of this experience.[4] And this selection and systematization involves relating experience to concepts, including general concepts which serve as the basis of judging what *elements* of the raw experience are significant to the whole. This is as true of the social as of the natural sciences.

It is interesting to note that there is one type of phenomenon which can apparently be grasped with an immediacy approaching that which the intuitionist claims—that of the rationality of

---

[1] *Wissenschaftslehre*, p. 96; von Schelting, *op. cit.*, p. 200. The formulations in this part of the discussion follow mainly Dr. von Schelting, who has in certain respects gone beyond Weber's own in classification and systematization, though without essential alteration of meaning.

[2] *Wissenschaftslehre*, p. 111.

[3] *Erleben* and *Erkennen*. *Wissenschaftslehre*, pp. 105 *ff.*; von Schelting, *op. cit.*, p. 201.

[4] Weber might well have gone a step farther and pointed out that experience itself is never "raw" in that sense but is itself "in terms of a conceptual scheme." Raw experience is itself an abstraction of an *element* of knowledge.

action. But this is precisely because the conceptual element is already contained *explicitly* in the object of intuition itself.[1]

One thing Weber grants, that in our statements about human affairs the conceptual element often remains implicit, and the statements take a form suggesting immediate intuition.[2] This, Weber says, is owing to the fact that common knowledge in this field reaches so far, and above all covers so many of the aspects of interest to the social scientist, that to make them explicit would be superfluous; they are omitted on grounds of "economy." But this does not imply that they are logically irrelevant to the validity of the statements.

The fundamental point is that "immediate experience" is diffuse and not capable of precise formulation. It is only through concepts that such precision can be gained. Weber suggests here a principle in terms of which selection and systematization can be and is made—that of "relevance to value" (*Wertbeziehung*).[3]

Finally, Weber returns to his own treatment of *Verstehen*. It will be remembered that there he granted or, rather, maintained that experience with meaningful content had a special quality of immediate certainty (*Evidenz*). It is something not present in the sense data of natural events. Very obviously the intuitionist theories lay great stress on this fact. Here, however, Weber charges them with another confusion. The immediate certainty of perception of meaning is at most only *one* element in the proof of the validity of knowledge and cannot by itself be trusted. It must be checked by reference to a rationally consistent system of concepts.[4] Without this check one immediately certain intuition may give rise to an endless succession of "intuitional judgments" which depart farther and farther from reality.

This situation also is no different from that existing in the physical sciences. There immediate sense impressions cannot be trusted without theoretical, conceptual criticism. When a stick is thrust into a pool of still water there can be no doubt that the

---

[1] This case is a strong point against the "fiction" view of the nature of concepts (see below).

[2] This, again, is Dr. von Schelting's formulation which is more explicit than Weber's own.

[3] *Wissenschaftslehre*, p. 124; von Schelting, *op. cit.*, p. 204.

[4] *Wissenschaftslehre*, pp. 67 *ff.*, 88 *ff.* and many other passages; von Schelting, *op. cit.*, pp. 211 *ff.*

observer "sees" that the stick is bent at the water line; his sense impression is that of a "bent stick." When he judges that the stick is not "really" bent, but that the impression is an optical illusion, it does not mean that he does not really *see* what he describes, but that the description is corrected by reference to a general system of theoretical knowledge.[1]

Similarly in the field of *Verstehen*. Our immediate intuitions of meaning may be real and, as such, correct. But their interpretation cannot dispense with a rationally consistent system of theoretical concepts. Only in so far as they measure up to such criticism can intuitions constitute knowledge. And without such criticism the door is opened to any number of uncontrolled and unverifiable allegations. Weber had a very deep and strong ethical feeling on this point; to him the intuitionist position made possible the evasion of responsibility for scientific judgments.

Weber again, however, does not discard everything in the positions criticized. On the one hand, it is a fact that the social sciences have an interest in human action and its motivation from the subjective point of view and, on the other hand, that there is a specific quality of immediacy in the understanding of the subjective.[2] It is with the elaboration of the consequences of these facts, and their relation to systematic theoretical thinking that most of the rest of Weber's methodological work is concerned.

Before proceeding to this development it is well to stop a moment to point out the relevance of Weber's critical position to the methodological problems which have mainly occupied the general study thus far. It may be said that Weber's attack has been for the most part upon the methodology of radical empiricism.[3] It was because of the particular features of his own intellectual milieu that he attacked two particular forms of it and not the third. As has already been noted,[4] on a positivistic basis empiricism has generally involved "reification" of particular theoretical systems, such as that of the classical physics or of the classical economics—as Professor Whitehead calls it, the "fallacy of misplaced concreteness."

[1] Indeed if he did not see a bend in the stick, although it is not "really" there, there would be something wrong with his eyesight.
[2] *Wissenschaftslehre*, pp. 89, 126; von Schelting, *op. cit.*, p. 213.
[3] In the two idealistic forms discussed in Chap. XIII, not that of reification, though this also has been incidentally criticized.
[4] Chap. XIII.

The Kantian dualism and its consequences precluded this form of empiricism from playing an important role in the social sciences in Germany, since they were predominantly in the idealistic tradition. Hence Weber's immediate concern was with the two forms of radical empiricism possible on that basis—particularistic and collectivistic *Historismus*. In his critique he has on the whole left the natural sciences and the natural science model for the social on one side.

His critique has, however, had one very important result— it went a very long way toward bridging the hiatus which the idealistic methodology had created between the natural and the social sciences in a *logical* context. He concludes that both must involve systems of general theoretical concepts, for without them anything approaching logical proof is out of the question. But in neither case can this system of concepts possibly be conceived of as a literal representation of the total concrete reality of raw experience. Hence his critical position *did* react on the methodology of the natural sciences. It is interesting to note here a definite convergence on a common *logical* meeting ground with the movement of methodology from a positivistic basis, which has been seen most explicitly among the subjects of this study in Pareto. Pareto, it will be remembered, laid down a general methodological outline common to all empirical explanatory science, natural and social. But to make natural science methodology applicable to social subject matter it was necessary for him to divest it of certain positivistic-empiricist implications of earlier methodologies. Weber has come to the same result from the other side, and has seen the same implications for the natural sciences.

In fact the radical methodological hiatus between natural and social sciences in the idealistic tradition was primarily a result of its predominant empiricism with regard to *both* branches. The intuitionist theories, it must not be forgotten, however vague and metaphysical they may appear to those with positivistic leanings, are strictly *empiricist* theories.[1] And that there is perception of meaningful wholes can hardly be denied.[2]

---

[1] My colleague Professor O. H. Taylor has called this view, very aptly, "romantic empiricism."

[2] See the immense amount of work on perception by Gestaltists. The material is summarized in K. Koffka, *Principles of Gestalt Psychology*.

Given this empiricism on both sides, the fundamental reason for the hiatus is evident—there are basic substantive differences between concrete phenomena involved in the behavior of stars and of human beings. The attempt to fit the latter into a positivistic formula has uniformly failed. Weber's achievement has been to separate out these substantive differences of the order of fact from considerations of the logical character of scientific theory. While the former differ fundamentally, the latter remain fundamentally the same.

The fact that German methodological thought has been dominated by the Kantian-idealistic dualism and our own by positivistic monism has not been without its historical benefits. Certain fundamental elements of the theory of action have emerged from the positivistic tradition only by virtue of a painful process. But in the idealistic tradition these elements have been from the start in the center of the stage. Weber's task was not to vindicate their legitimacy, but to clarify their methodological status and relation to the logical structure of scientific theory.[1] *Verstehen*, value and the means-end schema are the fundamental elements peculiar to human action which for Weber are left over from his critical analysis. The question is, what did he do with them? It is clear he did not attain a fully satisfactory position. Two main difficulties arose.

Natural and Social Science

The first important question is that of the standards Weber would lay down for the selection out of the total flux of raw experience of elements which are significant for the concepts of the social sciences, since such selection is the necessary logical prerequisite of *knowledge* as distinguished from raw experience. The starting point is Weber's statement that these standards are to be found in the subjective "direction of interest" of the scientist. In interpreting what are in turn the determinants of this direction of interest in the two groups of sciences, Weber's position is not altogether clear and consistent, and hence it is here that the first serious methodological difficulty of his position arises.

[1] For this he was very widely called a positivist in Germany.

He holds that our interest in natural phenomena so far as it is a scientific interest[1] is centered in their aspects of abstract generality, not of concrete individuality. Hence the aim of the natural sciences is the formulation of a system of universally applicable general laws. For the natural sciences general concepts constitute an end in themselves. With the social sciences, on the other hand, this is not so. Our interest in human beings and their cultural achievements is not that of abstract generality but of individual uniqueness. They are not to us "cases" of general laws.[2] A man does not love "woman" but a particular woman; he is not fond of "pictures" but of particular paintings. Since in the social field interest is in the aspect of concrete individuality, general concepts cannot stand in the same relation to this interest; their formulation and verification cannot be an end in itself for the scientist's labor; they are only means to the elucidation and understanding of the particular, unique and individual phenomena. This is the formula Weber advances to cover the basic methodological distinction of the two groups of sciences. Can its grounds of justification be analyzed still farther?

In Weber's view, as far as it seems clear on this point, there is a common human basis for the interest in natural phenomena, that is, control. It is through the aspects formulable in terms of abstract general concepts that this is possible; in the application of science to technology, the forces of nature are subjected to the service of human ends. Hence the interest in them is in the general aspect, and is a uniform interest which can have, for all times and places, a common aim. Apart from this interest in control, natural phenomena are, as an object of science, indifferent to human values.

But this is just where the difference lies between natural phenomena and the social case. Human beings, their actions and cultural achievements are the embodiments of value toward which we must, in some degree, take a value attitude. Hence our interest in them is directly determined by their relevance to the values which either the scientist himself shares or which are significant to him by agreement with his own values or conflict with them.

---

[1] We may have others, such as an aesthetic interest, in natural phenomena, thus in the individuality of a sunset.

[2] *Wissenschaftslehre*, pp. 175–176, 178–179, 193. This is Weber's position, not the present writer's (see below, pp. 597 *ff.*).

It is this "relevance to value" (*Wertbeziehung*)[1] which constitutes the[2] selective organizing principle for the empirical material of the social sciences.

Even in this case, it is important to note, the concrete individuality in which our interest is centered is not that of "raw experience." There is no reason to deny such individuality to our experience of natural phenomena. It is rather a constructed, selected individuality. From the elements given in experience are selected a limited number which are important from the point of view of relevance to value. This process results in a constructed concrete phenomenon, what Weber calls the historical individual.

Now, unlike the natural science case, the important elements of the direction of interest are not here common to all humanity. For it is one of Weber's basic theorems that value systems are diverse; there is a plurality of different possible systems. In so far then, as the selection of material is determined by relevance to such systems the same concrete materials will give rise not to one historical individual but to as many as there are, in this sense, points of view from which to study it. It is, in turn, in tho process of analysis of the historical individual and comparison of it with others that general concepts are built up. It follows, then, that the process will not issue in one ultimately uniform system of general concepts but in as many systems as there are value points of view or others significant to knowledge. There can be no one universally valid system of general theory in the social sciences.[3] This is one of the main routes by which Weber arrives at his view of the "fictional" nature of social science concepts, so important to his doctrine of the ideal type.[4]

Before discussing this, however, it is necessary to prepare the ground by clarifying a number of related issues. In the first place, the principle of value relevance combined with that of the relativity of value systems introduces an element of relativity into the social sciences which raises in an acute form the question of their claim to objectivity. Does it not reduce their structures of so-called knowledge to mere "manifestations of sentiments?"

[1] *Wissenschaftslehre*, p. 178.
[2] For Weber. There are certainly others.
[3] *Wissenschaftslehre*, p. 184.
[4] Others will be discussed below, pp. 602–603.

In the first place, Weber distinguishes carefully between determination of scientific interest, through value relevance (and thus of the immediate objects of scientific study, the historical individuals) and the exercise of value judgments. Value judgments (*Wertungen*) cannot claim the objective validity of science, and science must, as a methodological ideal, be kept free from them. Even though a value element enters into the selection of the material of science, once this material is given it is possible to come to objectively valid conclusions about the causes and consequences of given phenomena free of value judgments and hence binding on anyone who wishes to attain truth, regardless of what other subjective values he may hold.

This is possible first because even though in describing a concrete phenomenon what is made the subject of scientific analysis is not the full totality of experienceable fact about it, but a selection, the facts included in the historical individual as it is constructed are objective, verifiable facts. The question whether a statement of fact is true is clearly distinguishable from that of its significance to value. The relativity of *Wertbeziehung* touches only the latter, not the former, question. Secondly, once a phenomenon is descriptively given, the establishment of causal relations between it and either its antecedents or its consequences is possible only through the application, explicitly or implicitly, of a formal schema of proof that is independent of any value system, except the value of scientific truth.[1] This formal schema is basic to all empirical science, and only in so far as they conform with it can scientific judgments that pretend to assert causal relationships be valid. It may be remarked in passing that this scheme involves the use of general concepts transcending the historical individual.[2] Thus in spite of the relativity introduced by the concept of *Wertbeziehung* Weber maintains both that it is possible to keep value judgments logically distinct from those claiming objective scientific validity, and that the latter judgments can be made with confidence, escaping the subjectivity inherent in all value judgments.

So far Weber's position is acceptable. It is not, however, possible to accept his view of the methodological relations of the

----

[1] See von Schelting, *op. cit.*, pp. 255 *ff*.

[2] Weber's historical individual is clearly simply a unit or combination adequately described for theoretical purposes within a frame of reference.

natural and the social sciences. It has been pointed out that his critique of the objectivist and intuitionist methodologies has gone a long way to bridge the gap between the two groups of disciplines created by the Kantian dualism. There are two main criticisms of this methodological position. The first is that he did not go far enough, but that in following Rickert in this distinction he attempted to stop at an unstable halfway point.[1] He should have gone all the way to the view that in a purely *logical* aspect there is no difference whatever. The differences all lie on a substantive level.

The first source of difficulty seems to lie in Weber's attempt to draw too rigid a distinction between the subjective directions of interest of the scientist in each of the two groups of sciences. There seems to be no reason to doubt the importance of the motive of control with reference to the phenomena of nature. But it is possible to doubt both the extent to which that is the exclusive or even dominant motive of interest in the natural science field and that it is as unimportant as Weber maintains by implication in the sociocultural field. Indeed in the latter case it is curious that Weber took the position that he did, for one of his major theses throughout his work was that of the importance of scientifically verifiable knowledge of human affairs as a guide to rational action. Moreover in just this connection he strongly emphasized the need for general, theoretical knowledge. In so far as this is the context in which social studies are considered it would seem that, on the cognitive level, the ultimate aim of research was the building up of one or more systems of valid general theory, which would be equally applicable to any concrete situations that might arise.

Indeed, with reference both to nature and to action and culture two main types of nonscientific motives of cognitive interest may be differentiated. One is the "instrumental" interest. This is manifested whenever the question arises of using elements of the situation of action as means, or adapting action to them as conditions. But surely in rational action generally the social environment looms at least as large as does the natural. Particularly in the field Weber had primarily in mind, that of political action, this seems to be the case. The other main type of nonscientific motive of cognitive interest is what may be called a "disinter-

---

[1] The second will be taken up below (see pp. 606 *ff*).

ested" value attitude. This is not a matter of using things, but of defining one's attitude toward them in themselves. It is here that the element of concrete individuality becomes most prominent and that the principle of value relevance as formulated by Weber is applicable. There is no reason to deny that this element is quantitatively much more important in the social situation. But even if this is true it is not sufficient ground to justify its being made the basis of a radical methodological distinction between the two groups of sciences.

There is indeed no reason to exclude radically a value interest in this sense from the field of the natural sciences. In so far as value relevance is made the basis for an element of relativism in the theoretical systems of science, it may well be suspected that this relativism enters into the natural science field to a much greater extent than Weber intimated. Indeed a comprehensive comparative study of the interpretations of nature to be found in different civilizations with widely differing value systems would almost certainly reveal that this relativity existed to a surprising extent.[1]

Moreover, there is no reason to believe that a value interest as distinguished from a control interest is always necessarily one which concentrates on the aspect of concrete individuality. Indeed Weber himself, in the *Protestant Ethic*, gives several hints of the existence of religious motivation in the promotion of natural science in the Puritan era, a view which has been substantiated by later studies.[2] This urge, to know God through his works, was directed to the element of order in the physical world, and thus to those aspects of it that could be formulated in abstract and general terms. Indeed it may be suspected that Weber's distinction, in the rigid form in which he advanced it, is itself the manifestation of a particular value attitude of its author. It has been held to be a protest against the bureaucratic tendency to fit human beings as cogs into a machine, in which their place is defined by impersonal capabilities and functions rather than by their unique personality. In addition it is probable that Weber

[1] For an important study of this character see M. Granet, *La pensée chinoise.*

[2] See especially the study of R. K. Merton on *Science, Technology and Society in Seventeenth Century England.*

was misled into an exaggerated view of the unity of all natural science by lingering vestiges in his thought of Kantian empiricism, which blinded him to the elements of relativism to be found there.

A further element seems not to have received sufficient consideration on Weber's part. It is that, whatever the motives of original interest may be, there is an inherent tendency for the theoretical structures of all science in whatever field to become logically closed systems. Then, in so far as there is an instrumental interest in the social field, the general conceptual products of this interest will tend to become integrated in the same systems as those issuing from the value aspect. Once this has happened to an appreciable degree there will exist, as has been emphasized throughout this study, a secondary basis of interest in concrete phenomena—that derived from the structure of the theoretical system itself. The interest to this extent will be directed to those aspects of concrete phenomena which are important to the theoretical system.

Indeed, throughout, Weber seems not to have laid sufficient emphasis on the fact that scientific knowledge involves not only the fact that a selection is made from the possible data of "raw experience," but that what is experienced is itself determined, in part, by what scientific knowledge we have and, above all, by the general conceptual schemes that have been developed. Observation is always in terms of a conceptual scheme.

In all these respects, then, there seems to be no basis for a radical distinction in principle between the natural and the social sciences with regard to the roles of individuality and generality. Quantitative differences of degree there may be, but these are not sufficient to justify such a distinction.

The principle of value relevance helps to explain the element of relativism, in scientific methodology, but it is applicable to both groups of sciences, not to one alone.

For the classification of the sciences the methodological arguments Weber has developed seem to indicate a basic division into two groups, substantially on the lines he has suggested, with a dominant direction of interest, on the one hand, toward the concrete individuality of one or a class of historical individuals and, on the other hand, toward a system of abstract general principles and laws. But this division does not coincide with that between the natural and the sociocultural sciences.[1] There are, rather, examples of both in each field. The first group may be called the historical sciences, which concentrate their attention on particular concrete phenomena, attempting as full an understanding of their causes and consequences as is possible. In doing this they seek conceptual aid wherever it may be found. Examples in the natural science field are geology and meteorology; in the social field, history, above all, but also anthropology as it has generally been conceived. The other group, the "analytical," sciences, is concerned primarily with building up systems of general theory verifiable in terms of and applicable to a wide range of concrete phenomena. To them the individual phenomenon is a "case." In the natural science field theoretical physics is the leading example, but chemistry and general biology may also be included; in the social sciences theoretical economics is by far the most highly developed, but it is to be hoped that theoretical sociology and certain others will find a place by its side.[2]

These two types of sciences cut across each other in their application to fields of concrete phenomena. The same historical science will necessarily draw theoretical aid from a number of different analytical sciences, for example geology from physics, from chemistry and, in explaining the origin of organic deposits like coal, from biology. Similarly history should draw on biology,

[1] Weber himself partially recognized this, but went much too far in identifying the two groups of sciences.

[2] Then for the historical sciences theoretical concepts are means to understanding the concrete historical individual. For the analytical sciences, on the other hand, the reverse is true; concrete historical individuals are means, "cases" in terms of which the validity of the theoretical system may be tested by "verification."

From this it follows that there are two different possible meanings of the term "theory" which are often confused. On the one hand, we speak of the total explanation of a given concrete phenomenon, a historical individual or class of them, as a "theory," thus a "theory of eclipses" or Weber's own "theory of modern capitalism." On the other hand, we may apply the term to systems of general concepts as such, thus the "Newtonian physics" or the "classical economics." Weber points out quite correctly that a theory in the second sense cannot *by itself* explain a *single* empirical fact. It requires *data* which are always empirically unique, are part of a concrete historical individual, for any concrete explanation or prediction. See *Wissenschaftslehre*, pp. 171–172.

psychology, economics, sociology and other sciences. On the other hand, the theoretical system developed by an analytical science will normally be applicable to a number of different classes of concrete phenomena, for example physics to celestial bodies and the behavior of terrestial objects; economics to human actions in the market place and, in a less crucial role, to the church and the state. A distinction between the natural and the social sciences is possible on both levels. Historically considered the latter group is confined to the concrete phenomena of human life in social groups, analytically to those conceptual elements which are applicable only to this concrete subject matter.

But the basic distinction between historical and analytical is not to be identified with that between the natural and the social sciences. Indeed on no account is it possible to identify the distinction with any classification of concrete phenomena, for the analytical sciences of necessity cut across all such classifications. From this point of view it may be said that to make this identification is the basic fallacy of all of what has here been called empiricism, common to all three of the varieties discussed above. The result is invariably a dilemma. On one hand, the class of concrete phenomena in question may be treated by the method of an analytical science. Then the result is "reification," the fallacy of misplaced concreteness, with all its consequences. Or, on the other hand it may be treated by the method of a historical science alone, in which case the result is, theoretically considered, irrationalism, the denial of the validity of general conceptualization at all. On an empiricist basis there is no escape from this dilemma. Weber made his way out of it to a great extent, failing only to take the final step.[1]

Before concluding this phase of the discussion it should be remarked that Weber's methodological work has succeeded to a notable degree in synthesizing, on the methodological plane, elements which are central to science and to action, indeed in establishing a very close solidarity between the two. The traditional methodology of science has tended to think of it in complete abstraction from action. Hence, whenever the close factual interdependence of the two has been brought to attention it has tended to result in a wave of scientific skepticism. Weber has

---

[1] It is true that he was in it in the first place because of his inherited philosophical preconceptions.

succeeded in bringing a much needed element of relativity into his methodology thus relieving it of the necessity of making claims to an empiricist absolutism which would place it in a vulnerable position. At the same time he has vindicated its claims, properly qualified, to objectivity. Above all he has established the logical independence of the standards of objectivity, the schema of proof, from the relativistic elements.

Finally, among the principal elements of relativity in science prove to be elements that are of central importance to the analysis of action—the value elements. Scientific investigation, then, takes its place as a mode of action to be analyzed in the same terms as any other, rather than as a class of actions set apart. At the same time not only is it possible to place the development of science in the context of action without destroying its claim to objectivity but also verifiable knowledge itself is seen, with great clarity, to be an indispensable element of action itself. For the norm of intrinsic rationality in relation to the means-end relationship is devoid of meaning unless there is valid knowledge as a guide to action. Thus the two are elements of the same fundamental complex; a knowledge of action and its elements is indispensable to ground the methodology of science and, vice versa, scientific knowledge itself constitutes an element indispensable to the analysis of action. This insight is basic to the analytical system that has been emerging in the course of the present study.

It is well to emphasize again just what the element of relativism introduced by Weber means for the objectivity of scientific knowledge. In the first place, it means that scientific interest in any given action setting is not in the full totality of knowable facts, even about the concrete phenomena studied, but in certain selected elements of the latter. Hence at any given time even the total body of knowledge is not a complete reflection of humanly knowable reality. But to counterbalance this relativism, once the direction of interest is given and the relevant historical individuals constructed and correctly described, the system of propositions is, so far as it meets the requirements of the logical schema of proof, verifiable and objective. It follows that even though values change and with them the direction of scientific interest, in so far as past investigation has yielded valid knowledge, it remains valid, a permanently valid precipitate of the process.[1]

[1] The fact that a later age may completely lose interest in parts of it does not make it any less true.

And however different from each other the conceptual schemes are, in terms of which such knowledge has been formulated, they must if valid be "translatable" into terms of each other or of a wider scheme. This implication is necessary to avoid a completely relativistic consequence that would overthrow the whole position.

Furthermore, it is one of Weber's basic theorems that while there is a plurality of possible ultimate value systems, their number is, in fact, limited. From this it follows that on Weber's own principles there is a limited number of possible constructions of historical individuals from the same concrete objects of experience, on the one hand, and of systems of theoretical concepts, on the other. From this it follows further that there is in principle a finite totality of humanly possible scientific knowledge. Even this totality would not by any means be a complete reflection of the totality of conceivable objective reality[1] but would stand, like all objective knowledge, as Weber often puts it, in a functional relation to it. That is, the development of scientific knowledge is to be regarded as a process of asymptotic approach to a limit. The concrete impossibility of actual attainment at any given time or at any predictable future time does not affect the principle. Thus Weber's principle of value relevance, while it does introduce an element of relativity into scientific methodology (and a much-needed one by comparison with all empiricist views), does not involve the skepticism that is the inevitable consequence of any really radical relativity.[2]

THE IDEAL TYPE AND GENERALIZED ANALYTICAL THEORY

But this still leaves certain questions of the relation of scientific concepts to reality highly problematical. They can best be discussed in relation to Weber's theory of the ideal type.

Dr. von Schelting in an earlier study,[3] has shown that Weber's own treatment of this subject was not altogether satisfactory, and that he failed to distinguish several different kinds of con-

---

[1] Which is, however, precisely on this account not itself an object of experience in the sense of scientific knowledge but an abstraction arrived at by implication. It has logical affinities with the Kantian *Ding an sich.*

[2] Involved equally in Durkheim's sociological epistemology, Mannheim's *Wissenssoziologie* and many other trends of thought.

[3] "Die logische Theorie der historischen Kulturwissenschaften von Max Weber . . . ," *Archiv für Sozialwissenschaft und Sozialpolitik*, Vol. 49, summarized in *Max Webers Wissenschaftslehre*, pp. 329 *ff.*

cepts that he included under the same term. This fact is not without significance here. It is important to distinguish some of these different possible types of concepts, to relate them to each other and to explain certain unsatisfying features of Weber's treatment.[1]

The most fruitful way to get at Weber's approach to the concept of ideal type is to do so in terms of the polemical situation in which he was placed. From this it will appear that, like other categories that have been discussed,[2] this type is defined negatively, by contrast with other things, and is hence a residual category. It is then not surprising that further analysis should reveal a lack of homogeneity. The elements most relevant to this discussion are the following:

1. Weber throughout emphasized that scientific concepts do not exhaust concrete reality but involve selection and are hence in this sense unreal.

2. In his insistence on the logical distinction of the natural and social sciences this was strongly accentuated for social science concepts. For if the end of its study is always and exclusively the understanding of concrete historical individuals, such concepts can only be means. And the relativity inherent in the principle of value relevance prevents their being considered as final concepts even within the logically possible limits of science.[3]

3. Weber's general polemical animus was directed at methodological views derived from idealistic philosophy, above all, the intuitionist theories. At the same time he made *Verstehen* a basic methodological postulate of the social sciences. This involved dealing with the subjective aspect of action, above all, ideas, norms and value concepts. In this polemical situation the most immediate danger was that of having his position confused with an idealistic one which identified these value elements with the totality of concrete reality as scientifically knowable, or regarded the latter as an emanation of such ideas. This circumstance drove him strongly in the direction of insisting upon the unreality of the concepts in terms of which such elements were formulated.[4] Weber was right in this polemical context; but in another context

[1] Without full textual criticism, for lack of space.
[2] Notably Pareto's nonlogical action.
[3] *Wissenschaftslehre*, p. 207.
[4] *Cf.* Chap. X, *supra*, p. 396.

his formulations might lead to unfortunate impressions of his position.

4. Finally, a more general point has already been noted. In his polemics, especially against the "objectivist" position, Weber again rightly, laid powerful stress on the fact that scientific concepts, particularly in the social sciences, did not reflect the totality of "raw experience," which was of infinite diversity and complexity. In this situation he was led to minimize the other side of the picture, that all concrete observation of empirical fact, above all rigorous scientific observation, takes place in terms of a conceptual scheme. "Raw experience" in Weber's sense is not a concrete actuality at all but a methodological abstraction. Hence again the emphasis on the unreality of concepts.

The combination of these four elements could not but have the effect of driving Weber strongly in the direction of a fiction theory of the logical nature and function of social science concepts, and of as strongly inhibiting him from any sort of realism that ran a risk of confusion with any or all of the empiricist positions against which he was fighting. Hence, besides the fact that it contains elements which have a subjective reference, the only positive characterization of the ideal type that Weber gives[1] is that it is a construction of elements abstracted from the concrete, and put together to form a unified conceptual pattern. This involves a one-sided exaggeration (*Steigerung*) of certain aspects of the concrete reality, but is not to be found in it, that is, concretely existing, except in a few very special cases, such as purely rational action. It is a Utopia.[2] On the other hand, Weber is quite clear what it is not: (1) It is not a hypothesis,[3] in the sense that it is a proposition about concrete reality which is concretely verifiable, and to be accepted in this sense as true if verified. In contrast to this sense of concreteness, it is abstract. (2) It is not a description of reality if by this is meant a concretely existing thing or process to which it corresponds. In this sense also it is abstract. (3) It is not an average[4] (*Gat-*

---

[1] The main discussion of the ideal type which Weber gives is in the essay "Die Objektivität sozialwissenschaftlicher Erkenntnis," *Wissenschaftslehre*, pp. 146 *ff.*, but especially pp. 185 *ff*. See also pp. 505 *ff*. reprinted from *Wirtsch. u. Ges.*, Chap. I.

[2] On all this see especially *Wissenschaftslehre*, p. 190.

[3] *Wissenschaftslehre*, p. 190.

[4] *Ibid.*, p. 201.

tungsbegriff, in one meaning) in the sense that we can say the average man weighs 150 pounds. This average man is not an ideal type. (4) Nor, finally, is it a formulation of the concrete traits *common* to a class of concrete things, for instance in the sense that having beards is a trait common to men as distinct from women—this is a *Gattungsbegriff* in a second meaning.

Dr. von Schelting[1] was the first to point out that under the term ideal type Weber included the two quite heterogeneous categories of generalizing and individualizing concepts. In his later work[2] Dr. von Schelting has also worked out the fundamental distinction between two subcategories of the latter. On the one hand are the concrete historical individuals which constitute the *objects* of causal analysis, such as, among the phenomena discussed in the previous two chapters—modern rational bourgeois capitalism, the Indian caste system, Chinese patrimonial bureaucracy. Here, it may be said that the element of abstract "unreality" is essentially a consequence of the selectiveness of scientific interest. It is precisely the statement in outline form of the aspects of the concrete situation which are *of interest* for explanatory purposes. If the historical individual is to be capable of causal analysis it must be oversimplified; it must be reduced to what is essential, omitting the unimportant. Thus in Indian caste the complex details of the hierarchical aspect of the caste structure are disregarded and only the fact of hierarchical relation to the Brahmans is kept in view. But though simplified, and in the sense involved in value relevance one-sided, such a concept is still definitely *individual;* there is one and only one Indian caste system. The construction of such historical individuals has the function of preparing and organizing the concrete material for causal analysis. While it is not descriptive in the sense of fully reproducing reality it is so in the sense that its application to the concrete reality *explains* nothing as such, but only states what is to be explained. Explanation, on the other hand, involves general concepts.

[1] VON SCHELTING, "Die logische Theorie der historischen Kulturwissenschaften von Max Weber, "*Archiv für Sozialwissenshaft und Sozialpolitik,* Vol. 49, summarized in *Max Webers Wissenschaftslehre,* pp. 329 *ff.;* see also pp. 333 *ff.*

[2] VON SCHELTING, *Max Webers Wissenschaftslehre,* final chapter. This distinction was not contained in the earlier study.

The second category of individual concept is very similar in its logical function but different in its content. The first contained at least elements of real phenomena—things and events in time—elements of social fact. The other contains another order of object—ideas. Such are for example, the Calvinistic theology, the Brahmanic philosophy of karma and transmigration. These are, of course, relevant to real process—otherwise this study would have no interest in them—but short of Hegelianism they cannot be identified with it. Indeed the problem of their relations is precisely the central problem of Weber's concrete sociological work.

But neither are they the actual concrete contents of the minds of all Calvinists or all Brahmans, to say nothing of all members of all castes not explicitly rejecting Brahmanic authority. On the contrary, these two are exaggerations, they are developments into the most clear-cut and consistent form of the general tendencies of religious thought to be found in the circles in question. Here the ideal type may actually concretely exist in the sense that the system of ideas is explicit in some one document, Calvin's *Institutes*, for instance.[1] But this is not methodologically necessary, and above all it is certain that, for instance, the mass influence of the Calvinistic theology cannot be limited to those persons who have had a completely clear intellectual grasp of the logical structure of the theological system in Calvin's statement. Such concepts are, in their sociological application at least, in a sense unreal.

At the present stage of the discussion it is the other kind of "ideal type," the generalizing concept, which is important. Quoting Dr. von Schelting[2] it may be said, "The causal explanation of an individual event requires an answer to the question what would, under certain hypothetical, hence unreal, but nevertheless 'possible'[3] assumptions, have happened." A general ideal type is such a construction of a hypothetical course of events with two other characteristics: (1) abstract generality and (2) the ideal-typical exaggeration of empirical reality. Without the first of these last two elements, the concept might be applicable

[1] For essentially the same reason that a purely rational act may be intuitively apprehended. See above, p. 588.

[2] *Max Webers Wissenschaftslehre*, pp. 329–330.

[3] Weber's conception of "objective possibility" will be discussed below, pp. 610 *ff*.

only to a single historical situation;[1] without the second it might be merely a common trait or a statistical average. It is neither of these, but is an ideal construction of a *typical* course of action, or form of relationship which is applicable to the analysis of an indefinite plurality of concrete cases, and which formulates in pure, logically consistent form certain elements that are relevant to the understanding of the several concrete situations. Since *these* are the general concepts necessarily involved in the logic of empirical proof, their methodological status is vital.

Weber himself was fond of using the general concepts of orthodox economic theory as an example. Since this is an example that has concerned this study already[2] and since it contains in clear-cut form all the elements of the problem except one, it will be used as the main basis for discussion. The main point[3] is that neither Weber nor Dr. von Schelting seems to see a central problem in the methodological status of these concepts of economic theory.[4]

This example is taken from the field of the social sciences and involves *Verstehen*, which Weber regarded as essential to the ideal type; its relation to natural science concepts is another matter. On this basis the concepts of economic theory all involve a normative element—what is usually referred to as the postulate of economic rationality. There is general agreement[5] on the proposition that action can only be explained in terms of economic principles in so far as it *in fact* approaches the expectations in terms of this norm. Departures from it must be due to other than economic factors. All this is common ground. The problem arises here: the concepts of economic theory may be held to state a type of action fully conforming to the norm, to state a course not of concretely observed action but of *hypothetical*[6] concrete action. That this

---

[1] See VON SCHELTING, *op. cit.*, footnote page 330. Indeed Weber referred to certain constructions of this character as ideal types.

[2] See above, especially Chap. IV, V, VI.

[3] To this study.

[4] This has been developed at some length in Talcott Parsons, "Some Reflections on the Nature and Significance of Economics," *Quarterly Journal of Economics*, May, 1934.

[5] In orthodox circles.

[6] Hypothetical not in the sense that a concrete course of events is expected which will exactly correspond to the construction but negatively in the sense that it describes a course of events which has not actually been observed exactly as described.

norm has perhaps never been fully attained,[1] may in fact be unattainable and is in that sense unreal, is not the point. It makes sense as a limiting case—in much the same way as the physical concept of a frictionless machine which would involve no transformation of mechanical energy into heat. On the other hand, these concepts may state certain *analytical elements* in a generalized system of action.[2]

If analysis is confined to the first kind of concept it leads, when applied to situations which are not ideal experimental conditions for the theory, to the dilemma: either an illegitimate reification of a *single* theoretical system, or a "fiction" theory of the role of concepts in science which does not really get away from the empiricist irrationalism of the objectivist and intuitionist positions. More specifically in the case of Professor Robbins analyzed in the above article,[3] it leads to reification.[4] Weber, since most of his general ideal types are of this character, is caught in the same dilemma, but because of his much greater methodological sophistication and empirical knowledge and insight his is a much subtler case. He is no naïve monist like Robbins. But his "pluralism" tends, by hypostatization of ideal types, to break up, in a sense not inherent in analysis as such, the organic unity both of concrete historical individuals and of the historic process. In its reification phase it issues in what may be called a "mosaic" theory of culture and society, conceiving them to be made up of disparate atoms.[5] This, with his use of the rational norm, is the source of what has often been referred to as his objectionable "rationalism" and of the iron-bound character of the process of rationalization that is such a prominent feature of his empirical work. It is the central methodological difficulty of Weber's position, and far more than any factual mistakes underlies whatever serious difficulties there may be in his empirical theories.

The difference of the two types of concepts and, above all, the consequences of their respective employment have already been shown. There can be no doubt that the norm of free enterprise

[1] In a total action system.
[2] The two may overlap in concrete content. *Cf.* Chap. I, p. 35, note 1.
[3] *Supra*, footnote 4, p. 606.
[4] Most evident in his deep laissez-faire bias. See Lionel Robbins, *An Essay on the Nature and Significance of Economic Science.*
[5] Defined as ideal-type units.

as used by Marshall, with all its main subsidiary concepts, corresponds to the above postulate of economic rationality. Free enterprise is, for Marshall, a hypothetical state where men actually would live up to this norm. But it is equally clear that in this hypothetical state as conceived by Marshall more than one analytical element[1] is involved. *Two* are important here— utility and activities[2]—but neither of these two is conceivable even hypothetically as a concrete type of action. The whole analysis has shown that the economic concept of utility makes sense only in terms of a *given* system of ultimate ends, on the one hand, and, on the other, of elements of a given situation as well as certain other elements. It is possible to speak even of hypothetical action as "determined by considerations of maximum utility," only in so far as the values of these other elements are given independently of utility considerations; that is, the utility element must be considered as independent of these others. But the same is true of the activities element.[3] It is quite clear that it is analytically separable from that of utility as any comparison with a distinctly different concrete situation from that which Marshall had in mind will show. For instance, the case that Weber deals with[4] under the heading of traditionalism, in which a rise in rate of pay leads to *less* work so that the same total amount as before is earned, is in no respect less an example of maximization of utility than that which Marshall had in mind. Put a little differently, the concept of maximization of utility is completely meaningless by itself. It simply cannot be reified without bringing in logically distinct elements, such as the nature of ultimate wants.[5] But the fact that in a plurality of different hypothetical (ideal-type) cases, for example Weber's traditionalism and Marshall's free enterprise, the same funda-

[1] In the sense of the previous discussion.

[2] This is not to be taken to mean that for all purposes these two variables are the only ones that it is significant to distinguish in these phenomena. Another choice of variables might cut across this. The present concern is merely to illustrate the *logical* distinction between elements and units.

[3] However inadequately defined it may be by Marshall for present purposes.

[4] *Supra*, Chap. XIV, p. 514.

[5] Hence the role in the utilitarian position of the conception of random ends. The value of an element *may* be capable of separate existence as a unit. The argument is directed against the implicit assumption that it *must* be.

mental element of rational maximization of utility is involved, and *logically indispensable* to the concept, proves that this element of utility is an independent variable relative to traditionalism and to activities. The two elements simply are not reducible to terms of one another in the sense that maximization of utility logically implies either maximization of traditionalism (in Weber's sense) or of activities (in Marshall's sense).

This is brought out clearly by considering the relation of Marshall's case to Pareto. Essentially the same elements which Marshall dealt with as the utility elements appear in Pareto's generalized system as at least part of the "interests." But it is quite clear that Pareto treats the interests as variable independently of the residues and the sentiments they manifest. For example these interests may operate as well in a system characterized by the predominance of the residues of persistence as in one where the residues of combination are particularly strong, but the concrete outcome will be very different in the two systems. Marshall suppresses this independence of variation by relating maximization of economic rationality to a particular class of residues, those involved in activities. This involves an implicit theorem which, as the work of all three others, Pareto, Weber and Durkheim, has shown, is not in harmony with the facts.

But either this or another theorem of corresponding rigidity is the inevitable logical outcome of the implicit methodological view that *all* the analytical concepts of a theoretical system must correspond to units of concrete systems the independent existence of which is conceivable. What has, in the previous discussion, been dissected out of the structure of systems of action as the economic element cannot be thought of as such a unit. It is a mode of relation of units in systems beyond a certain minimum degree of complexity by virtue of which they have certain emergent properties. Yet the foregoing example demonstrated that it is independently variable relative to certain other elements of the same system, namely the value elements. Robbins' course is, by postulating that it is adequately descriptive of a concrete type of action, to push the value element out of the concrete system altogether; ends become random. Thus the interdependence of the economic and value elements *cannot* be taken account of. Marshall, on the other hand, bound economic rationality to a particular value of the value complex. Weber tends to be guilty of still a third fallacy, the "mosaic" atomism discussed above. None of these courses is satisfactory.

That Weber should not have arrived explicitly at the distinction of these types of concept is not at all surprising in view of the fact that the positions from which he started were of a thoroughly empiricist character and that his main task was to vindicate the logical necessity of the use *at all* of general concepts in explanatory science. It was not unnatural, above all in view of his polemical relation to idealist methodologies, that he should in his explicit formulations stop at the type of general concept which was nearest an empirically descriptive one, namely the hypothetically concrete type of action or relationship.

THE LOGIC OF EMPIRICAL PROOF

The logic of the situation in Weber's thought can best be followed through in terms of his treatment of the conditions of objective proof of empirical propositions, for which he developed the categories of objective possibility and adequate explanation.

At the outset it must be remembered that Weber's discussions of proof and causal imputation concerned immediately the question, how is it possible to prove the existence of a causal relation between certain features of a given historical individual and certain empirical facts which have existed prior to it? It is as a result of following up the logic of this problem that he is led to analyze the role of general concepts.

Dr. von Schelting gives a convenient summary of the logical steps involved in the procedure of causal imputation.[1] It presupposes the construction and verification descriptively of a historical individual—the thing to be explained. Then the indispensable[2] steps are as follows: (1) Analysis of this complex phenomenon (or process) in such a way that it is broken down into elements of such a character that each of them may be subsumed under a general law (*Regel des Geschehens*). (2) There is presupposed previous knowledge of such general laws. (3) Hypothetical elimination or alteration of one or more factors of the process, concerning which it is wished to raise the question of its (or

---

[1] VON SCHELTING, *op. cit.*, p. 262.

[2] Dr. von Schelting adds four others which *may* be taken; for the sake of brevity they may be negelected here.

their) causal significance for the result. (4) Hypothetical construction of what would *then* (after the elimination or alteration) be the expected course of events (application of the category of objective possibility). (5) Comparison of the hypothetical conception of a possible development (really that which would *have been* possible had certain things happened differently) with the actual course of events. (6) On the basis of this comparison, the drawing of causal conclusions. The general principle is that, in so far as the two, the actual and the possible, courses of events differ, the difference may be causally imputed to the factors "thought away" or considered as changed. If, on the other hand, this hypothetical change fails to make a difference, the judgment is justified that the factors in question were not causally important.

This schema[1] contains all the main elements of the problem. The main questions that arise lie in interpreting: What is a factor, in the sense of an element of the problem which may be thought of as eliminated or altered for purposes of the hypothetical construction? What are the general laws under which it is to be subsumed (*Generelle Erfahrungsregeln* or *generelle Regeln des Geschehens*)? And finally what is the character of the general relations of these two apparently equally indispensable elements of scientific knowledge to each other?

The first statement to be made is that, for purposes of this schema a factor is an entity involving statements of concrete fact. The question of causality is that of the consequences for the ensuing course of events arising from the existence of these facts at the time and place that they existed, in the given total circumstances. Thus in the examples that Dr. von Schelting takes from Weber the factors are (*a*) the *fact that* the Persian advance was held up at Marathon for a certain time, (*b*) the *fact that* the young mother had had a dispute with her cook,[2] and (*c*) the *fact that* there existed in Western Europe at a given time among large numbers of people the complex of attitudes Weber called the ethic of ascetic Protestantism.[3] These are the factors the causal significance of which is to be tested. In each

---

[1] It is a perfectly valid statement of Weber's position in a form more convenient than any of his own.

[2] VON SCHELTING, *op. cit.*, p. 280.

[3] *Ibid.*, p. 281 *ff.*

instance they refer to concrete specific states of affairs or events.

But each of these in turn forms "part" of a historical individual. It would be nonsense to attribute the freedom of Hellenic culture from religious-priestly, traditionalistic rigidity to the outcome of the battle of Marathon had the social situation in Greece at the time of the battle been that of contemporary Egypt, or to attribute a part in the development of capitalism to the Protestant ethic had the social situation in Western Europe been that of India during the same period.

Both the factor to which causal importance is to be attributed (or denied) and the situation in which it occurs are concrete phenomena. The phenomena with which the causal analysis is concerned constitute a "real process." The problem is that of the part played in the determination of the concrete individuality of a later stage by the fact that the factor in question happened or existed at an earlier one. This question can only have a definite meaning if the factor is thought of as operating in terms of a given concrete situation. Moreover, the only way in which to arrive at a judgment of the causal significance of a factor is to ask what would have happened if the factor in question had not been present or had been altered, *e.g.*, if the Persians had not been stopped at Marathon at all. It is clear that this is nothing, in principle, but the logic of experiment. Where practical difficulties make it impossible actually to reproduce the initial situation, and alter the factor in question, and then see what would happen, recourse must be had to a mental experiment, the construction of an objectively possible course of events.

But any such historical individual, including the factor in which interest is centered, is an organic unity and can only be observed as such (in the absence of possible experimentation). Hence anything with which to compare it must be[1] a "construction." In so far as the whole was in any sense determined the process *had* to result as it actually did. The construction of what would have happened under different circumstances therefore requires knowledge of how certain elements of the situation would have developed. This involves, then, as stated in the schema, both analysis of the phenomenon into elements and, with respect to each element, ability to predict with more or less

[1] With one exception, to be noted, that of analogy.

accuracy its trends of development. It is as logically necessary prerequisites of this latter prediction of tendencies that general laws become involved.

But, what are the other elements into which the historical individual in question is to be analyzed? In the Marathon[1] example it is certain features of the social structure and situation at the time in Greece, on the one hand; of Persian interests and probable policy on the other. They may be stated as follows: In the religious situation of Greece, beyond the family cults, there were at the time two main structural elements: (1) the civic cults, administration of which was assimilated to ordinary public office, a situation definitely incompatible with the dominance of a hereditary professional priestly class; (2) a professional element, especially in the oracles such as Delphi but *outside* the structure of the polis. The central question was whether the first element should continue to develop in its secularizing direction or whether this tendency should be counteracted and suppressed by a shift in the balance of religious power to the other element. Weber, with Eduard Meyer, argues that a Persian victory would with a high degree of probability have brought about this latter outcome. The main reasons are (1) it would have destroyed the political autonomy of the polis and with it the whole development of citizenship with which the "state-religion" was bound up; (2) the professional religious element would have been very useful to a Persian regime as a means of domestication and hence the latter would have done everything to promote the former's influence (this happened in Judea).

The historical question cannot be pursued further. The present issue is what is meant by the elements and the general laws that are necessary to the schema of logical proof. Only one thing can be definitely gathered from Weber's treatment: they are *general* concepts or categories. When a factor in a given historical individual or its temporal antecedent is thought of as altered or eliminated, it can only be the specific facts which change. The elements referred to must be in some sense general categories, forms of which the facts in question constitute the particular

---

[1] Weber regarded the battle of Marathon as decisive in the first place because it gave the Athenians time to get together a fleet and withdraw it to Salamis. The real point here, however, is the failure of the Persians to gain permanent political control over Greece.

content. The alteration must be one of content within the same form. The question is, then, what, in the terminology of logic, is the universal, of which the specific facts in question constitute a particular?

This is where the dichotomy that has been discussed above becomes relevant. In the relation of a universal to the particular facts of a concrete situation can stand not one type of general category but two. Weber fails to make the distinction, to specify which of the two is meant or the relations the two bear to each other. It is here that it is necessary, in order to clarify the implications of his position, to go beyond Weber's own analysis.

One type of universal is logically related to the particulars of a class[1] of objects as the concept of man is related to the individual human being. In one sense man is an abstraction—there is, empirically, no such thing as man, but only particular men and aggregates of them. But in the concept man are brought together a certain number of criteria such that any concrete entity in relation to which all of them can be identified may be placed in the class man in common with all other concrete entities sharing, within certain limits of variation, the same features. As Weber's analysis has shown, there are a number of different possible ways in which general concepts of this class character may be related to the totality of concrete entities included within the class. The class may be formulated as an average, with a certain range of variation, such that particulars falling within the range may still be said to belong to the class. Thus man may be defined with reference to such a feature as average stature or body weight. Or, secondly, the class may be defined with reference to traits common to the particulars, as when man is defined with reference to a certain type of brain structure, erect posture, opposable thumb and the like, but not with reference to hair or skin color, cephalic index, etc. Finally, it may be defined as an ideal type.

There can be no doubt that the elements that play the principal part in Weber's schema of proof as the universals into which the particular facts of the alterable factor fit, are class concepts in this sense. The ideal-type mode of formulation is chosen rather than one of the others mentioned above mainly for two reasons: First, their scientific function lies in connection with

---

[1] In the logical sense.

understanding the normative orientation of action. For this purpose it is convenient to take the case where the norm in question is conceived as completely realized; in this way, as Weber often notes, it is easiest to determine the role of other factors in terms of departure of the concrete case from the state of realization of the norm. Second, the concrete historical individuals to which these concepts are to be applied are organic phenomena. The isolation of parts, or units, of them is thus attended with the abstraction always involved in such a procedure. Since they must be abstract anyway because the class concept cannot be adequately descriptive of the concrete phenomena, the ideal-type concept is more suitable than either of the other kinds.

Weber himself frequently lays down as a principal criterion of the correct formulation of an ideal type that the combination of features used to characterize it should be such as taken together are meaningful, make sense. What this means is clear—that they must adequately describe, in terms of a frame of reference, a potentially concrete entity, an objectively possible entity in Weber's sense. Not, to be sure, in the sense that a concrete entity exactly corresponding to the type must be demonstrable as actually existing, but that all the essential properties of a concrete entity are included.[1] Thus, in mechanics it would not make sense to describe a body that had mass and velocity but no location in space. Similarly an action system which has means and ends but no norm governing the means-end relationship is nonsensical. The ideal type as relevant to this context is, then, a hypothetically concrete entity, a state of affairs or a process or a unit in one of these. It is ideal only in the sense of being a construction with a fictitious simplification and exaggeration of certain features. Examples which Weber employs frequently are "handicraft," "bureaucracy," "feudalism," "church," "sect."

It is clear that this kind of ideal type is not necessarily an analytical element in the sense in which the term has been used in this study. An element is also a universal or combination of them of which the facts descriptive of a concrete entity or state of affairs may be the particulars. But it need not be a class universal at all. It may be what might be called a universal of

---

[1] Essential, as defined by the requirements of the frame of reference employed.

predication. It may refer to general properties or qualities of concrete phenomena the values of which are facts descriptive of the phenomena. Thus in mechanics mass is an element in this sense. Its concrete counterpart is not, however, any unit of a mechanical system, but the mass *of* a particular body. Both the class concept and the universal of predication are abstractions. Both are so in part because they are universals and not particulars. But it is clear that the abstraction involved is of a different sort in the two concepts. The particular corresponding to the one is a concrete entity, George Washington *was* a man. The particular corresponding to the other need not be a concrete entity but may be the concrete property or quality *of* such an entity. The sun *has* (not *is*) a given mass. The two only coincide when the latter includes the universals involved in all the facts necessary for an adequate description of a unit.

A concrete entity is always capable of description in terms of a certain number of predications about it. What and how many these are will be determined by the frame of reference in terms of which it is described. There is always, for such a frame of reference, a group of general properties, the values of which, taken together, constitute an adequate description of a concrete unit or entity. Thus, in the classical mechanics, to describe a particle or body adequately it is necessary to state its mass, velocity, position in space and direction of motion. The omission of one or more of these makes the description indeterminate.

These considerations make it possible to designate certain general relations between the ideal-type universal and the analytical-element universal. The former is a true universal and is thus applicable to an indefinite plurality of particular cases. It cannot, therefore, include in its formulation a set of specific values of the elements relevant to the description of particulars of the class. It contains no concrete facts.

What it does contain is a fixed set of relations (possibly including variation within certain limits) of these values of elements. Only in so far as these relations are maintained can the type in question be said to exist or be relevant to the concrete situation being analyzed.

This may best be brought out by reverting to the previous illustration. Economic rationality may be regarded as such a general property of action systems. It is a property of the type of action Weber has described as traditionalism. Indeed this type involves, as one essential predication, the maximization of economic rationality. But the maximization of economic rationality alone is not an adequate description of the type of action Weber has in mind. It is action which is economically rational relative to a traditionally fixed standard of living, that is, not relative to *any* given ends whatever but relative to a system of ends in which the property of traditional fixity is maximized. It is the *combination* of these two specific properties which defines the type. But so long as this condition is given there is room for wide variation in the concrete instances in other respects, as in the concrete content of the ends and the particular features of the situations. The example of the Silesian mowers is only one of the many possible examples of this type of action. The type is equally applicable to American miners whose consumption habits and whose situations, in so far as they are relevant to securing a fixed income, are widely different.

This is what was meant when it was stated above that in the ideal type the elements are related to each other in a particular combination. Traditionalism[1] exists only in so far as, if economic rationality is maximized, the fixity of the standard of living is also maximized at the same time. The *relations* between the values of the analytical elements which are important to the formulation of the type are always the same whatever may be their particular values and those of other elements. Ideal-type analysis provides no means of breaking down the rigidity of these fixed relations.[2]

There would be no objection to this were it true that in fact the relations in question always subsisted in concrete reality, but this is not necessarily so. This is vividly brought out by comparison with the case from Marshall already discussed, of wants adjusted to activities. There the property of economic rationality

---

[1] It should be noted that Weber also uses this term in a much broader sense. For a discussion of it, see next chapter.

[2] Whether or not it should be broken down is a question of scientific convenience, of fact. If the combination is best treated as a unit, ignoring the possibility of independent variation of its elements, the type concept may *also* serve as an element. It may, on the other hand, be convenient to break it down.

is maximized, but its maximization is not combined with fixity in the standard of living, of wants; on the contrary, it is correlated with a progressively rising standard of living. Thus Marshall's free enterprise is characterized by another action type in which the maximization of economic rationality is combined with that of the activities discussed at length above, one aspect of which is an increasing want scale.

There is no difference whatever in the element of economic rationality in the two types of action; the difference between the types is a matter of the way in which this element is related to others, in these examples to elements of the ultimate value complex. This fact is of fundamental methodological significance. The formulation of class concepts, including ideal types in Weber's sense, is an indispensable procedure. But it is not usually possible for scientific analysis to stop there. To do so would result in a type atomism—each type concept would be a unit of analysis by itself. But in reality these units are systematically related to one another. This is true because they are formulated in terms of combinations of relations between the values of a more limited number of properties, each property being predicable of a number of different type concepts.

Above all, the values of the general elements concerned are not always combined in the particular way that any one type concept involves; they are independently variable over a wider range. This has just been demonstrated for one case. Maximization of economic rationality is not rigidly bound to fixity of wants but is doubtless in various ways empirically compatible with their flexibility also. To employ only the type concept in analysis is to obscure these possibilities of independent variation.

Furthermore, such a use of the type concept is a violation of the basic methodological canon of scientific economy. For on the type basis it is necessary to have a separate general concept for every possible combination of relations between the values of the relevant elements, while in terms of an element analysis it is possible to derive all these types from a much more limited number of element concepts.

Indeed, it is impossible to work out a systematic classification of ideal types without developing at the same time, at least implicitly, a more general theoretical system. For the relations between the types in the classification can only be stated by employing the categories that comprise such a generalized system. Thus, by virtue of the fact that maximization of economic rationality is common to them, traditionalism and free enterprise belong, for certain purposes, in the same class.

But this more generalized theoretical systematization involves, as has been seen, two different kinds of possible conceptualization. The one with which this study has been mainly concerned is a generalized system of structural categories applicable to any system of social action. The other is a system of variables. Even ideal types in Weber's sense may sometimes be treated as variable elements, since they are genuine universals. The same is true of the structural categories with which this discussion has been occupied. But elements need not be identifiable with either of these—for instance, Pareto's category of residues is not.

An ideal type, as Weber uses the term, is always a generalized unit of a social system. But it is usually of a more specific and concrete character than any of the categories of our generalized system of structure. For example, a rational unit act might be more likely to be treated by Weber as an ideal type than the unit act as such. But the unit act in this sense *may* be an ideal type. The same is not, however, true of certain other structural categories. These describe modes of relation of the units and their elements in complex systems of action and are not even conceivable as independently existing apart from the other structural elements. They constitute what may be called structural aspects of concrete systems, and the properties of the systems dependent on them are emergent properties. In common with the element that is a universal of predication short of adequate description of a unit, these have the fact that they cannot be conceived as corresponding to a class of objectively possible entities. The economic sector of the intrinsic means-end chain is such a structural aspect.

Before leaving this phase of the discussion, it may be remarked that the employment of ideal-type concepts in place of more general analytical concepts, with the rigidity of combinations of relations between the values of the latter which this entails, is one of the principal sources of bias in empirical interpretation. Two conspicuous examples may be mentioned. In the first place, Marshall was right in interpreting increasing economic rationality as an inherent tendency of human action. But he failed to see that this trend need not lead to free enterprise; it is not in the least incompatible, for instance, with an Indian caste system. The latter may well differ from free enterprise in the scope of considerations brought within the range of economic calculation, but not necessarily in the degree to which the typical individual attains a norm of economic rationality within the scope of its application to him at all.[1] What Marshall does is to relate the value of economic rationality to the whole complex of other elements which he sums up as the progressive development of character. This is the ultimate logical basis of his linear evolutionism, culminating in free enterprise, and it is responsible for his view of the inevitability of the latter. The result is an empirical error of the first magnitude.

A somewhat different situation is to be found in another school of economic theory of which the views of Professor Robbins[2] furnish a convenient example. There the professed aim is to construct an abstract science of economics. But by merely refusing to discuss them, it is not possible to evade the questions of the relations of the elements formulated in economic theory to the other elements of a system of action. Ignoring these relations altogether amounts to the implicit assumption that they are random relative to the economic. With reference to ultimate ends this consequence puts Professor Robbins squarely in the utilitarian position. Since the problem of order in the Hobbesian sense is not faced, there enters the further implicit assumption of a natural identity of interests. The result is a profound laissez-faire bias which appears conspicuously in Professor Robbins' other works.[3]

To sum up: The factor which the schema of proof requires to be eliminated or altered is always a set of concrete facts descriptive of concrete historical individuals. The concrete historical

---

[1] For instance, for Westerners choice of occupation is included within that scope. In India, so far as castes have a hereditary occupation, it is necessarily excluded. In one sense, but not the present one, this is ground for attributing greater economic rationality to Westerners.

[2] L. Robbins, *op. cit.* See also Talcott Parsons, "Some Reflections on 'The Nature and Significance of Economics,'" *Quarterly Journal of Economics*, May, 1934.

[3] *Cf.* L. Robbins, *The Great Depression*. Here the thesis is maintained that the depression is entirely due to arbitrary outside interference with the working of the competitive system.

individual is thought of as capable of analysis into different concrete elements in such a way that it is possible to think of one of them as altered in value independently of the others.

But for this procedure to lead to proof of causal relationship, it must be possible to subsume these facts under general concepts. It is there that the difficulty arises. These general elements are not all of one kind; three kinds are possible. Weber's ideal type belongs to one: it is a hypothetically concrete unit or part of the historical individual in question, the combination of general features of which is shared with an indefinite plurality of other concrete historical individuals.

This is an abstraction like any class concept because it is a logical universal, not a particular. It is also abstract because it is an ideal type, not an average or a bundle of common traits. The other kinds of concept are on a more generalized analytical plane. They need not be units at all. The corresponding particulars may describe a concrete separate entity but may also be limited to the predication of a single property to one or more such entities, or designate a structural aspect of a system. Such concepts also are abstract in the sense of being universals, but not in the same sense as the ideal type.

All concrete phenomena, including the particulars corresponding to ideal types, are capable of description only in terms of a specific combination of the values of analytical elements. The ideal type, being a universal, does not involve a combination of specific values, but it does involve a fixed set of relations between the values of the analytical elements. These elements are, however, often independently variable beyond the range permitted by the definition of the types. Hence confining general conceptualization to ideal types introduces an element of rigidity that may issue in a methodological atomism. In so far as these types are reified the result is either a "mosaic" theory of history, or a rigid evolutionary scheme.[1] On this basis the only defense against both implications is to insist on the fictional character of the type concepts.[2]

The meaning of the general laws under which the factors are to be subsumed may be different in the different cases. Ideal-type

---

[1] Weber leaned to the former alternative, however, with an evolutionary element present in his process of rationalization.

[2] This does not really help, as it involves equally serious difficulties.

elements may, as units, be supposed to have typical modes of behavior under given circumstances. In this case the laws in question are generalizations about these modes of behavior. They are "empirical generalizations" in the sense of the previous discussion,[1] qualified only by the element of fictional abstraction inherent in the ideal-type concept. They are not general statements of what actually happens, but of what would happen were the actual facts in complete conformity with the ideal type. Thus, in an example Weber cites, Gresham's law is a generalization about the concrete behavior of men relative to two monetary elements of differing value.[2] In this case the actual course of events generally conforms closely to the law, a proof of the empirical importance of economic rationality since the law is formulated on the assumption of its maximization.

An analytical law, on the other hand, states a uniform mode of relationship between the values of two or more analytical elements. It is thus likely to be applicable beyond the range of any one ideal type.[3] At the same time the kind of generalization about the behavior of the ideal-type units just discussed cannot usually be arrived at by the application of any one analytical law, but only by the application of the combination of several.

The principal exception to this statement is that where there exist what have been called ideal experimental conditions. These are present when a given change in the concrete phenomena in question can be attributed to variation in the value of the one element or the small group of elements explicitly under consideration at the time. This is true only when the values of all others concretely relevant can be treated as constants throughout the process being studied, or when their values remain within a certain limited range. Thus the law of falling bodies applies without qualification when air resistance or friction is constant at zero.

The fundamental distinctions which the foregoing discussion has attempted to clarify have nothing to do with that between the natural and the social sciences. They belong to the strict logic of empirical science in general in which, as it has already been maintained, the two groups of sciences do not differ at all.

[1] *Supra*, p. 33.
[2] "The overvalued currency will disappear from circulation."
[3] Whenever the elements are not identical with the types.

Weber's failure to clarify the distinctions and their consequences for general theory and its empirical application seems to have been largely due to the rigidity of the methodological line that he attempted to draw between the two groups. It is in the natural sciences that generalized theory in the present sense has been most highly developed in the past, and his rigid separation prevented him from making the fullest possible use of the methodological achievements in that field. In this respect Pareto had a distinct advantage over Weber.

In these fundamental *logical* respects there is no difference between the physical and the social sciences. They differ as far as seems relevant to the present study in only three respects, none of them logical, all substantive. (1) The elements, both structural and variable, differ from each other in specific character, and hence the laws do also. To speak of an act as having mass is as meaningless as to speak of a star as rational. Indeed a theoretical system in the analytical sense may be defined as a unit when it involves such a body of interrelated elements as, with their relations, cannot be expressed in terms of another set, and refers to a concrete system of the corresponding generalized structure. (2) They differ in the character of empirical evidence for their application. The subjective point of view is a source of evidence for the one but not for the other. It makes possible a set of definable operations. (3) They differ in the degree of organicism of the concrete historical individuals with which they have to deal.[1] Even this, however, is more a matter of adequacy in relation to a concrete aim of knowledge than of intrinsic difference.[2]

A concrete, even a hypothetically concrete act or complex of action, may involve *all* the elements of action.[3] This is why the analytical sciences cut across the historical sciences as noted above. But another point should be emphasized. Any concrete type of act may involve all the elements of action, but in a speci-

---

[1] That is, in the possibility of isolating concrete type elements from their context without doing violence to their essential properties. *Cf.* Aristotle on the sense in which a hand separated from the living body is a hand only in an equivocal sense.

[2] See final chapter.

[3] Qualified by the distinction between elementary and emergent properties. The unit act involves only the former. See Chap. XIX, p. 738 *ff.*

fic combination of relations of their values. But precisely in so far as the values of these elements can vary independently of each other—and there is no other reason for distinguishing them as elements—this independent variation is inhibited by the particular combination involved in the type.

The key to the overcoming of the rigidity, involved in the "ties" of ideal-type theory, is given in the statement that several elements of action are involved in every concrete act on the one hand, that they may vary independently of each other on the other. Variation in this context has a specific meaning. A complete scientific theory is not attained until all possible concrete types of a class of historical individuals (or concretely thinkable type-parts[1] of them) can be thought of as exemplifying different combinations according to laws, of the same analytical and structural elements. Independent variation here means that the value of one element can change while the values of the others do not in the same way and proportion.[2] The only road, then, to the development of generalized theory on either plane is the comparative study of different actions and complexes of action, differing in respect to their observable properties. By a sufficiently long and laborious process of such comparison, taking cases similar in some respects, differing in others, it is possible to formulate the variable elements. In the case of activities versus traditionalism, it is clear that the rational allocation of means to ends is a property *common* to the two cases, while the specific character of the ends is not. Once such an element is formulated it is possible to construct the concrete results of its operation in various possible combinations with others.

ADEQUACY OF EXPLANATION

With this reference to construction, the discussion comes back to Weber's treatment of "adequate explanation" with its bearing on the relation of empirical generalization to analytical law. The thesis may be advanced (1) that the degree to which it is

---

[1] In the sense in which professional priesthood was an element of Greek society.

[2] The variables in a system are in functional relations to each other. Hence a change in one will have repercussions on the others defined by the laws of the system. But they are not simply "tied" to each other. They are both independent and interdependent.

necessary to push forward from empirical generalization to analytical law in order to attain adequate explanation is relative to the given empirical problem, and (2) that if it is necessary the "empirical abstraction" of Weber's ideal types is a necessary stage[1] in the process of attaining a definition of the elements, both analytical and structural, of a generalized system.

To revert to an example employed above:[2] A housewife boils a potato only fifteen minutes and then serves it to her husband. He declares it is hard and adds, "It was not cooked long enough." This is a perfectly adequate causal imputation for the purpose. His interest in the potato is only in its relative hardness or softness in relation to palatability. It is "generally known" that to make a potato soft it must be boiled about forty-five minutes. The point is that for this purpose it is not necessary to know the explanation of the complex chemical changes which go on within a potato in the process of being boiled, or the laws these follow. The one law is quite sufficient to make the explanation valid and adequate. It can be verified. Similarly in the field of action an inquirer may be told that the quickest way to get from Harvard Square in Cambridge to the South Station in Boston is to take the subway. All the elements of this statement can be verified in terms of generally known laws about everyday experience (to Bostonians). Without such general laws, indeed, all rational action itself would be unthinkable. Moreover, they are strictly comparable to scientific laws, are indeed themselves entirely adequate scientific laws *for the purposes for which they are used*.

From this pole of common sense there is a very gradual transition to such conceptions at the other end of the scale as the second law of thermodynamics. The transition is a matter of (1) the increasing complexity of the data which must be taken into account in arriving at a judgment of adequate explanation, (2) of the extent to which the hypothetical constructions involved in arriving at such a judgment transcend common sense and what is generally known and become judgments of probability involving highly technical formulations of elements, and rigorous deduction of the involved logical consequences of certain facts. In arriving at concrete judgments of probability the point is

---

[1] Where the subject matter is markedly organic in the above sense.

[2] Footnote, p. 65.

soon reached where the elements of a problem are so many that concrete certainty is impossible.

As the complexity of problems increases in this way explicit conceptual aid becomes necessary. First the number of possible data is so great, and the question of their relevance so difficult that it is necessary deliberately to construct a historical individual, which becomes the thing to be explained. Second, in describing it we must be able to refer parts of it to type concepts of a range of applicability beyond the particular case. Thus in describing modern capitalism, Weber uses the concept of bureaucracy. Finally, in our judgments of objective possibility we must attempt to formulate typical lines of development for these elements. All these three kinds of ideal-typical construction are prominent in Weber's work, and entirely proper and necessary.

But this cannot be all. If it is, the unfortunate result is to hold all explanatory concepts to be mere fictions which, since they are not empirically true, do not explain anything. Then against this skepticism and the fact that it fails to do justice to the actual situation, comes the reaction, their hypostatization, with the resulting "mosaic" theory of concrete society. This is due to the rigidity of the "ties" which bind the elements of action together, in specific combinations, in the ideal types. History then becomes a process of shuffling ideal types, as *units*. It comes to be held that instead of being a useful fiction the ideal type exists as a constant concrete unit through a long process. The only means of breaking this mosaic rigidity without recourse to skepticism is generalized theory which breaks down the particular element combinations in the ideal types, but by seeing in them a manifestation of common elements in constant modes of relationship with each other, transfers knowledge to a more flexible, yet at the same time more realistic basis.

It has already been noted that Weber did not really confine himself to ideal-type theory. Indeed he could not without leaving his types entirely unrelated to each other. The attempt, which constitutes the principal theoretical aspect of his work, to construct a systematic classification of ideal types, really involved him by implication in generalized analytical theory. His sociological theory is neither the one nor the other but a mixture of both.

The reasons for this mixture should be clear. General concepts were for Weber, methodologically, a residual category—because his polemical animus was against those who would deny their role altogether. Of possible general concepts there are the three main categories, hypothetical concrete types, generalized structural categories and variable elements.[1] The first may be types either of action or of relationship. Given Weber's *Historismus*, his strong sense of the individuality of cultures and culture phenomena,[2] it is not surprising that he concentrated on relationships. Hence one body of systematic theory, the most conspicuous in his work, is a classification of possible types of social relationship. It is probably the most complete and systematic in the literature, and an indispensable aid to concrete research. But the main interest of this study is not in it but rather in the generalized account of systems of action which is, for the most part implicitly, interwoven with it and, as would be expected, to a large extent forms its logical foundation.

The present discussion of the logical nature of general theory has become involved in some difficult questions. No claim is advanced that they have been all cleared up—very far from it. Nor is it proposed in this study even to attempt to push them farther. The justification of this lies in the general starting point of the study. The procedure throughout has been one of cautious advance from well-known and clearly formulable "islands" of theoretical knowledge—above all the conception of science in its relation to the rationality of action—bit by bit into the unknown. The guiding principles have been two: never to refuse to face unsolved methodological problems (on such a plea as that they are metaphysical) if their solution promised to be important to the study, and never to go farther than necessary. The conclusion cannot be evaded that the scheme of the structural elements of action, which has formed the principal subject matter of this study, makes logical sense *only* when it is conceived of as the framework in one aspect of a generalized system of theory. Hence it has been necessary to go into the method-

---

[1] Which may, in specific content, overlap.

[2] As distinct from the anhistorical classical economists, for instance. He does this because it is in the aspect of structure rather than function that concrete individuality is most prominent. Social relationship is above all a structural category.

ological status of general theory far enough to establish what relation it holds to empirical causal explanation and to the other types of theoretical concept relevant in this same context. For present purposes it is not necessary to go further than this. Before turning to the outline of Weber's scheme of the structure of action systems, however, it will be helpful to remark on a few special points in order to prevent misunderstandings and to point certain directions of analysis.

In the first place, the discussion may revert to the schema of causal imputation. It will be remembered that among the indispensable requirements of that schema were cited (1) the analysis of a historical individual into elements each of which could be subsumed under a general law and (2) knowledge of such laws. The upshot of the foregoing analysis is to force the recognition that the concepts element and law really conceal different things, which need to be distinguished. There are, on the one hand, type-units—such as bureaucracy, priesthood, handicraft, etc. On the other hand, there are generalized theoretical categories such as rationality of action. Correspondingly, the laws may be empirical generalizations, which are judgments of the probable behavior under certain given circumstances of these concrete type elements, or they may be analytical laws which are statements of the general modes of interrelation of the values of the analytical elements, independently of the particular values of the latter.

It is perfectly possible for adequate judgments of causal imputation to be arrived at in terms of concrete type-units and empirical generalizations alone. The decisive question is whether, as in most common-sense judgments, our empirical knowledge of the behavior of the type-units under the relevant circumstances is adequate to the scientific interest in question. This is so not only in everyday life, but in a very large number of cases of historical imputation. As the cases become more complex, however, it is necessary to resort to more and more sharp and explicit formulation of these types—as ideal types— and to explicit construction of lines of their development. Finally, when this does not alone serve the needs of adequacy the resort to more generalized concepts and laws becomes necessary. This does not, however, compel one to dispense with the other kind of concept. They are often indispensable preparatory measures in terms of which to formulate clearly and accurately the points of articulation between the generalized theoretical system and the concrete reality. In turn, however, analytical theory naturally serves as a most important check on the formulations of general empirical type concepts. And for concrete causal imputation these analytically corrected empirical concepts must be reemployed.

Closely related to the question of adequacy in causal imputation is the role of another important methodological concept of Weber's to which brief mention should be given, that of probability (*Chance*). When it is necessary to make a very complex judgment of causal imputation, as in the relation of the Protestant ethic to modern capitalism, the historical individual concerned must be analyzed into a larger number of type-units.[1] Each of these must be subjected to judgments of probability as to its line of development under the relevant circumstances. These judgments rest on construction. Hence the predictability of a hypothetical objectively possible concrete state is naturally subject to error, in the case of the construction of each element, to say nothing of the totality of elements.[2] Hence objective empirical certainty is out of the question; the judgment can be only one of probability. In this sense Weber speaks of adequacy when the great majority of the causally relevant type-units that *might* have influenced a given historical individual are favorable to the particular thesis. When this is the situation those few which are not favorable may be regarded as in this sense contingent[3] and may be disregarded.

[1] Bureaucracy, rational law, state, science, etc.

[2] Of course positive construction (that of the total concrete situation) is by no means always necessary. A negative construction of the *difference* made by a change in the element in question is often enough. See *Wissenschaftslehre*, p. 286; von Schelting, *op. cit.*, p. 267.

[3] *Zufällig*. See *Wissenschaftslehre*, p. 286; von Schelting, *op. cit.*, pp. 312 ff. This formulation of Weber's clearly shows the embarrassment growing out of the imperfect development of his analytical theory. It rests on the assumption of an equal causal value of all the elements thus formulated. In the absence of any positive criterion of importance this is safer than any other assumption. But it is unsatisfactory. Such positive criteria may in fact be derived from analytical theory. Thus economic theory tells us beyond doubt that under present conditions the decisions of those in control of central banking policy are more important to the functioning of the economic order than are those of a group of businessmen whose operations are purely local. Both are elements in Weber's sense.

Thus in the case of modern capitalism, the positive relations between the Protestant ethic and the spirit of capitalism were established, as were the negative relations of the latter to other religious ethics. The construction of the influence of the Protestant ethic, backed up on the way by evidence of intermediate stages, corresponded to the observed facts. Then comes the application of the category of objective possibility. This Weber does in the case in point mainly by the aid of analogies.[1] The thinking away of the Protestant-ethic factor is done by analyzing situations where it does not exist.[2] This involves a judgment on the probability that the remaining constellation of factors (the material factors) would be on the whole not much less favorable to the historical individual in question (modern Western capitalism) in the analogical cases, especially China and India, than it was in the West. Weber's judgment of probability that it was not markedly less favorable, confirms his historical imputation of an important positive role to the Protestant ethic.

"Probability" here means only an expression of our failure to attain completely accurate empirical knowledge. "Contingency" of a factor is not to be confused with absolute chance in the sense of the mathematical theory of probability.[3] It is entirely relative to the concrete problem in hand.

This concept of probability[4] Weber carries over into the definitions of his type concepts. Thus in *Wirtschaft und Gesellschaft* he defines most of them as a "social relationship in so far as there is a probability that . . . " a certain abstractly defined norm of behavior or relationship will be adhered to. This is a consequence of the peculiar kind of abstraction involved in the ideal-type concept. For, on the one hand, it is descriptive in the sense that it states a hypothetical concrete unit or part; on the other hand, it is abstract or unreal in that this unit does not, in its

---

[1] Point 10 of Dr. von Schelting's list. *Op. cit.*, p. 262.

[2] That is, where the type-form economic ethic of religion has a different factual content.

[3] *Wissenschaftslehre*, p. 204.

[4] It seems to me that Professor Abel (*Systematic Sociology in Germany*, Chap. IV) distinctly exaggerates the importance of this concept of probability in regarding it as Weber's *principal* contribution to the methodology of the social sciences. He thereby gives Weber's position a positivistic twist which is distinctly misleading and accentuates the fictional character of his concepts.

theoretical purity, really exist. The gap between it and the facts is bridged by the concept of probability. It is a measure of the fact that such concepts are always *empirically* lacking in precision and protects Weber against the danger of reification. On the other hand, it is to be noted that analytical concepts, in their strict theoretical formulation, do not require this qualification; they are not fictional in the same sense.

At this point a few words should be said about the application of the foregoing analysis to Weber's treatment of capitalism. Weber's failure to recognize explicitly the role of a generalized theoretical system is responsible for a certain atomism in this treatment. The most important point at which this is evident is in the rigidity of the separation, as *concrete* type-units, between rational bourgeois capitalism, on the one hand, adventurers' capitalism, on the other. Weber's distinction is undoubtedly the result of entirely sound insight and, above all by contrast with the complete reification of the latter element in most Anglo-American criticisms of Weber,[1] of the greatest usefulness in understanding the problems he raised.

Yet there is almost certainly a more intimate fusion of the two in concrete fact than Weber's conceptual scheme recognizes. And this fusion could be better accounted for if, instead of concrete *types* of capitalism, the distinction were made in terms of the relative values of the different elements of action in concrete capitalistic activities. Thus in adventurers' capitalism the element of *Zweckrationalität* has a high value relative to that of disinterested moral obligation,[2] while in the main in rational bourgeois capitalism the reverse is true. The essential point is that modern capitalism is one socioeconomic system, not two. Unfortunately it is not possible to discuss the question further here. It may, however, again be emphasized that this criticism does not touch the main empirical thesis of Weber's theory, the role in the modern economic order of the disinterested ascetic sense of moral obligation to an impersonal task.

Essentially the same considerations give a certain element of justification to Professor Sorokin's methodological criticism of Weber's general sociology of religion. Its substance is as fol-

---

[1] *Cf.* Robertson's economic individualism.

[2] This distinction of elements is formulated *ad hoc* for the immediate purpose. It is not a final one. Weber's concept of *Zweckrationalität* is discussed in the next chapter.

lows:[1] The economic ethic of a religion is a concrete phenomenon (in ideal-typical formulation). The religious factor in the genesis of it is only one of several possible ones—there will also, for instance, be economic influences. Hence the effects of the economic ethic on concrete economic life are not exclusively the product of religion. From this Professor Sorokin concludes:[2] "Weber's analysis does not show even tentatively what the share of the religious factor is in molding the *Wirtschaftsethik* and correspondingly, its share in conditioning the effects of the latter in the field of economic phenomena. Thus, after Weber's work we are as ignorant about the degree of efficiency of the religious factor as we were before."

The substance of the methodological point is correct—as Weber himself fully recognized. This does not, however, justify the conclusions. In the first place, on the level of analysis by means of concrete type-units Weber certainly accomplished a great deal.[3] Suffice it to say that Weber has immensely clarified the question of the kind of influence on concrete economic life it may reasonably be expected that religion will have; this question is clarified particularly with respect to his doctrine of religious interests and their relation to ideas. This is a necessary preliminary to any sort of general theory of the influence of a religious factor. Secondly, in the only case for which he claimed it (the case of the influence of Protestanism on capitalism) Weber has arrived at a judgment of historical imputation with a high degree of adequacy which is in no way shaken by the criticism. It is not a judgment of exact quantitative importance in percentage terms—such a judgment would be absurd. It does, however, say a great deal about the degree of efficiency of this factor— that without it the historical development would certainly have been radically different.

In fact, in making this a criticism Professor Sorokin measures Weber's work by a standard inapplicable to it. In principle it is impossible, except in a limiting case, for any concrete phenomenon to be explicable in terms of the empirical laws governing any one concrete type-unit such as the Protestant ethic. It is in principle

---

[1] P. A. SOROKIN, *Contemporary Sociological Theories*, pp. 690–691.

[2] *Ibid.*, p. 691.

[3] It has been summarized at the end of Chap. XV and need not be repeated here.

impossible by Weber's method to assess its exact quantitative importance. Weber was fully aware of this logical situation and met it by judgments of adequacy, of imputation in terms of probability. On this level no other procedure is possible. It would, however, be possible on an analytical level to remedy some of these defects and hence arrive at a more accurate judgment. This would take the form of analyzing Weber's hypothetically concrete religious and economic factor-types in terms of their elements, and applying the results of this analysis. There is no space here to go into this further, though certain suggestions will be given in the next chapter.

It is interesting to point out one aspect of the question of why Weber did not bring analytical concepts and their role explicitly into his range of methodological self-consciousness. The primary explanation is that his approach to the question of the role of general concepts was that of their vindication against a radical empiricist attack, and that his attention focused so nearly exclusively on this issue that they remained for him a residual category, not adequately analyzed. Closely related to this is the circumstance that his mistaken contrast of the role of general concepts in the natural and the social sciences led him to lay the principal stress in connection with the latter on those concepts which were fictional constructions. This was, in turn, closely related to the importance, in his approach, of scientific knowledge as a means of practical action—and hence a strong feeling against pushing abstraction too far.[1]

But his failure self-consciously to develop a generalized theoretical system was not entirely due to an unwillingness to go to impractical extremes of abstraction. On the contrary, there is, in connection with his conception of the role of individuality in the social sciences, a definite misconception of certain aspects of the question of abstraction. That is, he held, in Dr. von Schelting's formulation, that[2] "Generalizing knowledge of historical-cultural reality cannot seek *without limit* for more and more general concepts and laws. For it cannot except in a relatively limited degree allow the 'de-individualization' and 'atomization' of concretely qualitative reality which that involves." That

---

[1] See VON SCHELTING, *op. cit.*, Section I. Weber's ethical position was what he called *Verantwortungsethik.*

[2] VON SCHELTING, *op. cit.*, p. 339.

is, the interest in individuality implied in *Wertbeziehung* and the generality of laws and elements are logically incompatible if generalization is pushed too far.

This appears to be a misconception based on a failure to distinguish the different levels of generalization. It arises from thinking of general concepts as always *type*[1] concepts. It is true that the broader these are—that is, the more individual cases they can include—the more abstract and empty they become.[2] Hence pushing generalization indefinitely in this direction would lead to more and more abstract concepts that are out of touch with the concrete individuality of real phenomena. This would be atomization.

But this argument fails to note that both of the other types of general concepts do not necessarily constitute simply a farther step in abstraction beyond the type-part concept in the same direction, but that they are abstract in a different sense. In this, the direction of a general system of elements into which concrete phenomena are broken up, abstraction is on a different level —the elements need not be parts. Moreover, when given concrete phenomena are seen from a specific focus of attention there is a definite limit to the extent to which analytical abstraction can be pushed without doing violence to the phenomena. That is, according to our focus of attention, our interest will be in the aspects of a concrete phenomenon relevant to a given theoretical *system*.[3] In the case of motivated human action this is the system which has concerned this study, that of the "theory of action." Dr. von Schelting has hit upon this fact without, apparently, fully appreciating its significance when he notes that the limit to generalizing abstraction in the social sciences is set by the postulate of *Verstehen*.[4] Without the subjective point of view

[1] The term type itself suggests the hypothetically concrete, not the analytical element.

[2] VON SCHELTING, *op. cit.*, p. 241.

[3] Or, stated a little differently, the unit subdivision of concrete phenomena is limited by the frame of reference. Unit analysis beyond the point where the unit can as a concrete entity be located in terms of the frame of reference is meaningless for purposes of the theory in question. In the action frame of reference it is an element (means, end, condition, norm) of a unit act which is the ultimate meaningful unit. It may be further subdivided into atoms and the like, but these are not, as such, units of an action system.

[4] VON SCHELTING, *op. cit.*, p. 342.

the theory of action becomes meaningless. The ununderstandable may be analyzed in terms of (one or more) other systems of categories, but not of *this* system.

Failure to see this involves an empiricist-monistic fallacy—that there "is" a single system of ultimate elements of concrete reality which would be reached by pushing abstraction far enough, and which somehow is held to express its ultimate reality. In this argument of Weber's, the reification which he seemed to have exorcised so thoroughly comes creeping back by an inconspicuous back door. His failure to bring the role of a general theoretical system clearly into the limelight of methodology is really a failure completely to overcome the empiricist fallacy. Once this is done, however, there need be no fear of analytical abstraction on the score of its incompatibility with the concept of individuality. For the inherent nature of the frame of reference of a theoretical system sets a limit to the extent of abstraction which is possible or in any way admissible within the range of any given type of focus of interest. The structure of such systems is most intimately related to *Wertbeziehung*.

ACTION AND COMPLEXES OF MEANING

Dr. von Schelting in the final section of his book[1] analyzes another limit to Weber's own methodological self-interpretation which calls for brief comment here because of its relevance to certain points that will be taken up in the next chapter. It concerns the concept of *Verstehen* which as he says, was essentially unproblematical to Weber. It was a basic postulate of the social sciences and that was all.

Weber dealt with it almost entirely in the context of the causal analysis of action. Hence to him it meant essentially the accessibility of the subjective aspect of other people's action as a real process in time. The object of this *Verstehen* is to uncover motivations.

Weber did, to be sure, attempt in a few places to make a distinction between two kinds of *Verstehen*. The most notable is the distinction[2] between *aktuelles* and *motivationsmässiges Verstehen*. When he brings in the understanding of the meaning

[1] *Ibid.*, pp. 353 *ff.*
[2] *Wissenschaftslehre*, pp. 504 *ff.*

of a mathematical proposition (2 × 2 = 4) under the first heading it would seem that he had reference to an atemporal world of meanings in abstraction from concrete motivations. But this line of distinction is quickly lost again when Weber includes under the same category understanding of "what he is doing" when we see a man chopping wood. The latter case certainly involves elements of concrete motivation—it is impossible to interpret the movements observed without reference to an end to which they are related as means.

In fact analysis of this distinction shows that Weber apparently conceived it as a pragmatic one. We understand things *aktuell* in so far as, in terms of ordinary everyday experience, they are evident through the mere fact of being observed. Just as to one with a grammar school knowledge of arithmetic the meaning of the symbol combination 2 × 2 = 4 is evident, so is it evident when we see a man wielding an object that we call an ax in a certain way that he is chopping wood. On the other hand, it is not evident from these immediate facts either why the proposition 2 × 2 = 4 was enunciated at that time and place (whether it was a school demonstration, a figuring of accounts or something else) or why the man was chopping wood (for exercise or to earn a living). *Motivationsmässiges Verstehen* is understanding of the elements of motivation that are not evident in the particular concrete observation but remain problematical.

Thus Weber just missed the important distinction. It is between motivation considered as a real process in time and atemporal complexes of meanings as such (*irreale Sinngebilde*). As Dr. von Schelting shows, Rickert held *only* the latter to be capable of *Verstehen*. But without going to his extreme the distinction is none the less vital and Dr. von Schelting has done a great service in emphasizing it.

This distinction may be restated in a form that will bring out more vividly its relations to the problems of this study. Concrete motivation involves an intrinsic relation between the meaningful elements and the others in the action complex. One meaning system involved in rational action is scientifically valid knowledge which expresses at least hypothetical intrinsic relations between end, means and conditions. In motivation, considered as a real process in time, meanings cannot be divorced from intrinsic relationships of this, or an analogous character.

On the other hand, the real things or events that may be observed may be significant *only* as symbols with no intrinsic significance of their concrete properties. In this case *Verstehen* is necessarily limited to the meanings of the symbols as such without reference to any intrinsic relationships in the real world.

These two are polar types and in concrete reality naturally shade off into one another. But the distinction is analytically important. Complexes of meanings as such are significant for the analysis of action mainly at two points. Dr. von Schelting clearly shows that understanding of them in abstraction from motivation plays an important part in Weber's own empirical research at both points.

Attention has already been called to the way in which Weber's work necessitated the ideal-typical formulation of systems of ideas which are relevant to concrete motivation, those of Calvinist theology, Brahmanic philosophy, etc. These are systems of interrelated propositions, and must be understood as such. Only when they have been so understood can their relation to concrete motivation in the form of the canalization of religious interests be understood, in turn.

Secondly, a subtler point, to a certain degree Weber also treated complexes of concrete actions as such as meaningful systems. That is, concrete acts are not treated as intrinsically significant in a means-end context but as symbolic of a system of meanings. No attempt will be made to go into examples here. Its connection with the role of symbolism in Durkheim's later work is, however, evident. In the next chapter certain relations of this type of symbolic expression to a system of the structural elements of action will be shown. Here it was only necessary to note its point of articulation with the general methodological basis of the study.

Two consequences may be suggested of the solidarity of science and action which Weber's methodological work has done so much to clarify on the scientific side. The first involves the problem of the relativity of scientific knowledge, arising from the principle of *Wertbeziehung*. This relativity cannot be pushed to an extreme which would involve dispensing with the formal schema of logical, objective proof. This is the nonrelative point of reference which is needed to bring order into the mass of relative specific propositions that constitute concrete scientific knowledge.

Now does not the solidarity of scientific knowledge with rational action imply the existence of a formal schema of elements of action which is in a similar sense exempt from the relativity of concrete knowledge? This seems to be a legitimate interpretation of the passage from Weber placed at the head of this study.[1] At least the main formal outline of the means-end schema is *inseparable* from the conception of action. Relativity can only apply to the specific modes of its application and framework of values, etc., not to the formal scheme itself, so long as the conceptual scheme of action is employed at all.

Secondly, Weber laid very great stress on the freedom of science from value judgments, a position that has been violently attacked. It seems to the present author Weber was entirely right. The fundamental logical distinction between value judgments and judgments of objective fact is basic both to science and to the theory of action. Without it science cannot be distinguished from the manifestation of sentiments nor can the rationality of means-end relationships be established. But the solidarity of science and action here goes even farther. Schematically stated, on a positivistic basis which, as has been shown, eliminates the normative aspect of action, such a distinction is impossible, for all meaningful judgments become scientific. On an idealistic basis, on the other hand, the distinction is equally eliminated—all judgments become those of value. Of the three systems considered here, only a voluntaristic theory of action can make the distinction significant—but also necessary.

Like the above treatment of his theory of capitalism and sociology of religion, this discussion of Weber's methodology has done scant justice to the manifold problems raised by his thought. It has, however, brought out certain basically important points for present purposes. Above all Weber, almost alone in Germany, came near to completely overcoming the predominant idealistic empiricism in the social sciences. He definitely succeeded in vindicating the logical necessity of general concepts for valid empirical knowledge. Beside this great achievement even his failure to appreciate the role of a generalized system of theory

[1] *Wissenschaftslehre*, p. 179.

is a minor matter. And his critical reaction against idealism finally led him in a direction which is of basic importance here— toward a voluntaristic theory of action. With the development of the outline of its structural aspect in the next chapter the main task of this study will be complete. The process of convergence will have been demonstrated.

CHAPTER XVII

MAX WEBER, IV: SYSTEMATIC THEORY

Chapter XVI has shown that Weber's central methodological concern was to vindicate the necessity for general theoretical concepts in the sociohistorical sciences. But the only kind of general concept for which he provided an explicit methodological clarification was his general ideal type. This, it has been shown, is a hypothetically concrete type which could serve as a unit of a system of action or social relationships. But it was not, on a methodological plane, explicitly related to a generalized theoretical system in either of its two main aspects, as a structural outline of systems of action or as a system of elements. Weber did, however, attempt to build up a systematic classification of ideal types[1] starting from a conception of action closely similar to that dealt with throughout this study. It is a reasonable hypothesis that in so far as these types are empirically verified and their classification is logically coherent, the general framework of concepts underlying the classification should be closely related to a generalized theoretical system, even though its methodological status as such is not explicitly worked out. It will be the task of the present chapter to test this hypothesis by systematically analyzing the logical framework of Weber's classification with the general scheme of the structure of systems of action, which has already been developed, in mind.

THE TYPES OF SOCIAL ACTION

Weber's logical starting point is the concept of action: "We shall call 'action' (*Handeln*) any human attitude or activity (*Verhalten*) (no matter whether involving external or internal

[1] The system is all to be found in Part I of *Wirtschaft und Gesellschaft*. To appreciate its significance, however, it is necessary not only to read the abstract formulations but to see them in the context of both his methodological and his empirical work. Of the latter there is a vast mass in the other parts of *Wirtschaft und Gesellschaft* as well as in *Gesammelte Aufsätze zur Religionssoziologie*.

640

acts, failure to act or passive acquiescence) if and in so far as the actor or actors associate a subjective meaning (*Sinn*) with it."[1] *Social* action is "such action as, according to its subjective meaning to the actor or actors, involves the attitudes and actions of others and is oriented to them in its course."[2] Sociology, finally, is "a science which attempts the interpretive understanding (*deutend Verstehen*) of social action in order thereby to arrive at a causal explanation of its course and effects."[3]

These famous and fundamental definitions of Weber's call for brief comment. It is clear that Weber directly associates the concept of action with an accessible subjective aspect, with the postulate of *Verstehen*. In so far as human "behavior"[4] is not accessible to such understanding through the subjective point of view of the actor, it is not action and does not concern the formulation of Weber's systematic sociological theory. With this negative limitation the present study has no quarrel. The second point is that Weber's interest is in understandable aspects of behavior, that is in action, only in so far as it is relevant to the causal explanation of its course and effects. The concepts Weber is concerned with are thus those of an empirical explanatory science, not of any normative[5] or other related kind of discipline. Finally, it is quite clear from the discussion of the previous chapter that he did not consider *Verstehen* restricted to the rational case. The latter plays, as will be seen, a basically important part in his scheme but not the only part. The *Evidenz* of *Verstehen* may be, he says,[6] either rational or emotional (he sometimes says *affektuell*). For instance we can understand an outburst of anger, even though when seen in terms of the situation of the actor it be strictly irrational.

[1] *Wirtsch. u. Ges.*, p. 1. The "in so far as" suggests that he is dealing with an abstract system and not a class of phenomena.

[2] *Ibid.*

[3] *Ibid.* This chapter will not be concerned with Weber's particular concept of the scope of sociology. See Chapter XIX.   Translations of Weber's text quoted in this chapter are by the author.

[4] "Action" is much to be preferred as a translation of Weber's *Handeln* because it fits Pareto's usage, and because it does not have the behavioristic connotations of the term behavior, which Professor Abel (*op. cit.*) uses. Behavior here may be taken to be the broader category.

[5] Which, for instance, he interpreted systematic jurisprudence to be.

[6] *Wirtsch. u. Ges.*, p. 2.

For any science of action nonsubjective processes and objects are not altogether excluded from consideration, but have a place as occasion, condition, result, favoring or hindering circumstance of human action.[1] It is possible that things which appear to a given investigator as explicable in subjective terms will in the end turn out to be the product of the laws of nonsubjective systems,[1] that is, the meaningful aspect may be epiphenomenal. Where a subjective explanation, *e.g.*, adequate motivation, cannot be discovered it may be possible to fall back on regularities which, however great their probabilities of correctness, still remain *unverstehbar*. A motive is "a meaningful complex (*Sinnzusammenhang*), which appears to the actor himself or to the observer to be an adequate (*Sinnvoll*) ground for his attitudes or acts."[2] A correct causal interpretation of concrete action implies "that the outward course and the motive are each correctly grasped and that their relation to each other is 'understandable.' "[3]

It is unnecessary for present purposes to go further into Weber's explicit methodological basis for the concept of action since the foregoing is sufficient to show it is substantially the concept dealt with all through this study. He proceeds immediately to give a classification of social as of other action which is the starting point of his systematic differentiation of types. The relevant passage[4] in full is as follows:

Like all action, that which is social may be determined: (1) *Zweckrational*[5]—by expectations of the behavior of objects of the external environment and of other persons, and through use of these expectations as "conditions" or as "means" for rational ends, rationally weighed and pursued. (2) *Wertrational*[5]—through conscious belief in the *absolute value in itself*—whether to be interpreted as ethical, aesthetic, religious or otherwise—of a given line of conduct purely for its own sake, quite independently of results. (3) "Affectual"[6]—especially

[1] *Ibid.*, p. 3.

[2] *Ibid.*, p. 5.

[3] *Ibid.* Error and/or other modes of lack of correspondence between the subjective and objective aspects of action are of course often understandable.

[4] *Ibid.*, p. 12.

[5] These two terms are purposely left untranslated. It is hoped that their meaning will become clear in the course of the discussion.

[6] *Affektuell.*

emotional, through given affects and states of feeling. (4) Traditional—through the habituation of long practice.

Weber introduces these four concepts as ways in which action may be determined, leaving the question of their methodological status undecided. The way in which he uses these concepts leads to the general conclusion that in definition they are primarily ideal types of concrete action, but their later use tends to set them in a different context. This situation is the source of much confusion.

In the first place, the distinction between the first two as stated in the passage quoted seems definitely to refer to types of concrete action. At first sight it might look as if *Zweckrationalität* referred to the intermediate sector of the intrinsic means-end chain of the previous analysis; *Wertrationalität*, on the other hand, to the element of ultimate ends. This will not, however, meet Weber's definitions, since in them each describes a complete type of action including both means-end relationships and ultimate ends. Both are ideal-type concepts.

The key to Weber's meaning is given in the distinction that Dr. von Schelting discusses[1] between the two possible "formal" types of ethical attitude which Weber calls *Verantwortungsethik* and *Gesinnungsethik*.[2] *Zweckrationalität* is the normative type of action logically implied by the former position, and *Wertrationalität* by the latter. The distinction is essentially as follows: The actor either recognizes a plurality of legitimate directions of value achievement, though perhaps all are not equally important, or he orients his total action to a single specific value, *e.g.*, salvation, which is absolute in the sense that all other potential values become significant only as means and conditions, possible aids or hindrances, to the attainment of this central value.[3]

In the first case one must not only be concerned with the choice of means to a particular end—this is common to both—

[1] VON SCHELTING, *Max Webers Wissenschaftslehre*, Part I. It is taken from Weber. See "Politik als Beruf" in *Gesammelte Politische Schriften*.

[2] These terms are difficult to translate; perhaps tentatively they may be translated as "ethics of responsibility" and "ethics of absolute value."

[3] Another relation to other values is possible: they may be incompatible with the supreme value, directly antagonistic to it, so that the indicated attitude is one of disinterested moral hostility. Thus to a dogmatic religion it is a duty to combat heresy.

but also with the weighing of values, *i.e.*, ultimate ends, against each other, and the possible effects of a given course of action, not only in relation to the achievement of its own immediate, or ultimate end in a direct chain, but also directly or through indirect channels on other values.[1] Hence the urge of the man in this position for objective knowledge is particularly strong, for only by possessing this can he make such judgments rationally. His action must be directed to the achievement of a harmony, a maximization of value achievement in a number of fields according to their relative urgency. In this connection Weber was very far indeed from believing in a preestablished harmony with no real conflicts between different possible values. On the contrary, he took a tragic view of the situation, maintaining the existence of very deep conflicts between the different possible value spheres[2] and especially emphasizing the tragic effect of the unanticipated indirect effects of action (*Schicksal, die Paradoxie der Folgen*).

The other position is concerned, as has been said, with the conditions of action only as means and conditions to attainment of the particular absolute value. Of course the actor is obligated to pursue such an absolute value with every possible effort, but he is not concerned with the success (*Erfolg*) of his action. Whether he can succeed or not has no relation to whether he should try—for there is no other value to compete or to compensate for lack of success. If success is impossible in the objective situation "martyrdom" is the only acceptable course. On the other hand, he is not in the least concerned with the effect of his action on the prospects of realizing other values (for himself or others), for other values simply do not count, or if they do they are to be regarded as dangerous competitors of the supreme value.[3] The matter of the results of his action is left to God,[4] it is no responsibility of the actor's.

[1] See *Wirtsch. u. Ges.*, p. 13.

[2] *Cf. Religionssoziologie*, Vol. I, pp. 554 *ff.* on the *Spannungen* of a rationalized religious view in relation to other values. *Cf.* also Weber's *Politische Schriften*.

[3] The basis of ascetic practices in a mystical religious position.

[4] The author is much indebted to personal conversations with Dr. von Schelting for clarification of this distinction and its relation to Weber's two types of rational action. Dr. von Schelting is not, however, responsible for the views expressed here. The resemblance of this distinction to that of

Hence in the terms employed in this study the distinction between the two types of rational action is to be regarded as resting on that between two polar types of ultimate-end systems. There are, of course, all manner of possible transition types between them, especially mitigations of the rigor of the extreme absoluteness of a single value. Every hierarchy of values involves an element of *Gesinnungsethik*, while the opposite extreme is, for instance, the position taken by Bentham in the famous formula, "Pushpin is as good as poetry." Not only each individual but each value counts as "one and only one."

In respect to the means-end relationship the difference is not in its logical character, but in its "extensity." Certain considerations of the relations of means and ends which are essential to action of the *zweckrational* type become entirely irrelevant at the *wertrational* pole. But there is nothing in Weber's types in any way in conflict with the above scheme of the structural elements of rational action. His distinction cuts across this analysis of structure having to do especially with differences in types of concrete ultimate-end system. The present concern is not to criticize the distinction, which, on the contrary, is most useful, but merely to point out its differences from the scheme developed in this study.[1]

Even though he splits it into two types Weber's rational action involves positively defined normative elements. It differs from Pareto's "logical action" in that Weber's concepts refer to hypothetically concrete complete types and hence include the ultimate-end element, as well as ultimate means and conditions. It is not confined to the mode of means-end relationship as such, as is Pareto's concept (in the above interpretation). Hence residual elements of action if they exist for Weber—and they do— are to be approached in a somewhat different way from that in which Pareto would approach them. But the matter is further complicated by the fact that Weber positively defined another

Pareto between skepticism and faith is striking. There are however, also significant differences. See above, Chap. VII, pp. 284 *ff.*

[1] Weber's actual usage does not seem to be by any means consistent. *Zweckrationalität* often comes to be thought of in abstraction from any ultimate ends. But the above is the only clear meaning which can be extracted from his definitions. Departures from it can be interpreted as due to the pressures inherent in the logical situation toward bringing out the structure of a generalized system as well as types. See below, p. 660.

type of norm besides his two rational types—the traditional. It is necessary to discuss this before approaching the question of residual elements.

It has already been shown that the concept of traditionalism plays a very important part in Weber's empirical sociological work. In the passage quoted above he gives it only an extremely cursory definition—action is determined traditionally "through the habituation of long practice (*durch eingelebte Gewohnheit*)." This might even suggest that traditionalism for Weber was simply the expression of the psychological mechanism of habit. But, however important habit may be in explaining the *mechanisms* of a traditional order it seems to be quite clear that this interpretation is not by itself acceptable. In the first place, the example that was used extensively in the last chapter shows that traditionalistic fixation need not apply to the total complex of action—the term does not designate sheer "automatism" but relates only to certain *normative* aspects, in this case the fixed standard of living. On the other hand, by definition the adaptation of means to ends is, within these limits, rational. Traditional action is apparently a type of total action, its traditionalism consisting in the fixity of certain essentials, their immunity from rational or other criticism.

Weber nowhere gives a fuller definition of *traditional action* as such. He does, however, give further specification of the more general concept of traditionalism, which can throw light on the question. In his discussion of the concept of legitimate order[1] he holds that the legitimacy of an order may be attributed to it by the actors on account of tradition.[2] Tradition, then, serves as a sanction of what is definitely and explicitly a normative aspect of a social system. There is absolutely nothing normative about habit as such. It is either a mechanism or a concrete pattern of actual behavior, not a way men should act.

Moreover, in his fundamentally important discussion of types of authority (*Typen der Herrschaft*), one of the three main types of *legitimate* authority is the traditional. His definition may be quoted in full: "Authority will be called traditional, in so far as its legitimacy rests upon the sanctity (*Heiligkeit*) of an order,

[1] *Wirtsch. u. Ges.*, pp. 16 *ff*. This concept will be discussed at length below as it is of basic importance for present purposes.
[2] *Ibid.*, p. 19.

and this sanctity of the order and that of positions of authority within it, are believed in because they have come down from the past [have always existed]."[1] The interesting point for present purposes is the use of the term sanctity which combined with legitimacy again brings out the normative aspect. No habit as such is sacred. This strongly suggests the attitude of moral obligation found to be so central to Durkheim's thought. Finally, it may be recalled that Weber established a close connection between traditionalism and symbolism and ritual in his discussion of primitive religion.[2]

From all this it is legitimate to conclude, first, that traditionalism has little theoretically to do with the psychological concept of habit; second, that it has a great deal to do with the normative aspect of action. Its intimate relation to legitimacy and to sanctity establishes that beyond question. It is not, however, profitable to pursue the question farther until these concepts and the closely related one of charisma have been considered. It seems evident, however, that traditionalism is not one of the ultimate structural (or other) elements of action systems. It is rather formulated on a more descriptive level. Moreover, traditional action is defined as a *type*, though in this case even more than in the case of the two rational types, the difficulties of this procedure become apparent. In Weber's actual usage the more general concept seems to appear in two main contexts: (1) as the concrete content of norms taken over without rational criticism from the past (tradition) and (2) as a quality or property of certain concrete actions or relationships (the traditionalism of the piece-rate mowers or of authority). There seems to be an inherent difficulty in adequately describing a *total* concrete system of action by the one term traditional in the sense involving norms, which probably accounts for the suggestion of "habit" in Weber's definition.

Finally a few words must be said about the category of affectual action. The difficulties of considering this an adequate definition of a concrete ideal type seem to be even greater than those involved in the definition of "traditional." Apparently Weber had in mind such examples as an outburst of anger which was "irrational" seen in terms of the interests of the actor in his given

[1] *Ibid.*, p. 130.
[2] *Supra*, Chap. XV, pp. 565–566.

situation. There is, of course, no doubt that such instances occur and that it is possible to construct ideal types of specifically irrational action including them. But such ideal types, to be on the same level as the two rational types, would have to be positively defined. It is an important fact that Weber's definition here as in the definition of "traditional" is very sketchy and indefinite, in marked contrast to his treatment of the two rational types. Moreover, still more important, there is nowhere a positive *use* of the concept in Weber's empirical work at all comparable with the use even of traditionalism.

The obvious conclusion seems to be that affectual action is to be regarded as a residual category. This is the more likely since Weber nowhere states that the classification of the four types of action was not meant to be exhaustive. The path by which he probably arrived at this concept may be described as follows: His real starting point, as was Pareto's, was the concept of rationality of action. At the same time his methodological position pushed him in the direction of formulating type concepts. Then the two possible types of formal ethical attitude led him to the distinction of the two types of rational action—each thought of as a complete, though normatively ideal, type.

Apparently the traditional stereotyping of certain aspects of action and relationships was essentially an impressive empirical fact that he was continually encountering in his concrete researches. Being precluded by his methodological approach from relating it to a generalized system of action he simply took it as an ultimate irreducible fact. Largely in conflict with his empirical usage he tried to fit it, not altogether successfully, into a logically symmetrical scheme of types of action. This left over certain nonrational aspects of action which were at the same time not traditional. The positive approach to them was to be found in Weber's view that understandability is not confined to the rational.[1] Affect was accessible to an observer—for example, as an outburst of anger. Hence this nonrational, nontraditional residuum is formulated as the distinguishing criterion of a fourth type of action. No attempt will be made here to develop further what elements may be found to be included in it. It may be merely noted as a caution that especially in view of the residual character of the concept it is just as illegitimate to jump to the conclusion

[1] *Supra,* p. 641.

that it stands for psychological irrationality in the case of the outburst of anger, an expression of an instinct of pugnacity, for instance, as it was to identify traditionalism with habit. Psychological elements may well be involved, but *certainly* do not exhaust the matter. Above all, it is interesting to note that the basically important concept charisma makes no appearance at all in the four types of action. It may well prove to have something to do with the interpretation of affectual action.

From the four types of action Weber proceeds to the concept of social relationship.[1] This is defined as "a state of attitudes (*Sichverhalten*)[2] of a plurality of persons which according to their subjective meaning are mutually concerned with each other and oriented by virtue of this fact. The social relationship thus *consists* entirely and exclusively in the probability that there will in certain circumstances be social action of a meaningfully predictable sort, without reference to the grounds of this probability." It is not necessary to go into an analysis of this definition here, but only to note a few things about it. It comprises another way of looking at the same facts involved in the schema of action; it is, in fact, simply a way of looking at certain complexes of action. It is important because it is the unit in terms of which Weber later builds up most of his more complex categories. This course involves departure from the strict schema of action as such, though it involves it by implication.[3]

But in his treatment of social relationships there is implied the existence of elements of regularity in action itself in order that there may be a significant probability of such kinds of action occurring as to constitute a definable relationship.

MODES OF ORIENTATION OF ACTION

Among the elements of regularity those which interest Weber are the ones that are understandable in terms of subjective categories. He then takes a still further step in narrowing the range of consideration by confining his attention to what he calls "modes of orientation" of action. This form of expression

---

[1] *Wirtsch. u. Ges.*, p. 13.

[2] *Verhalten* and *Sichverhalten* are exceedingly difficult terms to translate. "Attitude" is a rough rendering.

[3] This is one important reason why the scheme of structure of systems of action remained implicit in Weber.

strongly suggests a focus of interest on the normative aspect of action systems, an impression which is strengthened by the general character of Weber's approach to the problems of action.

This is obviously the case with two of the three categories which Weber puts forward in this connection. Action may, he says, be oriented in terms of (a) usage (*Brauch*), (b) interest (*Interessenlage*) or (c) legitimate order.[1] "Interest" is the category in which uniformities are understandable in terms of the rational (*zweckrational*) orientation of the actors to similar expectations. The concept of legitimate order, on the other hand, involves the orientation of action to the idea (*Vorstellung*) on the part of the actors of the existence of such an order as a norm. A few further remarks relative to these two categories are in order here. The stability of regularities of action based on interest lies, he says, in the fact that any actor who does not consider the interest of the others in his action thereby calls forth their resistance, which becomes an obstacle to the attainment of his own ends.[2] Also, orientation to a legitimate order is not limited to the extent to which its rules are lived up to, but also includes their evasion and defiance. The point is, of course, that the existence of the order *makes a difference* to the action and that this difference may be imputed to understandable motives.

The normative character of these two elements of regularity is thus clear: With respect to one it is attributed to a norm of rationality in the pursuit of given ends; with respect to the other it is attributable to rules involving an element of legitimacy, or obligation. The status of the third category, usage, is more doubtful in this respect. Indeed Weber's own formulation, which is very brief, suggests that this is a catchall for non-normative elements. He says that usage involves uniformity of action "in so far as it is given as a matter of actual practice" (*durch tatsächliche Uebung*). This suggests the psychological mechanism of habit as the primary point that he has in mind. His actual treatment, however, shows beyond doubt that here also normative elements are involved. But they are involved in a manner that has not yet been analyzed in this study. Hence explicit discussion of the interpretation of this category will be postponed

[1] *Wirtsch. u. Ges.*, p. 15.
[2] *Ibid.*, p. 16.

until the two more closely related to the foregoing discussion have been dealt with.

The exact logical status of these three concepts is not very clear in Weber's own treatment. Two of them are qualified in his own definitions by the phrase "in so far as." The third is merely stated "Action . . . may be oriented to the idea of a legitimate order." It is possible to consider them as three ideal *types* of action. But why should there be a second classification of these in addition to the first without a word as to the relation of the two or as to why a second should be necessary? The most plausible interpretation seems to be that what Weber was really doing was putting forward, as a general framework for his classification of ideal types, an outline of the generalized structure of systems of action. If this interpretation is correct none of them would be, for the most part, meant as descriptions of even hypothetically concrete types of action.[1]

Usage in this connection seems at first sight to be defined only negatively. It is merely the way "things are done." All Weber says is that there is a distinction between things "being done" because they have "always been done that way" (*Sitte*) and because "it is the newest way to do it" (fashion). But in the descriptive characterization no specific motive—no means-end relationship[2]—appears to be involved. This is not in the least the same as saying that these uniformities will not turn out to be understandable as the results of complexes of motivation.[3]

The other two involve specific norms; the efficient adaptation of means to ends, on the one hand—norms of efficiency; the norm of legitimacy, or moral obligation, on the other. There is no reason whatever why these two, and usage as well, should not all be involved in the same concrete situation; indeed they so frequently are involved that when there is complete absence of any one of them from any concrete complex of action it is to be regarded as a limiting case. To avoid confusion one distinction

---

[1] The principal motive for introducing these concepts is probably, as was intimated in the last chapter, that he needed a framework for his systematic classification of ideal types. Methodologically he did not seem to be clear as to the significance of what he was doing in the context of interest here.

[2] There appears to be only some such element as what Pareto calls *la besoin d'uniformité*, a diffuse entity, not a motive.

[3] See above, Chap. X, on Durkheim.

should be pointed out,[1] that between the fact of *orientation* to a legitimate order and the motives for acting in relation to it. The two elements of interest and legitimacy are interwoven in a complex way. The fact that an order is legitimate in the eyes of a large proportion of the community makes it *ipso facto* an element of the *Interessenlage* of any one individual, whether *he* himself holds it to be legitimate or not. Supposing he does not, his action, to be rational, must be none the less oriented to this order. This ground has been thoroughly gone over in the discussion of Durkheim.

It seems, then, that the best interpretation that can be placed on these concepts is that they are parts of a structural framework of action. Weber's approach to them, however, is somewhat different from that worked out in the analysis of Pareto. It is more like Durkheim's approach. That is, the element of legitimacy, which undoubtedly directly corresponds to Durkheim's moral obligation, does not first appear in the form of an ultimate end of a particular means-end chain, but as a property of an *order*, that is, a system of norms, to which particular actions are oriented, but which stands in the relation of "condition" rather than means or end to the unit act. The attitude of the actor to these norms may vary; that is, they may, on the one hand, be morally neutral conditions to which he orients his action, as he would to the availability of any technical means, or, on the other hand, his attitude may be a "moral" one of acceptance and hence an obligation to live up to them, or rejection and a corresponding obligation to combat them.

This is in all essentials the same as Durkheim's approach to the same phenomena. It may, following the previous terminology,[2] be called the institutional approach as distinct from the direct action-element approach of Pareto. There emerge, then, by this approach three elements: the apparently non-normative merely factual element of order, usage, the efficiency-norm element and the legitimacy-norm element. A total concrete order normally involves all three.[3] The main task now is to analyze each of these to see if it is, in turn, further reducible to elements and in what relation these stand to the scheme of the

[1] Weber himself makes it quite clearly. *Cf. Wirtsch. u. Ges.*, p. 16.
[2] *Supra*, Chap. X, pp. 399 *ff*.
[3] *Cf*. especially *Wirtsch. u. Ges.*, p. 17.

structure of action already developed. But before embarking on this analysis it is well to remark on the nature of Weber's own course from here on.

He proceeds to develop step by step a system of ideal types of social relationship.[1] Starting with three elementary relations— conflict (*Kampf*), *Vergemeinschaftung* and *Vergesellschaftung*[2]— he builds them up into more and more complex structures culminating in such concepts as church and state. It is almost needless to say that this is not generalized theory in the present sense at all, but is the development of the other possibility of generalizing conceptualization—that of a system of ideal-type concepts. The unit of this systematization is the social relationship. The result is a scheme of "objectively possible" types of social structure. As such it is a monumental work, unique of its kind in its scope and refinement, and a mine for almost any kind of empirical research. It has, in the empirical uses to which Weber himself put it, the important result of bringing out into clear relief the structural differentiation of institutions. Where Durkheim saw clearly only the functional side of institutions, their relation to the determination of individual action, Weber saw their structural aspect on a tremendous "architectonic" panorama. It was the finest product of the historical relativism of the idealistic tradition. There is no space here to follow through this extraordinary type system. Certain aspects of it will be discussed later in illustrating the importance of the consequences of the alternative analysis. But the latter is the main concern now.

It is not necessary to dwell at any considerable length upon the analysis of what has been called the efficiency-norm element. But it is worth while to make certain points, above all that Weber made, even if in slightly different form, all the main distinctions of structural elements which have appeared in the foregoing analysis. In the first place, his definition of *Interessenlage* associates it directly with *Zweckrationalität*. This means that action is determined by interest only in so far as it involves adaptation of means to given ends, according to objective standards. It

---

[1] See *Wirtsch. u. Ges.*, pp. 20–30 for the bold outline, but throughout Part I carried out in more special respects.

[2] Explicit consideration of these two concepts will be postponed until the note appended to this chapter in connection with Toennies.

may be said that this is what orientation to efficiency-norms is. It is true that Weber's concept of *Zweckrationalität* does not directly abstract from the ultimate-end element. But in *this* connection his use of it involves no reference to any specific type of ultimate-end system, nor to its specific role. The reference is wholly to the character of the means-end relationship in a given situation, whatever the ultimate ends may be. These are not considered as variables for the present purposes. Hence it may be concluded that this structural *element* differs from the *zweckrational type* precisely in omitting consideration of the character of ultimate ends. It then becomes equivalent[1] to the intermediate intrinsic means-end sector.

But this is not all. The internal differentiation of this sector worked out above is also to be found, in essentials, in Weber. As would be expected this is clearest in connection with his discussion of the status of the economic element. Action is, he says, "economically oriented, in so far as it is concerned, according to its subjective meaning, with provision for the desire for 'utilities' (*Nutzleistungen*)."[2] "Economic action (*Wirtschaften*) is a *peaceful* exercise of power (*Verfügungsgewalt*) which is primarily economically oriented."[3] The second definition especially has a strong concrete-type leaning. But, in the first place, it explicitly excludes force as a means to economic action—possibly other modes of coercion. Secondly, the orientation to acquisition of utilities exactly corresponds to the above analysis. It is interesting to note that Weber still more explicitly excludes the specific nature of the ultimate ends of this utility-seeking element by stating that it must not be taken to be confined to consumption wants, since that would rule out "naked acquisition." The essential thing is that utilities are actually sought after, not why.[4] The importance of this distinction for the treatment of capitalism is obvious. Capitalistic acquisitiveness, its specific limitless character, is not to be explained on economic grounds alone.

Moreover, Weber draws essentially the same distinction between the economic and the technological elements which has

[1] Since it also abstracts from the character of any *specific* situation.
[2] *Wirtsch. u. Ges.*, p. 31.
[3] *Ibid.*
[4] *Ibid.* Unfortunately he does not work out the concept of utility further.

been made above.[1] He says: "Not every action which is rational with respect to means should be called economic. Above all 'economy' is not identical with 'technology.'"[2] Rational technique is any employment of means which is consciously oriented to experience and its analysis. There is thus a technique of every kind of action,[3] *i.e.*, it is an element, not a type of action. An economic element enters in only in so far as the comparative scarcity of alternative means to a given end becomes relevant to the choice between them. This is always a consideration in addition to the technological, not in place of it. It means that the costs of use of a given means for a given end are considered. This, in turn, means that their comparative urgency for this and alternative ends becomes involved.[4] Thus the fundamental economic facts are scarcity, adaptation of means to alternative ends and cost. The economic element involves the weighing of the relative urgency of different uses of a given scarce means, which the technological does not.

This gives all the main lines of distinction. The only qualification is that the status of the distinction as a matter of structural elements, though strongly suggested, is not clarified. This is related to the fact noted in the last chapter that Weber took the concepts of economic theory as his leading case for the general ideal type, hence involving all the methodological difficulties found to be inherent in that concept. But considering this, and the fact that Weber originally approached economics with the antitheoretical biases of the historical school, he achieved a remarkable degree of methodological clarification of the logical status of economic theory—distinctly superior it may be said, to the majority of present-day orthodox economists.

The status of coercive power in Weber in relation to the economic factor is a more complicated question than that of the technological element. A fairly clearly definable line can, however, be discerned. In the first place, by limiting "economic action" to peaceful means Weber, as has been seen, explicitly excluded the use of force.[5] For the rest in his systematic treatment he

---

[1] Chap. VI.

[2] *Ibid.*, p. 32.

[3] Including, for instance, prayer and mystical contemplation.

[4] *Wirtsch. u. Ges.*, p. 33. This is surely an unexpected place to find an apparently independent version of the opportunity-cost doctrine.

[5] See also *Wirtsch. u. Ges.*, p. 32.

clearly separated in different chapters, The Sociological Fundamentals of Economic Life[1] and Types of Authority.[2] It is worth while, then, to investigate his concept of authority (*Herrschaft*), which he clearly did not think of as an economic category. He defines it as "the probability of securing obedience to specific commands on the part of a given group of persons."[3] It is a narrower concept than that of power (*Macht*) which is "the probability within a social relationship of being able to secure one's own ends, even against opposition."[4] In this widest sense power is by no means excluded from the economic element of relationships, but authority is. In so far as a social relationship involves economic considerations it is a matter of agreement, not of command, on the one side; obedience, on the other.

Of course agreement in this sense by no means excludes inequality of bargaining power, hence coercion.[5] At the same time it is perfectly possible to enter into a relationship that involves submission to authority by voluntary agreement. Thus Weber strongly emphasizes that the subjection to discipline in the capitalistic enterprise is, in the strictest sense, subordination to authority—although over a limited range. The worker must obey orders.[6] But all this does not affect the central fact that authority is a specific form of the exercise of power, involving the possibility of coercion.

The concept of the "political" Weber makes still narrower, tying it to authority exercised within a given geographical area, on the one hand, and involving the application or threat of physical coercion in case of need, on the other.[7] The important distinction between political and economic elements cannot for present purposes be found this far away from the central concern of economics.

If then, the concept of authority be taken as the clear line that Weber draws at the point where economic power stops[8] it

---

[1] *Ibid.*, pp. 31 *ff.*
[2] *Ibid.*, pp. 122 *ff.*
[3] *Ibid.*, pp. 28, 122. Irrespective of whether the obeyer likes the particular content of the command or not.
[4] *Ibid.*, p. 28.
[5] *Ibid.*, p. 123.
[6] *Ibid.*
[7] *Ibid.*, p. 29.
[8] The exercise of authority for Weber may be either *Wirtschaftsorient-*

leaves the following situation: Once activities in pursuit of the acquisition and distribution of utilities take place in a situation involving social relationships, the question arises of the determination of the power relationships of the participants in the concrete activities. From the situation involving complete equality of bargaining power which seems to have been the starting point of the earlier classical economists,[1] there is a whole series of degrees involving more and more possibility of coercion of one party to such a relationship by the other parties.

Of these power relationships two types may be roughly distinguished. On the one hand, the departure from the completely economic norm may be due to the employment of what may be called noneconomic means. These may be defined as force, fraud and the exercise of authority (in Weber's sense). The upshot of Weber's treatment would seem to be to draw, in these terms, the line between economic and noneconomic power, taking authority as the "mildest" of these means.[2] On the other hand, this still leaves open the possibility of inequalities of power, not as a direct result of greater productivity, but entering in as a result of taking advantage of a better situation, *e.g.*, monopoly, etc., or of greater shrewdness and foresight in the use of economic means, that is, the securing of voluntary agreements to exchange goods and services.[3]

It is over this question that differences about the role of the power element play their principal part in the history of economic thought. At one pole stands the main classical position resting on the postulate of the "natural identity of interests," a position which altogether eliminates the coercive element. At the other is the Marxian type of economic theory, one of several theories that make it the *central* element. Weber leans rather to the latter

---

iert, concerned with securing utilities, or *Wirtschaftsrelevant*, affecting the distribution of utilities in the community, but it is not *Wirtschaften* as such. The distinction of these three things is very useful for concrete research.

[1] As Professor F. H. Knight says, the great discovery that lay at the basis of this development was that of mutual advantage in exchange. See his "Freedom as Fact and Criterion," *International Journal of Ethics*, Vol. 39, pp. 129 *ff.*

[2] Weber seems to have little concern with fraud in his conceptual framework. It is impossible to go into the question here.

[3] What Weber aptly calls "dominance through a constellation of interests." *Wirtsch. u. Ges.*, pp. 604–606.

than to the former school.[1] For the present purpose (which is the distinction of the principal structural elements of action) the issue is one of expediency rather than of fundamental principle. The exclusion of the noneconomic means from the positions of variables in the system of *economic* theory seems clearly indicated.[2] On the other hand, it is clearly possible to formulate such a system on the postulate of the natural identity of interests. Whether the elements of economic coercion should be used to define the same system, broadening its scope, or whether they require separate systematic formulation can be decided only in terms of the results of actual attempts to do the former. There is no space here for critical analysis of what attempts have been made.

In the meantime it must be sharply emphasized that considerations of the logical simplicity of a system of economic theory that excludes coercion should not be allowed to obscure the enormous empirical importance of coercion in actual economic life. In the work of the great majority of liberal economists this has been conspicuously the case.[3] Weber is not subject to this criticism. He had a deep, almost tragic, consciousness of the importance of coercion in human affairs. Any study of his political writings is sufficient to convince one of this.[4]

LEGITIMATE ORDER, CHARISMA AND RELIGION

It is time to return to the concept of legitimate order, or as it has been put above, legitimacy norms, in relation to action. The way in which Weber deals with this is of central interest. In the first place he makes two classifications, the distinction between which is not at first sight evident. The first[5] is of modes in which "the legitimacy of an order may be guaranteed." The

---

[1] Of course he had no concern at all with the specific technicalities of Marxian economic theory, such as labor theory of value, surplus value, etc.

[2] As Weber says, "Das Pragma der Gewaltsamkeit ist dem Geist der Wirtschaft sehr stark Entgegengesetzt." *Wirtsch. u. Ges.*, p. 32.

[3] *Cf.* especially the remarks about Robbins and Souter in this respect in Talcott Parsons, "Some Reflections on the Nature and Significance of Economics," *Quarterly Journal of Economics*, May, 1934. Marshall is another conspicuous example.

[4] See Weber's *Gesammelte Politische Schriften*.

[5] *Wirtsch. u. Ges.*, p. 17.

second[1] is of reasons why binding legitimacy is attributed to the order by the actors.

The basis of the distinction emerges from consideration of the actual content of the classifications. The guarantee spoken of in connection with the first may be purely subjective (*innerlich*), in which case it is (*a*) affectual, (*b*) *wertrational* or (*c*) religious. Or it may be external, which means in terms of "interest," certain expectations of external consequences. The terminology here used seems somewhat objectionable, but the essential meaning is clear. It is a classification of types of motive, hence of forces, by which actual adherence to the norms of the order in question is to be explained. In the terminology of this study it is preferable to say that these motives may be classified as disinterested and interested. In the one case the order is looked upon as an expression of values, hence to be lived up to because it is valued for itself or for the values it expresses.[2] In the other, its existence is part of the situation in which one must act—it takes the role of morally neutral means or conditions for the actor's own ends. Thus a communist who personally does not believe in free speech may invoke the right to free speech in court to keep himself out of jail and thus further his own cause. Such a right[3] is part of the legitimate order of present society, which he uses as means to his own ends. Weber may be interpreted as pointing out that even though interests may morally be quite neutral to the order they none the less may play a part in guaranteeing it, that is, in maintaining its function.

The other classification is on a different plane—it is that of the motives for which *legitimacy* is ascribed to the order, not why the order is upheld in action. Negatively the conspicuous fact is that interest drops out entirely. While interest may be a very important reason for conforming to an order, it has nothing to do with ascribing legitimacy—or illegitimacy—to it. Here only the disinterested motive elements have a place. But Weber's subclassification of these is somewhat different from the above. It is (*a*) traditional, (*b*) affectual, (*c*) *wertrational* and (*d*) held to be legal by positive institution (*Satzung*). It does not seem important enough to inquire here why Weber eliminated religious

[1] *Ibid.*, p. 19.
[2] Or combated for disinterested motives.
[3] Under certain restrictions.

motives and added traditional. On this last it may be noted only that he says, "The legitimacy of an order by virtue of the *santification* of tradition is everywhere the most universal and original case."[1] This linking of traditionalism with *sanctity* is a conspicuous feature of his treatment of the former throughout.

It is interesting to note here a shift from the original meaning of *wertrational,* directly corresponding to that previously noted in *zweckrational.* Though the term absolute occurs,[2] in the context the important thing seems to be not the absoluteness but the "ultimacy" (in the sense of this study) of the value. This is evident from the fact that *zweckrational* has become identified with interest—concern with a thing or person only in so far as it or he may be usable as a means or should be taken account of as an intrinsically relevant condition. *Wertrational,* on the other hand, becomes here identified with the disinterested attitude of valuation of a thing for its own sake or as a direct expression or embodiment of an ultimate value, which hence cannot, in so far, simply be "used" as a means. In other words the distinction of *zweckrational* and *wertrational,* originally one of hypothetically concrete *types* of rational action, has stepped over into one of structural elements of action systems, recognizable as properties of attitudes. Occuring in the context where it appears this cannot but be significant.

The fourth category, positive institution of norms held to be legal, may from the present point of view be regarded as a category of derived legitimacy. The belief in legality implies that the instituting agency has a right to institute such norms. It falls for Weber into two subtypes—agreement and imposition (*Oktroyierung*). In the former case, it should be noted, the mere fact that persons with interests come to an agreement is not enough. In order that there may be legitimacy there must be an obligation assumed to carry out the terms of the agreement. This will be found to involve one or more of the other three elements, above all *Wertrationalität* (in the new sense). The connection of this with Durkheim's analysis of relations of contract is obvious. The element of legitimacy in agreements is a part of Durkheim's "non-contractual element of contract."[3] Thus purely voluntary

[1] *Wirtsch. u. Ges.,* p. 19.
[2] Both here and in the classification in *Wirtsch. u. Ges.,* p. 17.
[3] *Supra,* Chap. VIII.

agreement is the limiting case where the element of legitimacy is reduced to a minimum. But this by no means implies that it is eliminated.

At the present moment it is not proposed to go further into the mutual relations of tradition, affect and *Wertrationalität* (in the *second* sense, which will be employed from now on). But already the analysis has gone far enough to justify certain conclusions. Legitimacy is for Weber a quality of an order, that is, of a system of norms governing conduct, or at least to which action may (or must) be oriented. This quality is imputed to the order by those acting in relation to it. Doing so involves taking a given type of attitude toward the norms involved which may be characterized as one of disinterested acceptance. To put the matter somewhat differently, for one who holds an order to be legitimate, living up to its rules becomes, to this extent, a matter of moral obligation.

Thus Weber has arrived at the same point Durkheim reached when he interpreted constraint as moral authority. Moreover, Weber has approached the question from the same point of view, that of an individual thought of as acting in relation to a system of rules that constitute conditions of his action. There has emerged from the work of both men the same distinction of attitude elements toward the rules of such an order, the interested and the disinterested. In both cases a legitimate order is contrasted with a situation of the uncontrolled play of interests.[1] Both have concentrated their special attention on the latter element. Such a parallel is not likely to be purely fortuitous.[2]

But the parallel extends much farther. The question arises whether it is necessary to leave the analysis of the motive elements involved in legitimacy at the pluralism of the three mentioned in Weber's classification[3] or whether it is possible to find in Weber any indication of a more general unifying conception in terms of which all three may be related to each other. Such a unifying principle is undoubtedly present in the concept of charisma.

---

[1] *Cf. Wirtsch. u. Ges.*, p. 648.

[2] The fact that both had juristic training probably has something to do with the similarity of their approaches in so far as they differ from that of Pareto.

[3] Tradition, affect, *Wertrationalität.*

Weber himself deals with this concept in a number of different contexts[1] which involve rather sharp differences of emphasis. There is, however, a definite thread of continuity running through them all which consists precisely in the relation of charisma to the concept of legitimacy. Tracing this will involve some interpretation beyond simple exposition, but it is of the sort that is unavoidable in such a situation.

The conception has already been dealt with briefly in connection with Weber's religious typology.[2] There it was noted that Weber takes as his point of departure the contrast with routine (*Alltag*). Charisma is, then, a quality of things and persons by virtue of which they are specifically set apart from the ordinary, the everyday, the routine.[3] It is interesting to note that Weber on several occasions specifically contrasts charisma with the economic element. It is, as such, "*spezifisch wirtschaftsfremd.*"[4]

This apartness is what characterizes charismatic things or persons. It is hence not immediately related as such to action— it is a quality of concrete things, persons, acts, etc. But a hint of the relation to action is given in the kind of attitude men take toward charismatic things or persons. Weber applies a number of terms, but two may be singled out. Applied to a person the charismatic quality is exemplary (*vorbildlich*)[5]—something to be imitated. At the same time recognition of it as an exceptional quality lending prestige and authority is a duty.[6] The charismatic leader never treats those who resist him or ignore him, within the scope of his claims, as anything but delinquent in duty. On the basis of this characterization it seems legitimate to conclude that charisma implies a specific attitude of respect, and that this respect is like that owed to a recognized duty. It is clearly the ritual attitude of Durkheim: charismatic authority is a phase of moral authority.

[1] The principal points are: *Wirtsch. u. Ges.*, pp. 140–148; 227 *ff;* 250–261; 642–649; 753–778; *Religionssoziologie*, Vol. I, pp. 268–269.

[2] *Supra*, Chap. XV, pp. 564 *ff.*

[3] Routine here clearly does not mean that habitually performed but rather "profane." Morning prayers, though carried out daily, are not *Alltag*.

[4] *Wirtsch. u. Ges.*, p. 142. Compare Durkheim's statement, "Labor is the profane activity par excellence," quoted above, Chap. XI.

[5] *Wirtsch. u. Ges.*, p. 140.

[6] *Ibid.*

In other words, charisma is directly linked with legitimacy, is indeed the name in Weber's system for the source of legitimacy in general. The principal difficulty of the concept arises from the fact that he did not, apparently, originally conceive it in these general terms in relation to a scheme of the structure of action. It was, rather, conceived of in terms of a much more specific theory of social *change* and developed from there. There has already been occasion to develop the theory in terms of its most important empirical example for Weber, the role of the prophet.[1]

The main context is that of a break in a traditional order. Hence two of the most prominent aspects of the concept charisma —its association with antitraditionalism as its revolutionary character[2] and its particularly close association with a specific person, a leader. The prophet is thus the leader who sets himself explicitly and consciously against the traditional order—or aspects of it—and who claims *moral* authority for his position, whatever the terms in which he expresses it, such as divine will. It is men's duty to listen to him and follow his commands or his example. In this connection it is also important to note that the prophet is one who feels himself to be reborn. He is qualitatively different from other men in that he is in touch with or the instrument of a source of authority higher than any which is established or any to which obedience can be motivated by calculation of advantage.

If the concept of charisma is oriented to this particular context, then the essential problem is that of the relation of prophetic charisma to the legitimacy of the orders which govern everyday life. In *this* revolutionary sense, Weber holds, charisma is in the nature of the case a temporary phenomenon. For the message of the prophet to become embodied in a permanent everyday structure, to become institutionalized, it must undergo a fundamental change. In this process the authority that the prophet exercises by virtue of his personal *charisma* may develop in one of two directions—a traditionalized or a rationalized structure.[3]

The crucial point in the concrete development comes with the question of succession at the passing of the original charismatic

---

[1] *Supra*, Chap. XV, pp. 567 *ff*.

[2] *Wirtsch. u. Ges.*, p. 759.

[3] See in general *ibid.*, Part III, Chap. X, *Die Umbildung des Charisma*.

leader. It is not necessary to go into the various concrete ways in which the situation may, more or less successfully, be met. Only the two main outcomes will be noted. In the one case the charismatic quality is transferred according to one of a number of possible rules, from one concrete person (or group of persons) to another. The most usual, though by no means the only possible, instance is hereditary charisma (*Erbcharisma*).[1] Then the element of sacredness, the qualification for certain functions, inheres in the particular concrete person by virtue of his birth, an act within the given sphere becomes legitimate by virtue of the fact that *he* performs it.

The correlate of this is some definition of the norm embodying the prophet's mission. In this case it takes the form of a traditionalized system of norms (a sacred law) which carry the same quality of sanctity, of charisma, as the person of the ruler. In this way there arise what are for Weber the two main characteristics of traditional authority[2]—a traditional body of norms held sacred and unalterable and, *within* the margin of freedom left open by these and the possibility of their interpretation, an area of arbitrary personal authority of the ruler, legitimized by his generally charismatic personal quality. By this process, from being the specifically revolutionary force charisma becomes, on the contrary, the specific sanction of immobile traditionalism.[3]

The alternative to this mode of routinization is a line of development which involves thinking of the charismatic quality as objectified and hence capable of divorce from the particular concrete person. It then becomes either[4] (*a*) transferable or (*b*) obtainable by a person by his own efforts or, finally, (*c*) not a quality of a person as such at all but of an office, or of an institutional structure without reference to personal qualities. The first two still tie it to particular persons, even though they are not independent prophets or blood descendants of them. In the third case, however, charisma becomes inherent only in the office or the objective system of rules. It is hardly necessary to note that this is the road which leads to bureaucratic organization and

---

[1] *Gentilcharisma* is a subtype of this.
[2] *Cf. Wirtsch. u. Ges.*, pp. 130 *ff.*
[3] *Ibid.*, p. 774.
[4] *Ibid.*, p. 771.

"legality" as the standard of legitimacy. The essential point is that the quest of the source of legality always leads back to a charismatic element, whether by apostolic succession, revealed law (Calvin's *Geneva*), divine right or a general will.

Thus it is evident that what changes in the shift from revolutionary prophecy to traditional or rational everyday authority is not the quality charisma as such but its concrete modes of embodiment[1] and its relations to other elements of the particular concrete complex. Indeed Weber's fullest treatment of legitimacy[2] leaves no doubt that there is no *legitimate* order without a charismatic element. In traditionalism this is always given in the sanctity of tradition.[3] This involves more than the mere fact that things simply *have been* done in a certain way and people consider it "a good thing" to continue in the same way. There is a definite *duty* to do them in the traditional way. Similarly in a rational bureaucratic structure there must always be a source of the legality of its order which is, in the last analysis, charismatic. Finally, the same is true of preprophetic traditionalism.[4]

Thus defined charisma covers a field considerably broader than what is generally called religion. But it has already been noted that the probable genesis of the conception in Weber's own mind started from the role of the prophet in the more specifically religious sense. What then, is its relation to religion? To answer this question it is necessary to go back to the place of charisma in primitive religion. As was noted[5] in that connection the special apartness of the quality of charisma is correlated with the conception of a world of supernatural entities in the specific sense of the above discussion.[6] Indeed, this sense of the supernatural is nothing but the ideological correlate of the attitude of respect. Corresponding to the dualism of attitude, which has been found running through the thought of both Durkheim and Weber, between that of morally neutral utilitarian use and moral or

---

[1] Regarded as a variable, the element itself remains unchanged through a range of different values.

[2] *Ibid.*, pp. 642 *ff*. This section is probably unfinished, as are many in this work.

[3] In speaking of traditionalism Weber almost always uses the term sacred (*heilig*).

[4] *Supra*, Chap. XV, pp. 565–566.

[5] *Supra*, Chap. XV, p. 565.

[6] And, note, *only* in this specific sense.

ritual respect, is one of "worlds" or systems of entities—in this most general sense, one of nature and the supernatural.[1]

Weber has defined religious action as action in relation to supernatural entities thus conceived. Then in the broadest possible sense religious ideas might be defined as any conceptions men have of these supernatural entities and their relations to man and to nature. Then on the symbolic level the question of meaning begins to be involved. Events do not merely "happen" and "happen to" men, but they may be interpreted as having a meaning in the sense of symbolizing or expressing the actions, will or other aspects of supernatural entities.

One further logical link is necessary to complete the chain. The discussion of Durkheim's treatment of religion brought out the central role of the active attitude of men toward the non-empirical aspects of the universe. In terms of Weber's ideas this relation may be analyzed somewhat further. Weber's religious "interests"[2] may be held to be another name for these active attitudes. The religious elements of action are concerned with men's relations to supernatural entities. Religious interests define the directions of these activities, the ends men may hope to accomplish by means of these acts.

On the "primitive" level religious actions remain a more or less unintegrated series of acts in pursuit of particular interests. The world of supernatural entities is not itself integrated into a fully rationalized system.[3] According to the exigencies of life as they arise and to the supernatural facilities provided in the traditional culture, these interests are defined and pursued. Here the question of the influence of religious ideas[4] is a difficult one. It is probably safest to speak of ideas, interests, value attitudes and acts as a single complex in which relations of priority

[1] When Durkheim rejected the definition of religion as concerned with supernatural things, the concept of supernatural was a different one from that used here. The latter is, as should be evident, entirely consistent with Durkheim's theoretical position.

[2] The use of this term in both this context and the above context where it is contrasted with disinterested is confusing. It is retained here because it is Weber's own usage. Interest in the religious context, however, is equivalent to a combination of the transcendental ends and ultimate-value attitudes of the above discussion.

[3] This is naturally a matter of degree. A completely unintegrated system would scarcely constitute a religion. Cf. Durkheim's definition.

[4] Which are primarily of the order of "myth." Cf. supra, Chap. XI, p. 425.

are exceedingly difficult to establish. Weber does not make a very great contribution to this question.

On the prophetic level, however, he has contributed very greatly to clarifying the relationships.[1] He has shown that, once the attempt to rationalize the meaning of the world into a rationally consistent system has been started in a given direction, there is an immanent dialectic of this process of rationalization. It may go at a more or less rapid pace; in one or several respects it may in a given development be carried to more or less radical conclusions or stopped at different points. But the main outline is clear. There is a limited number of mutually exclusive possibilities.

In the discussion of Durkheim religious ideas were treated in the main negatively, as ideas concerned with the nonempirical aspects of the world. Weber's results make it possible to define them more closely. They are ideas concerning not merely *how* the world works, but *why* in a teleological sense; they concern the "meaning" of the world. From this point of view religious ideas are inseparably bound up with human interests and vice versa. Weber has shown how the problem of evil, especially suffering, forms a central starting point for the formulation of the question of meaning. Conversely, what human religious interests *can* be, comes to be defined in terms of the conception of the meaning of the world.

This mutual relation is not altogether a completely relativistic circle. It is possible to say, in general, what kind of meaning and of interest is involved. The meaning is just that involved in the above teleological sense. If a friend is killed in an automobile accident the "how" is usually fairly clear in a scientifically satisfying sense. It is true that our knowledge of the physiology of death is by no means complete—and the friend of the deceased is not likely to be in possession of more than a small fraction of that knowledge. But this is not what is problematical to him. It is rather the "why" in a sense relative to a system of values. The question is, what purpose or value could his death serve? In this sense such an occurrence is apt to be felt as particularly meaningless.

The "meaning" in question, then, is that which is relevant to a teleological value context, not to a scientific explanatory context. The interests are those in the ultimate-value achieve-

[1] *Cf.* note appended to Chap. XIV, *supra*.

ments with which we identify ourselves. In this connection it must be noted that the religious ideas Weber is primarily concerned with are not as such exclusively value ideas, or ends of action. They are rather rationalized interpretations of the meaning of the world, including a complete metaphysical system. Out of these fundamental metaphysical postulates, then, is to be derived what meaning the world *can* have for man and, from this, in turn, what his ultimate values can "meaningfully" be.

It is rather that such ideas canalize religious interests—hence define ultimate ends and through them influence action. Their functional role may be thought of as analogous to that of institutions.[1]

They do not themselves constitute ends of action but rather a framework of ideal conditions under which ends may be pursued. What concrete ends will make sense depends on what is the structure of this framework. But for it to exert an influence on action it presupposes certain typical interests of men. The principal one relevant in the present context is the interest in giving their life a meaning. Correlative with this is the fact that all men respect or hold sacred certain things. The variations are not in this basic fact itself but in the concrete content of the sacred.

While the quest for a meaning of the world leads to one of the possible metaphysical positions, this is most emphatically not to be interpreted to mean that either the attitude of respect or the human interests correlative with such a theory are metaphysical entities. They are strictly observable empirical facts. Man is an entity that in relation to his nature and the kind of situation in which he is placed is known to develop metaphysical interpretations of his world. But whether he is this kind of entity or is placed in this kind of situation is not a metaphysical question but a question of fact. The position taken here, derived above all from Durkheim and Weber, is to be criticized and defended on empirical grounds.

It is now possible to make a reinterpretation of charisma. It is the quality which attaches to men and things by virtue of their relations with the "supernatural," that is, with the nonempirical aspects of reality in so far as they lend teleological "meaning" to men's acts and the events of the world. Charisma is not a

[1] In Weber's terms definable as "forms of legitimate order."

metaphysical entity but a strictly empirical observable quality of men and things in relation to human acts and attitudes.

Though its scope is broader than the religious in the usual sense there is inherent in the concept a religious reference. That is, men's ultimate-value interests are in the nature of the case inseparably linked to their conceptions of the supernatural, in this specific sense. It is hence through this religious reference that charisma may serve as the source of legitimacy. That is to say, there is an inherent solidarity between the things we respect (whether they be persons, or abstractions) and the moral rules governing intrinsic relations and actions. This solidarity is connected with the common reference of all these things to the supernatural and our conceptions of our own ultimate values and interests that are bound up with these conceptions of the supernatural. The distinction between legitimacy and charisma can be stated, in general terms as follows: Legitimacy is the narrower concept in that it is a quality imputed only to the norms of an order, not to persons, things or "imaginary" entities, and its reference is to the regulation of action, predominantly in its intrinsic aspects. Legitimacy is thus the *institutional* application or embodiment of charisma.

In concluding this discussion it is interesting to point out explicitly the extraordinarily close correspondence of Durkheim with Weber both in approach to this range of problems and in treatment of them. In spite of their differences—Weber's absorbtion in the problems of social dynamics and Durkheim's almost complete indifference to them, Weber's concern with action and, Durkheim's with knowledge of reality—in the basic conceptual framework at which they arrive their results are almost identical. The identity applies at at least two strategic points—the distinction of the moral and non-moral motives of action in relation to norms, and the distinction between the quality of norms as such (Weber—legitimacy; Durkheim—moral authority) and the broader element of which this is a "manifestation" (Weber—charisma; Durkheim—sacredness). The correspondence is the more striking in that the two started from opposite poles of thought—Weber from historical idealism, Durkheim from highly self-conscious positivism. Moreover, there is no trace whatever of mutual influence. There is not a single reference in the works of either to those of the other. It may be suggested that such an agreement is most readily explained as a matter of correct interpretation of the same class of facts.

Finally the correspondence extends to the sociologistic theorem, not only the theorem itself but the particular mode of its statement. It will be remembered that Durkheim's views on this subject were charged with being "made in Germany."[1] It has already been noted how extremely unlikely that is. But in the present context the relevant fact is that Weber was in conscious and explicit revolt against most of the prevailing organicism of German social theory which he largely identified with the intuitionist methodology that he criticized so severely. As against the realism of this trend, he was almost a militant social nominalist. A great deal of the German polemic against him has been based on this fact.[2]

Weber ruthlessly discarded from his work all nonempirical entities. The only *Geist* with which he will have anything to do is a matter of empirically observable attitudes and ideas which can be directly related to the understandable motivation of action. But in spite of this fact he definitely takes a sociologistic position. For one of his most fundamental results is that of the dominant social role of religious ideas and value attitudes— specific embodiments or values of charisma—which are *common* to the members of a great social movement or a whole society. Indeed only in so far as the attitudes derived from the doctrines of karma and transmigration are common to all Hindus is caste legitimized, and only in so far as the Protestant ethic was common to large numbers was there adequate motivation to rational ascetic mastery over everyday life. A society can only be subject to a legitimate order, and therefore can be on a non-biological level something other than a balance of power of interests, only in so far as there are *common* value attitudes in the society.

This, again, is exactly where Durkheim emerged in his interpretation of the possible meaning of the social reality. It is what is *left* after Weber's criticism of the historical organicism of German idealistic thought. Weber's individualistic treatment of charisma in connection with the role of the prophet in no way touches this

[1] *Supra*, Chap. VIII, p. 307.

[2] The most extreme case is Spann's review of *Wirtschaft und Gesellschaft*. See his *Tote und lebendige Wissenschaft*.

fundamental point. It merely serves to correct the principal defect which has been found in Durkheim's own statement due to his lingering sociologistic positivism. This was the implication that the empirical role of the value element was confined to sanctioning the institutional *status quo*. Weber, on the contrary, through his theory of prophecy and of the processes of routinization of charisma shows still another side of the picture. His position is not in the least in conflict with Durkheim's, but merely provides a further extension of its application which Durkheim failed to develop. This advance was due, above all, to Weber's comparative perspective and his correlative preoccupation with problems of social change.

Two other points should be mentioned before leaving the concept of charisma. It has already been noted[1] that Weber did not hold that the fully rationalized systems of ideas with which his comparative analysis of religion were concerned were, in the sharply formulated ideal-typical form in which he presents them, actually present in the minds of the great masses of the people he claims have been influenced by them. These rationalizations constitute polar-type cases—"exaggerations" almost—of the meaningful tendencies implicit in mass attitudes. This circumstance gives a clue to the general direction of interpretation of his views on the role of ideas and value elements. It will be remembered that among the motives of attribution of legitimacy to an order[2] he distinguished affectual and *wertrational*. The latter may be interpreted as referring to the formulation of the rational-type case. In harmony with the residual character of the category of affect, the affectual motive may be interpreted at least to include value elements in so far as they fall short of complete and consistent rational formulation.

This is particularly indicated by the close relation between the terms in which "affectuality" and charisma are characterized,[3] which makes it legitimate to conclude that Weber's "affect" is, in this respect, the counterpart of Pareto's "sentiment" and the ultimate-value attitude employed in this study. The distinction between this concept and *Wertrationalität* is the

---

[1] See Chap. XVI, p. 605.

[2] *Supra*, p. 659.

[3] "Affectual faith" is in the "validity of the newly revealed or the exemplary." *Wirtschaft. u Ges.*, p. 19.

counterpart of that in Pareto between the polar type of "residue," which is a principle clearly formulated and unambiguous, and a "sentiment," or in the terminology used here, an ultimate end and an ultimate-value attitude. The principal importance of this distinction is to note that it means that for Weber also the role of the value elements is *not* limited to the exceptional case of the clear, logical formulation of metaphysical ideas and ultimate ends. Departures from the rational norms are not to be interpreted *ipso facto* as evidence of the role of psychological factors. Indeed the concept charisma is so formulated as specifically not to involve this limitation.

Unfortunately, Weber does not give any extended analysis of the relations involved. To a certain extent doubtless ideas must be regarded as manifestations of the same basic elements as are attitudes and acts. But they are not wholly a function of sentiments. The cognitive element is certainly an indispensable independent element, however imperfectly rationalized. It is a function of true, not purely imaginary aspects of reality. But even less so than in the case of scientific ideas is it *wholly* this. As Weber shows, in the direction of interest and of the ways of putting the problems of the meaning of the world, a subjective element is involved. In working this out a concept of *Wertbeziehung* would become involved. Indeed this is the starting point for a *Wissenssoziologie* of metaphysical and religious ideas, as the concept of *Wertbeziehung* in his scientific methodology was for one of scientific ideas. The most general statement is that non-empirical reality (with particular reference to the teleological problem of meaning), our cognitive conceptions of it, nonrationalized value attitudes and the structure of the situations in which we act and about which we think, are elements in a relation of mutual interdependence upon each other. But this is more a statement of the problem than a solution. Such a solution would be beyond the scope of this study. It is one of the most fundamental fields for future analytical and empirical study.[1] Weber's importance lies in opening it up and formulating the elements of the problem in a way that promises to lead to tangible results. It lay on the frontiers of his thought.[2]

---

[1] No further analysis is attempted here. A broad statement of the problem of the role of ideas is made in the note appended to Chap. XIV, *supra*.

[2] As the residual character of the concept of affect shows.

Ritual

The one great exception to the remarkable correspondence of Weber and Durkheim in the basic categories of their sociological treatment of religion, is that of ritual. This element, so central for Durkheim has, curiously enough, no explicit place in Weber's system of concepts. It would, indeed, be a serious blow to the thesis of the essential similarity of the conceptual schemes of these two men if it turned out either that Weber had ignored the empirical facts of ritual entirely, or that he had put an interpretation on them radically inconsistent with that of Durkheim.

This is not, however, the case. On the contrary, though these elements are not explicitly brought together by Weber to constitute a theory of ritual, there are present in his thinking all the principal elements of a theory very close to that of Durkheim. All of them have been encountered in previous parts of the discussion. It remains here to discuss them in their relevance to this particular phenomenon.

In the first place, a glance back over the above treatment of Weber's comparative sociology of religion will immediately show that he by no means ignored the empirical facts of ritual, above all magic, but was vitally concerned with them. One of his two main directions of rationalization lay in the elimination of magical elements.[1] In his discussion of the failure of both the Chinese and the Indian religious ethics to develop a thoroughgoing rationalization of practical conduct, he laid great stress on the fact that both failed to attack the great mass of popular magic even though the elite themselves abstained from participation. The Puritan ethic, on the other hand, was characterized by a deep-rooted hostility, especially to magic, but also to ritual in general. To attribute sacredness to the means invoked was idolatry, and magic challenged the finality of the divine order which was an expression of God's will. Only where interference with it was revealed, as in the actions of predestined saints, was it to be assumed. The only rituals allowed to remain were those thought to be directly sanctioned by revelation, namely, baptism and communion.[2]

[1] *Entzauberung der Welt.* See especially *Religionssoziologie*, Vol. I, pp. 512–513.

[2] The Asiatic religious ethics may well have *transcended* magic. They never turned against it to root it out.

Secondly this failure to root out ritual, especially magic, is unquestionably very closely connected in Weber's mind with the failure to break through traditionalism.[1] This is so evidently the case that it may well be suspected that traditional action is the principal category in Weber's thinking where ritual is to be found hiding. But is this merely a suspicion, or is there further evidence for it?

There unquestionably is evidence of this. In the first place, it has several times been noted that Weber frequently applies the adjective sacred[2] to tradition. Indeed it is scarcely possible to speak of traditionalism as an element of his thought without this reference, for only with it does it become a form of *legitimate* order. Also it is only in this connection that it plays an important role in Weber's analytical scheme. For Durkheim ritual practices were "practices in relation to sacred things." Since sacredness, or the ritual attitude, is an essential characteristic of ritual, one source of the sacredness of tradition may well be that part of it, at least, is ritual tradition.

But the analysis may be pushed still farther. The concept of charisma, which is almost another name for sacredness, or for its source, is directly associated with both preprophetic and post-prophetic traditionalism. The traditionalization of a prophetic doctrine or message *is* precisely a process of transference of the charismatic quality from the person of the prophet to traditionalized norms and bearers of authority. The association of charisma and traditionalism is most intimate. There is no reason why this should not be applied to ritual.

But there is one final link in the chain. After the first, the mana stage of the embodiment of charisma, the question of meaning arises and with it symbolism enters into the picture. The things and events which have a meaning, then, are to be interpreted for this purpose as symbolic representations of supernatural entities. That is the source of the sanctity of these sacred things. They acquire, by virtue of this fact, a *charismatic* quality. Certainly among these "things" and events which are meaningful symbols of "supernatural" entities are included *actions*. In so far, then, is this not precisely Durkheim's definition of ritual as "actions in relation to sacred things"? Indeed this is just Weber's definition

---

[1] In the different branches of Christianity this relation is most striking.
[2] *Heilig.*

of a religious act except for the fact that Weber substitutes "supernatural entity" for "sacred thing"—that is, the thing symbolized for the symbol.[1] Moreover, fundamental to Weber's view is the most important thing in Durkheim's, the role of the symbolic relation. One could hardly ask for closer correspondence.

Finally, Weber holds that the first and universal effect of the entrance of symbolism into the situation is the stereotyping of tradition. Hence with this link with traditionalism the circle is closed. But why this intimate association between ritual, symbolism and traditionalism? Ritual involves both symbolism and sacredness. The element of sacredness forbids drawing an act into the ordinary utilitarian calculations of advantage—by virtue of that alone it would cease to be sacred.[2] Hence once a practice is "proved" efficacious, it becomes immediately stereotyped. Moreover, the symbolic element, especially in so far as it enters into the means-end relationship, makes it highly undesirable that it be subjected in intrinsic terms to rational criticism. For in so far as the relationship *is* symbolic it will by definition fail to meet such criticism.

In a context of action, which inherently implies the attempt to achieve ends, it may safely be assumed that the idea that it does not matter what ends are employed is deeply repugnant to the actor.[3] In the field of rational techniques an element of stability is provided by the objective intrinsic elements of the means-end relationship and the character of means and ends. At the same time there is no *inherent* obstacle to the alteration of such techniques in response to increasing knowledge of these intrinsic relationships. When ritual elements enter in there is a different situation. The sacredness, or meaning of sacred things is not an intrinsic, empirically observable property of them but something superimposed, a symbolic meaning. Similarly in so far as the means-end relationship is symbolic, there is then *no* intrinsic stabilizing element. These symbols can only function when the convention is accepted, that is, when they are traditionally

---

[1] In one possible symbolic relation. *Supra,* Chap. V, p. 211; XI, p. 419.

[2] *Cf.* "The sacred is that which is specifically unalterable," cited above from *Wirtschaft u. Ges.*, p. 231.

[3] That would be a "frivolity" incompatible with the "vie sérieuse" of which Durkheim speaks. *Formes élémentaires*, p. 546.

stereotyped. Traditionalism is the stabilizing element of symbolic relationships.[1]

This and not any incompatibility of philosophical doctrine is, it may be suggested, the main basis of the conflict between science and religion. The spirit of science is inherently that of critical skepticism in intrinsic empirical terms while, on the other hand, religion cannot do without symbolism.[2]

But, however this may be, there is undoubtedly a place in Weber's system for an element of the structure of action which involves charisma, and at the same time falls outside the ordinary intrinsic means-end analysis, above all through the fact that it involves symbolic elements in particular ways. These are the essential features of Durkheim's treatment of ritual for purposes of analysis of the structure of action. The correspondence between the two is complete.[3]

It is true that Weber did not develop a theory of the function of ritual at all comparable to Durkheim's. This and the fact that its analytical place was implicit rather than explicit is due primarily to Weber's focus of empirical interest. That is, he was concerned primarily with the dynamic aspect of religion embodied in the two aspects of charisma (in its prophetic embodiment) and rationalization. In this context the significance of traditionalism was mainly negative. It was that which stood in the way of these dynamic forces. He was not particularly concerned with "why"; to establish the fact that traditionalism had this effect was adequate for his purposes. Hence he did not pursue the analysis of traditionalism very far. It is significant that the lines of thought that have furnished the material for the above interpretation have been taken mainly from the section on the sociology of religion in *Wirtschaft und Gesellschaft*, where Weber attempted a systematic discussion of religion. Had he pursued this farther on the basis of a generalized system of theory, this conception of ritual would undoubtedly have become explicit. But he did not. And for the purposes of his empirical research on the relations of

---

[1] In the case of language as in every other.

[2] The application of this to Pareto's cycles is obvious. See above, Chap. VII.

[3] It should be obvious that the relation Durkheim established between ritual and the social, *i.e.*, the common value element, also applies to Weber. The above discussion of charisma is sufficient evidence.

religious ethics and capitalism, he did not need to. The results of this analysis only serve to confirm his conclusions in that context, not to alter them.

It almost goes without saying that for Weber as for the other writers here dealt with the factors formulable in nonsubjective terms, heredity and environment, play their part in the determination of concrete action. This is true both in the role of ultimate means and conditions of action and in the role of the sources of ignorance and error—the nonrational psychological factors in failure to attain and deviations from the rational norm. Nowhere does Weber take an extreme position denying the possibility of an important actual role for these elements. His own attention, however, is not focused on the analysis of this role, but on that of the other elements which have been discussed. It is merely mentioned here for the sake of completeness and to protect Weber against the unfounded charge of denying their role. He combated at many points exaggerated claims to complete determinism in terms of these factors. But he was open-minded as to the possibility of their providing significant elements of explanation on any particular problem.[1]

MATTERS OF TASTE

Finally, before this part of the discussion is brought to a close attention may be called to one further question which lies on the frontier of both the present analysis and that of all the writers treated in this study. Here it will only be introduced; it will receive some further consideration in the note appended to this chapter, in connection with Toennies. It will be remembered that Weber's scheme, with which this main analysis of his systematic theory started, contained not only two elements, efficiency norms of rationality and legitimacy norms, but also a third, usage (*Brauch*). Is this merely a chance formulation or will it repay investigation? Apparently being peripheral to Weber's own interest it is not central to any of his major concepts or conclusions. But none the less one line of thought associated with it is worth a brief development.

It will be remembered that the term usage was used to refer to uniformities of action in so far as they could not be held to involve either of the above two types of norm. The probability of a

[1] See especially *Wirtschaft. u. Ges.*, pp. 6 *ff.*

uniformity is given "purely through actual practice."[1] This is, like the definitions of affectual and traditional action, a somewhat indefinite formulation.

It might be inferred that it applied primarily to the uniformities of "automatism," the results of instinct, habit, etc. This interpretation, however, seems to be excluded by the fact that Weber quite explicitly limits his conceptual scheme to action in so far as it can be referred to subjectively understandable motives, that is, to action, in his technical sense. Usage, he quite explicitly says, is a "uniformity in the orientation of *social action*."[2] He is perfectly frank to admit that this regularity passes imperceptibly over into those oriented to a legitimate order—in this case, "convention."[3]

But this still leaves the problem unsolved. The principal example Weber uses is that of "tastes" in the time, modes and conditions of taking food. In Germany the "continental breakfast" is usage. It is what is "generally done." But there is nothing to prevent one having bacon and eggs or shredded wheat if he wishes—no sanctions will be visited on one who departs from the usage.[4] This gives the clue. Within the limits that are acceptable to the legitimate order of the society and are compatible with the needs of "efficiency," *e.g.*, physiologically adequate food at not excessive cost, there are elements of regularity which may be referred to as "matters of taste."

It is to be particularly noted that this element also involves *orientation to norms*. There are not merely factual regularities of action (as Weber's formulation would seem to imply) but standards of "good taste" in a society. The factual regularities, so far as they obtain, are to be interpreted as arising from common (or like) orientation to common norms. Reflection will show that this element has an extremely wide application in social life. It applies not only to matters of food, dress, daily personal habits, etc., but is a very prominent element in "art," "recreation," etc.

How is this to be interpreted in terms of the present scheme? In the first place this normative aspect alone radically shuts out a

[1] *Ibid.*, p. 15.

[2] *Ibid.*

[3] Which Weber distinguishes as a form of order enforced through diffuse sanctions of "disapproval" as opposed to "law," enforced through sanctions of coercion by a specially authorized *agency* of enforcement. See *ibid.*, p. 17.

[4] Within limits, of course.

"naturalistic" interpretation. There is every reason to believe that value elements are involved. On the other hand, it is a normative aspect of a distinctly different character from those thus far considered. The most conspicuous difference is the absence of a certain "binding" quality of the norms—at least in the same sense.

Efficiency norms and legitimacy norms are norms of action in a specific sense. They denote standards of the "right" relations of means and ends in a given context or the "right" modes of doing things with reference to binding values. Ritual, also, in its subjective aspect is to be regarded strictly as a means of accomplishing specific ends. The ritual manipulations are binding in the sense that they constitute the "right"—and the only "right" —way of achieving the end. But in practically all concrete acts, whether their principal context is predominantly utilitarian or ritual, there is to be found an element of embellishment in respects referable to standards of taste.

It may serve to clarify the question if an example is taken from each of these two fields. For the ancient Maori of New Zealand[1] bird snaring was one of the principal modes of gaining a livelihood. It is a universal fact that their bird snares are decorated with elaborate carving which demonstrably has absolutely no relevance to the efficiency of the snare in catching birds. There is a ritual aspect to this, since the carvings have magical significance, but, as the next example will show, this does not exhaust the question. Secondly, the Catholic mass is a typical ritual. But it may be performed in the most primitive circumstances with the simplest vestments of the priest, a wooden box for an altar, the rudest pottery for vessels. Or it may be performed with all the pomp and luxury of a great cathedral, the priest in rich, luxurious vestments, a highly decorated altar, vessels of gold studded with jewels, etc. The point is that the ritual element as such is conceived in both cases as exactly the same. The differences of appointments are precisely matters of taste. The pomp of the cathedral is not a bit more efficacious than the simplicity of a frontier or mission chapel.

Finally, there is a whole class of concrete acts that are spoken of normally as artistic creation and appreciation, on the one hand, and recreation, on the other, where the "taste" element

[1] *Cf.* R. FIRTH, *Primitive Economics of the New Zealand Maori.*

becomes predominant. It is true that all these activities involve "techniques"; once given a certain norm of taste, there are right and wrong ways of going about achieving it. These techniques may, then, be subjected to the ordinary means-end analysis. But the norm of taste is not itself a binding norm of the same character as the other two classes of norms discussed above.

It has already been noted that this normative character implies a value element. How is its relation to the other structural elements of action to be conceived? It seems that here the activities and their products are best regarded as modes of expression of value attitudes. The normative element is involved because of the fact that for these activities and their products to constitute an adequate expression they must in some sense be in conformity with the character of the values they express. But this conformity does not take the form either of subjection in the role of means or conditions to specific ends—considering the expressive activity as a total complex, in abstraction from the techniques involved, and from norms governing the means-end relationships—or of rules of legitimate order.[1]

It takes the form rather of meaningful correspondence between value attitude and concrete forms of activity and product. That is, these elements are to be interpreted as belonging together in a *Sinnzusammenhang* so that, on the one hand, the concrete activities and their products—works of art, etc.—constitute in this sense a coherent *Gestalt* and, on the other, motivational interpretation of them involves demonstrating their adequacy as expressions of the attitudes concerned. It is in this sense and only this that the style of Gothic architecture may be interpreted as an expression of the medieval Catholic *Geist* as formulated, for instance, in the *Summa* of Thomas Aquinas.[2]

In principle any and all attitudes can be expressed in terms of norms of taste in this sense and action oriented to them. But it should be evident that value attitudes[3] and above all common

[1] Involving moral sanctions.

[2] This is, I take it, what Professor Sorokin is fond of calling the "jigsaw method."

[3] Understood as the value element of concrete attitudes of course. Such elements belong together in a logical-meaningful unity. See P. A. Sorokin, "Forms and Problems of Culture Integration," *Rural Sociology*, June and September, 1936. Reprinted as Vol. I, Chap. I, of his *Social and Cultural Dynamics.*

ultimate-value attitudes will in general find expression in this mode as well as in the other relations to action which have been outlined. Conversely, any and all concrete action may be found to involve an element of this character—it is by no means confined to "art" in the popular sense.

This conclusion involves a most important methodological point. At the end of Chap. XVI was mentioned Dr. von Schelting's distinction between the understanding (*Verstehen*) of concrete motivational processes, on the one hand; of atemporal *Sinnzusammenhänge*, on the other. Dr. von Schelting shows that Weber's explicit methodological attention was confined to the former, but that at the same time he actually employed the latter in his empirical researches.

Its employment in the working out of systems of ideas as such is not relevant to the present context. But its further extension to concrete complexes of action is. This may, indeed, be interpreted precisely as the methodological counterpart of the empirical role of norms of taste and the action complexes oriented to them.[1] It is true that Weber's central interest, both analytical and methodological, was not in these phenomena but in the role of the other two types of norm. But on the periphery of his thinking it emerged on both levels—through the logical necessities of interpreting the empirical subject matter.

The place of this aspect of action systems—for it fully deserves to be called such—is, along with that of common ultimate values in the other context, the grain of truth in the intuitionist-emanationist social theories. It is no accident that such theories have always laid particular stress on this aspect of social life and have attempted to fit all the other aspects into the same schema. Weber's obliviousness to it is primarily to be explained in terms of his polemical attack on these theories, and his consequent concentration on the aspects of action they had patently misinterpreted. Its re-emergence from his own work is all the more significant on this account.

It may be emphasized that this sketch makes no pretense to being an exhaustive or adequate account of the role of norms of taste or still less to providing an adequate key to the understanding of such concrete phenomena as art, to which its applica-

[1] Though not alone of these. See note appended to this chapter, the discussion of *Gemeinschaft*, for another application.

tion is particularly obvious. Its purpose has been to characterize a part of the structure of action which impinges directly on those with which the previous analysis has been concerned. And, true to the general methodological character of the study, it has been dealt with precisely *in its relations* with the previous categories. This fact lends it an unavoidable residual character of which the reader by this time will have learned to be suspicious as it is probable that it covers up essential distinctions. It does not, however, seem expedient to attempt to press the analysis further at the present juncture. In the note appended to this chapter, however, something will be said in connection with the concept of *Gemeinschaft* about a class of concrete phenomena in which another element of the same type is prominently involved. The above sketch will serve as an introduction to this treatment.

The catalogue of the structural elements of action discernible in or directly inferable from Weber's systematic scheme of ideal types has now been completed. It has proved possible to identify and assign to a clear and definite role in the general scheme every single element of the previous analysis, especially as gained from the study of the work of Pareto and Durkheim. Moreover, every one of these elements, if it emerges in their work in clear-cut form at all, can be given a formulation that will fit both the theoretical schemes and the empirical interpretations of all three writers and do justice to what, according to the best interpretation a careful analysis has been able to put upon them, these writers themselves meant by their theories.[1] This definitely and finally establishes the convergence that it has been the principal object of this study to demonstrate. Finally, in Weber there has emerged still another structural element, the orientation of forms of expression to norms of taste, which fills a gap left in the other schemes.

It is not proposed here to enter upon the implications of the establishment of this generalized scheme of the structure of action for the problem of the construction of systems of general theory. A tentative essay in that direction will be attempted in the final chapter. Nor is it proposed to pursue the comparison of the three farther, or to recapitulate the essentials of the scheme.

---

[1] Put somewhat differently, making allowance for differing focuses of interest, the three conceptual schemes can be directly translated into terms of each other without essential change of meaning.

That will be attempted in the first of the two concluding chapters.

In closing this treatment of Weber it is essential merely to re-emphasize and make explicit beyond any possibility of doubt one thing. That is, Weber's whole position is definitely and fundamentally a voluntaristic theory of action, and neither a positivistic nor an idealistic theory. This has been found to be true at every essential point.

In the first place, his treatment of capitalism, of Protestantism and capitalism and more generally of the social role of religious ideas is understandable only on this basis. The role both of ideas and of the ultimate values associated with them is fundamental to Weber's thought. But equally so is the fact that these elements do not stand alone but in complex interrelations with other independent factors. Without the independence of heredity and environment, without the complex interrelations of ultimate values, ideas, attitudes, norms of different sorts with each other and with heredity and environment, concrete social life and action as we empirically know it, and as Weber treats it, is simply not conceivable or thinkable at all.

Secondly, the discussion of Weber's methodology has completely confirmed this interpretation of his empirical work. His methodological interest has been found to be focused mainly on those aspects of the logic of science which are significant for the understanding of action and neither of "nature" nor of atemporal complexes of meaning.[1] And, deeper still, Weber has demonstrated that the conception of objective scientific knowledge in any sense, of any empirical subject matter, is indissolubly bound up with the reality both of the normative aspect of action and of obstacles to the realization of norms. Science itself cannot be methodologically grounded without reference to the value element in the relation of *Wertbeziehung*. Without it there can be no determinate selection of *relevant* data, hence of objective knowledge in distinction from the "stream of consciousness." The very conception of science itself implies action.[2] Furthermore it is this basic solidarity of science and action which is the ultimate justification of the starting point of this whole study, the role in action of the norm of rationality in the sense of a scientifically verifiable intrinsic means-end relationship. If,

[1] See Chap. XIX, p. 727.

[2] This is, as has been noted, one grain of truth in pragmatism.

then, there is to be science at all there must be action. And if there is to be a science of action it *must* involve the norm of intrinsic rationality in this sense; it must, in fact, revolve about this as the pivotal point. Denial of this fundamental relationship from either side inevitably leads sooner or later to subjectivism and skepticism which undermine both science and responsible action.[1]

There is another aspect of Weber's methodology which has been briefly touched upon which fits directly into the present context; that is, one principal aspect of the ideal type is its normative character. It is not, of course, a norm for the observer, but the observer understands action partly in terms of the norms he has evidence for imputing to the actor as binding for the latter's action. Weber uses for explanatory purposes mainly rational-type cases but in any case pure type cases, which imply hypothetical full realization of the norm. It is further instructive to recall that in his polemical opposition to intuitionist theories Weber took special pains to emphasize the *unreality* of ideal types in this sense.

The above disagreement with Weber over the ideal type did not affect this normative character at all, but only the fact that Weber failed to distinguish concrete norms (the hypothetically concrete type-element) from normative elements of a generalized theory of action, and confined his explicit methodological attention to the former category. But from his point of view his insistence on their unreality was perfectly sound, and the strongest possible indication that he was dealing in terms of a voluntaristic theory of action. For while the normative elements are absolutely indispensable to action it is equally true and important that they cannot stand alone but can only acquire their meaning in their relations to non-normative elements; the reification of these ideal types, that is, the normative elements, *ipso facto* disposes of action itself—the theory becomes idealistic.[2]

Third, the discussion of the present chapter has shown that there is, at least as far as the present analysis has gone, a complete

---

[1] A recognition of this fundamental truth, though not always clearly, is one of the principal merits of Professor W. Y. Elliott's interesting *Pragmatic Revolt in Politics*. This paragraph may be regarded as a philosophical excursion rather than part of the strictly scientific argument.

[2] *Cf.* supra Chap. XI, in connection with Durkheim.

account of the structure of action systems identifiable in Weber's own conceptual scheme. And this is true in spite of the fact that his methodology had not clarified the logical nature of a generalized theoretical system. This total system of structural elements cannot acquire meaning at all except in the context of a voluntaristic theory of action; on the other hand, it is also to be maintained that such an approach inevitably leads to these elements in some form.

Finally, another emergent aspect of Weber's theory may be remarked upon which was passed over earlier because it was not in the center of his attention. It is, however, highly significant in the present context, indeed finally clinches the proof both that his position was a voluntaristic theory of action and that once such a theory is built up certain empirical conclusions flow from it. The above treatment of the problem of social change has followed Weber's central interest in the mutual relations of prophecy, rationalization and traditionalization.

There is, however, another aspect of social change, an account of a radically different kind of process to be discerned in his work —which may be called "secularization." The most prominent point at which it is evidenced is in his conception of adventurers' capitalism. The emergence of this phenomenon is due to a process of emancipation from ethical control, the setting free of interests and impulses from normative limitations, traditional or rationally ethical. It appears in the mitigation of ascetic rigor in the later stages of the development of the Protestant ethic—in general in the process of accomodation on both Protestant and Catholic bases. It appears in what Weber refers to as the "secularizing influence of wealth," which he emphasizes so strongly in the *Protestant Ethic.*[1] It appears finally in other spheres than the economic, for instance in the development of erotic enjoyments into a fine art.[2]

This is the centrifugal "bombardment of interests and appetites," their tendency to escape control, which has already been referred to at length. It is essentially the process involved in Pareto's process of transition from dominance of the residues of persistence to those of combination,[3] equally in Durkheim's

---

[1] *The Protestant Ethic and the Spirit of Capitalism*, p. 174, especially.

[2] *Cf. Religionssoziologie*, Vol. I, pp. 556 *ff.* especially.

[3] *Supra*, Chap. VII, pp. 284–285.

transition from solidarity or integration to *anomie*.[1] It is a process the possibility of which is inherent in the voluntaristic conception of action as such. Its complete absence from Weber's thought would have given grave reason to doubt the accuracy of the above analysis. But it is there. Only, like the explicit role of ritual, it is pushed out of the foreground of attention by the peculiarities of Weber's own empirical interest.

Unlike Pareto, Weber did not set out to build up a generalized theoretical system in the social field. Indeed there is little evidence that he had any clear conception either of the possibility of doing so or of its usefulness if it could be done. He was, rather, deeply absorbed in specific empirical problems and conceived theory directly as an aid to empirical research, never to be pursued for its own sake, but only as a means of forging tools for the empirical tasks directly in view. But his empirical research was not carried on with any dry-as-dust pedantry, investigating obscure and esoteric problems. He attacked the most significant questions he could find, with a range of perspective and an imaginative scope that few have equaled. It is indeed significant that in doing this he was in fact led, though without full self-consciousness, to develop the outline of a generalized theoretical system in at least one of its main aspects. The structural outline of a generalized system of action in his work is the most complete of any encountered thus far. It has previously been repeatedly emphasized that general theory, properly understood, is not sterile dialectical argument, but of the utmost consequence for the interpretation of empirical problems. The study of Max Weber shows most strikingly, conversely, that empirical research, if it has the scope and imagination to be genuinely important to the deeper problems of the time, leads directly into generalized theory with or without explicit methodological intention. The solidarity of general theory and empirical knowledge, one of the principal theses of this study, could scarcely be more impressively shown.

NOTE ON *Gemeinschaft* AND *Gesellschaft*[2]

After setting forth the classification that formed the main starting point for the analysis of the last chapter, of modes of orientation of action as to

---

[1] *Supra*, Chaps. VIII and X.

[2] These terms have become practically internationalized in their German form so it seems futile to attempt to translate them.

interest, legitimate order and usage, Weber proceeded to set up a further threefold classification, *Kampf* (conflict), *Vergemeinschaftung* and *Vergesellschaftung*, which is the primary basis of the subsequent system of relationship types. The above analysis was not pushed to this point, as it is here that Weber turns from direct consideration of action to that of social relationships. Moreover, what is theoretically significant for present purposes could be brought out without considering this. There is, however, one point which should be briefly elucidated—that the aspect of social systems which has been called above modes of expression of attitudes, is not confined to matters of taste but extends over into the institutional sphere. For the purpose of showing this, the phenomena designated by the concept of *Gemeinschaft* as it has been developed in German sociological literature are convenient. But it is more convenient to discuss these phenomena in terms of the formulations of Toennies[1] who introduced the concept, on which Weber modeled his own, than it is to follow Weber farther. Toennies employed this dichotomy as the basis of a classification of social relationships.

Both *Gemeinschaft* and *Gesellschaft* are what are sometimes referred to as positive types of social relationship, that is, modes in which individuals are bound together. Thus both types specifically exclude conflict elements—indeed, as has been noted, Weber made conflict a third basic relationship element. With this issue it will be unnecessary to be concerned.

Gesellschaft for Toennies is the type of social relationship which has been formulated in the utilitarian school of social thought. It is significant that in the personal history that led to his theory Toennies was much preoccupied with the thought of Hobbes and deserves much credit for helping to revive interest in Hobbes. Indeed Hobbes and Marx may be considered the writers who influenced most his formulation of the concept of *Gesellschaft*. Next to these influences is that of Sir Henry Maine's concept of contract.

The keynote of *Gesellschaft* is the "rational pursuit of individual self-interest." The relationship is to be regarded subjectively as a means by which the individual attains his own ends. The motive for entering into such a relationship is that it is the most efficient means to his end that is available in the situation. All this presupposes the essential *separateness* of the parties to the relationship with respect to their own systems of ends or values. At least in so far as the relationship is of the *Gesellschaft* type whatever the parties may have in common beyond the specific elements directly spoken of is irrelevant to this conceptual analysis. And a total system of relationships approaches the *Gesellschaft* type precisely in so far as in understanding it such common elements may in fact be disregarded.

Toennies divides relations roughly into those among equals (*genossenschaftlich*), on the one hand, and those involving authority (*herrschaftlich*), on the other. Of the former class the typical *Gesellschaft* relations are exchange and the voluntary limited-purpose association.[2] In the case of exchange the parties act in the relation of means to each other's ends. *A* can supply something that *B* wants and vice versa. In the association relation they

---

[1] See F. Toennies, *Gemeinschaft und Gesellschaft*, 5th ed.

[2] *Verein* in the German terminology.

share a common immediate end, but only in matters related directly to this specific limited end can they be said to have common interests. Finally, authority on a *Gesellschaft* basis takes the form of a hierarchical relationship of superiority and subordination within a specific limited sphere. Bureaucratic authority in Weber's sense is a type case.

In each of these three cases the specific characteristic of *Gesellschaft* is a fusion of interests over a specific, *positively defined* area. Within that area it involves a "compromise" of interests of the parties, but it only mitigates their deeper-lying separateness, which in essentials remains untouched. Toennies goes even farther, following Hobbes, to say that there remains a latent conflict which is only patched up by compromise within this specific limited area.[1]

Toennies does not state the concept of *Gesellschaft* in such a way as to exclude institutional elements. On the contrary, the Marxian influence on his thought is particularly prominent in this respect. The compromises of *Gesellschaft* are arrived at within a framework of rules and are not purely *ad hoc* agreements in the sense of the Spencerian contractual relations. But in a very important sense the institutional rules are external to the relations in question, regulating them from the outside. They constitute conditions according to which men must enter into agreements to exchange or associate themselves for a common end or submit themselves to authority.

Toennies, in view of the role of the institutional element in *Gesellschaft* and of the role of *Gemeinschaft* generally, is of course not to be considered as belonging to the utilitarian school of social thought. But, with the qualifications necessary to take account of the institutional element, it is in the category of *Gesellschaft* that the elements of action of which the utilitarian position takes account find their main formulation in his theory.[2] Of course Toennies does not postulate that ultimate ends are *in fact* random, merely that in so far as relationships are of the *Gesellschaft* type what other ends the individual parties may entertain besides those involved immediately in the relationships become irrelevant. In particular it is irrelevant whether the ultimate-value systems of the parties are integrated. When a man walks into a store in a strange city to make a purchase his only relevant relation to the clerk behind the counter concerns matters of kind of goods, price, etc. All other facts about both persons may be disregarded. Above all it is not necessary even to know whether the two have any further interests in common beyond the immediate transaction.

Over against this Toennies sets *Gemeinschaft*. He uses a number of terms to characterize it of which only a few need be employed here. Above all, it is a broader relationship of solidarity over a rather undefined general area of life and interests. It is a community of fate (*Schicksal*). One may say that

---

[1] The similarity of Toennies' characterizations to those of Durkheim in this connection is striking. Toennies' book (1887) antedated the *Division of Labor* (1893).

[2] *Gemeinschaft* and *Gesellschaft* are for him *concrete* types of relationship. Hence the intermediate sector of the intrinsic means-end chain is involved in *Gemeinschaft*, too, but in a different way.

within the area of the relationship the parties act and are treated as a unit of solidarity. They share benefits and misfortunes in common, not necessarily equally, because *Gemeinschaft* relations perfectly well admit both of functional and of hierarchical differentiation. But it is the specific field of application of the communistic principle, to each according to his needs, from each according to his abilities.

Toennies tended to lay stress in this connection on the involuntary character of adherence to such a relationship, taking that of parent and child, for instance, as a type case, by contrast with voluntary entrance into a contractual relationship. This does not seem to be the important line of distinction, but rather to confuse the issue, since both friendship and marriage are in our society entered into mainly voluntarily, yet are most definitely in "ideal" relationships of the *Gemeinschaft* type.

The main criterion seems to lie rather on another plane, that of the way in which it is possible to speak of the parties having a "purpose" in entering into or adhering to the relationship. In the *Gesellschaft* case it was a specific limited purpose, a specific exchange of goods or services, or a specific immediate end held in common. In the *Gemeinschaft* case it is never this.[1] If it is possible to speak of an "end" for which a party enters into the relation, or for which it exists, this is of a different character. In the first place, it is of a general, indefinite character comprising a multitude of subsidiary specific ends, many of them as yet entirely undefined. If one is asked "Why did you marry?" he will generally find it an exceedingly difficult question to answer in the usual teleological terms. If on the other hand, he were asked why he went into a certain store he would reply without hesitation, "To buy some cigarettes." But the case of marriage—one is in love, perhaps; one wants a home, would like to have children, companionship, the "psychic security" which goes with these things, the combination of receiving benefits and being responsible for one's own share in maintaining the common enterprise

In so far as such a relationship is entered into by voluntary agreement it is an agreement to pool interests over a certain more or less well-defined general area of life. There are usually certain rather definitely understood minimum points—thus in marriage, that there should be sexual relations and a common household maintained. But even these do not define the relationship in the same sense that the specific ends of the parties do in the contractual case.

Of course there is an institutional aspect to *Gemeinschaft* relations as well as *Gesellschaft*. But there is a specific and typical difference in at least two important respects. In the *Gesellschaft* relation the parties to the relationship are held to obligations, morally in the first instance, but enforced by sanctions if necessary. But in this case the obligations are typically limited by the terms of the contract, that is, in entering into the relationship a party has assumed certain specific, positively defined obligations.[2] And, above all, in any new situation that may arise the presumption is against the inclusion

---

[1] These are, of course, polar types so there is a transition between them.

[2] *Gesellschaft* relations do not by any means involve *only* the "interested" motives of the earlier discussion.

of a new obligation unless it can be shown to be "in the contract" or implied in its terms.[1] The burden of proof is on him who would require the performance of an obligation not obviously and explicitly assumed.

Gemeinschaft obligations, on the other hand, are typically unspecified and unlimited. If specified at all it is in the most general terms. Thus in the marriage oath each assumes the obligation to "love and cherish, for richer for poorer, in sickness and in health." It is a blanket obligation to help in whatever contingency may arise in the course of a common life. The burden of proof is on him who would evade an obligation arising in any such contingency. One of the most striking examples is care for sickness. On the basis of contractual relations one does not, in general, feel obligated to assume the burden of care for an employe, or a business associate or customer who falls sick and whose own resources will not suffice. If one does it is from other motives, such as friendship or charitable feeling, not those inherent in the business relationship as such. But for a member of one's own family such care is a first obligation even though the object of it has done nothing to deserve it and he is personally disliked.

Though the obligations attached to a *Gemeinschaft* are unspecified and in the above sense unlimited, in another they are limited. But it is an entirely different kind of limitation from that given in the *Gesellschaft* relation. This is a corollary of the fact that the same person stands in a plurality of *Gemeinschaft* relations and others involving ethical obligations. Hence the claims of any one are limited by the potentially conflicting claims of others. There is implied a hierarchy of values, and a *valid* reason for refusing an obligation claimed by the other party to a *Gemeinschaft* relation is its incompatibility with a higher obligation. Thus a husband may reject claims of his wife on his time and attention because, being a doctor, they would force him to neglect the interests of his patients. But the point is that the higher obligation here must be explicitly invoked; in the *Gesellschaft* case such considerations are irrelevant. If a storekeeper attempts to collect more than is owed him on his bill, it does not even matter if the debtor squanders the extra money on useless or even pernicious things, while the storekeeper "needs" it. The important thing is that the debtor's refusal to pay more would be upheld by the moral sanction of the community even without inquiry as to whether the storekeeper would put the money to better use than he, according to the standards of that community.

The second important difference in the institutional aspect lies in the point at which institutional norms apply. In the *Gesellschaft* relation the institutional norms constitute a body of contingent rules: *If* you enter into an agreement you are obligated to carry out its terms faithfully. You are equally obligated to remain within certain limits in securing assent of the other party, in refraining from fraud, duress, etc., even if you have the power to perpetrate them. All these rules touch the specific means, ends and conditions of the actions or complexes of them.

[1] Qualified by the considerations discussed by Durkheim. *Supra*, Chap. VIII.

The *Gemeinschaft* relation is essentially different. There is none the less a system of institutional control in this sphere. But it does not in general take the form of norms directly regulating the specific ends, means and conditions of actions within the relationship. Where this occurs it is generally at the periphery. Certain things will be regarded as indispensable minima for the relationship to exist at all. Thus in the case of marriage general condemnation will strike the wife who will not allow her husband sexual access to her, and the husband who deserts or is guilty of nonsupport. But in general, and these cases are not really exceptions, institutional sanction is concerned rather with attitudes than with specific acts. The latter are judged primarily as expressions of these attitudes. This is especially clear from a consideration of gossip as a mode of social control in such matters. What we enjoin primarily are attitudes such as "love," "respect," "filial piety" and the like. The acts formally forbidden are those held to be particularly incompatible with the "proper" attitudes, those formally enjoined a minimum expression of such an attitude.[1] In the *Gesellschaft* relation on the other hand, attitudes are specifically irrelevant. It is the sphere of "formal legality."

This brings out what is in the present context the central point. In the *Gesellschaft* case the specific relationships are, within a framework of institutional norms, *ad hoc* for the specific acts or complexes of action. In that sense they are to be regarded as resultants of the immediate action elements. In a certain sense, as Toennies often remarks, the relation is mechanistic. The *Gemeinschaft* relation is, on the other hand, in the corresponding sense, specifically organic. For in order to understand the specific acts they must be seen in the context of the wider total relationship between the parties which by definition transcends these particular elements.

The relationship, then, is not to be regarded as a resultant of these immediate elements alone but as involving a wider framework within which they are placed. What carries the relationship is not these *ad hoc* elements taken alone but the relatively permanent and deep-seated attitudes of which these may be held to be expressions. It is owing to this fact that we always inquire into the attitude behind an act within a *Gemeinschaft* relationship as we do not in the other case.

In one sense the category of *Gemeinschaft* is strictly "formal." There may be a wide variety of different content involved. For instance, within the family even today there is a considerable amount of economic exchange of services incident to the maintenance of a common household. But this cannot be isolated from the wider framework of relationships and attitudes into which it fits, as it can be in the case of an ordinary market. This is not to be taken to mean that economic categories of analysis are inapplicable to such a situation, only that they cannot be taken alone. This has, indeed, been rather widely recognized by economists.

At the same time, whatever the reasons for it, there are certain types of concrete action which normally appear in a *Gemeinschaft* framework which strong moral feelings inhibit from being radically carried over into the

---

[1] Another aspect of these will be spoken of presently.

Gesellschaft context. This seems to be particularly true, at least in our society. of the sexual relationship. The connotations that the term prostitution has acquired are particularly striking in this respect. In its original reference prostitution refers to sexual intercourse precisely in abstraction from such a wider context of relationship—as an *ad hoc* transaction. It does not matter how "honest" the parties are, how considerate, how free from a desire to exploit one another. There may be a strong element of "workmanship," a disinterested performance of service, but it is still prostitution.

This same example brings out another thing. In our society not all extra-marital sexual relations count as prostitution. We specifically distinguish from it those which occur in a context of friendship. No matter how severely the latter may be condemned in our mores they are never treated in the same way as prostitution. This is because friendship is also a *Gemeinschaft* type of relationship.

It follows that in so far as acts fall within such a system of *Gemeinschaft* relations they constitute particular modes of expression of deeper-lying, more permanent attitudes. This means *ipso facto* that they take on a symbolic significance in addition to the intrinsic significance. There can be no doubt of the enormous importance of this fact in social life. Sentiments cluster about such acts, they acquire a meaning for those who perform them. Without being able to discuss them with any fullness one or two of the specific applications may be mentioned.

In the first place it seems probable that this explains a large part of the relatively easy acceptance of tasks of drudgery. A woman doing housework will find tasks relatively bearable which are not intrinsically interesting when they are part of the necessary maintenance of her own family. The same tasks would probably appear much more as sheer drudgery if she were performing them as a hired maid in someone else's house.[1]

The sexual relation brings out a somewhat different aspect. Here its symbolic aspect in terms of a wider relation, in marriage, for instance, gives it a "meaning" which is, of course, not usually necessary as an incentive for people to enter into it. But this framework serves in most important ways as a mode of controlling what are in themselves strong impulses difficult to manage. These impulses are, both in marriage and in friendship, canalized in specific directions which, in so far as the control is effective, prevent their development into dangerously all-absorbing modes of hedonistic gratification.[2]

The role of symbolism in this as in other contexts involves that of traditionalism. Toennies often remarks on the close connection between *Gemeinschaft* and traditionalism. From the analysis of the previous chapter the reasons for the connection should be evident. In turn, there is a particularly

[1] For a related case, see the very interesting monograph by Roethlisberger and Dickson, *Technical vs. Social Organization in an Industrial Plant*, Harvard School of Business Administration, Studies in Industrial Research, 1934. See also T. N. Whitehead, *Leadership in a Free Society*.

[2] Romanticism, in this context, may be regarded as an exaggeration of this symbolic aspect of sexual relations.

close relationship between *Gemeinschaft* and religion owing primarily to the fact that common to both is a certain type of attitude, of disinterested devotion involved in a fusion of interests over an area, and the prominent role of symbolism. This comes out with especial clearness with reference to the relations of religion and the family, a major though by no means the only concrete field of *Gemeinschaft* relations. It may be stated[1] as an empirical generalization that religious and family interests may be very closely integrated with each other, or may be acutely opposed; they are never mutually indifferent.

The most important point is that here in the phenomena of *Gemeinschaft* is to be found another case where acts may best be interpreted as modes of expression of attitudes rather than as means to specific ends.[2] Thus *Gemeinschaft* norms are norms closely analogous to the norms of taste discussed in connection with Weber's concept of *Brauch*. They are, however, analogous and not identical. For the way in which Weber distinguished legitimate order and *Brauch* threw the moral element entirely over into the category of legitimate order. This, however, as was natural enough, he analyzed predominantly in terms of the institutional aspect of the intrinsic means-end schema.

It is quite clear, though, that *Gemeinschaft* involves the moral element, as the nature of community attitudes toward a breach of marriage customs, for instance, definitely proves. By this criterion, then, it is definitely institutional but in other respects it is closer to the norm of taste. The attitudes expressed within the framework of *Gemeinschaft* relationships though concrete attitudes, involve a value element, of which a major component, in turn, is that of value attitudes common to members of the same community. Adherence to the norms regulating *Gemeinschaft* relationships is by no means purely a matter of taste.

Then the category of "modes of expression" has been broadened out to include, in a different relation, the same elements that have been central to the intrinsic and the symbolic means-end relationships. This has the methodological implication that, like action oriented to norms of taste, action in a *Gemeinschaft* context must be understood by the jigsaw method. The concrete motivation elements must be placed in the wider context of the relation, or complex of them, as a whole.

This is the essential reason for the importance in this context of the relationship schema. Statement of the facts in its terms throws emphasis immediately and directly on the organic aspects of the phenomena in a way in which the action schema does not. Thus it provides an important corrective to any biases of perspective which may arise from exclusive concern with the action schema.

But it should be emphasized again that this importance of the relationship schema is primarily descriptive, not analytical. For Toennies, *Gemein-*

---

[1] This statement has already been made in another place. See Talcott Parsons, "The Place of Ultimate Values in Sociological Theory," *International Journal of Ethics*, April, 1935, p. 312.

[2] Always making allowance, as in the cases discussed in the last chapter, for techniques within such activities.

schaft and *Gesellschaft* are ideal types of *concrete* relationship. His scheme is in this sense a classification. Its importance here lies in its stating and classifying the facts in such a way as to bring out with especial clarity what are for the present analytical purposes highly significant points. Above all it shows the limitations of the understanding of complexes of action in terms of the immediate ends and situation of each particular act taken alone.

But for the explanation of *Gemeinschaft* as well as *Brauch* the generalized theory derived by developing the action schema is the most important. The conception of modes of expression is not a repudiation of the schema of the structure of action but an *extension* of it into what were for its less extended forms residual categories. Above all, what is "expressed" is the same attitudes that have been encountered before, with ultimate-value attitudes as the component of greatest theoretical interest. The fact that this leads, methodologically, into channels that have been used most by theories on another basis than the voluntaristic theory of action, that is, idealistic theories, is not to be wondered at nor objected to. As has been seen, in this as in other respects, both the general positions with which this study has been concerned (but with which it differs) have left permanently valid precipitates, both empirical and methodological, which it has been possible to incorporate into another scheme. The fact that this element is here made use of does not constitute putting forward either an idealistic or a positivistic theory.

Weber, it has been noted, used a concept closely related to Toennies' *Gemeinschaft*. He used it, however, mainly on a descriptive level, and its implications that are important for present purposes do not come out so clearly in his case as they do in the case of Toennies. Hence it has seemed preferable to use Toennies' work as a basis for this discussion. But its main conclusions may be applied directly to Weber[1] and tied in with the previous analysis of this work.

But this discussion of *Gemeinschaft* and *Gesellschaft* should not be taken to mean that these concepts are unreservedly acceptable as the basis for a general classification of social relationships or, indeed, that it is possible to start from *any* dichotomy of only two types. The basic types cannot be reduced to two, or even to the three that Weber used. To attempt to develop such a scheme of classification would be definitely outside the scope of the present study. Such an attempt would, however, have to make a critical examination of the schemes of Toennies, Weber and some others one of its main tasks.

However, the aspects of Toennies' classification with which this discussion has been concerned do involve distinctions of basic importance for any such scheme and would hence have to be built into the wider scheme, which would probably involve considerable alteration in their form of statement. For the present purpose, however, that of demonstrating another application of the concept of mode of expression of attitudes, their formulation in Toennies' terms has sufficed.

[1] Weber, of course, in his discussion of these problems owed much to Toennies.

PART IV
CONCLUSION

CHAPTER XVIII

EMPIRICALLY VERIFIED CONCLUSIONS

In the first chapter it was stated that this study should be considered as an attempted empirical verification, in a particular case, of a theory of the process by which scientific thought develops, the theory that was there outlined. The point may here be reiterated with all possible emphasis. This study has attempted throughout to be an *empirical* monograph. It has been concerned with facts and the understanding of facts. The propositions set forth have been based upon facts, and direct references to the sources for these facts have been given throughout in footnotes.

That the phenomena with which the study has been concerned happen to be the theories that certain writers have held about other phenomena does not alter matters. Whether or not they have held, as here interpreted, the theories that have been discussed is just as much a question of fact as any other, to be verified by the same method, that of observation. The facts in this case have reference to the published works of these writers. They belong to a class of facts, linguistic expressions, about which there has been necessarily a good deal of discussion. Observation of this class of phenomena involves interpretation of the meanings of the linguistic symbols employed in these works. It must be granted that this is empirical observation, otherwise not only this study but all the works of the writers here discussed, and all others which involve the subjective aspect of action, must be denied scientific status. After the discussion of the previous chapters there is no need to insist upon this point further. But short of radical and consistent behaviorism the status of the material as observable empirical fact can scarcely be doubted.

It is true that this study has not been concerned with theories only as empirical phenomena; it has also done some explicit theorizing on its own account. But according to the view of science here maintained, not only is this right and proper in an empirical monograph, it is altogether indispensable. The facts do not tell their own story; they must be cross-examined. They must be carefully analyzed, systematized, compared and interpreted. As is the case with all empirical studies this one has had as much to do with working out the implications of certain facts as with the establishment of the original facts. Observation and theoretical analysis have stood in close relations of interdependence. Without a theory of interpretation many of the facts about these writers' theories on which the greatest stress has been laid would not have been important and, if they had been observed at all, would have led to no theoretical conclusions. But equally the theory would have remained sterile if it had not been continually verified by observation. Of course, in the process of development of the study the theory itself has undergone continual modification and restatement. As is usual in such studies only the final version has actually been stated.

In these terms, then, the concluding remarks will be divided into two parts. The present chapter will be devoted to a statement of the evidence for certain conclusions which it will be maintained have been definitely established on empirical grounds by the foregoing study. The following, the final, chapter will be concerned with developing a few of their methodological implications. These are, as far as can now be seen, legitimate implications of the empirical conclusions arrived at. But it is not claimed that they are established by empirical evidence in the same sense. Hence the two groups of conclusions should be kept clearly distinct.

SUMMARY OUTLINE OF THE STRUCTURE OF ACTION

But before stating the first group of conclusions, empirical demonstration of which is claimed, it will be well for the last time to summarize briefly the main line of analytical argument of the study as a whole. Thus the reader will have all the main points of the evidence freshly in mind and be in a better position to judge whether the theses stated are adequately proved.

Rationality and Utilitarianism

The starting point, both historical and logical, is the conception of intrinsic rationality of action. This involves the fundamental elements of "ends," "means" and "conditions" of rational action and the norm of the intrinsic means-end relationship. The rationality of action in terms of the latter is measured by the conformity of choice of means, within the conditions of the situation, with the expectations derived from a scientific theory[1] applied to the data in question and stated, as Pareto puts it, in the "virtual" form. Action in these terms is rational in so far as there is a scientifically demonstrable probability[2] that the means employed will, within the conditions of the actual situation, bring about or maintain the future state of affairs that the actor anticipates as his end.

Historically, this concept of rationality of action, not always clearly and unambiguously stated, has played the central role in what has been called the utilitarian branch of the positivistic tradition. In spite of differences due to varying assumptions about the environment in which rational action operates, it has been, in its essential structure, a constant structural element of the systems of thought considered here. The two radically positivistic polar positions do, however, alter its status in essential respects. The rationalistic position does so by erasing the distinctions between ends, means and conditions of rational action, making action a process only of adaptation to given conditions and predictions of their future state. The anti-intellectualistic position in its really radical form alters the status of rationality still more fundamentally; at the pole, indeed, eliminating it altogether. Both radical positivistic positions, however, involve insuperable difficulties—methodological and empirical.

The utilitarian type of theory concentrated on the means-end relationship and left the character of ends on the whole uninvestigated. This was sound. But in so far as it tended to become a closed system on a positivistic basis it was forced to the assumption that ends were random relative to the positivistically determinate elements of action. On this basis any attempt to bring order into this random variation led in the direction of radical positivistic determinism. In the cases of hedonism, the theory of natural selection, etc. several of these attempts have been reviewed and their consequences worked out. The utilitarian

---

[1] However elementary and empirical.

[2] This mode of statement makes allowance for error due to limitations of available objective knowledge.

assumption, explicit or implicit, of random ends is the only possible way to uphold on a positivistic basis the voluntaristic character of action, the independence of ends and the other normative elements of the structure of action from determinism in terms of heredity and environment.

Within the range of the utilitarian tradition and variations from it in the direction of the radical positivistic pole, there have appeared all the main relations of the norm of intrinsic rationality to the elements formulated in the radical positivistic theories, that is, to heredity and environment.[1] These may be seen in two main contexts. In so far as action is conceived as a process of rational adaptation of means to ends, they appear in the role of ultimate means and conditions of action. The qualification "ultimate" is made necessary by the fact that what are means and conditions to any given concrete actor may be in large part results of the other action elements of other individuals. To avoid reasoning in a circle it is necessary to think in terms of what are ultimate analytical conditions of action in general, abstracting from the concrete conditions of a particular concrete act. Failure clearly to make this distinction has been shown to be a prolific source of confusion. Another warning of the same order may be repeated. The same elements of heredity and environment play a part in determining the concrete ends of action. Such a concrete end is an anticipated concrete state of affairs, involving elements of the external environment and of heredity. Hedonism clearly illustrates this situation. Pleasure as an end of action was plausible because the psychological mechanisms that produce pleasurable feelings in certain circumstances are, in fact, expected to operate in the process leading to the desired state of affairs. But this has nothing to do with the analytical concept of end as part of a generalized system. It is a feature of the organism which we know by experience we can count on to operate in certain ways, and which hence belongs analytically to the conditions of action. To speak of ends as determined by the mechanism of pleasure is to that extent to eliminate ends from the generalized theoretical system.

[1] Used here, it will be remembered, in the technical sense defined in Chap. II, as a convenient summary for those elements bearing on action capable of formulation in terms of nonsubjective categories.

Secondly, the same elements of heredity and environment appear in relation to failure to attain the rational norm. From the objective point of view they appear mainly as reasons why action either falls short of or deviates from the norm, what have been called the resistant and the deviating factors, respectively. Subjectively the same factors in the same role appear as the sources of ignorance and error. Error in this sense is not random, but rather the existence of a bias of error in a particular direction is *ipso facto* evidence that a nonrational deviating factor is at work. Above all, within the positivistic framework, departures from the norm of rationality must be reducible, from the subjective point of view, to terms of ignorance or error or both.

Finally, it is not to be forgotten that there may well be hereditary elements which "drive" behavior in conformity with a rational norm but without the independent agency of the actor which is basic to the voluntaristic conception of action. In so far as this is true, whatever subjective aspect there is to action will turn out, on thorough investigation, to be reducible to terms of nonsubjective systems.[1] The test is always whether an adequate explanation of the concrete behavior in question can be attained without reference to the elements formulated in concepts with an inherent subjective reference.

Thus it is seen that both the norm of intrinsic rationality itself, and its main relations to heredity and environment in all three of the modes just outlined, could on the whole be adequately formulated within the general framework of the positivistic theoretical system, so long as it does not go over to the radical positivistic pole. It has, however, been shown that the utilitarian position is inherently unstable, and that in order to maintain it within a positivistic framework it is necessary to employ an extrapositivistic, metaphysical prop, which in the cases analyzed here has taken the form of the postulate of the natural identity of interests. Hence the more rigorously and systematically the implications of the positivistic position have been carried through, the more precarious has become the status of the normative elements of action which could find adequate formulation within a positivistic framework.

[1] It was noted above, Chap. XVII, p. 642, that Weber explicitly took account of this.

Indeed it may be held that the growing pressure of this increasingly rigorous systematization of the remoter implications of the positivistic approach to the study of human action has played an important part in the movement of thought which has occupied this study. The form of primary interest here is an increasingly sharp presentation of the "utilitarian dilemma": either a really radical positivistic position or the strictly utilitarian. The former course involved abandoning completely the means-end schema as analytically indispensable, the latter meant increasing dependence on extrascientific metaphysical assumptions. In the generally positivistic state of opinion all the weight of "hard-boiled" scientific prestige seemed to lie on the radically positivistic side. But at the same time the utilitarian tenets rested on sound empirical insight which could not readily be explained away. Hence the stage was set for a radical theoretical reconstruction that would transcend the dilemma altogether. Part II has been concerned with analyzing three different processes by which this reconstruction has occurred. They may be reviewed briefly.

Marshall

Marshall[1] took only one step, and that he took without clear self-consciousness of what he was doing. He inherited the conceptual scheme of the utilitarian tradition. And precisely the elements of it in which this study has been interested were central to his own further development of it in his utility theory. The conceptions of utility, of marginal utility and the principle of substitution are all completely dependent on the means-end schema, rational choice and the analytical independence of ends. This alone is sufficient to account for his failure to follow the trend, so important in his day, to radical positivism.

But at the same time he was quite clear about the inadequacy of a rigidly utilitarian position for explaining certain facts of economic life, those relating to the phenomena of free enterprise. The course he took was partly determined by his sound empirical insight, partly by his own ethical predilections. He broke through a rigidly utilitarian theory of economic life mainly at two points. First, he refused to accept the assumption of independence of wants even for the heuristic purposes of

[1] Analyzed in Chap. IV.

economic theory. This assumption he held applicable only to one class of wants, which he called, with a strongly derogatory connotation, "artificial" wants. For the class he was primarily interested in, "wants adjusted to activities," it would not hold. Secondly, he refused to accept the view that the concrete actions of economic life should be considered solely as means to want satisfaction, even for purposes of economics. They are at the same time fields for the "exercise of faculties" and the "development of character."

These two departures from the utilitarian schema are brought together under the concept of activities. This is not very clearly defined by Marshall; indeed, in relation to his inherited conceptual scheme, it is mainly a residual category. Certain things can, however, be said about it. It is quite clearly not primarily a new form of statement of the elements of heredity and environment. The explicit distinction between wants adjusted to activities and biological needs excludes this interpretation in one direction; it is excluded in a second direction by the clear impossibility of making out Marshall as a hedonist; and in still a third direction by his complete failure to question the rationality of action in the name of antirationalist psychology.

There can then be no doubt that activities constitute a residual category in the value direction. Both the wants adjusted to activities and the modes of activity themselves are to be regarded in the terms of this study primarily as manifestations of a single, relatively well-integrated system of value attitudes. The extraordinarily close resemblance of these attitudes to those involved in Weber's spirit of capitalism, particularly in its ascetic aspect, has been remarked upon.

"Activities" in this sense become for Marshall an important empirical element of the economic order. Along with increasing rationality and the accumulation of empirical knowledge, the development of this value system becomes to him the primary moving force of social evolution. But here Marshall stops. His consideration of integrated value systems as distinct from random ends is limited to this one system. He fails to develop the logical possibilities of there being others in other societies. He also fails to develop the theoretical possibilities of its relation to concrete action beyond the two points where it impinged directly on his utility theory. Thus the theoretical importance of his departure from tradition, and the empirical implications of a further development in this direction remained hidden, both to himself and to his followers. But in spite of this limitation he did take the crucial step, introducing an integrated value system, common to large numbers, which had no place in either the utilitarian or the radical positivistic framework.

Pareto

In the treatment of Pareto the same problems were considered from a different point of view. In the first place, his general methodological position cleared the way for the explicit development of a voluntaristic theory of action. For his skepticism had divested scientific methodology of the implication that a theory, to be methodologically acceptable, had to be positivistic. Indeed, of the four writers Pareto, in his general methodological requirements of scientific theory,[1] came much the closest to formulating a view that can be considered acceptable for the purposes of this study. Above all he thoroughly disposed of the fallacy of misplaced concreteness which has so persistently dogged the footsteps of positivistic social theory.

Pareto also was an eminent economist and as such developed essentially the same kind of utility theory as did Marshall. He furthermore shared with Marshall the conviction of its inadequacy for the scientific explanation of concrete human action even within the economic field. But his way of dealing with this situation was different from Marshall's. Rigidly limiting economic theory to the utility element he proceeded to supplement it with a broader synthetic sociological theory.

In his explicit conceptual scheme he did this by a double use of residual categories. The starting point is the positively defined concept of logical action. It is concrete action *in so far as* it consists of "operations logically united to their end" from the points of view both of the actor and of an outside observer. Nonlogical action, on the other hand, is definitely a residual category— action in so far as it fails, for whatever reason, to meet the logical criteria. Finally the concept of logical action is explicitly broader than the economic, but there is no positive systematic treatment of the noneconomic logical elements. They are enumerated, not defined. The principal task of further analysis

[1] As distinct from those peculiar to the theory of action.

of Pareto's work lies in following out what happens to both these residual categories in a structural context.

Pareto's explicit analysis of nonlogical action may first be summarized.[1] It is inductive and starts with a distinction of two classes of concrete data—overt acts and linguistic expressions. Pareto is directly concerned only with the latter and as a result of the analysis of nonscientific "theories" in this sense arrives at the categories of residue and derivation, the relatively constant and variable elements of these theories respectively. Thus the residue is a *proposition.*

Pareto developed the conception of the residues and derivations directly as variable elements in a theoretical system without explicit reference to the problem of structure. Having defined the concepts he proceeded to classify their values, without attempting, until a much later stage, to consider concrete systems of action. The concern of this study has, on the other hand, been to work out the implications of his treatment for the structure of the systems to which Pareto's analysis of elements is applicable.

In the first place, it was shown that the way in which he defined the concepts was such as to cut across what has been the major dichotomy of the present study, the distinction of the normative and the conditional aspects of systems of action. In particular, the residues must be held to manifest not one but both of these categories of elements. The result would be, in Pareto's own terms, to introduce into his classification of the residues, another basis, cutting across those he used. Many of Pareto's secondary interpreters have held that his "sentiments" were essentially the drives or instincts of antirationalist psychology. But the study of the way in which he approached his analysis has shown that there is no warrant in the logic of his position for this exclusive interpretation, and it has been shown to be specifically incompatible with certain important features of his work, particularly with his treatment of Social Darwinism and of the question, Do the residues correspond to the facts?[2]

This general bifurcation of structural elements is the basis for the further analysis.[3] The conception of logical action was the starting point for investigating the general question, What

[1] Treated in Chap. V.
[2] Treated in Chap. VI, pp. 219 *ff.*
[3] *Supra*, Chap. VI, pp. 228 *ff.*

are its implications for the structure of the total system of action in which it has a place? First, one element in the residues is that of the ultimate ends of action in the intrinsic means-end chain which, at the fully rationalized pole, is a clearly formulated, unambiguous principle[1] guiding action. The fact that ultimate ends belong in the nonlogical category makes it possible to interpret logical action as the intermediate sector of the intrinsic means-end chain. It has been possible to verify this interpretation of one element of the residues in terms of the role Pareto assigns to "faith" in the residues of persistence of aggregates. On no other hypothesis known to the present writer is this aspect of his cyclical theory understandable.

Secondly, it appears quite clearly that the value element is not exhausted by that of this particular type of residues, but that this is a rationalized polar-type case. Short of this there is a vaguer, less determinate value element discernible in the sentiments which is manifested in other residues, in derivations and in various ways in overt behavior. To designate this element and distinguish it from others involved in Pareto's sentiments the term ultimate-value attitudes has been introduced. Similarly to distinguish the residues that constitute governing principles of rational action from others they have been called ultimate ends. Here has appeared a distinction between two elements within the broader value category which was not contained in Marshall's concept of activities.

Third, it has turned out that logical action, or the intermediate intrinsic means-end sector is not, in systems of action structurally homogeneous but must be subdivided. On the basis of an analysis of the implications of Pareto's concept of logical action for such systems distinctions have been made between three such elements of the intermediate sector. On the principle of the progressive introduction of the broader relations of a given act to the rest of an action system there have been distinguished the technological, economic and political subsectors. It has also been possible to verify these lines of distinction in most striking fashion in terms of Pareto's theory of social utility. The hierarchical series of different levels on which he holds that the utility problem may be considered is the statement of the same distinctions

---

[1] "Le principe qui existe dans l'homme" as Pareto himself put it at one point.

in a somewhat different form. It is significant that these distinctions emerged in the synthetic part of Pareto's work where he is considering action systems as a whole, while they are not to be found in his explicit analytical scheme where only isolated unit acts are considered. Thus in place of a mere enumeration of the content of logical action has been introduced a scheme of systematically related structural elements.

Finally, to crown the hierarchy, in connection with the same theory of social utility there has been found to emerge a version of the sociologistic theorem. At the rationalized pole, with which Pareto is there concerned, it takes the form of the conception of the "end a society should pursue by means of logico-experimental reasoning." This may be restated to the effect that the actions of the members of a society are to a significant degree oriented to a single integrated system of ultimate ends common to these members. More generally the value element in the form both of ultimate ends and of value attitudes is in a significant degree common to the members of the society. This fact is one of the essential conditions of the equilibrium of social systems.

Thus as a result of Pareto's explicitly non-positivistic methodology and the much higher degree of historical relativism in his empirical views there is to be found implicit in his thought a differentiation of the structural elements of action systems far beyond the point to which Marshall carried it. The latter did not even clearly distinguish analytically the norm of intrinsic rationality from the value element—they were treated together in his conception of free enterprise. This distinction is explicit in Pareto—the one is logical, the other nonlogical. With this goes the clear differentiation of the ultimate-end element from the intermediate means-end sector. The latter, in turn, becomes differentiated into three subsectors, the lines of distinction of which did not come out at all clearly in Marshall. He tended to fuse them all with activities in his economic category, and thereby to suppress the element of coercive power entirely. Then the ultimate-value element itself differentiates into three distinguishable aspects, ultimate ends as such, value attitudes and both in so far as they are common to members of a community. Finally, there appears on the horizon a phenomenon as yet not explicitly analyzed but of great empirical importance to Pareto, which became analytically central for Durkheim, namely, ritual. Thus, though Pareto's starting point was not markedly different from that of Marshall, yet, by analyzing the stage that he reached, it is possible, from the present viewpoint, to make an enormous advance beyond Marshall.

Durkheim

Durkheim, in relation with Pareto, provides the first impressive example of convergence. It is true in a sense that they were both, even from the beginning, concerned with a very closely related set of problems. But the terms in which they approached these problems were so radically different that, prior to the present study, they have been thought to have little in common except that they were both sociologists.

Durkheim never dealt at all with matters of economic theory in the technical sense. But it has been shown that in his earlier empirical work he was greatly interested in the questions of economic individualism. Moreover, the theoretical terms in which Durkheim dealt with these problems have very much to do with the status of the utilitarian position. But here the immediate resemblance stops.

In one sense Durkheim's approach is through the action schema, but it was used in a peculiar way. The methodological counterpart of his empirical criticism of the utilitarian theories, in respect both to the *Division of Labor* and to the *Suicide,* is the assertion that they rest on an unsound teleology. In the terms of this study this means essentially that he thinks in terms of the utilitarian dilemma and having decisively rejected the utilitarian solution he is thrown back on the radical positivistic alternative. In subjective terms this means that the decisive factors must appear as facts of the external world to the actor, hence as conditions of his action. This is the genesis of "exteriority" and "constraint" as criteria of "social facts."

But with the extension in the *Suicide* of his empirical criticism from the utilitarian position to the whole group of theories involving the factors of heredity and environment a further set of problems developed. For the criteria of exteriority and constraint clearly included these elements as facts to the actor. Social facts became a residual category arrived at by elimination. This included the nonutilitarian aspects of action—that is, facts to the actor which were *not* a matter either of heredity or of the nonhuman environment. They constituted hence another kind of environmental factor, the *milieu social*.

The formulas to which Durkheim's name is still most widely attached—that "society is a reality *sui generis*," that it is a "psychic" entity and that it consists of "collective representations"—were framed, as has been seen, in the effort to define this residual category. All these efforts, but especially the synthesis argument, represent indirect attacks on the problem rather than developments out of the schema of action, which was his starting point.[1] In respect to this he remained in an impasse.

This impasse was finally broken through. The decisive step was the distinction of *social* constraint from naturalistic causation. The social milieu constitutes a set of conditions beyond the control of a given concrete individual, but not beyond the control of human agency in general. In fact from this point of view its most conspicuous aspect turns out to be a system of normative rules backed by sanctions.

Up to this point, having rejected utilitarian teleology, Durkheim still thinks of the actor passively on the analogy of a scientist studying the conditions of his situation. He entirely fails to consider the voluntaristic aspect of action and the role of ends. The next step, however, radically alters this situation. It is the recognition that fear of sanctions constitutes only the secondary motive for adherence to institutional norms; the primary is the sense of moral obligation. With this the primary meaning of constraint becomes moral obligation and a clear-cut distinction is drawn between social constraint and that of natural facts. The social reality has ceased to be merely a residual category.

But this brings Durkheim back to the voluntaristic aspect of the action schema which he had apparently deserted with his rejection of the utilitaran position. It is literally the synthesis that transcends both thesis and antithesis. For the sense of moral obligation toward a norm is clearly a value attitude in the above sense. Moreover, since the social milieu for Durkheim involves an integrated system of such norms, his position involves the existence of a common system of ultimate-value attitudes. The individualism of the utilitarian position has been transcended,

---

[1] It has been shown that the concept of collective representations did arise out of this schema, but in the particular rationalistic form Durkheim gave it rather than from a means-end analysis like that developed in Chap. VI.

but after this is done, the value element can return. Durkheim, having enunciated the sociologistic theorem at the beginning, has arrived by a process of its progressive reinterpretation, at essentially the same version as Pareto's; the social element involves the existence of a common value system.[1]

There is, however, one important difference. Pareto, approaching the problem through the direct development of the means-end schema and its generalization at the rational pole, formulated the social element as the "end a society should pursue." Durkheim's approach was different. Instead of generalizing the means-end schema for systems of action he thought of the individual acting in a social environment and went on to analyze the elements of this environment. Here he encountered a common system of normative rules as one of its principal features. Then he came to the sense of moral obligation first as a motive for individual obedience to a given rule, and at last he came to see that the maintenance of a common system of rules rested on a set of common values.

Thus Durkheim illuminated the institutional aspect of action systems, one which had been latent in Pareto's analytical thought, though there were strong suggestions of its role in his empirical work. But Durkheim brings it into clear relief as a distinct feature of the structure of action systems approached in terms of the intrinsic means-end schema. It turns out that action in the intrinsic means-end chain has at least a double normative orientation, as with Weber, both to efficiency norms and to legitimacy norms.

This new orientation has the further effect of bringing utilitarian elements back into the picture in the form of "interests" tending centrifugally to escape normative control. The most conspicuous formulation of this kind of conception in Durkheim's work so far considered is in the concept of *anomie*.[2] It bears a striking resemblance to Pareto's conception of the "interests" in relation to the residues of combinations. But on the whole relatively little of Durkheim's attention was centered on the intrinsic means-end schema as such, above all, on its intermediate sector. Hence the distinctions of elements in the latter which were found to be implicit in Pareto's work remained latent in

---

[1] Stated in Chap. X, pp. 381 *ff*.
[2] *Supra*, Chap. VIII, pp. 334 *ff*.

Durkheim's. His own further development of the action schema was of revolutionary importance but it lay in another direction, in aspects which had remained for Pareto, theoretically speaking, latent.

This important new development came in Durkheim's study of religion.[1] Considering his peculiar previous use of the subjective point of view it is not surprising that he started with the question of what "reality," that is, empirical reference of a class of facts to the actor, underlay religious ideas. But though his question is formulated in the same terms as before, his answer had revolutionary consequences. In the problem of institutions he gradually moved in his interpretation of the social milieu from considering it a set of facts of "nature," to a set of rules of moral obligation. But such rules are still empirical facts the importance of which lies in their intrinsic relation to action as agencies of control.

The specific objects of religious ideas, however, he found to be entities with one property in common—they were "sacred." Those with which theories of religion had been primarily concerned were mainly "imaginary" entities, gods, spirits, etc. But Durkheim showed that this property was shared with a large group of concrete objects and also actions, persons in certain circumstances, etc. Then the question arises, what is there in common between all sacred things which accounts for the common property of sacredness? The previous attempt had been to find an intrinsic source of this property. Durkheim takes a radically different course. The only property common to all sacred things is sacredness, and this does not lie in their intrinsic properties at all, but they have it only by virtue of the particular attitude men take toward them, the attitude of "respect."

If this be true, then, men respect sacred things not for themselves but because of their relations to something else they respect. What, then, is the character of this relation? It cannot be derived from the intrinsic properties of sacred things, but it is symbolic. Sacred things are sacred because they are symbols with a common symbolic reference to a source of sanctity. This symbolic relationship is something entirely new in the theory of action as considered up to this point.[2]

[1] Treated in Chap. XI.

[2] It was introduced in the discussion of Pareto, but he did not explicitly consider it in a systematic theoretical context.

Then arises the question, what is this common reference? It must be, says Durkheim, something we can respect in this specific sense, and in this sense we respect *only* moral authority. Hence the source of the sacredness of sacred things is the same as that of obligation to moral rules. It is "society." This synthesis of what had been before regarded as quite disparate aspects of human life was a stroke of genius on Durkheim's part—of revolutionary importance.

But this position is in need of further interpretation to clear up the difficulties left by Durkheim's lingering positivism. Society in this context is not a concrete entity; it is, above all, not the concrete totality of human beings in relation to each other. It is a "moral reality." The further analysis has shown that religious ideas have to do with men's cognitive relations with certain nonempirical aspects of the world, what has been called in a *special* sense, in the study of Weber, the "supernatural." Associated with these ideas are certain "active attitudes," as Professor Nock calls them, in part determined by these ideas but in part determining them, in turn. These active attitudes turn out to be the ultimate-value attitudes of the previous discussion, and, in so far as they constitute "society" in Durkheim's sense, are common value attitudes. The *source* of sacredness is the supernatural; our symbolic representations of it are sacred things; the attitude of respect to them is, along with respect for moral obligations, a manifestation of our ultimate-value attitudes which are social in so far as they are common.

But this is not all. The active attitudes associated with religious ideas are manifested not only in "ideas" but in certain actions or "behavior," and these actions share the quality of sacredness and involve relations to sacred entities. This whole class of "actions in relation to sacred things" Durkheim calls rituals. They are actions in the strictest sense, modes for the actor of attaining specific ends. As Durkheim puts it, they are part of the *vie sérieuse*.[1] But they differ in two fundamental respects from the actions the analysis has previously been concerned with. They are sacred and hence carried out only under special conditions, specifically removed from the ordinary utilitarian calculations of advantage—they are performed with the "ritual attitude." Further, they involve the manipulation

[1] See *Formes élémentaires*, p. 546.

of sacred symbols, what has been called a symbolic means-end relationship. In both these respects, measured by the standard of the intrinsic norm of rationality, they are not *ir*rational but *non*rational. The standard simply does not apply.

Finally, ritual to Durkheim was not merely a manifestation of value attitudes, but of great functional importance in relation to social "solidarity," a mode of revivifying and strengthening the common value elements, which are ordinarily more or less latent in the course of profane activities. In this connection the centrifugal tendencies of "interests" make a striking reappearance in Durkheim's thought. Ritual is one of the fundamental defense mechanisms of society against the tendency to *anomie*.

There was thus a steady process of development in Durkheim's thought about society. From a concrete reality it became a complex of elements of action existing only "in the minds of individuals." From a category of the "facts of nature," in the role of conditions of human action, it became a common value system involving a nonempirical reference. This latter tendency culminated in his sociological epistemology. This constituted the final break with the methodology of positivism, but brought new difficulties of its own. It represented a trend of Durkheim's thought in a definitely idealistic direction which in his final phase was warring with the voluntaristic theory of action. Reinterpreted in terms of the latter its essential truth is that which came out in more acceptable form in Weber's concept of *Wertbeziehung*, introducing as it did an element of relativity into knowledge and at the same time providing a point of departure for analysis of the social factors in its development.

It should be emphasized that in the respects relevant to the present context there is *nothing* important in the theories of Pareto which is incompatible with those of Durkheim, and vice versa. Their differences are complementary, lying in the different points at which they differentiated the elements of the structure of action. Pareto brought out,[1] as Durkheim did not, the internal differentiation of the intermediate intrinsic sector and the ultimate-value element so far as it is not integrated in a common system. Durkheim, on the other hand, brought into clear relief the role of the institutional element in relation to the intrinsic means-end chain and carried out a much further

[1] In the theory of social utility.

differentiation of the structure and modes of manifestation of the ultimate-value system, which for Pareto had remained residual.

This was done in the concepts of the sacred, of the role of symbolism and of their relations to ritual action and its function. In the concept of the sacred there is implied the nonempirical reference of ultimate values, and hence the relation of value attitudes to "ideas" is much more clearly evident than in Pareto. Furthermore, the symbolic relationship, which is central to representations of the supernatural turns out, along with the concept of sacredness, to provide the analytical key essential to the understanding of a whole class of actions, ritual, which had been highly important to Pareto empirically but for his systematic theory had remained residual. These concepts of Durkheim's are to be regarded as a further specification of the content of Pareto's categories of nonlogical action and sentiment.

That the conceptual elements which have been differentiated in the course of analyzing the work of Pareto and of Durkheim really do belong to the *same* theoretical system, and that the work of the two really did converge, is conclusively demonstrated by the fact that it has been possible to show that *all* of them and one other are to be found in the work of Weber. This is true in spite of the fact that Weber's work was entirely independent of that of either of the other two, and that Weber's methodological position was such as seriously to obscure the status of a generalized theoretical system. It is, above all, remarkable that a German historical economist should have come to a conception of the place of the economic element almost identical with that of the neoclassicist Pareto and that Weber, an idealist (in background), should have come to a *point-for-point* correspondence in the distinctly complex system of structural categories relating to religious ideas, institutions, ritual and value attitudes, with the outspoken positivist Durkheim. It is legitimate to maintain that in these fundamental respects the convergence has not merely been suggested or made to seem likely but has been *demonstrated* as a matter of empirical fact. It can only be doubted on the ground that the work of the three men has here been radically misinterpreted, and that is a question of fact.

Weber

The work of Weber should be sufficiently fresh in the reader's mind for it to be unnecessary to give it more than a very brief recapitulation. Empirically his main attack was on Marxian historical materialism which, as has been shown, constituted, analytically considered, in essentials a version of the utilitarian position, placed in a historical context. Over against this he placed a theory of the role of value elements in the form of a combination of religious interests, *e.g.*, value attitudes, in their relation to systems of metaphysical ideas. This was, however, placed in the context of a voluntaristic theory of action, not of idealistic emanationism. Value elements for Weber exert their influence in complex processes of interaction with the other elements of a system of action, not by simply "becoming real." All this was worked out in great detail in his empirical studies of the relations of religious ethics to economic life.[1]

The methodological counterpart of his refusal to regard the social influence of religious ideas as a process of emanation was his attack on the methodological views growing out of idealistic philosophy.[2] Their common characteristic was a denial of the possibility or validity of general concepts in the field of human action. As against them Weber sharply vindicated the indispensability of general theoretical concepts for the demonstration of any objective empirical proposition in any field.

While sharply rejecting their views of the logic of social science he salvaged out of the wreckage certain elements of basic importance to his own substantive position. Idealistic theories of intuition were sound in suggesting the subjective reference of the theory of action, the indispensability of the subjective point of view. The freedom argument left the norm of intrinsic rationality as basic to action. The organic aspect of intuitionism left the concept of a value element in its double relation, in *Wertbeziehung*, as methodologically indispensable to theory and as central to action itself. Above all the methodological vindication of general concepts is essential to the concept of action since science and rationality of action are indissolubly bound up together.

At the same time, due to circumstances which have been reviewed, there were from the present point of view two serious limitations in Weber's methodological position. First, in trying to defend a line of distinction between the *logical* character of the natural and the social sciences, which has here been held to

---

[1] Treated in Chaps. XIV and XV.
[2] *Supra*, Chap. XVI, pp. 581 *ff*.

be indefensible, he was driven to a fictional view of the nature of general concepts in these fields which tended to obscure the role of the essentially nonfictional generalized system of theory. Secondly, this and the circumstance that general concepts were for him a residual category obscured what is for this study the vital distinction between his hypothetically concrete type concepts and their empirical generalization, on the one hand, and the categories of a generalized theoretical system, on the other. Only the former are fictional in the social field, a fact that is due to the important degree of organicism of the subject matter.

Thus his explicit systematic theorizing tended to run off in a direction different from that of the main present interest, that of a systematic classification of structural ideal types of social relationship.[1] But in spite of these methodological limitations it has been possible to elicit by analysis a definite scheme of the structure of a generalized system of action which appears at the most strategic points of Weber's work and, though he did not clearly recognize its logical nature, this scheme was absolutely essential to Weber's specific results both empirical and theoretical. Thus the complexities in the category of general concepts brought to light by the previous analysis have been verified by the demonstration that *in fact* his actual systematic theorizing involves the different types that would be expected if the analysis is correct. It is not necessary to recapitulate the structural outline of this generalized system and the ways by which Weber arrived at its elements so fully as has been done in regard to Marshall and Pareto. The logical starting point is again the standard of intrinsic rationality embodied in the norm of efficiency. This involves essentially the same relations to heredity and environment which have been found to exist in every case. The intermediate sector of the intrinsic means-end chain is differentiated in essentially the same way as was worked out in the study of Pareto.[2] The line between the technological elements and the economic is the same as that drawn before and is perfectly explicit. That between economic and political involves more complex questions but, in drawing it as Weber did

---

[1] This is formal sociology in Simmel's sense. See G. SIMMEL, *Soziologie*, Chap. I.

[2] *Supra*, Chap. XVII, pp. 653 *ff.*

with the use of the concept of authority, there is both a clear recognition of the importance of coercive power as exercised by a variety of means, and a recognition that there is a definite limit to the extent to which these may be made to fit into ordinary economic categories of analysis.

The ultimate-value element came into Weber's work in the first instance with the systems of value attitudes associated with religious ideas. Its status in the role of ultimate ends of the intrinsic means-end chain comes out theoretically in connection with the types of rational action, *zweckrational* and *wertrational*. Its institutional relation to the intrinsic means-end chain is expressed in the concept of legitimate order, the direct equivalent of Durkheim's rules possessing moral authority. Its nonempirical "religious" reference is formulated in the concept of charisma, corresponding to Durkheim's sacred. By analyzing this it was possible to clarify the reciprocal relation between value attitudes, generally called by Weber in this context religious interests, and religious ideas. Consideration of the question of "meaning" in relation to these ideas, and to things and events in the world, leads to the central role of symbolism, and for Weber undoubtedly there was a class of actions to an eminent degree involving both charisma and symbolism, that is, ritual. This was not explicitly analyzed as by Durkheim but all the elements of Durkheim's analysis are present.

In all these respects there is a remarkable point-for-point correspondence between Weber and Durkheim.[1] There are, in this range of questions three main differences, none of them disagreements but all differences of emphasis. The categories relating to ritual, which were explicit and central for Durkheim, were largely implicit for Weber. On the other hand, the mutual relations of value attitudes and ideas of the supernatural, which had to be worked out by inference from Durkheim's position, are quite explicit in Weber, in a way that directly verifies the inferences made from Durkheim's position. Third, the role of value elements in dynamic processes of change from the *status quo*, which was almost completely latent in Durkheim, comes into the center of the stage for Weber in his theory of prophecy, thus correcting a seriously one-sided impression given by Durkheim as he himself left his work.

[1] *Supra*, Chap. XVII, pp. 661 *ff*.

Finally, in Weber is to be found another emergent aspect of action systems, that which has been called "modes of expression" of value attitudes, which has nowhere else been found. It turns out to be emergent on both the methodological and the theoretical levels. In the study of Weber it has been analyzed in one context, that of orientation of action to norms of taste. But in the discussion of Toennies the same kind of analysis is found to be applicable to institutional phenomena in the case of *Gemeinschaft*, where the norms in question contain a moral element and are not merely matters of taste.

The elements of structure of a generalized system of action thus outlined are seen to fall into three relatively well-defined groups. The first is heredity and environment, seen subjectively as the ultimate means and conditions of action and as the sources of ignorance and "determinate" error. These are the elements the scientific understanding of which is possible in terms of categories not involving a subjective reference.[1] They constitute data for the sciences of action.[2] Knowledge of their nature and behavior is the "permanently valid precipitate" for the theory of human action, left behind by the radically positivistic social theories.

The second is the group included in the intermediate intrinsic means-end sector. This group constitutes the permanently valid precipitate of the utilitarian theories. The atomistic character of utilitarian thought prevented the internal differentiation of this sector from coming out clearly, but the lines can be discerned. The general concept of rationality of action, common to them all, formulates the technological element. Utilitarian theories on a social level under the postulate of the natural identity of interests have formulated the economic element. In conceptual refinement this has reached its culmination in the marginal-utility analysis of modern economic theory since Jevons and Marshall. Finally, the element of coercive power received its classic formulation on a utilitarian basis with Hobbes and has since appeared in various forms whenever the postulate of the natural identity of interests has been broken down.

The third is the whole group of elements clustering about the ultimate-value system in so far as it is integrated and not reduc-

---

[1] Qualified for the psychological elements to be discussed in the next chapter.

[2] See the next chapter.

ible to the random ends of utilitarianism. It is, as has been shown, emergent from the positivistic tradition and the process of its emergence is that of the breakdown of the positivistic tradition in its transition to a voluntaristic theory of action. In some form it has always been indigenous to the idealistic tradition and for the development of the theory of action, this is the permanently valid idealistic precipitate. But until recently the positivistic-idealistic dualism of modern social thought has created, both methodologically and theoretically, a hiatus which has prevented its integration with the other elements into the description of a single comprehensive general system of action. Only the corresponding breakdown of the idealistic methodology which has been traced in the study of Weber has made possible the bridging of this hiatus and the convergence of the two developments.

Finally, there is an element which does not fall within any of these three structural groups as such but serves rather to bind them together. It is that which has been encountered at various points and called "effort." This is a name for the relating factor between the normative and the conditional elements of action. It is necessitated by the fact that norms do not realize themselves automatically but only through action, so far as they are realized at all. It is an element the analytical status of which in the theory of action is probably closely analogous to that of energy in physics.

Verified Conclusions

It may be submitted that the propositions included in the above outline and the discussions in the body of the study of which they form a brief summary, constitute, with one exception, adequate proof of the five theses about to be stated. The one exception is that within the scope of this study it has been impossible to include all the empirical evidence on which the theories under discussion have been based. In the above outline none could be included, but in the body of the study the attempt has been made to bring forward a fair sample of this evidence, and the reader who is sufficiently interested can turn to the works of the writers themselves for the rest. The five theses are:

1. That in the works of the four principal writers here treated there has appeared the outline of what *in all essentials*, is the

same system of generalized social theory, the structural aspect of what has been called the voluntaristic theory of action. Theoretically important differences between these writers can be reduced to three circumstances: (*a*) Differences of terminology, different names for the same thing (for instance Pareto calls "logical" what Weber calls "rational"). (*b*) Differences in the point to which the structural analysis has been carried in order to arrive at the explicit distinction of all the major elements. In this respect Marshall represents hardly more than a beginning of the advance beyond the utilitarian position. But it is a beginning at such a strategic point as to be of great interest here. (*c*) Differences in mode of statement due to the different empirical centers of attention and theoretical approaches of the different writers. Thus the moral element appeared for Pareto first as ultimate ends, one element of the residues; for Durkheim as institutional norms.

2. That this generalized system of theoretical categories common to the writers here treated is, taken as a total system, a *new* development of theory and is not simply taken over from the traditions on which they built. It is not, of course, a creation *ex nihilo* but was arrived at by a gradual process of critical re-examination of certain aspects and elements of the older systems, a process standing in closest relation to empirical observation and verification. Indeed, given the diversity of starting points, the fact alone that it is essentially the same system precludes its being simply taken over from the older systems. Above all, it does not contain only elements common to all the previous traditions. Though every one of its major groups of elements had some place in at least one of the other traditions as something more than part of a residual category, this is not true of the system as a whole looked at as a specific total structure of conceptual elements. The completed structure is at some vital point incompatible with each of these older systems.

3. That the development of this theoretical system has in each case stood in the closest relation to the principal empirical generalizations which the writer in question formulated. First, negatively, the closeness of Marshall's empirical views to those dominant in the utilitarian tradition is possible only by virtue of the relatively slight extent of his departure from their theoretical system. To take only one crucial instance, if from his

insight into the role of one common value system he had come to see the possibilities of different value systems, he could not have upheld linear evolutionism in the sense he did. In the cases of Pareto and Durkheim their departures from all the major positivistic empirical theories, such as linear evolutionism, *laissez faire*, Social Darwinism, religion and magic conceived as pre-science, are most intimately related to the voluntaristic theory of action. In part, their development of this theory is due to the criticism of positivistic theories which has followed from their new empirical discoveries and insights; in part, their new theoretical ideas have led them to new factual insights. The same is true of Weber, with the exception that he was fighting on two fronts—on the one side against idealistic, emanationist views and the empirical theories associated with them; on the other against the positivistic tendencies of Marxian historical materialism.

Above all, the important empirical interpretations of none of the three thinkers could be adequately developed or stated in terms of either a positivistic or an idealistic conceptual scheme. It is to be remembered that their "theories" in this sense are not merely such bald propositions as "Social change follows in certain respects a cyclical pattern" or "There are social factors in suicide" or "The Protestant ethic had an important effect on Western economic development." All these propositions could be fitted into other schemes. The "empirical interpretations" here spoken of are rather their specific accounts of the modes, processes and relations of elements of the phenomena concerned, which underly these most general propositions. The more deeply one goes into the detail of their explanations of these things the more central do the categories of the voluntaristic theory of action become.

4. That one major factor in the emergence of the voluntaristic theory of action lies in correct observation of the empirical facts of social life, especially corrections of and additions to the observations made by proponents of the theories against which these writers stood in polemical opposition. It has naturally been impossible, within the scope of this study, to present all the empirical evidence which each writer studied brought forward himself or which could be introduced. Hence the possibilities of empirical proof of this proposition have not been exhausted. The

evidence that has been presented is, however, adequate. In the first place a considerable amount of this evidence has been cited and on the whole found to be sound. Secondly, various criticisms brought against these empirical theories have been considered and found to be lacking in conclusiveness. Finally, there is the very impressive fact of convergence, that the work of these men who started from markedly different points of view converges upon a single theory.

It is, of course, conceivable that the convergence does not exist at all, but that its appearance in this study is the result of an accumulation of errors of interpretation by the present author. It is also conceivable, though very improbable, that it is the result of an accumulation of random errors on the part of the various theorists themselves. If either of these possibilities is to be considered, it might be instructive to calculate the probabilities that this might occur, considering the number of different elements and their combinations to be taken into account.

That it is due to a congruence of purely personal sentiments seems highly improbable in view of the great diversity of the four men in these respects which was noted in the first chapter. For instance, the anticlerical, radical humanitarianism that was at the basis of Durkheim's personal values was the commonest target for Pareto's biting irony. Finally, the diversities of individualistic positivism, sociologistic positivism and the idealistic social theories as conceptual schemes are so great as to eliminate as an adequate explanation the immanent development of previous theoretical systems without reference to the facts. Each of these theoretical systems could have developed in any one of several different ways— there was no general predetermination in favor of a voluntaristic theory of action. Above all, the utilitarian position could have developed, and did develop, into radical positivism, especially the theory of natural selection and psychological anti-intellectualism. Equally a critique of Marxian historical materialism in favor of the role of "ideas" could perfectly well have developed into a radically idealistic emanationist theory, and, with Sombart, did so develop.

In the matter of convergence, then, there remain two other possible explanations. One is the determination of the convergence by the adequacy of the theories to the facts. The other is that it is due to certain features of the total movement of European thought, independent of the facts observed by scientists, but common to all the intellectual traditions considered here out of which the voluntaristic theory of action has emerged. It is by no means argued that the latter element cannot be involved at all—it certainly is involved—but only that, taken by itself, it cannot serve as the exclusive or an adequate explanation.[1] In addition to the evidence already presented the following may be noted: Eliminating observation of the facts as an important element in the development of the theory of action really amounts to eliminating action itself, unless there be a purely fortuitous harmony between the outline of the theory and the facts to which it refers. For action itself in the relevant sense is not conceivable without some degree of correctness in observation of facts. This would place the whole problem of the nature of science itself, to say nothing of this particular set of scientific ideas, on so radically different a footing from the position taken here that the whole study would fall to the ground.[2]

This is, then, the basic thesis of the study. On it the whole structure must stand or fall. There is no possible explanation of

---

[1] It is presumably the common source of the similarity of *Wertbeziehung* which is essential to such a theoretical agreement.

[2] The thesis that there has been convergence between the theorists treated in this study on the structure of the same generalized system of social action is so crucial that, at the risk of boring the reader by repetition, he may here be referred to the principal points at which the main stages of its demonstration are to be found. In the first place, the distinction of the two principal elements of Marshall's work, utility theory and activities as genuinely independent rather than, as Marshall himself treated them, as tied together in the development of free enterprise, is verified directly by the results of structural analysis as applied to Pareto's system, in Chap. VI, pp. 264 *ff.* In Chap. IX (pp. 343 *ff.*) it is shown that the analysis of action from the subjective point of view in terms of the methodological schema of science is applicable to Durkheim as well as to Pareto. Indeed all the main thread of analysis of Durkheim's theoretical development has been couched in these terms. By following this it has been demonstrated (Chap. X, pp. 381 *ff.*) that the independence of the value elements from those of the intermediate sector of the intrinsic means-end chain is a necessary basis for interpreting Durkheim's later position. The analysis of the internal differentiation of the intrinsic means-end chain, developed independently of any of the writers, was verified by its correspondence with Pareto's analysis of social utility (Chap. VI, pp. 241 *ff.*). Durkheim's mode of treatment of religious ideas and ritual, and the version of the sociologistic theorem at which he arrived were shown to be consistent with the same elements considered in relation to

this convergence into a single theoretical system which does not include the proposition that correct observation and interpretation of the facts themselves constitutes a major element.

This conclusion is particularly important for the following reason: If this be true, and it is reasonable to think that it has been demonstrated, then the concepts of the voluntaristic theory of action must be sound theoretical concepts. It is not, of course,

---

Pareto. In the former connection, however, Pareto did not develop the main distinctions explicitly. (Compare Chap. VI, pp. 256 *ff.* and Chap. XI, pp. 414 *ff.* See also Chap. X, pp. 386 *ff.*)

Finally, in Chap. XVII it has been possible to show in detail that Weber's analysis of the intrinsic means-end system corresponds directly with that developed and verified in relation to Pareto (Chap. VI) while the general categories dealing with religion correspond point for point with those to be found in Durkheim (Chap. XI). Though some of the structural elements important to this study are explicit in some writers, others in others, it can be said that, with the exception of Marshall, who hardly began the transition from the utilitarian position, no element has been identified and found to be verifiable in the scheme of one writer which could not be fitted into that of the others. In so far as the interpretation of all three makes any sense it follows that, in the respects important to this study, the three writers all use the same generalized system. It has, however, been necessary to disregard certain aspects of the work of some of them in order clearly to bring out this consequence.

To avoid all possible misunderstanding a word may be said about the possible meaning of the term demonstration. In the most rigorous sense a conclusion may be said to be demonstrated (1) when every statement of fact on which it logically depends can be verified by a completely determinate, unambiguous operation and (2) when every step in logical inference can be derived with mathematical rigor. It cannot be claimed that this convergence has been demonstrated in quite so rigorous a sense. That the writers in question have actually written what it is claimed they have written can be verified by a perfectly definite operation—reading their texts. But the total number of relevant statements of fact is very large and unfortunately it is impossible to apply mathematical methods to the logical inferences from these facts. The problem is one of fitting these facts into a general pattern which makes sense. Short of mathematical demonstration there is no way of convincing a critic who simply refuses to see the facts in relation to the total pattern here presented and stubbornly asserts that this is the wrong interpretation of them. But it is claimed that no other interpretation of these facts, taken all together, which could be seriously considered has ever been put forward, though some of them may well fit into other schemes. Seen in terms of the scheme employed here the facts fall into a consistent pattern such that the evidence for convergence is adequate. No one who considers all the facts *together in relation to this scheme* can evade this conclusion.

asserted that they are in the present formulation final and will never develop further. But they have been through the test and proved to constitute a conceptual scheme usable in empirical research. Hence they furnish a feasible starting point for further theoretical work, since science always develops further from a given theoretical point of departure. To advocate the use of this scheme, then, is not to lay down a Utopian program of what the social sciences should do but never have done. It is, on the contrary, to take the position that what has proved useful in the past and has greatly contributed to the attainment of important empirical results is likely to continue to do so in the course of its future use and development.

5. That the four above conclusions, taken together, constitute the hoped-for empirical verification, for this particular case, of the theory of the development of scientific theory stated in the first chapter. It is, indeed, impossible to understand the processes of scientific change which have been demonstrated on any other basis. In particular it has been shown that this change cannot be understood adequately (*a*) as the resultant of a process of accumulation of new knowledge of empirical fact arrived at independently of the statement of problems and the direction of interest inherent in the structure of the initial theoretical systems; (*b*) as resulting from processes of the purely "immanent" development of the initial theoretical systems without reference to the facts; (*c*) as only the result of elements external to science altogether such as the personal sentiments of the authors, their class position,[1] nationality,[2] etc. That leaves the mutual interdependence of the structure of the theoretical systems with observation and verification of fact in a position of great, though by no means exclusive, importance.[3]

---

[1] A Marxian might say that since no proletarian is included this element has not been eliminated. Granted; but that could make no difference to the general conclusion. There is too much positive evidence for the importance of elements other than class position.

[2] It need hardly be recalled that all four writers were of different nationalities.

[3] It may be explicitly pointed out that this conclusion goes beyond the thesis that the scheme is empirically valid. It maintains that the fact of its empirical validity has been demonstrated to constitute *one* important factor in the explanation of why it has developed. Many other factors are involved of course, but it is here claimed that had it not been for the fact

It is worth while pointing out that if the last conclusion be accepted, especially in combination with the other four, this study has a legitimate claim to be considered, not only as a contribution to the understanding of certain social theories and their processes of development, but also as a contribution to social dynamics. For in view of its exceedingly close relations to rational action, which have constituted a main theme of the study as a whole, the development of empirical knowledge must be considered a factor of major importance in social change; the rationalistic positivists erred only in making it of exclusively dominating importance. This is as true of knowledge of human action as it is of that of nature. Hence an understanding of the kind of processes by which such knowledge, particularly in the form of science, develops is an indispensable preliminary to any accurate comprehension of its social role. Of course this study has not solved these problems, but it may lay claim to have contributed to their solution.

---

that its authors observed correctly, and reasoned cogently about their observations, the theory, as it has here been presented, would not have developed.   Only by virtue of this thesis can the study claim to make a contribution to social dynamics.

CHAPTER XIX

TENTATIVE METHODOLOGICAL IMPLICATIONS

It would, indeed, be rash to maintain that the outline of the structure of action presented in the last chapter was complete, even in the mere enumeration of distinguishable elements, to say nothing of the modes of relation between them. This can only be decided as a result of the continual testing of the theory in actual scientific use over a long period. It is in far too early a stage of development for any claim to be made that a definitive statement of it in either of these two respects has here been attained. It is not proposed to attempt in this study to carry these questions any farther. The limited task set for it has already been accomplished.

The development of the system has, however, been traced far enough to establish definitely its identity as a system, and as one distinct from other systems prominent in the thinking of contemporary social scientists, particularly those by modification of which its development has taken place. Whether in its present state it is a logically closed system, only time and much critical analysis can tell.[1] Above all, the main concern here has been with the definition of structural elements. This has naturally involved a great deal of reference to their mutual interrelations. But there has definitely been no attempt to investigate this latter question systematically, even to the extent to which the works of these writers could throw light on it. And this would be necessary before the question of logical closure could be settled even on the structural level.

All this must be left for the future; it transcends the scope of this study. Before closing it will, however, be advisable to

[1] Could it be stated as a system of simultaneous equations, this would be easy to tell. But even though the variables can be satisfactorily defined, it is quite another thing to attempt to state a sufficient number of demonstrated modes of relationship between them to furnish such a test. This study has been confined to certain preliminaries without even attempting such a statement.

attempt to do two things. In the first place certain methodological questions have run through the study as a whole. The reader will be left with a clearer impression if these are brought together in the form of a more systematic statement of the issues than has been provided in the body of the study, since there discussion of each of these issues has been limited by its relevance to the immediate questions of interpretation under consideration at the time. Second, the study considered in its earlier chapters the problem of the status of the conceptual scheme of one of the principal social sciences—economic theory. The problem of its status was, it was seen, of crucial methodological importance. At other points various other questions relating to the status of other social sciences have been mentioned. Hence it will be instructive to inquire, now that all the evidence has been presented, whether a basis is available for further systematic clarification of these issues.

Empiricism and Analytical Theory

Though this has been explicitly claimed to be a scientific, not a philosophical study, it has not been possible, for the reasons discussed in the first chapter, to avoid the consideration of certain philosophical problems. One group of these problems which has been touched upon at several points is a phase of the epistemological problem, that of the status of scientific concepts in relation to reality. In particular, it has been necessary to criticize, in terms of their unfortunate empirical implications, a group of views which have been brought together under the term empiricism.

It will be remembered that under this heading three different positions have been included. The first has been called positivistic empiricism and consists in the reification of general theoretical systems of the logical type of the classical mechanics. This means either that the concrete phenomena to which the theory is applicable are held to be exclusively understandable in terms of the categories of the system, or, in the less radical version, that all changes in such phenomena must be predictable from knowledge of the values of the variables of the system. The latter position makes room for certain constants, that is, assumptions necessary for the concrete application of the theory. But in so far as the empiricist position is adopted these constants are held to be constant not merely for the immediate scientific purposes in hand, but as part of the "nature" of the phenomena in question. In other words, the theory applies only when the "experimental conditions" are given in which predictions from its "laws" alone work out with concrete exactitude. The law of falling bodies is held to apply only in a vacuum. The most conspicuous example of such reification in the social field is the interpretation of the classical economics as a theory applicable only to a regime of perfect competition. The heuristic assumptions necessary for the doctrine of maximum satisfaction then become the constants, which are asserted, in the extreme case, to be necessary truths about concrete reality.

The other two modes of empiricism involve the repudiation of the validity of general theoretical concepts in this sense for any purpose in relation to the concrete phenomena in question. One form is what has been called particularistic empiricism, the doctrine that the only objective knowledge is that of the details of concrete things and events. It is impossible to establish causal relationships between them which are analyzable in terms of general concepts. They can only be observed and described, and placed in temporal sequence. It is clear that this is the methodological counterpart of Hume's skepticism in epistemology. It is quite clear that such a view is unacceptable here, since it would destroy the whole purpose of this study, which is to work out the outline of just such a system of general theoretical categories, having demonstrable empirical validity.

The third form of empiricism is what has been called (following Dr. von Schelting) intuitionist empiricism. It permits a conceptual element in social science, but maintains that this can be only of an individualizing character; it must formulate the unique individuality of a concrete phenomenon, such as a person or a culture complex. Any attempt to break down this phenomenon into elements that can be subsumed under general categories of any sort destroys this individuality and leads not to valid knowledge but to a caricature of reality. It is equally clear that this view is unacceptable for purposes of the present study since it denies to its central task any legitimacy as a scientific aim.

The first form, reification, is unacceptable for a different reason. It is correct in insisting on the scientific legitimacy of general theoretical concepts, but wrong in its interpretation of their status in relation to concrete reality. This study has presented abundant evidence for the view that the understanding of human action involves a plurality of such theoretical systems. There can be no doubt of the applicability of the systems of the physical sciences to human action, but attempts to exhaust its explanation in such terms have broken down. More narrowly, conclusive evidence has been presented to show that the assumptions necessary for a theory of economic *laissez faire* cannot, for the general purposes of social science, be assumed to be constant features of all social systems, but such systems are found to vary in ways subject to analysis in terms of other, noneconomic elements of the theory of action. In so far as this is the case, the single system of economic theory is inadequate to the broader theoretical task.

A fourth attitude toward scientific concepts and their relation to reality which has been encountered in the study is that they are not reflections of reality, but "useful fictions." The principal example was Weber's own formulation of the status of his ideal-type concepts, a formulation that was arrived at in conscious reaction against all three of the forms of empiricism just outlined. There is, as has been shown, an element of truth in this view as applied to certain types of concepts but, when applied, as Weber was inclined to apply it, to all general concepts of social or any other science, it also is untenable.

In opposition to all four of these untenable views may be set the epistemological position that seems to be implied throughout this study—analytical realism. As opposed to the fiction view it is maintained that at least some of the general concepts of science are not fictional but adequately "grasp" aspects of the objective external world. This is true of the concepts here called analytical elements. Hence the position here taken is, in an epistemological sense, realistic. At the same time it avoids the objectionable implications of an empiricist realism. These concepts correspond, not to concrete phenomena, but to elements in them which are analytically separable from other elements. There is no implication that the value of any one such element, or even of all those included in one logically coherent system, is completely descriptive of any particular concrete thing or event. Hence it is necessary to qualify the term realism with "analytical." It is the possibility of making this qualification which renders the resort to fictionalism unnecessary.

The mere statement of the general position which seems to be implied in the findings of this study and its relation to the other possibilities rejected, is not, however, enough. It is necessary to consider further what analytical realism means when it is applied to a detailed consideration of the conceptual structure of the theoretical system here developed, the voluntaristic theory of action, and the various kinds of concepts which must be discriminated in understanding how it is to be applied to problems of empirical research. This will involve taking up again the thread of the discussion of types of concepts which was begun in the first chapter.

THE ACTION FRAME OF REFERENCE

It has been seen throughout the study that it is necessary to distinguish two different levels on which the schema of action with all its main features may be employed; these have been called the descriptive level and the analytical level. Any concrete phenomenon to which the theory is applicable may be described as a system of action, in the concrete sense. Such a system is always capable of being broken down into parts, or smaller subsystems. If breakdown, or analysis, is followed far enough on this plane, it will eventually arrive at what has been called the unit act. This is the "smallest" unit of an action system which still makes sense as a part of a concrete system of action.

Though this unit act is the ultimate unit which can be thought of as a subsystem of action it is still not, from the point of view of the theory of action, an unanalyzable entity but is complex. It is to be thought of as composed of the "concrete" elements of action. It takes a certain number of these concrete elements to make up a complete unit act, a concrete end, concrete conditions, concrete means, and one or more norms governing the choice of means to the end. All these concepts have been discussed before and there is no necessity to repeat. It need only be noted that while each of these is, in a sense, a concrete entity, it is not one that is relevant to the theory of action unless it can be considered a part of a unit act or a system of them. A chair is, for instance, in a physical context a complex of molecules and atoms; in an action context it is a means, "something to sit on."

It is essential to distinguish from the concrete use of the theory of action, in this sense, the analytical. An end, in the latter sense, is not the concrete anticipated future state of affairs but only the difference from what it would be, if the actor should refrain from acting. The ultimate conditions are not all those concrete features of the situation of a given concrete actor which are outside his control but are those abstracted elements of the situation which cannot be imputed to action in general. Means are not concrete tools or instruments but the aspects or properties of things which actors by virtue of their knowledge of them and their control are able to alter as desired.

The fundamental distinction of these two different applications of the theory of action raises the problem of their relations to each other. This may be put most generally by saying that they involve a common frame of reference. This frame of reference consists essentially in the irreducible framework of relations between these elements and is implied in the conception of them, which is common to both levels, and without which talk about action fails to make sense. It is well to outline what the main features of this frame of reference are.

First, there is the minimum differentiation of structural elements, end, means, conditions and norms. It is impossible to have a meaningful description of an act without specifying all four, just as there are certain minimum properties of a particle, omission of any one of which leaves the description indeterminate. Second, there is implied in the relations of these elements a normative orientation of action, a teleological character. Action must always be thought of as involving a state of tension between two different orders of elements, the normative and the conditional. As process, action is, in fact, the process of alteration of the conditional elements in the direction of conformity with norms. Elimination of the normative aspect altogether eliminates the concept of action itself and leads to the radical positivistic position. Elimination of conditions, of the tension from that side, equally eliminates action and results in idealistic emanationism. Thus conditions may be conceived at one pole, ends and normative rules at the other, means and effort as the connecting links between them.

Third, there is inherently a temporal reference. Action is a process in time. The correlate of the teleological character is a time coordinate in the relation of normative and non-normative elements. The concept end always implies a future reference, to an anticipated state of affairs, but which will not necessarily exist without intervention by the actor. The end must in the mind of the actor be contemporaneous with the situation and precede the "employment of means." And the latter must, in turn, precede the outcome. It is only in temporal terms that the relations of these elements to each other can be stated. Finally, the schema is inherently subjective, in the sense of the above discussion. This is most clearly indicated by the fact that the normative elements can be conceived of as "existing" only in the mind of the actor. They can become accessible to an observer in any other form only through realization, which precludes any analysis of their causal relation to action. From the objective point of view alone all action is, it will be remembered, "logical."

These underlying features of the action schema which are here called the "frame of reference" do not constitute "data" of any empirical problem; they are not "components" of any concrete system of action. They are in this respect analogous to the space-time framework of physics. Every physical phenomenon must involve processes in time, which happen to particles which can be located in space. It is impossible to talk about physical processes in any other terms, at least so long as the conceptual scheme of the classical physics is employed. Similarly, it is impossible even to talk about action in terms that do not involve a means-end relationship with all the implications just discussed. This is the common conceptual framework in which all change and process in the action field is grasped.

Thus the action frame of reference may be said to have what many, following Husserl,[1] have called a "phenomenological" status. It involves no concrete data that can be "thought away," that are subject to change. It is not a phenomenon in the empirical sense. It is the indispensable logical framework in which we describe and think about the phenomena of action.[2]

This is not true of the components of concrete action systems, or of the values of analytical elements, the specific content of ends and the like. They are of the empirical order of existence and are subject to analysis in terms of causality and concrete empirical process. The distinction between the action frame of reference and the concrete data is vital.

---

[1] E. HUSSERL, *Logische Untersuchungen.*
[2] So long as the conceptional scheme employed here is used at all.

The fact that wherever the general action schema is used at all phenomena are described in terms of this common frame of reference means that whatever level of analysis is employed there is a common structure of all systems of action. It is this common structure which it has been the main task of this study to analyze. The ultimate unit is always the unit act with the fundamental structure of the elements that make it up. Then there are inherent in the frame of reference a certain number of "elementary" relations between the various unit acts in any system. These are mainly derived from the fact that the existence of other units in the same system is necessarily a feature of the situation in terms of which any one unit is to be analyzed. Finally there are the emergent relations of units in systems. These are not logically inherent in the concept of a system as such, but they are empirically shown to exist in systems beyond certain degrees of complexity. Indeed, by contrast with the utilitarian system, it is primarily recognition of the empirical importance of these emergent aspects of total systems which characterizes the voluntaristic theory of action. The primary interest of the preceding analysis has been in them.

This elucidation of the status of the frame of reference of action in its relation to the structure of systems makes it possible to state a needed qualification of the term concrete, as applied to such systems and their components. This leads to certain questions of the nature of the data of science and their relation to a theoretical system. The descriptions of even the concrete components of action systems, unit acts, their parts and aggregations, do not comprise all the possible facts that can be known about the phenomenon in question, but only those which are relevant within the action frame of reference. But even these facts, the data of the theory of action, fall into two classes. The distinction and the relations between the classes can best be elucidated in terms of an example showing the mutual interrelations of two alternative frames of reference for statement of the facts about the same phenomenon, the spatiotemporal and that of action.

In dealing with a case of suicide by jumping off a bridge, the *social* scientist will describe it as an "act"; the physical scientist as an "event." For the social scientist it has a "concrete" end, death by drowning—the actor anticipates "himself, dead in the water." The means is "jumping." The "conditions" include the height of the bridge, the depth of water, the distance of the point of striking from shore, the physiological effects of impact, of the filling of the lungs with water, etc. The actor "orients" himself to phenomena understandable in terms of the physical-spatial schema. He knows that *if* he jumps he will fall, and *if* he does not swim he will drown. When the facts are stated in terms of the action schema these physical facts are assumed as "data." But *given* these data the problems set for the social scientist lie in the "ifs" italicized above. The reasons why, *if* he jumps, the man will fall, do not interest the social scientist. He is interested only in the facts *that* the man will fall, *that* the would-be suicide knows it and knows the probable consequences to himself.[1]

To the *physical* scientist studying this particular phenomenon interest is focused on the "event" of the fall. He will apply to it the law of falling bodies, etc. *That* the man jumped is to him a *given* fact, he does not inquire why. Or if he does, in terms of "motive," he is no longer talking in terms of a "physical" frame of reference. That is, he is no longer describing his data in terms relevant to the particular theoretical system, of physics.

Then in the descriptions of concrete action are included facts relevant to theoretical systems other than that of action. In fact, they must be if the action frame of reference is to be considered capable of serving as a descriptive schema. But they are stated differently from their mode of statement in another schema for other theoretical purposes. This difference may be stated broadly as follows: The scientific function of a descriptive frame of reference is to make it possible to describe phenomena in such a way as to distinguish those facts about them which are relevant to and capable of explanation in terms of a given theoretical system from those which are not. The latter enter into the descriptions as one class of "data." To the social scientist it is a relevant but unproblematical fact that if a suicide jumps he falls. What is problematical is *why* he jumps. To the physicist, on the other hand, it is a relevant but unproblematical fact that the suicide *does* jump. What is problematical to him is why, having jumped, he fell as he did, with the rate of acceleration, the velocity and momentum on striking the water, etc. For the statement of "data" in this sense there is only the requirement that they should be "adequate" to the context. Both the social

---

[1] *Cf.* Durkheim's definition of suicide which is precisely as an "act," in this sense.

scientist and the suicide must know enough about the "physical aspect" to be able to predict that the jump will probably result in death. Otherwise the term suicide is meaningless as applied to the act. This may be called "motivationally relevant adequacy" of physical data. Similarly, the physicist must know enough about the jump to know that the jumper was actually detached from the bridge and *would* fall. This would constitute physically relevant adequacy of knowledge of the action data of the physical problem. To yield empirically valid conclusions every theoretical system must be able to describe these data as facts "adequately," in this sense. But, beyond establishing this adequacy, it need not pursue inquiry into why the data are as they are.[1]

This does not, however, exhaust the category of data of a science, if by that is meant all the observed facts about a concrete phenomenon describable within a given frame of reference, as is the general usage. It includes, rather, only what is usually referred to in the physical sciences as the constants of a problem. In addition there are the values of the variables. In the case of the suicide the physically relevant values are distance from the place of the jumping to the water line, etc. The socially relevant values are certain particular features of the situation of the actor, his ends and the like.[2] These data, like the constants, are always given in any particular concrete situation. They can never be deduced from theoretical concepts, but must be determined by observation. All deduction from theory can do is to help us mutually to verify different sets of data by drawing their respective implications for each other. And if, for example, we have the values in a given case for three variables out of four in the system we can, given the requisite logical or mathematical technique, deduce that of the fourth.

Thus the data of any concrete problem fall into the two classes, "constant" data and the values of variables. One of the most important functions of the frame of reference is to enable the distinction to be drawn.[3] Constants can *only* be described in terms of this frame of reference; their further analysis requires

[1] For *its* theoretical purposes.

[2] They are analyzed in Durkheim's monograph. See also *supra*, Chap. VIII.

[3] It is not, however, enough, as Marshall's experience shows.

a different set of terms. The description of values of variables, on the other hand, is the starting point for analysis.[1] This brings the discussion to the next step.

SYSTEMS OF ACTION AND THEIR UNITS

This concerns the construction *within* the frame of reference of concrete historical individuals and their various possible modes of subdivision into parts or units, on the one hand, and, on the other, the various objectively possible combinations of these units into more and more complex structures. In this connection a large number of exceedingly complex methodological problems are raised which it is impossible even to begin to discuss adequately here. Such discussion would require an extensive methodological treatise of its own. Only a few points essential to the immediate context can here be touched upon.

In the first place, if the above view of the essential role of the frame of reference is correct, it follows that the criterion of relevance to such a schema sets a definite limit to the extent of useful subdivision of the phenomena into units or parts. It is to be remembered that such a unit must be a "part" of the phenomenon in the sense that it can be conceived of as concretely existing in isolation from the other parts; whether or not it is practically possible to carry out the isolation experimentally *in concreto* is not methodologically important. In the classical physics, at least, it is safe to say that a unit of matter had to be conceived as itself a physical body, a particle. In the unit sense all physical bodies must be thought of as made of such particles and all physical processes must be conceived of as changes that "happen to" these units or combinations of them.[2]

In the case of phenomena describable in terms of the action schema, the "smallest" unit which can be *conceived* of as concretely existing by itself is the "unit act." This further involves the minimum "concrete elements" that have been spoken of—a concrete end, concrete means, concrete conditions (including

---

[1] Hence to make the distinction the variables must also be defined, that is, the analytical elements.

[2] The present author does not feel competent to say what difference the quantum theory may have made in this respect. The impression is that there has been a *correlative* change in conceptions both of the unit of matter and of the frame of reference in terms of which physical "bodies" and processes are described. If this be true it confirms the general view presented here.

institutional rules) and a concrete norm governing the means-end relationship. These are, in a sense, concrete units but they cannot be thought of in a form relevant to the action schema except as elements or parts of an act,[1] which further implies an "actor," that is, a "personality," the identity of which transcends any one of its particular acts.

Description of the same phenomena in terms that isolate these elements or, in turn, further subdivided parts of them, from their relation to an act in this sense, destroys the relevance to the action schema so that if the facts are relevant to any scientific theory it must be a theoretical system other than that of action. Thus in the suicide example the bridge, which in several respects constitutes a condition of the act, may from a physical point of view be "broken down" into parts all the way from towers, suspension cables, etc., on a macroscopic level to the molecules and atoms of the chemical substances of which the steel and concrete are composed. These units are relevant to the schema of action only in the particular concrete combination that we call a "bridge." Indeed the word bridge in everyday speech gets its primary meaning precisely from its relation to the action schema. It is a structure over a body of water or some other barrier, over which people or vehicles may go. It is defined functionally by its relation to action not physically as an aggregation or as a determinate structure of atoms.

This is the limitation on abstraction in one direction which was mentioned above.[2] A definite limit to the scientifically useful subdivision of concrete phenomena into units or parts is set by their relevance to the frame of reference. In the theory of action it is their capability of being thought of as acts or concrete elements of acts. One principal criterion of this capability is that the subjective point of view can be employed. Failure to see this was one of the main reasons why Weber was so afraid of abstraction and hence did not even attempt to develop a generalized theoretical system.

It will be asked whether breaking up concrete phenomena into parts or units in this sense is a process of abstraction at all.

---

[1] Abstracted from this they can all be placed in other descriptive frames of reference. Thus a tool which in the action schema is a "means" may also be described as a physical object.

[2] *Supra*, Chap. XVI, p. 633 *ff.*

The answer is that it is so precisely in so far as the phenomenon in question is organic. This is preeminently true of systems of action as they have been treated in this study. It is true that in the last analysis all such systems are "composed" of unit acts. But it is necessary to be careful in interpreting what this means. It does not mean that the relation of the unit act to the total system is closely analogous to that of a grain of sand to the heap of which it is a part. For it has been shown that action systems have properties that are emergent only on a certain level of complexity in the relations of unit acts to each other. These properties cannot be identified in any single unit act considered apart from its relations to others in the same system. They cannot be derived by a process of direct generalization of the properties of the unit act.[1] In so far as this is true, the conceptual isolation of the unit act, or of other parts constituting combinations of them, is a process of abstraction. This is the type of concept which is really and necessarily fictional, in the sense that Weber attributed to his ideal types. The questions of the organicism of systems of action, of the place of emergent properties of such systems which is a corollary and of the sense in which unit or part concepts that omit consideration of these properties are abstract need further elucidation.

It is best to begin with the simplest example of an emergent property which has been encountered in this discussion. It is impossible, from the data describing a single rational act with a single clearly defined immediate end and a specific situation with given conditions and means, to say whether or in what degree it is economically rational. The question is meaningless, for the economic category involves by definition the relation of scarce means to a plurality of different ends. Economic rationality is thus an emergent property of action which can be observed only

---

[1] "Direct" generalization may be taken to mean, the implications of the mere fact of the presence of a plurality of units in the same concrete system, derivable from the fact that certain relations between units, if there are more than one, are inherent in the frame of reference. A system composed of unit acts with only these elements of generalization is an atomistic system.

It is true, as was noted in the first chapter (footnote 1, p. 32), that mechanical systems have properties as wholes which the parts do not have in isolation. But in such a case all such properties (such as entropy) can be derived from those of the units with the aid of the considerations just discussed.

when a plurality of unit acts is treated together as constituting an integrated system of action. To carry unit analysis to the point of the conceptual isolation of the unit act is to break up the system and destroy this emergent property. So long as analysis is confined to the unit act, in talking of the rationality of action it is impossible to mean anything but the technological aspect of the property of rationality.

Thus, on the one hand, unit analysis is limited by the relevance of the unit formulated to the frame of reference being employed. On the other hand, so far as this mode of analysis is used, it is not, when applied to organic phenomena limited in the same sense, but must be used with caution because it involves a certain kind of abstraction. This abstraction consists in the progressive elimination, as the breaking down into parts is carried farther, of the emergent properties of the more complex systems. Limiting observation of the concrete phenomenon, then, to the properties that have a place in the unit act or other subsystem leads to indeterminacy in the theory when empirically applied to complex systems. This indeterminacy, a form of empirical inadequacy, is the fundamental difficulty of atomistic theories when applied to organic phenomena. They cannot do justice to properties such as economic rationality which are not properties of "action as such," that is, of isolated unit acts or of atomistic systems, but only of organic systems of action beyond a certain degree of complexity.

The methodological problem is thus a matter of the relation of the unit or part concept to the analysis of systems. The abstraction involved in the former consists in the impossibility of taking account of certain features of the latter and the concrete effects of variation in them in terms of such units and of the unduly simple elementary relations between them alone. The problem may be further clarified by reversion to a figure employed earlier in the study. It will be remembered that when the conception of an integrated system of rational action was outlined the figure of a "web" of interwoven strands was used. This provides a mode of visualizing what is meant by the organic character of systems of action. Thinking of such a system as made up of unit acts in the atomistic sense would involve the possibility of unraveling the web into concretely separable threads. Dropping the metaphor, means-end relations would be identifiable only as connecting a given concrete act with one ultimate end through a single sequence of acts leading up to it. In fact, however, the same concrete immediate end may be thought of as a means to a variety of ultimate ends, so that from this point ahead the "threads" branch out in a number of different directions.[1]

A given concrete unit act is to be thought of, then, as a "knot" where a large number of these threads come momentarily together only to separate again, each one to enter, as it goes on, into a variety of other knots into which only a few of those with which it was formerly combined enter with it.[2]

Even here, however, the metaphor may be misleading in one respect. A concrete web of threads can, in fact, be untied, the threads unraveled from each other. In the present case, and, if Professor Jennings is right, the genetic case, this cannot be done even conceptually. The web must be thought of as composed only of analytically, not in any sense concretely, separable units.

[1] This may be illustrated graphically:

$$\text{Time} \uparrow \quad \text{Unit act}$$
$$\underset{\uparrow}{\text{Means–end chains}}$$

[2] A close parallel to the logic of this situation in another science is that involved in the principle of segregation, in genetics. Here the hereditary constitution of a given individual organism is to be regarded as the meeting point of a large number of analytically identifiable "strands," that is, genes, which are relatively constant through a large number of generations. Looking back from a given individual the sources of these gene elements segregate out into more and more numerous elements, the number doubling with each generation to which the analysis is pushed back. Similarly looking forward in the progeny of the individual they will be *re-segregated* out with each successive generation. It is only by tracing a sufficient number of generations that the units can be identified. See H. S. Jennings, *The Biological Basis of Human Nature*.

Professor Jennings' account suggests a further extension of the parallel. What he calls the unit character theory of inheritance reified these gene elements by identifying them with concrete somatic characters of the mature organism. This led to the logical difficulties of the "mosaic" theory of development that he so clearly brings out. The atomism just warned against is a strict parallel to this. It involves the *identification* of the analytical elements of action with the concrete action elements of unit acts; it is logically the same kind of reification. The result is similarly a "mosaic" theory of action systems. We have seen (*supra*, Chap. XVI) Weber falling into a similar "mosaic" fallacy. The difference is that he uses another much more complex unit than the unit act.

The unraveling is a process of making *analytical* distinctions and following through the relations of the values of the elements thus arrived at in a series of concrete cases.

But if certain of these elements can only be given values by describing emergent properties of organic systems, what is the empirical basis of their inclusion at all in a scientific theory? Is it not true that only units really exist? The answer is to be found in the fact of independent variation. The basis for distinguishing the economic from the technological elements of rationality is the fact that they vary in value independently of one another. A maximization of either one does not imply a corresponding maximization of the other. But how is this independent variation to be demonstrated? It is possible only through comparison of different concrete cases. This is not true of the description of a unit which can be formulated independently of comparison.

The role of comparison in distinguishing elements is best brought out by a specific case. Given comparable technologically relevant conditions there is no essential difference between the technological efficiency of producing electric power by water power on the Colorado River (Boulder Dam) and, for instance, on the Ohio River near Pittsburgh. But the fact that Boulder Dam is a very long distance from coal supplies while Pittsburgh is in the center of a great coal field is reflected in the fact that near Pittsburgh it is cheaper to produce electric power by steam. Many further qualifications would have to be made to make the two cases strictly comparable, but the principle is clear. In each of these cases there are available two acceptable technological methods of attaining an end—electric power by water power or by steam. In any two different cases the choice between them might be made differently, not on technological but on economic grounds. The immediate economically relevant fact is the lower cost of coal at one place, its higher cost at the other. By spending less money at Boulder Dam for water-power electricity than for electricity produced from coal, there is involved less sacrifice of satisfaction of other wants than if the same amount of power were produced, delivered at the same point, by steam. This comparison demonstrates independent variation of the technological and the economic aspects of rationality of action.

Thus can be seen the essential methodological basis for not merely the validity, but the indispensability of the comparative method for all the analytical sciences. Experiment is, in fact, nothing but the comparative method where the cases to be compared are produced to order and under controlled conditions. Weber's insistence on comparative study, by contrast for instance with Sombart's genetic method, was thus deeply symptomatic. Without the comparative method there can be no empirical demonstration of the independent variation of the values of analytical elements.

Before leaving the question of the status of the descriptive unit or type-part concept in the sciences of action, a brief sketch may be made of some of the different kinds of such concepts the social scientist may be expected to encounter and of their relations to each other. Two preliminary remarks are in order. First, that causal explanation, as has been seen in connection with Weber, *always* involves breaking down a historical individual into structural units or parts, on the one hand, perhaps also into values of analytical elements, on the other. Precisely in so far as a phenomenon is indivisible, in either or both of these two senses, it must be considered inaccessible to science. Second, it has been shown that systems in the social field are to a highly important degree organic and hence certain of their properties are only identifiable when there are present sufficiently complex combinations of the more elementary units. It is as different ways of looking at these relatively complex combinations that the different possible descriptive schemata applicable to human society may be distinguished.

It has already been stated that the smallest elementary unit of human action which is still relevant to the action schema is what has been called the unit act. These unit acts may be conceived of as combined to constitute more and more complex concrete systems of action. These systems are organic in the sense that they have structurally and analytically important emergent properties which disappear when the breakdown of the systems into units or parts is carried far enough. Neither economic rationality nor value integration is a property of unit acts apart from their organic relations to other acts in the same action system. But allowing for this organic character the action schema may, descriptively, be carried out to the highest conceivable degree of complexity of concrete action systems.

When a certain degree of complexity is reached, however, to describe the system in full in terms of the action schema would involve a degree of elaboration of detail which would be very laborious and pedantic to work out. This is true even if description is limited to "typical" unit acts and all the complex detailed variations of the completely concrete acts are passed over. Fortunately, as certain degrees of complexity are reached, there emerge other ways of describing the facts, the employment of which constitutes a convenient "shorthand" that is adequate for a large number of scientific purposes.

This takes the form of confining attention to what may be called "descriptive aspects" of the concrete action system. These can be held to be functionally dependent on the concrete action system so that substituting them for the full concreteness is not, within certain limits, a source of error. This isolation of descriptive aspects can take place in two main directions which, in this particular case,[1] may be called the "relational" and the "aggregational." They are complementary, not exclusive.

The first has already been dealt with in connection with Weber. There it has been seen that the acts and action systems of different individuals, in so far as they are mutually oriented to one another, constitute social relationships. In so far as this *inter*action of the action systems of individuals is continuous and regular these relationships acquire certain identifiable, relatively constant properties or descriptive aspects. One of them is the structural.[2] Another is involved in the relative priority of *Gemeinschaft* and *Gesellschaft*. No attempt will be made here to give it a specific name as a property.[3]

The important thing is that so far as the relationship schema is employed for the observation and description of the facts of human life in society it sets a standard of what are adequate observations. It is not necessary to observe *all* the acts of the parties to a relationship, or all their attitudes, etc., but only enough to establish what is for the purposes in hand the relevant "character" of the relationship. For such observation to be facilitated as much as possible, there should be available in each relevant descriptive aspect a classification of types with adequate

---

[1] Perhaps more generally. No attempt will be made to go into this.

[2] Simmel's "form."

[3] In the earlier stages of defining quantitatively variable analytical elements the tendency is to give different names to the *poles* of variation. Thus, bodies are "light" or "heavy." Science tends to substitute for this a single entity, as "mass," thought of as capable of variation in value within a range.

criteria so that the observer may fit his observations into a conceptual scheme. Precisely in so far as such classifications have become established and verified is it possible to limit observation to a small number of "identifying" facts. How much observation is necessary for identification can, however, never be laid down a priori but depends on the particular facts and the current state of knowledge of the field in question. But the tendency of scientific progress is to *reduce* them continually. This takes place by a double process. First, some facts can be eliminated as irrelevant. Thus for purposes of the theory of gravitation the density of a body is irrelevant and need not be measured. Second, it is possible to establish connections between the relevant facts so that when some are observed it may be inferred that others exist without the trouble of observing them. Thus to identify an object as in a biological sense a "man" it is not necessary to open his skull to see whether he actually has a human brain.

Thus the primary function of such a secondary descriptive schema as that of social relationship is one of scientific economy, of reducing the amount of labor of observation and verification required before adequate judgments may be arrived at. A second function has already been noted, to state the facts in a way that will prevent carrying unit analysis to a point where it would destroy relevant emergent properties. That the relationship schema is secondary to that of action is proved by the following consideration: It is quite possible to isolate (conceptually) unit acts from a social relationship. But it is quite impossible to isolate even conceptually a social relationship from the actions of the parties. It is a descriptive aspect of action systems involving a plurality of individuals and their acts.

Attention has already been called to the fact that the schema of action implies an actor. This is as fundamental to the concept of action as is the assumption of a knowing subject to that of knowledge. It is impossible even to conceive of "knowledge" except as something *known by* a subject. Similarly action is a series of acts *of* one or more actors. It is not necessary for present purposes to become involved in the exceedingly difficult philosophical problems relative to the concept of the ego or self. A very few considerations will suffice in the present context.

First it may be noted that this implication of the concept of action points again to the organic property of action systems.

From the present point of view the implication of an actor constitutes a mode of relation of different unit acts to each other. In so far as it holds, the knowledge of the intrinsic properties of a conceptually isolated unit act is not enough for understanding it. It is necessary, in addition to know whose act it is and what relation it bears to other acts of the same actor. Thus in describing any given concrete action system one possible principle of descriptive organization of the units is their grouping according to the actor whose acts they are.

Thus arises the concept of an individual or a personality. The logic of the situation here is essentially the same as in the case just discussed. For present purposes, then, the concept of "personality" is to be regarded as a descriptive frame of reference for stating the facts of human action. In this sense a personality is nothing but the totality of observable unit acts described in their context of relation to a single actor. But this is to a greater or less degree an organic system of action and as such has in its totality emergent properties not deducible from those of the unit acts taken atomistically.

In so far as this is true, it is possible to employ a similar kind of descriptive "shorthand" to that employed in connection with the relationship schema. It is not necessary to observe all the unit acts of the person in question but only enough to identify him as a given theoretically relevant kind of person. Objectively these identifying properties may be referred to as character traits, subjectively as attitudes. They will be identifiable in terms of a classification as in the relationship schema. Thus for present[1] purposes the personality schema is another secondary descriptive schema of action. It is an organized system of unit acts brought together by their common reference to the same actor.

This process of "aggregation" can, however, be pushed forward another step. When action systems involving a plurality of actors are present they may be described as groups; that is, a larger aggregate may be thought of as made up of persons as their unit. The person, in this context, becomes a member of a group. There is no reason to doubt that groups, in this sense, also have emergent properties not derivable from those of persons

---

[1] This is, above all, not necessarily the same as the psychological concept of personality.

taken in conceptual isolation from their group membership. In any event, group properties can certainly be described without detailing all the character traits and attitudes of their members, hence further descriptive economy is achieved.

It is true that the individual person is the unit of composition of group structure. But it does not follow that the same person cannot at the same time be a member of a plurality of groups. On the contrary he generally is a member of many at the same time. Thus his whole personality is not involved in any one group. At the same time there are, of course, limitations to the compatibility of different group memberships. One cannot be a member of both the Catholic and the Baptist churches at the same time. This is a question of the particular concrete groups or of types of groups, and the relations of their characters to each other.

At the same time in the present context the group schema is also to be regarded as secondary to the action schema. There are no group properties that are not reducible to properties of *systems* of action and there is no analytical theory of groups which is not translatable into terms of the theory of action. The case of Durkheim is most striking. His analysis of the nature of social groups led directly to the schema of action and the generalized theory of action.

After what has already been said, it is unnecessary to insist that the generalization of these unit or part concepts[1] on all these levels can, with proper precautions and for properly limited purposes, yield empirical generalizations adequate to explain many things. The principal cautions are two. These concepts can hold only for ranges of variation of circumstances not too large to invalidate the assumption that for practical purposes the particular constant relations between the values of analytical elements which these type concepts in the concrete case represent, will not be so unreal as to exceed an acceptable margin of error. Second, it has been stated repeatedly that precisely in so far as the whole is organic its parts or units are not real entities but abstractions. Hence their use requires a particularly high degree of caution to avoid the kind of reification which creeps in when

[1] That is, not only unit acts, but social relationships, persons and groups may serve as units of social systems.

this is forgotten and these units are treated as constant real parts through complicated processes of change. The result is to reduce the organic wholes to a "mosaic" of unit parts.

Enough has been said to show the very close relation of the unit concept at all these different levels of complexity to the frame of reference of action. Such concepts have no meaning for the theory of action unless they are capable of description in terms of the latter—as concrete elements of action, as unit acts in some combination. This has been found to be true even though the facts are not stated directly in terms of the action schema but in that of the relationship, personality or group schemata. For all three of these are here held to be secondary to the action schema in the sense stated. The requirements of the frame of reference set a definite limit to the meaningful subdivision of historical individuals into unit parts, for they cease to be meaningful for the theory of action as soon as they lose their relevance to its frame of reference. In this sense it sets a limit to abstraction.

THE ROLE OF ANALYTICAL ELEMENTS

At a number of points in the foregoing discussion phases of the role of analytical elements have been encountered. On this subject only a very few words are called for. In the first place, it should be repeated with emphasis that element analysis and unit analysis are not stages of scientific abstraction but two different *kinds* of abstraction on two different planes. To use Simmel's figure of speech, they draw "lines through the facts" not in the sense that the first is the sector of the same line farthest from the concrete, the second, nearest, nor that the lines are parallel, but that they cut across each other. To use another figure, unit analysis unravels the warp of empirical reality, element analysis the woof.

From the point of view of element analysis every unit or part, concretely or conceptually isolated, constitutes a specific *combination* of the particular values of one or more analytical elements. Every "type" is a constant set of relations of these values. The element, on the other hand, may be the universal (1) of which the particular unit as a whole is a particular, (2) of which one or more facts describing it are particulars, (3) which corresponds to one or more emergent properties of complex combinations of such units. Any atomistic system that deals

only with properties identifiable in the unit act or any other
unit will of necessity fail to treat these latter elements adequately
and be indeterminate as applied to complex systems.

A word should also be said about the sense in which the term
emergent is here used since it has acquired various connotations
elsewhere. Here it has a strictly empirical meaning, designating
general properties of complex systems of phenomena which are,
in their particular values, empirically identifiable and which can
be shown by comparative analysis to vary, in these particular
values, independently of others. So far they are no different
from any other general properties. What distinguishes the
emergent from the elementary properties is *only* the fact that
upon unit analysis of the system in question beyond a certain
point they evaporate and are no longer observable. This has
been amply illustrated for the case of economic rationality.
The existence and empirical importance of emergent properties
in this sense is, as has been seen, a measure of the organicism
of the system. They are basically important to action systems.

Above all, it is not to be inferred that in some sense the ultimate
relevant unit, in the present case the unit act, with its elementary
properties, alone is "real" and the emergent properties are in
some sense "derived" or "fictitious." That would be a definite
departure from the empirical basis of science.[1] In distinguishing
analytical elements the facts must be taken as they are found.
The criterion is always empirically verifiable independent variation in values. Where this is demonstrable there is a "real"
element whether it be elementary or emergent. Indeed in science
there is no other criterion of reality. It is just as possible to argue
that the unit act is a fiction. Like Aristotle's concept of hand,
the unit act is a "real part" of an action system "only in an
equivocal sense." There is no mysticism whatever about this
concept of emergence. It is simply a designation for certain
features of the observable facts.

It can now be understood how analytical elements tie in with
the other two kinds of conceptualization which have been
discussed. Every actually or hypothetically concrete entity,
described in terms of a frame of reference, must have properties.
This is one of the ultimate necessities of thinking about empirical
reality, a phenomenological fact. Within a given frame of refer-

---

[1] A *metaphysical* atomism.

ence there will be found to be a limited number of these properties which, taken together, are adequate[1] to the description of the phenomenon in question. The number of those necessary for adequacy may in organic phenomena increase with the complexity of the phenomena.

The element of order in concrete phenomena, seen from the analytical point of view, consists in the fact that though these are, in their particular values, variable properties, their values stand in certain constant modes of relation to each other. The order consists in these modes of relation plus the constancy of definition of the elements of the theoretical framework within their range of variation.

Now the values of analytical elements are concrete data, facts of observation or combinations of facts. The processes of their variation are processes of concrete change in time. Hence the action schema in its form of a framework of analytical elements takes on a different meaning from that which it has as a descriptive schema. Its elements have causal significance in the sense that variation in the value of any one has consequences for the values of the others. Above all, the means-end schema becomes the central framework for the causal explanation of action. Furthermore it is the specific peculiarity of this schema that it has a subjective reference. It involves a real process in the mind of the actor, as well as external to it.

On this level then the action schema, including its central means-end component becomes more than phenomenological, it takes on not merely descriptive but also causal significance, and in so doing involves references to "real subjective processes" of motivation. It becomes, in Husserl's sense, "psychological."[2] But its phenomenological aspect, as a frame of reference, does not

---

[1] The standard of "adequacy" is set by the questions which, within the framework of the theoretical system, must be answered in order to attain a determinate solution of the problem in hand.

[2] *Cf.* HUSSERL, *op. cit.* This meaning is certainly not the one that can be involved in the definition of any analytically distinguishable science of psychology. It implies only (1) that the existence of the phenomena is empirical not "ideal" as is, for instance, that of a mathematical proposition; (2) that they are accessible to analysis in terms of subjective categories, in the sense employed throughout this study. To make psychology the science of psychological phenomena, in Husserl's sense, would be to make it the synthesis of all the sciences of action.

disappear; it remains implicit in any use of the action schema. Indeed it is this element which binds the descriptive action schema and the analytical action schema together. For purposes of explanation the analytical theory of action is applicable only to systems the facts about which can be stated in terms of the descriptive action schema or of one of its secondary derivative schemata, and so to phenomena ultimately divisible by unit analysis into unit acts and systems of them. Thus all three kinds of conceptualization are most intimately bound together.

It has repeatedly been stated that this study has not attempted a systematic treatment of what is, in this sense, the analytical aspect of the theory of action. It has been limited, rather, to working out the structural outline of the generalized systems of action to which such an analytical theory would be applicable. The two modes of conceptualization often overlap, however, so there has had to be much talk of variables, of analytical elements. But no attempt has been made to consider the problem of setting up a *system* of variables. The other has proved to be a quite sufficiently formidable task without the additional complications which the inclusion of the latter would have entailed. Moreover, it provides certain indispensable preliminaries to the systematic prosecution of the other task. Among other things, by showing that the conception of a generalized system is useful in its structural aspect, it has demonstrated that the task of setting up a corresponding system of elements and their relations is not logically impossible.[1]

In order not to leave the reader feeling that the formulation of analytical laws on the basis of the system here worked out is in the structural context impossible, it may be useful to suggest tentatively that there already exists the basis for the formulation of such a law of wide scope and high significance. The law may be tentatively formulated as follows: "In any concrete system of action a process of change so far as it is at all explicable in terms of those elements of action formulated in terms of the intrinsic means-end relationship can proceed only in the direction of approach toward the realization of the rational norms conceived as binding on the actors in the system." That is, more briefly, such a process of action can proceed only in the direction of increase in the value of the property rationality.

[1] Weber would, it has been shown, have held a contrary opinion.

Stated in this way this brings immediately to mind a striking analogy to the second law of thermodynamics. That also is a statement of the directionality of change in a system, this time a physical system; it must be in the direction of increasing entropy. Potential energy is converted into kinetic energy, into action, in the physical sense. Rationality occupies a logical position in respect to action systems analogous to that of entropy in physical systems (at least on the basis of classical physical theory). Effort energy is, in the processes of action, converted into realization of ends, or conformity with norms. Rationality is one, at least, of the properties in terms of which the extent of this change is to be measured for any *given* system at any given point in the process of change.

This conception of a law of increasing rationality as a fundamental generalization about systems of action is, of course, not original. It is the most fundamental generalization that emerges from Weber's work, his conception of the process of rationalization. Action systems do not, in his view, differ with regard to this basic character. The principal differences which he takes account of are two: the concrete content of the ends and norms toward the realization of which action is rationalized, and the formidability of the obstacles to the progress of the process. It is to be noted, though, that the latter differences, formulated by Weber mainly in the concept of traditionalism, are differences touching only the *rate* of the process of rationalization, not its direction.[1]

There is a further interesting parallel between Weber's process of rationalization and the second law of thermodynamics. In the framework of the classical physics this law has been made the basis of fatalistic conclusions about the "running down" of the physical universe. It is a striking fact that Weber's process of rationalization was both by himself and by his interpreters thought to lead to closely analogous fatalistic conclusions. These have taken a parallel form; in Weber's terms a stock of charismatic energy, as it were, was in process of being consumed in the course of a rationalization process and would leave behind it at the end a "dead mechanism."

---

[1] Weber's generalization is in need of qualification, for the fact that the intrinsic means = end relationship is not the only norm governing action systems in this general way.

It may be suggested very tentatively that the fatalistic conclusions in both cases go back to the same order of causes, to reification of theoretical systems. Professor Whitehead has shown the effects of this, the fallacy of misplaced concreteness, for the classical physics. It has been seen above how Weber similarly tended to reify his ideal type concepts. There can be little doubt of the connection of this tendency with the fatalistic interpretation of the process of rationalization. There is unfortunately no space here for further discussion of this interesting parallel.

The General Status of the Theory of Action

Having indicated the general epistemological position implied in the results of this study, that called analytical realism, and discussed its application to the various forms of theoretical conceptualization, this part of the methodological discussion may be concluded by a brief word about the most general philosophical status, usually called ontological, of the type of scientific theory considered here.[1] The position is realistic, in the technical epistemological sense. It is a philosophical implication of the position taken here that there is an external world of so-called empirical reality which is not the creation of the individual human mind and is not reducible to terms of an ideal order, in the philosophical sense.

The systems of scientific theory under consideration are obviously not this external reality itself, nor are they a direct and literal representation of it, such that one and only one such representation is in any sense valid. They stand, rather, in a functional relation to it, such that for certain scientific purposes they are adequate representations of it. It is possible to indicate a few of the features of this relation.

In the first place, the applicability to it of scientific theory implies that empirical reality in this sense is a factual order. Furthermore its order must be of a character which is, in some sense, congruent with the order of human logic. Events in it

---

[1] This discussion is, in strictness, outside the scope of the study, but it is inserted so that the reader who is interested in the possible philosophical implications of the position taken here may be able better to relate it to a philosophical universe of discourse. None of the empirical conclusions of the study depend on the following considerations.

cannot occur simply at random, in the sense which is the negation of logical order. For a common feature of all scientific theory is the logicality of the relations between its propositions.

But, in the second place, scientific theory is not itself an empirical entity; it is an ideal representation of empirical phenomena or aspects of them. It is thus subject to the limitations inherent in this fact. It is not a justified assumption that reality is exhausted by its congruence with the kind of ideal systems accessible to the human mind in its scientific phase, such as what we call logic. The same kind of argument may be applied to limitations inherent in the humanly available mechanisms of observation. If the term be interpreted broadly enough it is correct to say that factual elements can find a place in science only when there is a humanly possible operation by which they can be determined. The limitations to which human observation is subject may well be purely fortuitous seen in relation to the totality of external reality.

For both these reasons it may be inferred that humanly possible knowledge is not identical with that conceivably possible to a mind freed from these human limitations. But at the same time the fact of verification, that scientific theory "works," is proof that, though limited, the propositions of human science are not completely arbitrary but are adequately relevant to significant aspects of reality. There is and must be as a limiting concept a totality of humanly possible scientific knowledge which is not that of "external reality itself" but adequate to a significant part of it. In so far as science progresses actual knowledge approaches this limit asymptotically.

But in addition to the limitations on complete realism necessitated by common human limitations, there are others which determine the fact that knowledge at any given time in any given field is less than this totality of humanly possible knowledge. These may be said to be of two orders: those inherent in the nature of the cognitive aspect of the human mind and those owing to the fact that this cognitive aspect is never completely isolated from the other aspects; man is never exclusively Homo sapiens.

In the first connection the concrete entities dealt with by the scientist are never "fully" concrete even in the humanly possible sense but are what Weber called historical individuals. They are constructed entities, the construction being determined by the

THE GENERAL STATUS OF THE THEORY OF ACTION 755

structure of the frame of reference employed. Hence the realism
of the description of concrete entities must be modified to take
account of this element of descriptive selection. Secondly, in so
far as description in this sense is applied not to a total concrete
system, but to parts or units of it isolated from their context, a
further element of abstraction enters in to the extent that the
system is organic and has emergent properties. There is no
a priori reason to limit the number of important emergent properties as such systems increase in complexity. Finally there is the
abstraction involved in the concept of an analytical element.
The empirical reference of such a concept is not necessarily a
concrete phenomenon even in the above relative sense, but may
be one aspect of it; the particulars corresponding to the general
concept may constitute only a small part of the many facts
ascertainable about the phenomenon in question.

Hence a given system of generalized theory must be interpreted
in the light of this threefold abstraction from the totality of
humanly possible knowledge. It is capable of explaining only
part of the facts important within the given frame of reference.
The others, the values of constants, can be explained, if at all,
only in terms of other analytical systems. But the facts that are
important in terms of a given frame of reference are by no
means all those which can be known about the concrete phenomenon. Only when it has been adequately described in terms of all
known frames of reference, and all the data subsumed under
analytical concepts of some system, and all these different ways
of analyzing it systematically related to one another, can it be
said to have been as fully explained as is possible in the state
of scientific knowledge of the time. But these various levels of
abstraction do not imply unreality, in the fictional sense. This is
proved by the fact that the results of analysis on the different
levels, in terms of the various frames of reference, etc., are capable
of being integrated into a coherent body of knowledge which, as a
whole, has the realistic implications that have been outlined.
In so far as this happens the various parts of this body of knowledge serve to reinforce each other and to strengthen the evidence
in favor of any one proposition in it.

At the same time, evidence has been presented in this study
that though scientific knowledge is an independent variable in
human action it is interdependent with the other variables. In so

far as the others determine the human limitations on the knowability of reality which have been mentioned, they have already been taken account of. But there are, at the same time, other limitations. Those connected with the direction and limitations of scientific interest in relation to value systems are, perhaps, the most significant. In so far as the range of empirical interest has, in fact, been limited by these factors it may be inferred that the humanly possible approaches to empirical phenomena have not been exhausted. But as the possible variation of human values is actually approached, the scientific range is also broadened. It has been noted that if this element of relativism in science is not to lead to skeptical consequences, it is necessary to postulate that in this sense the possible points of view are of a limited number. With the accumulation of value experience the totality of knowledge approaches the asymptote.

The particular ontological status of the system of the theory of action is to be understood as a special application of these general considerations.

In the first place the action frame of reference is certainly one of those in which certain of the facts of human action can be for certain scientific purposes adequately described. It is not the only one of which this is true, but the critical results of this study show that, for certain purposes, which cannot but be considered scientifically legitimate, it is more adequate than any of the alternative frames of reference which have been considered here, such as the natural science schema of space-time and the idealistic schema. Within that frame of reference it has been possible to work out systematically points of articulation with both these other frames of reference through considering the status of the constant data of the problems of action. Furthermore it has been demonstrated that within the range of what must be considered variables from the point of view of the action system, there are several subgroups that constitute relatively independent subsystems. The necessity of taking account of all of these for concrete purposes has been shown.

It cannot be maintained either that in the formulation attained in the present study this theoretical system is complete, or that it will not, with the further development of the social sciences, be superseded by one as radically different from it as it is from the systems from which it has emerged. But its empirical usefulness as recounted in this study is such that it is quite safe to say that if and when it is superseded it will be found to have left a substantial permanently valid precipitate of knowledge which, with the appropriate restatement, it will be possible to incorporate into the future broader system. This, and this only, is the sense in which it is claimed that it has given us valid knowledge of empirical reality.

THE CLASSIFICATION OF THE SCIENCES OF ACTION

The general position regarding the relation of theoretical concepts to concrete phenomena which is implied in the findings of this study has been called analytical realism. In one respect this view is contrasted with the empiricist reification of theoretical systems. The latter view implied that only *one* system of analytical categories could be applicable to the understanding of any given concrete class of phenomena. By contrast with this implication the position taken here involves the theorem that the adequate understanding of many concrete phenomena may require the employment of analytical categories drawn from more than one such system, perhaps from several.

Secondly, this study has considered at length one particular case of a theoretical system with reference to which the problem of reification, in this sense, has been acute in much scientific discussion, that of orthodox economic theory. The conclusion reached is that, as Pareto rightly saw, it must be interpreted as the formulation of the relations of a limited group of analytical elements in the broader concrete system of action. Concrete phenomena, even those capable of description in terms of supply and demand, involve other variables not included in the system of economic theory. Empirical evidence has been presented sufficiently ample to prove this point beyond question. Furthermore it has been possible to go farther than merely to state that this group of elements is abstract, one among several in concrete social phenomena. In the sense used by Pareto and in one part of Marshall's theory, it has been placed in systematic logical relations to the other elements in the structure of the wider system here called action.

This wider system, the voluntaristic theory of action, has, in turn, been found to involve at another remove a similar kind of abstraction. In particular, its concrete application has been found to involve constant data that are capable of description, but not analytical explanation in terms of the action frame of reference. One set of these data fit into another of the broader frames of reference of contemporary science, called in the broadest sense the "physical," which describes phenomena as spatio-temporal things or events. Indeed one of the main polar positions with which the analysis here has had to be concerned is that at which the action schema loses explanatory relevance altogether and becomes merely descriptive. When this happens it turns all data into constants in the above sense. And at one pole, the radical positivistic, analytical treatment of these data involves the physical frame of reference, the positive criterion of which is spatiality, the negative criterion, analytical irrelevance of subjective categories. Complementary to this tendency for the theory of action under certain circumstances to slip over to a radically positivistic theory, is the tendency for it to slip over to the opposite, the idealistic pole. Ideas may be said to be constant data for the theory of action in the same methodological sense as are physical data. They are not, as such, variables of the action system.

Finally, in discussing Weber's methodology there has been encountered the bifurcation of scientific interest, in the one direction toward the understanding of concrete individual phenomena as such, in the other to the building of theoretical systems of general validity.

Consideration of all these questions has been necessary to the elaboration of the conceptual structure of this study. Each of them is important to the structure at some point. Moreover in connection with several there has had to be raised the question of the status, in relation to the whole, of a more restricted conceptual scheme, which is widely referred to as constituting the theoretical aspect of a specific science. Thus the economic theory in question is the theoretical preoccupation of economic science as a unified discipline. Also the question of the physical data of action systems has involved, in some sense or other, that of the relation of the natural and the social sciences.

A great deal of the confusion into which this study has attempted to introduce some order has been due to the failure of scholars clearly to discriminate between these various conceptual schemes and adequately to investigate their mutual

THE CLASSIFICATION OF THE SCIENCES OF ACTION

logical relations. Wherever, in any empirical problem, more than one of them becomes involved, it is essential in the interest of clarity that the student of the problem should know what he is doing; to know when he is employing one scheme, when another and what the shift from one to another implies. If a basic theorem of the present discussion be accepted, that in a large proportion of empirical problems in the action field more than one of these theoretical systems is involved, it follows that the questions of their relations cannot be evaded; they are scientifically important questions in the strict sense.

It is clear what this means: the study of these relations is the attempt to develop a systematic classification of the empirical sciences and an outline of this, so far as it bears upon the problems of the present study, is the final task to be undertaken.

There is a great deal of current protest against attempts to set up boundaries between the sciences, to divide them into neat compartments. We are told that all knowledge is one, that the way of progress is to break down divisions, not to set them up. It is possible to sympathize generally with the spirit of this protest. For concrete empirical research it is clearly impossible to adhere to any neatly separated fields. The empirical scholar will follow his problems wherever they may lead and refuse to be deterred by any signs which read, "Foreign Territory." Indeed this study, by demonstrating the extent to which different conceptual schemes must be called upon to unravel the complexities of the same empirical field, has given a direct justification to the advocacy of such scientific *Wanderlust*. But, at the same time, such an attitude, pushed to the extreme of refusing even to discuss the problems of systematic relationship of theoretical systems involved in the classification of the sciences, becomes a case of the kind of empiricist evasion of theoretical problems which has been shown again and again to be scientifically disastrous. It is an excellent thing to travel in many countries, but the traveler who refuses to take any cognizance of the local peculiarities and customs of the countries he visits is likely to get into trouble. Many a traveler has lost his life through sheer ignorance of these things. Such an attempt, then, is not mere pedantry; it is a deduction from the general scientific precept, "It is a good thing to know what you are doing." The attempt is further justified here by the fact that these problems have been touched upon in fragmentary fashion at various points in this study, and in these connections have been shown to be important to it. Their systematic treatment will provide an opportunity to bring out with greater clarity than before the main outline of the conceptual structure which has emerged as the principal outcome of the study as a whole. It will place its results in a clearer perspective than has been attainable in the summary contained in the previous chapter.

All the distinctions that will be made use of have already been encountered; it is necessary only to point out their relation to the present context. The first to be recalled is the line between the historical and the analytical sciences. The object of the first group is to attain the fullest possible understanding of a class of concrete historical individuals or of one of the class. This distinction holds regardless of whether the historical individual concerned is a natural object or event, a human individual, an act or system of acts, a system of social relations or a type of social group. In each case the explanation in question will involve, by implication if not explicitly,[1] reference to the theoretical categories of one or more analytical sciences. How many and what ones will depend on the particular scientific purpose in hand, the aspects of the phenomenon, changes in which require explanation. One such system may prove adequate but in no case is there an a priori presumption of such adequacy. Full explanation may be found to involve all the theoretical categories of all the analytical sciences.

On the other hand, there are the analytical sciences, the aim of which is to develop logically coherent systems of general analytical theory. The unit of reference for such sciences is not a particular historical individual nor a class of them, which may for purposes of the science in question be considered essentially the same, but a closed system of theory. Wherever such a closed system exists which is not translatable into terms of another it is possible to speak of an independent science.

The role of what has been called the frame of reference introduces a complication into this classification. For its use necessitates a distinction, implicit or explicit, between two classes

[1] Depending on whether, for empirical adequacy, it is necessary to go beyond structural or unit analysis. Only if it is necessary to do so does the distinction of analytical systems involved have to become explicit.

of data—those which are problematical and those which are unproblematical to the corresponding analytical system, the values of variables and of constants, respectively. On this basis it is best to distinguish between a "fully" and a "relatively" historical discipline. To illustrate: most history is written in terms of the action schema and its secondary derivatives. The data, for instance, of the geographical environment are taken simply as unproblematical data, are noted and their consequences worked out for the particular historic process in mind. This is a relatively historical procedure. It would become a fully historical one in so far as the historian attempted to explain changes in these data in terms of geology, climatology, etc., as well as the data of heredity, race, for instance, in terms of natural selection. Most actual historical disciplines are, in this sense, relatively rather than fully historical. Thus history generally confines its problems to data relevant to the action schema, meteorology to those relevant to the schemata of physics and chemistry. If, for instance, a meteorologist finds that smoke in or near a large city significantly alters the climate there, he takes the smoke production for the area as a fact without attempting to enter into an economic or a sociological explanation of it. He merely works out its meteorological consequences.

Unit or part concepts as such can hardly constitute the basis of independent sciences. In their descriptive and nonanalytical explanatory use they are adjuncts to the historical sciences. Further analysis of them, on the other hand, leads over to the analytical sciences. They constitute the principal conceptual link between the two.

It is not difficult to see that an empiricist methodology favors (1) the general classification of the sciences on a "historical" basis, according to the classes of concrete systems dealt with; (2) the limitation of the development of theory to the type-part concept and its empirical generalization. Any attempt at analytical theory on an empiricist basis leads to the reification of the theoretical system. Where, as in physics, the main concrete historical individuals studied are scientifically interesting to men almost entirely in the respects relevant to such a theory, for example the stars, and the processes going on in laboratories for atomic research, the consequences may not become serious until an advanced stage in the analysis. Where, as in the field of human behavior, almost any concrete historical individual is a meeting ground for the application of a number of such systems, the consequences become serious at an early stage. The fate of orthodox economic theory faced with institutionalist criticism is a vivid case in point. On an empiricist basis there is a complete deadlock.

On an analytical basis it is possible to see emerging out of this study as a whole a division into three great classes of theoretical systems. They may be spoken of as the systems of nature, action and culture.[1] It should be further noted that the distinction is one of theoretical systems, not one of classes of concrete historical individuals. Only the first two are systems of *empirical* scientific theory in the usual sense; the third occupies a special status.

This is because an empirical science is concerned with *processes in time*. The problematical data of the theories of both the nature systems and the action systems concern such processes; those of the culture systems do not. The line of distinction which may

---

[1] The closest approach to this classification is that of Freyer (*Soziologie als Wirklichkeitswissenschaft*) into *Naturwissenschaft, Wirklichkeitswissenschaft* and *Logoswissenschaft*. The present formulation owes a good deal to his scheme, though it differs in certain respects.

It will be noted that in this final classification the qualifying adjective, "voluntaristic" as applied to the theory of action has been dropped and reference is made simply to the sciences of action as distinguished from those of nature and of culture. It is true that in this study the conception of a positivistic theory of action has been employed and has been useful in analyzing and classifying theories. It has been applied to theories stated in terms of the action schema, but having positivistic implications. Here, however, the object is not to analyze others' theories but to set up the most nearly correct classification which is at present attainable.

It is a legitimate conclusion from the analysis of this study that in the sense of having independent causal importance there can in the last analysis be no such thing as a radically positivistic theory of action. It is always possible to state the facts in terms of the action frame of reference, but when the advance from description and unit analysis to element analysis is made, it turns out that the action categories are not analytically significant. The causally relevant variables can always be adequately stated in terms of a natural science system. In this sense a positivistic position always reduces the explanation of action to natural science terms.

It follows that if a theory of action is to have the status of an independent analytical system at all, it must, in the nature of the case, be a voluntaristic theory. Hence the qualifying adjective, originally introduced to distinguish the system this study was concerned with from a positivistic theory, becomes superfluous and can be dropped from the final classification.

THE CLASSIFICATION OF THE SCIENCES OF ACTION

be drawn between the first two is that the nature systems involve time in relation to space in the frame of reference, the action systems in relation to the means-end schema. Physical time is a mode of relationship of events in space, action time a mode of relation of means and ends and other action elements. *All* known empirical scientific theory apparently involves one or the other of these two basic frames of reference, physical space-time or the means-end schema of action. Action is *non*-spatial[1] but temporal.

The culture systems are distinguished from both the others in that they are *both* non-spatial and atemporal. They consist, as Professor Whitehead says, of *eternal* objects, in the strict sense of the term eternal, of objects not of indefinite duration but to which the category of time is not applicable. They are not involved in "process."

Concrete spatial objects and temporal events may have a cultural aspect, in this sense, but in so far as they are physically understandable it can only be as symbols. Eternal objects constitute the meanings of symbols. As objects they exist only "in the minds" of individuals.[2] They in themselves are not to be found by external observation, only their symbolic manifestations.

It cannot, however, be denied that the cultural systems have the status of science if by that is meant a body of objectively verifiable propositions. For if it is granted, as it must be, that the meanings of symbols are observable, it is necessary also to grant that there is verifiable knowledge of eternal objects. But this cannot take the form of causal understanding of events. Beyond the grasp of the immediate meaning of a particular isolated symbol it can only mean a grasp of the interrelations of eternal objects in meaningful systems.

Of these systems there are presented to our experience many kinds which it is not possible here to attempt to analyze and classify. The reader may, however, be reminded that the systems of scientific theory with which this study has been so intensively concerned are among such systems. As such they are neither physical objects nor events. There are also other kinds of culture systems as of "ideas," "art forms" and many more.

---

[1] Of course every *concrete* event occurs in space, *too*. But this fact is an unproblematical datum to the analytical *sciences* of action.

[2] Or "embodied" in systems of symbols the "understanding" of which implies a mind.

The relations of culture systems to action are highly complex. Here it is necessary to state only that they may, on the one hand, be considered as *products* of processes of action; on the other, as conditioning elements of further action, as for instance is true of scientific and other "ideas." The sciences of action can no more avoid concern with them than they can with "physical" facts. But the logical relation is essentially the same. They constitute unproblematical data, knowledge of which is essential to the solution of concrete problems.[1]

On both sides there is one exception. Though these three kinds of systems must be clearly distinguished from each other, they all constitute parts of a consistent whole of objective knowledge. Hence the presumption is that there exist important interrelations. It goes without saying that a vast number of physical objects may be considered in part products of processes of action.[2] Action, that is, changes the physical world as well as being conditioned by it. Similarly, culture systems are in part[3] products of action as well as in turn conditioning action. Both these borderline cases would naturally give rise to borderline disciplines. On the borderline between action and culture there is already a quite well-developed and recognized discipline, generally known in Germany as *Wissenssoziologie*. Its concern is with culture systems as products of action, the influence of action elements upon them and their concrete processes of development.

Leaving aside the "sciences" of culture[4] the empirical analytical sciences may then be divided into the two great groups of the natural sciences and the sciences of action. The latter are distinguished negatively by the irrelevance of the spatial frame of reference, positively by the means-end schema and by the indispensability of the subject aspect, hence of the method

---

[1] It should be noted that physical phenomena are also often the products of action.

[2] Usually called *artefacts*.

[3] From the causal point of view we must grant to them the relation to action a certain *Eigengesetzlichkeit*. A thought process which *is* a process of action is canalized by logical considerations. The system of logic, a culture system, is a causal element in the concrete result.

[4] Such as logic, mathematics, systematic jurisprudence, etc. One great branch constitutes what are sometimes called normative sciences. This term should be taken cautiously, however.

of *Verstehen*,[1] which is specifically irrelevant to the natural sciences.

Each of these groups constitutes in a sense *one* great system since there is a common basic frame of reference and in all probability a definite systematic relation of all the analytical and structural elements relevant to this frame of reference. But within each of these groups there have developed well-marked subsystems that enjoy a degree of independence of each other. It can be said with some definiteness what is the main principle of subdivision in the action group; with much less definiteness, in the natural science group. The main principle is that, with increasing complexity of concrete systems, there appear successively new emergent properties which give rise to new theoretical problems not relevant to the more elementary systems. No attempt will here be made to enter into the question as it concerns the natural sciences except to note that a somewhat similar doctrine of "emergence" is rather widely held among biologists. According to this doctrine what is peculiar to biological theory is the problems raised by the properties of organisms which are not to be found in their constituent physicochemical elements or parts. And surely the line between the physicochemical and the biological group is the clearest line of subdivision within the natural sciences.

But in the action group it is possible to be much more specific. It has been seen that certain fundamentals are to be posited of the elementary unit act. The first emergent property that arises with increasing complexity of action systems is, in one direction, that of economic rationality. Now the whole methodological discussion of this study in this connection has started with the fact that the ramifications of this element in its various relations to the concrete facts of action have given rise to a well-integrated theoretical system, that of economic theory. If one such emergent element can be made the basis of a coherent theoretical system there seems to be no clear prima-facie reason why others should not also, if others there be.

For it must be evident that, if the analysis is pushed no farther, the results of the discussion of the status of economic theory are

---

[1] Culture systems are obviously *only* understandable by this method. In the sciences of action we combine *both Verstehen* and observation of "behavior," that is, of the external spatial course of events.

anomalous. This is well illustrated by the position in which Pareto left the question. He is quite clear that what he called pure economics is to be regarded as an abstract theoretical system. Its status is precisely that which has been accorded here to an analytical system. But he leaves it as the *only* positively defined analytical science applicable to action. The only other social science he mentions is sociology, which, though he explicitly refused to define it rigorously, appears to include two aspects. One is an analytical aspect, the analysis of the nonlogical elements of action, the other a synthetic, the total account of concrete action generally, including the economic element. It is clear that sociology for Pareto must be considered, in the analytical sense, a residual science since it is concerned with a residual category of action elements.[1] On this basis it surely could not hope to be a closed system in the sense that mechanics has long been. From this it seems legitimate to conclude, either that the course Pareto took in defining the status of economic theory was wrong and an entirely different basis must be found or that it is necessary to proceed from his position, which involves only one positively defined analytical science of action, to the construction of a coherent system of the analytical sciences of action. Since the economic element of Pareto's treatment has a definite place in the wider scheme of elements of action here developed, it is reasonable to think that the latter will provide a practicable basis for the more comprehensive scheme of classification. This study is naturally definitely committed to Pareto's view of the status of economics.

Thus the principle employed is to classify analytical sciences according to which structural element or group of elements of a generalized system of action constitutes the focus of attention of the science in question. It must be remembered that this structural analysis may or may not coincide with the most convenient selection of analytical elements or variables. Thus, in the economic case, the relevant subsystem of the theory of action will include all the variables that are most significant in accounting for changes in actions attributable to the fact that these systems are economically rational to a high degree. One of these

[1] This may be, and probably was regarded by Pareto as, a first approximation. As such it was a great advance on the position for instance, of Marshall. Now, fortunately, it is possible to proceed to a second approximation.

may be the valid knowledge of their situation possessed by the actors. But in so far as the same systems are rational in respects other than the economic, namely the technological and the political, the same variable will probably be included in other subsystems. Though the analytical systems are, as a whole, distinct from each other, it does not follow that in the choice of particular variables they are mutually exclusive. On the contrary, they are almost certain to overlap. Any group of variables may constitute an analytical system which it is convenient to treat together in relation to empirical problems. Since the main structural features of the differentiation of action systems with which this study has been occupied form some of the most conspicuous features of the concrete phenomena of action, it is probable on general grounds that the variables which are the most closely related to each in the manner outlined will have a set of such close mutual interrelations that it is for many purposes convenient to treat them together as a system. This general presumption is greatly strengthened by the fact that the most closely articulated analytical system in the action field, that of economic theory, does, in fact, fit very closely one of these main distinguishable structural aspects of action systems.

The economic concept makes sense only for systems of action, but it is applicable to the system of action of a particular individual—"Crusoe economics."[1] The next conceptually important step in increasing complexity of systems of action comes with the inclusion of a plurality of individuals in the same system. This has a double consequence. On the one hand, it introduces the possibility of coercive power entering into the relations of the individuals within the system. This is a property not included in the economic concept. The action system of an individual may have not only economic rationality but also coercive rationality.

But this coercive rationality has a peculiar characteristic. It cannot be a property of the *total* action system[2] involving a plurality of individuals; it can only apply to some individuals or groups within such a system *relative* to others. Coercion is an

[1] All its fundamental conceptual elements are to be found on this level.

[2] In this respect it is analogous to the economic conception of value. The idea of a "general level of values" is nonsensical because value is a *relative* concept. Power is also a relative concept.

exercise of power over others. At the same time this possibility of coercion opens up a new set of problems, the problems of social order stated in classic form by Hobbes as a result of his exploration of the consequences of an unlimited struggle for power. In order that there may be a stable system of action involving a plurality of individuals there must be normative regulation of the power aspect of the relations of individuals within the system; in this sense, there must be a distributive order. This double aspect of *social* action systems, the problem of power relations and order in so far as it may be regarded as a solution of the struggle for power, gives another relatively well-marked set of emergent properties of action systems. These may be called the political action elements.

THE PLACE OF SOCIOLOGY

Third, it has been seen that the solution of the power question, as well as of a plurality of other complex features of social action systems, involves a common reference to the fact of integration of individuals with reference to a common value system, manifested in the legitimacy of institutional norms, in the common ultimate ends of action, in ritual and in various modes of expression. All these phenomena may be referred back to a single general emergent property of social action systems which may be called "common-value integration." This is a clearly marked emergent property readily distinguishable from both the economic and the political. If this property is designated the sociological, sociology may then be defined as "the science which attempts to develop an analytical theory of social[1] action systems in so far as these systems can be understood in terms of the property of common-value integration."

Thus, in terms of the emergent properties of action systems beyond those attributable to the elementary unit act, it is possible to distinguish three well-defined emergent levels. With each of these is associated a group of emergent properties that, on the one hand, disappear when the system is broken down by unit analysis beyond this level of complexity and, on the other hand, can no longer be thought of as standing alone when the construction of such systems is carried beyond the given stage of com-

[1] Involving a plurality of actors mutually oriented to each other's action.

plexity. Thus the three analytical social sciences of organized action systems, economics, politics[1] and sociology may reasonably be distinguished by their respective relations to these three emergent properties of such systems.

This leaves the unit act. In itself its basic properties do not constitute the subject matter of an independent analytical science. They constitute, rather, the common methodological basis of all the sciences of action, for it is really these basic elementary properties of the unit act in their mutual interrelations which constitute the common frame of reference of all the sciences of action. It is no more true that the unit act defines an independent science of action than that there is an independent natural science of space-time.

At the same time there are two points at which systematic theorizing in connection with action is not exhausted by the three systematic sciences just mentioned. In the first place, nothing has been said about the problems arising from the fact that action elements and processes involve a reference to an actor. This is another organic aspect of action systems not included in the three sets of emergent properties so far discussed. It has already been mentioned in connection with the aggregational organization of action systems, involving the concept of personality.

Reflection shows that concrete personality can be in part explained in terms of the analytical systems of these three social sciences. That aspect may be called the social component of personality. Application of this social analysis will, however, leave a residuum unexplained within the limits of relevance of the action frame of reference. In so far as this residuum can be abstracted from the specific content of the concrete ends and norms of unit acts, which is environmental, it will be found to be referable to heredity. There are, then, certain emergent properties of action systems, in part at least, understandable with reference to the hereditary basis of personality. There is an important place for a systematic analytical science concerned with these properties. In no other way can psychology be defined in terms of the general scheme employed here—as an

[1] In arriving at this conception of the place of politics the present author has been greatly influenced by discussions with Professor C. J. Friedrich of Harvard University. He is not, however, responsible for the above specific formulation.

analytical, not a historical[1] science. It would then be the analytical science concerned with the variable properties of action systems derivable from their reference to the hereditary basis of personality.

This makes psychology definitely a science of action and, in spite of the common reference to heredity, draws a clear line between it and biology.[2] Its categories refer to properties of action systems with special reference to the subschema of personality. They are thus *non*-spatial. They are modes of function of the organism as a whole. But they abstract from social relationships, and hence from the properties of action systems that emerge only on the social level.

Secondly, the general properties of the unit act, in abstraction from economic, political and sociological considerations, may be studied with special reference to the concrete content of immediate ends, norms and knowledge. Since the general properties of the unit act do not constitute the basis of an independent analytical science but, rather, the common basis of all the sciences of action, there will arise out of this study not so much one discipline as a plurality of disciplines according to classes of concrete ends.[3] These disciplines may be called the technologies. They will be highly important concretely, but they add relatively little to the systematic analytical theory of action.

Common to all these five analytical disciplines is the basic action schema on both the descriptive and the analytical level. The facts relevant to them all can be translated into terms of the action schema as a frame of reference. But, at the same time, it is in general convenient to operate, for most of their purposes, with more specialized subschemata. In regard to economics it is primarily the supply-and-demand schema. In the political discipline it is primarily the social-relationship schema in the special form of power relationships, secondarily the group[4] schema. In sociology the relationship and group schemata are particularly suitable. In psychology the personality schema is

---

[1] Two of the current definitions quite definitely make it a historical science in our sense as, the science of "behavior" and the science of "mind," or of "subjective processes."

[2] *Supra*, note appended to Chap. II, pp. 85–86.

[3] Such as industrial, military, scientific, erotic, ritual, ascetic, contemplative, artistic, etc.

[4] As for instance in the theories of political pluralism.

obviously central.[1] Finally, the technologies can in the nature of the case operate only in terms of the elementary means-end action schema.

History may be regarded primarily as the general historical science concerned with human action.[2] As has already been pointed out it tends to be a relatively rather than a fully historical discipline. Besides its subdivisions according to periods and concrete social units, peoples, nations, etc., it also tends to subdivide into the study of classes of concrete fact *particularly* relevant to one or another of the analytical sciences of action. Thus there are economic history, political history, social (perhaps, sociological) history, biography and histories of the various concrete technologies. History of religions would for obvious reasons, be included primarily in the sociologically relevant group. The main criterion of distinction between these various branches of history would be consideration of the facts in terms of one or another of the descriptive subschemata of action. Thus a biography is the history of a personality. It should be noted that history is here treated *only* so far as it claims empirical scientific status; in other words in so far as it attempts to arrive at empirically verifiable judgments of fact and of causal relationships. Any other aspect of concrete historical works, as works of art, for instance, is beyond the scope of the present discussion.

While in the interest of clear thinking it is essential to maintain the logical distinctions between the various analytical sciences of action, it is none the less true and important that since they all constitute subsystems of the same great and inclusive system of theory their interrelations are exceedingly close and the working scientist cannot afford to neglect them.[3] Above all, there seems to be no possibility that scientific work on a high level can be done by a man in any one of them who does not have a working knowledge of the others. This becomes particularly true at the

---

[1] Thus a basic psychological concept is that of attitudes. But it is quite clear that concrete attitudes are not the exclusive concern of psychology, but are relevant to all the sciences of action.

[2] As distinguished from what, reviving an old term, may be called natural history, on the one hand, history of ideas and other cultural systems, on the other.

[3] These interrelations will naturally give rise to borderline fields analogous to physical chemistry and biochemistry, *e.g.*, social psychology, social economics, etc.

higher levels of emergence. A sociologist can no more hope to do satisfactory work, empirical or theoretical, without a knowledge of psychology, economics and politics than can a biologist without a knowledge of physics and chemistry. The reasons are much the same. The "mechanisms" of the processes that a sociologist is interested in will always prove to involve crucially important elements on these "lower" levels. This fact has been largely obscured by empiricist methodology and the closely related elementary level of analytical thinking in the sciences of action. Over against this has to be set the fact that in these fields common sense is by no means of negligible value. Good common sense often yields better results than bad theoretical analysis.[1]

It will be noted that the place given to sociology in this classification makes it a special analytical science on the same level as economic theory. This procedure runs counter to the bulk of methodological tradition in the matter. The dominant view in the past has been the encyclopedic, which would make sociology a fully historical science in the above sense. Weber, defining it as the science of social action would make it either a relatively historical science, or a synthetic analytical science of action, including economics and politics.

The starting point from which this conclusion has been reached is the view of economic theory as a special analytical science, at which Pareto arrived. Once this is accepted it is, as has been stated, anomalous to stop there for purposes of more than first approximation and speak of only one such science in the action field. This is particularly true since other structural elements of action have been defined which are part of the same broader system as the economic and occupy methodologically the same logical status as emergent properties of action systems. The logical course, then, seems to be to carry the analysis through to the point of outlining a complete system of the special analytical sciences of action. The only alternative would be to go back to the empiricist basis of classification which has become, as a result of the preceding analysis, untenable.

The procedure here is not, however, altogether without precedent. Simmel's[2] was, perhaps, the first serious attempt

---

[1] Which does not prove its results are better than would be those of *good* theoretical analysis.

[2] SIMMEL, *Soziologie*, Chap. I.

to gain a basis for sociology as, in this sense, a special science. His formula is unacceptable for reasons that cannot be gone into here. But it was founded on sound insight and the view just stated may be regarded as a restatement of its sound elements in more acceptable terms. The main difficulty for Simmel was that the view he took of the other social sciences precluded relating his concept of sociology to other analytical social sciences on the same methodological level. To him sociology was the only abstract analytical science in the social field.[1]

Moreover, Durkheim's thought was progressing to a point where, had his conception of action continued to develop in the voluntaristic direction he might well have reached a similar outcome. Long before the close of his career his concept of society as a "reality *sui generis*" could no longer be considered a concrete entity but only an abstract element or group of elements of concrete reality. His conception of society also tallied well with the above view of emergence. Finally, its specific content in his thought makes it quite legitimate to identify it with the emergent property of common-value integration. The view taken here is the logical outcome of placing Durkheim's substantive results in a systematic scheme of the structure of action.[2]

It can easily be seen why such a view has had to wait upon a relatively full development of the generalized theory of action. This concept of sociology could not develop on a positivistic basis. For at the radical positivistic pole all empirical sciences become natural sciences in the above sense. Short of that, on a utilitarian basis action systems could only be considered on levels at which the property of common-value integration was not yet emergent, or, in concrete application, was present at best as a residual category, taking the form generally of implicit assumptions such as that of the natural identity of interests. If anything beyond psychology, economic theory and political theory of the Hobbesian type was to be given a place at all it had to be as a "synthetic" science.[3]

[1] It is interesting to compare this opinion with the corresponding status given to economics in Pareto's scheme.

[2] Another view similar in a number of respects, is that set forth by Professor Znaniecki in his *Method of Sociology*.

[3] Spencer's system is so definitely utilitarian that this may serve as an explanation of why he regarded sociology as an encyclopedic science.

On an idealistic basis, on the other hand, the *facts* of value integration were clearly seen, but the inherent tendency was to assimilate them to culture systems in the above sense, and thus to end up in some kind of emanationist theory. Freyer, in his book cited above, has analyzed this tendency with great acumen. Thus, as long as social thought has remained divided between the positivistic and the idealistic systems there has been no place for an analytical sociological theory in the sense in which it has just been defined. The possibility of giving it a place is, perhaps, the deepest symptom of the great change in social thinking the process of convergence here traced has brought about.

One final word. There has been of late a strong current of pessimism in the thought of students of the social sciences, especially those who call themselves sociologists. We are told that there are as many systems of sociological theory as there are sociologists, that there is no common basis, that all is arbitrary and subjective. To the present writer this current of sentiment has two equally unfortunate implications. On the one hand, it encourages the view that the only sound work in the social field is detailed factual study, without benefit of theory. On the other hand, for those who refuse to be satisfied with this, it encourages a dangerous irrationalism which lets go of scientific standards altogether. We are told sociology is an art, that what is valuable in it is to be measured by the standards of intuition and inspiration, that it is not subject to the canons of rigorous logic and empirical verification.

It is to be hoped that this study may contribute to the combating of both these dangerous tendencies. It may claim to do so in two principal respects. First, it has shown that, within the field it has covered, the differences are not so great as they appear at first sight. There is a substantial common basis of theory if we will but take the trouble to dig deep enough to find it. The opinion may, indeed, be ventured that it will be found to be the more substantial the more eminent the men whose work is studied. It would be quite possible to cite the four men here studied as examples of this lack of agreement. Yet it is a legitimate conclusion from the evidence here presented that this would be a superficial judgment. Their agreement far outweighs the differences that occur on the more superficial levels. What has happened in the minds of these men is not the appearance of an unorganized mass of arbitrary subjective judgments. It is part of a great deep stream of the movement of scientific thought. It is a movement of major proportions extending far beyond the works of the few men here considered.

Secondly, if the interpretation of the nature of scientific development here formulated be accepted even only in its application to this particular case, another conclusion follows. What has been traced is not merely a movement of thought of major proportions; it is scientific progress; indeed, notable scientific progress. One of its main aspects is a clearer, sounder understanding of a broad range of the facts of human action. The whole theoretical work here reviewed is oriented to and justified by this achievement. It could not have been done without the systematic theoretical thinking which forms the basis and is the subject of this study.

It is not, therefore, possible to concur in the prevailing pessimistic judgment of the social sciences, particularly sociology. If attention is centered not on the average achievement but, as is fully justified in such a case, on the best, we certainly need not be ashamed of our science. Notable progress on both empirical and theoretical levels has been made within the short space of a generation. We have sound theoretical foundations on which to build.

BIBLIOGRAPHY[1]

CHAPTER I. INTRODUCTORY

ARISTOTLE: *Politics*, trans. by B. Jowett, Oxford, Clarendon Press, New York, 1885.

BRIDGMAN, P. W.: *The Logic of Modern Physics*, The Macmillan Company, New York, 1927.

BRINTON, C. CRANE: *English Political Thought in the Nineteenth Century*, Ernest Benn, Ltd., London, 1933.

COHEN, MORRIS R.: *Reason and Nature*, Harcourt, Brace & Company, New York, 1931.

DURKHEIM, ÉMILE: *Les règles de la méthode sociologique*, 7th ed., F. Alcan, Paris, 1919.

HENDERSON, LAWRENCE J.: "An Approximate Definition of Fact," *University of California Publications in Philosophy*, Vol. 14, pp. 179–200, University of California Press, Berkeley, Calif., 1932.

―――― *Pareto's General Sociology: A Physiologist's Interpretation*, Harvard University Press, Cambridge, 1935.

Memorials of Alfred Marshall, ed. by A. C. Pigou, Macmillan & Company, Ltd., London, 1925.

PARETO, VILFREDO: *Traité de sociologie générale*, French ed. by P. Boven, 2 vols. Payot et Cie, Paris, 1917.

VON SCHELTING, ALEXANDER: *Max Webers Wissenshaftslehre*, J. B. C. Mohr (P. Siebeck), Tübingen, 1934.

"A Symposium on Pareto's Significance": WILLIAM W. McDOUGALL: "Pareto as a Psychologist," pp. 36–52; CARL MURCHISON: "Pareto and Experimental Social Psychology," pp. 53–63; JAMES H. TUFTS: "Pareto's Significance for Ethics," pp. 64–77; FLOYD N. HOUSE: "Pareto in the Development of Modern Sociology," pp. 78–89, *Journal of Social Philosophy*, Vol. 1, 1935–1936.

WEBER, MAX: *Gesammelte Aufsätze zur Wissenschaftslehre*, J. C. B. Mohr (P. Siebeck), Tübingen, 1922.

WHITEHEAD, ALFRED N.: *Science and the Modern World*, The Macmillan Company, New York, 1925.

---

[1] This bibliography is not meant to be exhaustive. It includes three classes of works: (1) The principal works of the authors treated. No attempt is made to include all their minor articles and book reviews. (2) A selected list of secondary references dealing with each author's work. (3) Other works which the present writer has either actually cited in the text or found particularly useful in connection with the subject matter. Though not exhaustive it is quite sufficient to lead any interested reader into any phase of the field he wishes to investigate further.

ZNANIECKI, FLORIAN: *The Method of Sociology*, Farrar & Rinehart, Inc., New York, 1934.

CHAPTER II. THE THEORY OF ACTION

VON GIERKE, OTTO: *Das deutsche Genossenschaftsrecht*, 4 vols., Weidmann, Berlin, 1868–1913.

PARSONS, TALCOTT: "The Place of Ultimate Values in Sociological Theory," *International Journal of Ethics*, Vol. 45, pp. 282–316, 1935.

———— "Society," *Encyclopedia of the Social Sciences*, Vol. XIV, The Macmillan Co., New York, 1934.

———— "Sociological Elements in Economic Thought. I. Historical," *Quarterly Journal of Economics*, Vol. 49, pp. 414–453, 1934–1935.

———— "Sociological Elements in Economic Thought. II. The Analytical Factor View," *Quarterly Journal of Economics*, Vol. 49, pp. 646–667, 1934–1935.

———— "Some Reflections on 'The Nature and Significance of Economics'," *Quarterly Journal of Economics*, Vol. 48, pp. 511–545, 1933–1934.

TROELTSCH, ERNST: *Die Bedeutung des Protestantismus für die Entsethung der modernen Welt*, R. Oldenburg, Munich, 1911.

———— *The Social Teaching of the Christian Churches*, trans. by Olive Wyon. 2 vols., The Macmillan Company, New York, 1931.

ZNANIECKI, FLORIAN: *The Laws of Social Psychology*, University of Chicago Press, Chicago, 1925.

———— *Social Actions*, Farrar & Rinehart, Inc. (for the Polish Sociological Institute), New York, 1936.

CHAPTER III. THE DEVELOPMENT OF INDIVIDUALISTIC POSITIVISM

BOBER, MANDELL M.: *Karl Marx's Interpretation of History*, Harvard University Press, Cambridge, 1927.

BONAR, JAMES: *Malthus and His Work*, Macmillan & Company, Ltd., London, 1885.

HALÉVY, ÉLIE: *La formation du radicalisme philosophique*, 3 vols., F. Alcan, Paris, 1901–1904; trans. by Mary Morris, Faber & Groger, London, 1928.

HENDERSON, LAWRENCE J.: *The Fitness of the Environment*, The Macmillan Company, New York, 1913.

HOBBES, THOMAS: *Leviathan*, J. M. Dent & Sons, Ltd., London, 1928.

KEYNES, JOHN M.: *The End of Laissez-faire*, L. & V. Woolf, London, 1926; New Republic, Inc., New York, 1926.

———— *Essays in Biography*, Macmillan & Company, Ltd., London, 1933.

KNIGHT, FRANK H.: "Freedom as Fact and Criterion," *International Journal of Ethics*, Vol. 39, pp. 129–147, 1928–1929.

LINDSAY, ALEXANDER D.: *Karl Marx's Capital: an Introductory Essay*, Oxford University Press, London, 1925.

LOCKE, JOHN: *Of Civil Government; Two Treatises*, J. M. Dent & Sons, Ltd., London, 1924.

MALTHUS, THOMAS R.: *Essay on the Principle of Population*, 1798, reprinted, Macmillan & Company, Ltd. (for the Royal Economic Society) London, 1926.

MILL, JOHN STUART: *Principles of Political Economy*, ed. with an introduction by W. J. Ashley, Longmans, Green & Company, London, 1909.

MITCHELL, WESLEY C.: "Human Behavior and Economics: A Survey of Recent Literature," *Quarterly Journal of Economics*, Vol. 29, pp. 1–47, 1914–1915.

—— "The Rationality of Economic Activity," *Journal of Political Economy*, Vol. 18, 1910, Part I, pp. 97–113; Part II, pp. 197–216.

PARETO, VILFREDO: *Les systèmes socialistes*, 2 vols., Giard, Paris, 1902–1903.

PARSONS, TALCOTT: "Malthus," *Encyclopedia of the Social Sciences*, Vol. X, The Macmillan Company, New York, 1933.

—— "Sociological Elements in Economic Thought. I. Historical," *Quarterly Journal of Economics*, Vol. 49, pp. 414–453, 1934–1935.

RICARDO, D.: *Letters of David Ricardo to Thomas Robert Malthus*, ed. by James Bonar, Oxford, Clarendon Press, New York, 1887.

—— *The Principles of Political Economy and Taxation*, J. M. Dent & Sons, Ltd., London, 1911.

SMITH, ADAM: *An Inquiry into the Nature and Causes of the Wealth of Nations*, ed. by Edwin Cannan, 2 vols., Methuen & Company, Ltd., London, 1904.

STEPHEN, LESLIE: *The English Utilitarians*, 3 vols., Duckworth & Co., London, 1900.

TAUSSIG, FRANK W.: *Wages and Capital*, D. Appleton-Century Company, Inc., New York, 1896.

TAYLOR, O. H.: "Economic Theory and Certain Non-economic Elements in Social Life," *Explorations in Economics, Essays in Honor of F. W. Taussig*, McGraw-Hill Book Company, Inc., New York, 1936.

—— "Economics and the Idea of Natural Law"; "Economics and the Idea of 'Jus Naturale,'" *Quarterly Journal of Economics*, Vol. 44, pp. 1–39, November, 1929; pp. 205–241, February, 1930.

TROELTSCH, ERNST: *The Social Teaching of the Christian Churches*, trans. by Olive Wyon, 2 vols., The Macmillan Company, New York, 1931.

VEBLEN, THORSTEIN: "The Preconceptions of Economic Science, I, II, III," *Quarterly Journal of Economics*, Vol. 13, pp. 121–150, 396–426, 1898–1899; Vol. 14, pp. 240–269, 1899–1900; reprinted in *The Place of Science in Modern Civilization*, Viking Press, New York, 1919.

CHAPTER IV.   ALFRED MARSHALL

A. Works

A full bibliography of Marshall's works compiled by J. M. Keynes is provided in the volume *Memorials of Alfred Marshall* (see reference below).

MARSHALL, ALFRED: *Industry and Trade*, Macmillan & Company, Ltd., London, 1919.

—— *Money, Credit and Commerce*, Macmillan & Company, Ltd., London, 1923.

—— *Official Papers*, Macmillan & Company, Ltd. (for the Royal Economic Society), London, 1926.

—— *Principles of Economics*, 8th ed., Macmillan & Company, Ltd. London, 1925.

—— and MARY PALEY MARSHALL: *The Economics of Industry*, Macmillan & Company, Ltd., London, 1879.

Memorials of Alfred Marshall, ed. by A. C. Pigou, Macmillan & Company, Ltd., London, 1925.

B. *Secondary Sources and Other Relevant Works*

DAVENPORT, HERBERT J.: *The Economics of Alfred Marshall*, Cornell University Press, Ithaca, N. Y., 1935.

HENDERSON, HERBERT D.: *Supply and Demand*, Nisbet & Co., Ltd., London, 1922; Cambridge Economic Handbook I, Harcourt, Brace & Company, New York, 1922.

HOMAN, PAUL T.: *Contemporary Economic Thought*, Harper & Brothers, New York, 1928.

KNIGHT, FRANK H.: *The Ethics of Competition*, Harper & Brothers, New York, 1935.

—— "Relation of Utility Theory to Economic Method in the Work of William Stanley Jevons and Others," in *Methods in Social Science*, pp. 59–69, ed. by Stuart A. Rice, University of Chicago Press, Chicago, 1931.

LÖWE, ADOLF: *Economics and Sociology*, Allen & Unwin, Ltd., London, 1935.

MILL, JOHN STUART: *Principles of Political Economy*, ed. with an introduction by W. J. Ashley, Longmans, Green & Company, London, 1909.

MITCHELL, WESLEY C.: "The Rationality of Economic Activity," *Journal of Political Economy*, Vol. 18, 1910, Part I, pp. 97–113; Part II, pp. 197–216.

PARSONS, TALCOTT: "On Certain Sociological Elements in Professor Taussig's Thought," *Explorations in Economics, Essays in Honor of F. W. Taussig*, McGraw-Hill Book Company, Inc., New York, 1936.

—— "Sociological Elements in Economic Thought. I. Historical," *Quarterly Journal of Economics*, Vol. 49, pp. 414–453, 1934–1935.

—— "Sociological Elements in Economic Thought. II. The Analytical Factor View," *Quarterly Journal of Economics*, Vol. 49, pp. 646–667, 1934–1935.

—— "Some Reflections on 'The Nature and Significance of Economics,'" *Quarterly Journal of Economics*, Vol. 48, pp. 511–545, 1933–1934.

—— "Wants and Activities in Marshall," *Quarterly Journal of Economics*, Vol. 46, pp. 101–140, 1931–1932.

—— "Economics and Sociology: Marshall in Relation to the Thought of His Time," *ibid.*, pp. 316–347.

RICARDO, D.: *Letters of David Ricardo to Thomas Robert Malthus*, ed. by James Bonar, Oxford, Clarendon Press, New York, 1887.

—— *The Principles of Political Economy and Taxation*, J. M. Dent & Sons, Ltd., London, 1911.

ROBBINS, LIONEL: *An Essay on the Nature and Significance of Economic Science*, 2d ed., Macmillan & Company, Ltd., London, 1935.

ROBERTSON, DENNIS H.: *Economic Fragments*, P. S. King & Son, Ltd., London, 1931.

Schumpeter, J. A.: "Epochen der Dogmen- und Methodengeschichte," *Grundriss der Sozialökonomik*, Vol. 1, 2d ed., J. C. B. Mohr (P. Siebeck), Tübingen, 1924.

Souter, R. W.: "'The Nature and Significance of Economic Science' in Recent Discussion," *Quarterly Journal of Economics*, Vol. 47, pp. 377–413, 1932–1933.

—— *Prolegomena to Relativity Economics*, Columbia University Press, New York, 1933.

Taussig, F. W.: "Alfred Marshall," *Quarterly Journal of Economics*, Vol. 39, pp. 1–14, 1924–1925.

The Trend of Economics, ed. by Rexford G. Tugwell, Alfred A. Knopf, Inc., New York, 1928.

Walsh, J. R.: "The Capital Concept Applied to Man," *Quarterly Journal of Economics*, Vol. 49, pp. 255–285, 1934–1935.

Weber, Max: *Gesammelte Aufsätze zur Religionssoziologie*, 3 vols., J. C. B. Mohr (P. Siebeck), Tübingen, 1920–1921.

—— *Gesammelte Aufsätze zur Wissenschaftslehre*, J. C. B. Mohr (P. Siebeck), Tübingen, 1922.

—— *The Protestant Ethic and the Spirit of Capitalism*, trans. by Talcott Parsons, George Allen & Unwin, Ltd., London, 1930.

Young, Allyn A.: "Economics as a Field of Research," *Quarterly Journal of Economics*, Vol. 42, pp. 1–25, 1927–1928.

—— "The Trend of Economics, as Seen by Some American Economists," *Quarterly Journal of Economics*, Vol. 39, pp. 155–183, 1924–1925.

Chapters V to VII. Vilfredo Pareto

A. Works

A full bibliography of Pareto's works is printed in G. H. Bousquet's *Vilfredo Pareto, sa vie et son oeuvre* (see reference under section *B* below).

Pareto, Vilfredo: *Cours d'économie politique professé à l'Université de Lausanne*, 2 vols., F. Rouge Lausanne, Pichon, Paris, 1896–1897.

—— *Fatti e Teorie*, Vallecchi, Florence, 1920.

—— *Manuel d'économie politique*, trans. of Italian edition by Alfred Bonnet (reviewed by the author), V. Giard et E. Brière, Paris, 1909.

—— *The Mind and Society*, ed. by Arthur Livingston; trans. by Andrew Bongiorno and Arthur Livingston, 4 vols., Harcourt, Brace & Company, New York, 1935.

—— *Le mythe vertuïste et la littérature immorale.* Études sur le dévenir social, V, M. Rivière et Cie., Paris, 1911.

—— *Les systèmes socialistes*, Cours professé à l'Université de Lausanne, 2 vols., V. Giard et E. Brière, Paris, 1902–1903.

—— *Traité de sociologie générale*, French ed. by Pièrre Boven (reviewed by the author) 2 vols., Payot et Cie., Lausanne, Paris, 1917–1919.

—— *Trasformazione della Democrazia.* Corbaccio, Milan, 1921.

—— *Trattato di Sociologia generale*, 1st ed., 2 vols., G. Barbéra, Florence, 1916.

B. *Secondary Sources*

BONGIORNO, ANDREW: "A Study of Pareto's Treatise on General Sociology," *American Journal of Sociology*, Vol. 36, pp. 349–370, 1930–1931.

BORKENAU, FRANZ: *Pareto*, John Wiley & Sons, Inc., New York, 1936.

BOUSQUET, GEORGES HENRI: *Vilfredo Pareto, sa vie et son oeuvre*, Payot et Cie., Paris, 1928.

——— *The Work of Vilfredo Pareto.* Trans. by McQuilkin De Grange, The Sociological Press, Minneapolis, 1928.

CARLI, FILIPPO: "Paretos soziologisches System und der 'Behaviorismus,'" *Kölner Vierteljahrshefte für Soziologie*, Heft 3–4, pp. 273–285, 1925.

FARIS, ELLSWORTH: *The Nature of Human Nature*, Chap. XVI, "An Estimate of Pareto," McGraw-Hill Book Company, Inc., New York, 1937.

Giornale degli Economisti, Vol. 44, 1924. The February issue is devoted to Pareto. A bibliography of Pareto's works is also given.

HANDMAN, MAX S.: "The Sociological Method of Vilfredo Pareto," in *Methods in Social Science*, ed. by Stuart A. Rice, pp. 139–153, University of Chicago Press, Chicago, 1931.

HENDERSON, L. J.: *Pareto's General Sociology: A Physiologist's Interpretation*, Harvard University Press, Cambridge, 1935.

HOMANS, GEORGE C. and CHARLES P. CURTIS, JR.: *An Introduction to Pareto, His Sociology*, Alfred A. Knopf, New York, 1934.

MICHELS, ROBERT: *Bedeutende Männer*, pp. 109 *ff.* Quelle & Meyer, Leipzig, 1927.

MURCHISON, CARL: "Pareto and Experimental Social Psychology," *Journal of Social Philosophy*, Vol. 1, pp. 53–63, 1935–1936.

PARSONS, TALCOTT: "Pareto," *Encyclopedia of the Social Sciences*, Vol. XI. The Macmillan Company, New York, 1933.

——— "Pareto's Central Analytical Scheme," *Journal of Social Philosophy*, Vol. 1, pp. 244–262, 1935–1936.

——— Review of Pareto's "The Mind and Society," *American Sociological Review*, Vol. 1, pp. 139–148, February, 1936; reviewed also in *American Economic Review*, Vol. 25, pp. 502–508, 1935.

PERRY, CHARNER M.: "Pareto's Contribution to Social Science," *International Journal of Ethics*, Vol. 46, pp. 96–107, 1935–1936.

SOROKIN, PITIRIM A.: *Contemporary Sociological Theories*, Chap. I, "The Mechanistic School," pp. 3–62; see especially pp. 37–62 on Pareto; Harper & Brothers, New York, 1928.

ZIEGLER, H. O.: "Ideologienlehre," *Archiv für Sozialwissenschaft und Sozialpolitik*, Vol. 57, pp. 657–700, 1927.

C. *General References*

MACHIAVELLI, N.: "Discourses on Livy," Vol. 2 of *The Historical, Political, and Diplomatic Writings of Nicolo Machiavelli*, trans. by C. E. Detmold, J. R. Osgood & Co., Boston, 1882.

——— *The Prince*, Oxford University Press, London, 1935.

MACIVER, ROBERT M.: *Society, Its Structure and Changes*, Ray Long & Richard R. Smith, Inc., New York, 1931.

PARSONS, TALCOTT: "Some Reflections on 'The Nature and Significance of Economics,'" *Quarterly Journal of Economics*, Vol. 48, pp. 511–545, 1933–1934.

ROBBINS, LIONEL: *An Essay on the Nature and Significance of Economic Science*, 2d ed., Macmillan & Company, Ltd., London, 1935.

SOUTER, RALPH W.: *Prolegomena to Relativity Economics*, Columbia University Press, New York, 1933.

TAYLOR, O. H.: "Economic Theory and Certain Non-economic Elements in Social Life," *Explorations in Economics, Essays in Honor of F. W. Taussig*, McGraw-Hill Book Company, Inc., New York, 1936.

WEBER, MAX: *Gesammelte Aufsätze zur Religionssoziologie*, 3 vols., J. C. B. Mohr (P. Siebeck), Tübingen, 1920–1921.

ZNANIECKI, FLORIAN: *The Method of Sociology*, Farrar & Rinehart, Inc., New York, 1934.

CHAPTERS VIII TO XI.   ÉMILE DURKHEIM

A. Major Works

DURKHEIM, ÉMILE: "Deux lois de l'évolution pénale," *L'année sociologique*, Vol. 4, pp. 65–95, 1899–1900.

—— *De la division du travail social.* F. Alcan, Paris, 1893.

—— *On the Division of Labor in Society*, trans. by George Simpson, The Macmillan Company, New York, 1933.

—— *L'éducation morale*, avertissement by Paul Fauconnet. F. Alcan, Paris, 1925.

—— *Les formes élémentaires de la vie religieuse*, Bibliothèque de philosophie contemporaire, F. Alcan, Paris, 1912; 2d ed., 1925; *The Elementary Forms of the Religious Life*, trans. by Joseph Ward Swain, George Allen & Unwin, Ltd., London; The Macmillan Company, New York, 1915.

—— *Les règles de la méthode sociologique*, F. Alcan, Paris, 1895.

—— *Le socialisme*, ed. by M. Mauss, F. Alcan, Paris, 1928.

—— *Sociologie et philosophie*, with a preface by C. Bouglé, Chap. I, "Représentations individuelles et représentations collectives," pp. 1–48; Chap. II, "Détermination du fait moral," pp. 41–90; Chap. III, "Résponses aux objections"; Chap. IV, "Jugements de valeur et jugements de réalité, pp. 91–176; Paris, F. Alcan, 1924.

—— *Le suicide*, F. Alcan, Paris, 1897; new ed., 1930.

—— and M. MAUSS. "De quelques formes primitives de classification," *L'année sociologique*, Vol. 6, pp. 1–72, 1901–1902.

—— (ed.): *L'année sociologique*. F. Alcan, Paris, 1896-1912.

B. Less Important Works

DURKHEIM, ÉMILE: "Le contrat social de Rousseau," *Revue de métaphysique*, Vol. 25, pp. 1–23, 129–161, 1918.

—— "De la définition des phénomènes religieux," *L'année sociologique*, Vol. 2, pp. 1–28, 1897–1898.

———— "Les études de science sociale," *Revue philosophique*, Vol. 22, pp. 61–80, 1886.

———— "La famille conjugale," *Revue philosophique*, Vols. 91–92, pp. 1–14, 1921.

———— "Introduction à la sociologie de la famille," *Annales de la faculté du lettres de Bordeaux*, Vol. 10, pp. 257–282, 1888

———— "De la méthode objective en sociologie," *Revue de synthèse historique*, Vol. 2, pp. 1–17, 1901.

———— "La pédagogie de Rousseau," *Revue de métaphysique*, Vol. 26, pp. 153–180, 1919.

———— "Pédagogie et sociologie," *Revue de métaphysique*, Vol. 30, pp. 37–54, 1903.

———— "Le problème réligieux et la dualité de la nature humaine," *Bulletin de la société française de philosophie*, Vol. 13, pp. 63–111, 1913.

———— "La prohibition de l'incest et ses origines," *L'année sociologique*, Vol. 1, pp. 1–70, 1896–1897.

———— "On the Relation of Sociology to the Social Sciences and to Philosophy," *Sociological Papers*, pp. 197–200, Macmillan & Company, Ltd. (for the Sociological Society), London, 1904.

———— Review of Fouillée, Belot and Landry, Section on Methodology, *L'année sociologique*, Vol. 10, pp. 352–369, 1905–1906.

———— Discussion of his own "Formes élémentaires de la vie réligieuse" and of Lévy-Bruhl's "Fonctions mentales dans les sociétés inférieures," *L'année sociologique*, Vol. 12, pp. 33–37, 1909–1912.

———— "La sociologie," *La science française*, Vol. 1, pp. 39–49, Ministère de l'instruction publique et des Beaux-Arts, Paris, 1915.

———— "Sociologie réligieuse et théorie de la connaissance," *Revue de métaphysique*, Vol. 17, pp. 733–758, 1909.

———— "Sur le totemisme," *L'année sociologique*, Vol. 5, pp. 82–121, 1900–1901.

C. Secondary Sources

ALLPORT, F. H.: "The Group Mind Fallacy in Relation to Social Science," *Journal of Abnormal and Social Psychology*, Vol. 19, pp. 60–73, 1924.

BARNES, H. E.: "Durkheim's Contribution to the Reconstruction of Political Theory," *Political Science Quarterly*, Vol. 35, pp. 236–254, 1930.

BARTH, P.: *Philosophie der Geschichte als Soziologie*, pp. 600–613, O. R. Reisland, Leipzig, 1897.

BELOT, G.: "La religion comme principe sociologique," *Revue philosophique*, Vol. 49, pp. 288–299, 1900.

———— "Une théorie nouvelle de la religion," *Revue philosophique*, Vol. 75, pp. 329–379, 1913.

———— "L'utilitarisme et ses nouveaux critiques," *Revue de métaphysique*, Vol. 2, pp. 404–464, 1894.

BOUGLÉ, C.: "Die philosophischen Tendenzen der Soziologie Durkheims," *Jahrbuch für Soziologie*, Bd. 1, 1925.

———— Review of Durkheim's "Représentations individuelles et représentations collectives," *L'année sociologique*, Vol. 2, pp. 152–155, 1897–1898.

BRANFORD, V. V.: "Durkheim: a Brief Memoir," *Sociological Review*, Vols. 9–10, pp. 77–82, 1916–1918.

CONZE, E.: "Zur Bibliographie der Durkheim-Schule," *Kölner Vierteljahrshefte für Soziologie*, Vols. 5–6, pp. 279–283, 1925–1926.

DAVY, G.: *Émile Durkheim*, Louis-Michaud, Paris, 1911.

—— "Émile Durkheim," *Revue de métaphysique*, Vol. 26, pp. 181–198, 1919; Vol. 27, pp. 71–112, 1920.

DENNES, WILLIAM R.: *The Methods and Presuppositions of Group Psychology*, Chap. III. Durkheim, *University of California Publications in Philosophy*, Vol. 6, No. 1, University of California Press, Berkeley, Calif., 1924.

DEPLOIGE, SIMON: *Le conflit de la morale et de la sociologie*, Institut Supérieur de Philosophie, Louvain, 1911.

DUPRAT, GUILLAUME L.: *Auguste Comte et Émile Durkheim*. Sonderabdruck Sozialwissenschaftliche Bausteine, Vol. 4, ed. by Prof. Fritz Karl Mann, Gustav Fischer, Jena, 1932.

ESSERTIER, D.: *Philosophes et savants français du XXe siècle, V. La Sociologie*, F. Alcan, Paris, 1930.

—— *Psychologie et sociologie*, F. Alcan, Paris, 1927.

FAUCONNET, P.: "The Durkheim School in France," *Sociological Review*, Vol. 10, pp. 15 20, 1927.

—— "L'oeuvre pédagogique de Durkheim," *Revue philosophique*, Vol. 93, pp. 93–94, 185–209, 1922.

GEHLKE, CHARLES E.: "Émile Durkheim's Contribution to Sociological Theory," *Studies in History, Economics and Public Law*, ed. by the Faculty of Political Science of Columbia University, Vol. 63, No. 1, Columbia University Press, New York, 1915.

GOLDENWEISER, A. A.: "Religion and Society: a Critique of Durkheim's Theory of the Origin and Nature of Religion," *Journal of Philosophy, Psychology and Scientific Method*, Vol. 14, pp. 113–124, 1917.

—— Review of "Les formes élémentaires de la vie religieuse," *American Anthropologist*, Vol. 17, pp. 719–735, 1915.

HALBWACHS, MAURICE: *Les causes du suicide. Travaux de L'année sociologique. Bibliothèque de philosophie contemporaine.* F. Alcan, Paris, 1930.

—— "La doctrine d'Émile Durkheim," *Revue philosophique*, Vol. 85, pp. 353–411, 1918.

HÖFFDING, H.: Review of "Les formes élémentaires de la vie religieuse," *Revue de métaphysique*, Vol. 22, pp. 828–848, 1914.

LACOMBE, R.: "L'interprétation des faits matériels dans la méthode de Durkheim," *Revue philosophique*, Vol. 99, pp. 369–388, 1925.

—— *La méthode sociologique de Durkheim*, F. Alcan, Paris, 1926.

—— "La thèse sociologique en psychologie," *Revue de métaphysique*, Vol. 33, pp. 351–377, 1926.

LOWIE, ROBERT H.: *Primitive Religion*. New York: Boni & Liveright, 1924.

MALINOWSKI, BRONISLAW: *Crime and Custom in Savage Society*, Harcourt, Brace & Company (for International Library of Psychology, Philosophy and Scientific Method), New York, 1926.

——— "Magic, Science and Religion," in *Science, Religion and Reality*, ed. by Joseph Needham, The Macmillan Company, New York, 1925.

MARICA, GEORGE E.: *Émile Durkheim: Soziologie und Soziologismus*, p. 174, Gustav Fischer, Jena, 1932.

MARITAIN, JACQUES: *Religion et culture*, Desclée, de Brouwer & Cie., Paris, 1930.

MAUCHAUSSAT, G.: "Sur les limites de l'interprétation sociologique de la morale," *Revue de métaphysique*, Vol. 35, pp. 347–379, 1928.

MAUSS, M.: "In memoriam, l'oeuvre inédite de Durkheim et des ses collaborateurs," *L'année sociologique*, new series, Vol. 1, pp. 7–29, 1923–1924; Vol. 2, pp. 9–19, 1925.

MAYO, ELTON: *The Human Problems of an Industrial Civilization*, The Macmillan Company, New York, 1933.

MERTON, ROBERT K.: "Durkheim's Division of Labor in Society," *American Journal of Sociology*, Vol. 40, pp. 319–328, 1934–1935.

PÉCAUT, FÉLIX: "Auguste Comte et Durkheim," *Revue de métaphysique*, Vol. 28, pp. 639–655, 1921.

——— "Émile Durkheim," *Revue pédagogique*, Vols. 72–73, pp. 1–20, 1918.

PIAGET, J.: "Logique génétique et sociologie," *Revue philosophique*, Vols. 105–106, pp. 167–205, 1928.

——— *The Moral Judgment of the Child*, trans. by Marjorie Gabain (*International Library of Psychology, Philosophy and Scientific Method*), K. Paul, French, Trubner & Co., Ltd., London, 1932.

RADCLIFFE-BROWN, A. R.: *The Andaman Islanders*, The University Press, Cambridge, England, 1922.

——— "The Sociological Theory of Totemism," reprinted from the *Proceedings of the Fourth Pacific Science Congress*, Java, 1929.

REINACH, SALOMON: "Extrait de L'année sociologique," Vol. 5, pp. 81–121, 1902 (on Durkheim's "Sur le totemisme"), *L'anthropologie*, Vol. 13, pp. 664–669.

——— "Extrait de L'année sociologique," Vol. 6, pp. 1–72 (on Durkheim and Mauss's "De quelques formes primitives de classification") *L'anthropologie*, Vol. 14, pp. 601–603, 1903.

RICHARD, G.: "Auguste Comte et Émile Durkheim," *Revue internationale de sociologie*, Vol. 40, pp. 603–612, November–December, 1932.

——— "Le conflit de la sociologie et de la morale philosophique," *Revue philosophique*, Vol. 59, 1905.

——— "La pathologie sociale d'Émile Durkheim," *Revue internationale de sociologie*, Vol. 38, p. 113, 1930.

——— *La sociologie générale*, Octave Doin et Fils, Paris, 1912.

DE ROBERTY, E.: "Les nouveaux courants d'idées dans la sociologie contemporaine," *Revue philosophique*, Vol. 77, pp. 1–31, 1914

SOROKIN, PITIRIM A.: *Contemporary Sociological Theories*, pp. 463–480, Harper & Brothers, New York, 1928.

TARDE, GABRIEL: *Études de psychologie sociale*, V. Giard et E. Brière Paris, 1898.

TOSTI, G.: "The Delusions of Durkheim's Sociological Objectivism," *American Journal of Sociology*, Vol. 4, pp. 171–177, 1898–1899.

WEBB, CLEMENT C. J.: *Group Theories of Religion and the Individual*, George Allen & Unwin, Ltd., London; The Macmillan Company, New York, 1916.

WORMS, R.: *La sociologie, sa nature, son contenu, ses attaches*, M. Giard & Cie, Paris, 1921.

D. *Other Relevant Works*

ALLPORT, FLOYD H.: *Institutional Behavior*, University of North Carolina Press, Chapel Hill, N. C., 1933.
——— "The Nature of Institutions," *Social Forces*, Vol. 6, pp. 167–179, 1927–1928.

FIRTH, RAYMOND W.: *Primitive Economics of the New Zealand Maori*, Chap. IV., "Magic in Economics," E. P. Dutton & Company, Inc., New York, 1929.

ROUSSEAU, JEAN JACQUES: *Du contrat social*, ed. by C. E. Vaughan, University Press, Manchester, 1918.

CHAPTER XIII. THE IDEALISTIC TRADITION

COHEN, MORRIS R.: *Reason and Nature*, Harcourt, Brace & Company, New York, 1931.

DILTHEY, WILHELM: *Einleitung in die Geisteswissenschaften*, Duncker und Humblot, Leipzig, 1883.

FREYER, HANS: *Soziolozie als Wirklichkeitswissenschaft: Logische Grundlegung des Systems der Soziologie*, B. G. Teubner, Leipzig, 1930.

VON GIERKE, OTTO: *Das deutsche Genossenschaftsrecht*, 4 vols., Weidmann, Berlin, 1868–1913.

GRÜNWALD, ERNST: *Das Problem der Soziologie der Wissens*, W. Braumüller, Vienna and Leipzig, 1934.

VON JHERING, RUDOLF: *Der Geist des Römischen Rechts*, 2 vols., 2d edition, Breitkopf & Härtel, Leipzig, 1866–1869.

MEINECKE, FRIEDRICH: *Die Entstehung des Historismus*, 2 vols., R. Oldenbourg, Munich, 1936.

PARSONS, TALCOTT: "'Capitalism' in Recent German Literature: I, Werner Sombart," *Journal of Political Economy*, Vol. 36, pp. 641–661, 1928.

ROTHACKER, ERICH: *Einleitung in die Geisteswissenschaften*, J. C. B. Mohr (P. Siebeck), Tübingen, 1920.

SOMBART, WERNER: *Der Bourgeois; Zur Geistesgeschichte des modernen Wirtschaftsmenschen*, Duncker und Humblot, Munich, 1913.
——— "Capitalism," *Encyclopedia of the Social Sciences*, Vol. III, The Macmillan Co., New York, 1930.
——— *Die drei Nationalökonomien*, Duncker und Humblot, Munich and Leipzig, 1930.
——— *Die Juden und das Wirtschaftsleben*, Duncker und Humblot, Leipzig, 1911.
——— *Der moderne Kapitalismus*, 3 vols., 2d ed., Duncker und Humblot, Leipzig, 1916.
——— *Der proletarische Sozialismus*, 2 vols., G. Fischer, Jena, 1924.

—— The Quintessence of Capitalism, trans. and ed. by M. Epstein, E. P. Dutton & Company, Inc., New York, 1915.

TROELTSCH, ERNST: Der Historismus und seine Probleme, Vol. III of Gesammelte Schriften, J. C. B. Mohr, Tübingen, 1922.

WHITEHEAD, ALFRED N.: Science and the Modern World, The Macmillan Company, New York, 1925.

WINDELBAND, WILHELM: Präludien, J. C. B. Mohr (P. Siebeck), Tübingen, 1884.

CHAPTERS XIV TO XVII.   MAX WEBER

A. Works

A complete bibliography of Weber's works is contained in Marianne Weber's Max Weber, Ein Lebensbild (see reference below).

WEBER, MAX: General Economic History, trans. by F. H. Knight, George Allen & Unwin, Ltd., London, 1927.

—— Gesammelte Aufsätze zur Religionssoziologie, 3 vols, J. C. B. Mohr (P. Siebeck), Tübingen, 1920–1921.

—— Gesammelte Aufsätze zur Sozial- und Wirtschaftsgeschichte, J. C. B. Mohr (P. Siebeck), Tübingen, 1924.

—— Gesammelte Aufsätze zur Soziologie und Sozialpolitik, J. C. B. Mohr (P. Siebeck), Tübingen, 1924.

—— Gesammelte Aufsätze zur Wissenschaftslehre, J. C. B. Mohr (P. Siebeck), Tübingen, 1922.

—— Gesammelte Politische Schriften, Drei Masken Verlag, Munich, 1921.

—— Grundriss der Sozialökonomik. III. Abteilung: Wirtschaft und Gesellschaft, 2 vols., J. C. B. Mohr (P. Siebeck), Tübingen, 1925.

—— The Protestant Ethic and the Spirit of Capitalism, trans. by Talcott Parsons, George Allen & Unwin, Ltd., London, 1930.

—— Wirtschaftsgeschichte, ed. by S. Hellman and M. Palyi, Duncker und Humblot, Munich, 1923,

WEBER, MARIANNE: Max Weber, Ein Lebensbild, J. C. B. Mohr (P. Siebeck), Tübingen, 1926.

B. Secondary Sources

1. Religion and Capitalism

BARKER, ERNEST: Church, State and Study, Methuen & Company, Ltd., London, 1930.

BRENTANO, LUJO: Die Anfänge des moderne Kapitalismus, K. Bayrische Akademie der Wissenschaften, Munich, 1916.

—— Der wirthschaftende Mensch in der Geschichte, F. Meiner, Leipzig, 1923.

BRODRICK, JAMES: The Economic Morals of the Jesuits: An Answer to Dr. H. M. Robertson, Oxford University Press, London, 1934.

FANFANI, AMINTORE: Cattolicisimo e Protestantesimo nella formazione storica del capitalismo, Società editrice "Vita e pensiero," Milan, 1934.

—— Protestantism, Catholicism and Capitalism. Sheed & Ward, London and New York, 1935.

FRIEDRICH, CARL J. and TAYLOR COLE: *Responsible Bureaucracy*, Harvard University Press, Cambridge, 1932.

FULLERTON, KEMPER: "Calvinism and Capitalism," *Harvard Theological Review*, Vol. 21, pp. 163–195, 1928.

HALBWACHS, M.: "Les origines puritaines du capitalisme moderne," *Revue d'histoire et philosophie réligieuses*, Vol. 5, pp. 132–134, 1925.

HALL, THOMAS C.: *The Religious Background of American Culture*, Little, Brown & Company, Boston, 1930.

HAUSER, HENRI: *Les débuts du capitalisme*, F. Alcan, Paris, 1927.

HONIGSHEIM, PAUL: "Zur Religionssoziologie des englischen Protestantismus," *Kölner Vierteljahrshefte für Soziologie*, Vol. 11, pp. 401–411, 1932, 1933.

KNIGHT, FRANK H.: "Historical and Theoretical Issues in the Problem of Modern Capitalism," *Journal of Economic and Business History*, Vol. 1, pp. 119–136, 1928.

KRAUS, JOHANN B.: *Scholastik, Puritanismus und Kapitalismus*, Duncker and Humblot, Munich and Leipzig, 1930.

MAURER, H. M.: "Studies in the Sociology of Religion. I. The Sociology of Protestantism," pp. 257–286, II. "Religion and American Sectionalism. The Pennsylvania German," pp. 408–438, *American Journal of Sociology*, Vol. 30, 1924.

MERTON, R. K.: *Science, Technology and Society in Seventeenth Century England*, to be published in *Osiris, History of Science Monographs*, Vol. IV, ed. by George Sarton, Cambridge.

OFFENBACHER, MARTIN: *Konfession und soziale Schichtung*, J. C. B. Mohr, Tübingen, 1901.

PARSONS, TALCOTT: " 'Capitalism' in Recent German Literature. II. Max Weber," *Journal of Political Economy*, Vol. 37, pp. 31–51, 1929.

——— "H. M. Robertson on Max Weber and His School," *Journal of Political Economy*, Vol. 43, pp. 688–696, 1935.

PIRENNE, HENRI: *Les périodes de l'histoire sociale du capitalisme*, Hayez, Brussels, 1914.

RACHFAHL, FELIX: "Kalvinismus und Kapitalismus," *Internationale Wochenschrift*, Bd. III, pp. 1217–1238, 1249–1267, 1287–1299, 1319–1334, 1347–1366, 1909.

ROBERTSON, HECTOR M.: *Aspects of the Rise of Economic Individualism: a Criticism of Max Weber and His School*, University Press (John Wilson & Son, Inc.), Cambridge, England, 1933.

VON SCHULZE-GAEVERNITZ, G.: "Die geistesgeschichtlichen Grundlagen der anglo-amerikanischen Weltsuprematie, III. Die Wirtschaftsethik des Kapitalismus," *Archiv für Sozialwissenschaft und Sozialpolitik*, p. 61.

SEÉ, H.: "Dans quelle mesure Puritains et Juifs ont-ils contribué au progrès du capitalisme modérne?", *Revue historique*, Vol. 154, pp. 57–68, 1927.

——— *Les origines du capitalisme moderne*, A. Colin, Paris, 1926.

SOMBART, W.: *The Jews and Modern Capitalism*, trans. by M. Epstein, T. F. Unwin, London, 1913.

TAWNEY, RICHARD H.: *Religion and the Rise of Capitalism*, Harcourt, Brace & Company, New York, 1926, 2d ed., 1929.

TROELTSCH, ERNST: *Die Bedeutung des Protestantismus für die Enstehung der moderne Welt*, R. Oldenburg, München, 1911.

—— *The Social Teaching of the Christian Churches*, trans. by Olive Wyon, 2 vols., The Macmillan Company, New York, 1931.

WOOD, H. G.: "The Influence of the Reformation on Ideas Concerning Wealth and Property," *Property; Its Duties and Rights, Historically, Philosophically and Religiously Regarded*, with an introduction by the Bishop of Oxford (Charles Gore), Macmillan & Company, Ltd., London, 1913.

2. *Methodological and General*

ABEL, THEODORE F.: "Systematic Sociology in Germany," *Studies in History, Economics and Public Law*, edited by the Faculty of Political Science of Columbia University, No. 310, Columbia University Press, New York, 1929.

BENNION, L. L.: *Max Weber's Methodology*, Dissertation, University of Strasbourg, Imprimatur, Les presses modernes, Paris, 1933.

BIENFAIT, W.: *Max Webers Lehre vom geschichtlichen Erkennen*, Ebering, Berlin, 1930.

ENGEL-REIMERS, CHARLOTTE: "Der Methodenstreit in der Soziologie," *Schmollers Jahrbuch*, Vol. 56, pp. 87–103, February, 1932.

FECHNER, ERICH: "Der Begriff des kapitalistischen Geistes bei Werner Sombart und Max Weber und die soziologischen Grundkategorien Gemeinschaft und Gesellschaft," *Weltwirtschaftliches Archiv*, Vol. 30, pp. 194–211, 1929.

—— "Der Begriff des kapitalistischen Geistes und das Schelersche Gesetz vom Zusammenhang der historischen Wirkfaktoren (Vergleich und Ausgleich zwischen Sombart und Max Weber)," *Archiv für Sozialwissenschaft und Socialpolitik*, Vol. 63, pp. 93–120, 1930.

FREYER, HANS: *Soziologie als Wirklichkeitswissenschaft*, B. G. Teubner, Leipzig, 1930.

GINSBERG, MORRIS: "Recent Tendencies in Sociology," *Economica*, February, 1933.

GRAB, HERMANN J.: *Der Begriff des Rationalen in der Soziologie Max Webers*, Sozialwissenschaftliche Abhandlungen, Vol. III, Karlsruhe, 1927.

HALBWACHS, MAURICE: "Max Weber, un homme, une oeuvre," *Annales d'histoire économique et sociale*, Vol. 1, pp. 81–88, January, 1929.

HINTZE, OTTO: "Max Webers Soziologie," *Schmollers Jahrbuch*, Vol. 50, pp. 83–95, 1926.

HONIGSHEIM, PAUL: "Max Weber als Soziologie," *Kölner Vierteljahrshefte für Soziologie*, Vols. 1–2, pp. 32–41, 1921.

—— "Der Max Weber-Kreis in Heidelberg," *Kölner Vierteljahrshefte für Soziologie*, Vols. 5–6, pp. 270 ff., 1925–1926.

JASPERS, KARL: *Max Weber*. Rede bei der von den Heidelberger Studentenschaft veranstalteten Trauerfeier, J. C. B. Mohr (P. Siebeck), Tübingen, 1921.

—— *Max Weber. Deutsches Wesen im politischen Denken, im Forschen und Philosophieren*, G. Stalling, Oldenburg, 1932.

KELSEN, HANS: *Der soziologische und der juristische Staatsbegriff, kritische Untersuchung des Verhältnisses von Staat und Recht,* J. C. B. Mohr (P. Siebeck), Tübingen, 1928.

KLÜVER, H.: "Max Weber's Ideal Type in Psychology," *Journal of Philosophy,* Vol. 23, pp. 29–35, 1926.

LANDSHUT, S.: *Kritik der Soziologie,* Duncker und Humblot, Munich, 1929.

——— "Max Webers geistesgeschichtliche Bedeutung," *Neue Jahrbücher für Wissenschaft und Jugendbildung.,* Vol. VII, pp. 507–516, 1931.

LENNERT, RUDOLF: *Die Religionstheorie Max Webers,* Kohlhammer, Stuttgart, 1935.

LIEBERT, ARTHUR: "Max Weber," *Preussische Jahrbücher,* Vol. 210, pp. 304–320, 1927.

LÖWITH, KARL: "Max Weber und Karl Marx," *Archiv für Sozialwissenschaft und Sozialpolitik,* Vol. 67, pp. 53–99, 175–214, 1932.

MEINECKE, FRIEDRICH: *Staat und Persönlichkeit,* E. S. Mittler und Sohn, Berlin, 1933.

MEITZEL, E. P. C.: "Max Weber," *Handwörterbuch der Staatswissenschaften,* 4th ed., vol. VIII, p. 926, Lieferungen 102–112.

VON MISES, L.: "Soziologie und Geschichte," *Archiv für Sozialwissenschaft und Sozialpolitik,* Vol. 61, pp. 465–512, 1929 (on Weber, pp. 470–497).

OPPENHEIMER, HANS: *Die Logik der soziologischen Begriffsbildung mit besonderer Berücksichtigung von Max Weber,* J. C. B. Mohr, Tübingen, 1925.

PALYI, MELCHIOR (ed.): *Erinnerungsgabe für Max Weber,* 2 vols., Munich: Duncker und Humblot, 1923.

PARSONS, TALCOTT: Review of von Schelting's "Max Webers Wissenschaftslehre," *American Sociological Review,* Vol. 1, pp. 675–681, 1936.

RICKERT, HEINRICH: "Max Weber und seine Stellung zur Wissenschaft," *Logos,* Vol. 15, pp. 222–237, 1926.

SALOMON, ALBERT: "Max Weber's Methodology," *Social Research,* Vol. 1, pp. 147–168, 1934.

——— "Max Weber's Political Ideas," *Social Research,* Vol. 2, pp. 368–384, 1935.

——— "Max Weber's Sociology," *Social Research,* Vol. 2, pp. 60–73, 1935.

SCHELER, MAX: *Schriften zur Sociologie und Weltanschauungslehre,* P. Reinhold, Leipzig, 1923.

VON SCHELTING, ALEXANDER: "Die logische Theorie der historischen Kulturwissenschaften von Max Weber und im besonderen sein Begriff des Idealtypus," *Archiv für Sozialwissenschaft und Sozialpolitik,* Vol. 49, pp. 623 ff., 1922.

——— *Max Webers Wissenschaftslehre,* J. C. B. Mohr (P. Siebeck), Tübingen, 1934.

SCHUHMACHER, H.: "Max Weber, Nationalökonom," *Jahrbuch der deutschen biographie,* Deutschen Verlags-Aust., pp. 593–615, Stuttgart.

SCHÜTZ, ALFRED: *Der sinnhafte Aufbau der sozialen Welt,* Julius Springer, Vienna, 1932.

Sorokin, Pitirim A.: *Contemporary Sociological Theories*, Harper & Brothers, New York, 1928.

Spann, Ottmar: *Tote und lebendige Wissenschaft*, 2d ed., Gustav Fischer, Jena, 1925.

Stoltenberg, H. L.: " 'Tote und lebendige Wissenschaft' (on Ottmar Spann and Max Weber)," *Zeitschrift für die Gesamte Staatswissenschaft*, Vol. 85, pp. 133–141, 1928.

Troeltsch, Ernst: *Der Historismus und seine Probleme*, Vol. III of *Gesammelte Schriften*, J. C. B. Mohr (P. Siebeck), Tübingen, 1922.

――― "Max Weber," *Deutscher Geist und Westeuropa*, J. C. B. Mohr (P. Siebeck), Tübingen, 1925.

Wach, Joachim: "Max Weber als Religionssoziologe" (appendix to his *Einführung in die Religionssoziologie*), J. C. B. Mohr (P. Siebeck), Tübingen, 1931.

Walther, Andreas: "Max Weber als Soziologe," *Jahrbuch für Soziologie*, Vol. II, pp. 1–65, 1926.

Wilbrandt, R.: "Max Weber als Erkenntniskritiker der Sozialwissenschaften," *Zeitschr. für die Gesamte Staatswissenschaft*, Vol. 79, pp. 583–674, 1925.

Wolf, Erich: "Max Webers ethischer Kritizismus und das Problem der Metaphysik," *Logos*, Vol. 19, pp. 359–375, 1930.

C. Other Relevant Works

Blunt, E. A. H.: *The Caste System of Northern India*, Oxford University Press, London, 1931.

Devereux, E. C., Jr.: "Gemeinschaft and Gesellschaft in Tokugawa Japan," unpublished thesis, Harvard University, 1934.

Elliott, William Y.: *The Pragmatic Revolt in Politics; Syndicalism, Fascism, and the Constitutional State*, The Macmillan Company, New York, 1928.

Granet, M.: *La pensée chinoise*, La Renaissance du Livre, Paris, 1934.

Grünwald, Ernst: *Das Problem der Soziologie des Wissens*, Wilhelm Braumüller, Vienna and Leipzig, 1934.

Knight, Frank H.: "Freedom as Fact and Criterion," *International Journal of Ethics*, Vol. 39, pp. 129–147, 1928–1929.

Koffka, Kurt: *Principles of Gestalt Psychology*, Harcourt, Brace & Company, New York, 1935.

Mannheim, Karl: *Ideologie und Utopie*, F. Cohen, Bonn, 1929; trans. by Louis Wirth and Edward Shils, Harcourt, Brace & Company, New York, 1936.

Parsons, Talcott: "Some Reflections on 'The Nature and Significance of Economics,'" *Quarterly Journal of Economics*, Vol. 48, pp. 511–545, 1933–1934.

Rickert, Heinrich: *Uber die Grenzen der naturwissenschaftlichen Begriffsbildung*, 5th ed., J. C. B. Mohr, Tübingen, 1929.

Robbins, Lionel: *The Great Depression*, Macmillan & Company, Ltd., London, 1934.

Roethlisberger F J and W. J. Dickson: *Management and the Worker; Technical vs. Social Organization in an Industrial Plant*, Harvard

School of Business Administration, Studies in Industrial Research, Boston, 1934.
SOROKIN, PITIRIM A.: "Forms and Problems of Culture Integration," *Rural Sociology,* Vol. 1, pp. 121–141, 344–374, 1936; Reprinted as Chap. I of his *Social and Cultural Dynamics,* 3 vols., American Book Company, New York, 1937.
TÖNNIES, FERDINAND: *Gemeinschaft und Gesellschaft,* Fues's Verlag (R. Reisland), Leipzig, 1887.
VEBLEN, THORSTEIN: *The Instinct of Workmanship,* The Macmillan Company, New York, 1914.
WHITEHEAD, T. N.: *Leadership in a Free Society,* Harvard University Press, Cambridge, 1936.

CHAPTERS XVIII AND XIX, CONCLUSION

FREYER, HANS: *Soziologie als Wirklichkeitswissenschaft,* B. G. Teubner, Leipzig, 1930.
FRIEDRICH, C. J.: *Constitutional Government and Politics,* Harper & Brothers, New York, 1936.
HUSSERL, EDMUND: *Logische Untersuchungen,* 2 vols, M. Niemeyer, Halle, 1900–1901.
JENNINGS, HERBERT SPENCER: *The Biological Basis of Human Nature,* W. W. Norton & Company, New York, 1930.
SIMMEL, GEORG: *Soziologie,* Duncker und Humblot, Leipzig, 1908.
WHITEHEAD, A. N.: *Science and the Modern World,* The Macmillan Company, New York, 1925.
ZNANIECKI, FLORIAN. *The Method of Sociology,* Farrar & Rinehart, Inc., New York, 1934.

INDEX

Data, 71, 117, 223, 393, 734 *ff.*, 750, 758, 761
  (*See also* Constants; Elements, analytical; Fact; Facts, social)
Definitiveness of study, lack of, 40
Demonstration, meaning of, 724
  (*See also* Causal relationships; Proof, logic of)
Dennes, W. S., 447
Density, dynamic, 321
  material, 322
  (*See also* Labor, division of)
Dependence, emotional *vs.* economic, 319
Dependent variables, 25
Deploige, S., 307, 409
Derivations, 227, 259, 456
  definition of, 198
  (*See also* Nonlogical action; Residues)
Descartes, René, 449
Desire, 387, 402
  (*See also* Ends; Motives; Wants)
Determinism, economic, 491, 493
  (*See also* Materialism, historical)
  empirical, 70, 344, 476
  logical, 10, 185
Dharma, 557–558
Dialectic, 110, 488
  (*See also* Change, social; Hegel, G. W. F., Marx, Karl; Materialism, historical)
Differentiation, social, 318 *ff.*, 512, 567
  (*See also* Labor, division of; Specialization)
Dilthey, Wilhelm, 476, 480, 484
Discipline, 285, 335, 384, 507, 515, 522
  (*See also* Bureaucracy; Constraint; Control, social; Institutions; Punishment)
Discovery of fact, 6
Disinterestedness, 164, 659 *f.*
  (*See also* Authority, moral; Moral element; Respect, attitude of; Value element)

Division of labor (*see* Labor, division of)
Dogma, 273, 558
  (*See also* Ideas, religious; Ideas, role of)
Drives, 222, 225
  (*See also* Darwinism, social; Instinct; Positivism, anti-intellectual)
Durkheim, Émile, 13, 17, 20, 74, 81, 84, 124, 202, 211, 248, 258, 261, 288, 293, 301 *ff.*, 453, 460 *ff.*, 487, 501–502, 529, 537, 550, 579, 609, 637, 647, 652, 660–661, 665–666, 682, 685–686, 688, 708–714, 717–718, 736
  convergence with Weber, 669–671, 673 *ff.*
Duty, 387, 662
  (*See also* Constraint; Obligation, moral; Respect, attitude of)
Dynamics, social, 726
  (*See also* Change, social)

E

Economic element, 233, 240, 243, 297–298, 619, 654–655, 658, 691, 704–705, 714, 716, 718, 739–740, 742–743, 765–766
  (*See also* Competition; Contract, relations of; Logical action)
Economic interpretation of history (*see* Materialism, historical)
Economic man (*see* Economic motives)
Economic motives, 161 *ff.*
  (*See also* Competition; Contract, relations of; Logical action)
Economic theory, status of, 13, 95 *ff.*, 165 *ff.*, 180, 183, 243, 264 *ff.*, 310, 452–455, 466, 476, 499, 598, 606 *ff.*, 616–618, 728, 757–758, 765, 769, 772
  (*See also* Competition; Contract, relations of; Logical action)

Motives, of suicide, 324
  (*See also* Subjective point of
  view; *Verstehen*)
Murchison, Carl, 190, 374
Mysticism, 523, 534, 562–563, 569 *ff.*
  (*See also* Buddhism; Hinduism;
  Pantheism; Taoism; Tradi-
  tionalism)
Myth, 273
  (*See also* Ideas, religious)

N

Nature, deterministic, law of, 88
  niggardliness of, 105, 107
  normative, law of, 88, 96, 119
  order of, 159 *ff.*, 523
  sciences of, 762
  state of, 90, 96, 100, 108, 151, 320
  (*See also* Identity of interests;
  Order, problem of)
Naturism, 414 *ff.*
Necessity, 185
  (*See also* Closure of theoret-
  ical systems; Determinism;
  Reification)
Newton, Sir Isaac, 88
Nock, A. D., 424, 425, 430, 431, 501,
  566, 712
Nominalism, 287
Nonempirical reality, 421 *ff.*, 431,
  467, 712
  (*See also* Charisma; Meaning,
  problem of; Ideas, religious;
  Sacredness)
Nonlogical action, 18, 192 *ff.*, 250 *ff.*,
  295, 456 *f.*, 705 *f.*, 714
  (*See also* Heredity and environ-
  ment; Irrationality; Non-
  scientific ideas; Rationality
  of action; Value elements)
Non-normative elements, 253
  (*See also* Conditions of action;
  Heredity and environment)
Nonscientific ideas, 26, 269 *ff.*
  (*See also* Ideas, religious; Ide-
  ology; Nonempirical reality)

Nonspatial categories, 45, 85, 444,
  763
  (*See also* Frame of reference of
  action)
Nonsubjective categories, 64, 67–68,
  82–84, 114, 202, 217, 222, 642,
  677, 701
  (*See also* Behaviorism; Heredity
  and environment)
Norm, 396–397
  definition, 75
  status of rational, 65
  systems of, 251
  types of, 679–680
  (*See also* Moral elements; Normative orientation; Rationality of action; Value elements)
Normality, social, 372 *ff.*
  (*See also* Integration; Pathol-
  ogy, social; Type, social)
Normative, to actor *vs.* observer, 75
  concept of, 74–77
  (*See also* Rationality; Subjective
  point of view; Value elements; Voluntaristic theory of
  action)
Normative order, 91 *ff.*
Normative orientation of action,
  44–45, 76, 206–207, 217, 295,
  370, 374–375, 377–378, 382,
  394, 396–398, 405–406, 456
  ff., 464, 483, 602, 615, 646,
  647, 650 *ff.*, 678 *ff.*, 701, 710,
  732
  (*See also* Rationality; Subjective
  point of view; Value elements; Voluntaristic theory
  of action)

O

Obedience (*see* Authority)
Objective point of view, 46, 187, 345
  (*See also* Behaviorism; Non-
  subjective categories)
Objectivism, 190, 327, 348–349, 356,
  581 *ff.*, 603, 729
  (*See also* Behaviorism)